JUVENILE DELINQUENCY

JUVENILE DELINQUENCY
Historical, Theoretical, and Societal Reactions to Youth

Editors

PAUL M. SHARP
Auburn University at Montgomery

BARRY W. HANCOCK
Indiana University at South Bend

PRENTICE HALL, ENGLEWOOD CLIFFS, NEW JERSEY 07632

Library of Congress Cataloging-in-Publication Data

Juvenile delinquency : historical, theoretical, and societal reactions
   to youth / [compiled by] Paul M. Sharp, Barry W. Hancock
         p.   cm.
      ISBN 0-13-103680-7
      1. Juvenile delinquency—United States.   I. Sharp, Paul M.
   II. Hancock, Barry W.
   HV9104.J845   1995
   364.3′6′0973—dc20
                                                    94-19804
                                                       CIP

Acquisitions editor: Nancy Roberts
Editorial/production supervision and
     interior design: Serena Hoffman
Cover designer: Carol Ceraldi
Production coordinator: Mary Ann Gloriande
Editorial assistant: Pat Naturale

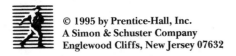

© 1995 by Prentice-Hall, Inc.
A Simon & Schuster Company
Englewood Cliffs, New Jersey 07632

Printed in the United States of America
10   9   8   7   6   5   4   3   2

ISBN 0-13-103680-7

Prentice-Hall International (UK) Limited, *London*
Prentice-Hall of Australia Pty. Limited, *Sydney*
Prentice-Hall Canada Inc., *Toronto*
Prentice-Hall Hispanoamericana, S.A., *Mexico*
Prentice-Hall of India Private Limited, *New Delhi*
Prentice-Hall of Japan, Inc., *Tokyo*
Simon & Schuster Asia Pte. Ltd., *Singapore*
Editora Prentice-Hall do Brasil, Ltda., *Rio de Janeiro*

Contents

PART III
The Social Context of Juvenile Delinquency 200

Preface

*I*n assembling this collection of readings in juvenile delinquency, we tried to satisfy professors and students in both undergraduate and graduate programs in courses on the subject of delinquency. We are especially proud that there is no particular ideological agenda followed in this collection. We have tried to create a comprehensive work that includes both classics in the field and contemporary research articles. We incorporated some much-needed historical materials yet wanted the text to be nonencyclopedic in presentation.

We approached the collection with several goals in mind. First, we wanted a book of readings that was more comprehensive and in-depth and yet more readable than any currently available. We have produced an anthology that may be used alone or to supplement a text in courses on juvenile delinquency and other crime-related courses. The combination of historical pieces with classic and contemporary theoretical articles, and the inclusion of more materials concerning females, gangs, violence among teens, and societal reactions to youth, are brought together in one work for the first time.

Second, we wanted to create pedagogical materials to facilitate the student's understanding of the articles, to aid the professor in the presentation of the subject, and to serve as an avenue toward further discussions and applications of the key concepts and ideas. We achieved this by creating three sections at the end of each article that draw materials, ideas, and terms from the article as well as from the larger body of delinquency literature. The questions for discussion, applications, and key terms make the book easy to use as a primary text, and these exercises are a unique feature of this anthology.

Third, we wanted more articles and information concerning female delinquency, legal issues in delinquency, and public policy information. The addition of this type of information challenges traditional old-school approaches to the study of delinquency. Omission of these materials in many texts is indicative of, as we see it, an ideological myopia balanced in favor of the author and not the reader.

Fourth, the measurement and magnitude of delinquency in this collection is not covered in the traditional sense of the official sources for offenses, court statistics, or huge national studies or data banks. Many of these issues are covered directly or indirectly in several of the articles. We feel most professors can teach the source materials for official and unofficial delinquency much better in lectures than we could by providing articles which typically argue strengths or weaknesses of collection techniques. The methodological issues of measurement, estimates, and trends in delinquency-related behaviors are complex and create some of the most highly debated issues in the field. A base for understanding data sources must come, we feel, from the instructor, with strengths, weaknesses, and possible solutions being part of the discussion concerning the collection as well as the uses of these data.

Juvenile Delinquency: Historical, Theoretical, and Societal Reactions to Youth is organized into five parts. The first, History of the Legal and Social Definitions of Juvenile Delinquency, presents five articles that set a solid foundation for understanding historical definitions of youth statuses and behavioral expectations in light of today's juvenile justice system. We selected these articles to serve as a backdrop to understanding the dynamics of the historical definitions and subsequent legal and societal reactions to youth and youth behavior. This historical treatment is a unique feature, not found in many anthologies of this kind, and rarely presented except in encyclopedic formats.

Part II, Theories of Juvenile Delinquency, presents classic as well as contemporary theoretical ideas of delinquency. Certainly, one could create a book dedicated exclusively to theory and nothing more. Our goal, however, has been to present articles that represent some of the most outstanding theoretical genre dealing with crime and delinquency. These readings, combined with the articles concerning history, challenge the reader to broaden the concept of delinquency and vividly expose the confusion in dealing with youth statuses, behavioral expectations, self-concept, youth culture, and theoretical attempts at explanation.

Part III, The Social Context of Delinquency, presents some of the livelier readings in the collection. Families, schools, subcultural groups, youth culture, the idea of "crime as play," and drug use are addressed in articles squarely in the social-problems area of the delinquency field. This collection ranges from traditional to contemporary approaches to understanding youth and delinquency issues.

In Part IV, Institutional Responses to Juvenile Delinquency, we traverse to some of the most important concepts and issues in delinquency research: the legal and formal institutional actions and reactions toward youth and delinquency. The legal processes of restricting rights and then extending rights, along with the differential treatment of youths and adults, makes this section vitally important. The differential responses of formal organizations based on status rather than behavior is central to understanding delinquency as well as the broader societal reactions to youth.

Finally, Part V, Juvenile Delinquency and Public Policy, presents four problemsolution arguments, which range from social science research to justice system overhaul. Hopefully, these selections add fuel to the debates about future directions in delinquency research and social-problem solutions. The selections here point out the difficulties experienced in solution–directed research. Public policy debate, after all, is often balanced on a fine line between the rights of individuals and the rights of society.

ACKNOWLEDGMENTS

We would like to extend our appreciation to several people who assisted us in preparing *Juvenile Delinquency: Historical, Theoretical, and Societal Reactions to Youth.* Nancy Roberts, editor-in-chief at Prentice Hall, and her staff and production team were invaluable in assisting with the development and production of this text-reader. It is simply a pleasure to have this sort of professional working relationship. We extend our thanks to the following reviewers for helpful critiques of the manuscript: Jim Embree, Sacramento City College; Lawrence Travis, III, University of Cincinnati; Lin Huff-Corzine, Kansas State University; and Jerry Bayer, McCook Community College. In addition, we would like to extend a big thank you to Lynn Sharp, Jamie Barter, and Michelle Chen for their time, advice, and patience; and to some special friends, Fluffy, Lamby Pie, Rockie and Oozie, Ali, Tippy, Smokie Joe Man, and Sir Hogie.

Our sincere thanks go out to all of those individuals concerned with the welfare of our young people, regardless of the scope and depth of their caring and involvement. Finally, to our many students who voiced their opinions that studying original sources added greatly to their learning experiences, we extend our gratitude.

Paul M. Sharp
Barry W. Hancock

JUVENILE DELINQUENCY

I

HISTORY OF THE LEGAL AND SOCIAL DEFINITIONS OF JUVENILE DELINQUENCY

*I*t would be impossible to understand the topic of juvenile delinquency without first becoming familiar with the historical underpinnings which gave rise to the terms *juvenile delinquency*. Statuses and the behavioral expectations related to age are powerful social forces in every society and have created many ideals of child-hood and young adulthood that are in constant conflict with the dynamic changes from the rapid modernization of the last two centuries. The age at which one acquires the status of adult and what constitutes delinquency are two of the most poignant issues that have shaped the definitions, research, and societal reactions to youth in the modern world. In many ways, the societal reactions to youth have had more bearing on the current definitions, attitudes, and responses to the delin-quency issue than any other source. Almost universally, children are considered to be different from adults and to require special kinds of care and treatment. In fact, our current concept of childhood grew out of the fertile philosophical debates in Europe during the Enlightenment. A new concern for the moral and social welfare of children was forged in lieu of the exploitation and manipulation considered acceptable practice prior to that time.

The reform that began in Europe gave momentum to the formalization process of the justice system and eventually to the creation of a separate system for youth. We have selected five articles for Part I in hopes that today's students of delinquency will more clearly understand the antecedents of contemporary soci-etal reactions to youth.

We begin with Paul Lerman's "Delinquency and Social Policy: A Historical Perspective," which strikes at the heart of justice in a democracy. Lerman contends the ideal of justice for all has not been subsequently realized in practice, and espe-cially not in the juvenile justice system, where social control is more determinative than justice or correction.

In our second selection, "The Child-Saving Movement and the Origins of the Juvenile Justice System," Anthony Platt traces the development of the juvenile justice system to the ideology of the movement and its fundamental preoccupation with the control of youth. The emergence of the juvenile court, the state as "superparent," and the reformatory movement are superbly handled. Platt argues, as do others, that the movement achieved success in rationalizing the dependent status of youth.

The first two articles blend well with the third article by Robert M. Mennel, "Attitudes and Policies toward Juvenile Delinquency in the United States: A Historiographical Review," which is critical of the policy-making process and the historical accounts of juvenile delinquency. With some of the most famous works in the history of delinquency studies cited, this article provides excellent references for further study.

"The Crime of Precocious Sexuality: Female Juvenile Delinquency in the Progressive Era," is a historical essay by Steven Schlossman and Stephanie Wallach. It implicitly draws relevant parallels to our contemporary juvenile justice system, which mirrors the Progressive era practices of discrimination and unequal treatment. Again, the societal reactions to the person's status rather than behavior should serve to remind us that the ideology that shaped the past has influenced today's juvenile justice system.

We conclude Part I with "The Watershed of Juvenile Justice Reform," by Barry Krisberg, Ira M. Schwartz, Paul Litsky, and James Austin. They argue that the watershed period we are currently experiencing may well reform the juvenile justice system to be more fair, humane, and cost-effective. Their conclusion that building more juvenile correctional facilities will not solve the system's problems is shared by many in juvenile justice. Alternatives to incarceration, especially the creative experimental alternatives, hold the promise of real reform. Most reformers realize that selective incapacitation is a reality when dealing with extreme forms of violence among young people. However, it is also true that most know the majority of our young people are in need of a helping hand and guidance.

1

Delinquency and Social Policy: A Historical Perspective

Paul Lerman

Graduate School of Social Work, Rutgers University

The American belief system has traditionally emphasized the ideals of liberty, justice for all, and freedom from arbitrary authority. An examination of our response to delinquent youth, from a historical perspective, reveals a profound discrepancy between these ideals and our societal practices. The issue of liberty is related to the traditional overreach of the American definition of delinquency. The issue of justice is related to the American failure to specify a correspondence between degrees of delinquency and degrees of correctional response. Restraint from arbitrary authority is related to the broad discretion that permits more youth to be detained than to be adjudicated in a court of law. An examination of recent data and trends indicates that the American system can be characterized more accurately as a juvenile social control system than as a justice or correctional system.

Last year, during the Bicentennial celebration, we heard a great deal about the ideals of liberty, justice for all, and freedom from arbitrary authority. One useful way of testing our adherence to these ideals is to assess America's response to its delinquent youth, from a historical perspective.

"Delinquency and Social Policy: A Historical Perspective," *Crime and Delinquency* (October 1977), pp. 383–393. Reprinted by permission of the publisher, Sage Publications, Inc.

Delinquency Definition and the Ideal of Liberty

Many Americans, when they think about delinquency, probably conjure up an image of criminal behaviors. However, the actual American definition of delinquency, as revealed by our correctional practices and statutes, ever since the founding of the Plymouth Bay Colony, has always included other reasons for legally punishing or incarcerating youth.

As might be expected, the colonists used the law of their native land as a basis for forming an American response to wayward youth. According to English law, juveniles above the age of seven were subject to criminal statutes and sanctions; however, both in England and in the colonies, youth under fifteen were usually treated less severely than adults. Beginning about 1660, the laws of the Massachusetts colony began to invoke the criminal process to support adult authority. A preamble to one of the 1660 laws stated:

> It appeareth, by too much experience, that diverse children and servants doe behave themselves disobediently and disorderly, towards their parents, masters, and Governors. . . .[1]

The law gave a magistrate the power to summon before him "any such offender, and upon conviction of such misdemeanors, . . . sentence him to endure such corporal punishment, by whipping or otherwise, as in his judgment the merit of the fact shall deserve, not exceeding ten stripes for one offense."[2]

The laws of 1660 also made lying by children and failure to observe the Sabbath punishable offenses. Besides these laws, Massachusetts and other colonies had special laws regarding indentured servants and apprentices, so that masters could apply to the courts for measures to control youth who fornicated, contracted to marry, or gambled at cards or dice. In addition to these special restrictions on youth, juveniles were also subject to the Poor Laws which condemned idleness, begging, and vagrancy and used criminal penalties to enforce obedience.

These kinds of behaviors were included in the first attempt at a correctional definition of "delinquency" by the House of Refuge founded in 1825, the first institution specifically designed for juvenile offenders. In a memorial to the public appealing for funds, the Society for the Reformation of Juvenile Delinquents, the founding organization, stated:

> The design of the proposed institution is, to furnish, in the *first place*, an asylum, in which boys under a certain age, who become subject to the notice of our Police, either as vagrants, or houseless, or charged with petty crimes, may be received . . . [and] subjected to a course of treatment, that will afford a prompt and energetic corrective of their vicious propensities. . . .[3]

New York legislation granted the institution of a state charter and gave the self-perpetuating managers the right to "receive and take into the House of Refuge . . . all such children as shall be taken up or committed as vagrants or convicted of criminal offenses. . . ."Committing bodies could include judges, police magistrates, and the commissioner of the Almshouse and the Bridewell, providing the youth were "proper objects."[4] The New York legislature thereby concurred in the broad correctional definition set forth by the reformers in their public appeal.

In 1826 Boston established a House of Reformation for Juvenile Offenders. The incorporation act gave the House directors the power,

. . . at their discretion, to receive and take into said house all such children who shall be convicted of criminal offenses or taken up and committed under and by virtue of an act of this Commonwealth "for suppressing and punishing of rogues, vagabonds, common beggars, and other idle, disorderly and lewd persons," and who may . . . be proper objects therefore. . . .[5]

Both the Boston and the New York statutes authorized the use of jails and prisons for youth who were not deemed "proper objects." However, by 1857, when the first national convention of refuge superintendents (from New York, Boston, Rochester, Cincinnati, Philadelphia, New Orleans, Baltimore, Pittsburgh, Chicago, and St. Louis) met in New York, there were seventeen juvenile reformatories, housing about 20,000 children admitted under policies and statutes that comprehended virtually every childhood misfortune.[6]

By the onset of the Civil War, a juvenile classified as a "proper object" of reformation could be covered by statutes that stemmed from three sources: (1) American adaptation of Elizabethan poor laws that covered idleness, begging, vagrancy, and destitution; (2) Puritan-inspired definitions of offenses peculiar to childhood and the apprentice status—in modern sociological language, juvenile status offenses; and (3) state adaptations of common-law criminal offenses. These three sources contributed, in actual correctional practice, to the lack of clear distinction between the problems of poverty, child welfare, and crime. In general, young America used the coercive power and punitive sanctions of the criminal law to handle many problems that were clearly noncriminal. In the nineteenth century, the reformatory performed the social functions of a juvenile almshouse, a workhouse, and a house of correction.

Sympathy for the plight of children whose fathers had been killed in the Civil War fostered a movement to build special asylums for poor and homeless youth, thereby diverting some youth from a reformatory experience. In addition, the "placing out" system, particularly in rural areas, was used to rescue children from "corrupting" living conditions.

The spread of the free common schools also served to occupy some idle youth during the day. While these efforts may have diverted many idle and dependent youth from reformatories, the earlier statutes remained on the books in the older states, and the new Midwest and Western states, early in their statehood, enacted a broad correctional conception of delinquency through a variety of statutes that legitimated institutionalization in specific facilities.[7]

With the creation of the first juvenile court in Chicago, at the turn of the twentieth century, there was an attempt to codify existing Illinois statutes by adding a dependency and neglect category distinct from a criminal delinquency classification. In actual practice, however, distinctions among dependents, neglected children, status youth, and criminal offenders were often blurred: all categories could be—and actually were—detained in the same institution, even though the legislation and some judges gave a new emphasis to reforming "worthy" children in their own homes. The 1899 law, for example, made it possible for a youth to be held in detention or sent to a state training school if he was destitute; or if he was homeless, abandoned, or dependent; or if he had improper parental care; or if he was begging or receiving alms; or if he was living in a house of ill fame or with any vicious or disreputable person; or if he was in an unfit place.[8]

Following the lead of Illinois, other states also made certain that the jurisdiction of the court was sufficiently broad to encompass, as a "proper object" for detention or reformation in a training school, a broad array of poor law, juvenile status, and criminal characteristics. These broad terms were justified in 1901 by a Chicago child-saving committee, which urged that the legal definition of "condition of delinquency" be amended to include items that were implicit in the original dependency and neglect category or had been used in practice—"incorrigible"; "growing up in idleness and crime"; or "knowingly associating with thieves or vicious or immoral persons." The committee argued that "the amendment is intended to include all children that are in the need of government and care."[9] Since the use of local jails and prisons was forbidden, any separate juvenile correctional facility was deemed to be a place of government and care of the incorrigible and idle as well as a place of custody for the criminal offender. The reformers were successful in enacting a statutory definition of delinquency that had been implicit in practice for about 250 years.

The reformers believed that by deliberately equating the delinquent with any child "in need of government and care" they could use the police powers of the state to save children who might escape a narrow legal construction of dependency and neglect. To provide this control and care, they pushed through the legislature the creation of the first all-juvenile detention facilities, establishment of a truancy and parental school, provisions for paid probation officers, and state subsidies to existing religious institutions. They also initiated, before World War I, the creation of small pensions for worthy widows to allow them to keep their children at home. The court, with its broad jurisdictional boundaries, was primarily designed to serve the intake functions of a coercive welfare agency within the context of a modern juvenile quasi-criminal court.

Until the early 1960's, no statute in any state explicitly acknowledged the legal or correctional difference between status offenders and criminal offenders. About fifteen years ago a new legal category, Person In Need of Supervision, known as PINS, was created in New York and California as a noncriminal basis of juvenile court jurisdiction, distinct from a narrower definition of dependency and child neglect. By 1974 thirty-four states distinguished between criminal-type delinquency and at least some of the status offenses, but only eleven states explicitly prohibited institutionalizing status offenders in state training schools that housed criminal offenders.

The movement to remove the vestiges of Poor Law and juvenile status characteristics from the correctional definition of "delinquency" recently received added support from the federal Juvenile Justice and Delinquency Prevention Act of 1974. A state receiving block grants under the Act must give assurance that, within a specified time, no status offender will be detained in or committed to an institution set up explicitly for criminal delinquents. While this movement to narrow the boundaries of delinquency definitions and practices is laudable, whether youth will actually fare better under the new labels is still uncertain. Recent evidence indicates that PINS youth are more likely than delinquent youth to be detained in a facility as part of their court processing, are detained longer, and, if institutionalized, stay for longer periods. Whether America can learn to treat all arrested truant, idle, incorrigible, promiscuous, and runaway youth less harshly than their truly delinquent brothers and sisters is still uncertain at this time.[10] In a country that prizes the ideal of liberty, it is ironic that youth can still lose their freedom so easily, and for such lengthy periods, for behaviors that are clearly not criminal and that would not even be admitted before an adult criminal court.

Delinquency and Justice for All

The evidence that noncriminal delinquents can be, have been, and are dealt with harshly is related to another American theme, "justice for all." Since 1824, when the House of Refuge was empowered to institutionalize a variety of youth—without distinction between the criminal and the noncriminal—for indeterminate periods, American juvenile laws and practices have flouted two basic components of a reasonable conception of justice: (1) Any deprivation of liberty, or other state-imposed penalty, should be graded proportionately to the degree of social harm a person has done or clearly threatens to do to members of a community. (2) Offenses or harms that are comparable should be dealt with by punishments that are equal.[11]

Before the Revolution of 1776, juveniles were treated like adults. In the reform legislation that swept the former colonies immediately after the War of Independence, imprisonment and fines replaced the pillory, the stocks, and other forms of corporal punishment. Borrowing ideas from European classical criminology (associated with Beccaria) and the general environment of the

Enlightenment, Americans reformed their criminal codes with the aim of securing equality of judicial handling. Children benefited from these reforms, even though they were also thrust into the same local jails and prisons as adults.[12]

About 1820, when the House of Refuge was under discussion, administrators of the local Bridewell were trying to separate youth from adults during the day, furnish some in-jail instruction in reading and writing, and care differently for their younger charges.[13] According to the keeper of the Bridewell, the period of confinement ranged from a few days to a year or more, with many remaining several months. Though the charges were mainly for "trifling offenses," many remained longer than customary "because of a want of residence."[14]

Instead of seeking residences for the vagrant, apprenticeships for the unemployed, and schools for the ignorant, the Society for the Reformation of Juvenile Delinquents decided to attack the problems of child welfare, poverty, and delinquency with a new social invention—an all-purpose workhouse and reformatory designed to reshape moral character coercively and render children obedient to their superiors. Only after a child had met the strict reform standards of the Refuge superintendent— during a stay ranging from a year to three years—would he be bound out as a laboring apprentice or sent out on a whaling ship. The reformers argued that agents of government should be the "fathers of the people," should "stand towards the community in the moral light of guardians of virtue."[15] In carrying out their guardianship inside the Refuge, they were not reluctant to use the stripes, solitary confinement, bread and water, and other correctional penalties.

In exchange for receiving a new and quite punitive "father," juveniles gave up their traditional rights under criminal law. Commitment to the Refuge meant that vagrancy and "trifling offenses" could be dealt with the same as more serious offenses since they could be viewed as signs of "vicious propensities." Many resolutions were proposed at the first national convention of House of Refuge superintendents in 1857 but only one was chosen for adoption—for fear of stifling any autonomous correctional initiatives. Not surprisingly, the superintendents agreed that they should have "unqualified control over the treatment and disposition of inmates for the length of their minority."[16] Children were deprived of legal restraints on the type, degree, and duration of punishment that agents of government could impose, and all parental rights were abrogated for the duration of the child's minority. In many cases, parents did not even know where youth had been placed after a long stay at Refuge.

Juvenile court legislation at the turn of the twentieth century continued this tradition of deliberately refraining from establishing any definition of degrees of delinquency or limits on the type, degree, and duration of penalties. When the indeterminate sentence has, in some jurisdictions, given way to eighteen-month renewable placements (or sentences) or three-year dispositions, no state has enacted legislation that limits its power in accordance with traditional norms of justice.

The historical legacy continues to confound the handling of juvenile status and trivial, petty offenders, the bulk of the delinquency population, and it neutralizes the common-sense moral distinction made by most Americans when they compare the harm done by a mugger of the elderly to a shoplifting spree at a local store. We have devised a system when the serious offense can be treated much too lightly and the trivial much too seriously. We now have 150 years of evidence that relinquishing substantive justice in exchange for a correctional regime that does not correct is a bad bargain. Even if our institutional programs were effective, one could still argue that just dispositions should take precedence over efforts at reformation. Recognition of the legal and moral concept of degrees of criminal delinquency could promote the ideal of "justice for all," including children.

The Modern Social Control System: The Ideal and the Actual

The overreach of the delinquency definition and the failure to specify degrees of offense highlight the profound discrepancy between formal declarations of liberty and justice and our societal practices. This disparity between the ideal and the actual deserves to be examined further, since the current degree of discrepancy tells us a good deal about the modern American approach to controlling, regulating, and treating delinquency.

Enforcement of the law in America is local and has always varied in scope and degree. As a result, many youthful misbehaviors have been overlooked by police or ignored by judges. In practice, police and judges have exercised discretion in softening the breadth and harshness of our laws. Until recently, reformers were usually not satisfied with this tendency toward underenforcement since identifying, correcting, and reforming youth at the earliest possible age was deemed important. The founders of the House of Refuge complained that local judges were reluctant to convict youth because they were unwilling to mix the young with older, hardened criminals. Seventy-five years later, when the modern juvenile justice system was created in Chicago, reformers complained that judges were reluctant to correct youth because they had to send youngsters to jails pending disposition of their cases. If the laws were not strictly enforced how could "guardians of virtue" become "fathers of the people" or take legal control of all children "in need of government and care"?

Both of these important movements in juvenile reform, the refuge movement and juvenile court movement, did help to separate youth from workhouse and criminal adults. But in the process of doing this, they created new forms of broad social control over youth. It is quite likely that *more* youth were incarcerated *after* each reform than *before* it. The Refuge Movement founders were the initiators of our reformatories, industrial and training schools, truancy and parental schools, and other *long-term* juvenile correctional facilities. The juvenile court movement founders were the initiators of *short-term* detention facilities, where youth could be properly studied and governed before a determination of whether they needed longer government and care.

Given the breadth of our nation's definition of juvenile delinquency and a continual growth in youth population, the juvenile court's available resources were continually strained to meet the demand for coercive child-saving. Under enforcement, informal adjustment of cases, and high probation case-loads were adaptive mechanisms utilized to deal with the fundamental problems of a potentially limitless demand for reformation of the young and the limited supply of resources. Other aids to the overburdened juvenile social control system were inadvertently provided in the support programs of Aid to Dependent Children, mental health, and child welfare, which siphoned off Poor Law and juvenile status offenders who comprised part of the potential "delinquent" population. States and counties, of course, have varied in their use of alternative resources and under-enforcement mechanisms, so that many juvenile facilities still house a mixed population of delinquent, dependent, neglected, and status offense children.

Accompanying all of these diverse trends have been assertions by correctional leaders that we have moved progressively from a policy of revenge and restraint to rehabilitation and reintegration of the juvenile offender. Some academics also have given support to this assessment.[17] Unfortunately, the disparity between these lofty intentions and actual practice is much greater than we have wished to believe. In 1967 the nation was presented with the results of the first nation-wide study of correction. The data provide a means of understanding how our juvenile policy operates from a national perspective.[18]

The figures of this national study clearly indicate that about *one-half* of the youth formally reported as arrested by local police departments were not sent to court—these cases were informally adjusted by the police. However, approximately *two-thirds* of arrested youth experienced a detention lockup for an average stay of twelve days. This means, of course, that more youth were detained than appeared on an official court calendar to have the charges formally assessed. The number of detention lockups surpassed the number of children appearing in court and the number receiving probation treatment. We can reasonably infer that *short-term restraint* (social control), not rehabilitative and reinte-

grative service, is the actual dominant public policy response toward youth.

This dominance of community-based institutionalization was first measured with 1965 data. However, it could not have occurred without the intervention of a new social control device, the specially constructed local juvenile detention facility associated with the rise of the juvenile court. This multipurpose facility has a variety of euphemistic names—reception center, diagnostic clinic, juvenile hall, and receiving home—but its essential quality is quite familiar to youth: it is a juvenile version of the local jail.

Recent data suggest that a greater emphasis on due process inside the courtroom and a verbal commitment to diversion and community-based programs have not halted the growth and reliance on detention lockups. A recently completed survey conducted by Rosemary Sarri and her team of University of Michigan researchers disclosed that in 1973 at least 100,000 children spent at least one day in an adult jail and that nearly 500,000 other youth were admitted to local detention facilities[19]—an increase of 50 per cent over the 1965 figure, much more than the growth in the youth population facing the risk of detention.

A recent study offers some clues to the difficulty of trying to reverse the steady rise in local detention rates. In 1967, the chief judge of the Cuyahoga County (Cleveland, Ohio) juvenile court launched a determined effort to reduce detention. He comments about his efforts as follows:

> Social workers, probation officers and police officers, who had previously for all practical purposes made the decision as to the necessity of detaining the child, reacted strenuously to our screening process. . . .
>
> Naturally, these criticisms, those from within the court and more especially those from outside agencies, militated against acceptance of our new policy. . . .
>
> The social agencies which staunchly proclaimed their non-punitive philosophy wanted us to detain children as part of their "treatment" process. . . .
>
> Helpful in discouraging one of the social agencies from the overuse of detention was our new requirement that an official com-

plaint must be filed concerning each child placed in the detention home. . . .

It had been a common practice for a probation officer to place a child in detention who was uncooperative, who failed to keep appointments, who truanted from school, or who, upon a complaint of the parents, was considered out of control at home. . . . The 380 children admitted by probation officers in 1967 was reduced to 125 in 1971, a reduction of 60 percent. . . .

As we began our initial effort to reduce population, we found that many children were being detained, a waiting acceptance by various state, county, and private facilities who, often arbitrarily and for their own convenience, imposed quotas and admission requirements on the court.[20]

This unusually frank report indicates that detention can be used as a multipurpose resource for a variety of arbitrary social control and administrative reasons. For three years (1967–69) Judge Whitlatch was unable to demonstrate empirically that the chief judge could administratively regulate the use of detention by police, probation officers, treatment agencies, and correctional organizations. Finally, in 1970 and 1971, his detention reduction policy began to show signs of success—particularly with police and his own probation staff. However, a separate reading of the 1971 Annual Report of the Cuyahoga County Court reveals that more local youth still received detention compared to formal probation—3,439 to 2,387.[21]

Summary and Conclusions

We continue to compound the original delinquency problem by permitting systems of juvenile control to expand under broad laws that operate under arbitrary discretionary standards. Many of the standards and the outcomes appear unreasonable and unjust when subjected to close scrutiny. Left to operate according to the unstated policy, the system tends to result in a dominance of social control. Merely adding more fiscal and organizational resources to the existing system—as during the last decade—can only further the relative dominance of social control over efforts at treatment. This incremen-

tal policy of merely adding more resources has resulted in excessive expense—in both dollars and social values—without offsetting benefits.

The community treatment strategy attempts to control one discretionary part of the social control system—institutionalization at the state level—while adding additional resources to other parts of the system. The evidence provided above indicates that this well-intentioned but limited approach can yield unintended and undesirable consequences. There can be no impact on definitional boundaries, total institutionalization rates from all sources, balance between sanctions and treatment, and duration of sanctions without addressing *all* of the critical discretionary decision points. A limited policy of rolling back or freezing the boundaries and the admission rates of all types of institutional usage could be a useful first step accompanying a revised community-treatment strategy. However, this would probably involve the creation of a monitoring, regulating, reporting system directed at police, judges, probation officers, and detention intake workers. Even if a consensus about narrower deviance and detention standards were obtained, actual compliance would have to be monitored at all decision points.

A broader strategy of changing the definitional boundaries and promoting justice could, quite reasonably, focus on eliminating the vestiges of Poor Law and status offenses from the jurisdiction of the juvenile courts and paying attention to degrees of delinquency. In addition, decreasing the coercive dominance of the total system could be coupled with a policy of searching for less extreme forms of social control and less costly forms of treatment. However, a strategy of rigorously reducing the boundaries of deviance definition and modifying institutional forms of sanctions need not be rationalized by claiming a rehabilitative technology where none has been scientifically demonstrated. The reduction of excessive social and fiscal costs, associated with unreasonable and unjust uses of institutionalization, possesses a social value that is superior to pursuing relatively ineffective modes of treatment. From an empirical perspective, a better case can be made for reducing the total system's unnecessary social and fiscal costs than for treatment strategies that contribute to increasing these costs. In practice this means that our juvenile system could become less costly if we concentrated less on expanding involuntary treatment and more on reducing the rationale and practices associated with unnecessary or unjust deprivation of liberty. The delivery of noncoercive treatment, limited as its impact may be, might begin to expand as the social and fiscal dominance of institutionalization at state and local levels actually diminished. If we are not clear about the priorities, we will unwittingly continue to incur unnecessary social and fiscal costs and leave the system essentially unchanged.

Signs of progress should not be too difficult to discern. Two of them are changes in the rates of total institutionalization and in length of stay. We can also find out whether the rates of formal complaints, formal adjudications, and probation dispositions exceed the rates of local and state institutionalization. Progress can also be noted by decreases in the arrests and coercive processing of cases of delinquent tendencies, juvenile status offenses, or children in need of supervision. In monitoring this last indicator of progress, analysts may have to assess new alternative societal responses toward the new legal category, juveniles in need of supervision (or JINS, PINS, MINS, and CINS, depending on the jurisdiction). Since this category of youth is most likely to be detained, to remain in detention longer, and to be institutionalized in state and private institutions for a greater length of stay, it is possible that programs operated under new sponsorship or child welfare titles may re-create traditional, costly examples of restraining institutions.[22] It is useful to remember, too, that reforms initiated at the turn of the century also began by creating an alternative community-based response to the traditional system of social control.

During the first seventy-five years of this century, we created a modern juvenile control system to regulate the conduct and character of America's youth. We accomplished this while believing that we were primarily engaged in saving or rehabilitating youth. The image of a nonrestraining society was set forth while we constructed new institutions that were classified as detention facilities, residential schools, diagnostic centers, and reception clinics. During this time we also created probation and other less coercive services, but the dominance of our continued reliance on institutionalization is clearly revealed by national and state data. In the last quarter of this century will we continue to maintain the discrepancy between reality and our intentions or will we begin the troublesome tasks of determining where arbitrary social control ends and justice and noncoercive help begin?

Notes

1. Joseph M. Hawes, *Children in Urban Society: Juvenile Delinquency in Nineteenth Century America* (New York: Oxford University Press, 1971), p. 14.

2. *Id.*, p. 41.

3. Society for the Reformation of Juvenile Delinquents, *House of Refuge Documents* (New York: Mahlon Day, 1832), p. 21. Hereafter cited as *Refuge Documents*.

4. Hawes, *op. cit. supra* note 1, p. 41; Robert S. Pickett, *House of Refuge* (Syracuse, N.Y.: Syracuse University Press, 1969), p. 58.

5. R. H. Bremner, J. Barnard, T. K. Hareven, and R. M. Mennel, *Children and Youth in America: A Documentary History*, 2 vols. (Cambridge, Mass.: Harvard University Press, 1970), Vol. I, p. 681.

6. David Rothman, *The Discovery of the Asylum* (Boston: Little, Brown, 1971), p. 209.

7. Bremner et al., *op. cit. supra* note 5, Vols. I, II.

8. *Id.*, Vol. II, p. 507.

9. Hawes, *op. cit. supra* note 1, p. 185.

10. P. Lerman, "Child Convicts," *TransAction*, July–August 1971, pp. 35–44, 72.

11. P. Lerman, "Beyond *Gault*: Injustice and the Child," in Paul Lerman, ed., *Delinquency and Social Policy* (New York: Praeger, 1970), p. 237.

12. Rothman, *op. cit. supra* note 6, pp. 30–57.

13. Pickett, *op. cit. supra* note 4, p. 57.

14. *Refuge Documents*, *op. cit. supra* note 3, p. 15.

15. *Id.*, p. 13.

16. Rothman, *op. cit. supra* note 6, p. 293.

17. L. T. Empey, *Alternatives to Incarceration* (Washington, D.C.: U.S. Dept. of Health, Education and Welfare, 1967).

18. President's Commission on Law Enforcement and Administration of Justice, *Task Force Report: Corrections* (Washington, D.C.: U.S. Govt. Printing Office, 1967), pp. 121, 129.

19. *Youth Reporter* (monthly newsletter, Youth

Development Office, U.S. Dept. of Health, Education and Welfare), November 1973, p. 2.

20. W. C. Whitlatch, "Practical Aspects of Reducing Detention Home Population," *Juvenile Justice*, August 1973, pp. 21, 22, 23.

21. *Cuyahoga County Juvenile Court Annual Report*, 1971, pp. 26–27.

22. Lerman, *supra* note 10.

QUESTIONS FOR DISCUSSION

1. For what offenses could children be punished in Colonial America?

2. What laws, codes, and norms have contributed to the juvenile justice statutes of today?

3. According to Lerman, we as a nation have "150 years of evidence that relinquishing substantive justice in exchange for a correctional regime that does not correct is a bad bargain." Discuss why this is a bad bargain and cite evidence to support your response.

4. Has the juvenile justice system evolved into a system of coercive social control rather than a system with rehabilitative and reintegrative goals?

APPLICATIONS

1. Historically, a persistent problem has emerged about defining at what age a juvenile should be considered an adult. Consider that at age sixteen a person may obtain a driver's license, at eighteen a person may vote and be drafted into the military, and at twenty-one a person may consume alcoholic beverages.

   a. At what age do you think a juvenile should be considered an adult?

   b. Is there a difference between biological maturity and psychological maturity?

   c. Should the justice system's legal definition take into account biological and/or psychological maturity when rendering decisions about whether to try a juvenile as an adult?

   d. Are there any acts committed by juveniles that should not be considered illegal (e.g., truancy, incorrigibility, idleness, runaway, promiscuity)?

2. Consider the Poor Laws of the 1600s. Are any laws today similar to Poor Laws?

   a. Choose a law that is similar to a poor law of Colonial America. List the poor law and the contemporary law and explain how they are alike and what their intended purposes are.

KEY TERMS

classical criminology a criminological perspective suggesting that (1) people have the free will to choose criminal or conventional behavior; (2) people choose to commit crime for reasons of greed or personal need; and (3) crime can be controlled by criminal sanctions, which should be proportionate to the guilt of the perpetrator.

discretion having the freedom to act or judge on one's own; a latitude of choice or action.

Enlightenment a philosophical movement of the eighteenth century, concerned with the critical examination of previously accepted doctrines and institutions from the point of view of rationalism.

incorrigible incapable of correction or reform. As applied to juveniles, this means parents or guardians cannot control an adolescent's behavior.

institutionalization the involuntary admission of a person to a confining environment with others exhibiting like attributes.

jurisdiction the right, power, and extent to which an authority may interpret and apply the law.

juvenile delinquency antisocial and/or criminal behavior exhibited by children or adolescents.

Poor Laws Colonial American law which condemned idleness, begging, and vagrancy and used criminal penalties to reinforce obedience.

positivist criminology a criminological perspective that uses scientific methods of the natural sciences and suggests that human behavior is a product of social, biological, psychological, or economic forces.

2

The Child-Saving Movement and the Origins of the Juvenile Justice System

Anthony Platt

Traditional Perspectives on Juvenile Justice

The modern system of crime control in the United States has many roots in penal and judicial reforms at the end of the nineteenth century. Contemporary programs which we commonly associate with the "war on poverty" and the "great society" [of the 1960s] can be traced in numerous instances to the programs and ideas of nineteenth century reformers who helped to create and develop probation and parole, the juvenile court, strategies of crime prevention, the need for education and rehabilitative programs in institutions, the indeterminate sentence, the concept of "half-way" houses, and "cottage" systems of penal organization.

The creation of the juvenile court and its accompanying services is generally regarded by scholars as one of the most innovative and idealistic products of the age of reform. It typified the "spirit of social justice," and, according to the National Crime Commission, represented a progressive effort by concerned reformers to alleviate the miseries of urban life and to solve social problems by rational, enlightened and scientific methods.[1] The juvenile justice system was widely heralded as "one of the greatest

advances in child welfare that has ever occurred" and "an integral part of total welfare planning."[2] Charles Chute, an enthusiastic supporter of the child-saving movement, claimed that "no single event has contributed more to the welfare of children and their families. It revolutionized the treatment of delinquent and neglected children and led to the passage of similar laws throughout the world."[3] Scholars from a variety of disciplines, such as the American sociologist George Herbert Mead and the German psychiatrist August Aichhorn, agreed that the juvenile court system represented a triumph of progressive liberalism over the forces of reaction and ignorance.[4] More recently, the juvenile court and related reforms have been characterized as a "reflection of the humanitarianism that flowered in the last decades of the 19th century"[5] and an indication of "America's great sense of philanthropy and private concern about the common weal."[6]

Histories and accounts of the child-saving movement tend either to represent an "official" perspective or to imply a gradualist view of social progress.[7] This latter view is typified in Robert Pickett's study of the House of Refuge movement in New York in the middle of the last century:

> In the earlier era, it had taken a band of largely religiously motivated humanitarians to see a need and move to meet that need. Although much of their vision eventually would be supplanted by more enlightened

"The Child-Saving Movement and the Origins of the Juvenile Justice System," in Richard Quinney (Ed.), *Criminal Justice in America* (Boston: Little Brown, 1974), pp. 362–383. © 1974 by Anthony Platt.

policies and techniques and far more elaborate support mechanisms, the main outlines of their program, which included mild discipline, academic and moral education, vocational training, the utilization of surrogate parents, and probationary surveillance, have stood the test of time. The survival of many of the notions of the founders of the House of Refuge testifies, at least in part, to their creative genius in meeting human needs. Their motivations may have been mixed and their oversights many, but their efforts contributed to a considerable advance in the care and treatment of wayward youth.[8]

This view of the nineteenth century reform movement as fundamentally benevolent, humanitarian and gradualist is shared by most historians and criminologists who have written about the Progressive era. They argue that this reform impulse has its roots in the earliest ideals of modern liberalism and that it is part of a continuing struggle to overcome injustice and fulfill the promise of American life.[9] At the same time, these writers recognize that reform movements often degenerate into crusades and suffer from excessive idealism and moral absolutism.[10] The faults and limitations of the child-saving movement, for example, are generally explained in terms of the psychological tendency of its leaders to adopt attitudes of rigidity and moral righteousness. But this form of criticism is misleading because it overlooks larger political issues and depends too much on a subjective critique.

Although the Progressive era was a period of considerable change and reform in all areas of social, legal, political and economic life, its history has been garnished with various myths. Conventional historical analysis, typified by the work of American historians in the 1940s and 1950s, promoted the view that American history consisted of regular confrontations between vested economic interests and various popular reform movements.[11] For Arthur Schlesinger, Jr., "liberalism in America has been ordinarily the movement of the other sections of society to restrain the power of the business community."[12]

. . . Conventional histories of progressivism argue that the reformers, who were for the most part drawn from the urban middle classes, were opposed to big business and felt victimized by the rapid changes in the economy, especially the emergence of the corporation as the dominant form of financial enterprise.[13] Their reform efforts were aimed at curbing the power of big business, eliminating corruption from the urban political machines, and extending the powers of the state through federal regulation of the economy and the development of a vision of "social responsibility" in local government. They were joined in this mission by sectors of the working class who shared their alienation and many of their grievances.

. . . The political and racial crises of the 1960s, however, provoked a reevaluation of this earlier view of the liberal tradition in American politics, a tradition which appeared bankrupt in the face of rising crime rates, ghetto rebellions, and widespread protests against the state and its agencies of criminal justice. In the field of criminology, this reevaluation took place in national commissions such as the Kerner Commission and President Johnson's Commission on Law Enforcement and the Administration of Justice. Johnson's Crime Commission, as it is known, included a lengthy and detailed analysis of the juvenile justice system and its ineffectiveness in dealing with juvenile delinquency.

The Crime Commission's view of the juvenile justice system is cautious and pragmatic, designed to "shore up" institutional deficiencies and modernize the system's efficiency and accountability. Noting the rising rate of juvenile delinquency, increasing disrespect for constituted authority and the failure of reformatories to rehabilitate offenders, the Commission attributes the failures of the juvenile justice system to the "grossly overoptimistic" expectations of nineteenth century reformers and the "community's continuing unwillingness to provide the resources—the people and facilities and concern—necessary to permit [the juvenile courts] to realize their potential. . . ."[14]

. . . In the following pages we will argue that the above views and interpretations of juvenile justice are factually inaccurate and suffer from a serious misconception about the functions of modern liberalism. The prevailing myths about the juvenile justice system can be summarized as follows: (1) The child-saving movement in the late nineteenth century was successful in humanizing the criminal justice system, rescuing children from jails and prisons, developing humanitarian judicial and penal institutions for juveniles, and defending the poor against economic and political exploitation. (2) The child-savers were "disinterested" reformers, representing an enlightened and socially responsible urban middle class, and opposed to big business. (3) The failures of the juvenile justice system are attributable partly to the overoptimism and moral absolutism of earlier reformers and partly to bureaucratic inefficiency and a lack of fiscal resources and trained personnel.

These myths are grounded in a liberal conception of American history which characterizes the child-savers as part of a much larger reform movement directed at restraining the power of political and business elites. In contrast, we will offer evidence that the child-saving movement was a coercive and conservatizing influence, that liberalism in the Progressive era was the conscious product of policies initiated or supported by leaders of major corporations and financial institutions, and that many social reformers wanted to secure existing political and economic arrangements, albeit in an ameliorated and regulated form.

The Child-Saving Movement

Although the modern juvenile justice system can be traced in part to the development of various charitable and institutional programs in the early nineteenth century,[15] it was not until the close of the century that the modern system was systematically organized to include juvenile courts, probation, child guidance clinics, truant officers, and reformatories. The child-saving movement—an amalgam of philanthropists, middle-class reformers and professionals—was responsible for the consolidation of these reforms.[16]

The 1890s represented for many middle-class intellectuals and professionals a period of discovery of "dim attics and damp cellars in poverty-stricken sections of populous towns" and "innumerable haunts of misery through-

out the land."[17] The city was suddenly discovered to be a place of scarcity, disease, neglect, ignorance, and "dangerous influences." Its slums were the "last resorts of the penniless and the criminal"; here humanity reached the lowest level of degradation and despair.[18] These conditions were not new to American urban life and the working class had been suffering such hardships for many years. Since the Haymarket Riot of 1886, the centers of industrial activity had been continually plagued by strikes, violent disruptions, and widespread business failures.

What distinguished the late 1890s from earlier periods was the recognition by some sectors of the privileged classes that far-reaching economic, political and social reforms were desperately needed to restore order and stability. In the economy, these reforms were achieved through the corporation which extended its influence into all aspects of domestic and foreign policies so that by the 1940s some 139 corporations owned 45 percent of all the manufacturing assets in the country. It was the aim of corporate capitalists to limit traditional laissez-faire business competition and to transform the economy into a rational and interrelated system, characterized by extensive long-range planning and bureaucratic routine.[19] In politics, these reforms were achieved nationally by extending the regulatory powers of the federal government and locally by the development of commission and city manager forms of government as an antidote to corrupt machine politics. In social life, economic and political reforms were paralleled by the construction of new social service bureaucracies which regulated crime, education, health, labor and welfare.

The child-saving movement tried to do for the criminal justice system what industrialists and corporate leaders were trying to do for the economy—that is, achieve order, stability and control while preserving the existing class system and distribution of wealth. While the child-saving movement, like most Progressive reforms, drew its most active and visible supporters from the middle class and professions, it would not have been capable of achieving significant reforms without the financial and political support of the wealthy and powerful. Such support was not without precedent in various philanthropic movements preceding the child-savers. New York's Society for the Reformation of Juvenile Delinquents benefited in the 1820s from the contributions of Stephen Allen, whose many influential positions included Mayor of New York and president of the New York Life Insurance and Trust Company.[20] The first large gift to the New York Children's Aid Society, founded in 1853, was donated by Mrs. William Astor.[21] According to Charles Loring Brace, who helped to found the Children's Aid Society, "a very superior class of young men consented to serve on our Board of Trustees; men who, in their high principles of duty, and in the obligations which they feel are imposed by wealth and position, bid fair hereafter to make the name of New York merchants respected as it was never before throughout the country."[22] Elsewhere, welfare charities similarly benefited from the donations and wills of the upper class.[23] Girard College, one of the first large orphanages in the United States, was built and furnished with funds from the banking fortune of Stephen Girard,[24] and the Catholic bankers and financiers of New York helped to mobilize support and money for various Catholic charities.[25]

The child-saving movement similarly enjoyed the support of propertied and powerful individuals. In Chicago, for example, where the movement had some of its most notable successes, the child-savers included Louise Bowen and Ellen Henrotin who were both married to bankers.[26] Mrs. Potter Palmer, whose husband owned vast amounts of land and property, was an ardent child-saver when not involved in the exclusive Fortnightly Club, the elite Chicago Woman's Club or the Board of Lady Managers of the World's Fair;[27] another child-saver in Chicago, Mrs. Perry Smith, was married to the vice-president of the Chicago and Northwestern Railroad. Even the more radically-minded child-savers came from upper-class backgrounds. The fathers of Jane Addams and Julia Lathrop, for example, were both lawyers and Republican senators in the Illinois legislature. Jane Addams' father was one of the richest men in north-

ern Illinois, and her stepbrother, Harry Haldeman, was a socialite from Baltimore who later amassed a large fortune in Kansas City.[28]

The child-saving movement was not simply a humanistic enterprise on behalf of the lower classes against the established order. On the contrary, its impetus came primarily from the middle and upper classes who were instrumental in devising new forms of social control to protect their privileged positions in American society. The child-saving movement was not an isolated phenomenon but rather reflected massive changes in productive relationships, from laissez-faire to monopoly capitalism, and in strategies of social control, from inefficient repression to welfare state benevolence.[29] This reconstruction of economic and social institutions, which was not achieved without conflict within the ruling class, represented a victory for the more "enlightened" wing of corporate leaders who advocated strategic alliances with urban reformers and support of liberal reforms.[30]

Many large corporations and business leaders, for example, supported federal regulation of the economy in order to protect their own investments and stabilize the marketplace. Business leaders and political spokesmen were often in basic agreement about fundamental economic issues. . . . "Few reforms were enacted without the tacit approval, if not the guidance, of the large corporate interests." For the corporation executives, liberalism meant "the responsibility of all classes to maintain and increase the efficiency of the existing social order."[31]

Progressivism was in part a businessmen's movement and big business played a central role in the Progressive coalition's support of welfare reforms. Child labor legislation in New York, for example, was supported by several groups, including upper-class industrialists who did not depend on cheap child labor. According to Jeremy Felt's history of that movement, "the abolition of child labor could be viewed as a means of driving out marginal manufacturers and tenement operators, hence increasing the consolidation and efficiency of business."[32] The rise of compulsory education, another welfare state reform, was also closely tied to the changing forms of industrial production and social control. Charles Loring Brace, writing in the mid-nineteenth century, anticipated the use of education as preparation for industrial discipline when, "in the interests of public order, of liberty, of property, for the sake of our own safety and the endurance of free institutions here," he advocated "a strict and careful law, which shall compel every minor to learn and read and write, under severe penalties in case of disobedience."[33] By the end of the century, the working class had imposed upon them a sterile and authoritarian educational system which mirrored the ethos of the corporate workplace and was designed to provide "an increasingly refined training and selection mechanism for the labor force."[34]

While the child-saving movement was supported and financed by corporate liberals, the day-to-day work of lobbying, public education and organizing was undertaken by middle-class urban reformers, professionals and special interest groups. The more moderate and conservative sectors of the feminist movement were especially active in anti-delinquency reforms.[35] Their successful participation derived in part from public stereotypes of women as the "natural caretakers" of "wayward children." Women's claim to the public care of children had precedent during the nineteenth century and their role in child rearing was paramount. Women, generally regarded as better teachers than men, were more influential in child-training and discipline at home. The fact that public education also came more under the direction of women teachers in the schools served to legitimize the predominance of women in other areas of "child-saving."[36]

The child-saving movement attracted women from a variety of political and class backgrounds, though it was dominated by the daughters of the old landed gentry and wives of the upper-class nouveau riche. Career women and society philanthropists, elite women's clubs and settlement houses, and political and civic organizations worked together on the problems of child care, education and juvenile delinquency. Professional and political women's groups regarded child-saving as a problem of women's rights, whereas their opponents seized upon it as an opportunity to keep women in their "proper place." Child-saving became a reputable task for any woman who wanted to extend her "housekeeping" functions into the community without denying anti-feminist stereotypes of woman's nature and place.[37]

For traditionally educated women and daughters of the landed and industrial gentry, the child-saving movement presented an opportunity for pursuing socially acceptable public roles and for restoring some of the authority and spiritual influence which many women felt they had lost through the urbanization of family life. Their traditional functions were dramatically threatened by the weakening of domestic roles and the specialized rearrangement of the family.[38] The child-savers were aware that their championship of social outsiders such as immigrants, the poor and children, was not wholly motivated by disinterested ideals of justice and equality. Philanthropic work filled a void in their own lives, a void which was created in part by the decline of traditional religion, increased leisure and boredom, the rise of public education, and the breakdown of communal life in large, crowded cities. "By simplifying dress and amusements, by cutting off a little here and there from our luxuries," wrote one child-saver, "we may change the whole current of many human lives."[39] Women were exhorted to make their lives useful by participating in welfare programs, by volunteering their time and services, and by getting acquainted with less privileged groups. They were also encouraged to seek work in institutions which were "like family-life with its many-sided development and varied interests and occupations, and where the woman-element shall pervade the house and soften its social atmosphere with motherly tenderness."[40]

While the child-saving movement can be partly understood as a "symbolic crusade"[41] which served ceremonial and status functions for many women, it was by no means a reactionary and romantic movement, nor was it supported only by women and members of the old gentry. Child-saving also had considerable instrumental significance for legitimizing new career openings for women. The new role of social worker combined elements of an old and partly fictitious role—defender of family life—and elements of a new role—social servant. Social work and professional child-saving provided new opportunities for career-minded women who found the traditional professions dominated and controlled by men.[42] These child-savers were members of the emerging bourgeoisie created by the new industrial order.

It is not surprising that the professions also supported the child-saving movement, for they were capable of reaping enormous economic and status rewards from the changes taking place. The clergy had nothing to lose (but more of their rapidly declining constituency) and everything to gain by incorporating social services into traditional religion. Lawyers were needed for their technical expertise and to administer new institutions. And academics discovered a new market which paid them as consultants, elevated them to positions of national prestige and furnished endless materials for books, articles and conferences.

. . . While the rank and file reformers in the child-saving movement worked closely with corporate liberals, it would be inaccurate to simply characterize them as lackeys of big business. Many were principled and genuinely concerned about alleviating human misery and improving the lives of the poor. Moreover, many women who participated in the movement were able to free themselves from male domination and participate more fully in society. But for the most part, the child-savers and other Progressive reformers defended capitalism and rejected socialist alternatives. Most reformers accepted the structure of the new industrial order and sought to moderate its cruder inequities and reduce inharmonies in the existing system.[43] Though many child-savers were "socialists of the heart" and ardent critics of society, their programs were typically reformist and did not alter basic economic inequalities.[44] Rhetoric and righteous indignation were more prevalent than programs of radical action.

Images of Crime and Delinquency

. . . The child-savers viewed the "criminal classes" with a mixture of contempt and benevolence. Crime was portrayed as rising from the "lowest orders" and threatening to engulf "respectable" society like a virulent disease. Charles Loring Brace, a leading child-saver, typified popular and professional views about crime and delinquency:

> As Christian men, we cannot look upon this great multitude of unhappy, deserted, and degraded boys and girls without feeling our responsibility to God for them. The class increases: immigration is pouring in its multitudes of poor foreigners who leave these young outcasts everywhere in our midst. These boys and girls . . . will soon form the great lower class of our city. They will influence elections; they may shape the policy of the city; they will assuredly, if unreclaimed, poison society all around them. They will help to form the great multitude of robbers, thieves, and vagrants, who are now such a burden upon the law-respecting community. . . .[45]

This attitude of contempt derived from a view of criminals as less-than-human, a perspective which was strongly influenced and aggravated by nativist and racist ideologies.[46] The "criminal class" was variously described as "creatures" living in "burrows," "dens," and "slime"; as "little Arabs" and "foreign childhood that floats along the streets and docks of the city—vagabondish, thievish, familiar with the vicious ways and places of the town";[47] and as "ignorant," "shiftless," "indolent," and "dissipated."[48]

The child-savers were alarmed and frightened by the "dangerous classes" whose "very number makes one stand aghast," noted the urban reformer Jacob Riis.[49] Law and order were widely demanded:

> The "dangerous classes" of New York are mainly American-born, but the children of Irish and German immigrants. They are as ignorant as London flashmen or costermongers. They are far more brutal than the peasantry from whom they descend, and they are much banded together, in associations, such as "Dead Rabbit," "Plug-ugly," and various target companies. They are our *enfant perdus*, grown up to young manhood. . . . They are ready for any offense or crime, however degraded or bloody. . . . Let but Law lift its hand from them for a season, or let the civilizing influences of American life fail to reach them, and, if the opportunity offered, we

should see an explosion from this class which might leave this city in ashes and blood.[50]

These views derived considerable legitimacy from prevailing theories of social and reform Darwinism which . . . proposed that criminals were a dangerous and atavistic class, standing outside the boundaries of morally regulated relationships. Herbert Spencer's writings had a major impact on American intellectuals and Cesare Lombroso, perhaps the most significant figure in nineteenth century criminology, looked for recognition in the United States when he felt that his experiments on the "criminal type" had been neglected in Europe.[51]

Although Lombroso's theoretical and experimental studies were not translated into English until 1911, his findings were known by American academics in the early 1890s, and their popularity, like that of Spencer's works, was based on the fact that they confirmed widely-held stereotypes about the biological basis and inferior character of a "criminal class." A typical view was expressed by Nathan Allen in 1878 at the National Conference of Charities and Correction: "If our object is to prevent crime in a large scale, we must direct attention to its main sources—to the materials that make criminals; the springs must be dried up; the supplies must be cut off."[52] This was to be achieved, if necessary, by birth control and eugenics. Similar views were expressed by Hamilton Wey, an influential physician at Elmira Reformatory, who argued before the National Prison Association in 1881 that criminals had to be treated as a "distinct type of human species."[53]

Literature on "social degradation" was extremely popular during the 1870s and 1880s, though most such "studies" were little more than crude and racist polemics, padded with moralistic epithets and preconceived value judgments. Richard Dugdale's series of papers on the Jukes family, which became a model for the case-study approach to social problems, was distorted almost beyond recognition by anti-intellectual supporters of hereditary theories of crime.[54] Confronted by the evidence of Darwin, Galton, Dugdale, Caldwell and many other disciples of the bio-

logical image of behavior, many child-savers were compelled to admit that "a large proportion of the unfortunate children that go to make up the great army of criminals are not born right."[55] Reformers adopted and modified the rhetoric of social Darwinism in order to emphasize the urgent need for confronting the "crime problem" before it got completely out of hand. A popular proposal, for example, was the "methodized registration and training" of potential criminals, "or these failing, their early and entire withdrawal from the community."[56]

Although some child-savers advocated drastic methods of crime control—including birth control through sterilization, cruel punishments, and life-long incarceration—more moderate views prevailed. This victory for moderation was related to the recognition by many Progressive reformers that short-range repression was counter-productive as well as cruel and that long-range planning and amelioration were required to achieve economic and political stability. The rise of more benevolent strategies of social control occurred at about the same time that influential capitalists were realizing that existing economic arrangements could not be successfully maintained only through the use of private police and government troops.[57] While the child-savers justified their reforms as humanitarian, it is clear that this humanitarianism reflected their class background and elitist conceptions of human potentiality. The child-savers shared the view of more conservative professionals that "criminals" were a distinct and dangerous class, indigenous to working-class culture, and a threat to "civilized" society. They differed mainly in the procedures by which the "criminal class" should be controlled or neutralized.

Gradually, a more "enlightened" view about strategies of control prevailed among the leading representatives of professional associations. Correctional workers, for example, did not want to think of themselves merely as the custodians of a pariah class. The self-image of penal reformers as "doctors" rather than "guards," and the medical domination of criminological research in the United States at that time facilitated the acceptance of "therapeutic" strategies in prisons and reformatories.[58] Physicians gradually provided the official rhetoric of penal reform, replacing cruder concepts of social Darwinsim with a new optimism. Admittedly, the criminal was "pathological" and "diseased," but medical science offered the possibility of miraculous cures. Although there was a popular belief in the existence of a "criminal class" separated from the rest of humanity by a "vague boundary line," there was no good reason why this class could not be identified, diagnosed, segregated, changed and incorporated back into society.[59]

By the late 1890s, most child-savers agreed that hereditary theories of crime were overfatalistic. The superintendent of the Kentucky Industrial School of Reform, for example, told delegates to a national conference on corrections that heredity is "unjustifiably made a bugaboo to discourage efforts at rescue. We know that physical heredity tendencies can be neutralized and often nullified by proper counteracting precautions."[60] E. R. L. Gould, a sociologist at the University of Chicago, similarly criticized biological theories of crime as unconvincing and sentimental. "Is it not better," he said, "to postulate freedom of choice than to preach the doctrine of the unfettered will, and so elevate criminality into a propitiary sacrifice?"[61]

Charles Cooley, writing in 1896, was one of the first American sociologists to observe that criminal behavior depended as much upon social and economic circumstances as it did upon the inheritance of biological traits. "The criminal class," he observed, "is largely the result of society's bad workmanship upon fairly good material." In support of this argument, he noted that there was a "large and fairly trustworthy body of evidence" to suggest that many "degenerates" could be converted into "useful citizens by rational treatment."[62]

Although there was a wide difference of opinion among experts as to the precipitating causes of crime, it was generally agreed that criminals were abnormally conditioned by a multitude of biological and environmental forces, some of which were permanent and irreversible. Strictly biological theories of crime were modified to incorporate a devel-

opmental view of human behavior. If, as it was believed, criminals are conditioned by biological heritage and brutish living conditions, then prophylactic measures must be taken early in life. "We must get hold of the little waifs that grow up to form the criminal element just as early in life as possible," exhorted an influential child-saver. "Hunt up the children of poverty, of crime, and of brutality, just as soon as they can be reached."[63] Efforts were needed to reach the criminals of future generations. "They are born to crime," wrote the penologist Enoch Wines, "brought up for it. They must be saved."[64] New institutions and new programs were required to meet this challenge.

Juvenile Court and the Reformatory System

The essential preoccupation of the child-saving movement was the recognition and control of youthful deviance. It brought attention to, and thus "invented" new categories of youthful misbehavior which had been hitherto unappreciated. The efforts of the child-savers were institutionally expressed in the juvenile court which, despite recent legislative and constitutional reforms, is generally acknowledged as their most significant contribution to progressive penology. There is some dispute about which state first created a special tribunal for children. Massachusetts and New York passed laws, in 1874 and 1892 respectively, providing for the trials of minors apart from adults charged with crimes. Ben Lindsey, a renowned judge and reformer, also claimed this distinction for Colorado where a juvenile court was, in effect, established through an educational law of 1899. However, most authorities agree that the Juvenile Court Act, passed by the Illinois legislature in the same year, was the first official enactment to be recognized as a model statute by other states and countries.[65] By 1917, juvenile court legislation had been passed in all but three states and by 1932 there were over 600 independent juvenile courts throughout the United States.[66]

The juvenile court system was part of a general movement directed towards developing a specialized labor market and industrial discipline under corporate capitalism by creating new programs of adjudication and control for "delinquent," "dependent" and "neglected" youth. This in turn was related to augmenting the family and enforcing compulsory education in order to guarantee the proper reproduction of the labor force. For example, underlying the juvenile court system was the concept of *parens patriae* by which the courts were authorized to handle with wide discretion the problems of "its least fortunate junior citizens."[67] The administration of juvenile justice, which differed in many important respects from the criminal court system, was delegated extensive powers of control over youth. A child was not accused of a crime but offered assistance and guidance; intervention in the lives of "delinquents" was not supposed to carry the stigma of criminal guilt. Judicial records were not generally available to the press or public, and juvenile hearings were typically conducted in private. Court procedures were informal and inquisitorial, not requiring the presence of a defense attorney. Specific criminal safeguards of due process were not applicable because juvenile proceedings were defined by statute as civil in character.[68]

The judges of the new court were empowered to investigate the character and social background of "predelinquent" as well as delinquent children; they concerned themselves with motivation rather than intent, seeking to identify the moral reputation of problematic children. The requirements of preventive penology and child-saving further justified the court's intervention in cases where no offense had actually been committed, but where, for example, a child was posing problems for some person in authority, such as a parent or teacher or social worker.

The role model for juvenile court judges was doctor-counselor rather than lawyer. "Judicial therapists" were expected to establish a one-to-one relationship with "delinquents" in the same way that a country doctor might give his time and attention to a favorite patient. Juvenile courtrooms were often arranged like a clinic and the vocabulary of its participants was largely composed of medical metaphors. "We do not know the child without a thorough examination," wrote Judge Julian Mack. "We must reach into the soul-life of the child."[69] Another judge from Los Angeles suggested that the juvenile court should be a "laboratory of human behavior" and its judges trained as "specialists in the art of human relations." It was the judge's task to "get the whole truth about a child" in the same way that a "physician searches for every detail that bears on the condition of the patient."[70] Similarly, the judges of the Boston juvenile court liked to think of themselves as "physicians in a dispensary."[71]

The unique character of the child-saving movement was its concerns for predelinquent offenders—"children who occupy the debatable ground between criminality and innocence"—and its claim that it could transform potential criminals into respectable citizens by training them in "habits of industry, self-control and obedience to law."[72] This policy justified the diminishing of traditional procedures and allowed police, judges, probation officers and truant officers to work together without legal hindrance. If children were to be rescued, it was important that the rescuers be free to pursue their mission without the interference of defense lawyers and due process. Delinquents had to be saved, transformed and reconstituted. "There is no essential difference," noted a prominent child-saver, "between a criminal and any other sinner. The means and methods of restoration are the same for both."[73]

The juvenile court legislation enabled the state to investigate and control a wide variety of behaviors. As Joel Handler has observed, "the critical philosophical position of the reform movement was that no formal, legal distinctions should be made between the delinquent and the dependent or neglected."[74] Statutory definitions of "delinquency" encompassed (1) acts that would be criminal if committed by adults; (2) acts that violated county, town, or municipal ordinances; and (3) violations of vaguely worded catch-alls—such as "vicious or immoral behavior," "incorrigibility," and "truancy"—which "seem to express the notion that the adolescent, if allowed to continue, will engage in more serious conduct."[75]

The juvenile court movement went far beyond a concern for special treatment of adolescent offenders. It brought within the ambit of government control a set of youthful activities that had been previously ignored or dealt with on an informal basis. It was not by accident that the behavior subject to penalties—drinking, sexual "license," roaming the streets, begging, frequenting dance halls and movies, fighting, and being seen in public late at night—was especially characteristic of the children of working-class and immigrant families. Once arrested and adjudicated, these "delinquents" became wards of the court and eligible for salvation.

It was through the reformatory system that the child-savers hoped to demonstrate that delinquents were capable of being converted into law-abiding citizens. Though the reformatory was initially developed in the United States during the middle of the nineteenth century as a special form of prison discipline for adolescents and young adults, its underlying principles were formulated in Britain by Matthew Davenport Hill, Alexander Maconochie, Walter Crofton and Mary Carpenter. If the United States did not have any great penal theorists, it at least had energetic administrators—like Enoch Wines, Zebulon Brockway and Frank Sanborn—who were prepared to experiment with new programs.

The reformatory was distinguished from the traditional penitentiary in several ways: it adopted a policy of indeterminate sentencing; it emphasized the importance of a countryside location; and it typically was organized on the "cottage" plan as opposed to the traditional congregate housing found in penitentiaries. The ultimate aim of the reformatory was reformation of the criminal, which could only be achieved "by placing the prisoner's fate, as far as possible, in his own hand, by enabling him, through industry and good conduct to raise himself, step by step, to a position of less restraint. . . ."[76]

Based on a crude theory of rewards and punishments, the "new penology" set itself the task of re-socializing the "dangerous classes." The typical resident of a reformatory, according to one child-saver, had been "cradled in infamy, imbibing with its earliest natural nourishment the germs of a depraved appetite, and reared in the midst of people whose lives are an atrocious crime against natural and divine law and the rights of society." In order to correct and reform such a person, the reformatory plan was designed to teach the value of adjustment, private enterprise, thrift and self-reliance. "To make a good boy out of this bundle of perversities, his entire being must be revolutionized. He must be taught self-control, industry, respect for himself and the rights of others."[77] The real test of reformation in a delinquent, as William Letchworth told the National Conference of Charities and Correction in 1886, was his uncomplaining adjustment to his former environment. "If he is truly reformed in the midst of adverse influences," said Letchworth, "he gains that moral strength which makes his reform permanent."[78] Moreover, reformed delinquents were given every opportunity to rise "far above the class from which they sprang," especially if they were "patient" and "self-denying."[79]

Reformation of delinquents was to be achieved in a number of different ways. The trend from congregate housing to group living represented a significant change in the organization of penal institutions. The "cottage" plan was designed to provide more intensive supervision and to reproduce, symbolically at least, an atmosphere of family life conducive to the resocialization of youth. The "new penology" also urged the benefits of a rural location, partly in order to teach agricultural skills, but mainly in order to guarantee a totally controlled environment. This was justified by appealing to the romantic theory that corrupt delinquents would be spiritually regenerated by their contact with unspoiled nature.[80]

Education was stressed as the main form of industrial and moral training in reformatories. According to Michael Katz, in his study on nineteenth-century education, the reformatory provided "the first form of compulsory schooling in the United States."[81] The prominence of education as a technique of reform reflected the widespread emphasis on socialization and assimilation instead of cruder methods of social control.

But as Georg Rusche and Otto Kirchheimer observed in their study of the relationship between economic and penal policies, the rise of "rehabilitative" and educational programs was "largely the result of opposition on the part of free workers," for "wherever working-class organizations were powerful enough to influence state politics, they succeeded in obtaining complete abolition of all forms of prison labor (Pennsylvania in 1897, for example), causing much suffering to the prisoners, or at least in obtaining very considerable limitations, such as work without modern machinery, conventional rather than modern types of prison industry, or work for the government instead of for the free market."[82]

Although the reformatory system, as envisioned by urban reformers, suffered in practice from overcrowding, mismanagement, inadequate financing and staff hiring problems, its basic ideology was still tough-minded and uncompromising. As the American Friends Service Committee noted, "if the reformers were naive, the managers of the correctional establishment were not. Under the leadership of Zebulon R. Brockway of the Elmira Reformatory, by the latter part of the nineteenth century they had co-opted the reformers and consolidated their leadership and control of indeterminate sentence reform."[83] The child-savers were not averse to using corporal punishment and other severe disciplinary measures when inmates were recalcitrant. Brockway, for example, regarded his task as "socialization of the anti-social by scientific training while under completest governmental control."[84] To achieve his goal, Brockway's reformatory became "like a garrison of a thousand prisoner soldiers" and "every incipient disintegration was promptly checked and disinclination of individual prisoners to conform was overcome."[85] Child-saving was a job for resolute professionals who realized that "sickly sentimentalism" had no place in their work.[86]

"Criminals shall either be cured," Brockway told the National Prison Congress in 1870, "or kept under such continued restraint as gives guarantee of safety from further depredations."[87] Restraint and discipline were an integral part of the "treatment" program and not merely expediencies of administration. Military drill, "training of the will," and long hours of tedious labor were the essence of the reformatory system and the indeterminate sentencing policy guaranteed its smooth operation. "Nothing can tend more certainly to secure the most hardened and desperate criminals than the present system of short sentences," wrote the reformer Bradford Kinney Peirce in 1869.[88] Several years later, Enoch Wines was able to report that "the sentences of young offenders are wisely regulated for their amendment; they are not absurdly shortened as if they signified only so much endurance of vindictive suffering."[89]

Since the child-savers professed to be seeking the "best interests" of their "wards" on the basis of corporate liberal values, there was no need to formulate legal regulation of the right and duty to "treat" in the same way that the right and duty to punish had been previously regulated. The adversary system, therefore, ceased to exist for youth, even as a legal fiction.[90] The myth of the child-saving movement as a humanitarian enterprise is based partly on a superficial interpretation of the child-savers' rhetoric of rehabilitation and partly on a misconception of how the child-savers viewed punishment. While it is true that the child-savers advocated minimal use of corporal punishment, considerable evidence suggests that this recommendation was based on managerial rather than moral consideration. William Letchworth reported that "corporal punishment is rarely inflicted" at the State Industrial School in Rochester because "most of the boys consider the lowering of their standing the severest punishment that is inflicted."[91] Mrs. Glendower Evans, commenting on the decline of whippings at a reform school in Massachusetts, concluded that "when boys do not feel themselves imprisoned and are treated as responsible moral agents, they can be trusted with their freedom to a surprising degree."[92] Officials at another state industrial school for girls also reported that "hysterics and fits of screaming and of noisy disobedience, have of late years become unknown. . . ."[93]

The decline in the use of corporal punishment was due to the fact that indeterminate sentencing, the "mark" or "stage" system of rewards and punishments, and other techniques of "organized persuasion" were far more effective in maintaining order and compliance than cruder methods of control. The chief virtue of the "stage" system, a graduated system of punishments and privileges, was its capacity to keep prisoners disciplined and submissive.[94] The child-savers had learned from industrialists that persuasive benevolence backed up by force was a far more effective device of social control than arbitrary displays of terrorism. Like an earlier generation of penal reformers in France and Italy, the child-savers stressed the efficacy of new and indirect forms of social control as a "practical measure of defense against social revolution as well as against individual acts."[95]

Although the child-saving movement had far-reaching consequences for the organization and administration of the juvenile justice system, its overall impact was conservative in both spirit and achievement. The child-savers' reforms were generally aimed at imposing sanctions on conduct unbecoming "youth" and disqualifying youth from the benefit of adult privileges. The child-savers were prohibitionists, in a general sense, who believed that social progress depended on efficient law enforcement, strict supervision of children's leisure and recreation, and enforced education. They were primarily concerned with regulating social behavior, eliminating "foreign" and radical ideologies, and preparing youth as a disciplined and devoted work force. The austerity of the criminal law and penal institutions was only of incidental concern; their central interest was in the normative outlook of youth and they were most successful in their efforts to extend governmental control over a whole range of youthful activities which had previously been handled locally and informally. In this sense, their reforms were aimed at defining, rationalizing and regulating the dependent status of youth.[96] Although the child-savers' attitudes to youth were often paternalistic and romantic, their commands were backed up by force and an abiding faith in the benevolence of government.

The child-saving movement had its most direct impact on the children of the urban poor. The fact that "troublesome" adolescents were depicted as "sick" or "pathological," imprisoned "for their own good," addressed in paternalistic vocabulary, and exempted from criminal law processes, did not alter the subjective experiences of control, restraint and punishment. It is ironic, as Philippe Ariès observed in his historical study of European family life, that the obsessive solicitude of family, church, moralists and administrators for child welfare served to deprive children of the freedoms which they had previously shared with adults and to deny their capacity for initiative, responsibility and autonomy.[97]

Notes

1. See, for example, The President's Commission on Law Enforcement and Administration of Justice, *Juvenile Delinquency and Youth Crime* (Washington, D.C.: U.S. Government Printing Office, 1967), pp. 2–4.

2. Charles L. Chute, "The Juvenile Court in Retrospect," 13 *Federal Probation* (September, 1949), p. 7; Harrison A. Dobbs, "In Defense of Juvenile Court," *Ibid.*, p. 29.

3. Charles L. Chute, "Fifty Years of the Juvenile Court," *National Probation and Parole Association Yearbook* (1949), p. 1.

4. George H. Mead, "The Psychology of Punitive Justice," 23 *American Journal of Sociology* (March, 1981), pp. 577–602; August Aichhorn, "The Juvenile Court: Is It a Solution?" in *Delinquency and Child Guidance: Selected Papers* (New York: International Universities Press, 1964), pp. 55–79.

5. Murray Levine and Adeline Levine, *A Social History of Helping Services: Clinic, Court, School, and Community* (New York: Appleton-Century-Crofts, 1970), p. 156.

6. Gerhard O. W. Mueller, *History of American Criminal Law Scholarship* (New York: Walter E. Meyer Research Institute of Law, 1962), p. 113.

7. See, for example, Herbert H. Lou, *Juvenile Courts in the United States* (Chapel Hill: University of North Carolina Press, 1927); Negley K. Teeters and John Otto Reinmann, *The Challenge of Delinquency* (New York: Prentice-Hall, 1950); and Ola Nyquist, *Juvenile Justice* (London: Macmillan, 1960).

8. Robert S. Pickett, *House of Refuge: Origins of Juvenile Reform in New York State, 1815–1857* (Syracuse: Syracuse University Press, 1969), p. 188.

9. See, for example, Arthur M. Schlesinger, Jr., *The*

American as Reformer (Cambridge: Harvard University Press, 1950).

10. See, for example, Richard Hofstadter, *The Age of Reform* (New York: Vintage Books, 1955), and Joseph R. Gusfield, *Symbolic Crusade: Status Politics and the American Temperance Movement* (Urbana: University of Illinois Press, 1963).

11. R. Jackson Wilson (Ed.), *Reform, Crisis, and Confusion, 1900–1929* (New York: Random House, 1970), especially pp. 3–6.

12. Arthur M. Schlesinger, Jr., *The Age of Jackson* (Boston: Little, Brown, 1946), p. 505.

13. Hofstadter, *op. cit.*, chapter IV.

14. The President's Commission on Law Enforcement and Administration of Justice, *op. cit.*, pp. 7, 8.

15. For discussions of earlier reform movements, see Pickett, *loc. cit.* and Sanford J. Fox, "Juvenile Justice Reform: An Historical Perspective," 22 *Stanford Law Review*, (June, 1970), pp. 1187–1239.

16. The child-saving movement was broad and diverse, including reformers interested in child welfare, education, reformatories, labor and other related issues. This paper is limited primarily to child-savers involved in anti-delinquency reforms and should not be interpreted as characterizing the child-saving movement in general.

17. William P. Letchworth, "Children of the State," *National Conference of Charities and Correction, Proceedings* (St. Paul, Minnesota, 1886), p. 138.

18. R. W. Hill, "The Children of Shinbone Alley," National Conference of Charities and Correction, *Proceedings* (Omaha, 1887), p. 231.

19. William Appleman Williams, *The Contours of American History* (Chicago: Quadrangle Books, 1966), especially pp. 345–412.

20. Pickett, *op. cit.*, pp. 50–55.

21. Committee on the History of Child-Saving Work, *History of Child-Saving in the United States* (National Conference of Charities and Correction, 1893), p. 5.

22. Charles Loring Brace, *The Dangerous Classes of New York and Twenty Years' Work Among Them* (New York: Wynkoop and Hallenbeck, 1880), pp. 282–83.

23. Committee on the History of Child-Saving Work, *op. cit.*, pp. 70–73.

24. *Ibid.*, pp. 80–81.

25. *Ibid.*, p. 270.

26. For more about these child-savers, see Anthony Platt, *The Child-Savers: The Invention of Delinquency*, (Chicago: University of Chicago Press, 1969), pp. 75–100.

27. Louise C. Wade, *Graham Taylor: Pioneer for Social Justice, 1851–1938* (Chicago: University of Chicago Press, 1964), p. 59.

28. G. William Domhoff, *The Higher Circles: The Governing Class in America* (New York: Random House, 1970), p. 48, and Platt, *op. cit.*, pp. 92–98.

29. "The transformation in penal systems cannot be explained only from changing needs of the war against crime, although this struggle does play a part. Every system of production tends to discover punishments which correspond to its productive relationships. It is thus necessary to investigate the origin and fate of penal systems, the use or avoidance of specific punishments, and the intensity of penal practices as they are determined by social forces, above all by economic and then fiscal forces." Georg Rusche and Otto Kirchheimer, *Punishment and Social Structure* (New York: Russell & Russell, 1968), p. 5.

30. See, for example, Gabriel Kolko, *The Triumph of Conservatism: A Reinterpretation of American History, 1900–1916* (Chicago: Quadrangle Books, 1967); James Weinstein, *The Corporate Ideal in the Liberal State, 1900–1918* (Boson: Beacon Press, 1969); Samuel Haber, *Efficiency and Uplift: Scientific Management in the Progressive Era, 1890–1920* (Chicago: University of Chicago Press, 1964); and Robert H. Wiebe, *Businessmen and Reform: A Study of the Progressive Movement* (Cambridge: Harvard University Press, 1962).

31. Weinstein, *op. cit.*, pp. ix, xi.

32. Jeremy P. Felt, *Hostages of Fortune: Child Labor Reform in New York State* (Syracuse: Syracuse University Press, 1965), p. 45.

33. Brace, *op. cit.*, p. 352.

34. David K. Cohen and Marvin Lazerson, "Education and the Corporate Order," 8 *Socialist Revolution*, (March–April, 1972), p. 50. See also Michael B. Katz, *The Irony of Early School Reform: Educational Innovation in Mid-Nineteenth Century Massachusetts*, (Cambridge: Harvard University Press, 1968), and Lawrence A. Cremin, *The Transformation of the School: Progressivism in American Education, 1876–1957* (New York: Vintage, 1961).

35. It should be emphasized that child-saving reforms were predominantly supported by more privileged sectors of the feminist movement, especially those who had an interest in developing professional careers in education, social work and probation. In recent years, radical feminists have emphasized that "we must include the oppression of children in any program for feminist revolution or we will be subject to the same failing of which we have so often accused men: of not having gone deep enough in our analysis, of having missed an important substratum of oppression merely because it didn't directly concern *us*." Shulamith Firestone, *The Dialectic of Sex: The Case for Feminist Revolution*, (New York: Bantam, 1971), p. 104.

36. Robert Sunley, "Early Nineteenth Century American Literature on Child-Rearing," in Margaret Mead and Martha Wolfenstein (Eds.), *Childhood in Contemporary Cultures* (Chicago: University of Chicago Press, 1955), p. 152; see, also, Orville G. Brim, *Education for Child-Reading* (New York: Free Press, 1965), pp. 321–49.

37. For an extended discussion of this issue, see Platt, *loc. cit.* and Christopher Lasch, *The New Radicalism in America, 1889–1963: The Intellectual as a Social Type* (New York: Alfred A. Knopf, 1965), pp. 3–68.

38. Talcott Parsons and Robert F. Bales, *Family, Socialization and Interaction Process* (Glencoe, Illinois: Free Press, 1955), pp. 3–33.

39. Clara T. Leonard, "Family Homes for Pauper and Dependent Children," Annual Conference of Charities, *Proceedings* (Chicago: 1879), p. 175.

40. W. P. Lynde, "Prevention in Some of Its Aspects," *Ibid.*, pp. 165–66.

41. Joseph R. Gusfield, *Symbolic Crusade, loc. cit.*

42. See, generally, Roy Lubove, *The Professional Altruist: The Emergence of Social Work as a Career, 1880–1930* (Cambridge: Harvard University Press, 1965).

43. Williams, *op. cit.*, p. 373 and Weinstein, *op. cit.*, p. 254.

44. Williams, *op. cit.*, pp. 374, 395–402.

45. Committee on the History of Child-Saving Work, *op. cit.*, p. 3.

46. See, generally, John Higham, *Strangers in the Land: Patterns of American Nativism, 1860–1925* (New York: Atheneum, 1965).

47. Brace, *op. cit.*, pp. 30, 49; Bradford Kinney Peirce, *A Half Century with Juvenile Delinquents* (Montclair, New Jersey: Patterson Smith, 1969, originally published 1869), p. 253.

48. Nathan Allen, "Prevention of Crime and Pauperism," Annual Conference of Charities, *Proceedings* (Cincinnati, 1878), pp. 111–24.

49. Jacob A. Riis, *How the Other Half Lives* (New York: Hill and Wang, 1957, originally published in 1890), p. 134.

50. Brace, *op. cit.*, pp. 27, 29.

51. See, for example, Lombroso's comments in the Introduction to Arthur MacDonald, *Criminology* (New York: Funk and Wagnalls, 1893).

52. Allen, *loc. cit.*

53. Hamilton D. Wey, "A Plea for Physical Training of Youthful Criminals," National Prison Association, *Proceedings* (Boston, 1888), pp. 181–93. For further discussion of this issue, see Platt, *op. cit.*, pp. 18–28 and Arthur E. Fink, *Causes of Crime: Biological Theories in the United States, 1800–1915* (New York: A. S. Barnes, 1962).

54. Richard L. Dugdale, *The Jukes: A Study in Crime, Pauperism, Disease, and Heredity* (New York: G. P. Putnam's Sons, 1877).

55. Sarah B. Cooper, "The Kindergarten as Child-Saving Work," National Conference of Charities and Correction, *Proceedings* (Madison, 1883), pp. 130–38.

56. I. N. Kerlin, "The Moral Imbecile," National Conference of Charities and Correction, *Proceedings* (Baltimore, 1890), pp. 244–50.

57. Williams, *op. cit.*, p. 354.

58. Fink, *op. cit.*, p. 247.

59. See, for example, Illinois Board of State Commissioners of Public Charities, *Second Biennial Report* (Springfield: State Journal Steam Print, 1873), pp. 195–96.

60. Peter Caldwell, "The Duty of the State to Delinquent Children," National Conference of Charities and Correction, *Proceedings* (New York, 1898), pp. 404–10.

61. E. R. L. Gould, "The Statistical Study of Hereditary Criminality," National Conference of Charities and Correction, *Proceedings* (New Haven, 1895), pp. 134–43.

62. Charles H. Cooley, " 'Nature' in the Making of Social Careers," National Conference of Charities and Correction, *Proceedings* (Grand Rapids, 1896), pp. 399–405.

63. Committee on the History of Child-Saving Work, *op. cit.*, p. 90.

64. Enoch C. Wines, *The State of Prisons and of Child-Saving Institutions in the Civilized World* (Cambridge: Harvard University Press, 1880).

65. Helen Page Bates, "Digest of Statutes Relating to Juvenile Courts and Probation Systems," 13 *Charities* (January, 1905), pp. 329–36.

66. Joel F. Handler, "The Juvenile Court and the Adversary System: Problems of Function and Form," 1965 *Wisconsin Law Review* (1965), pp. 7–51.

67. Gustav L. Schramm, "The Juvenile Court Idea," 13 *Federal Probation* (September, 1949), p. 21.

68. Monrad G. Paulsen, "Fairness to the Juvenile Offender," 41 *Minnesota Law Review* (1957), pp. 547–67.

69. Julian W. Mack, "The Chancery Procedure in the Juvenile Court," in Jane Addams (Ed.), *The Child, the Clinic and the Court* (New York: New Republic, 1925), p. 315.

70. Miriam Van Waters, "The Socialization of Juvenile Court Procedure," 21 *Journal of Criminal Law and Criminology* (1922), pp. 61, 69.

71. Harvey H. Baker, "Procedure of the Boston Juvenile Court," 23 *Survey* (February, 1910), p. 646.

72. Illinois Board of State Commissioners of Public Charities, *Sixth Biennial Report* (Springfield: H.W. Rokker, 1880), p. 104.

73. Frederick H. Wines, "Reformation as an End in Prison Discipline," National Conference of Charities and Correction, *Proceedings* (Buffalo, 1888), p. 198.

74. Joel F. Handler, *op. cit.*, p. 9.

75. Joel F. Handler and Margaret K. Rosenheim, "Privacy and Welfare: Public Assistance and Juvenile Justice," 31 *Law and Contemporary Problems* (1966), pp. 377–412.

76. From a report by Enoch Wines and Theodore Dwight to the New York legislature in 1867, quoted by Max Grünhut, *Penal Reform* (Oxford: Clarendon Press, 1948), p. 90.

77. Peter Caldwell, "The Reform School Problem," National Conference of Charities and Correction, *Proceedings* (St. Paul, 1886), pp. 71–76.

78. Letchworth, op. cit., p. 152.

79. Committee on the History of Child-Saving Work, *op. cit.*, p. 20.

80. See Platt, *op. cit.*, pp. 55–66.
81. Katz, *op. cit.*, p. 187.
82. Rusche and Kirchheimer, *op. cit.*, pp. 131–132.
83. American Friends Service Committee, *op. cit.*, p. 28.
84. Zebulon R. Brockway, *Fifty Years of Prison Service* (New York: Charities Publication Committee, 1912), p. 393.
85. *Ibid.*, pp. 310, 421.
86. *Ibid.*, pp. 389–408.
87. *Ibid.*
88. Peirce, *op. cit.*, p. 312.
89. Enoch Wines, *op. cit.*, p. 81.
90. On informal cooperation in the criminal courts, see Jerome H. Skolnick, "Social Control in the Adversary System," 11 *Journal of Conflict Resolution* (March, 1967), pp. 52–70.
91. Committee on the History of Child-Saving Work, *op. cit.*, p. 20.
92. *Ibid.*, p. 237.
93. *Ibid.*, p. 251.
94. Rusche and Kirchheimer, *op. cit.*, pp. 155–156.
95. *Ibid.*, p. 76. For a similar point, see American Friends Service Committee, *op. cit.*, p. 33.
96. See, generally, Frank Musgrove, *Youth and the Social Order* (London: Routledge and Kegan Paul, 1964).
97. Philippe Ariès, *Centuries of Childhood: A Social History of Family Life* (New York: Vintage Books, 1965).

QUESTIONS FOR DISCUSSION

1. According to the author, there are three "prevailing myths" about the juvenile justice system. List these myths and discuss how they developed.

2. In what ways did economics and social class dimensions affect the evolution of the child-saving movement?

3. One of the outcomes of the child-saving movement was the creation of the reformatory. What were the goals of the reformatory? By what specific means did the reformatory attempt to achieve these goals?

APPLICATIONS

1. The child-saving movement in America began in the nineteenth century and has continued, in some respects, to the present day. In contemporary America we speak of "at risk" children and adolescents when describing young people who for various reasons have an enhanced probability of being socially dysfunctional.
    a. How are at risk children similar and/or dissimilar to the children of the nineteenth century?
    b. Discuss several ways in which society has changed since the nineteenth century?
    c. What challenges and difficulties did you face as a child that were significantly different than those faced by children of the nineteenth century?

2. After reading this article, it should be clear that policies about the appropriate handling of children are influenced by several major social institutions in America.
    a. In your opinion, how do the following entities affect the way children are treated today?
        (1) politics
        (2) religion
        (3) schools
        (4) families

KEY TERMS

bureaucracy   typically a governmental group characterized by specialization of functions, adherence to fixed rules, and a hierarchy of authority.

constituency   a group or geographical area of people who are represented by an elected official.

humanistic   an attribute that stresses an individual's dignity, worth, and capacity for self-realization through the use of logic and reason.

laissez–faire a doctrine opposing governmental interference in economic affairs beyond the minimum necessary for the maintenance of peace and property rights.

liberalism a philosophy based on a belief in progress, the essential goodness of the human race, individual autonomy, and the protection of political and civil liberties.

nouveau riche a person with newly ascribed or achieved wealth.

parens patriae a judicial doctrine that allows the court, acting on behalf of the government, to intervene into family relations whenever a child's welfare is threatened.

philanthropic dispensing money or other resources as aid for humanitarian purposes. May include giving food, clothing, and other items to charitable organizations.

progressivism the belief in moderate political change and social improvement by governmental action.

rhetoric a speech or discourse. Often this word is used to indicate insincere or grandiloquent language.

social class a grouping of people based on one or more common characteristics. May include groupings by economic strength, social status, or political power.

3

Attitudes and Policies toward Juvenile Delinquency in the United States: A Historiographical Review

Robert M. Mennel

During the past decade, the history of juvenile delinquency has attracted considerable scholarly attention. This reflects both the recent popularity of social history and the desire of some historians to become involved in the policymaking process. Generally, interpretations have emphasized the social-control motives of the founders of institutions and the juvenile court while portraying the delinquents themselves as victims of social and economic discrimination. Recent research has neglected case studies and the comparative approach. Several recent works have uncovered some popular support for institutions and shown American policies, at least in the nineteenth century, to be less disadvantageous than European formulations. These studies have also stressed the significant differences between programs and institutions in the United States. Future research can profitably examine the post–World War II era, focusing particularly on the influence of legal changes, professional study, and government policy on programs and institutions. Scholars undertaking this work can make their contributions more useful by declining to view themselves as policymakers.

The American juvenile justice system remains a topic of national concern. Peter Prescott's *The Child Savers* (1981), a bleak portrait of

"Attitudes and Policies toward Delinquency in the United States," *Crime and Justice: An Annual Review of Research,* 4 (Chicago: University of Chicago Press 1982), pp. 191–224. Reprinted by permission of the publisher.

the New York City Family Court, is the latest in a long series of indictments. A representative sampling might include Howard James, *Children in Trouble* (1970), Albert Deutsch, *Our Rejected Children* (1952), Clifford Shaw, *The Jack-Roller* (1930), and John Peter Altgeld, *Our Penal Machinery and Its Victims* (1886) and perhaps might begin with Elijah Devoe's 1848 exposé of the New York House of Refuge. Prescott popularizes the principal policy implication of sociological labeling theory, that is, that the more fortunate youths were those who slipped off the official blotter and escaped future treatment. Traditionally, scholars and reformers who have condemned one approach have always had a new institution or mode of treatment on hand. Thus, critics of congregate reform schools promoted cottage and farm schools. Scientists distrustful of the determinism of Lombrosian criminology advocated psychological study. Even today, most of us resist the notion that little can be done or, even worse, that institutions and programs have been created in the knowledge that they will fail. We would rather think of juvenile delinquency as a symptom of larger disjunctions and inequalities in American life, of problems thus far unsolved but not insoluble.

This critical but hopeful spirit has animated the "new" social history that has been the vogue of the profession in the 1960s and

1970s. The fundamental premise, epitomized by Tamara K. Hareven, ed., *Anonymous Americans: Explorations in Nineteenth-Century Social History* (1971), was that historians had ignored "ordinary" people and vulnerable or disadvantaged groups such as women, children, and minorities. Traditional history was also indicted for minimizing ideological conflict in order to persuade readers of the benevolence and indispensability of existing institutions and power relationships. The novelty of this perspective has been questioned. More than fifty years ago, Charles and Mary Beard's *The Rise of American Civilization* exalted common people and castigated "robber barons," while Mary Beard's collection of documents, *America through Women's Eyes* (1933), helped inaugurate women's history. The Beards, however, were mavericks in a small, genteel profession, whereas contemporary social historians occupy dominant positions in a vastly larger and more complex enterprise. The difference is important and has implications for writing on the history of delinquency and correctional institutions.

The American Historical Association's recent survey of historical writing (Kammen 1980) reveals a specialized and increasingly compartmentalized discipline. One is amazed by the variety of research but sobered by the fact that a growing number of chronological and topical experts communicate more within subgroups than among them. In this context the history of crime and delinquency is but a chapter of social history. I prefer to think of it as a wave—a separate entity yet one that is inextricably connected to other topics such as the history of law, social welfare, education, and the family. Understanding of the origins of the concept of juvenile delinquency, for example, owes much to Bernard Bailyn's *Education in the Forming of American Society* (1960), which linked institutional development of all sorts to the effect of socioeconomic forces upon family government in the late eighteenth century. Thus, historians have been attracted to the topic of delinquency because of its interstitial qualities. As scholars, it challenges them to utilize a wide range of related historical work. As potential reformers, it offers a means of cooperation with presentist and

policy-oriented social scientists who share their view that history is a tool to promote change. An illustrative way to date the beginning of the current era may be to note the simultaneous appearance in 1960 of Cloward and Ohlin's *Delinquency and Opportunity* (1960), a cornerstone of the War on Poverty, and Griffen's *Their Brothers' Keepers: Moral Stewardship in the United States, 1800–1865* (1960), which stressed the social control motives of urban elites responsible for the first wave of asylums, prisons, and reform schools.

This essay examines historical works on juvenile delinquency and juvenile correctional institutions. Since the literature, with several notable exceptions, is not widely known, section I briefly notes the principal scholars and includes a paragraph about my own background. Section II identifies some general characteristics and conceptual problems of contemporary scholarship. For the rest of the essay, I have adopted an approach that is both chronological and analytical. Section III begins with a discussion of interpretations of the origins and treatment of juvenile delinquency in the nineteenth century. The advent of the juvenile court is a natural midpoint (section IV), and challenges to the benevolent purposes of the court in the 1960s and the concomitant deinstitutionalization movement form section V. In crossing this terrain, I hope to offer the reader a summary view of developments, indicate interpretive controversies, and also suggest opportunities and strategies for future research.

I. Scholarship

The most prominent American historian focusing upon juvenile delinquency is David Rothman, whose two volumes, *The Discovery of the Asylum* (1971) and *Conscience and Convenience* (1980), relate definitions and institutional expressions of criminal justice, juvenile justice, and mental health to the major changes in American society from the colonial era to the eve of World War II. My own work, *Thorns and Thistles: Juvenile Delinquents in the United States, 1825–1940* (Mennel 1973b), is narrower in scope but attempts a similar transit. Joseph Hawes,

Children in Urban Society: Juvenile Delinquency in Nineteenth Century America (1971), is yet more confined and episodic, though it does include a chapter on juvenile delinquency in children's literature.

Several studies develop their effect by utilizing the case study approach: Robert Pickett, *House of Refuge: Origins of Juvenile Reform in New York State, 1815–1854* (1969), is self-explanatory. Anthony Platt's *The Child Savers: The Invention of Delinquency* (1977a) studies child-saving philanthropy in late-nineteenth-century Chicago as a preface to an explanation of the beginning of the Illinois juvenile court, the first of its kind; Steven Schlossman, *Love and the American Delinquent: The Theory and Practice of "Progressive" Juvenile Justice, 1825–1920* (1977), follows a general analysis of doctrine with a detailed examination of the Wisconsin system and the early juvenile court in Milwaukee; Jack Holl, *Juvenile Reform in the Progressive Era: William R. George and the Junior Republic Movement* (1971), investigates an important private institution that attempted to reform children by requiring them to participate in a model "free enterprise" system. Miriam Langsam, *Children West: A History of the Placing Out System of the New York Children's Aid Society, 1853–1890* (1964), examines the leading example of anti-institutional reformism. Michael Gordon, *Juvenile Delinquency in the American Novel, 1905–1965* (1971), surveys a variety of scenarios.

Assessment of the juvenile court is an important aspect of the studies cited above and has attracted separate attention as well. Ellen Ryerson, *The Best Laid Plans: America's Juvenile Court Experiment* (1978), is a general study of reformer's attitudes, while Charles Larsen, *The Good Fight* (1972), recounts the life of Ben Lindsey, America's most famous juvenile court judge.

These represent only the major studies. Examples of related works include documentary collections (Abbott 1938; Bremner 1970–74; Sanders 1970), articles (Fox 1970; Mennel 1980a, 1980b; Parker 1976a, 1976b; Teeters 1960; Wohl 1969; Zuckerman 1976), dissertations (Brenzel 1978; Pisciotta 1979; Schupf 1971; Stack 1974; Stewart 1980; Wirkkala 1973); studies with major chapters

on delinquency (Katz 1968; Leiby 1967; Levine and Levine 1970); and the principal works of earlier generations (Beaumont and Tocqueville 1835; Brace 1872; Burleigh and Harris 1923; Folks 1902; Healy 1915; Hurley 1907; Reeves 1929; Shaw 1929; Snedden 1907; Thomas 1923; Thrasher 1927; Thurston 1942; Van Waters 1925; Wines and Dwight 1867, 1880).

My research interest developed from participation in the Child and State Project directed by Robert H. Bremner of Ohio State University. This work, funded by the federal government and administered by the American Public Health Association, took its name and inspiration from Grace Abbott's two-volume documentary history (1938) covering most aspects of child-state relations. The new volumes, *Children and Youth in America: A Documentary History* (Bremner 1970–74), represented a thorough restudy and expansion of the original. I edited the juvenile delinquency documents and in the process gathered material for my dissertation (Mennel 1969), which was expanded to *Thorns and Thistles* (Mennel 1973b).

II. Historiographical Issues

Michael Ignatieff's thoughtful article (1981) on the historiography of punishment raises basic issues that can help shape consideration of this topic as well. His dialectic begins with Whiggish accounts that portray the creation of systematic law codes and penitentiaries as the enlightened activity of altruistic citizens who eventually triumphed over the foul conditions and "barbaric" punishment characteristic of the medieval period and early modern age. The reformers' accomplishments were described as monuments to their benevolent intent and also harbingers of future and presumable equally reformative programs. In the 1960s, historians joined others in questioning the wisdom of some of these initiatives (psychosurgery and behavior modification, for example) and in reflecting doubts about "the size and intrusiveness of the modern state." Ignatieff notes, "The prison was thus studied not for itself, but for what its rituals of humiliation could reveal about a society's ruling conceptions of power, social obligation and human malleability" (Ignatieff 1981). Of late, however, "antirevisionists" or "counterrevisionists" have appeared on the scene to attack these accounts "for over-schematizing a complex story, and for reducing the intentions behind the new institution to conspiratorial class strategies of divide and rule." Counterrevisionism, charges Ignatieff, "abdicates from the task of historical explanation altogether," since it "merely maintains that historical reality is more complex than the revisionists assumed, that reformers were more humanitarian than revisionists made them out to be, and that there are no such things as classes." The task of future research thus becomes the development of a historiography "which accounts for institutional change without imputing conspiratorial rationality to a ruling class, without reducing institutional development to a formless *ad hoc* adjustment to contingent crisis, and without assuming a hyper-idealist, all triumphant humanitarian crusade."

Ignatieff's essay challenges revisionists including himself ("a former though unrepentant member of the revisionist school") to undertake their future research on the basis of a renewed appreciation for the volitional bases of human activity. Revisionists should question their faith that "the state enjoys a monopoly of the primitive sanction, that its moral authority and practical power are *the* binding sources of social order and that all social relations can be described in the language of power and domination." Ignatieff dismisses "counterrevisionists," generally identified as authors of case studies of French and English institutions, because they minimize the significance of the penitentiary by stressing local resistance to the rationalist ideas that produced it. Future history will be accomplished by revisionists who have seen the light.

The historiography of delinquency runs parallel to Ignatieff's account in some respects. There was a period when historians linked nineteenth-century institution founding and certainly the juvenile court to the march of American progress (Faulkner 1931; Tyler 1944). And certainly the predominant emphasis of 1960s scholarship reflected the egalitarian values and social anger of that era. The coerciveness of the elites who founded the institutions is stressed, and sympathy for the children designated delinquents is widespread. The titles of the monographs convey the message. Who "loves" a delinquent? No one. What happens to the "best laid plans"? They go astray, of course. What did the "child savers" do? They "invented" a pathology. Also like Ignatieff's scholars, historians of juvenile delinquency seldom venture beyond 1940. Whether this stems from the general tendency of the discipline to relegate the recent past to journalism or from the proliferation and complexity of government programs and professional study is impossible to say. The paucity of work is clear, however, and makes a trenchant analysis such as John Moore's article (1969) on early federal policy all the more valuable.

There have also been substantial disagreements between scholars of delinquency. Rothman's review (1974) of my book and Platt's review (1977b) of Schlossman's illustrate the sharp tone of the debate. Scholarly dialogue has been limited. My study commends certain approaches, particularly the environmentalism of the early children's aid societies and the Chicago sociologists of the 1920s. "Tony" Platt, editor of *Crime and Social Justice*, regards variations between programs expressing the nature or the nurture philosophy as less significant than the controlling inequalities of capitalist society. These are differences between a moderate and a radical, but Platt probably views the gap as unbridgeable.

Platt, Rothman, and others have acted upon their convictions and become involved in preventive work. David and Sheila Rothman, for example, are codirectors of the Project on Community Alternatives for the mentally disabled. These are commendable efforts. But in the dominant ahistoricism of contemporary life, the historian/policymaker faces a dilemma beyond the bureaucratic frustrations and resource problems common to most social programs. To illustrate: Prescott's study (1981) bears the same title as Platt's, originally published in 1969 and revised in 1977. This shows bad manners but is not surprising. The modern world has little time for historians. The point here is that historians can make their most useful contribution by writing better history. How then should this be done?

In contrast to Ignatieff, I suggest that the demanding task is to "merely maintain" the complexity of historical reality. To do so, the historian must be primarily concerned with shaping the data of the past into a plausible representation of reality. The important skills are preciseness in describing events, sensitivity to distinctions, fairness in appraising individuals and groups, and enthusiasm in collecting and relating material. These count more than assertiveness or conviction in propounding a particular view. Such an approach does not require, in the case at hand, the conclusion that reformers were humanitarian or that social classes were illusory. Nor does it pretend to objectivity in the manner of Leopold von Ranke and the German school of the late nineteenth century. We are the products of our own age and will surely reflect it in our writing. But we must protest this fact. For, just as Horace Mann proclaimed himself the lawyer of the next generation, so historians are or should be the lawyers for generations gone by. Theory can be helpful in addressing this work, but it must always be ready to yield to the experiences of people who are now dead.

From this perspective there are two major shortcomings that characterize the historical literature on juvenile delinquency: (1) the failure to utilize the comparative approach, (2) the shortage of comprehensive case studies linking institutions and programs to the society that produced and sustained them. The reasons for these deficiencies are not hard to find. The language skills of American historians, never great, have followed the general downward trend of recent years. Even studies of European subjects written in English are ignored. Although there have been several case studies, they are vulnerable to the objection that they are unrepresentative. For the incipient policymaker, generalizations on the national level are important. Consequently, the preferred method is to gather a few facts and opinions on many programs rather than to accept the inherent contingency of the case study in exchange for the possible reward of an understanding that is both concrete and illustrative.

III. The Nineteenth Century

Let us start by summarizing the inception of efforts to define and treat juvenile delinquency. The term itself was almost never used before 1800 because public authorities relied upon family government to correct or at least contain children who misbehaved or committed crimes. Early law codes and commentaries, such as Blackstone's, recognized mitigating circumstances for accused children, but the purpose of these statutes was not to exonerate or to categorize youthful wrongdoing but to sustain the family-based system of discipline. Colonial laws commanded parents to punish their children so that court officials would not have to intervene. By the late eighteenth century, however, the ability of family government to serve as the keystone of social control came to be doubted as villages developed into commercial towns and cities and as work left the home for the shop and factory. Families could no longer absorb vagrant youths as servants and apprentices. The children of poorer families left home, or were cast loose, to seek their way as deprived individuals. They became the source material for new definitions of crime, poverty, and juvenile delinquency.

The initial definers were established male citizens of the major East Coast cities, New York, Philadelphia, and Boston. Their sense of duty as well as their fear of impoverished, unfamiliar faces and anonymously committed crime led them to create a variety of institutions—almshouses, insane asylums, penitentiaries. They hoped these would not only isolate troublesome and indigent individuals but also provide them with the habits necessary to function as law-abiding individuals in a volatile capitalistic society.

Neglected and delinquent children were the objects of special attention because their behavior was more likely to be viewed as the product of environmental stimuli than as a sign of innate depravity. The basic fear was that children who were convicted of crimes suffered corruption by mixing with adult criminals, as did children who were released by sympathetic judges and juries. Thus, special institutions for children proliferated. These were first called houses of refuge, then reform schools, to indicate emphasis upon the growing enthusiasm for common schooling in the mid-nineteenth century. As this occurred, the concept of juvenile delinquency was born and began to come of age. Beyond describing the criminal and vagrant status of certain children, it announced the institutions that would correct, educate, and socialize apart from the ministrations of family government.

A word about the institutions themselves. The houses of refuge and many of the early reform schools were organized on a congregate basis; that is, the children lived in cells or large dormitories and followed rigid schedules based upon contract labor in central workshops. Surrounded by high walls and characterized by harsh discipline, the refuges resembled the adult penitentiaries of the day. After lengthy incarcerations, the children were considered trained "for usefulness" and were released or apprenticed, the boys to local artisans and farmers, the girls to domestic service. The proliferation of these institutions in the mid-nineteenth century was marked. In 1867, Wines and Dwight noted seven state reform schools outside of New York and local refuges and reform schools in nine eastern and midwestern cities. By 1900 all states and major cities outside the Deep South had boys' reform schools and, in most cases, separate institutions for girls as well.

By this time an alternative strategy for preventing delinquency had developed. Epitomized by the work of Charles Loring Brace and his New York Children's Aid Society (1853), this approach emphasized noninstitutional solutions such as placing out. Brace agreed with reform-school founders that the temptations of the volatile urban environment were the basis for delinquency, but, unlike them, he believed that children were born with a disposition to do good and hence did not require lengthy incarceration. "The best of all asylums for the outcast child is the *farmer's home*," said Brace, and until the agrarian depression of the late 1880s he sent railroad cars full of "street arabs" to the western states.

Brace's ideas found institutional expression with the opening of the Massachusetts Industrial School for Girls (1856) and the Ohio Reform Farm (1857). The cottage or family plan reformatory, with its agrarian location and routine and its "elder brothers," "elder sisters," or surrogate parents supervising youths divided into "families," became the dominant type of reform school in the late nineteenth century. The family organization maintained its popularity even when vocational programs shifted from farm chores to industrial training in the twentieth century.

The end result was hardly a smooth-running system. Institutionalists and advocates of placing out bickered constantly. Nativist Protestants expressed their preferences, thus hastening the development of Roman Catholic institutions. Delinquent girls did institutional housework and often were sexually abused when placed out. Negro children were initially more fortunate, since few institutions accepted them. Once admitted, they were usually segregated. By the Civil War, several institutions had experienced rioting and incendiarism, which usually began in the workshops where contract labor encouraged exploitation.

But it was a legitimized system. Institution founders and public authorities successfully defended themselves against the claims of parents who regarded reform schools and children's aid societies as usurpers of family government. In the precedent-setting decision *Ex Parte Crouse* (4 Wharton 9, Pennsylvania [1838]), the Pennsylvania Supreme Court denied the attempt of a father to free his daughter on a writ of habeas corpus from the Philadelphia House of Refuge saying, "The right of parental control is a natural, but not an inalienable one. . . . The infant has been snatched from a course which must have ended in confirmed depravity; and, not only is the restraint of her person lawful, but it would be an act of extreme cruelty to release her from it."

Historians' accounts of these developments are deficient in several respects. They gloss over the colonial era, describing the rudimentary state of institutions but relating this mainly to the still-powerful Calvinist ideology that resisted the concept of malleable human nature. They utilize the comparative method, but only to indicate the presence of seemingly similar reform activity in Europe; American institutions are usually presented as indigenous responses to the physical and social mobility of the Jacksonian era.[1] Also, scholars tend to rely upon the social control desires of elites as a sufficient causal explanation, and this blurs the variety of the institutional impulse. Of course these generalizations cannot be uniformly applied. Rothman (1971) and Mennel (1973b), for example, treat the colonial period, but in summary form. Neither gives concrete illustrations of shifting patterns of crime and family life that might have set the stage for institution building. Schlossman (1974, 1977) relates reform schools to emerging instrumentalist definitions of education, law, and even polite advice literature. The general criticisms hold, however, and can be best demonstrated by referring to a variety of studies and sources in addition to the principal monographs.

The colonial period is thinly treated because family history has become, in good measure, the property of colonial scholars, hence "warning out" modernists. Lawrence Stone's recent survey (1981) shows the increasing complexity of the subject and the intensity of its application in the pre-1800 era. He summarizes that, while the family was a key mediator in the change from traditional to modern society, it displayed a variety of types, by class, region, and religious affiliation, substantially limiting efforts to reach general conclusions. The difficulty peculiar to the study of delinquency is that the literary evidence is heavily weighted toward memoirs of genteel family life, thus favoring the definers of social problems and founders of institutions and relegating the inarticulate—that is, the clients and inmates—to demographic accounts.

This barrier may be more apparent than real. A number of studies (Ariès 1965; Bremner 1970–74; Jones 1938; Laslett 1965;

Pinchbeck and Hewitt 1969–73) have confirmed important trends such as the decline of household-based apprenticeship and the proportionately increasing number of unattached young wage laborers living in cities, all of which precipitated planning for schools, missions, and houses of refuge. Moreover, the accounts of the elite bear closer reading, since they link the anxieties of affluent parents about their own children to their fears about the children of the poor. Allan Horlick (1975) has used such materials to show how New York businessmen of the 1840s, reflecting both the uncertainties of their own climb to power and the difficulty of limiting the aristocracy of the next generation to young men who endorsed charitable activity, created remedies and screening groups in the form of moralistic literature and the YMCA. The memoirs of the men who founded the first houses of refuge demonstrate that they conceived of the institutions as serving not only the court system but also a broad range of families who requested or were offered their assistance as patriarchs and neighbors (Pickett 1969; Mennel 1980a). The refuge founders placed substantial authority in the hands of the superintendents, whose conduct they expected would further exemplify their ideal of a society cemented by patriarchal families. The neighborhood orientation and local scope of the institutions (only New York and Philadelphia had refuges), as well as their quasi-public organization (state chartered but privately managed and funded by combinations of donations and public revenues), suggest a limited comparison with English institutions such as the Philanthropic Society's reformatory (1788) in London (Carlebach 1970; Heale 1976; Owen 1964; Pinchbeck and Hewitt 1969–73). The Anglo-American connection, as illuminated by family history, provides an additional way to demarcate the first years of definition and treatment.

In the later nineteenth century, the increasing number and variety of institutions made more apparent, though it did not originate, philosophical differences on the nature and requirements of childhood. Even the management of the refuges alternated between proponents of Benthamite rationalism, who drew their inspiration from the disciplinary routines of the penitentiaries, and advocates of the Swiss pedagogue Johann Pestalozzi, who believed that children were unique individuals who became socialized by appeals to their inherently good sentiments and thoughts (Lewis 1965; Mennel 1973b; Pickett 1969; Schlossman 1977; Slater 1970). The rationalists prevailed in the refuges, but the romantic ideal, fueled by religious evangelicalism, reappeared in the family reform schools and childrens' aid societies and also animated other reform activity such as the urban missions (Banner 1973; Langsam 1964; Rosenberg 1971; Smith 1957; Sutherland 1976; Wohl 1969).

The differences between silent obedience and emotional allegiance to adult values may appear moot to some contemporary observers, but they mattered greatly to nineteenth-century people and thus appeared in related facets of American life. The trend toward instrumentalism in law, for example, reflected the rationalist faith that human conduct could be improved by public policy (Horwitz 1971; Schlossman 1974). The growing genre of children's literature increasingly portrayed the young as disposed toward the path of virtue and receptive to confirmation through adult kindness and personal attention (Kiefer 1948; Wishy 1968). Education, like juvenile reform, stood at the crossroads. Many urban schools, with their hierarchical monitorial systems and emphasis upon rote learning and compulsory attendance, displayed the social control philosophy (Kaestle 1973; Kaestle and Vinovskis 1980; Katz 1968; Lazerson 1971). But in other schools the influence of Horace Mann's ideas liberated students and teachers alike from the narrow curriculum and harsh discipline of the colonial past, and they responded eagerly to the possibilities of learning (Cremin 1961; Messerli 1973). Reform school founders conceived of their institutions as midpoints between the common school and the penitentiary. They rejected serious offenders and utilized both rationalist and romantic approaches in their attempt to change young people (Fox 1970; Mennel 1973b).

The significance of early reform schools is best revealed in a comparative setting.

Pedagogues such as Horace Mann and Henry Barnard publicized the development of European institutions, giving special prominence to two family schools: Johann H. Wichern's Rauhe Haus, founded in Hamburg in 1833, and Frederic A. DeMetz's "La Colonie Agricole" in Mettray, France (1839). American institution founders visited to study their agricultural routines and the cottage organization where "elder brothers" utilized various combinations of merit badges, military drill, singing, and close personal supervision to seek the allegiance of the *colóns* to the values of their keepers. The transfer of techniques is interesting, but the comparative approach is most informative in noting differences and omissions. In the 1850s, for example, western states often ignored European innovations and copied the congregate institutions of the East, while even those who undertook pilgrimages to Mettray or Hamburg did so with only hazy knowledge of Mann's or Barnard's work (Foucault 1978; May 1973; Mennel 1980a, 1980b; Thavenet 1976).[2]

I used the comparative perspective in a case study of the Ohio Reform School for Boys (1857), one of the first cottage and farm institutions. The "Farm" was organized with reference to Mettray and other European schools, but differed from them in operation and reformatory goals. In Ohio, literacy and individual attainment were encouraged; nearly all of the entering boys could read, and half could write and cipher. Most could do all three upon release. They also had the opportunity to participate in dramatics and both solo and group singing. Education at Mettray was limited to thirty minutes a day and spent mostly on reading the catechism. Dramatics were not performed, and the boys were allowed to sing only as a group. Released *colóns* were often illiterate or could only read. Former Mettray inmates were carefully placed, usually in the army or in menial farm labor with families other than their own. They were then kept in these positions by the supervision of local notables or the military. Ohio boys were usually released to the care of parents or friends or left to their own devices; farm labor apprenticeships were regarded as confining. The parents of

American delinquents were treated permissively in another respect. Local committing jurisdictions did not pursue them to pay individual maintenance costs despite administrative and legislative injunctions to do so. European, especially English, institutions forced parents to contribute to institutional income (Carlebach 1970; Mennel 1980a, 1980b; Pinchbeck and Hewitt 1969–73).

Institutional hierarchies and sociopolitical allegiances also present striking contrasts. At Mettray, all officers were trained, with a classical education, at the institution's Ecole Préparatoire. *Colóns* could serve as monitors *(frères âinés)* but could not aspire to higher positions. Ohio "elder brothers" were not required to have special training. Inmates could and did achieve these positions, and a few even became superintendents of other institutions. The chief obstacle to such advances was the disposition of superintendents and trustees to hire their own friends and relatives. European institutions underwrote hereditary power and privilege. Wichern consistently supported the German monarchy, while DeMetz demonstrated his loyalty by sending a contingent of *colóns* to help the national guard crush the republican forces in the revolution of 1848. On the other hand, boys and officers from the Ohio Reform Farm joined the Union army in large numbers, in part because they opposed slave-owning (Mennel 1980a, 1980b; Muller 1976; Shanahan 1954).

The comparative method helps to show some of the salient characteristics of American institutions. Americans took selective readings of European schools, purposefully or unintentionally ignoring their hierarchical characteristics and lauding their agricultural routine and small-group organization. But this is what one should expect from a country where social relations were dynamic, where urbanism was a growing but disagreeable trend, and where racism and nativism coexisted with dedication to the ideal of equal opportunity.

The further significance of American reform schools is that they were broadly publicized and, at least at first, popularly supported. Ohio Farm annual reports were printed in German and English and summa-

rized in local newspapers. Didactic children's literature and journals of education spoke well of the institutions but also used them to caution their juvenile audience. There was only minor political opposition to the founding of the schools; in the sea of turmoil that was Ohio politics in the 1850s, the reform school was an island of consensus. During the first two decades of operation there was a waiting list, and large numbers of parents and guardians committed their own children. Boys who were released, and even some who escaped, wrote letters on their own volition praising the institutions. Discharge papers were valued because they "proved character." In the early 1870s there was even an alumni association that returned for an annual picnic (Mennel 1980a, 1980b).

What this suggests is not that reform schools were idyllic retreats, but that they may have met the needs of a variety of people, not all of whom were founders of institutions. Other scholars have contended the same thing about the juvenile court, and John Hagan has noted that truly unpopular social control movements, such as Prohibition, are repealed (Hagan 1980; Schlossman 1977; Schultz 1973). Paul Boyer's recent study (1978) has urged us to be sensitive to nineteenth-century reformers who sought to defuse broad-based fears of disorder that gained their lethal force from combining with equally popular suspicion of institutional solutions. The reform school's opponents were not academicians but country people ("Jacksonians") who regarded them as "soft" boarding schools. Labor groups complained about the contract system, while agricultural organizations such as the Patrons of Husbandry refused to cooperate with the farm reform schools because they were afraid that the status of farming would be degraded (Mennel 1980a, 1980b; Pickett 1969).

Eventually, of course, the institutions lost whatever value they had as redemptive agencies. The reasons are various. Gradual though grudging popular acceptance of industrialization secured the workshop as an organizational form and limited the development of farm schools. Workshops had been sore points from the beginning, especially when outside contractors were used. But even though the institution staff ran the shops by the 1880s, the rate of work-related death and injury continued to increase, and most fires were set there (Mennel 1973b; Pickett 1969; Rothman 1971). Thomas Bender has related the changing character of charity societies to the passing of the generation of founders who had daily contact with the presumed objects of their beneficence. Their successors, perhaps because they tended to accept more easily the prevalent social divisions, relied upon paid subordinates to organize the daily work (Bender 1975). The same trend was evident in reform schools, where the demands for routinized operation were even greater. Superintendents and staff increasingly functioned as buffers, which meant keeping the children in, since the outside world no longer viewed the institutions as novelties (National Conference of Charities and Correction 1893). Serious politicians and distinguished foreign visitors like Alexis de Tocqueville and Charles Dickens no longer came to call. However, the schools did serve occasionally as party spots for sporting trustees and state legislators. Reform school officials, emulating their superiors, began to insulate themselves from their inmates. Attendance at summer schools and charity conferences came to count more for advancement than time spent with the children. The Ohio superintendent visited the Rauhe Haus and proclaimed his allegiance to its warm personal style and humble cottages. To implement this ideal, he requested an appropriation to build large Gothic residence halls and an administration building, thus permitting the demolition of the original farm cottages.[3]

Conflict continued, but the institutions endured. And why not? Their rise had occurred in a society where economic and social change had rendered ambiguous the scope and authority of existing institutions, particularly the patriarchal family. In their early careers, the schools had accomplishments to be proud of, and even in decline they served as conveniences that society was unwilling to abandon. But they were blatant advertisements for social control, inappropriate for a society that increasingly valued elaborate though unspecific warnings, particularly to the young. Thus the opposition that began to form came less from the inmates and their parents than from the young middle-class men and women who promoted a more decentralized system, one that promised broader though less intense surveillance as well as the opportunity to apply social and psychological therapies. This interpretation has stressed popular acceptance of the institutions and of gradual efforts to change them and suggests that recent studies have overemphasized the power and coerciveness of those who founded and managed the schools.

Before discussing the juvenile court and its influence, special mention should be made of two research areas: local studies on crime, order, and police and works on female delinquency. Recent crime and police studies have excelled in analyzing the ecology and etiology of lawbreaking and disorder (Johnson 1973, 1979; Lane 1967; Laurie 1973; Monkkonen 1975; Richardson 1970; Schneider 1980). Boys and young men appear here as gang members and fire laddies, some of whom were surely sent to institutions. But examination of reform school records reveals that only a minority of inmates arrived via local criminal courts. County common pleas and probate courts were more likely venues, and disputes within families were often precipitating factors (Mennel 1980b). Local court studies could clarify the extent to which courts and institutions served families seeking to commit their children or citizens fearing crime and disorder. The implication is that gangs, particularly when they were affiliated with local political organizations, may have been able to protect their members from classification as delinquents, while young people who conflicted with their parents and had no peer groups to support them were prime candidates for reform school.

The relative scarcity of recent studies on the history of female delinquency (Manton 1976; Brenzel 1975, 1978; Schlossman and Wallach 1978) may be explained in part by the challenges they pose on perplexing and controversial issues in the writing of women's history. On the one hand, to the degree that institutions confined women and girls on morals charges, they require censure, since these were unpunished male offenses. But criticism must be tempered for several reasons. First, as Barbara Brenzel has shown (1978, 1980), the schools did provide a degree of care and protection for homeless and abused girls. Second, and more important, women administrators took charge of female institutions in the late nineteenth century, which may be interpreted as a sign of progress in the narrative of women's history.

A complicating factor, raised though certainly not encompassed by female reform schools, is the meaning of sexual behavior. Homosexuality and lesbianism were regular features of life in juvenile institutions. After 1900, a few adult female reformatories had permissive attitudes toward lesbian relationships (Freedman 1981). In general, however, extraordinary efforts were made to suppress sexual activity, of which there was plenty. The matron at the Western House of Refuge (New York) complained that she could not prevent black and white girls from "[getting] together in bed." An 1891 investigation of the Ohio Reform School discovered many boys with venereal sores on the mouth and noted the superintendent's practice of personally applying a blistering fluid to the sexual organs of boys who were caught masturbating (Mennel 1973b, 1980b). Historians might profitably relate adult attitudes to the imperatives of the economy, which condoned gluttony and overdressing while frowning upon sex and desire. The trick is to convey the ways contemporary mores encouraged as well as dampened libidinal drives and to do so without succumbing to the vogue of intimate self-revelation and imposing one's own preferences upon the reader.

IV. The Juvenile Court

The first juvenile court opened in Illinois in 1899, and the idea spread rapidly to other states; by 1912 twenty-two states had passed juvenile court legislation, and all but two had done so by 1932. In one sense the court represented the culmination of efforts to reform children without committing them to reform school or sending them to jail. The Illinois law combined the concept of probation, first developed in Massachusetts (1869), where children's aid societies supervised children who were awaiting trial or who had been sentenced, with several New York laws providing for separate trial sessions and detention facilities. As courts developed their own probation staffs, detention homes, and investigative services, the reform schools were relegated to places of "dernier resort," in the words of one superintendent (Mennel 1972).

The juvenile court was more than a systematic alternative to incarceration, however; Jane Addams claimed that it signified "almost a change in mores." She referred not only to the legal innovations but also to the fact that the court's leverage—that is, its administrative power to gather case histories and its generally urban location—made it a key weapon in the Progressive campaign to get government to assume a greater responsibility for social welfare (Flexner and Baldwin 1912; Lou 1927). The social and psychological facts about the children appearing before the court offered the most compelling evidence for the adoption of child labor laws, mothers' pensions, municipal playgrounds, compulsory school attendance, public health care for children, and rigorous regulation of tenement-building. Thus the popularity of the juvenile court derived in some measure from the fact that it served as a laboratory for the professional study of delinquency. Theoretical works based on empirical research flourished, with the ecological approach of the University of Chicago sociologists and the psychological studies of William Healy becoming ancestors of the type. In the daily operation of the court, this trend was manifested in the eclipse of voluntary probation officers by civil service professionals trained in the "art" of gathering desired information and supervising a client population (Levine and Levine 1970; Lubove 1965; Mennel 1973b).

An important result of this activity was to rescue the *parens patriae* doctrine from the reform schools, where its credibility was being seriously undermined. By expressing a preference for diagnosis and probation, the court implicitly downgraded incarceration, yet retained it as a judicial option. Court decisions soon ratified the new arrangement.

Commonwealth v. Fisher (213 Pennsylvania 48 [1905]), a decision upholding the parental character of the Pennsylvania juvenile court, became the most often cited precedent, concluding, "the legislature surely may provide for the salvation of . . . a child, if its parents or guardians be unable or unwilling to do so, by bringing it into one of the courts of the state without any process at all, for the purpose of subjecting it to the state's guardianship and protection."

The court did not lack criticism even in its early days (Eliot 1914). This stemmed mostly from its imprecise, encompassing jurisdiction, a situation that was addressed by the development of family and domestic relations courts. Occasional studies such as Sheldon and Eleanor Glueck's *One Thousand Delinquents* (1934) faulted the effectiveness of the court and its agencies but did not question the institution's benevolent intent. After World War II, however, a number of investigations accused local and state governments of not providing entitled services to wards of the court. In time, legal decisions ratified this disillusion by according children who appeared in court most of the rights of adults accused of crimes (Bremner 1970–74; Mennel 1973b).

Research on the modern era is complicated by a new obstacle but characterized by traditional defects. Confidentiality of records poses the additional problem. Archivists and institution officials are understandably edgy about providing access to the records of living persons. Of course they must also take into account the possibility of objections from descendants of nineteenth-century delinquents. In either case, the scholar's promise to use pseudonyms or initials can sometimes allay official doubts. As noted earlier, however, the importance of the issue is deflated because few historians are interested in the case study approach, which makes the heaviest demands upon archival holdings where confidentiality is likely to be a consideration. Rather, they are content to sample published works from a variety of locations and generalize therefrom. These points can be illustrated by referring to the literature.

We begin with the exception that proves the case. Stephen Schlossman's *Love and the American Delinquent* (1977) is the most useful study because of its case study orientation. Schlossman uses court and institution records to systematically link the failures of the Wisconsin reform school to the later flounderings of the Milwaukee Juvenile Court and to put both into the context of the larger reform movements of their times. Thus the cottage school was connected to the domestic advice literature of Lydia Maria Child and Catharine Beecher, which sanctified the family as a refuge against social and economic disorder. And the juvenile court, like the playground movement, mothers' pensions, and home economics programs, reflected the greater optimism of the Progressive era. All of the latter were designed to strengthen and discipline the families of the poor with minimal reference to institutional sanctions. Yet, as Schlossman notes, the court no less than the institution set aside "affectional discipline" in favor of a more expeditious approach. The detention center became a jail, and judges browbeat children and punished them for offenses unrelated to those that brought them into court. Reformatory and court authorities showed little interest in establishing personal relationships with the children but eagerly counted as successes those who dropped out of sight. These officials, Schlossman emphasizes, were not members of a status-conscious local elite but rather shared the disadvantaged origins of their clients (Schlossman 1977).

The only incongruous note is Schlossman's conclusion that a child-centered approach, epitomized to him by Ben Lindsey's Denver Juvenile Court, is possible. Schlossman's evidence, however, sketches fundamentally shallow and manipulative adult personalities clearly incapable of effecting such a transformation. The contradiction may not be that serious. Lindsey was a master of public relations, as much absorbed in the creation of his own image as a crusader as in spending time talking to children. Like "Daddy" George, founder of the George Junior Republic ("nothing without labor"), he gave affection to people of all ages in the course of a life filled with many interests. What set Lindsey apart was his insatiable curiosity and encompassing humanity, rare traits in any field of endeavor. But he did share some of the less attractive characteristics of Schlossman's little-known court authorities (Holl 1971; Larsen 1972; Mennel 1973b).

Like Schlossman, David Rothman is concerned with the rift between humanitarian rhetoric and neglectful practice. He utilizes conscience and convenience to describe the division in order to emphasize the pridefulness of early twentieth century reformers, particularly their faith that the new social and behavioral sciences would provide a theory of treatment based upon "individual justice." Convenience signifies the ease with which political and bureaucratic interests frustrated these ideals. Rothman shares with Schlossman (and with the reform school and juvenile court founders themselves) a belief that the downward direction of historical change is not inevitable, though neither is specific about desirable therapies or about strategies for institutionalizing them. Ryerson, reflecting the more limited view of the juvenile court implicit in the *Gault* decision (*In Re Gault*, 387 U.S. 1[1967]), is more cautious but, like Rothman and Schlossman, believes that somewhere in the vast array of delinquency prevention programs is one that not only works but can be generally applied (Rothman 1980; Ryerson 1978; Schlossman 1977).

This faith is commendable in that it encourages at least the mention of various programs extant in given periods. It resists the determinism characteristic of other accounts such as Anthony Platt's *The Child Savers* (1977a) and Christopher Lasch's *Haven in a Heartless World* (1977). Platt's analysis of child-saving philanthropy in late nineteenth century Illinois caricatures the role of middle-class women from Hull House who helped to create the first juvenile court, presenting them as agents of corporate capitalism primarily intent on diminishing the civil liberties and privacy of lower-class and immigrant youth. Lasch portrays social workers and psychologists as absorbed in creating therapeutic jargon in order to secure themselves as professional groups by making their audiences expert-dependent. Both of these works deny altruism as a cause of welfare activity. Lasch's, however, is more interesting, since it documents a strain of intolerance among professional groups advocating egalitarian social policies (Lasch 1973, 1977). De Tocqueville first made this connection after observing Jacksonian democracy. Lasch is intrigued by the hostility of most social scientists to the suggestion that their work, even when publicly supported, may contribute little to the diminution of crime, delinquency, and mental illness.[4]

Rothman's work deserves separate treatment here since it is the best known. *Conscience and Convenience* has a moderate appearance, being neither as harshly skeptical as Lasch and Platt nor as partial to early social workers and juvenile court proponents as a number of studies (Chambers 1963, 1971; Davis 1967; Leiby 1967; Trattner 1968). But Rothman is unpersuasive, at least insofar as his treatment of delinquency is concerned, because he does not utilize the relevant work of other scholars or respect the complexity of his subjects' thoughts and actions.[5] For example, Rothman presents the psychologist G. Stanley Hall as a key influence in the development of the juvenile court because of his supposed enthusiasm for individual case study and environmental causation. But a reading of Dorothy Ross's excellent though difficult study (1972) shows Hall's greatest interest to be the development of a neo-Darwinist philosophy of human development in which youthful misbehavior was a "stage" that could be little influenced by institutions. And Miriam Van Waters, the foremost figure in female corrections from 1920 to 1950, walked out of Hall's seminar after disputing his contention that a prostitute was a "type" (Mennel 1973b).

Rothman's discussion of Dr. William Healy, founder of the first mental hygiene clinic for juvenile court children, best illustrates the problem. To Rothman, the essence of Healy's representativeness was his aimless experimentalism. Supposedly, Healy dabbled with Freud but propounded no particular psychological theory in amassing *The Individual Delinquent* (1915), the book for which he is best known. This may be a proper charge to level against someone who was styling himself as a social psychologist, but Rothman has an obligation to discuss the term. Healy was clearly influenced by the studies of George Mead and Charles Cooley, who rejected the determinisms of Freud and John B. Watson and described the self as originating both in the social process and in the images that the individual constructed of other persons and objects. The premise of *The Individual Delinquent* was that human behavior was shaped largely by the self-concept the individual acquired from society. Moreover, as John Burnham has shown (1961), Healy's work marked the beginning of a more open-ended approach to the scientific study of delinquency by repudiating the monocausism of eugenicists and Lombrosian criminologists. Healy himself had first studied delinquents by taking anatomical measurements to see whether youthful offenders conformed to Lombroso's description of the born criminal. Finally, Healy's lukewarm Freudianism developed later, after the Glueck's study (1934) reported a high rate of recidivism among children treated at the Judge Baker Center (Boston) where Healy was director. This cast general doubt upon the usefulness of community mental health clinics, a movement popularized by Healy in the 1920s, and thus encouraged him to stress the familial causes of delinquency (Mennel 1973b).

Rothman's incomplete analysis of Healy's ideas is matched by his failure to probe the broader significance of the Judge Baker Center's mediocre record. No thorough study of the subject exists, but it is not difficult to speculate on the quality of the relationship that existed between the Protestant psychologists from the center and the Roman Catholic judges, politicians, and social workers in the Boston Juvenile Court.[6] How were they supposed to react to the demand of Augusta Bronner, Healy's lifelong collaborator and second wife, for greater authority to remove delinquent children from their homes in order "to make over unworthy or stupid parents, to teach them the principles of child psychology, to alter in very fundamental ways a considerable share of mankind"? In Rothman's narrative, Catholic aid societies exist mainly to play cooperative roles (as they did in the Chicago Juvenile Court) in the emergence of the powerful secular state. His disinclination to discuss the recrudescent character of religious and cultural conflict is ironic, since his own style resembles the jeremiad of the Puritan preacher. For the mid-twentieth century believer, therapy replaces religion to sustain the faithful in an error-prone world and nurtures the possibility that they may inherit the earth. Nothing dates Rothman's work more than the contemporary revival of interest in the religiocultural bases of life.

Rothman makes some interesting points but generally does not follow through with sustained analysis. He notes, for example, that district attorneys favored the juvenile court because it uncluttered their calendars. To what degree was this so? Rothman does not pursue this issue or related questions such as the role of local bar associations in the formation and operation of the court. On another subject, he establishes that reformatory superintendents favored military drill over psychiatric treatment as the prime agent of reform. Rothman sees this preference as a reflection of their army careers but also as a necessity, given low staff wages that attracted purportedly unskilled applicants. A complete discussion, however, would probe the connection between reform schools and military enlistment and note the high esteem that military forces then enjoyed. Doubtless some of the reform school staff were former enlisted men and therefore skilled in teaching calisthenics and drill. Morris Janowitz (1978) has noted that war and peacetime drafts were important integrators of American society in the fifty years before Vietnam. Reformatory institutions complemented this development in a minor way. The point here is not to praise reform school militarism but to explain it in the context of earlier twentieth century history instead of judging it from the inclinations of the age of therapy.

The strangest thing about Rothman's book is that is contains no analysis at all of the crime and delinquency studies of the Chicago school of sociology. Clifford Shaw's Chicago Area Project (1934) stressed the inevitability of delinquency in slum areas and the need to channel the energies of delinquent gangs into legitimate community and neighborhood groups that could apply pressure for better services on municipal and state welfare bureaucracies (Shaw and McKay 1942). This approach influenced a later generation of planners, especially those organizing the Community Action Programs in the War on Poverty (Marris and Rein 1973). One would think that Rothman might want to search out other anti-institutional enthusiasts even though his own interests focus upon mental patients rather than delinquent gangs.

Chicago sociologists were also great believers in the importance of the delinquent youth's own account of his life and troubles, with Shaw's *The Jack-Roller* (1930) being the model of the type. Contemporary social scientists and historians, by contrast, are interested mainly in clinical case histories, which is a pity since the major autobiographies of delinquents are among the more revealing documents of modern times. Brendan Behan's *Borstal Boy* (1959), an acid portrayal of the class hatreds embedded in British reformatory policy, can profitably be compared with the endorsement of Borstals by Healy and Bendict Alper (1941), which shows how Americans, who refused to acknowledge the existence of social classes, expressed opinions about them. The account of Josiah Flynt Willard (1908) and Jean Genêt (1966) are equally shattering in their effect because they put society rather than the individual youth under the microscope.

To conclude, the reader interested in gaining a comprehensive understanding of the origins of modern delinquency programs ought to supplement the accounts mentioned above with more general histories of social welfare activity. Trattner's biography (1968) of the social-work executive Homer Folks and Chambers's biography (1971) of Paul Kellogg, editor of the *Survey*, show reformers with broad interests, reflective attitudes toward their own policies, and distrust of panaceas, such as eugenics, that minimized human capacity to change. Allen Davis's study (1967) of the settlement house movement presents young men and women, often with sheltered upbringings, motivated by their compassion for the trials of recent immigrants and their confidence that the new biological and statistical sciences could improve urban life for everyone. The juvenile court was but one part of this hope, and, like related causes (child labor and consumer protection laws, etc.), it suffered from the general disillusion with social explanation that flowed from World War I and its aftermath. Roy Lubove (1965) traces this shift within social work as early practitioners defined the profession on the basis of social diagnostic skills, but later created an internal hierarchy enshrining psychoanalytic case work as "queen" in the 1920s. In all of these studies we see life through the eyes of decades other than our own and can easily imagine that some delinquents fared better than others.

V. Recent Study

Several histories touch one aspect or another of delinquency policy in the era since World War II, but there has been no interest comparable to earlier periods. The Bremner documents provide summary coverage to the early 1970s, and two political studies perceptively analyze the tangled underbrush of congressional study and Great Society policy (Bremner 1970–74; Marris and Rein 1973; Moore 1969). Some works discuss various social and psychological theories but suffer from limited knowledge of the range of therapies and of the particular reasons for the popularity of any one approach (Finestone 1976; Levine and Levine 1970; Ryerson 1978). As I noted earlier, the lack of interest may be attributed in part to disciplinary inhibitions and to the overwhelming volume and variety of programs encouraged by a welfare state that continued to expand until 1980.

There may be another, more significant reason for the lack of scholarly activity. In recent years the definition and treatment of delinquency has been most influenced by the alteration of the juvenile court following the *Gault* decision and by the growth of diversion programs predicated upon broad professional distrust of institutions. By conveying to juveniles most of the standards and safeguards of criminal law, *Gault* and related decisions undercut the court's reputation, which was both valid and hyperbolic, as a humanitarian agency. This reduction in authority was accelerated by the prevalent assumption of many community-based programs that delinquents were not guilty of crimes but were victims of social and economic deprivation (U.S. President's Commission on Law Enforcement and Administration of Justice 1967). The relevant point is that both developments accorded with the transcendental mood of historical scholarship in the late 1960s and 1970s. Current reticence, therefore, may derive from the fact that one generation's panaceas have not worked.

Why not? A standard reply is that they were never tried. The antipoverty initiatives of the Great Society were buried in Vietnam and the Middle East, and a series of conservative administrations ensured that there would be no resurrection. Such an explanation exemplifies what Charles Sanders Peirce called the method of tenacity, that is, settling doubt by adhering without reflection to original premises. A more flexible method of inquiry hints at uncomfortable truths. For example, the United States Comptroller General's Report (1975), detailing the failures and corruption of federal antidelinquency programs, would not surprise the student of early federal policy. Miriam Van Waters's report for the National Commission on Law Observance and Enforcement (1931) outlined the cruelty and neglect suffered by youthful violators of federal law. Moreover, any appraisal of recent federal programs, particularly in the area of children's rights, ought to recognize that their libertarian character left a mixed legacy. Formal rights were conveyed, but alternative policies based upon economic redistribution were frustrated.

The fundamental premise of libertarian reform was that families, group homes, and peer groups would provide suitable alternatives to the discredited courts and institutions. In fact, the family became libertarianism's most prominent victim, since the philosophy's basic expression was the quest for individual authenticity in the marketplace. In the study of social problems, this meant the atomistic proliferation of "fields" of study. The subjects were serious enough— child abuse, "parenting," and so forth—but the investigative results were often either obvious or wrong. Additionally, to the degree that study was animated by the desire to

make professional status a universal social goal, it put heavy pressure on families who dissented from it. The historians' culpability here is compounded because they gave deinstitutionalization a glamorous gloss by idealizing the colonial period because of its reliance upon family government.

Disillusion, deceit, and now political opposition have flowed inexorably from the contradictions of Great Society programs. Thus Margaret Rosenheim's *Justice for the Child* (1962) became *Pursuing Justice for the Child* (1976), expressing the increasing tentativeness of veteran social investigators. Malcolm W. Klein has noted (1979) that evaluations of programs designed to keep children out of institutions have shown that the programs develop strategies ("net widening" is the operative term) to maintain their client populations, presumably at the level necessary to secure continued funding. And surely, the Reagan administration's proposed policy of block-granting many social programs is based in part upon belief that sociological study may exacerbate rather than solve life's problems. The bet is that state and local governments agree and will fund programs whose constituent demands (day care and centers for the elderly, for examples) are more pressing than those of the advice-giving industry.

There is no cause for celebration here. We currently lack only the assurance of a high government official that the administration is not "antiyouth" to know for certain that valuable programs as well as dubious research will be eliminated. Indeed, the new age arrived before the 1980 election, with many states passing laws lowering the age and increasing the number of offenses for which juveniles could be sent to criminal court. The new conservatism appears harsher than that of Potter Stewart and Warren Burger, whose dissenting opinions in the *Gault* era were based upon the belief that conveying constitutional safeguards to youthful lawbreakers was less important than providing the juvenile court more resources to fulfill its mandate.

Popular reaction to forthcoming reductions in government services is still uncertain, but there is agreement that a half-century of growth in federal and state programs has ended. Historians may or may not be apprehensive about future developments, but they generally welcome watersheds because these help to organize and explain significant blocks of time. Some scholars regard periods mainly as conveniences, but others take seriously Hegel's injunction that the importance of things becomes apparent at the moment of their disappearance—or, as he put it, the Owl of Minerva flies only at dusk. The fact of flight should encourage historians to explore the recent past. Why did psychological study enjoy such a vogue in the 1940s and 1950s? To what extent did institutions incorporate psychoanalytic techniques? Did the revival of social theory in the 1960s make a similar impact? How did the two approaches interact at various levels of government and within particular institutions? In answering these and related questions, historians should utilize case studies, biographies, and the comparative approach.

As they conduct these investigations, historians should remind themselves of the essentials of their calling. Charles Rosenberg (1979) comments, "It is no more than a truism to observe that social scientists are trained to discern and formulate patterns that can be expressed in general terms, while the historian is tied by sensibility and socialization to the particular." If so, it bears repeating, because historians embarrass themselves when they forget. History succeeds when the author addresses readers in a suggestive rather than a didactic tone in order to vivify forces and lives beyond the audience's immediate experiences. Social investigators may enhance their own studies by appreciating the difference.

Notes

1. "Jacksonian reform" is one of those phrases that historians casually accept and shouldn't. Few of the individuals who built reformatory institutions supported Jackson; many more viewed his vigorous individualism as a prime cause of social disorder (Mennel 1973b). Furthermore, scholars do not use presidents' names to characterize reform in later periods. "Lincolnian" sounds awkward, as does "Rooseveltian," which is confusing as well. "Jacksonian" is euphonious, elastic (from the Battle of New Orleans to the Mexican War), but not very helpful to the matter at hand.

2. The low rate of emigration from France to the United States contributed to the fact that Mettray was never well understood. The Rauhe Haus fared better because it was known in the Lutheran settlements where Wichern's umbrella organization, die Innere Mission, was active. However, these communities were themselves fairly well insulated from the non-German-speaking community.

3. European institutions such as Red Hill (the Philanthropic Society's home), Mettray, and the Rauhe Haus have retained or replicated their original buildings. At Mettray the church occupies the central place reserved for the administration building in American reform schools.

4. See also Henrika Kuklick's review of a related work, Burton J. Bledstein, *The Culture of Professionalism* (1976), *Journal of American History* 68 (1981):152–53. Richard Sennett, *Families against the City* (1970), a study of one middle-class Chicago neighborhood's reaction to the Haymarket Massacre (1886), illustrates yet another determinism. On the basis of extremely limited evidence, Sennett contends that demands for more police protection came mainly from nuclear families who had isolated themselves from the diversity of the city as extended families had not.

5. The same has also been said about his discussion of mental health. See Gerald Grob's review of *Conscience and Convenience in Commentary* 70 (1980):75–77. See also Gerald N. Grob, "Abuse in American Mental Hospitals in Historical Perspective: Myth and Reality," *International Journal of Law and Psychiatry* 3 (1980):295–310.

6. Morris J. Vogel, *The Invention of the Modern Hospital: Boston, 1870–1930* (Chicago: University of Chicago Press, 1980), discusses the conflict between Protestant trustees of Boston City Hospital and Irish ward politicians.

References

ABBOTT, GRACE, ED.
1938   *The Child and the State.* 2 vols. Chicago: University of Chicago Press.

ALTGELD, JOHN P.
1886   *Our Penal Machinery and Its Victims.* Chicago: A. C. McClurg.

ARIÈS, PHILLIPE
1965   *Centuries of Childhood: A Social History of Family Life.* New York: Vintage Books.

BAILYN, BERNARD
1960   *Education in the Forming of American Society.* Chapel Hill: University of North Carolina Press.

BANNER, LOIS
1973   "Religious Benevolence as Social Control: A Critique of an Interpretation," *Journal of American History* 60:23–41.

BARNARD, HENRY
1854   *National Education in Europe.* Hartford: F. C. Brownell.

BEARD, CHARLES, AND MARY BEARD
1927   *The Rise of American Civilization.* New York: Macmillan.

BEARD, MARY, ED.
1933   *America through Women's Eyes.* New York: Macmillan.

BEAUMONT, GUSTAYE DE, AND ALEXIS DE TOCQUEVILLE
1835   *On the Penitentiary System of the United States.* Carbondale: Southern Illinois University: 1964 reprint edition.

BEHAN, BRENDAN
1959   *Borstal Boy.* New York: Alfred A. Knopf.

BENDER, THOMAS
1975   *Toward an Urban Vision: Ideas and Institutions in Nineteenth Century America.* Lexington: University Press of Kentucky.

BLEDSTEIN, BURTON J.
1976   *The Culture of Professionalism: The Middle Class and the Development of Higher Education in America.* New York: Norton.

BOYER, PAUL
1978   *Urban Masses and the Moral Order in America, 1820–1920.* Cambridge: Harvard University Press.

BRACE, CHARLES LORING
1872   *The Dangerous Classes of New York, and Twenty Years' Work among Them.* New York: Wynkoop and Hallenbeck.

BREMNER, ROBERT H.
1956   *From the Depths: The Discovery of Poverty in the United States.* New York: New York University Press.
1970–74 *Children and Youth in America: A Documentary History.* 3 vols. Cambridge: Harvard University Press.

BRENZEL, BARBARA M.
1975   "Lancaster Industrial School for Girls: A Social Portrait of a Nineteenth Century Reform School," *Feminist Studies* 3:40–53.
1978   "The Girls at Lancaster: A Social Portrait of the First Reform School for Girls in North America, 1856–1905." Ed.D. dissertation, Harvard University.
1980   "Domestication as Reform: A Study of the Socialization of Wayward Girls, 1856–1905," *Harvard Educational Review* 50:196–213.

BURLEIGH, EDITH N., AND FRANCES K. HARRIS
1923   *The Delinquent Girl.* New York: New York School of Social Work.

BURNHAM, JOHN C.
1961   "Oral History Interviews of William Healy and Augusta Bronner." Houghton Library, Harvard University.

CARLEBACH, JULIUS
1970   *Caring for Children in Trouble.* New York: Humanities Press.

CHAMBERS, CLARKE A.
1963   *Seedtime of Reform: American Social Service and Social Action, 1918–1933.* Minneapolis: University of Minnesota Press.
1971   *Paul U. Kellogg and the "Survey": Voices for Social Welfare and Social Justice.* Minneapolis: University of Minnesota Press.

CLOWARD, RICHARD, AND LLOYD OHLIN
1960   *Delinquency and Opportunity: A Theory of Delinquent Gangs.* New York: Free Press.

CREMIN, LAWRENCE
1961   *The Transformation of the School: Progressivism in American Education, 1876–1957.* New York: Alfred A. Knopf.

DAVIS, ALLEN F.
1967   *Spearheads for Reform: The Social Settlements and the Progressive Movement, 1890–1914.* New York: Oxford.

DEUTSCH, ALBERT
1952   *Our Rejected Children.* Boston: Little, Brown.

ELIOT, THOMAS D.
1914   *The Juvenile Court and the Community.* New York: Macmillan.

FAULKNER, HAROLD U.
1931   *The Question for Social Justice, 1898–1914.* New York: Macmillan.

FINESTONE, HAROLD
1976   *Victims of Change: Juvenile Delinquents in American Society.* Westport, Conn.: Greenwood Press.

FLEXNER, BERNARD, AND ROGER N. BALDWIN
1912   *Juvenile Courts and Probation.* New York: Century.

FLYNN, FRANK T.
1954   "Judge Merritt W. Pinckney and the Early Days of the Juvenile Court in Chicago," *Social Service Review* 28:20–30.

FOLKS, HOMER
1902   *The Care of Destitute, Neglected and Delinquent Children.* New York: Macmillan.

FOUCAULT, MICHEL
1978   *Discipline and Punish.* New York: Pantheon.

FOX, SANFORD J.
1970   "Juvenile Justice Reform: An Historical Perspective," *Stanford Law Review* 22:1187–1239.

FREEDMAN, ESTELLE B.
1981   *Their Sisters' Keepers: Women's Prison Reform in America, 1830–1930.* Ann Arbor: University of Michigan Press.

GENÊT, JEAN
1966   *Miracle of the Rose.* New York: Grove Press.

GLUECK, SHELDON, AND ELEANOR GLUECK
1934   *One Thousand Juvenile Delinquents.* Cambridge: Harvard University Press.

GORDON, MICHAEL
1971   *Juvenile Delinquency in the American Novel, 1905–1965: A Study in the Sociology of Literature.* Bowling Green, Ohio: Bowling Green University Popular Press.

GRIFFEN, CLIFFORD S.
1960   *Their Brothers' Keepers: Moral Stewardship in the United States, 1800–1865.* New Brunswick, N.J.: Rutgers University Press.

HAGAN, JOHN
1980   "The Legislation of Crime and Delinquency: A Review of Theory, Method and Research," *Law and Society Review* 14:603–28.

HAREVEN, TAMARA K., ED.
1971 *Anonymous Americans: Explorations in Nineteenth-Century Social History*. Englewood Cliffs, N.J.: Prentice-Hall.

HAWES, JOSEPH M.
1971 *Children in Urban Society: Juvenile Delinquency in Nineteenth Century America*. New York: Oxford.

HEALE, MICHAEL J.
1976 "From City Fathers to Social Critics: Humanitarianism and Government in New York, 1790–1860," *Journal of American History* 43:21–41.

HEALY, WILLIAM
1915 *The Individual Delinquent*. Boston: Little, Brown.

HEALY, WILLIAM, AND BENEDICT S. ALPER
1941 *Criminal Youth and the Borstal System*. New York: Commonwealth Fund.

HOLL, JACK M.
1971 *Juvenile Reform in the Progressive Era: William R. George and the Junior Republic Movement*. Ithaca: Cornell University Press.

HORLICK, ALLAN STANLEY
1975 *Country Boys and Merchant Princes: The Social Control of Young Men in New York*. Lewisburg: Bucknell University Press.

HORWITZ, MORTON J.
1971 "The Emergence of an Instrumental Conception of American Law," *Perspectives in American History* 5:287–328.

HURLEY, TIMOTHY D.
1907 *The Origin of the Juvenile Court Law*. Chicago: Visitation and Aid Society.

IGNATIEFF, MICHAEL
1978 *A Just Measure of Pain: The Penitentiary in the Industrial Revolution, 1750–1850*. New York: Pantheon.

1981 "State, Civil Society and Total Institution: A Critique of Recent Social Histories of Punishment." In *Crime and Justice: An Annual Review of Research*, vol. 3, ed. Michael Tonry and Norval Morris. Chicago: University of Chicago Press.

JAMES, HOWARD
1970 *Children in Trouble: A National Scandal*. New York: David McKay.

JANOWITZ, MORRIS
1978 *The Last Half-Century: Societal Change and Politics in America*. Chicago: University of Chicago Press.

JOHNSON, DAVID R.
1973 "Crime Patterns in Philadelphia, 1840–70." In *The Peoples of Philadelphia: A History of Ethnic Groups and Lower-Class Life, 1790–1940*, ed. Allen F. Davis and Mark H. Haller. Philadelphia: Temple University Press.

1979 *Policing the Urban Underworld: The Impact of Crime on the Development of the American Police, 1800–1887*. Philadelphia: Temple University Press.

JONES, MARY G.
1938 *The Charity School Movement: A Study of Eighteenth Century Puritanism in Action*. Cambridge: Cambridge University Press.

KAESTLE, CARL F.
1973. *The Evolution of an Urban School System: New York City, 1750–1850*. Cambridge: Harvard University Press.

KAESTLE, CARL F., AND MARIS A. VINOVSKIS.
1980 *Education and Social Change in Nineteenth-Century Massachusetts*. Cambridge: Cambridge University Press.

KAMMEN, MICHAEL, ED.
1980 *The Past before Us: Contemporary Historical Writing in the United States*. Ithaca: Cornell University Press.

KATZ, MICHAEL B.
1968 *The Irony of Early School Reform: Educational Innovation in Mid-Nineteenth Century Massachusetts*. Cambridge: Harvard University Press.

KIEFER, MONICA
1948 *American Children through Their Books*. Philadelphia: University of Pennsylvania Press.

KLEIN, MALCOLM W.
1979 "Deinstitutionalization and Diversion of Juvenile Offenders: A Litany of Impediments." In *Crime and Justice: An Annual Review of Research*, vol. 1, ed. Norval Morris and Michael Tonry. Chicago: University of Chicago Press.

LANE, ROGER
1967 *Policing the City: Boston, 1822–1885*. Cambridge: Harvard University Press.

LANGSAM, MIRIAM Z.
1964 *Children West: A History of the Placing out System of the New York Children's Aid Society, 1853–1890*. Madison: State Historical Society of Wisconsin.

LARSEN, CHARLES
1972 *The Good Fight: The Life and Times of Ben B. Lindsey*. Chicago: Quadrangle.

LASCH, CHRISTOPHER
1973 "Origins of the Asylum." In *The World of Nations: Reflections on American History, Politics, and Culture*, ed. Christopher Lasch. New York: Alfred A. Knopf.

1977 *Haven in a Heartless World: The Family Besieged*. New York: Basic Books.

LASLETT, PETER
1965 *The World We Have Lost: England before the Industrial Age*. New York: Charles Scribner's Sons.

LAURIE, BRUCE
1973 "Fire Companies and Gangs in Southwark: The 1840's." In *The Peoples of Philadelphia: A History of Ethnic Groups and Lower-Class Life, 1790–1940*, ed. Allen F. Davis and Mark M. Haller. Philadelphia: Temple University Press.

LAZERSON, MARVIN
1971 *The Origins of the Urban School*. Cambridge: Harvard University Press.

LEIBY, JAMES
1967 *Charity and Correction in New Jersey: A History of*

State Welfare Institutions. New Brunswick, N.J.: Rutgers University Press.

1978 *A History of Social Welfare and Social Work in the United States.* New York: Columbia University Press.

LEVINE, MURRAY, AND ADELINE LEVINE
1970 *A Social History of Helping Services.* New York: Appleton-Century-Crofts.

LEWIS, W. DAVID
1965 *From Newgate to Dannemora: The Rise of the Penitentiary in New York, 1746–1848.* Ithaca: Cornell University Press.

LOU, HERBERT H.
1927 *Juvenile Courts in the United States.* Chapel Hill: University of North Carolina Press.

LUBOVE, ROY
1965 *The Professional Altruist: The Emergence of Social Work as a Career, 1880–1930.* Cambridge: Harvard University Press.

MANTON, JO
1976 *Mary Carpenter and the Children of the Streets.* Exeter, N.H.: Heinemann.

MARRIS, PETER, AND MARTIN REIN
1973 *Dilemmas of Social Reform: Poverty and Community Action in the United States.* Rev. ed. Chicago: Aldine.

MAY, MARGARET
1973 "Innocence and Experience: The Evolution of the Concept of Juvenile Delinquency in the Mid-Nineteenth Century," *Victorian Studies* 18:7–29.

MENNEL, ROBERT
1972 "Origins of the Juvenile Court: Changing Perspectives on the Legal Rights of Juvenile Delinquents." *Crime and Delinquency* 18:68–78.

1973a "Juvenile Delinquency in Perspective," *History of Education Quarterly* 13:275–81.

1973b *Thorns and Thistles: Juvenile Delinquents in the United States, 1825–1940.* Hanover: University Press of New England.

1980a "The Family System of Common Farmers: The Early Years of Ohio's Reform Farm, 1858–1884," *Ohio History* 89:279–322.

1980b "The Family System of Common Farmers: The Origins of Ohio's Reform Farm, 1840–1858," *Ohio History* 89:125–56.

MESSERLI, JONATHAN
1973 *Horace Mann: A Biography.* New York: Alfred A. Knopf.

MOHL, RAYMOND
1970 *Poverty in New York, 1783–1823.* New York: Oxford.

MONKKONEN, ERIC H.
1975 *The Dangerous Class: Crime and Poverty in Columbus, Ohio, 1860–1885.* Cambridge: Harvard University Press.

MOORE, JOHN
1969 "Controlling Delinquency: Executive, Congressional and Juvenile, 1961–64." In *Congress and Urban Problems,* ed. Frederic N.

Cleaveland. Washington, D.C.: Brookings Institution.

MULLER, NORBERT
1976 "La Colonie Agricole Pénitentiare de Mettray." Memoire, Université de Tours.

NATIONAL COMMISSION ON LAW OBSERVANCE AND ENFORCEMENT
1931 *The Child Offender in the Federal System of Justice.* Washington, D.C.: U.S. Government Printing Office.

NATIONAL CONFERENCE OF CHARITIES AND CORRECTION
1893 *History of Child Saving in the United States.* Boston: n.p.

OWEN, DAVID
1964 *English Philanthropy, 1660–1960.* London: Oxford.

PARKER, GRAHAM
1976a "The Juvenile Court Movement." *University of Toronto Law Journal* 26:140–72.

1976b "The Juvenile Court: The Illinois Experience." *University of Toronto Law Journal* 26:253–306.

PICKETT, ROBERT S.
1969 *House of Refuge: Origins of Juvenile Reform in New York State, 1815–1857.* Syracuse: Syracuse University Press.

PINCHBECK, IVY, AND MARGARET HEWITT
1969–73 *Children in English Society.* 2 vols. London: Routledge and Kegan Paul.

PISCIOTTA, ALEXANDER W.
1979 "The Theory and Practice of the New York House of Refuge, 1857–1935." Ph.D. dissertation, Florida State University.

PLATT, ANTHONY M.
1974 "The Triumph of Benevolence: The Origins of the Juvenile Justice System in the United States." In *Criminal Justice in America,* ed. Richard Quinney. Boston: Little, Brown.

1977a *The Child Savers: The Invention of Delinquency.* 2d ed. Chicago: University of Chicago Press.

1977b Review of Schlossman, *Love and the American Delinquent, Crime and Social Justice* 8:80–83.

PRESCOTT, PETER S.
1981 *The Child Savers.* New York: Alfred A. Knopf.

REEVES, MARGARET
1929 *Training Schools for Delinquent Girls.* New York: Russell Sage.

RICHARDSON, JAMES F.
1970 *The New York Police: Colonial Times to 1901.* New York: Oxford.

ROSENBERG, CARROLL SMITH
1971 *Religion and the Rise of the American City: The New York City Mission Movement, 1812–1870.* Ithaca: Cornell University Press.

ROSENBERG, CHARLES
1979 "Toward an Ecology of Knowledge: On Discipline, Context and History." In *The Organization of Knowledge in Modern America, 1860–1920,* ed. Alexandra Oleson and John Voss. Baltimore: Johns Hopkins University Press.

ROSENHEIM, MARGARET K., ED.
1962 *Justice for the Child: The Juvenile Court in Transition.* New York: Free Press.

1976   *Pursuing Justice for the Child.* Chicago: University of Chicago Press.

ROSS, DOROTHY
1972   *G. Stanley Hall: The Psychologist as Prophet.* Chicago: University of Chicago Press.

ROTHMAN, DAVID J.
1971   *The Discovery of the Asylum: Social Order and Disorder in the New Republic.* Boston: Little, Brown.
1974   Review of Mennel, *Thorns and Thistles, American Historical Review* 79:244–45.
1980   *Conscience and Convenience: The Asylum and Its Alternatives in Progressive America.* Boston: Little, Brown.

RYERSON, ELLEN
1978   *The Best Laid Plans: America's Juvenile Court Experiment.* New York: Hill and Wang.

SANDERS, WILEY B., ED.
1970   *Juvenile Offenders for a Thousand Years: Selected Readings from Anglo-Saxon Times to 1900.* Chapel Hill: University of North Carolina Press.

SCHLOSSMAN, STEVEN L.
1974   "Juvenile Justice in the Age of Jackson," *Teachers College Record* 46:119–33.
1977   *Love and the American Delinquent: The Theory and Practice of "Progressive" Juvenile Justice, 1825–1920.* Chicago: University of Chicago Press.

SCHLOSSMAN, STEVEN L., AND STEPHANIE WALLACH
1978   "The Crime of Precocious Sexuality: Female Juvenile Delinquency in the Progressive Era," *Harvard Educational Review* 48:65–94.

SCHNEIDER, JOHN
1980. *Detroit and the Problem of Order, 1830–1880.* Lincoln: University of Nebraska Press.

SCHULTZ, J. LAWRENCE
1973   "The Cycle of Juvenile Court History," *Crime and Delinquency* 19:457–76.

SCHUPF, HARRIET W.
1971   "The Perishing and Dangerous Classes: Efforts to Deal with the Neglected, Vagrant and Delinquent Juvenile in England, 1840–1872." Ph.D. dissertation, Columbia University.

SENNETT, RICHARD
1970   *Families against the City.* Cambridge: Harvard University Press.

SHANAHAN, WILLIAM O.
1954   *German Protestants Face the Social Question.* South Bend: University of Notre Dame Press.

SHAW, CLIFFORD R.
1929   *Delinquency Areas.* Chicago: University of Chicago Press.
1930   *The Jack-Roller: A Delinquent Boy's Own Story.* Chicago: University of Chicago Press.

SHAW, CLIFFORD R., AND HENRY D. MCKAY
1942   *Juvenile Delinquency in Urban Areas.* Chicago: University of Chicago Press.

SLATER, PETER G.
1970   "Views of Children and of Child Rearing during the Early National Period: A Study in the New England Intellect." Ph.D. dissertation, University of California, Berkeley.

SMITH, TIMOTHY
1957   *Revivalism and Social Reform in Mid-Nineteenth Century America.* New York: Abingdon Press.

SNEDDEN, DAVID
1907   *Administrative and Educational Work of the American Reform School.* New York: Columbia University Press.

STACK, JOHN
1974   "Social Policy and Juvenile Delinquency in England and Wales, 1815–75." Ph.D. dissertation, University of Iowa.

STEWART, JOSEPH M.
1980   "A Comparative History of Juvenile Correctional Institutions in Ohio." Ph.D. dissertation, Ohio State University.

STONE, LAWRENCE
1981   "Family History in the 1980's," *Journal of Interdisciplinary History* 12:51–87.

SUTHERLAND, NEIL
1976   *Children in English-Canadian Society, 1880–1920.* Toronto: University of Toronto Press.

TEETERS, NEGLEY K.
1960   "The Early Days of the Philadelphia House of Refuge," *Pennsylvania History* 27:165–87.

THAVENET, DENNIS
1976   "'Wild Young "Uns" in Their Midst': The Beginning of Reformatory Education in Michigan." *Michigan History* 60:240–59.

THOMAS, WILLIAM I.
1923   *The Unadjusted Girl.* Boston: Little, Brown.

THRASHER, FREDERIC M.
1927   *The Gang: A Study of 1,313 Gangs in Chicago.* Chicago: University of Chicago Press.

THURSTON, HENRY W.
1942   *Concerning Juvenile Delinquency: Progressive Changes in Our Perspective.* New York: Columbia University Press.

TRATTNER, WALTER I.
1968   *Homer Folks: Pioneer in Social Welfare.* New York: Columbia University Press.

TYLER, ALICE FELT
1944   *Freedom's Ferment: Phases of American Social History to 1860.* Minneapolis: University of Minnesota Press.

U.S. COMPTROLLER GENERAL
1975   *Report to Congress: How Federal Efforts to Coordinate Programs to Mitigate Juvenile Delinquency Proved Ineffective.* Washington, D.C.: Government Printing Office.

U.S. PRESIDENT'S COMMISSION ON LAW ENFORCEMENT AND ADMINISTRATION OF JUSTICE
1968   *The Challenge of Crime in a Free Society.* Washington, D.C.: U.S. Government Printing Office.

VAN WATERS, MIRIAM
1925   *Youth in Conflict.* New York: New Republic.

VOGEL, MORRIS J.
1980   *The Invention of the Modern Hospital: Boston 1870–1930.* Chicago: University of Chicago Press.

WILLARD, JOSIAH FLINT [JOSIAH FLYNT]
1908   *My Life.* New York: Outing.

WINES, ENOCH C., AND THEODORE W. DWIGHT
1867   *Report on the Prisons and Reformatories of the United States and Canada.* Albany: Van Benthuysen.
1880   *The State Prisons and Child Saving Institutions in the Civilized World.* Cambridge, Mass.: J. Wilson.

WIRKKALA, JOHN
1973   "Juvenile Delinquency and Reform in Nineteenth Century Massachusetts." Ph.D. dissertation, Clark University, Worcester, Mass.

WISHY, BERNARD
1968   *The Child and the Republic.* Philadelphia: University of Pennsylvania Press.

WOHL, R. RICHARD
1969   "The 'Country Boy' Myth and Its Place in American Urban Culture," *Perspectives in American History* 3:77–158.

ZUCKERMAN, MICHAEL.
1976   "Children's Rights: The Failure of Reform," *Policy Analysis* 2:371–85.

QUESTIONS FOR DISCUSSION

1. The author is generally critical of the historical accounts of juvenile delinquency. What are his criticisms? Do you think these criticisms are valid?

2. What social changes of the late 1800s severely hampered the family unit's ability to govern and control youth?

3. Discuss the major differences between the juvenile delinquency policies of the 1960s and those of the 1980s. Name several reasons these changes occurred.

APPLICATIONS

1. Identify an individual who is over the age of forty. This could be a parent, a friend, a teacher, or another acquaintance. Using a tape recorder or a note pad, ask that person about his or her experiences as a youth. Ask specific questions such as the following:
    a. How has the world changed since you were a teenager? Are the social pressures any different?
    b. How are teenagers different now?
    c. Are today's teenagers more prone to break the law?

2. Let us assume that you are in charge of reviewing and making recommendations about policies that will decrease juvenile delinquency and improve the juvenile justice system. What would you recommend?

KEY TERMS

almshouse a privately financed home for the poor.

altruism unselfish regard for or devotion to the welfare of others.

determinism the theory or doctrine which maintains that acts of will, occurrences in nature, or social and/or psychological phenomena are caused by preceding events or natural law.

egalitarian a belief in human equality with respect to social, political, and economic rights and privileges.

eugenics a science that deals with improving a race or breed by controlling mating habits, genetic engineering, and hereditary qualities.

hierarchy a grouping of people by rank, according to economic, social, or professional standing.

historiography the writing of history based on the critical examination of sources.

ideology a systematic body of concepts about human life or culture.

mores the fixed, morally binding customs of a particular group; habits or mannerisms.

penitentiary an institution in which offenders of the law are confined for detention or punishment. Historically, offenders were to feel regret and sorrow for their deeds; repenting from their sins.

reformatory a penal institution to which young and first-time offenders are committed for training and reformation.

revisionism a movement in revolutionary Marxian socialism favoring evolutionary rather than revolutionary change.

4

The Crime of Precocious Sexuality: Female Juvenile Delinquency in the Progressive Era

Steven Schlossman
Radcliffe Institute, Harvard University

Stephanie Wallach
Simmons College

The juvenile justice system's discrimination against poor and minority children has been well documented, but the system's discrimination on the basis of gender has been less widely recognized. Drawing on neglected court records and secondary sources, Steven Schlossman and Stephanie Wallach show how girls bore a disproportionate share of the burden of juvenile justice in the Progressive era. The authors note that during the Progressive era female juvenile delinquents often received more severe punishments than males, even though boys usually were charged with more serious crimes. Schlossman and Wallach conclude that the discriminatory treatment of female delinquents in the early twentieth century resulted from racial prejudice, new theories of adolescence, and Progressive-era movements to purify society.

This essay is an historical inquiry into the practice of sexual discrimination against female juvenile delinquents. Although American public policy toward girl offenders first took shape in the middle decades of the nineteenth century—the Victorian era—we have decided to focus on the Progressive era of the early twentieth century. During this

latter period scientific and popular literature on female delinquency expanded enormously, and most states adopted the main components of modern correctional machinery. Our essay spotlights the differences between stated intentions, revealed preferences, and actual outcomes.[1] Although we attempt to develop a broad interpretation, we must emphasize the selectivity of our historical research. We do not pretend to have exhausted available sources, to have explored all possible interpretations of our evidence, or, certainly, to have written the definitive account. Instead, we offer a preliminary synthesis of untapped sources in an effort to call attention to a neglected subject, to encourage additional research on it, and to suggest ways of integrating the topic of female delinquency into the rapidly growing fields of women's history and the history of corrections.

Our essay speaks only indirectly to modern-day issues in juvenile justice. Continuities between past and present will often be apparent, to be sure, but we dare not draw them too explicitly for the simple reason that social scientists know very little about the theory and practice of female juvenile justice between the 1920s and the 1960s.[2] Nonetheless, we do believe it is possible to use history as a force for social change by laying bare the

roots and assumptions of anachronistic policies—policies, in this instance, that lag
behind our current attitudes toward female
sexuality and equal justice for women. Given
our reformist goals, it may be useful to
explain in advance why we focus on sexual
discrimination as opposed to other equally
blatant injustices in the correctional system.

Like other critics of American juvenile
justice, we decry practices that lead to unwarranted labeling and incarceration of children
and that discriminate against poor, minority
youth, regardless of sex.[3] We consider it
indisputable that, from the early nineteenth
century to the present, the juvenile justice
system has systematically singled out lower-
class children for punishment and ignored
middle- and upper-class youth.[4] In this essay,
however, our main concern is not with class,
ethnic, racial, or age bias, for we believe
those themes have been adequately treated
elsewhere. Rather, what most interests us
now is how, in a correctional system that dis-
criminates consistently against poor, minority
children as a whole, females carry a disproportionate share of the burden of injustice.

Discussion of female delinquency is conspicuously absent from most scholarly writing
on criminal justice. Despite a persistent hue
and cry during the last decade about spiral-
ing rates of delinquency, despite mounting
evidence demonstrating the ineffectiveness
of correctional programs, and despite the
women's rights movement, girl offenders are
largely ignored. Even as the number of
females processed through the juvenile
courts climbs steadily, an implicit consensus
remains that the male teenager defines the
delinquency problem in modern America
and suffers most egregiously from correctional injustices.[5]

We suggest two main reasons why girl
delinquents receive so little attention. First,
girls are accused primarily of so-called victim-
less crimes, that is, offenses that do not
involve clear-cut damage to persons or property. If committed by adults, these actions
would not be legally punishable; if committed by boys, the same acts would be interpreted less seriously and punished less
severely. Thus, rather ironically, the plight of
female delinquents receives little scrutiny

because they are accused of committing less
flagrant violations of legal codes. Second, traditional stereotypes of women as the weaker
and more dependent sex rationalize, indeed
even legitimate, discriminatory correctional
practices in the name of humanitarianism. As
the half-century struggle to enact the Equal
Rights Amendment makes abundantly clear,
one of the most tenacious beliefs in our society is that women require more comprehensive legal protection than do men. Society
justifies "preventive" intervention into the
lives of antisocial girls under the rationale
that they are especially vulnerable to evil
forces and temptations. This so-called chivalrous attitude leads to earlier intervention and
longer periods of supervision for delinquent
girls than delinquent boys.

The sparse historical writing about
female delinquency concentrates on reformatories, especially the pioneering nineteenth-century institutions, rather than on
the juvenile justice system as a whole.[6] Furthermore, several of the studies are uncritical
and Whiggish in their interpretations, seeing
a benign humanitarian spirit behind early
twentieth-century correctional innovations
for girls. Margaret Reeves, for example, conducted an exhaustive survey of girls' reformatory programs in the 1920s and concluded,
with few reservations, that they embodied the
triumph of social conscience in America and
the onward march of correctional science.[7]
Recently, Robert Mennel, in his ambitious
survey of juvenile correctional history,
described Progressive-era policies as "the first
sign of a more sympathetic attitude toward
female delinquents."[8]

On the basis of our research, we consider
the traditional interpretation to be lacking in
four principal respects: it offers little empirical evidence of benign or effective treatment
of girl offenders; it generally blurs the distinction between the stated intentions of correctional reformers and the actual outcomes
of their efforts; it deals inadequately with the
fears and prejudices underlying benevolent
programs for poor, immigrant children; and
it does little to illuminate, even obliquely, the
practice of sexual discrimination in the juvenile justice system today. We do not quarrel
with historians who emphasize the humani-

tarian spirit that guided such famous juvenile reformers as Jane Addams, Sophonisba Breckinridge, and Edith Abbott, or such lesser figures as Augusta Bronner, Mabel Elliott, Emma Lundberg, and Edith Burleigh.[9] But we do believe that the humanitarian schemes were often quite repressive in design and even more so in outcome.

Our main arguments can be sketched as follows. Although public response to female delinquency emerged in the Victorian era, not until the Progressive period was female delinquency widely perceived as a social problem requiring extensive governmental intervention. In the Progressive period the abundant literature on delinquency was riddled with stereotypical assumptions about women and, in particular, about immigrant women. These stereotypes laid a basis for more punitive treatment of delinquent girls than delinquent boys. Girls were prosecuted almost exclusively for "immoral" conduct, a very broad category that defined all sexual exploration as fundamentally perverse and predictive of future promiscuity, perhaps even prostitution. But while girls, unlike boys, were almost never accused of violating criminal statutes, they received stiffer legal penalties.

Discriminatory treatment of female delinquents was consistent with racial prejudices in the Progressive period. Ethnic girls—immigrants or daughters of immigrants—were seen as inherently more predisposed to immoral conduct than Yankee girls—daughters of native-born parents. Discriminatory correctional practices also embodied the new wisdom of the behavioral sciences, particulary the theories of adolescence generated by such pioneer psychologists as G. Stanley Hall. Finally, the practice of female juvenile justice reflected the quasi-utopian, but ultimately repressive, pursuit of Progressive-era reformers for a more "pure" society, as revealed in the eugenics, antiprostitution, and sex-education campaigns.

Female Delinquency: The Emergence of a Social Problem

Public response to female delinquency can be traced at least as far back as the Jacksonian period, although the traditional date of origin is 1856, when Massachusetts opened the nation's first reform school for girls. Well known in the latter half of the century, the Massachusetts example inspired emulation by diverse philanthropic organizations in the East and Midwest. Several state governments responded to the wishes of these organizations and built reformatories for girls. Compared to the huge reformatories for boys erected in the nineteenth century—by the 1850s the New York House of Refuge held over one thousand inmates—the institutions for girls were generally small and makeshift, often consisting of two or three converted farmhouses. Several of the girls' facilities were little more than receiving stations; their primary purpose was to facilitate the smooth operation of boys' reformatories after attempts to house both sexes in the same buildings had proved embarrassing failures.[10]

The female reformatories incorporated the evangelical spirit of Victorian religious revivalism. Until the end of the nineteenth century the image of the female delinquent remained mainly that of the individual "fallen woman."[11] This image contrasted sharply with that of the male delinquent, who was described less as a sinner than as a carefully nurtured young criminal.[12] To be sure, boys' delinquencies were routinely condemned but were rarely, as was often the case with girls', regarded as indications of innate moral perversity.

Nineteenth-century authors of crime literature wrote endlessly about delinquency—the classic presentation being Charles Loring Brace's *The Dangerous Classes of New York and Twenty Years' Work Among Them*[13]—but they paid very little attention to female delinquents. The "dangerous classes" against whom the reformers warned and about whom newspapers printed sensational stories were overwhelmingly male.[14] When the girl offender did appear in the literature, she was treated mainly as a footnote to the problem of boy delinquency. But early in the twentieth century—especially in the decade preceding the First World War—female delinquency began to attract increasing attention as a separate and pressing social problem.

The heightened public awareness of and growing governmental response to female delinquency in the Progressive era are well documented. Articles on girl offenders appeared in a wide range of popular and scholarly journals. The prestigious philanthropic organization, the National Conference of Charities and Correction, began to discuss female delinquency regularly for the first time since the organization's founding in the early 1870s. Several books were devoted in whole or in part to female criminality. While the mass media continued to emphasize the "boy problem," many civic groups began giving equal attention to the "girl problem." Local organizations such as PTAs, juvenile protective associations, women's clubs, and settlement houses sponsored lectures and discussions on the causes and cures of girls' delinquency; they also led campaigns to garner funds for such innovations as girls' clubs, YWCA summer camps, and, to a lesser extent, Girl Scouts.[15]

Governmental investment in the custody and treatment of female delinquents increased dramatically in the Progressive era. The decade between 1910 and 1920 was an especially prolific period for the creation of publicly sponsored reformatories for girls. Whereas between 1850 and 1910 an average of fewer than five new reformatories were created per decade, twenty-three new facilities opened between 1910 and 1920. Furthermore, older nineteenth-century reformatories were expanded in size, staff, and clientele in this decade. Equally important, a number of states took over private girls' reformatories.[16] In short, the involvement of government with female delinquency grew sharply in the Progressive period, reflecting the expanded discussion of the subject in the literature on juvenile crime.

The Practice of Sexual Discrimination

Before trying to explain the rising interest in female delinquency in the Progressive era, it is necessary to demonstrate that girls received discriminatory treatment in juvenile courts and reformatories. The historical sources for such an empirical study are vast but have never been tapped. We have examined the sources selectively and have chosen for close analysis those we believe are representative of three bodies of evidence.

First, we briefly analyze scattered statistical data to demonstrate that juvenile courts treated female delinquents more harshly than male delinquents. Second, we present an overview of cases in a single juvenile court to evoke the actual decision-making process and thereby show that sentimental notions of the "good girl" and conventional ideals of domesticity prefigured punitive treatment for girl delinquents. Third, we look synoptically at the rehabilitative goals and methods of female reformatories to illuminate further the discriminatory nature of treatment. Our goal is to provide empirical evidence for the contention, developed later in this essay, that the practice of female juvenile justice coincided with the ideology of treatment. Discrimination on the basis of sex was no accident, we believe, but rather was integral to both the theory and practice of Progressive-era juvenile justice.

The first body of evidence was derived from court records in Chicago, San Francisco, Milwaukee, and New Haven. Several points stand out most prominently from these data: the vast majority of delinquents, boy and girls alike, were poor, ghetto-dwelling children of recent immigrants; however, unlike males, females were brought to court almost exclusively for alleged early sexual exploration; and female offenders were treated more punitively than males.

The ethnic origins of both boy and girl delinquents are revealing. In Milwaukee, for example, more than 90 percent of the children brought into court were the offspring of European immigrants. Of these, three out of four were either German or Polish. In Chicago, San Francisco, and New Haven the ethnic background of delinquents was similar, although southeastern European countries were more frequently represented, reflecting the different patterns of immigrant settlement in these cities.[17]

That the delinquents were predominantly poor is evident in a number of ways. Although it is impossible to compare the incomes of families of delinquent and non-delinquent children or to assess the contributions of different family members to total income, we do have periodic salary data for the fathers of delinquent youth in Milwaukee. These data suggest the truth of the popular impression that delinquents were primarily from the working class. Their fathers' salaries were low, generally reported to be less than ten dollars per week. Moreover, the salaries were highly irregular: many fathers moved frequently from job to job; many were unemployed for long periods because of seasonal hiring, debilitating illnesses (particularly tuberculosis), and drinking bouts. In addition, an analysis of the occupations of delinquents' fathers, using city directories and addresses supplied in court to distinguish individuals with the same names, indicates that the majority were working class or lower on the economic scale, the single largest category being that of "laborer."[18] A further indication that delinquents came mainly from poor, ghetto families is their residence patterns. The majority of Milwaukee delinquents lived in the poorest immigrant neighborhoods surrounding the city's scattered railway network.

Although similar in their social and cultural backgrounds, girl and boy delinquents were treated very differently in court. Consider the types of crimes for which boys and girls made their first courtroom appearances. The majority of boys were charged with offenses that fell under the adult criminal code. In Chicago, for example, stealing accounted for more than half of the reported crimes.[19] The charges against girls were of an entirely different nature. The majority were charged under the loose heading of "immorality";[20] however, a charge of "immorality" did not mean that a girl had had intercourse or performed some other mature sexual act. Rather, a girl only had to show "signs" in her appearance, conversation, and bearing that she had probably had intercourse in the past or might do so in the near future. These criteria naturally opened the way to invidious judgments, especially because the delinquents were mainly daughters of immigrants, who were, according to contemporary racial mythology, instinctively emotional and lacking in self-restraint. Thus judges and probation officers would see precocious sexual activity where it did not exist, would prematurely regard unfamiliar cultural patterns of behavior and expression as signs of advanced sexual experience, and

would be more pessimistic about the implications of sexual exploration by ethnic than by Yankee girls.

In practice, an extraordinarily wide range of conduct was included under the label of immorality: staying away from home, associating with persons of dubious character, going to dance houses, fornicating, coming home late at night, masturbating, using obscene language, riding at night in automobiles without a chaperone, strutting about in a lascivious manner, and so forth. To the courts, being "on the road to ruin" was but one short step from being "ruined"; hence, so-called predelinquents were treated much like those who actually engaged in mature sexual relations. The ostensible purposes behind such a loose definition of crime were to root out the underlying causes of misconduct as soon as they became evident and to instruct ethnic girls that their Yankee counterparts upheld higher standards of sexual propriety than their own parents practiced or condoned.[21]

The different treatment of boy and girl delinquents was even more apparent in the disposition of cases. Far more frequently than girls, boys received the relatively noncoercive sanction of probation—supervision in the child's own home or in a surrogate home approved by the court. In Chicago, for instance, 59 percent of the boys who appeared in court between 1899 and 1909 were placed on probation, as compared to only 37 percent of the girls. Conversely, significantly higher proportions of girls than boys were incarcerated in reformatories for sentences that could last several years. In Milwaukee twice as many girls as boys were committed, and in Chicago one-half of the girl delinquents, as contrasted with one-fifth of the boy delinquents, were sent to reformatories.[22] In sum, girls appeared in juvenile court on noncriminal charges far more frequently than boys; nonetheless, girls received more punitive dispositions.[23]

We turn now to another body of evidence: the day-to-day experiences of girls in juvenile court. From the archival records of the Milwaukee Children's Court we have chosen several cases from between 1901 and 1920 for examination. Transcripts from actual hearings, we believe, provide the most vivid and dramatic demonstration of the assumptions that shaped the definition and treatment of female delinquency in the Progressive era.[24]

Alleged girl delinquents in Milwaukee had their private lives probed in fine detail so that judges and probation officers could assess the underlying causes of misbehavior. Whenever it could be demonstrated that a girl had used vile language, masturbated, or indulged in lascivious thoughts, the court freely employed some type of intervention, usually probation. Consider the case of Annagret Schmitt. Neither the hearing transcript nor the accompanying records provides a precise reason why Annagret was brought into court—a common occurrence, since it was assumed that some form of aberrant sexual expression was behind any specific accusation. Thus Annagret, like every girl who appeared in court, was subjected to a vaginal examination. The only proof of virginity was an intact hymen. To his own surprise the examining doctor concluded that Annagret was still a virgin, but he informed the court that irritation in her clitoral area indicated she was a regular masturbator. The probation officer, a woman, analyzed the situation as follows: "She masturbates, and she has somewhat injured herself in that way, and probably this is the cause of her conduct at home, and says things [sic] that are not true . . . . [Annagret] most likely is trying to imagine things, and then believes everything is true." Thus, according to the court, Annagret's masturbatory habits explained her penchant for fantasy and justified labeling her a delinquent and placing her under supervision.

In cases of advanced sexual misconduct, the court usually explored the circumstances in excruciating detail. The ostensible goals were to procure evidence against the male or males involved and to evaluate the girls' attitudes toward men and sex. At times, though, the immediate goal seemed to be nothing other than sheer titillation, much like the famous vice reports in this period. Such reports offered, in the names of science and social reform, pornographic scenes that would have been censored in the commercial media. In court, girls were required to recount, with some attempt to recreate the atmosphere, the steps that led to their sexual encounters, their physical experiences ("How far did he go into you; what did you feel; did you bleed?"), and their later subjective reactions. In pursuing this line of questioning the court's assumptions were transparent; it presumed that a girl's moral condition and potential for rehabilitation depended on just how much of her biological purity had been preserved and on how morally revolted she was by her experiences.

At the same time that the court avidly investigated the girls' sex lives, it preached a conventional code of Victorian morality, highlighting especially the virtues of chastity and the joys of marriage. With all good intentions the court lectured sexually precocious girls on how their behavior was endangering their later salability as wives. Without doubt many of the sexually active girls who appeared in juvenile court were immature and would have benefited from intelligent advice about sex. But the advice the court proffered must have struck these girls as naive and irrelevant to their current needs and past experiences. Consider, for example, one judge's advice to a girl who had contracted venereal disease:

> By and by, three or four years from now, some nice fellow will come along, and you love him, and he will love you, and you will get married, and live right. That ought to be the aim of a girl like you, to look forward to the time you have a good home and a good man.

Quaint moral admonitions like these were the court's main antidote to sexual precocity among girls and, if nothing else, reveal the cultural stereotypes that shaped the legal processing of female delinquents.

As observed earlier, juvenile courts did not distinguish between actual delinquency and predelinquency because they saw their mission as the treatment of underlying causes. The courts aimed to "save" girls once it became apparent they were "on the road to ruin." Consider the case of Sara Wadrewski. Sara's father had brought her into court on a charge of disobedience, alleging that she had refused to work, stayed out late, and gone to parties where the girls dressed like boys. As often happened, a probation officer was on hand to supplement the parents' charges by relating neighborhood gossip. Sara, he intimated, probably had had intercourse with several boys because she was seen lying on the grass with them in a local park. A group of neighbors made similar accusations. To the judge's question, "In what way is she a bad girl?" one neighbor responded, "Why, for the reason that she bums around and doesn't work, and doesn't bring no money home, and runs to parties, and then calls names, calls her brother names, he is a cripple." Sara roundly denied most of the allegations, particularly the charges that she had had group sex, or indeed, that she had ever had "connection." But her protestations of virginity were to no avail; shortly after the initial hearing she was committed to the local Catholic reformatory.

Juvenile court sessions were often like scenes from a Kafka novel. One could never be sure that the disposition of a case would be on the basis of the accusations or on the quality of evidence. Despite these uncertainties it was almost guaranteed that a girl would be sent to a reformatory if either she or her parents, especially her mother, were not blushingly contrite about the girl's sexual adventures. A classic case is that of fifteen-year-old Deborah Horwitz, who freely admitted staying out late at night with many boys and who casually flaunted her sexual desires. In addition to Deborah's self-incriminating testimony, efficient snooping by a probation officer into Deborah's bedroom bureau turned up even more incriminating evidence: five self-photos that the court considered racy (although Deborah got no more racy than opening the top button of her high-necked blouse and removing her hat); and a remarkably candid series of letters to a sailor friend that left no doubt about her initiation into the joys of sex.

In such cases the court's custom was to blame the mother for her daughter's actions. Mrs. Horwitz, however, would not stand for it: "I got lots of trouble with the other girl, she needs an operation, and I got lots of trouble with the other children." Nor would Deborah accept the court's harsh evaluation of her behavior. Thus the judge intoned:

Well, Deborah, this is a very serious matter. If you would live a good life you would be a good woman, and be useful to society, but you have started out very bad. There is only one way to reform you and this is to send you to an institution. I cannot let you go home to your parents. . . . How is it, can't you stop?

Deborah responded, "I can stop, of course I can." "Why don't you behave yourself, then?" the judge rejoined. "These boys tell me that you just coax them." "I never coaxed anybody," Deborah maintained. But to no effect. Precocious sexuality in a girl who would not at least feign repentance and whose parents would not at least feign shock was intolerable to the court. Deborah was committed forthwith to the state reformatory for girls.

As these excerpts reveal, the court defined female delinquency wholly in sexual terms and responded to girls on the basis of Victorian views of women's social role and sexuality. We shall have more to say later about the persistence of these Victorian assumptions in the Progressive period. For the present we will extend our study of actual treatment by examining the female reformatories, which, as noted earlier, expanded rapidly in the early twentieth century. Like the juvenile courts, the reformatories operationalized prevailing cultural stereotypes about women and transformed these stereotypes into tools for punishment and rehabilitation.

Female reformatories in the Progressive era had four principal goals. The basic one was the isolation from males of sexually precocious females, preferably in bucolic settings. Elaborate efforts were made to keep all men away from the institutions or, indeed, from anywhere near the girls. In California, for example, sponsors of the female reformatory concluded that the mile separating the male from the female institution was inadequate. A new facility far removed from males was essential to eliminate "the influences that mysteriously emanate from the proximity of the sexes."[25] The mere act of isolating delinquent girls came to be seen as a rehabilitative tool. As such, it served an important, latent economic function by rationalizing a minimal public investment in other, more positive, methods of treatment.

Not only were the institutions situated so as to eliminate sexual temptation, but they were also designed to serve a second long-range function. Safe custody was considered a spur to later marriage. By incarcerating delinquent girls the reformatories removed them from the unregulated sexual marketplace of ghetto streets and forced them to save their sexual favors, moral reputations, and health until they were of marriageable age. Most inmates of female reformatories were fifteen or sixteen years old, too young to marry in most states. A minimal stay of two to three years was therefore considered essential; upon release the girls would be of marriageable age and could seek legitimate gratification for their pent-up sexual energies. The institutions further promoted marriageability by placing the girls, after release, in new social settings where their moral improprieties were not common knowledge and where they could search anew for companionship.[26] Like the isolation of inmates from all contacts with men, the assumption that custodial care could have long-term therapeutic value underlay the marital goals of the reformatories. Thus, it could seriously be argued that custody in female reformatories was itself a form of treatment.[27]

Female reformatories did employ nominally rehabilitative programs, if only to give the girls something to do while their virtue was being protected. These programs embodied traditional stereotypes about women. The institutions attempted to instill in inmates the ideology of domesticity and the minimal skills necessary for its practice. According to correctional administrators, a girl's delinquency alone revealed that she had not learned to revere domestic pursuits. Instruction in domesticity was allied with the reformatories' marital goals: inmates would become so devoted to and skillful at domestic chores that they would easily attract husbands. It was as if, in the moral calculus of the juvenile reformers, a rigorous pursuit of domesticity would compensate for the girls' previous immoralities. Moreover, even if the girls failed to find mates shortly after release, they would at least be trained as domestics and so could support themselves while working in upright, middle-class households.[28]

Inmates were expected to take care of their reformatory cottages with the same pride that middle-class women lavished on their homes. Ideally, the girls would assimilate middle-class domestic values and lower-class domestic skills.[29] In each reformatory cottage, the matron served as the domestic educator, teaching girls both proper attitudes and skills. To increase public regard for the vocational-training programs, reformatory superintendents described them as if they were part of the larger home-economics movement that swept the country in the Progressive era.[30] Actually, the training rarely went beyond the chores necessary for personal hygiene and cottage upkeep, with a cooking class or two added for good measure. As one superintendent blithely argued,

> We never have taught typewriting and stenography. I find that in our community you can get about a dozen girls, who want to use a typewriter to one that wants to use a scrubbing brush. It seems to me that if you can get girls to understand that to be a homemaker is about the best thing that can come into the life of a woman, this is almost the best education they can have at the present time.[31]

Another superintendent was candid enough to admit what must often have been true in other reformatories that boasted "scientific" courses in home economics: "We teach the girls in practical cooking, as few are mentally capable of appreciating food values as taught in regular domestic science courses."[32]

The fourth and final goal of the female reformatories, surely their most ambitious, is implicit in the previous remark on inmates' mental limitations. The female reformatories were expected to play a central role in fulfilling the objectives of the eugenics movement, which achieved its greatest popularity at precisely the same time that governmental investment in female corrections significantly expanded.[33]

Eugenicists in the Progressive era sought to improve the "genetic fund" of the American population by discouraging and, if possible, forcibly preventing propagation by individuals considered innately inferior in culture and intellect. Almost by definition, the eugenicists identified recent immigrants from southeastern Europe as inferior. Relying on the rediscovery of Mendelian genetic theory in 1900, the eugenicists presented several key arguments: social conditions, such as poverty, and personality traits, such as laziness and courage, were discrete "unit characters" transmitted through heredity; unit characters were immutable; race was the primary determinant of human capacities; in some races socially undesirable unit characters predominated; and social legislation was necessary to encourage breeding of the racially fit and discourage breeding of the unfit. According to the eugenicists, persistent immorality among children was a sign of their genetic inferiority or racial degeneracy. To keep these degenerates from further diluting the nation's "genetic fund" and to prevent the nation from committing "race suicide," eugenicists insisted that permanent institutionalization and, if possible, sterilization were essential. The hereditarily degenerate threatened the eugenicists' vision of a more perfect and efficient world devoid of crime, poverty, and disease—a world quite consistent with the vision of many well-known reformers who outwardly were not eugenicists themselves.

Male and female reformatories were to play a special role in the larger eugenics campaign, as early detectors of innate criminality. In this role, however, the reformatories faced a unique problem: from a clientele composed mainly of children of racially inferior immigrants, how were they to identify those whose inheritance was so inferior as to warrant permanent incarceration or sterilization? By the 1910s the principal method of detection became mental testing, which rapidly evolved through a bewildering variety of forms, culminating in the 1916 Stanford revision of the Binet test—the intelligence quotient (IQ) test. With a seemingly precise instrument like the Stanford-Binet test in hand, psychologists and their helpers administered mental tests with virtual abandon to captive inmate populations. The tests were purported to identify those delinquents whose innate intelligence was so low that, in the judgment of the psychologists, they could never learn to control their instincts and

become civilized members of society. These defective delinquents, as they were commonly called, were to be transferred from the reformatories and incarcerated, if facilities permitted, in homes for feeble-minded children—institutions that proliferated in the Progressive era. In sum, the newly devised mental test legitimated eugenic goals by providing a scientific instrument for weeding out from the delinquent population those children whose antisocial behavior was inbred.[34]

Eugenic goals, as we noted, applied equally to male and female reformatories, and IQ and other mental tests were freely administered in both. But the literature on delinquency discussed feeble-mindedness among girls with a special urgency. In part this was because delinquent girls appeared at first to test at somewhat lower levels than delinquent boys.[35] More important, though, were the two widely held beliefs that women bore the primary moral responsibility for determining whether to have children and that women lacked the sexual drives of men. From this perspective, sexually precocious girls were morally and biologically perverse. When this view was joined with the belief that delinquent girls' intelligence was so far below normal that they could never learn to control their instincts, it becomes clear why the specter of female delinquency haunted the eugenics movement and why delinquent girls were more frequently incarcerated than delinquent boys.

Sexual Precocity and the Social Order in the Progressive Era

Having sketched the main elements of female juvenile justice in the Progressive era, we return to our earlier questions: why did public interest and investment in female delinquency burgeon so noticeably in this period, and why were girls treated more punitively than boys?

Perhaps the most obvious explanation of the rising interest in female delinquency in the Progressive period would be that the incidence of female delinquency grew until it simply could not be ignored. Much evidence could be marshaled to sustain this argument. One could turn, for example, to the remarkable data on family breakdown, cultural disintegration, and crime in urban immigrant communities documented in Thomas and Znaniecki's 1927 classic, *The Polish Peasant in America*.[36] Equally familiar are Jane Addams's poignant commentaries on the tensions and communication gulfs between mothers and daughters in *Democracy and Social Ethics* and *The Spirit of Youth and the City Streets*.[37] Similarly, one could assess the moral consequences of growing female participation in the work force. Did the increasingly familiar, "promiscuous" social relations of young men and women at work, mainly in the factory, encourage early sexual experimentation, as many contemporaries feared?[38] Finally, one could point to the pervasive image of the white-slave trade, as embodied in the work of the Chicago Vice Commission or Jane Addams's *A New Conscience and an Ancient Evil*.[39] The image of the white-slave trader fueled the era's antiprostitution campaigns and expressed metaphorically the common view that impoverished women were vulnerable to unscrupulous entrepreneurs. In short, the rising public investment in and sensitivity to female delinquency could be seen as a pragmatic response to a real and growing social problem.

Although this argument is appealing, two serious limitations, one methodological and the other conceptual, persuade us, while not ignoring or denying it, to focus our attention elsewhere. First, the argument encounters the methodological difficulties common to all attempts to calculate the actual incidence of crime, whether in the present or, especially, in the past. We agree with modern-day sociologists and criminologists that official crime data and popular impressions of crime waves are unreliable indices of illegal activity in any period.[40] Second, as Edwin Schur and others have argued, the traditional foci in criminological research on the incidence of crime and the personal characteristics of offenders have often obscured the fact that crime is a social and legal artifact.[41] Crime does not exist in the abstract; certain activities become illegal only when so labeled. This holds true particularly for juvenile delinquency because, as we have seen, its legal definition is extremely broad and imprecise.

To reiterate, we do not deny the possibility that rates of female delinquency were actually on the rise in the Progressive era, although it would be nearly impossible, given the broad definition of delinquency, to determine how to measure its incidence. Rather, our point is simply that the public agencies responsible for defining, prosecuting, and punishing antisocial behavior invariably shape a society's awareness of criminal conduct at any moment. Therefore, whatever the actual incidence of delinquency, it is essential to examine the cultural context in which delinquency was defined and the legal and penal context in which codes were enforced.[42]

We believe the heightened sensitivity to female delinquency and the growing governmental investment in correctional institutions can be best understood in relation to three developments that directly and indirectly affected social policies—eugenic solutions to social problems, increasing popularity of theories of adolescence, and the movement for "social purity." We have already dealt with the first development, the pervasive appeal of eugenics,[43] and so will proceed to the second development, the growing popularity of theories of adolescence.

Differential treatment of boy and girl delinquents did not represent a failure in implementation, we believe, but rather was an inevitable outcome of the sexually biased social-science theories of adolescence that matured in the Progressive era.[44] These theories gave the imprimatur of science to traditional Victorian views of women as weak, impressionable, emotional, and yet erotically impassive.[45] Moreover, these theories helped shape juvenile justice in two major ways: they invalidated the most optimistic features of the juvenile court movement as applied to girls, and they legitimated the creation of new reformatories for girls just when institutional care for boys was being widely challenged.

The central role of Clark University president G. Stanley Hall in developing and popularizing new ideas about adolescence has been well documented.[46] Following Hall's lead, reformers of various hues portrayed adolescence as at once the most malleable and the most problematic time of development. Adolescence represented a new stage of life: anything was possible, for better or for worse. Most important, during adolescence a child's permanent character took shape. Jane Addams captured the common viewpoint most poignantly in her paean to the "spirit of youth": in adolescence the human spirit bursts forth anew in unsuspecting children, enthralling them with the enchantment of life, confusing them with the rush of passion and idealism.[47] During this stage of life, the reformers admonished, children required especially solicitous parental care and creative social planning to help them cope safely with the potentials of adolescence.

Not surprisingly, most commentators believed that the female youngsters of poor immigrant families were particularly vulnerable. They grew up in slums, came from inferior racial stock, and were scarred by cultural norms that sanctioned the open display of male sexual interest. However, this concern for the vulnerability of ethnic girls did not lead to extensive social programs for them. The many organizations developed for children in the Progressive era, such as day and evening clubs, scouts, and summer camps, were promoted much less vigorously for girls than for boys.[48] This resulted, in part, because boys were a much more immediate social threat: their delinquencies posed a clear and present danger, whereas girls' delinquencies engendered more long-term fears. But the best explanation, we believe, lies in the fact that adolescent girls were considered much less malleable than adolescent boys. Institutions like girls' clubs and Girl Scouts received less support than their male counterparts because adolescence in girls, as a life stage, was regarded as a much less promising period for reshaping character. Rather than a new beginning, adolescence in girls was the time when character traits instilled earlier were put to the test. Most writers assumed that by the time girls reached puberty the most promising time for shaping their character had long since passed.[49] Thus, while the psychological theories of adolescence provided a new source of "scientific" optimism for preventing delinquency among boys, they gave no such hope for aiding girls.[50]

For similar reasons, we believe, the promise of the juvenile court movement was less widely acclaimed for girls than for boys. As Schlossman argues in his history of "progressive" juvenile corrections, the main rehabilitative tool of the court movement was probation.[51] Ideally, probation was to be a means of family education. Probation officers were to function less as agents of law enforcement than as visiting teachers who would instruct parents and children on how to eliminate family stress and how to use community resources to increase economic security and recreational enjoyment. The theory of probation was built firmly on the assumptions that most children became delinquent during their adolescent years, that adolescents were especially malleable, and that the successful rechanneling of youthful energies into lawful pursuits would motivate parents to modify their behavior toward their children and eliminate delinquency-producing conditions in the home. Probation epitomized the belief that adolescents merited several chances to become upright citizens.

Not so—or at least markedly less so—with erring adolescent girls.[52] Writers on female delinquency argued that, while a female's delinquencies were less criminally culpable, they were also less amenable to change through a relatively informal means of supervision like probation. Girls also received probation less frequently than boys because of the greater tendency to blame parents of delinquent girls. Unlike boys, it was argued, girls did not have places other than their homes in which to spend free time safely. Although writers on delinquency recognized that immigrant mothers and youth entered the work force because of poverty, they nonetheless held that rearing a girl imposed special moral responsibilities. Thus all mothers, regardless of economic circumstances, were obliged to keep their girls at home, when not in school or church, and to transform homes into refuges for protecting female virtue. This tendency to hold mothers more directly responsible for the behavior of girl delinquents than of boy delinquents further diminished the likelihood of probation for girls. If the female delinquent was considered less redeemable than her male counterpart, so too was her mother.

As probation was devalued for girl offenders, incarceration was judged more suitable. Earlier we examined the main rationales for female reformatories; here we will present additional justifications that illuminate why girl and boy delinquents were treated differently. One was the belief that girl delinquents, unlike boys, were not at all childlike in their behavior. By usurping the ultimate adult prerogative—sexual intercourse—female delinquents forfeited their right to be regarded merely as innocent, curious children. Moreover, precocious sexual exploration by girls threatened society's attempt to keep children innocent, chaste, and dependent until marriageable age. Female delinquents thereby subverted family government and had to be removed from their natural homes for the protection of neighborhood youth. Finally, imprisonment was seen as a boon to rehabilitation because of the speed with which neighborhood grapevines disseminated the reputations of "bad girls." One writer summed up these diverse rationales for more frequent incarceration of delinquent girls:

> And suppose a boy does bolt? He can try again. Suppose he "goes bad" a second or a third time, either through animal spirits or bad companions? He can begin all over again. Suppose he even stays out nights, and goes into lower forms of degradation? Even then if he can pull himself together physically and morally, he has not lost the chance for a decent manhood and a square deal. But is it so with any delinquent girl? No, a thousand times no! By the publicity of even the appearance in Court her reputation is tarnished, and with her reputation in question, her chance to retrieve herself in the same environment is very small. And in that eighty percent of crimes against the person, does my girl get a fair chance to "try again?" No, the world is against her, evil men are ready to tempt her further, the industrial situation helps to put her at their mercy, and even nature herself gives a last push towards the downward path when she physically handicaps herself. No! My girl who has once become delinquent finds it a 1000 times more difficult to straighten herself than the boy. The delinquent girl must be preserved against the *opportunities* of temptation which

are inevitably more fatal to her than to the boy.[53]

Clearly, then, the juvenile reformatory was the best possible place to treat delinquent girls—to protect society from them and them from society.

The third and final development behind growing awareness of female delinquency in the Progressive era was the movement for "social purity." More particularly, we want to analyze the relation of the purity ideal to what several historians have described as the "sexual revolution" of the Progressive era or the beginnings of "the modernization of sex." We believe that changes in sexual mores provided the cultural foundation for the burgeoning interest in female delinquency, the expansion of female reformatories, and the differential treatment of boy and girl delinquents. To explicate our position, we will first examine changing sexual mores in the Progressive era and then point up how they shaped new policies toward female delinquents.[54]

Increasing investment in reformatories for sexually precocious girls reflected a widespread revulsion against the growing frequency and legitimacy of sex as an everyday topic of discussion.[55] The expansion of the government's capacity to punish sexual promiscuity formed one phase of what we term a "sexual counterrevolution." The men and women who led this counterrevolution were, by and large, the same types of middle-class, nonethnic individuals who participated in the better-known political and social reforms of the period. For these men and women, the sexual counterrevolution represented a moral analogue to the cleansing of corruption in the political and economic arenas.[56]

To the counterrevolutionists the public's fascination with sex was inherently dangerous because it threatened the maintenance of conventional family life. They were particularly troubled by many recent changes: the flagrant commercialization of sex in the press; the demystification of sex by doctors, psychologists, and intellectuals; the increasingly open propaganda for dissemination of birth-control devices; and the moral dangers inherent in the discovery of new medical remedies for venereal disease. The counter-revolutionists urged that new strategies were essential to revitalize older sexual ideals, neutralize overstimulated sexual appetites, and purify social discourse on sex. If reticence was no longer possible, purity was.[57]

The counterrevolutionists engaged in three major "reform" campaigns: the wholesale destruction of prostitution; the widespread dissemination of sex education; and, our main subject, the punishment of sexually precocious girls. Each campaign had a number of concrete, functional goals, but each needs to be seen symbolically as well. Together, the campaigns represented a ritualistic protest against cultural changes, a spirited reaffirmation of older moral ideals, and an urgent call for creative new strategies to realize them.

The campaign against prostitution was, ironically, both a contribution to and a sharp reaction against what one author wittily called the arrival of "sex o'clock" in America.[58] Prostitution had been a widespread and fairly well-accepted part of American urban life. To be sure, moralists of many kinds had periodically demonstrated against the easy acceptance of prostitution and were probably responsible for insuring that only one brief effort was made, in St. Louis, to experiment with European methods of regulation.[59] By and large, though, prostitutes sold their services with little interference, and, all evidence indicates, remarkably large percentages of American males used them.[60]

In the Victorian years prostitution was silently tolerated for three principal reasons. For one, prostitutes thrived mainly in the poorer, immigrant neighborhoods, and the feeling was, then as now, that as long as prostitutes remained in the slums, more respectable communities need not worry unduly about them. Second, nineteenth-century popular opinion sanctioned the view that men possessed superabundant sexual energies that required frequent release for mental and physical health. We must be careful not to exaggerate here; for opposite beliefs on male sexuality were also held in the Victorian period. Several reformers argued, for example, that sexual indulgence destroyed men's bodies and minds and that men should be continent in their sexual expression.[61] In retrospect, though, what is remarkable is how easily these contradictory sentiments coexisted—the latter as ideology for public consumption, the former as an "underground" precept guiding actual behavior.[62]

The third reason for toleration of prostitution was the Victorian sentimentalization of womanhood.[63] "Respectable" women—the only kind men dared marry—were placed gingerly upon a pedestal and viewed as rarefied creatures without sexual motivation. By nature they were so innocent and gentle that it would have been cruel for husbands to impose their sexual lusts upon them. This viewpoint obviously facilitated public acceptance of prostitution: the practice was rationalized as a protection of the home and domestic life through the absorption of men's excess sexual energies.

In the reform campaigns of the Progressive era, the ambivalences and contradictions of Victorian sexual thinking gave way to the unyielding pursuit of purity and innocence. Under the leadership of the counterrevolutionists, city after city conducted elaborate studies of prostitution, revealing how openly prostitution flourished. Estimates varied, but it was conservatively calculated that well over half of American males from all social classes used or had used prostitutes and that many had contracted some form of venereal disease. Using these facts to support their position, the counterrevolutionists attacked regulation or even the toleration of prostitution as blasphemy. The wholesale destruction of prostitution became their goal, and, to a remarkable extent, they succeeded in wiping out many of the nation's most famous red-light districts in the years before the First World War.[64]

The metaphor of the white-slave trade fueled the antiprostitution campaign, but the extent to which prostitution was centrally organized was always uncertain.[65] Two other well-publicized arguments, though, helped sustain the fight against prostitution. The first resulted from several major scientific advances in detection and treatment of venereal disease. The counterrevolutionists drew grave moral implications from these scientific developments. On the one hand, they insisted, the physical devastation and easy communicability of venereal disease demanded rapid elimination of prostitution to safeguard family health. On the other hand, they asserted, the discovery of effective cures for venereal disease required quick destruction of prostitution, lest men be tempted to greater vice by the knowledge that they need not fear infection.[66]

The second rationale for destroying prostitution also drew upon medical opinion, although in this instance it was more a medical assertion than a demonstrable advance in scientific knowledge. The counterrevolutionists contended that a single standard of sexual behavior—that of continence—should prevail for men and women.[67] This ideal, as we observed, also had its supporters in the Victorian era. The twentieth-century proponents of continence did little to challenge the underground Victorian view that men's sexual appetites were ravenous. Instead, they emphatically urged continence as part of the larger Progressive-era moral revival, which included such other popular displays of conscience as the prohibition movement and the campaigns against child labor, dime novels, cheap movies, and the easy availability of narcotic drugs. Furthermore, the counterrevolutionists now gained the concerted support of powerful medical organizations against the underground doctrine of "sexual necessity." Three hundred of the nation's leading physicians, for example, issued a much-publicized manifesto in favor of male continence, which declared in part:

> In view of the individual and social dangers which spring from the widespread belief that continence may be detrimental to health, and of the fact that municipal toleration of prostitution is sometimes defended on the ground that sexual indulgence is necessary, we, the undersigned, members of the medical profession, testify to our belief that continence has not been shown to be detrimental to health or virility; that there is no evidence of its being inconsistent with the highest physical, mental, and moral efficiency; and that it offers the only sure reliance for sexual health outside of marriage.[68]

In sum, the counterrevolutionists, who led the antiprostitution campaign, relied heavily on medical opinion to persuade the American public that Victorian sexual liberties were sinful and unhealthy and that continence was possible through moral exertion and the removal of temptation. Paradoxically, then, at the very time when sex was becoming an accepted part of social discourse, a surprisingly effective campaign was led to eliminate one of the most common figures of nineteenth-century society, the prostitute.

Like the antiprostitution crusade, the sex-education movement drew heavily on medical science. Proponents of sex education saw themselves as progressive, fearlessly attacking the Victorian "conspiracy of silence" about sex. On closer inspection, though, sex education appears to have been anything but a modernizing influence. The sex educators fought mainly against imaginary adversaries, for sex was already an everyday topic of conversation. Moreover, the movement's rhetoric was largely puritanical, revealing deep fears about the moral impact of cultural change.[69]

The main goals of sex education were to purify discourse on sex, particularly in the popular press and among children, and to instill moral inhibitions against sexual gratification now that effective birth control and cures for venereal disease were becoming widely available. The sex educators were moral crusaders marching under the banners of medical and pedagogical science. They sought to develop instructional techniques for innocently conveying new medical knowledge abut sex to children and, at the same time, imbuing sex with older spiritual meanings. Sex education was a means of pedagogical warfare against the purveyors of sexual titillation. Far from encouraging freer discussion of sex, the sex educators wanted to discipline lust and channel it to conventional moral ends.[70]

While the sex educators claimed to bring discussion of sex into the open, their pedagogical approach was so indirect as to be obscurantist. About the only form of open sexual discussion they could tolerate, in fact, involved the mating of plants. The copulation of pistils and stamens served as a model for teaching children acceptable sexual emotion and was much preferred to analogies between human and animal sexuality.[71] To the extent that sex educators actually discussed human sex, it was always as a form of spiritual communion; intercourse was mainly a melding of chaste minds. The sex-education movement, then, is best conceived as part of a new strategy for realizing Victorian moral ideals in an era growing increasingly comfortable with sex. If adults in the Progressive period had become unduly attracted to sex, their children need not be.[72]

How is the sexual counterrevolution related to our main subject—female juvenile justice in the Progressive era? We believe the sentiments that motivated the antiprostitution and sex-education campaigns also inspired punitive treatment of female delinquents. The expansion of female reformatories was especially significant, for they played important instrumental and symbolic roles in the sexual counterrevolution. First, and most pragmatically, the female reformatories assisted in the medical effort to eliminate venereal disease. They isolated those girls who were assumed most likely to become disease carriers. If the girls were already carriers, the reformatories prevented them from spreading disease and made treatment possible. Second, and most presumptuously, the incarceration of sexually promiscuous girls was thought to facilitate the moral ideal of male continence. By removing from view a prime source of sexual temptation, the reformatories, it was earnestly hoped, would also eliminate a stimulant of sexual desire in ghetto communities, especially for teenage boys. Third, and most urgently, the reformatories took sexually active girls off the street during the age range when prostitutes were most commonly recruited.[73] Hence reformatories, aided by the juvenile courts' punitive attitude toward sexual precocity among girls, would contribute to the attack on prostitution by cutting off a likely supply of new recruits.

Finally, and most idealistically, the reformatories assumed a special symbolic role in the sexual counterrevolution. In an era becoming increasingly fascinated by all things sexual, reformatories offered a warn-

ing that society would still not tolerate girls who showed the same interest in sex as boys and reinforced the traditional belief that "normal" girls were sexually impassive. These sentiments seem to us to have represented, to a large extent, a rearguard defense against emerging modern views on the reality of female sexual desire. But if, in fact, the counterrevolutionists lost the war, they were a powerful enough force in the Progressive era to win important battles. We should not gauge their significance in the early twentieth century by their long-term defeat in the battle for sexual liberation.

In sum, we believe that female juvenile justice in the Progressive era was closely tied to the evolution of sexual mores. In an era of shifting cultural norms, new social policies emerged to defend older moral ideals. As we noted earlier, we do not deny the possibility that there may have been a real increase in female delinquency in the early twentieth century. But we insist that, whether the increase was real or imagined, the public response to female delinquency formed part of a larger cultural reaction, an attempt to revitalize Victorian morality and to punish women—prostitutes and sexually precocious girls alike—who impeded attainment of that goal.

Conclusion

We promised earlier not to draw glib comparisons between past and present because of the incomplete nature of our historical research. But our research unequivocally demonstrates that the roots of sexual discrimination in juvenile justice are indeed deep. Despite radically different attitudes today toward the social role and sexual desires of women, our correctional polices share many of the assumptions common in the nineteenth and early twentieth centuries.[74] Perhaps mainstream ideas about the proper role of women and of female sexuality have not changed as much as some may think;[75] perhaps correctional policies always lag behind changes in cultural perception; perhaps we as a society are trying unconsciously to relieve guilt about the passing of older moral standards by continuing to punish the most vulnerable group of females—poor, minority children who today, as in the past, predominate among incarcerated girls. We do not have a ready answer, but we do believe that there is an intimate relation between a society's correctional system and its deepest values and beliefs. And without doubt the values and beliefs that shaped a discriminatory system of juvenile justice in the Victorian and Progressive eras still dominate the administration of female juvenile justice today.

Notes

1. See Lawrence Cremin, "Foreword," in *American Education and Vocationalism*, eds. Marvin Lazerson and W. Norton Grubb (New York: Teachers College Press, 1974), p. ix.

2. One reason for the lack of scholarly attention to girl offenders in this period was the emphasis on gang delinquency, in which girls participated very little. There is, however, Paul Tappan's classic *Delinquent Girls in Court* (Montclair, N.J.: Patterson Smith, 1969), originally published in 1947.

3. See, for example, Lois Forer, "*No One Will Lissen*" (New York: Grosset and Dunlap, 1970); Patrick Murphy, *Our Kindly Parent . . . The State* (New York: Viking, 1974); Lisa Richette, *The Throwaway Children* (New York: Dell, 1969); and Ken Wooden, *Weeping in the Playtime of Others* (New York: McGraw-Hill, 1976).

4. See, for example, Michael Katz, *The Irony of Early School Reform* (Cambridge, Mass.: Harvard University Press, 1968); Anthony Platt, *The Child Savers* (Chicago: University of Chicago Press, 1969); Alexander Liazos, "Class Oppression: The Functions of Juvenile Justice," *The Insurgent Sociologist*, Fall 1974, **1**, 2–24; and Steven Schlossman, *Love and the American Delinquent* (Chicago: University of Chicago Press, 1977).

5. For exceptions see Don Gibbons, *Delinquent Behavior* (Englewood Cliffs, N.J.: Prentice-Hall, 1976), 2nd ed., pp. 169–189; William Sanders, *Juvenile Delinquency* (New York: Praeger, 1976), pp. 64–83; Rose Giallombardo, *The Social World of Delinquent Girls* (New York: Wiley, 1974); Meda Chesney-Lind, "Juvenile Delinquency: The Sexualization of Female Crime," *Psychology Today*, July 1974, **8**, 43–46; Meda Chesney-Lind, "Judicial Enforcement of the Female Sex Role: The Family Court and the Female Delinquent," *Issues in Criminology*, Fall 1973, **8**, 51–69; Kristine Rogers, " 'For Her Own Protection . . .': Conditions of Incarceration for Female Juvenile Offenders in the State of Connecticut," *Law and Society Review*, 1972, **7**, 223–246; Sarah Gold, "Equal Protection for Juvenile Girls in Need of Supervision in New York State," *New York Law Forum*, 1971, **17**, 570–598; Robert Terry, "Discrimination in the Handling of Juvenile Offenders by Social Control Agencies," in *Becoming Delinquent*, eds. Peter Garabedian and Don Gibbons (Chicago: Aldine, 1970), pp. 78–92; Freda Adler, *Sisters in Crime* (New York: McGraw-Hill, 1975), chap. 4; *Crime and Delinquency*, 1977, **23** (issue theme: "Criminal Justice to Women: Not Fair!"); and Paul Katzeff, "Equal Crime," *Boston Magazine*, December 1977, 107–108, 206, 208–210. For an estimate that girls now form nearly one-quarter of the juvenile court clientele, see Rosemary Sarri and Robert Vintner, "Justice for Whom? Varieties of Correctional Approaches," in *The Juvenile Justice System*, ed. Malcolm Klein, **v** (New York: Russell Sage, 1975), p. 171.

6. See the pioneering studies by Barbara Brenzel, "Lancaster Industrial School for Girls: A Social Portrait of a Nineteenth Century Reform School for Girls," *Feminist Studies*, Fall 1975, **3**, 40–53; and by Estelle Freedman, "Their Sisters' Keepers: The Origins of Female Corrections in America," Dissertation, Columbia University, 1976.

7. Margaret Reeves, *Training Schools for Delinquent Girls* (New York: Russell Sage, 1929).

8. Robert Mennel, *Thorns and Thistles* (Hanover, N.H.: University Press of New England, 1973), p. 172.

9. See especially Robert Bremner, *From the Depths* (New York: New York University Press, 1956); and Walter Trattner, *Crusade for the Children* (Chicago: Quadrangle, 1970).

10. Brenzel, "Lancaster"; Mennel, *Thorns and Thistles*, chap. 4; Freedman, "Their Sisters' Keepers," chaps. 3 and 4.

11. On the image of the "fallen woman," see Freedman, "Their Sisters' Keepers," chap. 2; for the emphasis on environmental causes behind male criminality, see David Rothman, *The Discovery of the Asylum* (Boston: Little, Brown, 1971).

12. Schlossman, *Love*, chaps. 2, 3, and 5.

13. Charles Loring Brace, *The Dangerous Classes of New York and Twenty Years' Work among Them* (New York: Wynkoop and Hallenbeck, 1872).

14. Miriam Langsam, *Children West* (Madison, Wis.: State Historical Society of Wisconsin, 1964); Thomas Bender, *Toward an Urban Vision* (Lexington, Ky.: University Press of Kentucky, 1975); and Steven Schlossman, "The 'Culture of Poverty' in Ante-Bellum Social Thought," *Science and Society*, 1974, **38**, 150–166.

15. These observations draw upon Schlossman's study of social-reform groups in Milwaukee and of parent-education organizations throughout the country. See Schlossman, *Love*, chap. 7, and "Before Home Start: Notes Toward a History of Parent Education in America. 1897–1929," *Harvard Educational Review*, 1976, **46**, 436–467. Also useful is David McLeod, "Good Boys Made Better: The Boy Scouts of America, Boys' Brigades, and YMCA Boys' Work, 1880–1920," Dissertation, University of Wisconsin, 1973.

16. Reeves, *Training Schools*, pp. 39ff; and Mennel, *Thorns and Thistles*, pp. 171–179.

17. For data on Milwaukee see Schlossman, *Love*, appendix 2, table 6. Our main source for Chicago is Sophonisba Breckinridge and Edith Abbott, *The Delinquent Child and the Home* (New York: Russell Sage, 1912); for San Francisco, Emily Huntington, Leona Jones, Donna Moses, and Ruth Turner, "The Juvenile Court," Bachelor of Arts Thesis, University of California at Berkeley, 1917; and for New Haven, Mabel Wiley, *A Study of the Problem of Girl Delinquency in New Haven* (New Haven, Conn.: Civic Federation of New Haven, 1915).

18. Schlossman, *Love*, pp. 143–144.

19. Breckinridge and Abbott, *The Delinquent Child*, pp. 28–35. See also Huntington et al., "The Juvenile Court," appendix.

20. Breckinridge and Abbott, *The Delinquent Child*, pp. 38–40; Huntington et al., "The Juvenile Court," appendix; Alida Bowler, "A Study of Seventy-Five Delinquent Girls," *Journal of Delinquency*, 1917, **2**, 157; Mabel Elliott, *Correctional Education and the Delinquent Girl* (Harrisburg, Pa.: Commonwealth of Pennsylvania Department of Welfare, 1928), pp. 34–35; Louise Ordahl and George Ordahl, "A Study of Delinquent and Dependent Girls," *Journal of Delinquency*, 1918, **3**, 34–35; and Wiley, *A Study of the Problem*, p. 11.

21. Bowler, "A Study of Seventy-Five Delinquent Girls," p. 159; Breckinridge and Abbott, *The Delinquent Child*, pp. 35–39; Elliott, *Correctional Education*, pp. 34–35; Ordahl and Ordahl, "A Study of Delinquent and Dependent Girls," pp. 55–59; and Wiley, *A Study of the Problem*, p. 9.

22. Breckinridge and Abbott, *The Delinquent Child*, p. 41; and Schlossman, *Love*, appendix 2, table 3.

23. In arguing that girls received more punitive treatment, we assume that incarceration is, by its very nature, a harsher form of punishment than probation. We are *not* saying, however, that the treatment of girls in reformatories was harsher than that of boys in reformatories.

24. These cases derive from Schlossman's sample of 1,200 cases in Milwaukee (10 percent of the total heard in this period). To the best of our knowledge, the Milwaukee court is the only one to have opened its early records for historical investigation; it is consequently impossible to say whether they are strictly representative of experiences in courts elsewhere. Although selected with an eye toward the exemplary and archetypal, each case was necessarily idiosyncratic because, obviously, no two children or their parents were exactly alike. The cases that follow should be appreciated much like opera highlights, as suggestive of a larger drama and of characteristic patterns of interaction among protagonists. To protect client anonymity we have changed the names of children and parents who appeared in court, although we have tried to retain their particular ethnic origins. For the same reason we have not cited the specific dates or docket numbers of individual cases.

25. Adina Mitchell, *Special Report on the Whittier State School* (Sacramento, Calif.: State Printing Office,

1896), p. 11. See also Mary Berry, "The State's Duty to the Delinquent Girl," National Conference on the Education of Truant, Backward, Dependent and Delinquent Children, *Proceedings* (1918), pp. 82–83; Mrs. Jennie Griffith, "The Training of Delinquent Girls," Conference of the National Committee on Prisons and Prison Labor, *Proceedings* (1919), pp. 15, 17; Miriam Van Waters, "Where Girls Go Right," *Survey Graphic*, 1922, **1**, 365; and Maine Industrial School for Girls, *Annual Report* (Waterville, Me.: Sentinel Publishing Co., 1909), pp. 7–8.

26. Breckinridge and Abbott, *The Delinquent Child*, p. 8; Huntington et al., "The Juvenile Court," appendix; Olga Bridgman, "An Experimental Study of Abnormal Children, with Special Reference to the Problems of Dependency and Delinquency," University of California, *Publications in Psychology*, 1918, **3**, 8; Berry, "The State's Duty," p. 87; Edith Burleigh and Frances Harris, *The Delinquent Girl* (New York: New York School of Social Work, 1923), pp. 32, 38–43; Mary Dewson, "Probation and Institutional Care of Girls," in *The Child in the City*, ed. Sophonisba Breckinridge (Chicago: Chicago School of Civics and Philanthropy, 1912), pp. 360–362; Martha Falconer, "Work of the Girls' Department, House of Refuge, Philadelphia," National Conference of Charities and Correction, *Proceedings* (1908), p. 393; and National Conference of Charities and Correction, *Proceedings* (1903), p. 517. Elliott's *Correctional Education*, a follow-up study of ex-inmates from the Sleighton Farms reformatory in Pennsylvania, left no doubt that marriage was the most important variable in explaining post-release behavior.

27. This argument was rarely advanced about the boys' reformatories. In fact, although historians have yet to provide adequate documentation, male reformatories apparently experimented with a variety of new correctional ideas in the Progressive era and participated tangentially in the "progressive education" movement. Elaborate vocational-training programs at a few of the larger reformatories became the envy of "progressive" educators such as David Snedden. In addition, many public reformatories experimented with self-government programs designed loosely along the lines suggested by William George in his famous Junior Republics; many adopted new forms of recreational and military training to improve health and discipline and upgraded their academic offerings for older inmates. Of course we do not believe that these newer correctional programs necessarily rehabilitated inmates. Our point is simply that levels of interest and public investment in rehabilitative programs were greater in boys' than girls' reformatories. For background on the relation between "progressive education" and juvenile corrections, see Walter Drost, *David Snedden* (Madison, Wis.: University of Wisconsin Press, 1967); and Jack Holl, *Juvenile Reform in the Progressive Era* (Ithaca, N.Y.: Cornell University Press, 1971).

28. A widely discussed social "problem" in the Progressive era was the declining availability of

trained domestic help; hence it can be argued that the reformatories' emphasis on domestic training was economically functional for the girls. It was also recognized, though, that domestics received wages so low that some were tempted to turn to prostitution for supplementary income.

29. Mary Berry, "Co-Ordination of Industrial and Vocational Work with Parole Administration," National Conference on the Education of Truant, Backward, Dependent and Delinquent Children, *Proceedings* (1902), pp. 52–60; Bowler, "A Study of Seventy-Five Delinquent Girls," pp. 156–157; Burleigh and Harris, *The Delinquent Child*, pp. 8–9; William Fairbanks, "Girls' Reformatories and Their Inherent Characteristics," National Conference of Charities and Correction, *Proceedings* (1901), pp. 254–262; Miss Mary Hinkley, "Problems of Administration: The Responsibilities of a School Toward its Girls," National Conference on the Education of Truant, Backward, Dependent and Delinquent Children, *Proceedings* (1920), pp. 20–23; Maine Industrial School for Girls, *Annual Report* (1909), p. 15; Griffith, "The Training of Delinquent Girls," p. 17; and Miss Elizabeth Mansell, "An Institution Program for Delinquent Girls," National Conference on the Education of Truant, Backward, Dependent and Delinquent Children, *Proceedings* (1917), p. 35.

30. See Emma Weigley, "It Might Have Been Euthenics: The Lake Placid Conference and the Home Economics Movement," *American Quarterly*, 1974, **26**, 79–96; and Barbara Ehrenreich and Deidre English, "The Manufacture of Housework," *Socialist Revolution*, October–December, 1975, **5**, 5–40.

31. National Conference of Charities and Correction, *Proceedings* (1901), p. 258.

32. California School for Girls, *Biennial Report* (Sacramento, Calif.: State Printing Office, 1918), p. 9.

33. For background on the eugenics movement we have relied especially on Mark Haller, *Eugenics* (New Brunswick, N.J.: Rutgers University Press, 1963); Donald Pickens, *Eugenics and the Progressive Era* (Nashville, Tenn.: Vanderbilt University Press, 1968); Rudolph Vecoli, "Sterilization: A Progressive Measure?" *Wisconsin Magazine of History*, 1960, **48**, 190–203; Peter Tyor, "Segregation or Surgery: The Mentally Retarded in America, 1850–1920," Dissertation, Northwestern University, 1972; and Allan Chase, *The Legacy of Malthus* (New York: Knopf, 1976).

34. *The Journal of Delinquency*, published in California, provided the principal forum for discussing this use of mental tests. Its articles were written mainly by psychologists, physicians, psychiatrists, and correctional workers. The *Journal* came especially under the influence of Lewis Terman and several of his students at Stanford, although other prominent members of its editorial board included William Healy, founder of the Juvenile Psychopathic Clinic in Chicago, and Arnold Gesell, the developmental psychologist from Yale.

35. See, for example, C. S. Bluemel, "Binet Tests on Two Hundred Juvenile Delinquents," *Training School Bulletin*, 1915, **12**, 191. Of all the drawbacks of the early IQ tests administered to delinquents, the most basic one was the leeway given to the examiner. The tests left much room for interpretation; often there was no clear-cut right or wrong answer. In such instances the examiners frequently came to dubious conclusions about inmates' mental ages. Consider the following example from Bluemel (p. 187), in which the examiner asked:

> "What is the difference between pride and pretension?" The first replies: "If you have too much pride, you go to certain places—cafes and dance halls. Some pretend to be proud but are poor." The second replies: "Pride means to be proud, and pretension means to pretend to be something that you are not." The third replies: "Pride is something in you that makes you—if you have enough of it—hold yourself a little above people that are without pride. Pretension is false pride." Obviously, these answers indicate that the three girls are at different mental levels. This fact is also attested by their answers to the other questions; and the answers in their totality permit one to make a fair estimate of their mental ages.

See also Ordahl and Ordahl, "A Study of Delinquent and Dependent Girls," pp. 41–73; and Jean Walker, "Factors Contributing to the Delinquency of Defective Girls," University of California, *Publications in Psychology*, 1925, **3**, 147–207.

36. William Thomas and Florian Znaniecki, *The Polish Peasant in America*, 2 vols. (New York: Knopf, 1927).

37. Jane Addams, *Democracy and Social Ethics* (New York: Macmillan, 1902); and *The Spirit of Youth and the City Streets* (New York: Macmillan, 1909).

38. For example, see "Are Low Wages Responsible for Women's Immorality?," *Current Opinion*, May 1913, **54**, 402.

39. Jane Addams, *A New Conscience and an Ancient Evil* (New York: Macmillan, 1913).

40. The previously cited texts of Gibbons and Sanders (see footnote 5) are especially sensitive to this difficulty. See also the essays collected under the heading, "The Data of Delinquency: Problems of Definition and Measurement," in *Juvenile Delinquency*, ed. Rose Giallombardo (New York: Wiley, 1966).

41. Edwin Schur, *Radical Non-Intervention* (Englewood Cliffs, N.J.: Prentice-Hall, 1973).

42. See especially Platt, *The Child Savers*; and Leon Radzinowicz, *Ideology and Crime* (New York: Columbia University Press, 1966).

43. The theories and policies proposed in the eugenics movement drew upon several long-term preoccupations of American social reformers. Hereditarian thinking and racial mythologies were staples of

American social thought throughout the nineteenth century, existing before the influence of Social Darwinism. Similarly, anti-immigrant hostility was common from the early nineteenth century onward, particularly in the large cities of the Northeast. We believe, nonetheless, that racial mythologies and anti-immigrant prejudice attained, in tandem, a new degree of legitimacy after the rediscovery in 1900 of Mendel's ideas, especially after these were popularized, and distorted, by social scientists whose influence on social policy grew enormously in the Progressive period. For example, Henry Goddard, one of the leading applied social scientists in the country and the first person to translate and adapt the Binet-Simon intelligence tests to American needs, wrote the best-selling bible of the eugenics movement, *The Kallikak Family* (New York: Macmillan, 1912) and led campaigns for literacy tests, restrictive marriage covenants, sterilization laws, and immigration restrictions. Even Jane Addams, a quintessential environmentalist, could endorse "the new science of eugenics" and "its recently appointed university professors" (*A New Conscience*, pp. 130–131). See Charles Rosenberg, "The Bitter Fruit: Heredity, Disease, and Social Thought," *Perspectives in American History*, 1974, **8**, 189–235; Ray Billington, *The Protestant Crusade, 1800–1860* (New York: Macmillan, 1938); and Oscar Handlin, *Boston's Immigrants* (Cambridge, Mass.: Harvard University Press, 1941). On the growing role of social scientists, see Julius Weinberg, *Edward Alsworth Ross and the Sociology of Progressivism* (Madison, Wis.: State Historical Society of Wisconsin, 1972); Barry Karl, *Charles E. Merriam and the Study of Politics* (Chicago: University of Chicago Press, 1974); Julia and Herman Schwendinger, *Sociologists of the Chair* (New York: Basic Books, 1974); and Chase, *The Legacy of Malthus*, pt. 2.

44. Although such theories were not nearly as new as their proponents claimed, they did exert considerable influence on Progressive-era social reformers. See Joseph Kett, *Rites of Passage* (New York: Basic Books, 1977), chap. 8; and Steven Schlossman, "G. Stanley Hall and the Boys' Club: Conservative Applications of the Recapitulation Theory," *Journal of the History of the Behavioral Sciences*, 1973, **9**, 140–147.

45. Two articles that advance the same argument as it applies to formal criminological theory are Doris Klein, "The Etiology of Female Crime: A Review of the Literature," *Issues in Criminology*, Fall 1973, **8**, 3–30; and Dale Hoffman-Bustamante, "The Nature of Female Criminality," *Issues in Criminology*, Fall 1973, **8**, 117–136.

46. See Dorothy Ross, *G. Stanley Hall* (Chicago: University of Chicago Press, 1972); Kett, *Rites of Passage*, chap. 8; and Schlossman, "G. Stanley Hall and the Boys' Club."

47. Addams, *The Spirit of Youth.*

48. On boys' clubs, see Schlossman, "G. Stanley Hall and the Boys' Club"; on camps, see McLeod, "Good Boys Made Better"; on Boy Scouts, see Jeffrey

Hantover, "Sex Role, Sexuality, and Social Status: The Early Years of the Boy Scouts of America," Dissertation, University of Chicago, 1976; and Peter Schmitt, *Back to Nature* (New York: Oxford University Press, 1969), chap. 10. For a more comprehensive synthesis of these and other organizations aimed at youth, see Kett, *Rites of Passage*, chaps. 7 and 8.

49. In reaching this conclusion we have relied especially upon: Augusta Bronner, "Effect of Adolescent Instability on Conduct," *Psychological Clinic*, 1915, **7**, 249–265; Burleigh and Harris, *The Delinquent Girl*; Mary Paddon, "A Study of Fifty Feeble-Minded Prostitutes," *Journal of Delinquency*, 1918, **3**, 1–11; Maude Miner, "The Woman Delinquent," New York City Conference of Charities and Correction, *Proceedings*, (1911), pp. 152–165; Rheta Dorr, "Reclaiming the Wayward Girl," *Hampton's Magazine*, January 1911, **26**, 67–78; Bridgman, "An Experimental Study of Abnormal Children"; Mary Moxcey, *Girlhood and Character* (New York: Abingdon, 1916); Winifred Richmond, *The Adolescent Girl* (New York: Macmillan, 1926); Ruth True, "The Neglected Girl," in *West Side Studies*, ed. Pauline Goldmark (New York: Survey Associates, 1914), pp. 1–134; Emily Lamb, "A Study of Thirty-Five Delinquent Girls," *Journal of Delinquency*, 1919, **4**, 75–85; Ordahl and Ordahl, "A Study of Delinquent and Dependent Girls"; Merritt Pinkney, "The Delinquent Girl and the Juvenile Court," in *The Child in the City*, ed. Breckinridge, pp. 349–354; Breckinridge and Abbott, *The Delinquent Child*; Wiley, *A Study of the Problem*; William Thomas, *The Unadjusted Girl* (Boston: Little, Brown, 1923): Miriam Van Waters, "Causes and Cure" and "The True Value of Correctional Education," in the Miriam Van Waters Papers, Box 11, Schlesinger Library, Radcliffe College; Falconer, "Work of the Girls' Department"; Elliott, *Correctional Education*; Huntington et al., "The Juvenile Court"; Walrek, "Factors Contributing to the Delinquency of Defective Girls"; Miss Vida Francis, "The Delinquent Girl," National Conference of Charities and Correction, *Proceedings* (1906), pp. 138–145; and Jane Rippin, "Social Readjustment as the Function of the Judge," Conference of the National Committee on Prisons and Prison Labor, *Proceedings* (1919), pp. 25–31.

50. We quote from Kett, *Rites of Passage*, p. 224; "Hall, moreover, had written very little about girls, a bias fully reflected in both the literature on boys-work after 1900 and in the masculine orientation and sexual segregation of scouting. . . . It was a boy's world, not a girl's and not a man's, a fact which prompted H. W. Gibson, a YMCA tractarian and boys-worker, to reduce all of adolescent psychology to something called 'boyology.' " A very useful compendium which nicely captures the differences in the theories is *Boy Training*, ed. John Alexander (New York: Association Press, 1915).

51. Schlossman, *Love*, chap. 4.

52. The citations in note 49 are all relevant here, espe-

cially Breckinridge and Abbott, *The Delinquent Child* pp. 35–38, 72–73, 169; Ordahl and Ordahl, "A Study of Delinquent and Dependent Girls," pp. 60–61; Van Waters, "Causes and Cure," p. 5; Paddon, "A Study of Fifty Feeble-Minded Prostitutes," p. 10; and True, "The Neglected Girl," p. 19.

53. Francis, "The Delinquent Girl," p. 140.

54. In the 1950s and 1960s the most common historical approach to the subject of morals and sex in the Progressive era was to emphasize its puritanical features. This approach flowed from the interpretation of social-reform movements epitomized by the work of Richard Hofstadter, especially *The Age of Reform* (New York: Knopf, 1955). In the past few years a different historical interpretation has emerged that stresses the loosening grip of Victorian morality on sexual attitudes and hold that "modern" attitudes toward sex first emerged in the Progressive era rather than, as is more commonly thought, in the 1920s. This view rests on several sources of evidence: the work of historical demographers, who argue that rates of premarital pregnancy rose markedly in this period; self-report studies, which indicate that dramatic increases in premarital intercourse occurred; and reexamination of literary sources, which suggests that social discourse in the Progressive era was a good deal less prudish than had been thought. As examples, see Linda Gordon, *Woman's Body, Woman's Right* (New York: Grossman, 1976), pt. 2; Paul Robinson, *The Modernization of Sex* (New York: Harper & Row, 1976); John Burnham, "The Progressive-Era Revolution in American Attitudes Toward Sex," *Journal of American History,* 1973, **59**, 885–908; James McGovern, "The American Woman's Pre-World War I Freedom in Manners and Morals," *Journal of American History,* 1968, **55**, 315–333; and Carl Degler, "What Ought to Be and What Was: Women's Sexuality in the Nineteenth Century," *American Historical Review,* 1974, **79**, 1467–1490.

While we agree with the historians who argue that the early twentieth century witnessed a marked increase in the public's willingness to discuss sex openly, we are uneasy about the tendency to locate the origins of sexual modernity in the Progressive era. This approach, we feel, exaggerates indications of the new morality and plays down evidence of older Victorian thinking. Most important for the history of female juvenile justice, this interpretation shifts attention away from major efforts in this period to reaffirm Victorian moral and sexual standards as well as to recast older religious commands into new secular, scientific language. Thus we both agree and disagree with the new interpretation.

55. On the scholarly side, the psychologist Helen Thompson Woolley noted that between 1910 and 1914 "the number of experimental investigations in the field [psychology of sex] has increased to such an extent that whereas it was difficult at that time [1910] to find anything to review, it is now impossible to review all that I could find" ("The Psychology of Sex," *The Psychological Bulletin,* 1914, **11**, 353). If scholars were having a field day with sex, so was the American public: "A wave of sex hysteria seems to have invaded this country," wrote the anonymous author of a piece which has since become an historical classic. "Our former reticence on matters of sex is giving way to a frankness that would even startle Paris." ("Sex O'Clock in America," *Current Opinion,* August 1913, **55**, 113).

56. This is our impression from reading the literature; we have not conducted empirical research on the social origins of the counterrevolutionists. Certainly Theodore Roosevelt was the most prominent of the individuals who engaged as fervidly in moral as in political reform. Roosevelt popularized the notion of "race suicide" and boasted that one of his greatest achievements was to have exercised enough will power to remain a virgin until marriage (William Harbaugh, *The Life and Times of Theodore Roosevelt* [New York: Oxford University Press, 1975], p. 15).

57. For general background see David Pivar, *Purity Crusade* (Westport, Conn.: Greenwood, 1973); and David Kennedy, *Birth Control in America* (New Haven, Conn.: Yale University Press, 1970).

58. "Sex O'Clock in America."

59. John Burnham, "Medical Inspection of Prostitutes in Nineteenth Century America—The St. Louis Experiment and Its Sequel," *Bulletin of the History of Medicine,* 1971, **45**, 203–218.

60. See Roy Lubove, "The Progressives and the Prostitute," *Historian,* 1962, **24**, 308–330; Robert Riegel, "Changing American Attitudes toward Prostitution (1800–1920)," *Journal of the History of Ideas,* 1968, **29**, 437–452; Keith Thomas, "The Double Standard," *Journal of the History of Ideas,* 1959, **20**, 195–216; Egal Feldman, "Prostitution, the Alien Woman and the Progressive Imagination, 1910–1915," *American Quarterly,* 1967, **19**, 192–206; Eric Anderson, "Prostitution and Social Justice: Chicago, 1910–15," *Social Service Review,* 1974, **48**, 203–228; Claudia Johnson, "That Guilty Third Tier: Prostitution in Nineteenth-Century American Theatres," in *Victorian America,* ed. Daniel Howe (Philadelphia: University of Pennsylvania Press, 1976), pp. 111–120; and James Wunsch, "Prostitution and Public Policy: From Regulation to Suppression, 1858–1920," Dissertation, University of Chicago, 1976.

61. A very useful introduction to the ideals and practices of sex in the Victorian period is *Primers for Prudery,* ed. Ronald Walters (Englewood Cliffs, N.J.: Prentice-Hall, 1974). See also Gordon, *Woman's Body,* chaps. 4 and 8; and Patricia Vertinsky, "Education for Sexual Morality: Moral Reform and the Regulation of American Sexual Behavior in the Nineteenth Century," Dissertation, University of British Columbia, 1974, sect. 2.

62. We borrow the term "underground" from Bryan Strong, who writes of the attempt in the early twentieth century "to counteract the underground belief in what was called the 'sexual necessity,' which declared that men must exercise their sexual

power lest their organs weaken or atrophy for want of use. Belief in a 'sexual necessity,' of course, was inconsistent with the ideal of chastity and continence" ("Ideas of the Early Sex Education Movement in America, 1890–1920," *History of Education Quarterly*, 1972, **12**, 145).

63. See, for example, Anne Scott, *The Southern Lady* (Chicago: University of Chicago Press, 1970); and Barbara Welter, "The Cult of True Womanhood: 1820–1860," *American Quarterly*, 1966, **18**, 151–174.

64. See Gordon, *Woman's Body*, p. 204. While we find her argument intriguing, we do not believe there is sufficient evidence to support Gordon's cause-effect contention that "the basis for the weakening of prostitution between 1910 and 1920 was not the conversion of men to purity; it was the conversion of women to 'indulgence'" (p. 192).

65. For example, see Clifford Roe, *The Prodigal Daughter: The White Slave Evil and the Remedy* (Chicago: L. W. Walter, 1911); and *War on the White Slave Trade*, ed. Ernest Bell (Chicago: Charles C. Thompson, 1909).

66. The principal medical spokesperson and organizational leader of the counterrevolutionists was Dr. Prince Morrow, whose activities are well treated in Burnham, "The Progressive Era Revolution."

67. See especially Thomas, *The Unadjusted Girl*; and Strong, "Ideas of the Early Sex Education Movement."

68. Quoted in Maurice Bigelow, *Sex-Education* (New York: Macmillan, 1918), p. 161.

69. We are especially indebted to the works of Pivar, Strong, and Vertinsky, "Education for Sexual Morality." The best primary sources, in our estimation, are *The Social Emergency*, ed. William Foster (Boston: Houghton-Mifflin, 1914); Bigelow, *Sex-Education*; and National Society for the Scientific Study of Education, *Education with Reference to Sex* (Chicago: University of Chicago Press, 1909).

70. Although the sex educators, by and large, wanted nothing to do with Freud, they were advocating a form of creative repression akin to the goals of the early conservative champions of Freud in America. See Nathan Hale, *Freud and the Americans* (New York: Oxford University Press, 1971).

71. For example, Bigelow writes in *Sex-Education*: "Like eating [sex] is a necessary function inherited from animals; but there has been an evolution of greater significance. In the animal world, sexual activity has only one function, reproduction; but human life at its highest has superadded psychical and social meaning to sexual relationships, and the result has been affection and the human family. If we reject this higher view of the double significance of sexuality in human life, and insist that only the necessary propagative function is worthy of recognition, it is almost inevitable that most people will continue to accept the hopeless view that human sexuality is on the same vulgar plane as that of the animals; in short, that it is only an animal function. This, I insist, is a depressing interpretation that will never help overcome the pre-vailing vulgar attitude toward sex" (p. 74).

72. For assessments of the influence of the sex-education movement, see Strong, "Ideas of the Early Sex Education Movement," pp. 152–153; and Vertinsky, "Education for Sexual Morality," chap. 9.

73. According to Jane Addams, "it has been estimated that at any given moment the majority of girls utilized by the trade are under twenty years of age and that most of them were procured when younger. . . . the average age of recruits to prostitution is between sixteen and eighteen years. . . . All the recent investigations have certainly made clear that the bulk of the entire traffic is conducted with the youth of the community, and that the social evil, ancient though it may be, must be renewed in our generation through its younger members. The knowledge of the youth of its victims doubtless in a measure accounts for the new sense of compunction which fills the community." *A New Conscience*, pp. 52, 142.

74. Richard Flaste, "Is Juvenile Justice Tougher on Girls Than on Boys?" *New York Times*, 6 September 1977, p. 48, cols. 1–4.

75. The classic argument, of course, is presented in Betty Friedan, *The Feminine Mystique* (New York: Norton, 1963). In addition to previously cited books and articles, the following historical works shed much light on continuities between past and present: Charles Rosenberg, "Sexuality, Class, and Role," *American Quarterly*, 1973, **25**, 131–153; Charles Rosenberg and Carroll Smith-Rosenberg, "The Female Animal: Medical and Biological Views of Women," *Journal of American History*, 1973, **60**, 332–356; Rosalind Rosenberg, "The Dissent from Darwin, 1890–1930: The New View of Woman among American Social Scientists," Dissertation, Stanford University, 1974; and Paula Fass, *The Damned and the Beautiful* (New York: Oxford University Press, 1977).

A Guide to Additional Primary-Source Materials on Female Juvenile Delinquency in the Early Twentieth Century

BOWEN, MRS. JOSEPH "The Delinquent Child of Immigrant Parents." National Conference of Charities and Correction, *Proceedings* (1909), pp. 255–261.

BRIDGMAN, OLGA "An Experimental Study of Abnormal Children with Special Reference to the Problems of Dependency and Delinquency." University of California, *Publications in Psychology*, 1918, **3**, 2–59.

BRONNER, AUGUSTA *A Comparative Study of the Intelligence of Girls*. New York: Teachers College Press, 1914.

BURLEIGH, EDITH "The Advantage of Parole Under a Separate Superintendent." National Conference on the Education of Truant, Backward, Dependent and Delinquent Children, *Proceedings* (1916), pp. 80–83.

BURLEIGH, EDITH "Some Principles for Parole for Girls." National Conference of Charities and Correction, *Proceedings* (1918), pp. 147–154.

DEBOLT, MRS. L. N. "Industrial Employment as a Factor in the Reformation of Girls." National Conference of Charities and Correction, *Proceedings* (1900), pp. 214–220.

DUMMER, MRS. W. F. "Introduction to Roundtable Discussion on the Delinquent Girl." The American Sociological Society, *Publications*, 1921, **16**, 185–186.

DYE, CHARLOTTE "The Defective Delinquent." National Conference on the Education of Truant, Backward, Dependent and Delinquent Children, *Proceedings* (1917), pp. 78–82.

FALCONER, MARTHA "The Culture of Family Life Versus Reformatory Treatment." National Conference of Charities and Correction, *Proceedings* (1914), pp. 108–110.

FALCONER, MARTHA "Reformatory Treatment for Women." National Conference of Charities and Correction, *Proceedings* (1914), pp. 253–256.

GODDARD, HENRY "The Treatment of the Mental Defective Who Is Also Delinquent." National Conference of Charities and Correction, *Proceedings* (1911), pp. 64–65.

HAMILTON, DR. ALICE "Venereal Disease in Institutions for Women and Girls." National Conference of Charities and Correction, *Proceedings* (1910), pp. 53–56.

HARRIS, DR. MARY "Preparing Delinquent Women for the New Citizenship." Conference of the National Committee on Prisons and Prison Labor, *Proceedings* (1919), pp. 6–14.

HARRIS, DR. MARY *I Knew Them in Prison.* New York: Viking, 1936.

HOAG, DR. ERNEST, AND DR. EDWARD WILLIAMS *Crime, Abnormal Minds and the Law.* Indianapolis, Ind.: Bobbs-Merrill, 1923.

HODDER, JESSIE "The Next Step in the Treatment of Girls and Women Offenders." National Conference of Charities and Correction, *Proceedings* (1918), pp. 117–121.

HOLSOPPLE, FRANCIS "Social Non-Conformity: An Analysis of 420 Delinquent Girls and Women." Dissertation, University of Pennsylvania, 1919.

KAUFFMAN, REGINALD *The Girl That Goes Wrong.* New York: Macaulay, 1911.

KENWORTHY, DR. MARION "The Logic of Delinquency." The American Sociological Society, *Publications*, 1921, **16**, 197–204.

LUNDBERG, EMMA "The Child-Mother as a Delinquency Problem." National Conference of Charities and Correction, *Proceedings* (1920), pp. 167–168.

MINER, MAUDE *Slavery of Prostitution.* New York: Macmillan, 1916.

MINER, MAUDE "The Individual Method of Dealing with Girls and Women Awaiting Court Action." Congress of the American Prison Association, *Proceedings* (1921), pp. 8–12.

MONTGOMERY, MISS SARAH "Discipline and Training of Girls in Industrial Schools." National Conference of Charities and Correction, *Proceedings* (1908), pp. 198–201.

MORROW, DR. LOUIS, AND DR. OLGA BRIDGMAN "Delinquent Girls Tested by the Binet Scale." *Training School Bulletin*, 1912, **9**, 33–36.

MORSE, MRS. FRANNIE "The Methods Most Helpful to Girls." National Conference of Charities and Correction, *Proceedings* (1904), pp. 306–311.

MURRAY, VIRGINIA "The Runaway Girl and the Stranded Girl." National Conference of Charities and Correction, *Proceedings* (1920), pp. 175–180.

NATIONAL CONFERENCE ON THE EDUCATION OF TRUANT, BACKWARD, DEPENDENT AND DELINQUENT CHILDREN, *Proceedings* (1915), pp. 49–53, and (1917), pp. 36–41, 82–90.

RENZ, EMILE "The Intelligence of Delinquents and the Eugenic Significance of Mental Defect." *Training School Bulletin*, 1914, **11**, 37–39.

RIPPIN, JANE "Municipal Detention for Women." National Conference of Charities and Correction, *Proceedings* (1918), pp. 132–139.

SESSIONS, DR. KENOSHA "Some Deductions from the Wasserman Test." National Conference on the Education of Truant, Backward, Dependent and Delinquent Children, *Proceedings* (1915), pp. 47–49.

SESSIONS, DR. KENOSHA "The Delinquent Girls as a Community Problem." National Conference on the Education of Truant, Backward, Dependent and Delinquent Children, *Proceedings* (1918), pp. 76–78.

SMITH, DR. CARRIE "The Unadjusted Girl." National Conference of Charities and Correction, *Proceedings* (1920), pp. 180–183.

TAFT, JESSIE "Some Problems in Delinquency—Where Do They Belong?" The American Sociological Society, *Publications*, 1921, **16**, 186–196.

VAN WATERS, MIRIAM "Juvenile Court Procedure as a Factory in Diagnosis." The American Sociological Society, *Publications*, 1921, **16**, 209–217.

WALD, MRS. LILLIAN "The Immigrant Young Girl." National Conference of Charities and Correction, *Proceedings* (1909), pp. 261–266.

WILSON, OTTO *Fifty Years' Work with Girls, 1883–1933.* Alexandria, Va.: National Florence Crittendon Mission, 1933.

WORTHINGTON, GEORGE, AND RUTH TOPPING *Specialized Courts Dealing with Sex Delinquency.* New York: Frederick H. Hitchcock, 1925.

QUESTIONS FOR DISCUSSION

1. Compared to delinquent boys, delinquent girls have received far less attention in historical literature and research studies. What two main reasons do the authors give for this?

2. The authors cite four principal reasons why the traditional interpretations of Progressive era policies regarding delinquent girls are lacking. List these reasons. Do you think the authors make a convincing argument? Why?

3. Discuss the four principal goals of female reformatories in the Progressive era. How and why did male reformatories differ from female reformatories?

APPLICATIONS

1. Set up an appointment with a member of the local judiciary, preferably a juvenile judge or probation officer. Ask this official about the differences in offenses committed by females and by males. Next, ask about the differences in the court sentences or treatment of these juveniles. Are there any disparities?

2. Do you believe that females and males should be treated differently for similar offenses? Why?

KEY TERMS

anachronistic   a person or thing that is out of place chronologically; a concept or theory from a former era that is incongruous or inapplicable to the present.

bucolic   refers to rural settings; relating to typical rural life.

chivalrous   marked by honor, generosity, and courtesy; tradionally high-minded consideration for women.

disposition   to deal with conclusively; to make a final decision or arrangement.

immutable   not capable of or susceptible to change.

legal artifact   an object that is created or results from a legal institution or activity (e.g., legal precedence, documents).

pragmatism   relating to matters in a practical way as opposed to an idealistic, intellectual, or artistic manner.

precocious   exhibiting unusually mature qualities at an early age.

Progressive era   that period from approximately 1900 to 1930 characterized by beliefs and attitudes of moderate social and economic reform by the government.

revivalism   a new presentation or publication of something old; a reviving or restoring of a past belief, attitude, or ideology. Typically a religious notion but can be applied to governmental philosophies.

Victorian era   that period from approximately 1870 to 1900 characterized by rigid moral standards, attitudes, and conduct; considered to be an especially repressive period with regard to dress and behavior; also characterized by stuffiness and hypocrisy.

5

The Watershed of Juvenile Justice Reform

Barry Krisberg
President of the National Council on Crime and Delinquency

Ira M. Schwartz
*Senior Fellow and Director of the Center for the Study of Youth Policy
at the Hubert Humphrey Institute of Public Affairs of the University of Minnesota*

Paul Litsky
Director of Analytic Research at the National Council on Crime and Delinquency

James Austin
Research Director at the National Council on Crime and Delinquency

This article presents an overview of current policy debates surrounding reform in the juvenile justice system. New data on trends in juvenile crime and the justice system are also presented. These data reveal that while juvenile arrests have declined, the juvenile justice system has become more formal and restrictive and more oriented toward punishment. The authors also present their views of policy implications and potential remedies.

The year 1984 marked the tenth anniversary of the federal Juvenile Justice and Delinquency Prevention Act of 1974 (JJDPA). This landmark piece of legislation was enacted by Congress and signed by President Gerald Ford after nearly six "years of exhaustive study on the part of the Senate Subcommittee to Investigate Juvenile Delinquency" (Krisberg and Schwartz, 1983: 335). In many respects, the legislation represents one of the most dramatic symbols of a lengthy national campaign to reform our system of juvenile justice. Another major reform symbol was the U.S. Supreme Court decision *In re Gault*,

"The Watershed of Juvenile Justice Reform," *Crime and Delinquency*, 32:1 (January 1986), pp. 5–38. Reprinted by permission of the publisher, Sage Publications, Inc.

which extended basic legal rights to children in the juvenile court.

There are many reasons why the JJDPA enjoys landmark status. Since the creation of the Children's Bureau in 1912, the federal government has played an increasingly active role in juvenile delinquency. However, the JJDPA of 1974 contained a broad mandate for reform and was the most comprehensive federal juvenile justice legislation ever enacted. For example, the Act called for such things as the "evaluation of all federally assisted juvenile delinquency programs," the provision of "technical assistance to public and private institutions," the development and implementation of training programs for juvenile justice professionals, paraprofessionals, and volunteers, the support for juvenile delinquency research, and the development and support for the "implementation of national standards for the administration of juvenile justice" (U.S. Senate Committee on the Judiciary, 1975: xi–xii). The JJDPA also called upon the federal government to provide "the necessary resources, leadership, and coordination (1) to develop and implement effective methods of preventing and reducing delinquency, (2) to develop and conduct effective programs to prevent delinquency, to divert juveniles from the traditional juvenile justice system and to provide critically needed alternatives to institutionalization, and (3) to improve the quality of juvenile justice in the United States" (U.S. Senate Committee on the Judiciary, 1975: xiii).

The JJDPA is significant in that it requires the achievement of specific and measurable objectives by states choosing to participate in its grant program. Some of these objectives, such as deinstitutionalization of status offenders and removal of minors from adult jails, continue to be extremely controversial policy goals. During their inquiry, the Senate Subcommittee to Investigate Juvenile Delinquency found that "almost 40 percent of all children involved in the juvenile justice system were status offenders and dependent and neglected youth" (U.S. Senate Committee on the Judiciary, 1975: 4). They were juveniles who had "not done anything which could be considered a violation of criminal law" (U.S. Senate Committee on the Judiciary, 1975: 4). The Act required that, "within two years after submission and approval of a state plan, states must stop the incarceration of such youth in secure juvenile detention or correctional facilities . . . in order to continue to receive federal juvenile crime control funds" (U.S. Senate Committee on the Judiciary, 1975: xxii). This requirement was subsequently modified by giving states five years to comply with this mandate (U.S. House of Representatives, 1980: 384).

Despite the controversial policy objectives of the JJDPA, it is worth recalling that the JJDPA enjoyed broad-based support from juvenile justice and child welfare professionals, public interest groups, national youth-serving organizations, child advocacy groups, and from the Congress itself. The JJDPA was passed in the House of Representatives by a vote of 329–20 (U.S. Senate Committee on the Judiciary, 1975: 7) and it passed in the Senate with only one dissenting vote (U.S. Senate Committee on the Judiciary, 1975: 7). The congressional support for this legislation was best expressed by Senator Mathias, ranking Republican member of the Senate Sub-

committee to Investigate Juvenile Delinquency, when he stated that it was an "act which had strong bipartisan support and which represented the best efforts of persons of all political persuasions" (U.S. Senate Committee on the Judiciary, 1975: 6).

Coincidentally, the tenth anniversary of the JJDPA arrived during the same year that the Act was critically debated and subsequently reauthorized with much less support from the Executive branch. Once again, juvenile justice professionals, public interest groups, child advocates, and congressional leaders forged a strong consensus during this legislative process. This coalition was also crucial to continued funding of the JJDPA because of repeated efforts by the Reagan Administration to "zero out" the budget of the Office of Juvenile Justice and Delinquency Prevention. Whereas the JJDPA survived serious political attacks, the reform movement that spawned it seemed in deep trouble. It is our contention that the current period represents a watershed in terms of reform. Further, a new reform agenda is being promoted that seeks to overturn some of the accomplishments of the past ten years.

A recent report of the National Advisory Committee for Juvenile Justice and Delinquency Prevention (NAC), entitled *Serious Juvenile Crime: A Redirected Federal Effort*, represents one of the best articulated statements of this new agenda. Submitting their report to the president and the Congress, the NAC stated that "the time has come for a major departure from the existing philosophy and activity of the federal government in the juvenile justice field" (NAC, 1984: iii). The NAC recommended that the "federal effort in the area of juvenile delinquency should focus primarily on the serious, violent, or chronic offender" (NAC, 1984: 9). Also, they recommended that federal initiatives be limited to such things as research, carefully designed and evaluated demonstration projects, "dissemination of information," and providing "training and technical assistance" (NAC, 1984: 11). They rejected basic components of the JJDPA, such as the continued provision of grants to states to accomplish deinstitutionalization of status offenders and jail removal.

The NAC's call for a more narrowly focused federal effort was, in large part, based on their conclusion that "federal anti-delinquency policy has been based on ideas whose vogue has run far ahead of solid knowledge" (NAC, 1984: 8). The NAC was critical of past congressional leaders and noted that the JJDPA "was passed at a time when its sponsors were more certain about the rightness of a particular philosophy than experience has warranted" (NAC, 1984: 6). For example, the NAC argued:

> Congressional sponsors and the coalition of youth-service agencies that were the Act's most prominent backers argued that the juvenile justice system itself was to blame for much delinquency. It labeled youth as delinquent, thereby causing a self-fulfilling prophecy. Or it sent youth to institutions, "schools for crime," where they learned to become smarter and inveterate criminals. Neither assertion had an empirical basis. Neither has acquired one in the past ten years. But these claims were repeated so often and so loudly that people assumed they were right. Unsubstantiated theory governed policy: minimize punishment of juveniles whenever possible, rely only on prevention rather than emphasize correction and deterrence to reduce delinquency [NAC, 1984: 7].

The NAC raised serious questions about the appropriateness of many of the priorities embodied in the JJDPA. For example, although noting that the deinstitutionalization (of status offenders) and separation of adult and juvenile offenders are admirable goals, they questioned whether such activities should be part of federal regulatory activity or whether these concerns should be addressed at the state and local level. For example, the NAC (1984: 13) noted that "California is currently experimenting with approaches that sometimes mix individuals in the age group 16–24 as a single institutional population and that federal policy should not discourage this kind of diversity and innovation."

The NAC statement is quite consistent with policy positions expressed by U.S. Department of Justice officials (see Regnery, forthcoming). These policies are also reflected in newly proposed regulations that offer broader latitude to states seeking compliance with the status offender and jail removal requirements of the JJDPA (*Federal Register*, February 13, 1985: 6098). Moreover, the Department of Justice has begun an ambitious program of discretionary research and action projects emphasizing the new reform agenda. These new areas include (1) more effective prosecution of serious and violent juvenile offenders, (2) prevention of the victimization of children, (3) reduction of school violence, (4) promoting concern for the victims of juvenile crime, and (5) restoring the concept of "accountability" or just deserts to the juvenile justice system. While many of these new goals are commendable, it will be important to examine if they supplant or come in conflict with the original JJDPA reform agenda.

Changes in federal policy are also reflected in the actions of state legislatures. For example, since 1978, legislation has been enacted in nearly half the states aimed at handling serious juvenile offenders in adult courts (Academy for Contemporary Problems, 1982: 211–212). These statutory changes fall into three categories: (1) making it easier to prosecute juvenile offenders in adult courts (California and Florida), (2) lowering the age of judicial waiver (Tennessee, Kentucky, and South Carolina), and (3) excluding certain offenses from juvenile court jurisdiction (Illinois, Indiana, Oklahoma, and Louisiana). In addition, a number of states have attempted to stiffen juvenile court penalties for serious juvenile offenders through (1) mandating minimum terms of incarceration (Colorado, New York, and Idaho) or (2) enacting a comprehensive system of sentencing guidelines (Washington). Other states have required the more active involvement of prosecutors in juvenile court (California) and others have increased the power of prosecutors to determine court positions (Colorado).

Besides legislative changes, there are other indices of the success of the new agenda. In most American communities there are grass-roots efforts to heighten public awareness about the hidden victimization of children. These campaigns have focused on the physical and sexual abuse of children and the plight of missing children. Parents and school officials are organizing programs to teach children how to protect themselves from harm. For example, many parents are volunteering to permit law enforcement agencies to fingerprint their children. This is a far cry from the earlier fears of "negative labeling" and reflects intensified lobbying efforts to alter traditional justice system practices to improve assistance to victims and promote harsher punishment for offenders.

In these same communities, there are increased efforts to combat disruptive behavior in schools and to suppress drug use on school grounds and in public recreation areas by increasing the presence of law enforcement and by referring more youth to the juvenile court.

There are also major signs of a national reassessment of the handling of status offenders. Many are calling for status offenders to be brought back under the jurisdiction of the juvenile justice system. These critics of the De-institutionalization of Status Offenders (DSO) movement assert that the hoped-for network of alternatives for status offenders never materialized and that many troubled youth are now left without needed help and protection. For example, juvenile court officials, law enforcement officers, educators, and parents in such states as Hawaii, Washington, California, Ohio, North Carolina, and Florida are advocating for more authority to arrest and detain status offenders. In California, some educators, juvenile justice professionals, and state policymakers are supporting efforts to establish secure "private disciplinary" schools for truants that would be licensed by the state superintendent of public schools and comply with the standards for juvenile training schools developed by the American Correctional Association. In addition, federal officials have recently advocated that the JJDPA be amended to allow status offenders to be detained in secure facilities for up to five days.

The recent U.S. Supreme Court decision in the *Schall v. Martin* (1984) case represents yet another example of the fundamental changes that may be under way. Originally, the plaintiffs filed a lawsuit in Federal District Court claiming that the New York Family Court Act was unconstitutional because of its vagueness and because it allowed for the preventive detention of juveniles.

The District Court struck down the statute as permitting detention without due process and ordered the release of all class members. The Court of Appeals affirmed, holding that since the vast majority of juveniles detained under the statute either have their cases dismissed before an adjudication of delinquency or are released after adjudication, the statute is administered, not for preventive purposes, but to impose punishment for unadjudicated criminal acts, and that therefore the statute is unconstitutional as to all juveniles (*Schall vs. Martin*, 1984: 4681).

However, the U.S. Supreme Court reversed the decision of the appeals court. Justice Rehnquist, writing the opinion for the majority, declared that the "preventive detention under the statute serves the legitimate state objective, held in common with every State, of protecting both the juvenile and the society from the hazards of pretrial crime" (*Schall v. Martin*, 1984: 4681). Although the ultimate impact of the Supreme Court's decision has yet to be felt, some experts believe the court's ruling may encourage a significant expansion in the use of secure detention.

We are already witnessing an intense ideological debate among proponents of the old and new agendas for juvenile justice reform. This debate is being waged at professional conferences, in legislative chambers, in the media, and in community meetings. These discussions are often quite heated because of deep concerns for the well-being of children as well as legitimate fears about the excessive level of serious and violent youth crime. We believe it is crucial that the debate be grounded in empirical data about how the nation's juvenile justice system is now handling youth referred to its care. Although the data are often less than ideal, they offer important clues as to the consequences of contemporary policy directions. These data also point to alarming trends, such as the growing disproportionate representation of minorities in juvenile correctional facilities, that should be carefully examined by juvenile justice professionals, policymakers, and concerned citizens.

Declining Youth Population and Juvenile Arrests

Between 1971–1982 the United States youth population that was eligible for juvenile court jurisdiction declined by 8.4%.[1] From 1979 to 1982, the eligible youth population declined by 4.4%. This decline is expected to continue throughout the decade of the 1980s. Thereafter, the increase in the U.S. birthrates during the last few years is anticipated to produce an upturn in the number of American teenagers in the mid-1990s or an echo "baby boom." These demographic trends have been experienced in many communities in terms of declining junior high school and high school enrollments and a reduction in the size of the American family. There are even newspaper reports that fast-food restaurants, a major employment source for teenagers, are experiencing labor shortages.

As the youth population has shrunk so have juvenile arrests been generally declining since 1975. For example, there were 1,927,120 juveniles arrested in 1975—the peak year for juvenile arrests. By 1982, the total number of juvenile arrests had dropped to 1,630,226—a decline of 15%. During this same time period (1975–1982) arrests of juveniles for murder, rape, robbery, and aggravated assault had also dropped by 15%. Arrests of juveniles for status offenses declined from 563,709 in 1975 to 204,803 (a decline of 64%).[2]

Increasing Police Referrals to Juvenile Court

At the same time that fewer juveniles were being arrested, the manner by which police handled arrested juveniles also changed. Using data presented in the FBI's Uniform Crime Reports, one observes a steady increase in the proportion of arrested juveniles who are referred to the juvenile court for further action. In the early 1970s, approximately half of juveniles taken into custody were referred to the juvenile court. By 1981, this proportion had increased to 58%. Likewise, the proportion of arrested juveniles whose cases were handled informally by law enforcement agencies dropped

from 45% to 34%. Police referrals of juveniles to welfare or other community agencies remained relatively unchanged from 1971–1981. This same period witnessed a sharp rise in juveniles being referred to adult courts. For example, in 1971 less than 1% of arrested juveniles were referred by police to adult courts. But in 1981, referrals to adult courts constituted 5% of all juvenile arrests.

The clear picture emerging from these data is of more formal and restrictive police responses to youth crime—even though the actual numbers of youth being arrested were declining. Some have speculated that the more formal law enforcement practices reflect the U.S. Supreme Court decisions extending more legal rights to juveniles. Others have argued that, as police stopped arresting status offenders and used diversion programs in lieu of arrests, the residual group of arrestees were charged with more serious offenses that required more restrictive dispositions. Yet another explanation of these police dispositional trends may be found in the increasing public support for "get tough" approaches to youth crime. Especially during the mid-1970s there were vocal critics of the alleged leniency of the juvenile justice system. Other observers have interpreted these data as evidence of agency equilibrium to maintain case loads. Although it is extremely difficult to sort out the most plausible explanation of changing police practices toward juveniles, it is important to trace the impact of these changed practices on the juvenile court.

Increasing Severity of Juvenile Court Sanctions

Table 1 presents data on the volume and rate of referrals to the nation's juvenile courts. The most obvious finding is the relatively stable number of cases throughout this period. For example, from 1975 to 1981 the number of cases declined by only 4%. The rate of cases handled per 100,000 youth was virtually unchanged. However, the data also show a small but steady downward trend in the volume of juvenile court cases from 1975–1979. Thereafter the trend was

TABLE 1 National Juvenile Court Statistics on Cases Handled in 1975 to 1981

	1975	1976	1977	Year 1978	1979	1980	1981
Cases disposed of							
Number	1,406,000	1,396,800	1,355,500	1,340,700	1,306,700	1,345,000	1,348,100
Rate*	4,786	4,780	4,664	4,638	4,545	4,717	4,793
Percentage of cases handled with a petition	47.0	—	48.3	49.8	45.7	43.1	46.8

SOURCE: Adapted from *Delinquency in the United States* (1979, 1981) National Center for Juvenile Justice.
*Rate per 100,000 youth age 10 to upper limit of juvenile court jurisdiction.

TABLE 2 National Juvenile Court Statistics on Offense at Referral, 1975 to 1981

Offense at Referral	1975 Total	%	1976 Total	%	1977 Total	%	1978 Total	%	1979 Total	%	1980 Total	%	1981 Total	%
Person	145,100	10.3	124,600	8.9	128,800	9.5	114,200	8.5	143,200	11.0	154,500	11.5	159,100	11.8
Property	588,400	41.8	641,200	45.9	632,100	46.6	614,200	45.8	644,400	49.3	658,500	49.0	661,900	49.1
Drugs	116,000	8.2	95,800	6.9	90,000	6.6	82,600	6.2	79,800	6.1	74,800	5.6	72,800	5.4
Public order	201,000	14.3	214,700	15.4	224,600	16.6	212,300	15.8	180,300	13.8	204,900	15.2	206,000	15.3
Status	355,600	25.3	320,500	22.9	280,000	20.7	317,400	23.7	259,000	19.8	252,300	18.8	248,300	18.4
Total	1,406,100	99.9	1,396,800	100.0	1,355,500	100.0	1,340,700	100.0	1,306,700	100.0	1,345,000	100.1	1,348,100	100.0

SOURCE: Adapted from *Delinquency in the United States* (1979, 1981), National Center for Juvenile Justice.
NOTE: Percentages may not add to 100 due to rounding.

reversed. The nation's juvenile courts witnessed a rise in cases disposed of between 1979–1981. It is important to examine these trends in light of the juvenile arrest statistics discussed above. Police were arresting fewer juveniles but they were sending a larger proportion of arrestees to court, creating a steady state in the volume of referrals and dispositions. The court was disposing of these cases via formal petitions in slightly less than half the cases. During 1975–1981 the percentage of court referrals resulting in a delinquency petition remained largely unchanged.

There were changes in the types of offenses for which youth were referred to the juvenile court. These data are summarized in Table 2. Referrals for status offenses declined by 30%. The number of referrals for public order offenses remained approximately the same and referrals for drug offenses declined by 37%. Whereas the juvenile court reviewed a smaller number of minor offenders, those cases involving more serious crimes actually

increased. Between 1975–1981, referrals for persons crimes increased by 10% and property crimes increased by 12%. This latter increase in referrals for property and person offenses (despite declining arrests for these crimes) reflects the changing way police were handling these cases.

One popular explanation of this phenomenon is that as status offenders were removed from court jurisdiction, the police felt more comfortable sending more serious cases for juvenile court handling. According to some observers of police behavior, law enforcement agencies were much more willing to pass cases on to the court. These data may also give partial evidence that some offenses, once designated as status or minor offenses, have been relabeled as more serious crimes. For example, in California arrests for status offenses dropped dramatically soon after the passage of legislation restricting the use of secure confinement for status offenders. But, arrests of juveniles for minor criminal offenses climbed during this same

TABLE 3 Dispositions of Cases Referred to Juvenile Court with and without Petitions in 1979 and 1981 (figures in percentages)

| | 1979 | | 1981 | |
	With Petition	Without Petition	With Petition	Without Petition
Waived to Criminal Court	1.4	0	1.9	0
Dismissed	24.1	72.0	26.0	72.5
Probation	47.0	23.4	33.9	23.2
Institution	10.4	0.1	13.6	0.1
Public or Private Agency	4.8	0.2	3.5	0.2
Other	12.3	4.4	21.2	4.0
Total Number	596,900	709,800	630,700	717,400

SOURCE: Adapted from *Delinquency in the United States* (1979, 1981), National Center for Juvenile Justice.

TABLE 4 Proportion of Juvenile Court Dispositions for Nondismissed Cases with Reason for Referral in 1979 and 1981 (in percentages)

| | Reason for Referral | | | | | | | | | | | |
Disposition	Person 1979	1981	Property 1979	1981	Drugs 1979	1981	Public Order 1979	1981	Status 1979	1981	Total 1979	1981
Waived to criminal court	3.6	5.9	1.3	2.3	1.0	1.7	1.3	2.2	0.0	0.0	1.3	2.5
Institution	16.5	22.9	10.2	18.3	5.1	12.7	10.9	19.3	4.7	14.0	9.7	18.3
Public or private agency	4.6	3.8	3.9	4.0	2.3	2.7	4.8	4.4	7.2	10.8	4.6	4.7
Probation	63.6	37.5	71.8	48.9	76.7	51.6	60.3	42.6	65.5	42.5	68.4	45.8
Other	11.6	30.0	12.8	26.5	14.8	31.4	22.8	31.5	22.7	32.7	16.0	28.6
Total*	99.9	100.1	100.0	100.0	99.9	100.1	100.1	100.1	100.1	100.0	100.0	99.9

SOURCE: Adapted from *Delinquency in the United States* (1979, 1981), National Center for Juvenile Justice.
*Totals may not sum to 100 due to rounding.

period. Another possibility is that the increased role of prosecutors in the juvenile court may be escalating the nature of referral charges. Whatever the hypothesized explanation for the changing nature of juvenile court offenses, many juvenile court judges perceived that they were handling a more serious type of delinquent behavior.

This perception of the increased seriousness of delinquent offenses is clearly reflected in juvenile court sentencing practices. Table 3 compares 1979 and 1981 in terms of different methods of case disposition. For cases handled without a delinquency petition (mostly minor offenses), the distribution of court dispositions was virtually unchanged. The vast majority of these cases were dismissed (72%), with the next most frequent category being informal probation. For cases handled via a delinquency petition, one sees a decline in the use of probation and an increase in institutional placements. As shown in Table 4, the increasing severity of court sanctions occurred for virtually all offense types. Also of importance was the growth in "other dispositions" that reflected the extensive use of restitution and fines as enhancements to traditional probation.[3]

In sum, national juvenile court statistics reveal a virtually constant case load despite the sharply declining juvenile arrest rate. The court continued to use petitions in slightly less than half the cases. As a result of combined police and prosecution practices, the nature of referral changes appeared more serious and the courts have employed more restrictive sanctions such as institutionalization and enhanced conditions of probation. One can easily anticipate that juvenile court policies that increasingly used more restrictive sanctions would inevitably result in an increase in the numbers of juveniles incarcerated across the country.

TABLE 5   United States Public Juvenile Detention and Training School Admissions, One-Day Counts, and Expenditures

	1971 Total	Rate per 100,000	% Change 71–74	1974 Total	Rate per 100,000	% Change 74–79	1979 Total	Rate per 100,000	% Change 79–82	1982 Total	Rate per 100,000	% Change 71–82
Detention Admissions	496,526	1,655	6.6	529,075	1,791	−14.6	451,810	1,571	−7.8	416,610	1,516	−16.1
Male	349,407	2,329	6.2	371,225	2,514	−4.1	356,167	2,477	−7.3	330,075	2,403	−5.5
Female	147,119	981	7.3	157,850	1,069	−39.4	95,643	665	−9.5	86,535	630	−41.2
Detention One-Day Count	11,767	39	−6.4	11,010	37	−3.0	10,683	37	22.1	13,048	47	10.9
Male	7,926	53	−2.9	7,698	52	15.6	8,901	62	21.7	10,833	79	36.7
Female	3,841	26	−13.8	3,312	22	−46.2	1,782	12	24.3	2,215	16	−42.3
Detention Expenditures												
In thousands of dollars	92,110	—	39.1	128,160	—	78.6	228,849	—	37.0	313,584	—	240.4
Adjusted for inflation	75,899	—	14.3	86,764	—	21.3	105,271	—	3.1	108,500	—	43.0
Training School Admissions	67,775	226	−0.5	67,406	228	−5.2	63,901	222	2.3	65,401	238	−3.5
Male	53,089	354	1.2	53,737	364	3.2	55,457	386	3.6	57,472	418	8.3
Female	14,686	98	−6.9	13,669	93	−38.2	8,444	59	−6.1	7,929	58	−46.0
Training School One-Day Count	35,960	120	−29.4	25,397	86	−8.7	23,200	81	8.1	25,071	91	−30.3
Male	27,874	186	−29.2	19,745	134	2.5	20,237	141	9.8	22,213	162	−20.3
Female	8,086	54	−30.1	5,652	38	−47.6	2,963	21	−3.5	2,858	21	64.7
Training School Expenditures												
In thousands of dollars	248,759	—	9.3	271,847	—	47.0	399,485	—	46.8	586,396	—	135.7
Adjusted for inflation	204,977	—	10.2	184,040	—	−0.2	183,763	—	10.4	202,893	—	−1.0
Eligible Youth Population	30,004,031	—	−1.6	29,534,890	—	−2.6	28,752,979	—	−4.4	27,476,521	—	−8.4

SOURCES: U.S. Census Bureau, Children in Custody; U. S. Bureau of Labor Statistics.

NOTE: Percentage change denotes change in number of admissions or one-day count.

*Adjusted for inflation denotes expenditures times consumer price index where one dollar = purchasing power of one dollar for all items in 1967.

INCREASING THE IMPRISONMENT OF CHILDREN

A biannual survey conducted by the U.S. Census Bureau provides the most comprehensive picture of how the nation's juvenile correctional system has been changing. This statistical series, popularly known as "Children in Custody," consists of a complete enumeration of all public juvenile correctional facilities and a somewhat less than complete but adequate survey of all private juvenile correctional institutions. The public facility survey was begun in 1971 and the private facility data were first gathered in 1974. Data from these surveys are summarized in Tables 5 and 6. (Table 5 includes only public detention centers and training schools. Table 6 includes other public facilities as well as detention centers and training schools, i.e., shelter care facilities.)

Detention: Fewer Admissions but Longer Lengths of Stay

The Children in Custody survey reveals a steady decline in detention admissions from 1974–1982. Total detention admissions declined by 21%. This decline was most dramatic for females for whom detention admissions dropped by 45%. Male admissions declined by 11%. The largest drop in detention admissions occurred between 1974 and 1979. Thereafter, detention admissions continued to decline, albeit at a slower rate. Decreasing numbers of detention admission

TABLE 6   United States Juveniles in Public and Private Correctional Facilities: Selected Data 1974–1982

	1974	1975	1977	1979	1982
A. Private Facilities					
Total Admissions	53,661	56,708	67,045	69,507	88,806
Male	33,364	38,119	40,315	40,251	54,439
Female	20,297	18,589	26,730	29,256	34,367
One-day counts	31,749	27,290	29,070	28,678	31,390
Male	22,104	19,152	20,387	20,505	22,242
Female	9,645	8,138	8,683	8,173	9,148
Expenditures*	294,036	273,644	384,327	456,046	718,993
Controlled for inflation**	199,062	169,659	211,764	209,781	248,772
Average length of stay (in days)	—	307	270	261	260
B. Public Facilities					
Total Admissions	647,175	642,403	612,931	567,129	529,897
Male	466,181	475,497	476,550	451,711	422,714
Female	180,994	166,905	137,381	115,418	107,183
One-day counts	44,922	46,980	43,882	43,234	48,701
Male	34,783	37,926	36,756	37,167	42,182
Female	10,139	9,054	7,126	6,067	6,519
Expenditures*	507,903	594,021	705,009	842,467	1,148,296
Controlled for inflation**	343,850	368,293	388,460	387,535	397,310
Average length of stay	181	174	161	161	171
C. Public and Private Facilities					
Admissions	700,836	699,110	680,976	636,636	618,703
One-day count	76,671	74,270	72,952	71,912	80,091
Expenditures*	801,939	867,665	1,089,336	1,298,513	1,867,289
Controlled for inflation**	542,913	537,952	600,224	597,316	646,082

SOURCES: U.S. Census Bureau, Children in Custody; U.S. Bureau of Labor Statistics.
* Expenditures in thousands of dollars.
** Based on Consumer Price Index for all items, Base Year is 1967.

are quite consistent with the juvenile justice data presented earlier. Admissions to detention were influenced by two factors: (1) the significant decline in juvenile arrests and (2) the nationwide effort to extract status offenders from secure detention. Indeed from 1974–1979, the height of the DSO movement, declining female detention admissions accounted for 80% of the total decline in admissions. Between 1979–1982 detention admissions were declining at a much slower rate and males accounted for 74% of the drop in detention admissions. These data suggest that great progress had already been accomplished in removing status offenders from detention. As noted earlier, federal juvenile justice policymakers were also beginning to question the wisdom of the DSO movement.

Whereas detention admissions have been dropping, the average length of stay of those detained has increased. In 1974, the average length of detention stay was 11.3 days; by 1982, length of stay had increased to 17.4 days. The effect of increasing detention stays was to maintain a high level of youth in detention (based on one-day counts) despite the dropping admissions. For example, from 1974–1979 the number of youth in detention centers on a given day declined by 3%. Moreover, this slight decline of youth in detention actually reflects a decrease of 1,530 females and an increase of 1,203 males found in a one-day count in 1974 compared to 1979. However, from 1979–1982, the detention one-day counts rose by 1,932 for males and 433 for females. Thus after a decade of reform efforts to limit the use of detention, the 1982 Children in Custody survey documented the highest number of youth residing in detention since 1971 despite fewer admissions. This may suggest agency policies designed to maintain current levels of staff and budget even as the youth population is declining.

Rising detention lengths of stay can be more directly attributed to two major developments. First, the increasing formality of juvenile justice processing and escalating penalties have led to more contested court proceedings and extended preadjudication stays. Youth who are waived to adult court are often housed in juvenile detention centers. Further, the increasing severity of juvenile court sanctions has led to more protracted adjudicatory processes. The increased focus on evidentiary reviews by prosecutors and the defense may also have contributed to increasing detention stays.

A second major factor in increasing detention lengths of stay has been the rapidly growing practice of sentencing juveniles to detention centers as a condition of their probation. This practice is similar to the "split sentence" in adult criminal courts. In 1977 there were 4,804 admissions to detention on a commitment or sentenced status. By 1979, this number had increased to 13,323 and, in 1982, there were 21,027 admissions to detention on a commitment status. These detention sentences are generally for 30–45 days, often followed by a probation term. Many public policy questions are raised by this new practice, which is increasing in legislative and judicial popularity. For instance, some have argued that these dispositions are overly harsh because they place relatively minor offenders in very secure facilities that possess minimal educational and counseling services. Another problem is that these committed youth are often mixed in with preadjudicatory detainees who may have committed more serious and violent offenses. Preliminary data suggest that females are more likely to receive the split sentence because of the general lack of dispositional options for them. Finally, it should be noted that detention stays are extremely expensive, averaging $90–$100 per day, and there is no credible evidence that this sanction has a positive effect on reducing recidivism.

There are some additional trends surrounding detention centers. Particularly alarming is the fact that black and Hispanic youth make up an ever larger proportion of the detention population. In 1977, blacks and Hispanics accounted for 41% of youth in detention but, by 1982, this proportion had risen to 51%. This growth does not appear to be the result of racial demographic trends or shifting arrest patterns. Further, the intense fiscal crisis of local government in the early 1980s reduced the real dollar expenditures for detention services. Whereas between 1974–1979 there was a 21.3% growth in detention expenditures adjusted for inflation, during 1979–1982 this growth figure was 3.1%. However, it is important to recall that during 1974–1979 detention populations were stable whereas during 1979–1982 the average daily detention population grew by 22%. Thus per youth detention expenditures were actually declining. Data on capital expenditures for detention reveal a similar picture of modest public investment during 1979–1982. These budgetary decisions resulted in many jurisdictions experiencing deteriorating physical plants, program restrictions and cutbacks in child care services. In short, the experience of detention during the watershed period became increasingly harsh for a growing number of confined youth.

Training Schools: More Youth Admitted and Longer Lengths of Stay

The profound changes affecting detention centers were also experienced by training schools. During 1974–1979 the nation's training schools had modestly declining admissions and small declines in one-day counts of their populations. But, thereafter, these trends were reversed and both admissions and one-day counts began to climb. For example, from 1979–1982, admissions increased from 63,901 to 65,401. During the same period one-day counts increased from 23,200 to 25,071. As with detention trends, the increased training school population was especially significant for males. In fact, females in training schools had dropped almost by half from 5,652 in 1974 to 2,963 in 1979. During the same time frame the male one-day count was virtually unchanged. During 1979–1982, however, there was a continuing but slow decline in females in training schools (4%) but a 10% increase in their male counterparts. These data reflect both the waning of the campaign to remove status offenders (primarily females) from training schools and an increased use of institutionalization for adjudicated male delinquents. Not only were more youth being sent to training schools, they were also staying longer. Whereas training school average length of stay declined from 260 days in 1974 to 238 days in 1979, length of stay rose back up to 256 days by 1982.

Similar to the findings about detention, the proportion of minority youth in the nation's training schools has increased. In 1977 whites made up 53% of the public training school population; by 1982 the proportion of whites in training schools had declined to 46%.

Expenditures for training schools kept pace with inflation from 1974–1979 and increased slightly from 1979–1982. Particularly alarming was the fact that the average daily population of training schools (25,071) was approaching their total bed capacity (27,182). Indeed, many jurisdictions such as Illinois, Colorado, and California were reporting severe crowding conditions in their training schools. The increased crowding of juvenile facilities in these jurisdictions was vastly overshadowed by the severe crisis of prison crowding. Thus few dollars were allocated by states to add more juvenile correctional bed capacity or to launch community-based alternative placements. Directors of state training-school systems were also reporting a growth in the number of inappropriate mental health cases being dumped into their correctional facilities. Overall the message was that the nation's training schools were becoming more crowded with more difficult to manage youth. At the same time, the resources available for educational, vocational, medical, and psychological services were drying up.

Jurisdictional Differences

There are clear indications that the initiative for juvenile justice reform has shifted from the federal level to state and local jurisdictions. States have always exercised leadership in correctional programming. In fact,

national-level trends showing increases in the number of youth in detention centers and training schools mask important differences between individual states. A previous study of the 1979 Children in Custody data noted large disparities between the states in admission rates, lengths of stay, confinement of youth in adult facilities, expenditures per youth, conditions of confinement, and the extent of chronic crowding in juvenile correctional facilities.

> What emerges is a highly complex and idiosyncratic pattern of correctional facility use among the states that is largely unexplained by youth crime factors . . . The current public policy debate must confront these findings and consider the prospects for needed reforms carefully [Krisberg et al., 1984: 179].

Examination of the 1982 Children in Custody survey shows that the vast disparity in correctional policies has continued.

For example, in 1982 the national juvenile detention admission rate was 1,516 youth per 100,000 age-eligible population. A total of 34 states had rates below the national average whereas 16 states and the District of Columbia were above it. Differences ranged from very low admission rates in some states (such as South Carolina, West Virginia, Wisconsin, Connecticut, New York, and North Carolina) to admission rates twice the national average in 4 states (California, Nevada, Utah, and Washington) and the District of Columbia.

The national detention center one-day count (incarceration rate) was 47 youth per 100,000 age-eligible youth. There were 35 states below the national average whereas 15 states were above it. Table 7 shows the top 10 states in detention incarceration rates in 1974, 1979, and 1982. Six states were in the top ten throughout the decade (California, Nevada, Michigan, Florida, Washington, and Arizona).

One might expect a close association between detention admission and juvenile arrests. In fact, Arizona, Florida, and Nevada do rank high in FBI Part I juvenile arrest rates. However, other factors appear to be causing the high detention incarcera-

TABLE 7   Top Ten States in Rate of Detention Incarceration*
1974, 1979, 1982

	1974			1979			1982	
Rank	State	Rate per 100,000	Rank	State	Rate per 100,000	Rank	State	Rate per 100,000
1	California	127	1	California	115	1	California	157
2	Nevada	81	2	Michigan	70	2	Nevada	125
3	Michigan	64	3	Nevada	67	3	Washington	94
4	Georgia	60	4	Washington	59	4	Florida	87
5	Florida	56	5	Florida	57	5	Georgia	67
6	Utah	55	6	Arizona	54	6	Michigan	61
7	Washington	54	7	Georgia	50	7	Ohio	58
8	Arizona	51	8	Virginia	49	8	Alaska	57
9	Kansas	48	9	Utah	46	9	Arizona	55
10	Delaware	43	10	Ohio	43	10	Delaware	55

SOURCE: U.S. Department of Census, Children in Custody Series.
* Based on one-day count and age-eligible youth population in state.

tion rates in California, Washington, Michigan, Georgia, and Alaska. One such factor is the increasing use of detention facilities for sentenced youth. In Washington, for example, 26% of the youth incarcerated in 1983 were on a sentenced status. The top 4 states in terms of sentencing youth to detention were Washington, California, Alaska, and Georgia.

Another disturbing trend is that the states with the highest detention incarceration rates showed little inclination to curtail their detention practices. Between 1979 and 1982 California experienced a 30% increase in the number of youth detained. Similar increases are noted for Nevada (115%), Washington (51%), Florida (49%), Georgia (31%), Ohio (26%), and Delaware (144%).

Whereas 30 states showed increases in the number of youth they incarcerated in detention centers between 1979 and 1982, 13 states experienced decreases. The most notable were Connecticut (43% decrease), District of Columbia (52% decrease), Idaho (68% decrease), Kansas (31% decrease), Michigan (17% decrease), Oregon (33% decrease), New York (11% decrease), and South Carolina (29% decrease). States such as Connecticut and South Carolina were already among the lowest states in detention incarceration rates in 1979. New York, Oregon, Michigan, and the District of Columbia experienced reductions in 1982 from relatively high rates

in 1979. Much of the decrease in New York, South Carolina, Michigan, and Kansas was attributed to policies reducing the number of detained status offenders.

The national training school admission rate in 1982 was 206 per 100,000 age-eligible youth. Half the states fell above and half below the national average. Among the states with the lowest admission rates were Vermont, Massachusetts, Michigan, New York, Pennsylvania, Utah, West Virginia, Kentucky, and Alabama. Both Massachusetts and Vermont had virtually closed down their training school facilities during the decade, substituting an array of community-based alternatives. Kentucky, West Virginia, Alabama, and Utah have similarly curtailed their reliance on large, congregate-care training schools. Michigan and New York retained low admission rates throughout the seventies. The highest training admission rates were found in Alaska, the District of Columbia, Maryland, New Hampshire, and Oregon.

Whereas national training school admissions rates remained relatively stable, one-day incarceration rates were dramatically increasing from 81 per 100,000 in 1979 to 91 in 1983. Much of this increase was due to the increase in the average length of stay, as noted previously. Table 8 shows the top 10 states in training school one-day rates in 1974, 1979, and 1982. Consistently among the top ten in each of these years were the District of

TABLE 8 Top Ten States in Rate of Training School Incarceration*
1974, 1979, 1982

	1974			1979			1982	
Rank	State	Rate per 100,000	Rank	State	Rate per 100,000	Rank	State	Rate per 100,000
1	District of Columbia	597	1	District of Columbia	408	1	District of Columbia	484
2	Nevada	303	2	Michigan	261	2	Delaware	262
3	Wyoming	210	3	Wyoming	256	3	Wyoming	248
4	New Hampshire	190	4	Alaska	248	4	Alaska	235
5	Alaska	190	5	Delaware	213	5	Nevada	225
6	Vermont	187	6	Oregon	176	6	Louisiana	205
7	Louisiana	176	7	Kansas	171	7	Montana	157
8	North Carolina	166	8	Louisiana	160	8	Kansas	154
9	South Carolina	161	9	New Hampshire	146	9	Oregon	152
10	Montana	157	10	Montana	143	10	Maryland	143

SOURCE: U.S. Department of Census, Children in Custody.
*Based on one-day count and age-eligible youth population state.

Columbia, Nevada, Wyoming, Alaska, Louisiana, and Montana. The District of Columbia's rate was more than five times the national average. Delaware, Wyoming, Alaska, Nevada, and Louisiana possessed incarceration rates double the national average.

On the other hand, there were few youth in training schools in Utah, Massachusetts, or West Virginia. Pennsylvania, Michigan, Kentucky, and Alabama also had training school incarceration rates far below the national average.

Although the overall number of youth incarcerated in the nation's training schools rose between 1979 and 1982, many states were significantly reducing their reliance on training schools. Youth incarcerated in Utah training schools decreased 57%, West Virginia reduced its training school population by 59%, Missouri by 49%, Kentucky by 32%, and Connecticut by 33%. These states were already below the national average training school incarceration rate. Only New Hampshire and South Carolina show significant decreases in their one-day training school rates, which were above the national average. States that consistently rank among the highest training school incarceration rates continued to increase their training school populations between 1979 and 1982. Among these states were California (32% increase), Illinois

(34% increase), Louisiana (22% increase), Maryland (32% increase), New Jersey (61% increase), and Ohio (36% increase). In California alone, there were 825 more youth incarcerated in 1982 than in 1979; in Ohio 524 more, and in Illinois 277 more.

The Private Sector of Juvenile Corrections

So far, we have been describing trends in public juvenile correctional facilities. But a second and less visible component of the juvenile justice system consists of privately operated correctional facilities. Most of these facilities are group homes but some also function as private training schools or correctional camp programs. The U.S. Census Bureau began surveying the private sector of juvenile corrections in 1974.

From 1974–1979, admissions to private facilities grew from 53,661 to 69,507—an increase of 30%. Male admissions increased by 21% and female admissions by 44%. From 1979–1982 private correctional admissions continued to grow by 28%. During this later period male admissions grew at a faster rate than females (35% versus 17%). One-day counts in private facilities remained virtually unchanged during the period 1974–1982. The growth of admissions was counterbalanced by a drop in the average length of stay in private facilities. Operating expenditures for private juvenile corrections reached almost $719 million in 1982, representing a 25% increase in real dollars when compared to expenditures in 1974.

It should be noted that growth of the private sector was actively advocated by juvenile justice reformers of the early 1970s. It was argued that smaller, privately operated programs could provide improved care to troubled youth. Indeed, the deinstitutionalization movement resulted in many youth, particularly female status offenders, being shifted from public training schools to private residential programs. Some now question whether this development represented significant progress. For example, private facilities traditionally spend less per youth than public facilities and youth reside in private programs much longer than in public facilities. Most important, the growth in the private correctional admissions did not offset growth in the public sector. Put differently, the number of delinquents admitted to both public and private facilities grew during the watershed period.

POLICY CONSIDERATIONS

National juvenile justice trends reveal a system growing more formal, restrictive, and punitive. Juvenile correctional facilities are increasingly filled with black and Hispanic youth. These changes are occurring even as the youth population and juvenile arrests are declining. Moreover, the changing nature of our juvenile justice system is occurring amidst an intense ideological debate over the value of previous reform efforts. It is apparent that the liberal reform thrust of the early 1970s has been replaced by a more conservative agenda. This watershed period provides a unique opportunity for policymakers, practitioners, and child advocates to examine and benefit from lessons learned from the earlier reform era. If, however, this reassessment is conducted solely on the basis of condemning past reform efforts, then it is unlikely that enlightened public policy will result. For even as past reformers made overblown claims for the results of their programs, perhaps current reformers are expecting too

much for the outcomes of their efforts to "get tough" with juvenile offenders.

Data presented in this article represent a summary of twelve years of national juvenile justice information. In our judgment, these data should prove to be useful to those interested in and responsible for the development of more effective juvenile crime control measures. Also, the data raise a number of issues that require urgent attention.

(1) Historically, states and local jurisdictions have been the principal sources of innovation and significant developments in juvenile corrections policy. Although there are some who feel that the deinstitutionalization movement essentially began with the enactment of the JJDPA of 1974, the best available evidence suggests that this movement started well before the Act was passed. Between 1969 and 1972, state officials in Massachusetts closed that state's large juvenile training schools. In their place were created a few small high security treatment units for violent and dangerous youth as well as a diverse network of community-based alternatives for other offenders. Also, between 1971 and 1974, the one-day counts in juvenile training schools dropped from 35,960 to 25,397, a drop of approximately 30%. The one-day counts further declined to 23,200 in 1979 and then began increasing up to 25,071 in 1982.

The data contained in this article as well in other studies indicate that many jurisdictions are continuing to exercise leadership in juvenile correctional programming. For example, the state of Massachusetts continues to rank lowest in the country with respect to admissions to public juvenile correctional facilities. Other states such as West Virginia, Michigan, Pennsylvania, Kentucky, Utah, and Alabama have managed to reduce their reliance on training schools substantially, without endangering public safety.

Also, the experiences in such places as Genessee County, Michigan, where the use of preadjudicatory detention has been reduced to the absolute minimum without increasing the risks to public safety (and at significant long-range cost savings) need to be studied. In FY 1983–1984, 307 juveniles were detained from Genessee County by the court and the state social service agency. Genessee County has a population of approximately 450,000 people and includes the industrialized city of Flint, Michigan.

Since the creation of the Children's Bureau in 1912, the federal government has attempted to play an increasingly active role in juvenile justice policy. Despite the growing federal presence, juvenile justice policy is still made at the state and local level and this is likely to be the case well into the future. Although the enactment of the JJDPA of 1974 created the prospects for federal leadership, the potential of the federal juvenile justice program has never been realized (U.S. Senate Committee on the Judiciary, 1975: XI-8). In the mid-1970s while federal juvenile justice reformers were actively pursuing the goals of diversion and deinstitutionalization of status offenders, virtually all the states were passing legislation designed to toughen their response to serious and violent juvenile offenders. Federal officials endorsed this trend only after it was well under way. Moreover, the impact of this state legislative activity is far more significant than the relatively small amounts of federal juvenile justice grant funds.

(2) Criticisms that the juvenile justice reforms of the past twenty years failed to respond to the issue of violent crime and repeat offenders are valid. Although various studies indicate that the number of juveniles meeting these criteria is relatively small, these offenders are of great concern to the public. As Ohlin predicted, failure to give adequate attention to this issue could prove to be "the Achilles heel of a reform process" (Coates, 1978: 190). In fact, the inability of reformers to provide meaningful programs and policies aimed at serious juvenile offenders resulted in the wave of "get tough" legislation that swept the nation during the 1970s.

Critics have also pointed out that many reform programs were not rooted in solid research findings (NAC, 1984: 6–7). Although the absence of research was a real problem, the reformers sought to rectify that problem by stimulating research via the JJDPA. For instance, the prestigious National Advisory Commission on Criminal Justice Standards and Goals recommended the development of community-based programs even though they acknowledged that the success of these programs in terms of public safety and costs was yet to be documented through research.

(3) It is important to recall that there were a number of issues during the late 1960s and 1970s over which there was great consensus that reforms were desperately needed. For example, there was the concern over the plight of children in jails. The Children's Defense Fund, after visiting nearly 450 jails in Florida, Georgia, Indiana, Maryland, New Jersey, Ohio, South Carolina, Texas, and Virginia, "found frequent instances in which juveniles were confined with adults charged with violent crimes" (Offices of Juvenile Justice and Delinquency Prevention, 1983: 2). They found most jails to be old, dirty, and decrepit, with insufficient sanitary, food, or medical facilities. Only 9.8% of the jails reported any educational activities; only 12.4% reported any recreational activities. Understaffed jails often relied on trustees—other adult inmates—to perform staff functions. There was growing concern over the high incidence of juvenile suicides in adult jails and concern that juveniles were often subjected to various forms of physical and sexual abuse (Flaherty, 1980: 10).

There was also increasing concern over the conditions in detention centers and training schools. For example, Howard James, the Pulitzer Prize-winning journalist, visited juvenile institutions and adult jails in 44 states. He found much boredom and idleness, widespread use of solitary confinement, and that juveniles were often beaten, flogged, locked in dungeon-like cells, and subjected to other forms of abuse (James, 1970: 107–133). Kenneth Wooden (1976: 30), another noted journalist, toured juvenile institutions in the early 1970s and concluded that "without public awareness a system that was designed to help children in trouble has become a tyrannical monster, destroying the very children it was mandated to save." Also, lawsuits in such states as Texas, Massachusetts, New York, Indiana, Missouri, and Rhode Island further documented the scandalous conditions in juvenile facilities (Piersma et al., 1977: 611–637). Concern was also expressed over the fact that "almost 40% of all children involved in the juvenile justice system were status offenders and, to a much lesser extent, dependent and neglected children" (U.S. Senate Committee on the Judiciary, 1975: 4). Often, these youth would "end up in institutions with hardened juvenile offenders and adult criminals" (U.S. Senate Committee on the Judiciary, 1975: 4).

Although considerable progress has been made in some of these areas, particularly in deinstitutionalizing status offenders, many of the deep-seated problems of juvenile justice have not been changed. For example, a recent Bureau of Justice Statistics study reported that the number of juveniles incarcerated in adult jails in 1982 was approximately the same as the number confined in such facilities in 1978 (Bureau of Justice Statistics, 1984). Moreover, recent litigation in Idaho, Oregon, Kentucky, Iowa, Ohio, Tennessee, Colorado, and New Mexico indicate that inadequate conditions of confinement, physical abuse, and suicides continue to be a major problem for juveniles housed in jails. Christopher Peterman, age 17, was arrested and placed in the Ada County Jail (Boise, Idaho) "for failure to pay $73 worth of traffic tickets and fines" (*Yellen v. Ada County*, 1983: 17). Christopher was placed in a cell with five other juveniles who had a history of violent behavior where he "was beaten and eventually tortured to death" (*Yellen v. Ada County*, 1983: 17).

Likewise there is growing evidence that harsh conditions of confinement continue to plague juvenile detention centers and training schools. For instance, a recent series of articles in the *Los Angeles Times* alleged that there were abusive practices in California Youth Authority (CYA) facilities and in local juvenile halls (detention centers). It was reported that "disruptive youngsters [in CYA institutions] . . . are spreadeagled on metal bed frames in isolation cells [with] . . . their wrists and ankles bound with leather cuffs" (Hurst, 1984: 1). "In Orange and San Diego County Juvenile Halls, obstreperous youngsters are strapped to their beds." In Los Angeles County, "Children as young as 11 are required to march in silence and eat their meals in silence" (Hurst, 1984: 3). Also, in Los Angeles County, juveniles were put in "the box" (isolation) for such minor offenses as "giggling when they were supposed to be quiet" (Hurst, 1984: 3).

In Oregon, a federal judge recently ruled that isolation was being used excessively and inappropriately at the Maclaren School for Boys (*Gary v. Hegstrom*, 1984: 11–12). Juveniles at the School were put in solitary confinement for such things as " 'mouthing off' to staff, refusing to obey an order or directive, yelling or swearing, getting out of bed at night without permission—behaviour generally considered typical for adolescents" (*Gary v. Hegstrom*, 1984: 13). Also, the court found "that the [isolation] cells were dirty and unsanitary" (*Gary v. Hegstrom*, 1984: 23). What was perhaps the most shocking was the fact that "physical restraints, including handcuffs, leg irons, and leather straps [were being used] . . . unnecessarily and as a substitute for adequate programming and adequate psychiatric services" (*Gary v. Hegstrom*, 1984: 27).

In Florida, a federal judge for the Northern District of Florida ordered that state human service and juvenile corrections officials take immediate steps to "discontinue hogtying [and] . . . shackling to fixed objects" (*Bobby M. v. Graham*, 1983: 1). Also, the court ordered the implementation of criteria and standards for the use and operation of isolation in the security units in the training schools (*Bobby M. v. Graham*, 1983: 1).

With a few notable exceptions, there continues to be a heavy reliance on the use of detention centers and training schools. Despite a declining youth population, declining serious juvenile crime rates, and the relatively high costs and limited benefits of institutional care, the number of juveniles incarcerated on a given day in detention centers and training schools is increasing. Also, juveniles are being confined in such facilities for longer periods of time. There is no solid evidence that these policies of increased juvenile incapacitation are positively affecting public safety. Incarceration policies are largely unrelated to rates of serious youth crime.

(4) It appears that juvenile detention centers are beginning to take on the charac-

ter of the adult jail. In 1982, 21,027 juveniles were committed to such facilities on a sentenced status. The states of California and Washington account for the bulk of the juveniles committed to detention centers, but the practice can be found in many states.

The practice of committing juveniles to detention centers should be of great concern to policymakers and practitioners. Detention centers are simply not designed to serve postadjudicatory population. Placing committed youth in the same facilities as those awaiting dispositions creates significant administrative, programmatic, and legal problems. In addition, most juvenile detention centers are maximum security facilities that are far more secure and restrictive than training school facilities. This means that commitment of juveniles to such facilities essentially amounts to placing them in secure confinement without adequate programs. A few states, such as Washington, have specific provisions in their juvenile statutes allowing for the commitment of juveniles to detention. This concept is gaining in popularity among lawmakers and juvenile justice professionals throughout the country.

(5) Since 1977, there has been a substantial increase in the proportion of minority youth incarcerated in juvenile detention centers and training schools. In fact, minority youth now make up over 50% of all juveniles incarcerated at any one time in such facilities. In contrast, approximately 65% of the juveniles placed in private juvenile correctional facilities are white. These trends suggest that a two-tiered juvenile correctional system is developing—one where minority youth end up in *public* institutions and white youth are placed in *private* facilities.

(6) More than one-third of the training schools in the United States were chronically overcrowded in 1982. The average daily population in training schools nationally almost equals the design capacity of the facilities and there is a great danger that the number of overcrowded juvenile institutions may increase significantly in the future. This, coupled with the fact that training school budgets have not kept pace with inflation, signals a potentially volatile situation because crowding and understaffing are considered key fac-

tors contributing to violence among confined youth, violence between youth and staff, and attempted suicides.

CONCLUSION

We are currently experiencing a watershed period in juvenile justice reform. A new agenda of reform is emerging and gathering political strength. The prior agenda of deinstitutionalization, diversion, and juvenile justice reform is being openly questioned and criticized. As this ideological debate rages, the nation's juvenile justice system has become more formal, more restrictive, and more oriented toward punishing serious offenders. Juvenile correctional facilities hold more youth than since the early 1970s and these facilities are increasingly crowded and understaffed. There are reports that some of the institutional abusive practices that motivated the reformers of the 1970s are still pervasive. Thus the watershed period presents a challenge to rethink and refocus the energies of all juvenile justice reformers.

It is essential that the old and new agendas not be placed in opposition. Legitimate concerns for child welfare and for the plight of victims are part of both reform movements. For example, few who decry child abuse would wish to tolerate the abuse of youth in juvenile facilities. Further, the heightened attention paid to serious youth crime should not imply a retreat from traditional goals of rehabilitation and prevention. The favored therapeutic approaches may have changed, but there remains a strong commitment to trying to return troubled youth to conventional lives. Each group of reformers has learned of the dilemmas of the public correctional system and has sought to encourage the development of privately operated correctional programs. Both old and new reformers seek a juvenile justice system that is fair, humane, and cost-effective.

The new and old reform agendas should not be made contradictory because the goals of the traditional reformers have not yet been fully achieved. A decade of reform has resulted in more youth being confined and in facilities that are deteriorating physically. Moreover, there is an urgent need to examine the programs and operational policies of juvenile facilities. In particular, it is extremely valuable to examine how states as diverse as Massachusetts and Utah have implemented the ideals of the proponents of the JJDPA. How do places such as Genessee County, Michigan, effectively manage the difficult problem of juvenile detention? We need to conduct detailed and careful studies of the "success stories" so that program and policy directions can be developed for other jurisdictions. We also need to know more about the impact of highly publicized reforms such as revision of Washington state's juvenile code. Far more than federal policy initiatives, the experience of state and local jurisdictions will continue to be most influential in shaping the future agenda of juvenile justice reforms.

Although long-range policy planning is required, there are a number of immediate steps that can alleviate some of the most obvious shortcomings of current juvenile justice practices. For example, in the area of removing juveniles from adult jails, several states have passed statutory prohibitions against this practice. Pennsylvania enacted such legislation in 1977. Since that time, Maryland, Rhode Island, and, most recently, Virginia and Missouri have banned the detention of youth in adult jails. Other states such as Colorado and Illinois have employed a combination of legislative and programmatic strategies to reduce vastly the number of juveniles who are jailed in these states.

Reducing the inappropriate incarceration of juveniles in detention centers and training schools will require specific attention to improved risk screening at several stages in the juvenile justice process. Implementing more objective screening instruments will help juvenile correctional officials make more valid decisions on which youth require secure care. In most jurisdictions more objective risk screening should result in more youth being placed in community-based programs.[4] Besides improving risk screening, juvenile justice policymakers must make an active commitment to create community programs that protect public safety and respond to individual youth needs. The KEY, Inc., program in Massachusetts and the High Impact Program in Pittsburgh, Pennsylvania, are excellent examples of alternatives to training schools that provide very intensive community supervision for chronic offenders. In Utah, programs such as Esperanza, Carousel, and Sojourn are excellent models of small, nonsecure residential programs for youth who were formerly placed in the Utah state training schools. These successful programs need to be replicated elsewhere.

Juvenile justice officials and concerned citizens also must develop meaningful programs for violent juvenile offenders. The OJJDP recently supported a national research and demonstration effort for violent juvenile offenders. This multisite program included a 6- to 12-month period of confinement, followed by 6 months of structured group home or supervised community living. Although the evaluation results are not yet completed, many of these programs report excellent progress with very serious offenders. Another model program for violent youth is the Weaversville Intensive Treatment unit in Pennsylvania. Run by RCA Corporation, Weaversville is a small secure facility (capacity 22) with a high staff–youth ratio. The program provides enriched counseling services and an excellent educational program. In Massachusetts, the Justice Resource Institute operates a network of small, secure units to house serious offenders and violent youth. These youth receive intensive treatment services from a highly skilled professional staff. Interestingly, all of these programs for violent offenders report costs per youth that are lower than typical state training school costs.

The programs and policies suggested above do not represent the panacea to all the problems of the juvenile justice system. Yet it is timely to experiment and refine these alternative approaches. As we mentioned earlier, demographic forces are now producing a decline in a number of youth being arrested. But in the next 7–10 years most jurisdictions will begin seeing the "Echo Baby Boomers" passing through their high risk years in terms of juvenile crime. Unless we restructure our juvenile justice programs now, this new wave of adolescents will produce even higher levels of incarceration than is currently the case. As with overcrowding in adult prisons and jails, it is foolish to believe we can simply build enough new juvenile correctional facilities to stay ahead of this problem.

Notes

1. This figure was computed by adding up estimates for each state of youth aged 10 years to the upper age of original juvenile court jurisdiction in that state.
2. During 1975–1982, juvenile arrests for burglary, larceny, and theft dropped by 22%. Juveniles arrested for minor offenses increased by 18%.
3. It is possible that some of the shift from probation to "other dispositions" may simply reflect changes in how courts are reporting these dispositions.
4. These risk models would also enhance public safety by selecting out those youth who should not be released from secure care.

References

ACADEMY FOR CONTEMPORARY PROBLEMS
1982   Major Issues in Juvenile Justice Information and Training, Youth in Adult Courts: Between Two Worlds. Washington, DC: Department of Justice.

BUREAU OF JUSTICE STATISTICS
1984   The 1983 Jail Census. Washington, DC: Government Printing Office.

COATES, R. B., A. D. MILLER, AND L. E. OHLIN
1978   Diversity in a Youth Correctional System. Handling Delinquents in Massachusetts. Cambridge, MA: Ballinger.

FLAHERTY, M. G.
1980   An Assessment of National Incidence of Juvenile Suicide in Adult Jails, Lockups, and Juvenile Detention Centers. Washington, DC: Government Printing Office.

HURST, J.
1984   "Unruly youths face shackles, isolation." Los Angeles Times (July 22): 1, 3, 28.

JAMES, H.
1970   Children in Trouble: A National Scandal. New York: David McKay.

JUVENILE JUSTICE AND DELINQUENCY PREVENTION ACTION OF 1974
1974   Pub. L. No. 93-415, 88 Stat. p. 1109.

KRISBERG, B. AND I. SCHWARTZ
1983   "Rethinking juvenile justice." Crime & Delinquency 29, 3: 333–364.

KRISBERG, B., I. SCHWARTZ, AND P. LITSKY
1984   "Youth in confinement: Justice by geography." J.
of Research in Crime and Delinquency 21, 2: 153–181.

NATIONAL ADVISORY COMMISSION ON CRIMINAL JUSTICE STANDARDS AND GOALS
1973   Corrections. Washington, DC: Government Printing Office.

NATIONAL ADVISORY COMMITTEE FOR JUVENILE JUSTICE AND DELINQUENCY PREVENTION (NAC)
1984   Serious Juvenile Crime: A Redirected Federal Effort. Washington, DC: Office of Juvenile Justice and Delinquency Prevention.

OFFICE OF JUVENILE JUSTICE AND DELINQUENCY PREVENTION
1983   It's Your Move: Juveniles in Adult Jails and Lockups. Washington, DC: Department of Justice.

PIERSMA, P., J. GANOUSIS, A. E. VOLENIK, H. F. SWANGER, AND P. CONNELL
1977   Law and Tactics in Juvenile Cases. Philadelphia: American Law Institute.

REGNERY, A.
XXXX   "Current federal juvenile justice policy." Crime & Delinquency.

SNYDER, H., T. FINNEGAN, AND J. L. HUTZLER
1981   Delinquency in the United States. Pittsburgh: National Center for Juvenile Justice.

SNYDER, H., T. FINNEGAN, J. L. HUTZLER, D. SMITH, N. FEINBERG, AND P. MCFALL
1979   Delinquency in the United States. Pittsburgh: National Center for Juvenile Justice.

UNITED STATES HOUSE OF REPRESENTATIVES, COMMITTEE ON EDUCATION AND LABOR
1980   Juvenile Justice Amendments of 1980. Washington, DC: Government Printing Office.

UNITED STATES SENATE COMMITTEE ON THE JUDICIARY
1975   Ford Administration Stifles Juvenile Justice Policy. Washington, DC: Government Printing Office.

WOODEN, K.
1976   Keeping in the Playtime of Others. New York: McGraw-Hill.

Legal Cases

Bobby M. v. Graham,
        Court Order on Use of Security Units and Lockup, No. TCA 83-7003 (N.D. Fla. July 5, 1983).

Bobby M. v. Graham,
        Court Order on Preliminary Injunction, No. TCA 83-7003, (N.D. Fla. July 14, 1985).

Gary v. Hegstrom,
        Docket no. 77-1039-BV (D. Oregonk unpublished opinion, 1984).

Schall v. Martin
        (1984), United States Law Review, 52(47), pp. 4681–4696.

Yellen v. Ada County,
        Second Amended Complaint, Civ. Action No. 83-1026, (D. Idaho 1983).

QUESTIONS FOR DISCUSSION

1. As the youth population has become smaller, juvenile arrests have generally been declining since 1975. Nevertheless, there has been an increase in the severity of juvenile court sanctions. Why has this increase occurred?

2. How will the "echo baby boom" affect the rates of juvenile crime and court responses over the next ten years?

3. Proportionately more minorities are in juvenile correctional facilities as the conservative crime control agenda increasingly dominates public policy. Do you think this trend will continue? Why?

APPLICATIONS

1. It comes as a surprise to many people that juvenile crime rates have declined. The public's fear of crime continues to far exceed the actual crime in our society. Why do you think this is so? What influences the public's fear of crime?

2. Let us assume that you are a juvenile court judge. For which kinds of offenses would you incarcerate a juvenile? For which offenses would you consider alternative measures?

KEY TERMS

adjudication a judicial decision or sentence; being under the formal constraint of a court of law.

demographic refers to the size, density, distribution, and vital statistics of a population.

detention a period of temporary custody prior to disposition by a court.

echo baby boom the period during the 1990s when an increase in the juvenile population will occur again as a result of the World War II "baby boomers' " children reaching adolescence.

hypothesized refers to making a tentative assumption in order to draw out and test its logical and empirical consequences.

phenomenon refers to any object or event that is perceived through awareness, the senses, or consciousness.

preventive detention incarcerating an offender prior to a court hearing in an effort to prevent the commission of further criminal acts.

PART

II

THEORIES OF JUVENILE DELINQUENCY

Many of the theoretical formulations concerning juvenile delinquency are also found in criminology, criminal justice, police science, public safety, and deviance courses. All theories of delinquency deal with human behavior in one way or another and hence are often found in related courses and fields.

Theory is speculation about the causes of an event or the nature of something. Although theory is somewhat abstract, it attempts to provide an explanation. An essential element of the study of delinquency is a solid grasp of the classic as well as the more contemporary theories of delinquency. Understanding how others have conceptualized delinquency and how they have created theoretical explanations for it will assist in your thinking critically about the subject. The student of delinquency research should remember that no theory is completely correct or accepted. There is always room for revision, expansion, and, if needed, a complete rejection of a particular theory. This rejection has occurred many times in the area of crime-related research wherein a major paradigmatic shift changes the fundamental approach of certain disciplines.

Some theories presented here are carefully structured in terms of causal statements and hypothetical derivations while others are eloquently simple. Part II is a collection of eight articles representing some of the most important theoretical explanations in delinquency research. Each work was selected as a representative of an important and major theoretical genre as well as for the historical importance of the article itself. Some of these works have been pivotal in determining the future direction of entire disciplines and the larger investigation of crime and deviance.

We begin with one of the more influential structural theories, Robert K. Merton's "Social Structure and Anomie," which questions the biological explanations of deviance and offers a sociological alternative that still affects deviance and criminological researchers of today. This theory is known as a *strain theory* because Merton argues that lower-class individuals especially experience frustration due to an inability to achieve cultural goals which have been blocked by differential opportunities. This frustration or "anomie" leads some individuals to achieve goals through deviant or criminal opportunities.

In "A Sociological Theory of Criminal Behavior," Edwin H. Sutherland and Donald R. Cressey present another remarkably important theory that attempts to explain crime—"differential association." They claim we learn crime just as we learn most everything else—through interaction in association with significant others. This learning may include criminal techniques as well as attitudes, rationalizations, and beliefs about these behaviors. Two of the most important ways in which we learn throughout our lives are by imitation and by moving from discomfort toward comfort. The real power of this theory has been to channel much of the thinking about crime and delinquency away from biological toward environmental explanations. One need not be a high-powered criminologist to apply Sutherland and Cressey's association idea to peer or reference groups.

Our third selection reverses the question of why individuals deviate and asks instead, "Why do people conform?" Travis Hirschi offers us "A Control Theory of Delinquency," in which he answers that the stronger the "bond to society," the less likely one is to deviate. The stronger our attachments to our parents, schools, and conventional society, the less likely we are to violate the rules of society. When the bonds are weak or broken, we are more likely to violate the rules.

In "Techniques of Neutralization: A Theory of Delinquency," Gresham M. Sykes and David Matza combine some elements of both the learning and control theories. These "techniques" serve as defenses to delinquency-related behaviors and provide a rationale that allows the person to "drift" into nonconformity and yet not transform his or her nondelinquent identity. These defenses allow the person to vacillate from conformity to delinquency and back again. As all of us can recall some clever rationalizations we have used to justify past behaviors, we should easily be able to understand this theory.

In "Lower Class Culture as a Generating Milieu of Gang Delinquency," Walter B. Miller identifies the elements of lower-class culture that he believes lead to the transmission of cultural values favoring gang delinquency.

Terence P. Thornberry, in "Toward an Interactional Theory of Delinquency," presents a blend of many of the previous theories. Yet, he places delinquency in the larger causal network of social factors which he claims is dynamic rather than static and develops over the individual's lifetime.

The fact that female delinquency has been all but ignored and that salient explanations of female deviance are next to nil is presented with clarity by Meda Chesney-Lind in "Girls' Crime and Woman's Place: Toward a Feminist Model of Female Delinquency." The societal reactions to female deviance or delinquency have too often been based on patriarchal ideology rather than viewed within the larger social context. Chesney-Lind makes many suggestions as to the directions of future theoretical formulations of delinquency.

Our final selection, "Foundation for a General Strain Theory of Crime and Delinquency," by Robert Agnew, is an excellent example of the more contemporary attempts at theoretical revisions based on updated thinking and knowledge. He argues that the revisions in the older strain models can make strain theories viable again as major explanations rather than as minor elements in some of the learning or control theories. Rather than blending several theories together, Agnew concentrates on elaborating strain theory as a general theory and accepts that it cannot be used as a full replacement of the earlier strain models.

6

Social Structure and Anomie

Robert K. Merton

There persists a notable tendency in socio-logical theory to attribute the malfunctioning of social structure primarily to those of man's imperious biological drives which are not adequately restrained by social control. In this view, the social order is solely a device for "impulse management" and the "social processing" of tensions. These impulses which break through social control, be it noted, are held to be biologically derived. Nonconformity is assumed to be rooted in original nature.[1] Conformity is by implica-tion the result of an utilitarian calculus or unreasoned conditioning. This point of view, whatever its other deficiencies, clearly begs one question. It provides no basis for deter-mining the nonbiological conditions which induce deviations from prescribed patterns of conduct. In this paper, it will be suggested that certain phases of social structure gener-ate the circumstances in which infringement of social codes constitutes a "normal" response.[2]

The conceptual scheme to be outlined is designed to provide a coherent, systematic approach to the study of sociocultural sources of deviant behavior. Our primary aim lies in discovering how some social structures *exert a definite pressure* upon certain persons in the society to engage in nonconformist rather than conformist conduct. The many ramifications of the scheme cannot all be dis-cussed; the problems mentioned outnumber those explicitly treated.

Among the elements of social and cul-tural structure, two are important for our purposes. These are analytically separable although they merge imperceptibly in con-crete situations. The first consists of cultur-ally defined goals, purposes, and interests. It comprises a frame of aspirational reference. These goals are more or less integrated and involve varying degrees of prestige and senti-ment. They constitute a basic, but not the exclusive, component of what Linton aptly has called "designs for group living." Some of these cultural aspirations are related to the original drives of man, but they are not deter-mined by them. The second phase of the social structure defines, regulates, and con-trols the acceptable modes of achieving these goals. Every social group invariably couples its scale of desired ends with moral or institu-tional regulation of permissible and required procedures for attaining these ends. These regulatory norms and moral imperatives do not necessarily coincide with technical or efficiency norms. Many procedures which from the standpoint of *particular individuals* would be most efficient in securing desired values, for example, illicit oil-stock schemes, theft, fraud, are ruled out of the institutional area of permitted conduct. The choice of expedients is limited by the institutional norms.

To say that these two elements, culture goals and institutional norms, operate jointly

"Social Structure and Anomie," *American Sociological Review*, 3 (October 1938), pp. 672–682.

is not to say that the ranges of alternative behaviors and aims bear some constant relation to one another. The emphasis upon certain goals may vary independently of the degree of emphasis upon institutional means. There may develop a disproportionate, at times, a virtually exclusive, stress upon the value of specific goals, involving relatively slight concern with the institutionally appropriate modes of attaining these goals. The limiting case in this direction is reached when the range of alternative procedures is limited only by technical rather than institutional considerations. Any and all devices which promise attainment of the all important goal would be permitted in this hypothetical polar case.[3] This constitutes one type of cultural malintegration. A second polar type is found in groups where activities originally conceived as instrumental are transmuted into ends in themselves. The original purposes are forgotten, and ritualistic adherence to institutionally prescribed conduct becomes virtually obsessive.[4] Stability is largely ensured while change is flouted. The range of alternative behaviors is severely limited. There develops a tradition-bound, sacred society characterized by neophobia. The occupational psychosis of the bureaucrat may be cited as a case in point. Finally, there are the intermediate types of groups where a balance between culture goals and institutional means is maintained. These are the significantly integrated and relatively stable, though changing, groups.

An effective equilibrium between the two phases of the social structure is maintained as long as satisfactions accrue to individuals who conform to both constraints, viz., satisfactions from the achievement of the goals and satisfactions emerging directly from the institutionally canalized modes of striving to attain these ends. Success, in such equilibrated cases, is twofold. Success is reckoned in terms of the product and in terms of the process, in terms of the outcome and in terms of activities. Continuing satisfactions must derive from sheer *participation* in a competitive order as well as from eclipsing one's competitors if the order itself is to be sustained. The occasional sacrifices involved in institutionalized conduct must be compensated by socialized rewards. The distribution of statuses and roles through competition must be so organized that positive incentives for conformity to roles and adherence to status obligations are provided *for every position* within the distributive order. Aberrant conduct, therefore, may be viewed as a symptom of dissociation between culturally defined aspirations and socially structured means.

Of the types of groups which result from the independent variation of the two phases of the social structure, we shall be primarily concerned with the first, namely, that involving a disproportionate accent on goals. This statement must be recast in a proper perspective. In no group is there an absence of regulatory codes governing conduct, yet groups do vary in the degree to which these folkways, mores, and institutional controls are effectively integrated with the more diffuse goals which are part of the cultural matrix. Emotional convictions may cluster about the complex of socially acclaimed ends, meanwhile shifting their support from the culturally defined implementation of these ends. As we shall see, certain aspects of the social structure may generate countermores and antisocial behavior precisely because of differential emphases on goals and regulations. In the extreme case, the latter may be so vitiated by the goal emphasis that the range of behavior is limited only by considerations of technical expediency. The sole significant question then becomes, which available means is most efficient in netting the socially approved value?[5] The technically most feasible procedure, whether legitimate or not, is preferred to the institutionally prescribed conduct. As this process continues, the integration of the society becomes tenuous and anomie ensues.

Thus, in competitive athletics, when the aim of victory is shorn of its institutional trappings and success in contests becomes construed as "winning the game" rather than "wining through circumscribed modes of activity," a premium is implicitly set upon the use of illegitimate but technically efficient means. The star of the opposing football team is surreptitiously slugged; the wrestler furtively incapacitates his opponent through ingenious but illicit techniques; university alumni covertly subsidize "students" whose talents are largely confined to the athletic field. The emphasis on the goal has so attenuated the satisfactions deriving from sheer participation in the competitive activity that these satisfactions are virtually confined to a successful outcome. Through the same process, tension generated by the desire to win in a poker game is relieved by successfully dealing oneself four aces, or, when the cult of success has become completely dominant, by sagaciously shuffling the cards in a game of solitaire. The faint twinge of uneasiness in the last instance and the surreptitious nature of public delicts indicate clearly that the institutional rules of the game *are known* to those who evade them, but that the emotional supports of these rules are largely vitiated by cultural exaggeration of the success-goal.[6] They are microcosmic images of the social macrocosm.

Of course, this process is not restricted to the realm of sport. The process whereby exaltation of the end generates a *literal demoralization*, i.e., a deinstitutionalization, of the means is one which characterizes many[7] groups in which the two phases of the social structure are not highly integrated. The extreme emphasis upon the accumulation of wealth as a symbol of success[8] in our own society militates against the completely effective control of institutionally regulated modes of acquiring a fortune.[9] Fraud, corruption, vice, crime, in short, the entire catalogue of proscribed behavior, becomes increasingly common when the emphasis on the *culturally induced* success-goal becomes divorced from a coordinated institutional emphasis. This observation is of crucial theoretical importance in examining the doctrine that antisocial behavior most frequently derives from biological drives breaking through the restraints imposed by society. The difference is one between a strictly utilitarian interpretation which conceives man's ends as random and an analysis which finds these ends deriving from the basic values of the culture.[10]

Our analysis can scarcely stop at this juncture. We must turn to other aspects of the social structure if we are to deal with the social genesis of the varying rates and types of deviate behavior characteristic of different societies. Thus far, we have sketched three ideal

types of social orders constituted by distinctive patterns of relations between culture ends and means. Turning from these types of *culture patterning*, we find five logically possible, alternative modes of adjustment or adaptation *by individuals* within the culture-bearing society or group.[11] These are schematically presented in the following table, where $(+)$ signifies "acceptance," $(-)$ signifies "elimination," and $(\pm)$ signifies "rejection and substitution of new goals and standards."

		Culture Goals	Institutionalized Means
I.	Conformity	+	+
II.	Innovation	+	−
III.	Ritualism	−	+
IV.	Retreatism	−	−
V.	Rebellion[12]	±	±

Our discussion on the relation between these alternative responses and other phases of the social structure must be prefaced by the observation that persons may shift from one alternative to another as they engage in different social activities. These categories refer to role adjustments in specific situations, not to personality *in toto*. To treat the development of this process in various spheres of conduct would introduce a complexity unmanageable within the confines of this paper. For this reason, we shall be concerned primarily with economic activity in the broad sense, "the production, exchange, distribution, and consumption of goods and services" in our competitive society, wherein wealth has taken on a highly symbolic cast. Our task is to search out some of the factors which exert pressure upon individuals to engage in certain of these logically possible alternative responses. This choice, as we shall see, is far from random.

In every society, Adaptation I (conformity to both culture goals and means) is the most common and widely diffused. Were this not so, the stability and continuity of the society could not be maintained. The mesh of expectancies which constitutes every social order is sustained by the model behavior of its members falling within the first category. Conventional role behavior oriented toward the basic values of the group is the rule rather than the exception. It is this fact alone which permits us to speak of a human aggregate as comprising a group or society.

Conversely, Adaptation IV (rejection of goals and means) is the least common. Persons who "adjust" (or maladjust) in this fashion are, strictly speaking, *in* the society but not *of* it. Sociologically, these constitute the true "aliens." Not sharing the common frame of orientation, they can be included within the societal population merely in a fictional sense. In this category are *some* of the activities of psychotics, psychoneurotics, chronic autists, pariahs, outcasts, vagrants, vagabonds, tramps, chronic drunkards, and drug addicts.[13] These have relinquished, in certain spheres of activity, the culturally defined goals, involving complete aim-inhibition in the polar case, and their adjustments are not in accord with institutional norms. This is not to say that in some cases the source of their behavioral adjustments is not in part the very social structure which they have in effect repudiated nor that their very existence within a social area does not constitute a problem for the socialized population.

This mode of "adjustment" occurs, as far as structural sources are concerned, when both the culture goals and institutionalized procedures have been assimilated thoroughly by the individual and imbued with affect and high positive value, but where those institutionalized procedures which promise a measure of successful attainment of the goals are not available to the individual. In such instances, there results a two-fold mental conflict insofar as the moral obligation for adopting institutional means conflicts with the pressure to resort to illegitimate means (which may attain the goal) and inasmuch as the individual is shut off from means which are both legitimate *and* effective. The competitive order is maintained, but the frustrated and handicapped individual who cannot cope with this order drops out. Defeatism, quietism, and resignation are manifested in escape mechanisms which ultimately lead the individual to "escape" from the requirements of the society. It is an expedient which arises from continued failure to attain the goal by legitimate measures and from an inability to adopt the illegitimate route because of internalized prohibitions

and institutionalized compulsives, *during which process the supreme value of the success-goal has as yet not been renounced.* The conflict is resolved by eliminating *both* precipitating elements, the goals and means. The escape is complete, the conflict is eliminated, and the individual is associalized.

Be it noted that where frustration derives from the inaccessibility of effective institutional means for attaining economic or any other type of highly valued "success," that Adaptation II, III, and V (innovation, ritualism, and rebellion) are also possible. The result will be determined by the *particular* cultural background, involved. Inadequate socialization will result in the innovation response whereby the conflict and frustration are eliminated by relinquishing the institutional means and retaining the success-aspiration; an extreme assimilation of institutional demands will lead to ritualism wherein the goal is dropped as beyond one's reach but conformity to the mores persists; and rebellion occurs when emancipation from the reigning standards, due to frustration or to marginalist perspectives, leads to the attempt to introduce a "new social order."

Our major concern is with the illegitimacy adjustment. This involves the use of conventionally proscribed but frequently effective means of attaining at least the simulacrum of culturally defined success—wealth, power, and the like. As we have seen, this adjustment occurs when the individual has assimilated the cultural emphasis on success without equally internalizing the morally prescribed norms governing means for its attainment. The question arises, Which phases of our social structure predispose toward this mode of adjustment? We may examine a concrete instance, effectively analyzed by Lohman,[14] which provides a clue to the answer. Lohman has shown that specialized areas of vice in the near north side of Chicago constitute a "normal" response to a situation where the cultural emphasis upon pecuniary success has been absorbed, but where there is little access to conventional and legitimate means for attaining such success. The conventional occupational opportunities of persons in this area are almost completely limited to manual labor. Given our cultural stigmatization of manual labor, and its correlate, the prestige of white collar work, it is clear that the result is a strain toward innovational practices. The limitation of opportunity to unskilled labor and the resultant low income cannot compete *in terms of conventional standards of achievement* with the high income from organized vice.

For our purposes, this situation involves two important features. First, such antisocial behavior is in a sense "called forth" by certain conventional values of the culture *and* by the class structure involving differential access to the approved opportunities for legitimate, prestige-bearing pursuit of the culture goals. The lack of high integration between the means-and-end elements of the cultural pattern and the particular class structure combine to favor a heightened frequency of antisocial conduct in such groups. The second consideration is of equal significance. Recourse to the first of the alternative responses, legitimate effort, is limited by the fact that actual advance toward desired success symbols through conventional channels is, despite our persisting open-class ideology,[15] relatively rare and difficult for those handicapped by little formal education and few economic resources. The dominant pressure of group standards of success is, therefore, on the gradual attenuation of legitimate, but by and large ineffective, striving and the increasing use of illegitimate, but more or less effective, expedients of vice and crime. The cultural demands made on persons in this situation are incompatible. On the one hand, they are asked to orient their conduct toward the prospect of accumulating wealth and on the other, they are largely denied effective opportunities to do so institutionally. The consequences of such structural inconsistency are psychopathological personality, and/or antisocial conduct, and/or revolutionary activities. The equilibrium between culturally designated means and ends becomes highly unstable with the progressive emphasis on attaining the prestige-laden ends by any means whatsoever. Within this context, Capone represents the triumph of amoral intelligence over morally prescribed "failure," when the channels of

vertical mobility are closed or narrowed[16] *in a society which places a high premium on economic affluence and social ascent for all its members.*[17]

This last qualification is of primary importance. It suggests that other phases of the social structure besides the extreme emphasis on pecuniary success must be considered if we are to understand the social sources of antisocial behavior. A high frequency of deviate behavior is not generated simply by "lack of opportunity" or by this exaggerated pecuniary emphasis. A comparatively rigidified class structure, a feudalistic or caste order, may limit such opportunities far beyond the point which obtains in our society today. It is only when a system of cultural values extols, virtually above all else, certain *common* symbols of success *for the population at large* while its social structure rigorously restricts or completely eliminates access to approved modes of acquiring these symbols *for a considerable part of the same population* that antisocial behavior ensues on a considerable scale. In other words, our egalitarian ideology denies by implication the existence of noncompeting groups and individuals in the pursuit of pecuniary success. The same body of success symbols is held to be desirable for all. These goals are held to *transcend class lines,* not to be bounded by them, yet the actual social organization is such that there exist class differentials in the accessibility of these *common* success symbols. Frustration and thwarted aspiration lead to the search for avenues of escape from a culturally induced intolerable situation; or unrelieved ambition may eventuate in illicit attempts to acquire the dominant values.[18] The American stress on pecuniary success and ambitiousness for all thus invites exaggerated anxieties, hostilities, neuroses, and antisocial behavior.

This theoretical analysis may go far toward explaining the varying correlations between crime and poverty.[19] Poverty is not an isolated variable. It is one in a complex of interdependent social and cultural variables. When viewed in such a context, it represents quite different states of affairs. Poverty as such, and consequent limitation of opportunity, are not sufficient to induce a conspicuously high rate of criminal behavior. Even the often mentioned "poverty in the midst of plenty" will not necessarily lead to this result. Only insofar as poverty and associated disadvantages in competition for the culture values approved for *all* members of the society are linked with the assimilation of a cultural emphasis on monetary accumulation as a symbol of success is antisocial conduct a "normal" outcome. Thus, poverty is less highly correlated with crime in southeastern Europe than in the United States. The possibilities of vertical mobility in these European areas would seem to be fewer than in this country, so that neither poverty *per se* nor its association with limited opportunity is sufficient to account for the varying correlations. It is only when the full configuration is considered, poverty, limited opportunity, and a commonly shared system of success symbols, that we can explain the higher association between poverty and crime in our society than in others where rigidified class structure is coupled with *differential class symbols of achievement.*

In societies such as our own, then, the pressure of prestige-bearing success tends to eliminate the effective social constraint over means employed to this end. "The-end-justifies-the-means" doctrine becomes a guiding tenet for action when the cultural structure unduly exalts the end and the social organization unduly limits possible recourse to approved means. Otherwise put, this notion and associated behavior reflect a lack of cultural coordination. In international relations, the effects of this lack of integration are notoriously apparent. An emphasis upon national power is not readily coordinated with an inept organization of legitimate, i.e., internationally defined and accepted, means for attaining this goal. The result is a tendency toward the abrogation of international law, treaties become scraps of paper. "Undeclared warfare" serves as a technical evasion, the bombing of civilian populations is rationalized,[20] just as the same societal situation induces the same sway of illegitimacy among individuals.

The social order we have described necessarily produces this "strain toward dissolution." The pressure of such an order is upon outdoing one's competitors. The choice of means within the ambit of institutional control will persist as long as the sentiments sporting a competitive system, i.e., deriving from the possibility of outranking competitors and hence enjoying the favorable response of others, are distributed throughout the entire system of activities and are not confined merely to the final result. A stable social structure demands a balanced distribution of affect among its various segments. When there occurs a shift of emphasis from the satisfactions deriving from competition itself to almost exclusive concern with successful competition, the resultant stress leads to the breakdown of the regulatory structures.[21] With the resulting attenuation of the institutional imperatives, there occurs an approximation of the situation erroneously held by utilitarians to be typical of society generally wherein calculations of advantage and fear of punishment are the sole regulating agencies. In such situations, as Hobbes observed, force and fraud come to constitute the sole virtues in view of their relative efficiency in attaining goals—which were for him of course, not culturally derived.

It should be apparent that the foregoing discussion is not pitched on a moralistic plane. Whatever the sentiments of the writer or reader concerning the ethical desirability of coordinating the means-and-goals phases of the social structure, one must agree that lack of such coordination leads to anomie. Insofar as one of the most general functions of social organization is to provide a basis for calculability and regularity of behavior, it is increasingly limited in effectiveness as these elements of the structure become dissociated. At the extreme, predictability virtually disappears and what may be properly termed cultural chaos or anomie intervenes.

This statement, being brief, is also incomplete. It has not included an exhaustive treatment of the various structural elements which predispose toward one rather than another of the alternative responses open to individuals; it has neglected, but not denied the relevance on the factors determining the specific incidence of these responses; it has not enumerated the various concrete responses which are constituted by combination of specific values of the analytical variables; it has omitted, or included only by implication, any consideration of the social functions performed by illicit responses; it has not tested the full explanatory power of the analytical scheme by examining a large number of group variations in the frequency of deviate and conformist behavior; it has not adequately dealt with rebellious conduct which seeks to refashion the social framework radically; it has not examined the relevance of cultural conflict for an analysis of culture-goal and institutional-means malintegration. It is suggested that these and related problems may be profitably analyzed by this scheme.

Notes

1. E.g., Ernest Jones, *Social Aspects of Psychoanalysis*, 28, London, 1924. If the Freudian notion is a variety of the "original sin" dogma, then the interpretation advanced in this paper may be called the doctrine of "socially derived sin."

2. "Normal" in the sense of a culturally oriented, if not approved, response. This statement does not deny the relevance of biological and personality differences which may be significantly involved in the *incidence* of deviate conduct. Our focus of interest is the social and cultural matrix; hence we abstract from other factors. It is in this sense, I take it, that James S. Plant speaks of the "normal reaction of normal people to abnormal conditions." See his *Personality and the Cultural Pattern*, 248, New York, 1937.

3. Contemporary American culture has been said to tend in this direction. See André Siegfried, *America Comes of Age*, 26–37, New York, 1927. The alleged extreme(?) emphasis on the goals of monetary success and material prosperity leads to dominant concern with technological and social instruments designed to produce the desired result, inasmuch as institutional controls become of secondary importance. In such a situation, innovation flourishes as the *range of means* employed is broadened. In a sense, then, there occurs the paradoxical emergence of "materialists" from an "idealistic" orientation. Cf. Durkheim's analysis of the cultural conditions which predispose toward crime and innovation, both of which are aimed toward efficiency, not moral norms. Durkheim was one of the first to see that "contrairment aux idées courantes le criminal n'apparait plus comme un être radicalement insociable, comme une sorte d'élément parasitaire, de corps étranger et inassimilable, introduit au sein de la société; c'est un agent régulier de la vie sociale." See *les Régles de la Méthode Sociologique*, 86–89, Paris, 1927.

4. Such ritualism may be associated with a mythology which rationalizes these actions so that they appear to retain their status as means, but the dominant pressure is in the direction of strict ritualistic conformity, irrespective of such rationalizations. In this sense, ritual has proceeded farthest when such rationalizations are not even called forth.

5. In this connection, one may see the relevance of Elton Mayo's paraphrase of the title of Tawney's well-known book. "Actually the problem is *not that of the sickness of an acquisitive society; it is that of the acquisitiveness of a sick society." Human Problems of an Industrial Civilization*, 153, New York, 1933. Mayo deals with the process through which wealth comes to be a symbol of social achievement. He sees this as arising from a state of anomie. We are considering the unintegrated monetary-success goal as an element in producing anomie. A complete analysis would involve both phases of this system of interdependent variables.

6. It is unlikely that interiorized norms are completely eliminated. Whatever residuum persists will induce personality tensions and conflict. The process involves a certain degree of ambivalence. A manifest rejection of the institutional norms is coupled with some latent retention of their emotional correlates. "Guilt feelings," "sense of sin," "pangs of conscience" are obvious manifestations of this unrelieved tension; symbolic adherence to the nominally repudiated values or rationalizations constitute a more subtle variety of tensional release.

7. "Many," and not all, unintegrated groups, for the reason already mentioned. In groups where the primary emphasis shifts to institutional means, i.e., when the range of alternatives is very limited, the outcome is a type of ritualism rather than anomie.

8. Money has several peculiarities which render it particularly apt to become a symbol of prestige divorced from institutional controls. As Simmel emphasized, money is highly abstract and impersonal. However acquired, through fraud or institutionally, it can be used to purchase the same goods and services. The anonymity of metropolitan culture, in conjunction with this peculiarity of money, permits wealth, the sources of which may be unknown to the community in which the plutocrat lives, to serve as a symbol of status.

9. The emphasis upon wealth as a success symbol is possibly reflected in the use of the term "fortune" to refer to a stock of accumulated wealth. This meaning becomes common in the late sixteenth century (Spenser and Shakespeare). A similar usage of the Latin *fortuna* comes into prominence during the first century B.C. Both these periods were marked by the rise to prestige and power of the "bourgeoisie."

10. See Kinglsey Davis, "Mental Hygiene and the Class Structure," *Psychiatry*, 1928, 1:esp.62–63; Talcott Parsons, *The Structure of Social Action*, 59–60, New York, 1937.

11. This is a level intermediate between the two planes distinguished by Edward Sapir; mainly, culture patterns and personal habits systems. See his "Contribution of Psychiatry to an Understanding of Behavior in Society," *Amer. J. Sociol.*, 1937, 42:862–870.

12. This fifth alternative is on a plane clearly different from that of the others. It represents a *transitional* response which seeks to *institutionalize* new procedures oriented toward revamped cultural goals shared by the members of the society. It thus involves efforts to *change* the existing structure rather than to perform accommodative actions *within* this structure, and introduces additional problems with which we are not at the moment concerned.

13. Obviously, this is an elliptical statement. These individuals may maintain some orientation to the values of their particular differentiated groupings within the larger society or, in part, of the conventional society itself. Insofar as they do so, their conduct cannot be classified in the "passive rejection" category (IV). Nels Anderson's description of the behavior and attitudes of the bum, for example, can readily be recast in terms of our analytical scheme. See *The Hobo*, 93–98, *et passim*, Chicago, 1923.

14. Joseph D. Lohman, "The Participant Observer in Community Studies," *Amer. Sociol. Rev.*, 1937, 2:890–898.

15. The shifting historical role of this ideology is a profitable subject for exploration. The "office-boy-to-president" stereotype was once in approximate accord with the facts. Such vertical mobility was probably more common then than now, when the class structure is more rigid. (See the following note.) The ideology largely persists, however, possibly because it still performs a useful function for maintaining the *status quo*. For insofar as it is accepted by the "masses," it constitutes a useful sop for those who might rebel against the entire structure, were this consoling hope removed. This ideology now serves to lessen the probability of Adaptation V. In short, the role of this notion has changed from that of an ideology, in Mannheim's sense.

16. There is a growing body of evidence, though none of it is clearly conclusive, to the effect that our class structure is becoming rigidified and that vertical mobility is declining. Taussig and Joslyn found that American business leaders are being *increasingly* recruited from the upper ranks of our society. The Lynds have also found a "diminished chance to get ahead" for the working classes in Middletown. Manifestly, these objective changes are not alone significant; the individual's subjective evaluation of the situation is a major determinant of the response. The extent to which this change in opportunity for social mobility has been recognized by the least advantaged classes is still conjectural, although the Lynds present some suggestive materials. The writer suggests that a case in point is the increasing frequency of cartoons which observe in a tragi-comic vein that "my old man says everybody can't be President. He says if ya can get three days a week steady on W.P.A. work ya ain't doin' so bad either." See F. W. Taussig and C. S. Joslyn, *American Business Leaders*, New York, 1932; R. S. and H. M. Lynd, *Middletown in Transition*, 67 ff., chap. 12, New York, 1937.

17. The role of the Negro in this respect is of considerable theoretical interest. Certain elements of the Negro population have assimilated the dominant caste's values of pecuniary success and social advancement, but they also recognize that social ascent is at present restricted to their own caste almost exclusively. The pressures upon the Negro which would otherwise derive from the structural inconsistencies we have noticed are hence not identical with those upon lower class whites. See Kinglsey Davis, *op. cit.*, 63; John Dollard, *Caste and Class in a Southern Town*, 66ff., New Haven, 1936; Donald Young, *American Minority Peoples*, 581, New York, 1932.

18. The psychical coordinates of these processes have been partly established by the experimental evidence concerning *Anspruchsniveaus* and levels of performance. See Kurt Lewin, *Vorsatz, Willie und Bedurfnis*, Berlin, 1926; N. F. Hoppe, "Erfolg und Misserfolg," *Psychol. Forschung*. 1930, 14:1–63; Jerome D. Frank, "Individual Differences in Certain Aspects of the Level of Aspiration," *Amer. J. Psychol.*, 1935, 47:119–128.

19. Standard criminology texts summarize the data in this field. Our scheme of analysis may serve to resolve some of the theoretical contradictions which P. A. Sorkin indicates. For example, "not everywhere nor always do the poor show a greater proportion of crime . . . many poorer countries have had less crime than the richer countries. . . . The [economic] improvement in the second half of the nineteenth century, and the beginning of the twentieth, has not been followed by a decrease of crime." See his *Contemporary Sociological Theories*, 560–561, New York, 1928. The crucial point is, however, that poverty has varying social significance in different social structures, as we shall see. Hence, one would not expect a linear correlation between crime and poverty.

20. See M. W. Royse, *Aerial Bombardment and the International Regulation of War*, New York, 1928.

21. Since our primary concern is with the socio-cultural aspects of this problem, the psychological correlates have been only implicitly considered. See Karen Horney, *The Neurotic Personality of Our Time*, New York, 1937, for a psychological discussion of this process.

QUESTIONS FOR DISCUSSION

1. Why does Merton object to attributing problems in society to "biological drives" that have not been adequately restrained?

2. What assumptions are made about cultural goals and institutionalized means in Merton's five-pattern scheme for adaptation?

3. In which of the five patterns do you think we might categorize most juvenile delinquents?

4. Can you think of any individuals or groups that may not fit into Merton's patterns?

5. In what way is the pattern of rebellion different from the other four patterns?

APPLICATIONS

1. On a sheet of paper make two columns. In column 1 list what you believe are the goals of our culture. In column 2 list what you believe are the institutionally approved means for achieving these cultural goals. Compare your responses to other classmates'.
   a. On what goals and means do your classmates agree? How do they disagree?
   b. Utilizing group discussion, attempt to arrive at a full consensus on what should be included as goals and means.
   c. In which of Merton's five patterns would you categorize yourself? Do you think a person could change from pattern to pattern depending on the social situation?

2. When an individual cannot achieve culturally approved goals and/or is denied institutional means for goal obtainment, a condition occurs which Emile Durkheim called *anomie* or normlessness. When an individual loses the attachment to social norms, the sources of social and self-restraint are dissolved. Social disorder is the result. Among individuals and groups, regard for normative and legal prescriptions is lacking or altered.
   a. When the Los Angeles police officers were first acquitted for the alleged beating of Rodney King, there was subsequent looting and arson. This is an example of social disorder. How might the concept of anomie be used to explain this phenomena?
   b. How might we apply Merton's five-pattern scheme in order understand this event?
   c. From your perspective, what changes should be invoked immediately and over the long term to maintain social order in urban areas?

KEY TERMS

anomie a state of normlessness in which the social control of individual behavior has become ineffective.

conceptual scheme a tool or model utilized for describing a particular phenomena.

culture the totality of socially transmitted behavior patterns, arts, beliefs, institutions, and all other products of human work and thought characteristic of a community or population.

folkways patterns of behavior common in and typical to a group.

macrocosm a universal system regarded as an entity containing subsystems or subgroups.

microcosm a system more or less analogous to a much larger system in constitution, configuration, or development.

ritualistic prescribing to any detailed method or procedure faithfully or regularly followed.

role the characteristics and expected social behavior of an individual.

social conflict the absence of harmony, equilibrium, order, or consensus. Disconsensual in terms of values, meanings, or resources.

status a position based on prestige and lifestyle.

7

A Sociological Theory of Criminal Behavior

Edwin H. Sutherland

Donald R. Cressey

The Problem for Criminological Theory

If criminology is to be scientific, the heterogeneous collection of multiple factors known to be associated with crime and criminality must be organized and integrated by means of explanatory theory which has the same characteristics as the scientific theory in other fields of study. That is, the conditions which are said to cause crime should be present when crime is present, and they should be absent when crime is absent. Such a theory or body of theory would stimulate, simplify, and give direction to criminological research, and it would provide a framework for understanding the significance of much of the knowledge acquired about crime and criminality in the past. Furthermore, it would be useful in minimizing crime rates, provided it could be "applied" in much the same way that the engineer "applies" the scientific theories of the physicist.

There are two complementary procedures which may be used to put order into criminological knowledge. The first is logical abstraction. Blacks, males, urban-dwellers, and young adults all have comparatively high crime rates. What do they have in common that results in these high crime rates? Research studies have shown that criminal behavior is associated, in greater or lesser

degree, with such social and personal pathologies as poverty, bad housing, slum-residence, lack of recreational facilities, inadequate and demoralized families, mental retardation, emotional instability, and other traits and conditions. What do these conditions have in common which apparently produces excessive criminality? Research studies have also demonstrated that many persons with those pathological traits and conditions do not commit crimes and that persons in the upper socio-economic class frequently violate the law, although they are not in poverty, do not lack recreational facilities, and are not mentally retarded or emotionally unstable. Obviously, it is not the conditions or traits themselves which cause crime, for the conditions are sometimes present when criminality does not occur, and they also are sometimes absent when criminality does occur. A generalization about crime and criminal behavior can be reached by logically abstracting the conditions and processes which are common to the rich and the poor, the males and the females, the blacks and the whites, the urban- and the rural-dwellers, the young adults and the old adults, and the emotionally stable and the emotionally unstable who commit crimes.

In developing such generalizations, criminal behavior must be precisely defined and carefully distinguished from noncriminal behavior. Criminal behavior is human behavior, and has much in common with noncriminal behavior. An explanation of criminal behavior should be consistent with a general

"A Sociological Theory of Criminal Behavior," *Criminology*, 10th ed. (Philadelphia: J.B. Lippincott Co., 1978), pp. 77–83. Reprinted by permission of the publisher.

theory of other human behavior, but the conditions and processes said to produce crime and criminality should be specific. Many things which are necessary for behavior are not important to criminality. Respiration, for instance, is necessary for any behavior, but the respiratory process cannot be used in an explanation of criminal behavior, for it does not differentiate criminal behavior from noncriminal behavior.

The second procedure for putting order into criminological knowledge is differentiation of levels of analysis. The explanation or generalization must be limited, largely in terms of chronology, and in this way held at a particular level. For example, when Renaissance physicists stated the law of falling bodies, they were not concerned with the reasons why a body began to fall except as this might affect the initial momentum. Galileo did not study the "traits" of falling objects themselves, as Aristotle might have done. Instead, he noted the relationship of the body to its environment while it was falling freely or rolling down an inclined plane, and it made no difference to his generalization whether a body began to fall because it was dropped from the hand of an experimenter or because it rolled off the ledge of a bridge due to vibration caused by a passing vehicle. Also, a round object would roll off the bridge more readily than a square object, but this fact was not significant for the law of falling bodies. Such facts were considered as existing on a different level of explanation and were irrelevant to the problem of explaining the behavior of falling bodies.

Much of the confusion regarding crime and criminal behavior stems from a failure to define and hold constant the level at which they are explained. By analogy, many criminologists and others concerned with understanding and defining crime would attribute some degree of causal power to the "roundness" of the object in the above illustration. However, consideration of time sequences among the conditions associated with crime and criminality may lead to simplicity of statement. In the heterogeneous collection of factors associated with crime and criminal behavior, one factor often occurs prior to another (in much the way that "roundness" occurs prior to "vibration," and "vibration" occurs prior to "rolling off a bridge"), but a theoretical statement can be made without referring to those early factors. By holding the analysis at one level, the early factors are combined with or differentiated from later factors or conditions, thus reducing the number of variables which must be considered in a theory.

A motion picture made several years ago showed two boys engaged in a minor theft; they ran when they were discovered; one boy had longer legs, escaped, and became a priest; the other had shorter legs, was caught, committed to a reformatory, and became a gangster. In this comparison, the boy who became a criminal was differentiated from the one who did not become a criminal by the length of his legs. But "length of legs" need not be considered in a criminological theory because it is obvious that this condition does not determine criminality and has no necessary relation to criminality. In the illustration, the differential in the length of the boys' legs apparently was significant to subsequent criminality or noncriminality only to the degree that it determined the subsequent experiences and associations of the two boys. It is in these experiences and associations, then, that the mechanisms and processes which are important to criminality or noncriminality are to be found.

Two Types of Explanations of Criminal Behavior

Scientific explanations of criminal behavior may be stated either in terms of the processes which are operating at the moment of the occurrence of crime or in terms of the processes operating in the earlier history of the criminal. In the first case, the explanation may be called "mechanistic," "situational," or "dynamic"; in the second, "historical" or "developmental." Both types of explanation are desirable. The mechanistic type of explanation has been favored by physical and biological scientists, and it probably could be the more efficient type of explanation of criminal behavior. As Gibbons said:

> In many cases, criminality may be a response to nothing more temporal than the provocations and attractions bound up in the immediate circumstances. It may be that, in

some kinds of lawbreaking, understanding of the behavior may require detailed attention to the concatenation of events immediately preceding it. Little or nothing may be added to this understanding from a close scrutiny of the early development of the person.[1]

However, criminological explanations of the mechanistic type have thus far been notably unsuccessful, perhaps largely because they have been formulated in connection with an attempt to isolate personal and social pathologies among criminals. Work from this point of view has, at least, resulted in the conclusion that the immediate determinants of criminal behavior lie in the person-situation complex.

The objective situation is important to criminality largely to the extent that it provides an opportunity for a criminal act. A thief may steal from a fruit stand when the owner is not in sight but refrain when the owner is in sight; a bank burglar may attack a bank which is poorly protected but refrain from attacking a well-protected bank. A corporation which manufactures automobiles seldom violates the pure food and drug laws, but a meat-packing corporation might violate these laws with great frequency. But in another sense, a psychological or sociological sense, the situation is not exclusive of the person, for the situation which is important is the situation as defined by the person who is involved. That is, some persons define a situation in which a fruit-stand owner is out of sight as a "crime-committing" situation, while others do not so define it. Furthermore, the events in the person-situation complex at the time a crime occurs cannot be separated from the prior life experiences of the criminal. This means that the situation is defined by the person in terms of the inclinations and abilities which he or she has acquired. For example, while a person could define a situation in such a manner that criminal behavior would be the inevitable result, past experiences would, for the most part, determine the way in which he or she defined the situation. An explanation of criminal behavior made in terms of these past experiences is a historical or developmental explanation.

The following paragraphs state such a developmental theory of criminal behavior on the assumption that a criminal act occurs when a situation appropriate for it, as defined by . . . the person, is present. The theory should be regarded as tentative, and it should be tested by all other factual information and theories which are applicable.

Developmental Explanation of Criminal Behavior

The following statements refer to the process by which a particular person comes to engage in criminal behavior:

1. *Criminal behavior is learned.* Negatively, this means that criminal behavior is not inherited, as such; also, the person who is not already trained in crime does not invent criminal behavior, just as a person does not make mechanical inventions unless he has had training in mechanics.

2. *Criminal behavior is learned in interaction with other persons in a process of communication.* This communication is verbal in many respects but includes also "the communication of gestures."

3. *The principal part of the learning of criminal behavior occurs within intimate personal groups.* Negatively, this means that the impersonal agencies of communication, such as movies and newspapers, play a relatively unimportant part in the genesis of criminal behavior.

4. *When criminal behavior is learned, the learning includes (a) techniques of committing the crime, which are sometimes very complicated, sometimes very simple; (b) the specific direction of motives, drives, rationalizations, and attitudes.*

5. *The specific direction of motives and drives is learned from definitions of the legal codes as favorable or unfavorable.* In some societies an individual is surrounded by persons who invariably define the legal codes as rules to be observed, while in others he is surrounded by persons whose definitions are favorable to the violation of the legal codes. In our American society these definitions are almost always mixed, with the consequence that we have culture conflict in relation to the legal codes.

6. *A person becomes delinquent because of an excess of definitions favorable to violation of law over definitions unfavorable to violation of law.* This is the principle of differential association. It refers to both criminal and anticriminal associations and has to do with counteracting forces. When persons become criminal, they do so because of contacts with criminal patterns and also because of isolation from anticriminal patterns. Any person inevitably assimilates the surrounding culture unless other patterns are in conflict; a southerner does not pronounce r because other southerners do not pronounce r. Negatively, this proposition of differential association means that associations which are neutral so far as crime is concerned have little or no effect on the genesis of criminal behavior. Much of the experience of a person is neutral in this sense, for instance, learning to brush one's teeth. This behavior has no negative or positive effect on criminal behavior except as it may be related to associations which are concerned with the legal codes. This neutral behavior is important especially as an occupier of the time of a child so that he or she is not in contact with criminal behavior during the time the child is so engaged in the neutral behavior.

7. *Differential associations may vary in frequency, duration, priority, and intensity.* This means that associations with criminal behavior and also associations with anticriminal behavior vary in those respects. Frequency and duration as modalities of associations are obvious and need no explanation. Priority is assumed to be important in the sense that lawful behavior developed in early childhood may persist throughout life, and also that delinquent behavior developed in early childhood may persist throughout life. This tendency, however, has not been adequately demonstrated, and priority seems to be important principally through its selective influence. Intensity is not precisely defined, but it has to do with such things as the prestige of the source of a criminal or anticrimi-

nal pattern and with emotional reactions related to the associations. In a precise description of the criminal behavior of a person, these modalities would be rated in quantitative form and a mathematical ratio would be reached. A formula in this sense has not been developed, and the development of such a formula would be extremely difficult.

8. *The process of learning criminal behavior by association with criminal and anticriminal patterns involves all of the mechanisms that are involved in any other learning.* Negatively, this means that the learning of criminal behavior is not restricted to the process of imitation. A person who is seduced, for instance, learns criminal behavior by association, but this process would not ordinarily be described as imitation.

9. *While criminal behavior is an expression of general needs and values, it is not explained by those general needs and values, since non-criminal behavior is an expression of the same needs and values.* Thieves generally steal in order to secure money, but likewise honest laborers work in order to secure money. The attempts by many scholars to explain criminal behavior by general drives and values, such as the happiness principle, striving for social status, the money motive, or frustration, have been, and must continue to be, futile, since they explain lawful behavior as completely as they explain criminal behavior. They are similar to respiration, which is necessary for any behavior, but which does not differentiate criminal from noncriminal behavior.

It is not necessary, at this level of explanation, to explain why persons have the associations they have; this certainly involves a complex of many things. In an area where the delinquency rate is high, a boy who is sociable, gregarious, active, and athletic is very likely to come in contact with the other boys in the neighborhood, learn delinquent behavior patterns from them, and become a criminal; in the same neighborhood the psychopathic boy who is isolated, introverted, and inert may remain at home, not become acquainted with the other boys in the neighborhood, and not become delinquent. In another situation, the sociable, athletic, aggressive boy may become a member of a scout troop and not become involved in delinquent behavior. The person's associations are determined in a general context of social organization. A child is ordinarily reared in a family; the place of residence of the family is determined largely by family income; and the delinquency rate is in many respects related to the rental value of the houses. Many other aspects of social organization affect the associations of a person.

The preceding explanation of criminal behavior purports to explain the criminal and noncriminal behavior of individual persons. As indicated earlier, it is possible to state sociological theories of criminal behavior which explain the criminality of a community, nation, or other group. The problem, when thus stated, is to account for variations in crime rates, which involves a comparison of the crime rates of various groups or the crime rates of a particular group at different times. The explanation of a crime rate must be consistent with the explanation of the criminal behavior of the person, since the crime rate is a summary statement of the number of persons in the group who commit crimes and the frequency with which they commit crimes. One of the best explanations of crime rates from this point of view is that a high crime rate is due to social disorganization. The term *social disorganization* is not entirely satisfactory, and it seems preferable to substitute for it the term *differential social organization.* The postulate on which this theory is based, regardless of the name, is that crime is rooted in the social organization and is an expression of that social organization. A group may be organized for criminal behavior or organized against criminal behavior. Most communities are organized for both criminal and anticriminal behavior, and, in that sense the crime rate is an expression of the differential group organization. Differential group organization as an explanation of variations in crime rates is consistent with the differential association theory of the processes by which persons become criminals.

Note

1. Don C. Gibbons, "Observations on the Study of Crime Causation," *American Journal of Sociology*, 77:262–78, 1971.

QUESTIONS FOR DISCUSSION

1. Discuss the two complementary procedures utilized to order criminological knowledge.

2. Describe the differences between mechanistic or situational and historical or developmental explanations of crime.

3. In your own words, list and discuss the nine main tenets of differential association.

4. Why do Sutherland and Cressey believe the term *social disorganization* should be replaced with the more accurate *differential social organization*?

APPLICATIONS

1. Sutherland and Cressey postulate that criminal behavior is learned in intimate groups and that media such as movies and newspapers are relatively unimportant.
   a. What intimate groups have affected your behavior? How?
   b. Do you think that criminal acts and violence on television and movies affect people's behavior? Why?

2. Consider those individuals in your high school who were rowdy or troublemakers. How did they differ from those individuals who were considered model students? What accounted for these differences, in terms of what the two groups of individuals had learned?

KEY TERMS

assimilate refers to accepting and conforming to the culture or mores of a group and/or population.

cultural conflict when a particular individual or group's norms, values, beliefs, and behaviors are in opposition to another group's or to the dominant culture of a society. Assuming that legal codes should represent the consensual culture of society, violation of such codes may be indicative of disconsensus by particular subcultures.

gregarious the tendency to associate with other people who are much like yourself.

heterogeneous consisting of dissimilar or diverse parts or constituents; as in a heterogeneous society that consists of a variety of norms, values, and beliefs.

mechanistic refers to the idea that behavior can be determined and understood by the rigid application of scientific law; the same behavior exhibited by two people is caused by the same antecedents.

pathology the structural and functional deviation from what is considered "normal." With regard to definitions of social deviance, pathology refers to a particularly aberrant individual.

psychopathic an emotionally and behaviorally disordered state characterized by a perception of reality that ignores social and moral responsibilities and is exhibited by substance abuse, sexual perversions, or criminal acts. Psychopaths, typically, may act concerned about other people. However, they engage in this facade for the purposes of manipulation and self-gain.

social disorganization the decline or disintegration of groups, institutions, communities, and societies; may occur because of poorly distributed resources, competition with other organizations, a loss of shared values, or pronounced social stratification.

8

A Control Theory of Delinquency

Travis Hirschi

Control theories assume that delinquent acts result when an individual's bond to society is weak or broken. Since these theories embrace two highly complex concepts, the *bond* of the individual to *society*, it is not surprising that they have at one time or another formed the basis of explanations of most forms of aberrant or unusual behavior. It is also not surprising that control theories have described the elements of the bond to society in many ways, and that they have focused on a variety of units as the point of control. . . .

ELEMENTS OF THE BOND

Attachment

In explaining conforming behavior, sociologists justly emphasize sensitivity to the opinion of others.[1] Unfortunately, . . . they tend to suggest that man *is* sensitive to the opinion of others and thus exclude sensitivity from their explanations of deviant behavior. In explaining deviant behavior, psychologists, in contrast, emphasize insensitivity to the opinion of others.[2] Unfortunately, they too tend to ignore variation, and, in addition, they tend to tie sensitivity inextricably to other variables, to make it part of a syndrome or "type,"

and thus seriously to reduce its value as an explanatory concept. The psychopath is characterized only in part by "deficient attachment to or affection for others, a failure to respond to the ordinary motivations founded in respect or regard for one's fellow";[3] he is also characterized by such things as "excessive aggressiveness," "lack of superego control," and "an infantile level of response."[4] Unfortunately, too, the behavior that psychopathy is used to explain often becomes part of the *definition* of psychopathy. As a result, in Barbara Wootton's words: "[The psychopath] is . . . *par excellence*, and without shame or qualification, the model of the circular process by which mental abnormality is inferred from anti-social behavior while anti-social behavior is explained by mental abnormality."[5]

The problems of diagnosis, tautology, and name-calling are avoided if the dimensions of psychopathy are treated as causally and therefore problematically interrelated, rather than as logically and therefore necessarily bound to each other. In fact, it can be argued that all of the characteristics attributed to the psychopath follow from, are effects of, his lack of attachment to others. To say that to lack attachment to others is to be free from moral restraints is to use lack of attachment to explain the guiltlessness of the psychopath, the fact that he apparently has no conscience or superego. In this view, lack of attachment to others is not merely a symptom of psychopathy, it *is* psychopathy; lack of conscience is just another way of saying the

"A Control Theory of Delinquency," *Causes of Delinquency* (Berkeley: University of California Press, 1969), pp. 16–26. Copyright ©1969 The Regents of the University of California.

same thing; and the violation of norms is (or may be) a consequence.

For that matter, given that man is an animal, "impulsivity" and "aggressiveness" can also be seen as natural consequences of freedom from moral restraints. However, since the view of man as endowed with natural propensities and capacities like other animals is peculiarly unpalatable to sociologists, we need not fall back on such a view to explain the amoral man's aggressiveness.[6] The process of becoming alienated from others often involves or is based on active interpersonal conflict. Such conflict could easily supply a reservoir of *socially derived* hostility sufficient to account for the aggressiveness of those whose attachments to others have been weakened.

Durkheim said it many years ago: "We are moral beings to the extent that we are social beings."[7] This may be interpreted to mean that we are moral beings to the extent that we have "internalized the norms" of society. But what does it mean to say that a person has internalized the norms of society? The norms of society are by definition shared by the members of society. To violate a norm is, therefore, to act contrary to the wishes and expectations of other people. If a person does not care about the wishes and expectation of other people—that is, if he is insensitive to the opinion of others—then he is to that extent not bound by the norms. He is free to deviate.

The essence of internalization of norms, conscience, or superego thus lies in the attachment of the individual to others.[8] This view has several advantages over the concept of internalization. For one, explanations of deviant behavior based on attachment do not beg the question, since the extent to which a person is attached to others can be measured independently of his deviant behavior. Furthermore, change or variation in behavior is explainable in a way that it is not when notions of internalization or superego are used. For example, the divorced man is more likely after divorce to commit a number of deviant acts, such as suicide or forgery. If we explain these acts by reference to the superego (or internal control), we are forced to say that the man "lost his conscience" when

he got a divorce; and, of course, if he remarries, we have to conclude that he gets his conscience back.

This dimension of the bond to conventional society is encountered in most social control-oriented research and theory. F. Ivan Nye's "internal control" and "indirect control" refer to the same element, although we avoid the problem of explaining changes over time by locating the "conscience" in the bond to others rather than making it part of the personality.[9] Attachment to others is just one aspect of Albert J. Reiss's "personal controls"; we avoid his problems of tautological empirical *observations* by making the relationship between attachment and delinquency problematic rather than definitional.[10] Finally, Scott Briar and Irving Piliavin's "commitment" or "stake in conformity" subsumes attachment, as their discussion illustrates, although the terms they use are more closely associated with the next element to be discussed.[11]

Commitment

"Of all passions, that which inclineth men least to break the laws, is fear. Nay, excepting some generous natures, it is the only thing, when there is the appearance of profit or pleasure by breaking the laws, that makes men keep them."[12] Few would deny that men on occasion obey the rules simply from fear of the consequences. This rational component in conformity we label commitment. What does it mean to say that a person is committed to conformity? In Howard S. Becker's formulation it means the following:

> First, the individual is in a position in which his decision with regard to some particular line of action has consequences for other interests and activities not necessarily [directly] related to it. Second, he has placed himself in that position by his own prior actions. A third element is present though so obvious as not to be apparent; the committed person must be aware [of these other interests] and must recognize that his decision in this case will have ramifications beyond it.[13]

The idea, then, is that the person invests time, energy, himself, in a certain line of activity—say, getting an education, building up a business, acquiring a reputation for virtue. When or whenever he considers deviant behavior, he must consider the costs of this deviant behavior, the risk he runs of losing the investment he has made in conventional behavior.

If attachment to others is the sociological counterpart of the superego or conscience, commitment is the counterpart of the ego or common sense. To the person committed to conventional lines of action, risking one to ten years in prison for a ten-dollar holdup is stupidity, because to the committed person the costs and risks obviously exceed ten dollars in value. (To the psychoanalyst, such an act exhibits failure to be governed by the "reality-principle.") In the sociological control theory, it can be and is generally assumed that the decision to commit a criminal act may well be rationally determined—that the actor's decision was not irrational given the risks and costs he faces. Of course, as Becker point out, if the actor is capable of in some sense calculating the costs of a line of action, he is also capable of calculational errors: ignorance and error return, in the control theory, as possible explanations of deviant behavior.

The concept of commitment assumes that the organization of society is such that the interest of most persons would be endangered if they were to engage in criminal acts. Most people, simply by the process of living in an organized society, acquire goods, reputations, prospects that they do not want to risk losing. These accumulations are society's insurance that they will abide by the rules. Many hypotheses about the antecedents of delinquent behavior are based on this premise. For example, Arthur L. Stinchcombe's hypothesis that "high school rebellion . . . occurs when future status is not clearly related to present performance"[14] suggests that one is committed to conformity not only by what one has but also by what one hopes to obtain. Thus "ambition" and/or "aspiration" play an important role in producing conformity. The person becomes committed to a conventional line of action, and he is therefore committed to conformity.

Most lines of action in a society are of course conventional. The clearest examples are educational and occupational careers. Actions thought to jeopardize one's chances in these areas are presumably avoided. Interestingly enough, even nonconventional commitments may operate to produce conventional conformity. We are told, at least, that boys aspiring to careers in the rackets of professional thievery are judged by their "honesty" and "reliability"—traits traditionally in demand among seekers of office boys.[15]

Involvement

Many persons undoubtedly owe a life of virtue to a lack of opportunity to do otherwise. Time and energy are inherently limited: "Not that I would not, if I could, be both handsome and fat and well dressed, and a great athlete, and make a million a year, be a wit, a bon vivant, and a lady killer, as well as a philosopher, a philanthropist, a statesman, warrior, and African explorer, as well as a 'tone-poet' and saint. But the thing is simply impossible."[16] The things that William James here says he would like to be or do are all, I suppose, within the realm of conventionality, but if he were to include illicit actions he would still have to eliminate some of them as simply impossible.

Involvement or engrossment in conventional activities is thus often part of a control theory. The assumption, widely shared, is that a person may be simply too busy doing conventional things to find time to engage in deviant behavior. The person involved in conventional activities is tied to appointments, deadlines, working hours, plans, and the like, so the opportunity to commit deviant acts rarely arises. To the extent that he is engrossed in conventional activities, he cannot even think about deviant acts, let alone act out his inclinations.[17]

This line of reasoning is responsible for the stress placed on recreational facilities in many programs to reduce delinquency, for much of the concern with the high school dropout, and for the idea that boys should be drafted into the army to keep them out of trouble. So obvious and persuasive is the idea that involvement in conventional activities is a major deterrent to delinquency that it was accepted even by Sutherland: "In the general area of juvenile delinquency it is probable that the most significant difference between juveniles who engage in delinquency and those who do not is that the latter are provided abundant opportunities of a conventional type for satisfying their recreational interests, while the former lack those opportunities or facilities."[18]

The view that "idle hands are the devil's workshop" has received more sophisticated treatment in recent sociological writings on delinquency. David Matza and Gresham M. Sykes, for example, suggest that delinquents have the values of a leisure class, the same values ascribed by Veblen to *the* leisure class: a search for kicks, disdain of work, a desire for the big score, and acceptance of aggressive toughness as proof of masculinity.[19] Matza and Sykes explain delinquency by reference to this system of values, but they note that adolescents at all class levels are "to some extent" members of a leisure class, that they "move in a limbo between earlier parental domination and future integration with the social structure through the bonds of work and marriage."[20] In the end, then, the leisure of the adolescent produces a set of values, which, in turn, leads to delinquency.

Belief

Unlike the cultural deviance theory, the control theory assumes the existence of a common value system within the society or group whose norms are being violated. If the deviant is committed to a value system different from that of conventional society, there is, within the context of the theory, nothing to explain. The question is, "Why does a man violate the rules in which he believes?" It is not, "Why do men differ in their beliefs about what constitutes good and desirable conduct?" The person is assumed to have been socialized (perhaps imperfectly) into the group whose rules he is violating; deviance is not a question of one group imposing its rules on the members of another group. In other words, we not only assume the deviant *has* believed the rules, we assume he believes the rules even as he violates them.

How can a person believe it is wrong to steal at the same time he is stealing? In the strain theory, this is not a difficult problem. (In fact, . . . the strain theory was devised specifically to deal with this question.) The motivation to deviance adduced by the strain theorist is so strong that we can well understand the deviant act even assuming the deviator believes strongly that it is wrong.[21] However, given the control theory's assumptions about motivation, if both the deviant and the nondeviant believe the deviant act is wrong, how do we account for the fact that one commits it and the other does not?

Control theories have taken two approaches to this problem. In one approach, beliefs are treated as mere words that mean little or nothing if the other forms of control are missing. "Semantic dementia," the dissociation between rational faculties and emotional control which is said to be characteristic of the psychopath, illustrates this way of handling the problem.[22] In short, beliefs, at least insofar as they are expressed in words, drop out of the picture; since they do not differentiate between deviants and nondeviants, they are in the same class as "language" or any other characteristic common to all members of the group. Since they represent no real obstacle to the commission of delinquent acts, nothing need be said about how they are handled by those committing such acts. The control theories that do not mention beliefs (or values), and many do not, may be assumed to take this approach to the problem.

The second approach argues that the deviant rationalizes his behavior so that he can at once violate the rule and maintain his belief in it. Donald R. Cressey had advanced this argument with respect to embezzlement,[23] and Sykes and Matza have advanced it with respect to delinquency.[24] In both Cressey's and Sykes and Matza's treatments, these rationalizations (Cressey calls them "verbalizations," Sykes and Matza term them "techniques of neutralization") occur prior to the commission of the deviant act. If the neutralization is successful, the person is free to commit the act(s) in question. Both in Cressey and in Sykes and Matza, the strain that prompts the effort at neutralization also provides the motive force that results in the subsequent deviant act. Their theories are thus, in this sense, strain theories. Neutralization is difficult to handle within the context of a theory that adheres closely to control theory assumptions, because in the control theory there is no special motivational force to account for the neutralization. This difficulty is especially noticeable in Matza's later treatment of this topic, where the motivational component, the "will to delinquency," appears *after* the moral vacuum has been created by the techniques of neutralization.[25] The question thus becomes: Why neutralize?

In attempting to solve a strain-theory problem with control-theory tools, the control theorist is thus led into a trap. He cannot answer the crucial question. The concept of neutralization assumes the existence of moral obstacles to the commission of deviant acts. In order plausibly to account for a deviant act, it is necessary to generate motivation to deviance that is at least equivalent in force to the resistance provided by these moral obstacles. However, if the moral obstacles are removed, neutralization and special motivation are no longer required. We therefore follow the implicit logic of control theory and remove these moral obstacles by hypothesis. Many persons do not have an attitude of respect toward the rules of society; many persons feel no moral obligation to conform regardless of personal advantage. Insofar as the values and beliefs of these persons are consistent with their feelings, and there should be a tendency toward consistency, neutralization is unnecessary; it has already occurred.

Does this merely push the question back a step and at the same time produce conflict with the assumption of a common value system? I think not. In the first place, we do not assume, as does Cressey, that neutralization occurs in order to make a specific criminal act possible.[26] We do not assume, as do Sykes and Matza, that neutralization occurs to make many delinquent acts possible. We do not assume, in other words, that the person constructs a system of rationalizations in order to justify commission of acts he *wants* to commit. We assume, in contrast, that the beliefs that free a man to commit deviant acts are *unmotivated* in the sense that he does not construct or adopt them in order to facilitate the attainment of illicit ends. In the second place, we do not assume, as does Matza, that "delinquents concur in the conventional assessment of delinquency."[27] We assume, in contrast, that there is *variation* in the extent to which people believe they should obey the rules of society, and, furthermore, that the less a person believes he should obey the rules, the more likely he is to violate them.[28]

In chronological order, then, a person's beliefs in the moral validity or norms are, for no teleological reason, weakened. The probability that he will commit delinquent acts is therefore increased. When and if he commits a delinquent act, we may justifiably use the weakness of his beliefs in explaining it, but no special motivation is required to explain either the weakness of his beliefs or, perhaps, his delinquent act.

The keystone of this argument is of course the assumption that there is variation in belief in the moral validity of social rules. This assumption is amenable to direct empirical test and can thus survive at least until its first confrontation with data. For the present, we must return to the idea of a common value system with which this section was begun.

The idea of a common (or perhaps better, a single) value system is consistent with the fact, or presumption, of variation in the strength of moral beliefs. We have not suggested that delinquency is based on beliefs counter to conventional morality; we have not suggested that delinquents do not believe delinquent acts are wrong. They may well believe these acts are wrong, but the meaning and efficacy of such beliefs are contingent on other beliefs and, indeed, on the strength of other ties to the conventional order.[29]

Notes

1. Books have been written on the increasing importance of interpersonal sensitivity in modern life. According to this view, controls from within have become less important than controls from without in *producing* conformity. Whether or not this observation is true as a description of historical trends, it is true that interpersonal sensitivity has become more important in *explaining* conformity. Although logically it should also have become more impor-

tant in explaining nonconformity, the opposite has been the case, once again showing that Cohen's observation that an explanation of conformity should be an explanation of deviance cannot be translated as "an explanation of conformity has to be an explanation of deviance." For the view that interpersonal sensitivity currently plays a greater role than formerly in producing conformity, see William J. Goode, "Norm Commitment and Conformity to Role-Status Obligations," *American Journal of Sociology*, LXVI (1960), 246–258. And, of course, also see David Riesman, Nathan Glazer, and Rouel Denney, *The Lonely Crowd* (Garden City, New York: Doubleday, 1950), especially Part I.

2. The literature on psychopathy is voluminous. See William and Joan McCord, *The Psychopath* (Princeton: D. Van Nostrand, 1964).

3. John M. Martin and Joseph P. Fitzpatrick, *Delinquent Behavior* (New York: Random House, 1964), p. 130.

4. *Ibid.* For additional properties of the psychopath, see McCord and McCord, *The Psychopath*, pp. 1–22.

5. Barbara Wootton, *Social Science and Social Pathology* (New York: Macmillan, 1959), p. 250.

6. "The logical untenability [of the position that there are forces in man 'resistant to socialization'] was ably demonstrated by Parsons over 30 years ago, and it is widely recognized that the position is empirically unsound because it assumes [!] some universal biological drive system distinctly separate from socialization and social context—a basic and intransigent human nature" (Judith Blake and Kingsley Davis, "Norms, Values, and Sanctions," *Handbook of Modern Sociology*, ed. Robert E. L. Faris [Chicago: Rand McNally, 1964], p. 471).

7. Emile Durkheim, *Moral Education*, trans. Everett K. Wilson and Herman Schnurer (New York: The Free Press, 1961), p. 64.

8. Although attachment alone does not exhaust the meaning of internalization, attachments and beliefs combined would appear to leave only a small residue of "internal control" not susceptible in principle to direct measurement.

9. F. Ivan Nye, *Family Relationships and Delinquent Behavior* (New York: Wiley, 1958), pp. 5–7.

10. Albert J. Reiss, Jr., "Delinquency as the Failure of Personal and Social Controls," *American Sociological Review*, XVI (1951), 196–207. For example, "Our observations show . . . that delinquent recidivists are less often persons with mature ego ideals or nondelinquent social roles" (p. 204).

11. Scott Briar and Irving Piliavin, "Delinquency, Situational Inducements, and Commitment to Conformity," *Social Problems*, XIII (1965), 41–42. The concept "stake in conformity" was introduced by Jackson Toby in his "Social Disorganization and Stake in Conformity: Complementary Factors in the Predatory Behavior of Hoodlums," *Journal of Criminal Law, Criminology and Police Science*, XLVIII (1957), 12–17. See also his "Hoodlum or Business

Man: An American Dilemma," *The Jews*, ed. Marshall Sklare (New York: The Free Press, 1958), pp. 542–550. Throughout the text, I occasionally use "stake in conformity" in speaking in general of the strength of the bond to conventional society. So used, the concept is somewhat broader than is true for either Toby or Briar and Piliavin, where the concept is roughly equivalent to what is here called "commitment."

12. Thomas Hobbes, *Leviathan* (Oxford: Basil Blackwell, 1957), p. 195.

13. Howard S. Becker, "Notes on the Concept of Commitment," *American Journal of Sociology*, LXVI (1960), 35–36.

14. Arthur L. Stinchcombe, *Rebellion in a High School* (Chicago: Quadrangle, 1964), p. 5.

15. Richard A. Cloward and Lloyd E. Ohlin, *Delinquency and Opportunity* (New York: The Free Press, 1960), p. 147, quoting Edwin H. Sutherland, ed., *The Professional Thief* (Chicago: University of Chicago Press, 1937), pp. 211–213.

16. William James, *Psychology* (Cleveland: World Publishing Co., 1948), p. 186.

17. Few activities appear to be so engrossing that they rule out contemplation of alternative lines of behavior, at least if estimates of the amount of time men spend plotting sexual deviations have any validity.

18. *The Sutherland Papers*, ed. Albert K. Cohen et al. (Bloomington: Indiana University Press, 1956), p. 37.

19. David Matza and Gresham M. Sykes, "Juvenile Delinquency and Subterranean Values," *American Sociological Review*, XXVI (1961), 712–719.

20. *Ibid.*, p. 718.

21. The starving man stealing the loaf of bread is the image evoked by most strain theories. In this image, the starving man's belief in the wrongness of his act is clearly not something that must be explained away. It can be assumed to be present without causing embarrassment to the explanation.

22. McCord and McCord, *The Psychopath*, pp. 12–15.

23. Donald R. Cressey, *Other People's Money* (New York: The Free Press, 1953).

24. Gresham M. Sykes and David Matza, "Techniques of Neutralization: A Theory of Delinquency," *American Sociological Review*, XXII (1957), 664–670.

25. David Matza, *Delinquency and Drift* (New York: Wiley, 1964), pp. 181–191.

26. In asserting that Cressey's assumption is invalid with respect to delinquency, I do not wish to suggest that it is invalid for the question of embezzlement, where the problem faced by the deviator is fairly specific and he can reasonably be assumed to be an upstanding citizen. (Although even here the fact that the embezzler's nonsharable financial problem often results from some sort of hanky-panky suggests that "verbalizations" may be less necessary than might otherwise be assumed.)

27. *Delinquency and Drift*, p. 43.

28. This assumption is not, I think, contradicted by the evidence presented by Matza against the existence of a delinquent subculture. In comparing the attitudes and actions of delinquents with the picture painted by delinquent subculture theorists, Matza emphasizes—and perhaps exaggerates—the extent to which delinquents are tied to the conventional order. In implicitly comparing delinquents with a supermoral man, I emphasize—and perhaps exaggerate—the extent to which they are not tied to the conventional order.

29. The position taken here is therefore somewhere between the "semantic dementia" and the "neutralization" positions. Assuming variation, the delinquent is, at the extremes, freer than the neutralization argument assumes. Although the possibility of wide discrepancy between what the delinquent professes and what he practices still exists, it is presumably much rarer than is suggested by studies of articulate "psychopaths."

QUESTIONS FOR DISCUSSION

1. List the major components of *control theory*. Discuss how these elements of the social bond explain delinquency or deviance.

2. Why is Hirschi critical of explanations of delinquency that focus on psychopathology and sociocultural definitions? Provide specific examples of Hirschi's criticisms.

3. According to Hirschi, whether or not a person commits delinquent acts is dependent on the relative strength or weakness of that person's ties to the conventional order. What is the "conventional order"? In a culturally diverse society, are there any problems with the definition of *conventional order*?

APPLICATIONS

1. Make a list of the people to whom you have a social bond. Why are you attached and committed to these people? Does this social bond affect the way you think and behave? Why?

2. Let us assume you are an expert in counseling delinquent youth. How might you use the concepts of control theory to augment behavioral changes?

KEY TERMS

conscience a sense of one's own blameworthiness with regard to conduct, intents, or character; produces a feeling of obligation to do right or be good. Also, that part of the superego which transmits commands and admonitions to the ego.

ego one of three divisions of the psyche (the others are the id and the superego), which serves as the conscious mediator between individual perception and social reality, according to psychoanalytic theory.

internalization the conscious or subconscious incorporation of particular values or patterns of culture as future guiding principles for thought and action.

neutralization refers to rationalizing delinquent behavior; A set of defense mechanisms that releases a youth from the constraints of moral norms (refer to the next article for an in-depth explanation of neutralization techniques).

superego one of three divisions of the psyche (the others are the id and the ego), which represents the internalization of parental conscience and the rules of society, according to psychoanalytic theory; functions to reward and punish through a system of moral attitudes.

syndrome a group of symptoms that occur together and characterize a particular abnormality; in psychology and the medical field the word *syndrome* is generally used to label a group of symptoms when the cause or pathology of the abnormality is unknown.

tautology refers to a needless repetition of an idea or statement; circular reasoning where the cause and effect of a phenomenon are interchangeable; we refer to tautologies as "pretzel logic" because of their circularity.

9

Techniques of Neutralization: A Theory of Delinquency

Gresham M. Sykes

David Matza

In attempting to uncover the roots of juvenile delinquency, the social scientist has long since ceased to search for devils in the mind or stigma of the body. It is now largely agreed that delinquent behavior, like most social behavior, is learned and that it is learned in the process of social interaction.

The classic statement of this position is found in Sutherland's theory of differential association, which asserts that criminal or delinquent behavior involves the learning of (a) techniques of committing crimes and (b) motives, drives, rationalizations, and attitudes favorable to the violation of law.[1] Unfortunately, the specific content of what is learned—as opposed to the process by which it is learned—has received relatively little attention in either theory or research. Perhaps the single strongest school of thought on the nature of this content has centered on the idea of a delinquent sub-culture. The basic characteristic of the delinquent sub-culture, it is argued, is a system of values that represents an inversion of the values held by respectable, law-abiding society. The world of the delinquent is the world of the law-abiding turned upside down and its norms constitute a countervailing force directed against the conforming social order. Cohen[2] sees the process of developing a delinquent sub-culture as a matter of building, maintaining, and reinforcing a code for behavior which exists

by opposition, which stands in point by point contradiction to dominant values, particularly those of the middle class. Cohen's portrayal of delinquency is executed with a good deal of sophistication, and he carefully avoids overly simple explanations such as those based on the principle of "follow the leader" or easy generalizations about "emotional disturbances." Furthermore, he does not accept the delinquent sub-culture as something given, but instead systematically examines the function of delinquent values as a viable solution to the lower-class, male child's problems in the area of social status. Yet in spite of its virtues, this image of juvenile delinquency as a form of behavior based on competing or countervailing values and norms appears to suffer from a number of serious defects. It is the nature of these defects and a possible alternative or modified explanation for a large portion of juvenile delinquency with which this paper is concerned.

The difficulties in viewing delinquent behavior as springing from a set of deviant values and norms—as arising, that is to say, from a situation in which the delinquent defines his delinquency as "right"—are both empirical and theoretical. In the first place, if there existed in fact a delinquent sub-culture such that the delinquent viewed his illegal behavior as morally correct, we could reasonably suppose that he would exhibit no feelings of guilt or shame at detection or confinement. Instead, the major reaction would tend in the direction of indignation or a sense of martyr-

"Techniques of Neutralization: A Theory of Delinquency," *American Sociological Review*, 22 (December, 1957), pp. 664–670.

dom.[3] It is true that some delinquents do react in the latter fashion, although the sense of martyrdom often seems to be based on the fact that others "get away with it" and indignation appears to be directed against the chance events or lack of skill that led to apprehension. More important, however, is the fact that there is a good deal of evidence suggesting that many delinquents *do* experience a sense of guilt or shame, and its outward expression is not to be dismissed as a purely manipulative gesture to appease those in authority. Much of this evidence is, to be sure, of a clinical nature or in the form of impressionistic judgments of those who must deal first hand with the youthful offender. Assigning a weight to such evidence calls for caution but it cannot be ignored if we are to avoid the gross stereotype of the juvenile delinquent as a hardened gangster in miniature.

In the second place, observers have noted that the juvenile delinquent frequently accords admiration and respect to law-abiding persons. The "really honest" person is often revered, and if the delinquent is sometimes overly keen to detect hypocrisy in those who conform, unquestioned probity is likely to win his approval. A fierce attachment to a humble, pious mother or a forgiving, upright priest (the former, according to many observers, is often encountered in both juvenile delinquents and adult criminals) might be dismissed as rank sentimentality, but at least it is clear that the delinquent does not necessarily regard those who abide by the legal rules as immoral. In a similar vein, it can be noted that the juvenile delinquent may exhibit great resentment if illegal behavior is imputed to "significant others" in his immediate social environment or to heroes in the world of sport and entertainment. In other words, if the delinquent does hold to a set of values and norms that stand in complete opposition to those of respectable society, his norm-holding is of a peculiar sort. While supposedly thoroughly committed to the deviant system of the delinquent sub-culture, he would appear to recognize the moral validity of the dominant normative system in many instances.[4]

In the third place, there is much evidence that juvenile delinquents often draw a sharp line between those who can be victimized and those who cannot. Certain social groups are not to be viewed as "fair game" in the performance of supposedly approved delinquent acts while others warrant a variety of attacks. In general, the potentiality for victimization would seem to be a function of the social distance between the juvenile delinquent and others and thus we find implicit maxims in the world of the delinquent such as "don't steal from friends" or "don't commit vandalism against a church of your own faith."[5] This is all rather obvious, but the implications have not received sufficient attention. The fact that supposedly valued behavior tends to be directed against disvalued social groups hints that the "wrongfulness" of such delinquent behavior is more widely recognized by delinquents than the literature has indicated. When the pool of victims is limited by considerations of kinship, friendship, ethnic group, social class, age, sex, etc., we have reason to suspect that the virtue of delinquency is far from unquestioned.

In the fourth place, it is doubtful if many juvenile delinquents are totally immune from the demands for conformity made by the dominant social order. There is a strong likelihood that the family of the delinquent will agree with respectable society that delinquency is wrong, even though the family may be engaged in a variety of illegal activities. That is, the parental posture conducive to delinquency is not apt to be a positive prodding. Whatever may be the influence of parental example, what might be called the "Fagin" pattern of socialization into delinquency is probably rare. Furthermore, as Redl has indicated, the idea that certain neighborhoods are completely delinquent, offering the child a model for delinquent behavior without reservations, is simply not supported by the data.[6]

The fact that a child is punished by parents, school officials, and agencies of the legal system for his delinquency may, as a number of observers have cynically noted, suggest to the child that he should be more careful not to get caught. There is an equal or greater probability, however, that the child will internalize the demands for conformity. This is not to say that demands for conformity cannot be counteracted. In fact, as we shall see shortly, an understanding of how internal and external demands for conformity are neutralized may be crucial for understanding delinquent behavior. But it is to say that a complete denial of the validity of demands for conformity and the substitution of a new normative system is improbable, in light of the child's or adolescent's dependency on adults and encirclement by adults inherent in his status in the social structure. No matter how deeply enmeshed in patterns of delinquency he may be and no matter how much this involvement may outweigh his associations with the law-abiding, he cannot escape the condemnation of his deviance. Somehow the demands for conformity must be met and answered; they cannot be ignored as part of an alien system of values and norms.

In short, the theoretical viewpoint that sees juvenile delinquency as a form of behavior based on the values and norms of a deviant sub-culture in precisely the same way as law-abiding behavior is based on the values and norms of the larger society is open to serious doubt. The fact that the world of the delinquent is embedded in the larger world of those who conform cannot be overlooked nor can the delinquent be equated with an adult thoroughly socialized into an alternative way of life. Instead, the juvenile delinquent would appear to be at least partially committed to the dominant social order in that he frequently exhibits guilt or shame when he violates its proscriptions, accords approval to certain conforming figures, and distinguishes between appropriate and inappropriate targets for his deviance. It is to an explanation for the apparently paradoxical fact of his delinquency that we now turn.

As Morris Cohen once said, one of the most fascinating problems about human behavior is why men violate the laws in which they believe. This is the problem that confronts us when we attempt to explain why delinquency occurs despite a greater or lesser commitment to the usages of conformity. A basic clue is offered by the fact that social rules or norms calling for valued behavior seldom if ever take the form of categorical imperatives. Rather, values or norms appear as *qualified* guides for action, limited in their applicability in terms of time, place, persons, and social circumstances. The moral injunction against killing, for example, does not apply to the enemy during combat in time of war, although a captured enemy comes once again under the prohibition. Similarly, the taking and distributing of scarce goods in a time of acute social need is felt by many to be right, although under other circumstances private property is held inviolable. The normative system of a society, then, is marked by what Williams has termed *flexibility*; it does not consist of a body of rules held to be binding under all conditions.[7]

This flexibility is, in fact, an integral part of the criminal law in that measures for "defenses to crimes" are provided in pleas such as nonage, necessity, insanity, drunkenness, compulsion, self-defense, and so on. The individual can avoid moral culpability for his criminal action—and thus avoid the negative sanctions of society—if he can prove that criminal intent was lacking. *It is our argument that much delinquency is based on what is essentially an unrecognized extension of defenses to crimes, in the form of justifications for deviance that are seen as valid by the delinquent but not by the legal system or society at large.*

These justifications are commonly described as rationalizations. They are viewed as following deviant behavior and as protecting the individual from self-blame and the blame of others after the act. But there is also reason to believe that they precede deviant behavior and make deviant behavior possible. It is this possibility that Sutherland mentioned only in passing and that other writers have failed to exploit from the viewpoint of sociological theory. Disapproval flowing from internalized norms and conforming others in the social environment is neutralized, turned back, or deflected in advance. Social controls that serve to check or inhibit deviant motivational patterns are rendered inoperative, and the individual is freed to engage in delinquency without serious damage to his self image. In this sense, the delinquent both has his cake and eats it too, for he remains committed to the dominant normative system and yet so qualifies its imperatives that violations are "acceptable" if not "right." Thus the delinquent represents not a radical opposition to law-abiding society but something more like an apologetic failure, often more sinned against than sinning in his own eyes. We call these justifications of deviant behavior techniques of neutralization; and we believe these techniques make up a crucial component of Sutherland's "definitions favorable to the violation of law." It is by learning these techniques that the juvenile becomes delinquent, rather than by learning moral imperatives, values or attitudes standing in direct contradiction to those of the dominant society. In analyzing these techniques, we have found it convenient to divide them into five major types.

The Denial of Responsibility. In so far as the delinquent can define himself as lacking responsibility for his deviant actions, the disapproval of self or others is sharply reduced in effectiveness as a restraining influence. As Justice Holmes has said, even a dog distinguishes between being stumbled over and being kicked, and modern society is no less careful to draw a line between injuries that are unintentional, i.e., where responsibility is lacking, and those that are intentional. As a technique of neutralization, however, the denial of responsibility extends much further than the claim that deviant acts are an "accident" or some similar negation of personal accountability. It may also be asserted that delinquent acts are due to forces outside of the individual and beyond his control such as unloving parents, bad companions, or a slum neighborhood. In effect, the delinquent approaches a "billiard ball" conception of himself in which he sees himself as helplessly propelled into new situations. From a psychodynamic viewpoint, this orientation toward one's own actions may represent a profound alienation from self, but it is important to stress the fact that interpretations of responsibility are cultural constructs and not merely idiosyncratic beliefs. The similarity between this mode of justifying illegal behavior assumed by the delinquent and the implications of a "sociological" frame of reference or a "humane" jurisprudence is readily apparent.[8] It is not the validity of this orientation that concerns us here, but its function of deflecting blame attached to violations of social norms and its relative independence of a particular personality structure.[9] By learning to view himself as more acted upon than acting, the delinquent prepares the way for deviance from the dominant normative system without the necessity of a frontal assault on the norms themselves.

The Denial of Injury. A second major technique of neutralization centers on the injury or harm involved in the delinquent act. The criminal law has long made a distinction between crimes which are *mala in se* and *mala prohibita*—that is between acts that are wrong in themselves and acts that are illegal but not immoral—and the delinquent can make the same kind of distinction in evaluating the wrongfulness of his behavior. For the delinquent, however, wrongfulness may turn on the question of whether or not anyone has clearly been hurt by his deviance, and this matter is open to a variety of interpretations. Vandalism, for example, may be defined by the delinquent simply as "mischief"—after all, it may be claimed, the persons whose property has been destroyed can well afford it. Similarly, auto theft may be viewed as "borrowing," and gang fighting may be seen as a private quarrel, an agreed upon duel between two willing parties, and thus of no concern to the community at large. We are not suggesting that this technique of neutralization, labelled the denial of injury, involves an explicit dialectic. Rather, we are arguing that the delinquent frequently, and in a hazy fashion, feels that his behavior does not really cause any great harm despite the fact that it runs counter to law. Just as the link between the individual and his acts may be broken by the denial of responsibility, so may the link between acts and their consequences be broken by the denial of injury. Since society sometimes agrees with the delinquent, e.g., in matters such as truancy, "pranks," and so on, it merely reaffirms the idea that the delinquent's neutralization of social controls by means of qualifying the norms is an extension of common practice rather than a gesture of complete opposition.

The Denial of the Victim. Even if the delinquent accepts the responsibility for his deviant actions and is willing to admit that his deviant actions involve an injury or hurt, the moral indignation of self and others may be neutralized by an insistence that the injury is not wrong in light of the circumstances. The injury, it may be claimed, is not really an injury; rather, it is a form of rightful retaliation or punishment. By a subtle alchemy the delinquent moves himself into the position of an avenger and the victim is transformed into a wrong-doer. Assaults on homosexuals or suspected homosexuals, attacks on members of minority groups who are said to have gotten "out of place," vandalism as revenge on an unfair teacher or school official, thefts from a "crooked" store owner—all may be hurts inflicted on a transgressor, in the eyes of the delinquent. As Orwell has pointed out, the type of criminal admired by the general public has probably changed over the course of years and Raffles no longer serves as a hero;[10] but Robin Hood, and his latter day derivatives such as the tough detective seeking justice outside the law, still capture the popular imagination, and the delinquent may view his acts as part of a similar role.

To deny the existence of the victim, then, by transforming him into a person deserving injury is an extreme form of a phenomenon we have mentioned before, namely, the delinquent's recognition of appropriate and inappropriate targets for his delinquent acts. In addition, however, the existence of the victim may be denied for the delinquent, in a somewhat different sense, by the circumstances of the delinquent act itself. Insofar as the victim is physically absent, unknown, or a vague abstraction (as is often the case in delinquent acts committed against property), the awareness of the victim's existence is weakened. Internalized norms and anticipations of the reactions of others must somehow be activated, if they are to serve as guides for behavior; and it is possible that a diminished awareness of the victim plays an important part in determining whether or not this process is set in motion.

The Condemnation of the Condemners. A fourth technique of neutralization would appear to involve a condemnation of the condemners or, as McCorkle and Korn have phrased it, a rejection of the rejectors.[11] The delinquent shifts the focus of attention from his own deviant acts to the motives and behav-

ior of those who disapprove of his violations. His condemners, he may claim, are hypocrites, deviants in disguise, or impelled by personal spite. This orientation toward the conforming world may be of particular importance when it hardens into a bitter cynicism directed against those assigned the task of enforcing or expressing the norms of dominant society. Police, it may be said, are corrupt, stupid, and brutal. Teachers always show favoritism and parents always "take it out" on their children. By a slight extension, the rewards of conformity—such as material success—become a matter of pull or luck, thus decreasing still further the stature of those who stand on the side of the law-abiding. The validity of this jaundiced viewpoint is not so important as its function in turning back or deflecting the negative sanctions attached to violations of the norms. The delinquent, in effect, has changed the subject of the conversation in the dialogue between his own deviant impulses and the reactions of others; and by attacking others, the wrongfulness of his own behavior is more easily repressed or lost to view.

The Appeal to Higher Loyalties. Fifth, and last, internal and external social controls may be neutralized by sacrificing the demands of the larger society for the demands of the smaller social groups to which the delinquent belongs such as the sibling pair, the gang, or the friendship clique. It is important to note that the delinquent does not necessarily repudiate the imperatives of the dominant normative system, despite his failure to follow them. Rather, the delinquent may see himself as caught up in a dilemma that must be resolved, unfortunately, at the cost of violating the law. One aspect of this situation has been studied by Stouffer and Toby in their research on the conflict between particularistic and universalistic demands, between the claims of friendship and general social obligations, and their results suggest that "it is possible to classify people according to a predisposition to select one or the other horn of a dilemma in role conflict."[12] For our purposes, however, the most important point is that deviation from certain norms may occur not because the norms are rejected but because other norms, held to be more pressing or involving a higher loyalty, are accorded precedence. Indeed, it is the fact that both sets of norms are believed in that gives meaning to our concepts of dilemma and role conflict.

The conflict between the claims of friendship and the claims of law, or a similar dilemma, has of course long been recognized by the social scientist (and the novelist) as a common human problem. If the juvenile delinquent frequently resolves his dilemma by insisting that he must "always help a buddy" or "never squeal on a friend," even when it throws him into serious difficulties with the dominant social order, his choice remains familiar to the supposedly law-abiding. The delinquent is unusual, perhaps, in the extent to which he is able to see the fact that he acts in behalf of the smaller social groups to which he belongs as a justification for violations of society's norms, but it is a matter of degree rather than of kind.

"I didn't mean it." "I didn't really hurt anybody." "They had it coming to them." "Everybody's picking on me." "I didn't do it for myself." These slogans or their variants, we hypothesize, prepare the juvenile for delinquent acts. These "definitions of the situation" represent tangential or glancing blows at the dominant normative system rather than the creation of an opposing ideology; and they are extensions of patterns of thought prevalent in society rather than something created de novo.

Techniques of neutralization may not be powerful enough to fully shield the individual from the force of his own internalized values and the reactions of conforming others, for as we have pointed out, juvenile delinquents often appear to suffer from feelings of guilt and shame when called into account for their deviant behavior. And some delinquents may be so isolated from the world of conformity that techniques of neutralization need not be called into play. Nonetheless, we would argue that techniques of neutralization are critical in lessening the effectiveness of social controls and that they lie behind a large share of delinquent behavior. Empirical research in this area is scattered and fragmentary at the present time, but the work of Redl,[13] Cressy,[14] and others has supplied a body of significant data that has done much to clarify the theo-

retical issues and enlarge the fund of supporting evidence. Two lines of investigation seem to be critical at this stage. First, then is need for more knowledge concerning the differential distribution of techniques of neutralization, as operative patterns of thought, by age, sex, social class, ethnic group, etc. On a priori grounds it might be assumed that these justifications for deviance will be more readily seized by segments of society for whom a discrepancy between common social ideals and social practice is most apparent. It is also possible however, that the habit of "bending" the dominant normative system—if not "breaking" it—cuts across our cruder social categories and is to be traced primarily to patterns of social interaction within the familial circle. Second, there is need for a greater understanding of the internal structure of techniques of neutralization, as a system of beliefs and attitudes, and its relationship to various types of delinquent behavior. Certain techniques of neutralization would appear to be better adapted to particular deviant acts than to others, as we have suggested, for example, in the case of offenses against property and the denial of the victim. But the issue remains far from clear and stands in need of more information.

In any case, techniques of neutralization appear to offer a promising line of research in enlarging and systematizing the theoretical grasp of juvenile delinquency. As more information is uncovered concerning techniques of neutralization, their origins, and their consequences, both juvenile delinquency in particular, and deviation from normative systems in general may be illuminated.

Notes

1. E. H. Sutherland, *Principles of Criminology*, revised by D. R. Cressey, Chicago: Lippincott, 1955, pp. 77–80.

2. Albert K. Cohen, *Delinquent Boys*, Glencoe, Ill.: The Free Press, 1955.

3. This form of reaction among the adherents of a deviant subculture who fully believe in the "rightfulness" of their behavior and who are captured and punished by the agencies of the dominant social order can be illustrated, perhaps, by groups such as Jehovah's Witnesses, early Christian sects,

nationalist movements in colonial areas, and conscientious objectors, during World War I and II.

4. As Weber has pointed out, a thief may recognize the legitimacy of legal rules without accepting their moral validity. Cf. Max Weber, *The Theory of Social and Economic Organization* (translated by A. M. Henderson and Talcott Parsons), New York: Oxford University Press, 1947, p. 125. We are arguing here, however, that the juvenile delinquent frequently recognizes *both* the legitimacy of the dominant social order and its moral "rightness."

5. Thrasher's account of the "Itschkies"—a juvenile gang composed of Jewish boys—and the immunity from "rolling" enjoyed by Jewish drunkards is a good illustration. Cf. F. Thrasher, *The Gang,* Chicago: The University of Chicago Press, 1947, p. 315.

6. Cf. Solomon Kobrin, "The Conflict of Values in Delinquency Areas," *American Sociological Review*, 16, (October, 1951), pp. 653–661.

7. Cf. Robin Williams, Jr., *American Society*, New York: Knopf, 1951, p. 28.

8. A number of observers have wryly noted that many delinquents seem to show a surprising awareness of sociological and psychological explanations for their behavior and are quick to point out the causal role of their poor environment.

9. It is possible, of course, that certain personality structures can accept some techniques of neutralization more readily than others, but this question remains largely unexplored.

10. George Orwell, *Dickens, Dali, and Others*, New York: Reynal, 1946.

11. Lloyd W. McCorkle and Richard Korn, "Resocialization Within Walls," The Annals of the American Academy of Political and Social Science, 293, (May, 1954), pp. 88–98.

12. See Samuel A. Stouffer and Jackson Toby, "Role Conflict and Personality," in *Toward a General Theory of Action*, edited by Talcott Parsons and Edward A. Shils, Cambridge: Harvard University Press, 1951, p. 494.

13. See Fritz Redl and David Wineman, *Children Who Hate*, Glencoe: The Free Press, 1956.

14. See D.R. Cressey, *Other People's Money*, Glencoe: The Free Press, 1953.

QUESTIONS FOR DISCUSSION

1. List and explain the four reasons why the authors do not believe that delinquent behavior arises "from a situation in which the delinquent defines his delinquency as 'right'."

2. What are the five major techniques of neutralization? In your own words, discuss each of them.

3. The authors suggest there are two pressing areas of research that need to be conducted to improve the understanding of neutralization techniques. What are they?

APPLICATIONS

1. Consider the five major techniques of neutralization. Which of these rationalizations have you used to justify your behavior? Do you think these rationalizations are used by all people at one time or another? Do these rationalizations help distinguish the delinquent from the nondelinquent? Why?

2. Think about a young person spray painting his or her name on a bridge or on the face of a building. Upon being apprehended, the police ask the youth why he or she spray painted the building. The youth replies, "Because it was fun!" How would a rationalization like this be explained by the theory of neutralization?

KEY TERMS

a priori refers to a condition or event that previously existed or occurred.

alchemy a power or process of transforming something common into something special.

countervailing refers to compensating or counteracting; offering an opposing opinion.

cynical being contemptuously distrustful of human nature or motives; disbelief in sincerity or integrity.

de novo refers to something new; creating anew.

imperatives actions or ideas that must not be avoided; necessary or obligatory.

indignation   anger aroused by something unjust, mean, or that is perceived to be unfair.

jurisprudence   the science or philosophy of law.

mala in se   behaviors, based on natural law, that are considered wrong in and of themselves; generally includes murder, rape, theft, arson, and other violent crimes.

mala prohibita   criminal behaviors that are considered wrong only because they are prohibited by law.

martyrdom   suffering or death that occurs because of adherence to a principle, a cause, or a belief.

paradoxical   characteristic of something that is seemingly contradictory or opposed to common sense and yet is perhaps true.

significant others   those other people who are most important for an individual in determining his or her behavior.

stigma   a mark of shame or discredit; an outcast by prevailing social standards.

10

Lower Class Culture as a Generating Milieu of Gang Delinquency

Walter B. Miller

The etiology of delinquency has long been a controversial issue, and is particularly so at present. As new frames of reference for explaining human behavior have been added to traditional theories, some authors have adopted the practice of citing the major postulates of each school of thought as they pertain to delinquency, and going on to state that causality must be conceived in terms of the dynamic interaction of a complex combination of variables on many levels. The major sets of etiological factors currently adduced to explain delinquency are, in simplified terms, the physiological (delinquency results from organic pathology), the psychodynamic (delinquency is a "behavioral disorder" resulting primarily from emotional disturbance generated by a defective mother-child relationship), and the environmental (delinquency is the product of disruptive forces, "disorganization," in the actor's physical or social environment).

This paper selects one particular kind of "delinquency"[1]—law-violating acts committed by members of adolescent street corner groups in lower class communities—and attempts to show that the dominant component of motivation underlying these acts consists in a directed attempt by the actor to adhere to forms of behavior, and to achieve standards of value as they are defined within

that community. It takes as a premise that the motivation of behavior in this situation can be approached most productively by attempting to understand the nature of cultural forces impinging on the acting individual as they are perceived *by the actor himself*—although by no means only that segment of these forces of which the actor is consciously aware—rather than as they are perceived and evaluated from the reference position of another cultural system. In the case of "gang" delinquency, the cultural system which exerts the most direct influence on behavior is that of the lower class community itself—a long-established distinctively patterned tradition with an integrity of its own—rather than a so-called "delinquent subculture" which has arisen through conflict with middle class culture and is oriented to the deliberate violation of middle class norms.

The bulk of the substantive data on which the following material is based was collected in connection with a service-research project in the control of gang delinquency. During the service aspect of the project, which lasted for three years, seven trained social workers maintained contact with twenty-one corner group units in a "slum" district of a large eastern city for periods of time ranging from ten to thirty months. Groups were Negro and white, male and female, and in early, middle, and late adolescence. Over eight thousand pages of direct observational data on behavior patterns of group members and other community resi-

"Lower Class Culture as a Generating Milieu of Gang Delinquency," *Journal of Social Issues*, 14:3 (1958), pp. 5–19. Reprinted by permission of the publisher.

dents were collected; almost daily contact was maintained for a total time period of about thirteen worker years. Data include workers' contact reports, participant observation reports by the writer—a cultural anthropologist—and direct tape recordings of group activities and discussions.[2]

Focal Concerns of Lower Class Culture

There is a substantial segment of present-day American society whose way of life, values, and characteristic patterns of behavior are the product of a distinctive cultural system which may be termed "lower class." Evidence indicates that this cultural system is becoming increasingly distinctive, and that the size of the group which shares this tradition is increasing.[3] The lower class way of life, in common with that of all distinctive cultural groups, is characterized by a set of focal concerns—areas or issues which command widespread and persistent attention and a high degree of emotional involvement. The specific concerns cited here, while by no means confined to the American lower classes, constitute a distinctive *patterning* of concerns which differs significantly, both in rank order and weighting from that of American middle class culture. The following table presents a highly schematic and simplified listing of six of the major concerns of lower class culture. Each is conceived as a "dimension" within which a fairly wide and varied range of alternative behavior patterns may be followed by different individuals under different situations. They are listed roughly in order of the degree of *explicit* attention accorded, each, and in this sense represent a weighted ranking of concerns. The "perceived alternatives" represent polar positions which define certain parameters within each dimension. As will be explained in more detail, it is necessary in relating the influence of these "concerns" to the motivation of delinquent behavior to specify *which* of its aspects is oriented to, whether orientation is *overt* or *covert, positive* (conforming to or seeking the aspect), or *negative* (rejecting or seeking to avoid the aspect).

The concept "focal concern" is used here in preference to the concept "value" for several interrelated reasons: (1) It is more readily

TABLE 10.1 Focal Concerns of Lower Class Culture

Area	Perceived Alternatives (state, quality, condition)	
1. *Trouble*:	law-abiding behavior	law-violating behavior
2. *Toughness*:	physical prowess, skill: "masculinity" fearless, bravery, daring	weakness, ineptitude; effeminacy; timidity, cowardice, caution
3. *Smartness*:	ability to outsmart, dupe "con": gaining money by "wits" shrewdness, adroitness in repartee	gullibility, "con-ability"; gaining money by hard work; slowness, dull-wittedness, verbal maladroitness
4. *Excitement*:	thrill; risk, danger; change, activity	boredom; "deadness," safeness; sameness, passivity
5. *Fate*:	favored by fortune, being "lucky"	ill-omened, being "unlucky"
6. *Autonomy*:	freedom from external constraint; freedom from superordinate authority; independence	presence of external constraint; presence of strong authority; dependency, being "cared for"

derivable from direct field observations. (2) It is descriptively neutral—permitting independent consideration of positive and negative valences as varying under different conditions, whereas "value" carries a built-in positive valence. (3) It makes possible more refined analysis of subcultural differences, since it reflects actual behavior, whereas "value" tends to wash out intracultural differences since it is colored by notions of the "official" ideal.

Trouble: Concern over "trouble" is a dominant feature of lower class culture. The concept has various shades of meaning; "trouble" in one of its aspects represents a situation or a kind of behavior which results in unwelcome or complicating involvement with official authorities or agencies of middle class society. "Getting into trouble" and "staying out of trouble" represent major issues for male and female, adults and children. For men "trouble" frequently involves fighting or sexual adventures while drinking: for women, sexual involvement with disadvantageous consequences. Expressed desire to avoid behavior which violates moral or legal norms is often based less on an explicit commitment to "official" moral or legal standards than on a desire to avoid "getting into trouble," e.g., the complicating consequences of the action.

The dominant concern over "trouble" involves a distinction of critical importance for the lower class community—that between "law-abiding" and "non law abiding" behavior. There is a high degree of sensitivity as to where each person stands in relation to these two classes of activity. Whereas in the middle class community a major dimension for evaluating a person's status is "achievement" and its external symbols, in the lower class, personal status is very frequently gauged along the law abiding -non law abiding dimension. A mother will evaluate the suitability of her daughter's boyfriend less on the basis of his achievement potential than on the basis of his innate "trouble" potential. This sensitive awareness of the opposition of "trouble-producing" and "non-trouble-producing" behavior represents both a major basis for deriving status distinctions, and an internalized conflict potential for the individual.

As in the case of other focal concerns, which of two perceived alternatives—"law-abiding" or "non law abiding"—is valued varies according to the individual and the circumstances; in many instances there is an overt commitment to the "law-abiding" alternative, but a covert commitment to the "non-law-abiding." In certain situations, "getting into trouble" is overtly recognized as prestige-conferring: for example, membership in certain adult and adolescent primary groupings ("gangs") is contingent on having demonstrated an explicit commitment to the law-violating alternative. It is most important to note that the choice between "law abiding" and "non law abiding" behavior is still a choice *within* lower class culture; the distinction between the policeman and the criminal, the outlaw and the sheriff, involves primarily this one dimension; in other respects they have a high community of interests. Not infrequently brothers raised in an identical cultural milieu will become police and criminals respectively.

For a substantial segment of the lower class population "getting into trouble" is not in itself overtly defined as prestige-conferring, but is implicitly recognized as a means to other valued ends, e.g., the covertly valued desire to be "cared for" and subject to external constraint, or the overtly valued state of excitement or risk. Very frequently "getting into trouble" is multi-functional, and achieves several sets of valued ends.

Toughness: The concept of "toughness" in lower class culture represents a compound combination of qualities or states. Among its most important components are physical prowess, evidenced both by demonstrated possession of strength and endurance and athletic skill; "masculinity," symbolized by a distinctive complex of acts and avoidances (bodily tattooing: absence of sentimentality; nonconcern with "art," "literature," conceptualization of women as conquest objects, etc.); and bravery in the face of physical threat. The model for the "tough guy"—hard, fearless, undemonstrative, skilled in physical combat—is represented by the movie gangster of the thirties, the "private eye," and the movie cowboy.

The genesis of the intense concern over "toughness" in lower class culture is probably related to the fact that a significant proportion of lower class males are reared in a predominately female household, and lack of consistently present male figure with whom to identify and from whom to learn essential components of a "male" role. Since women serve as a primary object of identification during pre-adolescent years, the almost obsessive lower class concern with "masculinity" probably resembles a type of compulsive reaction-formation. A concern over homosexuality runs like a persistent thread through lower class culture. This is manifested by the institutionalized practice of baiting "queers," often accompanied by violent physical attacks, an expressed contempt for "softness" or frills, and the use of the local term for "homosexual" as a generalized pejorative epithet (e.g., higher class individuals or upwardly mobile peers are frequently characterized as "fags" or "queers"). The distinction between "overt" and "covert" orientation to aspects of an area of concern is especially important in regard to "toughness." A positive overt evaluation of behavior defined as "effeminate" would be out of the question for a lower class male; however, built into lower class culture is a range of devices which permit men to adopt behaviors and concerns which in other cultural milieux fall within the province of women, and at the same time to be defined as "tough" and manly. For example, lower class men can be professional short-order cooks in a diner and still be regarded as "tough." The highly intimate circumstances of the street corner gang involve the recurrent expression of strongly affectionate feelings towards other men. Such expressions, however, are disguised as their opposite, taking the form of ostensibly aggressive verbal and physical interaction (kidding, "ranking," roughhousing, etc.).

Smartness: "Smartness," as conceptualized in lower class culture, involves the capacity to outsmart, outfox, outwit, dupe, "take," "con" another or others, and the concomitant capacity to avoid being outwitted, "taken" or duped oneself. In its essence, smartness involves the capacity to achieve a valued entity—material goods, personal status— through a maximum use of mental agility and a minimum use of physical effort. This capacity has an extremely long tradition in lower class culture, and is highly valued. Lower class culture can be characterized as "non-intellectual" only if intellectualism is defined specifically in terms of control over a particular body of formally learned knowledge involving "culture" (art, literature, "good" music, etc.), a generalized perspective on the past and present conditions of our own and other societies, and other areas of knowledge imparted by formal education institutions. This particular type of mental attainment is, in general, overtly disvalued and frequently associated with effeminancy; "smartness" in the lower class sense, however, is highly valued.

The lower class child learns and practices the use of this skill in the street corner situation. Individuals continually practice duping and outwitting one another through recurrent card games and other forms of gambling, mutual exchanges of insults, and "testing" for mutual "conability". Those who demonstrate competence in this skill are accorded considerable prestige. Leadership roles in the corner group are frequently allocated according to demonstrated capacity in the two areas of "smartness" and "toughness"; the ideal leader combines both, but the "smart" leader is often accorded more prestige than the "tough" one—reflecting a general lower class respect for "brains" in the "smartness" sense.[4]

The model of the "smart" person is represented in popular media by the card shark, the professional gambler, the "con" artist, the promoter. A conceptual distinction is made between two kinds of people: "suckers," easy marks, "lushes," dupes, who work for their money and are legitimate targets of exploitation; and sharp operators, the "brainy" ones, live by their wits and "getting" from the suckers by mental adroitness.

Involved in the syndrome of capacities related to "smartness" is a dominant emphasis in lower class culture on ingenious aggressive repartee. This skill learned and practiced in the context of the corner group, ranges in form from the widely prevalent semi-ritualized teasing, kidding, razzing, "ranking," so characteristic of male peer group interaction, to the highly ritualized type of mutual insult interchange known as "the dirty dozens," "the dozens," "playing house," and other terms. This highly patterned cultural form is practiced on its most advanced level in adult male Negro society, but less polished variants are found throughout lower class culture—practiced, for example, by white children, male and female, as young as four or five. In essence, "doin' the dozens" involves two antagonists who vie with each other in the exchange of increasingly inflammatory insults, with incestuous and perverted sexual relations with the mother as a dominant theme. In this form of insult interchange, as well as on other less ritualized occasions for joking, semiserious, and serious mutual invective, a very high premium is placed on ingenuity, hair-trigger responsiveness, inventiveness, and the acute exercise of mental faculties.

Excitement: For many lower class individuals the rhythm of life fluctuates between periods of relatively routine or repetitive activity and sought situations of great emotional stimulation. Many of the most characteristic features of lower class life are related to the search for excitement or "thrill." Involved here are the highly prevalent use of alcohol by both sexes and the widespread use of gambling of all kinds—playing the numbers, betting on horse races, dice, cards. The quest for excitement finds what is perhaps its most vivid expression in the highly patterned practice of the recurrent "night on the town." This practice, designated by various terms in different areas ("honky-tonkin'"; "goin' out on the town"; "bar hoppin'"), involves a patterned set of activities in which alcohol, music, and sexual adventuring are major components. A group or individual sets out to "make the rounds" of various bars or night clubs. Drinking continues progressively throughout the evening. Men seek to "pick up" women, and women play the risky game of entertaining sexual advances. Fights between men involving women, gambling, and claims of physical prowess, in various combinations, are frequent consequences of a night of making the rounds. The explosive potential of this type of adventure with sex and aggression, frequently leading to "trouble," is semi-explicitly sought by the individual. Since there is always a good likelihood that being out on the town will eventuate in

fights, etc., the practice involves elements of sought risk and desired danger.

Counterbalancing the "flirting with danger" aspect of the "excitement" concern is the prevalence in lower class culture of other well established patterns of activity which involve long periods of relative inaction, or passivity. The term "hanging out" in lower class culture refers to extended periods of standing around, often with peer mates, doing what is defined as "nothing," "shooting the breeze," etc. A definite periodicity exists in the pattern of activity relating to the two aspects of the "excitement" dimension. For many lower class individuals the venture into the high risk world of alcohol, sex, and fighting occurs regularly once a week, with interim periods devoted to accommodating to possible consequences of these periods, along with recurrent resolves not to become so involved again.

Fate: Related to the quest for excitement is the concern with fate, fortune, or luck. Here also a distinction is made between two states—being "lucky" or "in luck," and being unlucky or jinxed. Many lower class individuals feel that their lives are subject to a set of forces over which they have relatively little control. These are not directly equated with the supernatural forces of formally organized religion, but relate more to a concept of "destiny," or man as a pawn of magical powers. Not infrequently this often implicit world view is associated with a conception of the ultimate futility of directed effort towards a goal: if the cards are right, or the dice good to you, or if your lucky number comes up, things will go your way; if luck is against you, it's not worth trying. The concept of performing semi-magical rituals so that one's "luck will change" is prevalent; one hopes that as a result he will move from the state of being "unlucky" to that of being "lucky." The element of fantasy plays an important part in this area. Related to and complementing the notion that "only suckers work" (Smartness) is the idea that once things start going your way, relatively independent of your own effort, all good things will come to you. Achieving great material rewards (big cars, big houses, a roll of cash to flash in a fancy night club), valued in lower class as well as in other parts of American culture, is a recurrent theme in lower class fantasy and folklore; the cocaine dreams of Willie the Weeper or Minnie the Moocher present the components of this fantasy in vivid detail.

The prevalence in the lower class community of many forms of gambling, mentioned in connection with the "excitement" dimension, is also relevant here. Through cards and pool which involve skill, and thus both "toughness" and "smartness"; or through race horse betting, involving "smartness"; or through playing the numbers, involving predominantly "luck," one may make a big killing with a minimum of directed and persistent effort within conventional occupational channels. Gambling in its many forms illustrates the fact that many of the persistent features of lower class culture are multi-functional—serving a range of desired ends at the same time. Describing some of the incentives behind gambling has involved mention of all of the focal concerns cited so far—Toughness, Smartness, and Excitement, in addition to Fate.

Autonomy: The extent and nature of control over the behavior of the individual—an important concern in most cultures—has a special significance and is distinctively patterned in lower class culture. The discrepancy between what is overtly valued and what is covertly sought is particularly striking in this area. On the overt level there is a strong and frequently expressed resentment of the idea of external controls, restrictions on behavior, and unjust or coercive authority. "No one's gonna push *me* around," or "I'm gonna tell him he can take the job and shove it . . ." are commonly expressed sentiments. Similar explicit attitudes are maintained to systems of behavior-restricting rules, insofar as these are perceived as representing the injunctions, and bearing the sanctions of superordinate authority. In addition, in lower class culture a close conceptual connection is made between "authority" and "nurturance." To be restrictively or firmly controlled is to be cared for. Thus the overtly negative evaluation of superordinate authority frequently extends as well to nurturance, care, or protection. The desire for personal independence is often expressed in such terms as "I don't need *nobody* to take care of me. I can take care of myself!" Actual patterns of behavior, however, reveal a marked discrepancy between expressed sentiment and what is covertly valued. Many lower class people appear to seek out highly restrictive social environments wherein stringent external controls are maintained over their behavior. Such institutions as the armed forces, the mental hospital, the disciplinary school, the prison or correctional institution, provide environments which incorporate a strict and detailed set of rules defining and limiting behavior, and reinforced by an authority system which controls and applies coercive sanctions for deviance from these rules. While under the jurisdiction of such systems, the lower class person generally expresses to his peers continual resentment of the coercive, unjust, and arbitrary exercise of authority. Having been released, or having escaped from these milieux, however, he will often act in such a way as to insure recommitment, or choose recommitment voluntarily after a temporary period of "freedom."

Lower class patients in mental hospitals will exercise considerable ingenuity to insure continued commitment while voicing the desire to get out; delinquent boys will frequently "run" from a correctional institution to activate efforts to return them; to be caught and returned means that one is cared for. Since "being controlled" is equated with "being cared for," attempts are frequently made to "test" the severity or strictness of the superordinate authority to see if it remains firm. If intended or executed rebellion produces swift and firm punitive sanctions, the individual is reassured, at the same time that he is complaining bitterly at the injustice of being caught and punished. Some environmental milieux, having been tested in this fashion for the "firmness" of their coercive sanctions, are rejected ostensibly for being too strict, actually for not being strict enough. This is frequently so in the case of "problematic" behavior by lower class youngsters in the public schools, which generally cannot command the coercive controls implicitly sought by the individual.

A similar discrepancy between what is

overtly and covertly desired is found in the area of dependence-independence. The pose of tough rebellious independence often assumed by the lower class person frequently conceals powerful dependency cravings. These are manifested primarily by obliquely expressed resentment when "care" is not forthcoming rather than by expressed satisfaction when it is. The concern over autonomy-dependency is related both to "trouble" and "fate." Insofar as the lower class individual feels that his behavior is controlled by forces which often propel him into "trouble" in the face of an explicit determination to avoid it, there is an implied appeal to "save me from myself." A solution appears to lie in arranging things so that his behavior will be coercively restricted by an externally imposed set of controls strong enough to forcibly restrain his inexplicable inclination to get in trouble. The periodicity observed in connection with the "excitement" dimension is also relevant here; after involvement in trouble-producing behavior (assault, sexual adventure, a "drunk"), the individual will actively seek a locus of imposed control (his wife, prison, a restrictive job); after a given period of subjection to this control, resentment against it mounts, leading to a "break-away" and a search for involvement in further "trouble."

Focal Concerns of the Lower Class Adolescent Street Corner Group

The one-sex peer group is a highly prevalent and significant structural form in the lower class community. There is a strong probability that the prevalence and stability of this type of unit is directly related to the prevalence of a stabilized type of lower class child-rearing unit—the "female-based" household. This is a nuclear kin unit in which a male parent is either absent from the household, present only sporadically, or, when present, only minimally or inconsistently involved in the support and rearing of children. This unit usually consists of one or more females of child-bearing age and their offspring. The females are frequently related to one another by blood or marriage ties, and the unit often includes two or more gen-

erations of women, e.g., the mother and/or aunt of the principal child-bearing female.

The nature of social groupings in the lower class community may be clarified if we make the assumption that it is the *one-sex peer unit* rather than the two-parent family unit which represents the most significant relational unit for both sexes in lower class communities. Lower class society may be pictured as comprising a set of age-graded one-sex groups which constitute the major psychic focus and reference group for those over twelve or thirteen. Men and women of mating age leave these groups periodically to form temporary marital alliances, but these lack stability, and after varying periods of "trying out" the two-sex family arrangement, they gravitate back to the more "comfortable" one-sex grouping, whose members exert strong pressure on the individual *not* to disrupt the group by adopting a two-sex household pattern of life.[5] Membership in a stable and solidary peer unit is vital to the lower class individual precisely to the extent to which a range of essential functions—psychological, educational, and others, are not provided by the "family" unit.

The adolescent street corner group represents the adolescent variant of this lower class structural form. What has been called the "delinquent gang" is one subtype of this form, defined on the basis of frequency of participation in law-violating activity; this subtype should not be considered a legitimate unit of study per se, but rather as one particular variant of the adolescent street corner group. The "hanging" peer group is a unit of particular importance for the adolescent male. In many cases it is the most stable and solidary primary group he has ever belonged to; for boys reared in female-based households the corner group provides the first real opportunity to learn essential aspects of the male role in the context of peers facing similar problems of sex-role identification.

The form and functions of the adolescent corner group operate as a selective mechanism in recruiting members. The activity patterns of the group require a high level of intragroup solidarity; individual members must possess a good capacity for subordinating individual desires to general group interests as well as the capacity for intimate and persisting interaction. Thus highly "disturbed" individuals, or those who cannot tolerate consistently imposed sanctions on "deviant" behavior cannot remain accepted members; the group itself will extrude those whose behavior exceeds limits defined as "normal." This selective process produces a type of group whose members possess to an unusually high degree both the *capacity* and *motivation* to conform to perceived cultural norms, so that the nature of the system of norms and values oriented to is a particularly influential component of motivation.

Focal concerns of the male adolescent corner group are those of the general cultural milieu in which it functions. As would be expected, the relative weighting and importance of these concerns pattern somewhat differently for adolescents than for adults. The nature of this patterning centers around two additional "concerns" of particular importance to this group—concern with "belonging," and with "status." These may be conceptualized as being on a higher level of abstraction than concerns previously cited, since "status" and "belonging" are achieved *via* cited concern areas of Toughness, etc.

Belonging: Since the corner group fulfills essential functions for the individual, being a member in good standing of the group is of vital importance for its members. A continuing concern over who is "in" and who is not involves the citation and detailed discussion of highly refined criteria for "in-group" membership. The phrase "he hangs with us" means "he is accepted as a member in good standing by current consensus"; conversely, "he don't hang with us" means he is not so accepted. One achieves "belonging" primarily by demonstrating knowledge of and a determination to adhere to the system of standards and valued qualities defined by the group. One maintains membership by acting in conformity with valued aspects of Toughness, Smartness, Autonomy, etc. In those instances where conforming to norms of this reference group at the same time violates norms of other reference groups (e.g., middle class adults, institutional "officials"), immediate reference group norms are much more compelling since violation risks invoking the group's most powerful sanction: exclusion.

Status: In common with most adolescents in American society, the lower class corner group manifests a dominant concern with "status." What differentiates this type of group from others, however, is the particular set of criteria and weighting thereof by which "status" is defined. In general, status is achieved and maintained by demonstrated possession of the valued qualities of lower class culture—Toughness, Smartness, expressed resistance to authority, daring, etc. It is important to stress once more that the individual orients to these concerns *as they are defined within lower class society;* e.g., the status-conferring potential of "smartness" in the sense of scholastic achievement generally ranges from negligible to negative.

The concern with "status" is manifested in a variety of ways. Intra-group status is a continued concern, and is derived and tested constantly by means of a set of status-ranking activities; the intra-group "pecking order" is constantly at issue. One gains status within the group by demonstrated superiority in Toughness (physical prowess, bravery, skill in athletics and games such as pool and cards), Smartness (skill in repartee, capacity to "dupe" fellow group members), and the like. The term "ranking," used to refer to the pattern if intra-group aggressive repartee, indicates awareness of the fact that this is one device for establishing the intra-group status hierarchy.

The concern over status in the adolescent corner group involves in particular the component of "adultness," the intense desire to be seen as "grown-up," and a corresponding aversion to "kid-stuff." "Adult" status is defined less in terms of the assumption of "adult" responsibility than in terms of certain external symbols of adult status—a car, ready cash, and, in particular, a perceived "freedom" to drink, smoke, and gamble as one wishes and to come and go without external restrictions. The desire to be seen as "adult" is often a more significant component of much involvement in illegal drinking, gambling, and automobile driving than the explicit enjoyment of these acts as such.

The intensity of the corner group member's desire to be seen as "adult" is sufficiently great that he feels called upon to demonstrate qualities associated with adultness (Toughness, Smartness, Autonomy) to a much greater degree than a lower class adult. This means that he will seek out and utilize those avenues to these qualities which he perceives as available with greater intensity than an adult and less regard for the "legitimacy." In this sense the adolescent variant of lower class culture represents a maximization or an intensified manifestation of many of its most characteristic features.

Concern over status is also manifested in reference to other street corner groups. The term "rep" used in this regard is especially significant, and has broad connotations. In its most frequent and explicit connotation, "rep" refers to the "toughness" of the corner group as a whole relative to that of other groups; a "pecking order" also exists among the several corner groups in a give interactional area, and there is a common perception that the safety or security of the group and all its members depends on maintaining a solid "rep" for toughness vis-a-vis other groups. This motive is most frequently advanced as a reason for involvement in gang fights: "We *can't* chicken out on this; our rep would be shot!"; this implies that the group would be relegated to the bottom of the status ladder and become a helpless and recurrent target of external attack.

On the other hand, there is implicit in the concept of "rep" the recognition that "rep" has or may have a dual basis—corresponding to the two aspects of the "trouble" dimension. It is recognized that group as well as individual status can be based on both "law-abiding" and "law-violating" behavior. The situational resolution of the persisting conflict between the "law-abiding" and "law-violating" bases of status comprises a vital set of dynamics in determining whether a "delinquent" mode of behavior will be adopted by a group, under what circumstances, and how persistently. The determinants of this choice are evidently highly complex and fluid, and rest on a range of factors including the presence and perceptual immediacy of different community reference-group loci (e.g., professional criminals, police, clergy, teachers, settlement house workers), the personality structures and "needs" of group members, the presence in the community of social work, recreation, or educational programs which can facilitate utilization of the "law-abiding" basis of status, and so on.

What remains constant is the critical importance of "status" both for the members of the group as individuals and for the group as a whole insofar as members perceive their individual destinies as linked to the destiny of the group, and the fact that action geared to attain status is much more acutely oriented to the fact of status itself than to the legality or illegality, morality or immorality of the means used to achieve it.

Lower Class Culture and the Motivation of Delinquent Behavior

The customary set of activities of the adolescent street corner group includes activities which are in violation of laws and ordinances of the legal code. Most of these center around assault and theft of various types (the gang fight; auto theft; assault on an individual; petty pilfering and shoplifting; "mugging"; pocketbook theft). Members of street corner gangs are well aware of the law-violating nature of these acts; they are not psychopaths, nor physically or mentally "defective"; in fact, since the corner group supports and enforces a rigorous set of standards which demand a high degree of fitness and personal competence, it tends to recruit from the most "able" members of the community.

Why, then, is the commission of crimes a customary feature of gang activity? The most general answer is that the commission of crimes by members of adolescent street corner groups is motivated primarily by the attempt to achieve ends, states, or conditions which are valued, and to avoid those that are disvalued within their most meaningful cultural milieu, through those culturally available avenues which appear as the most feasible means of attaining those ends.

The operation of these influences is well illustrated by the gang fight—a prevalent and characteristic type of corner group delinquency. This type of activity comprises a highly stylized and culturally patterned set of sequences. Although details vary under different circumstances, the following events are generally included. A member or several members of group A "trepass" on the claimed territory of group B. While there they commit an act or acts which group B defines as a violation of its rightful privileges, an affront to their honor, or a challenge to their "rep." Frequently this act involves advances to a girl associated with group B; it may occur at a dance or party; sometimes the mere act of "trespass" is seen as deliberate provocation. Members of group B then assault members of group A, if they are caught while still in B's territory. Assaulted members of group A return to their "home" territory and recount to members of their group details of the incident, stressing the insufficient nature of the provocation ("I just *looked* at her! Hardly even said anything!"), and the unfair circumstances of the assault ("About *twenty* guys jumped just the *two* of us!"). The highly colored account is acutely inflammatory; group A, perceiving its honor violated and its "rep" threatened, feels obligated to retaliate in force. Sessions of detailed planning now occur; allies are recruited if the size of group A and its potential allies appears to necessitate larger numbers; strategy is plotted, and messengers dispatched. Since the prospect of a gang fight is frightening to even the "toughest" group members, a constant rehearsal of the provocative incident or incidents and the essentially evil nature of the opponents accompany the planning process to bolster possibly weakening motivation to fight. The excursion into "enemy" territory sometimes results in a full scale fight: more often group B cannot be found, or the police appear and stop the fight, "tipped off" by an anonymous informant. When this occurs, group members express disgust and disappointment; secretly there is much relief; their honor has been avenged without incurring injury; often the anonymous tipster is a member of one of the involved groups.

The basic elements of this type of delinquency are sufficiently stabilized and recurrent as to constitute an essentially ritualized pattern, resembling both in structure and expressed motives for action classic forms such as the European "duel," the American Indian tribal war, and the Celtic clan feud. Although the arousing and "acting out" of individual aggressive emotions are inevitably involved in the gang fight, neither its form nor motivational dynamics can be adequately handled within a predominantly personality-focused frame of reference.

It would be possible to develop in considerable detail the processes by which the commission of a range of illegal acts is either explicitly supported by, implicitly demanded by, or not materially inhibited by factors relating to the focal concerns of lower class culture. In place of such a development, the following three statements condense in general terms the operation of these processes:

1. Following the cultural practices which comprise essential elements of the total life pattern of lower class culture automatically violates certain legal norms.

2. In instances where alternate avenues to similar objectives are available, the non-law-abiding avenue frequently provides a relatively greater and more immediate return for a relatively smaller investment of energy.

3. The "demanded" response to certain situations recurrently engendered within lower class culture involves the commission of illegal acts.

The primary thesis of this paper is that the dominant component of the motivation of "delinquent behavior" engaged in by members of lower class corner groups involves a positive effort to achieve states, conditions, or qualities valued within the actor's most significant cultural milieu. If "conformity to immediate reference group values" is the major component of motivation of "delinquent" behavior by gang members, why is such behavior frequently referred to as negativistic, malicious, or rebellious? Albert Cohen, for example, in *Delinquent Boys* (Glencoe: Free Press, 1955) describes behavior which violates school rules as comprising elements of "active spite and malice, contempt and ridicule, challenge and defiance." He ascribes to the gang "keen delight in terrorizing 'good' children, and in general making themselves obnoxious to the virtuous." A recent national conference on social work with "hard-to-reach" groups characterized lower class corner groups as "youth groups in conflict with the culture of their (*sic*) communities." Such characterizations are obviously the result of taking the middle class community and its institutions as an implicit point of reference.

A large body of systematically interrelated attitudes, practices, behaviors, and values characteristic of lower class culture are designed to support and maintain the basic features of the lower class way of life. In areas where these differ from features of middle class culture, action oriented to the achievement and maintenance of the lower class system may violate norms of middle class culture and be perceived as deliberately non-conforming or malicious by an observer strongly cathected to middle class norms. This does not mean, however, that violation of the middle class norm is the dominant component of motivation; it is a by-product of action primarily oriented to the lower class system. The standards of lower class culture cannot be seen merely as a reverse function of middle class culture—as middle class standards "turned upside down"; lower class culture is a distinctive tradition many centuries old with an integrity of its own.

From the viewpoint of the acting individual, functioning within a field of well-structured cultural forces, the relative impact of "conforming" and "rejective" elements in the motivation of gang delinquency is weighted preponderantly on the conforming side. Rejective or rebellious elements are inevitably involved, but their influence during the actual commission of delinquent acts is relatively small compared to the influence of pressures to achieve what is valued by the actor's most immediate reference groups. Expressed awareness by the actor of the element of rebellion often represents only that aspect of motivation of which he is explicitly conscious; the deepest and most compelling components of motivation—adherence to highly meaningful group standards of

Toughness, Smartness, Excitement, etc.—are often unconsciously patterned. No cultural pattern as well-established as the practice of illegal acts by members of lower class corner groups could persist if buttressed primarily by negative, hostile, or rejective motives; its principal motivational support, as in the case of any persisting cultural tradition, derives from a positive effort to achieve what is valued within that tradition, and to conform to its explicit and implicit norms.

Notes

1. The complex issues involved in deriving a definition of "delinquency" cannot be discussed here. The term "delinquent" is used in this paper to characterize behavior or acts committed by individuals within specified age limits which if known to official authorities could result in legal action. The concept of a "delinquent" individual has little or no utility in the approach used here; rather specified types of *acts* which may be committed rarely or frequently by few or many individuals are characterized as "delinquent."

2. A three year research project is being financed under the National Institutes of Health Grant M-1414, and administered through the Boston University School of Social Work. The primary research effort has subjected all collected material to a uniform data-coding process. All information bearing on some seventy areas of behavior (behavior in reference to school, police, theft, assault, sex, collective athletics, etc.) is extracted from the records, recorded on coded data cards, and filed under relevant categories. Analysis of these data aims to ascertain the actual nature of customary behavior in these areas, and the extent to which the social work effort was able to effect behavioral changes.

3. Between 40 and 60 per cent of all Americans are directly influenced by lower class culture, with about 15 percent, or twenty-five million, comprising the "hard-core" lower class group—defined primarily by its use of the "female-based" household as the basic form of child-rearing unit and of the "serial monogamy" mating pattern as the primary form of marriage. The term "lower class culture" as used here refers most specifically to the way of life of the "hard core" group; systematic research in this area would probably reveal at least four to six major subtypes of lower class culture, for which the "concerns" presented here would be differently weighted, especially for those subtypes in which "law-abiding" behavior has a high overt valuation. It is impossible within the compass of this short paper to make the finer intracultural distinctions which a more accurate presentation would require.

4. The "brains-brawn" set of capacities are often paired in lower class folk lore or accounts of lower

class life, e.g., "Brer Fox" and "Brer Bear" in the Uncle Remus stories, or George and Lennie in "Of Mice and Men."

5. Further data on the female-based household unit (estimated as comprising about 15 per cent of all American "families") and the role of one-sex groupings in lower class culture are contained in Walter B. Miller, "Implications of Urban Lower Class Culture for Social Work." *Social Service Review,* 1959, *33,* No. 3.

QUESTIONS FOR DISCUSSION

1. List and discuss the focal concerns of lower-class culture. Which, if any, of these concerns are shared by middle- and upper-class cultures? Why?

2. Explain the lower-class concern with "trouble" potential.

3. Whether an act is considered to be delinquent or nonconforming so often is dependent on which individual or group creates the definition. Miller argues that lower-class groups conform to their immediate reference group values. Rather than being delinquent or nonconformists, lower-class youth are in fact conformists, though not to a middle-class standard. Do you agree with this line of reasoning? Why?

APPLICATIONS

1. Assuming that you are a middle-class student, what are the focal concerns of your culture? How do they differ from the concerns of the lower class?

2. Have you ever violated the law? If yes, how did you justify your behavior? In what ways did your cultural values and beliefs affect your decisions?

KEY TERMS

cathected having invested mental or emotional energy.

concomitant something that accompanies or is collaterally connected with something else.

epithet generally a disparaging word or phrase; a word or phrase used noxiously in place of another word or phrase.

etiology the cause or origin of a given thought, behavior, or event.

invective behavior or spoken words characterized by insult or abuse.

milieu the physical or social setting where social actions occur and develop.

ostensibly giving the appearance or acting as if something is true.

pejorative disparaging or belittling; saying something that has negative connotations.

repartee an exchange of clever and/or amusing words; a lighthearted debate or spar.

valence a value or weight given to an idea; giving a theory or concept a positive or negative valence means an implicit assumption has been made as to its correctness.

11

Toward an Interactional Theory of Delinquency

Terence P. Thornberry

Contemporary theories of delinquency are seen as limited in three respects: they tend to rely on unidirectional causal structures that represent delinquency in a static rather than dynamic fashion, they do not examine developmental progressions, and they do not adequately link processual concepts to the person's position in the social structure. The present article develops an interactional theory of delinquency that addresses each of these issues. It views delinquency as resulting from the freedom afforded by the weakening of the person's bonds to conventional society and from an interactional setting in which delinquent behavior is learned and reinforced. Moreover, the control, learning, and delinquency variables are seen as reciprocally interrelated, mutually affecting one another over the person's life. Thus, delinquency is viewed as part of a larger causal network, affected by social factors but also affecting the development of those social factors over time.

A variety of sociological theories have been developed to explain the onset and maintenance of delinquent behavior. Currently, three are of primary importance: social control theory (Hirschi, 1969), social learning theory (Akers, 1977), and integrated models that combine them into a broader body of explanatory principals (Elliott, Ageton, and Canter, 1979; Elliott, Huizinga, and Ageton, 1985).

"Toward an Interactional Theory of Delinquency," *Criminology*, 25:4 (1987), pp. 863–891. Reprinted by permission of The American Society of Criminology.

Control theory argues that delinquency emerges whenever the social and cultural constraints over human conduct are substantially attenuated. As Hirschi states in his classic presentation (1969), control theory assumes that we would all be deviant if only we dared. Learning theory, on the other hand, posits that there is no natural impulse toward delinquency. Indeed, delinquent behavior must be learned through the same processes and mechanisms as conforming behavior. Because of these different starting points, control and learning models give causal priority to somewhat different concepts, and integrated models capitalize on these complementary approaches. Muting the assumptive differences, integrated theories meld together propositions from these (and sometimes other theories—for example, strain) to explain delinquent behavior.

Although these approaches have substantially informed our understanding of the causes of delinquency, they and other contemporary theories suffer from three fundamental limitations. First, they rely on unidirectional rather than reciprocal causal structures. By and large, current theories ignore reciprocal effects in which delinquent behavior is viewed as part of a more general social nexus, affected by, but also affecting, other social factors. Second, current theories tend to be nondevelopmental, specifying causal models for only a narrow age range, usually midadolescence. As a result, they fail to capitalize on developmental patterns to explain the initiation, maintenance, and desistance of delinquency. Finally, contemporary theories tend to assume uniform causal effects throughout the social structure. By ignoring the person's structural position, they fail to provide an understanding of the sources of initial variation in both delinquency and its presumed causes. In combination, these three limitations have led to theories that are narrowly conceived and which provide incomplete and, at times, misleading models of the causes of delinquency.

The present article develops an interactional theory of delinquency that addresses and attempts to respond to each of these limitations. The model proposed here pays particular attention to the first issue, recursive versus reciprocal causal structures, since the development of dynamic models is seen as essential to represent accurately the interactional settings in which delinquency develops.

Origins and Assumptions

The basic premise of the model proposed here is that human behavior occurs in social interaction and can therefore best be explained by models that focus on interactive processes. Rather than viewing adolescents as propelled along a unidirectional pathway to one or another outcome—that is, delinquency or conformity—it argues that adolescents interact with other people and institutions and that behavioral outcomes are formed by that interactive process. For example, the delinquent behavior of an adolescent is formed in part by how he and his parents *interact* over time, not simply by the child's perceived, and presumably invariant, *level* of attachment to parents. Moreover, since it is an interactive system, the behaviors of others—for example, parents and school officials—are influenced both by each other and by the adolescent, including his or her delinquent behavior. If this view is correct, then interactional effects have to be modelled explicitly if we are to understand the social and psychological processes involved with initiation into delinquency, the maintenance of such behavior, and its eventual reduction.

Interactional theory develops from the same intellectual tradition as the theories

mentioned above, especially the Durkheimian tradition of social control. It asserts that the fundamental cause of delinquency lies in the weakening of social constraints over the conduct of the individual. Unlike classical control theory, however, it does not assume that the attenuation of controls leads directly to delinquency. The weakening of controls simply allows for a much wider array of behavior, including continued conventional action, failure as indicated by school dropout and sporadic employment histories, alcoholism, mental illness, delinquent and criminal careers, or some combination of these outcomes. For the freedom resulting from weakened bonds to be channeled to delinquency, especially serious prolonged delinquency, requires an interactive setting in which delinquency is learned, performed, and reinforced. This view is similar to Cullen's structuring perspective, which draws attention to the indeterminacy of deviant behavior. "It can thus be argued that there is an *indeterminate* and not a determinate or etiologically specific relationship between motivational variables on the one hand and any particular form of deviant behavior on the other hand" (Cullen, 1984: 5).

Although heavily influenced by control and learning theories, and to a lesser extent by strain and culture conflict theories, this is not an effort at theoretical integration as that term is usually used (Elliott, 1985). Rather, this paper is guided by what we have elsewhere called theoretical elaboration (Thornberry, 1987). In this instance, a basic control theory is extended, or elaborated upon, using available theoretical perspectives and empirical findings to provide a more accurate model of the causes of delinquency. In the process of elaboration, there is no requirement to resolve disputes among other theories—for example, their different assumptions about the origins of deviance (Thornberry, 1987:15-18); all that is required is that the propositions of the model developed here be consistent with one another and with the assumptions about deviance stated above.

Organization

The presentation of the interactional model begins by identifying the central concepts to be included in the model. Next, the underlying theoretical structure of the proposed model is examined and the rationale for moving from unidirectional to reciprocal causal models is developed. The reciprocal model is then extended to include a developmental perspective, examining the theoretical saliency of different variables at different developmental stages. Finally, the influence of the person's position in the social structure is explored. Although in some senses the last issue is logically prior to the others, since it is concerned with sources of initial variation in the causal variables, it is discussed last so that the reciprocal relationships among the concepts—the heart of an interactional perspective—can be more fully developed.

THEORETICAL CONCEPTS

Given these basic premises, an interactional model must respond to two overriding issues. First, how are traditional social constraints over behavior weakened and, second, once weakened, how is the resulting freedom channelled into delinquent patterns? To address these issues, the present article presents an initial version of an interactional model, focusing on the interrelationships among six concepts: attachment to parents, commitment to school, belief in conventional values, associations with delinquent peers, adopting delinquent values, and engaging in delinquent behavior. These concepts form the core of the theoretical model since they are central to social psychological theories of delinquency and since they have been shown in numerous studies to be strongly related to subsequent delinquent behavior (see Elliott et al., 1985, Chs. 1–3, for an excellent review of this literature).

The first three derive from Hirschi's version of control theory (1969) and represents the primary mechanisms by which adolescents are bonded to conventional middle-class society. When those elements of the bond are weakened, behavioral freedom increases considerably. For that freedom to lead to delinquent behavior, however, interactive settings that reinforce delinquency are required. In the model, those settings are represented by two concepts—associations with delinquent peers and the formation of delinquent values—which derive primarily from social learning theory.

For the purpose of explicating the overall theoretical perspective, each of these concepts is defined quite broadly. Attachment to parents includes the affective relationship between parent and child, communication patterns, parenting skills such as monitoring and discipline, parent-child conflict, and the like. Commitment to school refers to the stake in conformity the adolescent has developed and includes such factors as success in school, perceived importance of education, attachment to teachers, and involvement in school activities. Belief in conventional values represents the granting of legitimacy to such middle-class values as education, personal industry, financial success, deferral of gratification, and the like.

Three delinquency variables are included in the model. Association with delinquent peers includes the level of attachment to peers, the delinquent behavior and values of peers, and their reinforcing reactions to the adolescent's own delinquent or conforming behavior. It is a continuous measure that can vary from groups that are heavily delinquent to those that are almost entirely nondelinquent. Delinquent values refer to the granting of legitimacy to delinquent activities as acceptable modes of behavior as well as a general willingness to violate the law to achieve other ends.

Delinquent behavior, the primary outcome variable, refers to acts that place the youth at risk for adjudication; it ranges from status offenses to serious violent activities. Since the present model is an interactional one, interested not only in explaining delinquency but in explaining the effects of delinquency on other variables, particular attention is paid to prolonged involvement in serious delinquency.

THEORETICAL STRUCTURE

The present section develops the reciprocal structure of the interactional model by examining the interplay of the concepts just defined. It begins by describing (Figure 17.1) the way in which these variables are typically represented in predominately recursive theories of delinquency (see, for example, Johnson, 1979: Weis and Sederstrom, 1981; Elliott et al., 1985).

In these models, all the variables are temporally ordered; earlier ones affect later ones, but there is no provision for feedback or reciprocal causal paths. The unidirectional specification can be illustrated by examining the relationship between attachment to parents and associations with delinquent peers. According to the model, attachment to parents reduces the extent to which the child associates with delinquent peers, an assertion consistent with common observation and empirical research (for example, Poole and Regoli, 1979). Yet, by implication, the model also states that associations with delinquent peers exerts no causal influence on the extent to which the child is attached to parents. If peer associations were thought to influence attachment to parents, then this effect would have to be specified and estimated. As seen in Figure 17.1, reciprocal effects of this type are excluded by design.

The second feature to note about this model is that it treats delinquency entirely as an outcome of a social process rather than as an integral part of that process. Models such as this assert that various social factors cause delinquent behavior but ignore the possibility that delinquency and its presumed causes are part of a reciprocal causal structure, mutually influencing one another over the person's life span. For example, these models state that associations with delinquent peers increase the likelihood of delinquent conduct, an obviously reasonable assertion, but ignore the possibility that delinquent conduct affects the likelihood and intensity of associations with delinquent peers. Similar statements can be made for the other relationships in which delinquency is embedded.

It should be noted at the outset that there is nothing inherently incorrect with recursive models; if the causal processes are unidirectional, recursive models offer a correct specification and should be used. It is only when the causal processes are in fact reciprocal that models such as these lead to problems of misspecification and incorrect interpretations of causal effects. The remainder of this section develops the argument that unidirectional models are inadequate and that reciprocal models are required to understand the causes of delinquency, precisely because delinquency is embedded in an interactive social process, affected by and affecting other variables. As a starting point, the findings of three recent panel studies that examine both unidirectional and reciprocal models of delinquent conduct are considered.

Empirical Findings

Thornberry and Christenson (1984) estimated a reciprocal causal structure for unemployment and criminal involvement, both measured at the individual level, for a sample of young adult males. They found that unidirectional models, either from unemployment to crime or from crime to unemploy-

FIGURE 17.1 A Typical Recursive Causal Model of Delinquency

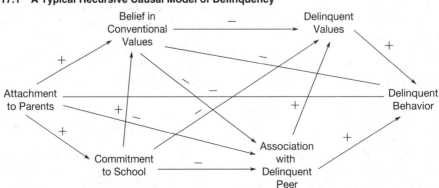

ment, were inadequate to model the causal process. Overall, their findings:

> offer strong support for a reciprocal model of crime causation. Consistent with our theoretical specification, unemployment has significant instantaneous effects on crime and crime has significant effects, primarily lagged effects, on unemployment (1984:408).

Liska and Reed (1985) studied the relationship among three control theory variables, attachment to parents, success in school, and delinquency. Although their results differed somewhat for blacks and whites, these variables appear to be embedded in a reciprocal causal loop. Overall, "the analysis suggests that parental attachment affects delinquency, that delinquency affects school attachment, and that school attachment affects parental attachment" (Liska and Reed, 1985:556–557).

Finally, Burkett and Warren (1987) estimate a panel model for four variables: religious commitment, belief in the sinfulness of marijuana use, associations with peers who use marijuana, and self-reported marijuana use. Their basic finding suggests that religious commitment and belief affect marijuana use indirectly, through association with delinquent peers. They also present consistent evidence that these four variables are reciprocally related over time. Marijuana use increases associations with delinquent peers, and associations with delinquent peers reduce religious commitments. In addition, marijuana use at time one significantly affects both religious commitment and beliefs at later times and "this, in turn, contributes to deeper involvement with marijuana-using peers and subsequent continued use in response to direct peer pressure" (1987:123).

All three of these studies derive primarily from a social control framework, but use different data sets, variables, and analytic techniques. Nevertheless, all provide empirical support for the improved explanatory power of reciprocal models. The pattern of relationships observed in these studies strongly suggests that reciprocal causal models are necessary to model adequately the social settings in which delinquent behavior emerges and develops.

These findings also suggest that previous tests of delinquency theories based on recursive causal structures are both incomplete and misleading. As Thornberry and Christenson (1984:399) point out, such tests:

> are incomplete since estimates for reciprocal paths simply cannot be obtained. More importantly, recursive tests can produce misleading results since estimates of unidirectional effects obtained from them may be in substantial error. Conceivably, recursive tests could indicate a unidirectional effect between two variables, i.e., $X \rightarrow Y$, when the actual relationship (as estimated from a nonrecursive model) could indicate either that the variables are reciprocally related, i.e., $X \leftrightarrow Y$, or that the direction of the causality is actually reversed, i.e., $X \leftarrow Y$ (see Heise, 1975:191–93; Hanushek and Jackson, 1977:79–86).

If any or all of these errors exist, and results of recent research suggest they do, then current theories of delinquency, which have been strongly influenced by the results of recursive studies, are inadequate to describe the actual processes in which delinquency is embedded. Because of this, it is important to develop and test interactional models that allow for reciprocal effects.

MODEL SPECIFICATION

A causal model allowing for reciprocal relationships among the six concepts of interest—attachment to parents, commitment to school, belief in conventional values, association with delinquent peers, delinquent values, and delinquent behavior—is presented in Figure 17.2. This model refers to the period of early adolescence, from about ages 11 to 13, when delinquent careers are beginning, but prior to the period at which delinquency reaches its apex in terms of seriousness and frequency. In the following sections the model is extended to later ages.

The specification of causal effects begins by examining the three concepts that form the heart of social learning theories of delinquency—delinquent peers, delinquent values, and delinquent behavior. For now we

FIGURE 17.2 A Reciprocal Model of Delinquent Involvement at Early Adolescence[a]

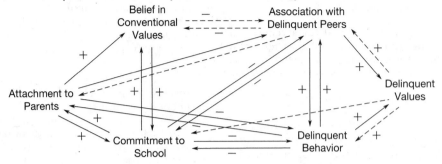

[a]Solid lines represent stronger effects; dashed lines represent weaker effects.

focus on the reciprocal nature of the relationships, ignoring until later variations in the strength of the relationships.

Traditional social learning theory specifies a causal order among these variables in which delinquent associations affect delinquent values and, in turn, both produce delinquent behavior (Akers, Krohn, Lanza-Kaduce, and Radosevich, 1979; Matsueda, 1982). Yet, for each of the dyadic relationships involving these variables, other theoretical perspectives and much empirical evidence suggest the appropriateness of reversing this causal order. For example, social learning theory proposes that associating with delinquents, or more precisely, people who hold and reinforce delinquent values, increases the chances of delinquent behavior (Akers, 1977). Yet, as far back as the work of the Gluecks (1950) this specification has been challenged. Arguing that "birds of a feather flock together," the Gluecks propose that youths who are delinquent seek out and associate with others who share those tendencies. From this perspective, rather than being a cause of delinquency, associations are the result of delinquents seeking out and associating with like-minded peers.

An attempt to resolve the somewhat tedious argument over the temporal priority of associations and behavior is less productive theoretically than capitalizing on the interactive nature of human behavior and treating the relationship as it probably is; a reciprocal one. People often take on the behavioral repertoire of their associates but, at the same time, they often seek out associates who share their behavioral interests. Individuals clearly behave this way in conventional settings, and there is no reason to assume that deviant activities, such as delinquency, are substantially different in this regard.

Similar arguments can be made for the other two relationships among the delinquency variables. Most recent theories of delinquency, following the lead of social learning theory, posit that delinquent associations lead to the formation of delinquent values. Subcultural theories, however, especially those that derive from a cultural deviance perspective (Miller, 1958) suggest that values precede the formation of peer groups. Indeed, it is the socialization of adolescents into the "lower-class culture" and its particular value system that leads them to associate with delinquent peers in the first place. This specification can also be derived from a social control perspective as demonstrated in Weis and Sederstrom's social development model (1981) and Burkett and Warren's social selection model (1987).

Finally, the link between delinquent values and delinquent behavior restates, in many ways, the basic social psychological question of the relationship between attitudes and behavior. Do attitudes form patterns or does behavior lead to attitude formation? Social psychological research, especially in cognitive psychology and balance models (for example, Festinger, 1957; Brehm and Cohen, 1962) points to the reciprocal nature of this relationship. It suggests that people indeed behave in a manner consistent with their attitudes, but also that behavior is one of the most persuasive forces in the formation and maintenance of attitudes.

Such a view of the relationship between delinquent values and behavior is consistent with Hindelang's findings:

> This general pattern of results indicates that one can "predict" a respondent's self approval [of illegal behaviors] from knowledge of that respondent's involvement/non-involvement [in delinquency] with fewer errors than vice-versa (1974:382).

It is also consistent with recent deterrence search which demonstrates that the "experiential effect," in which behavior affects attitudes, is much stronger than the deterrent effect, in which attitudes affect behavior (Paternoster, Saltzman, Waldo, and Chiricos, 1982; Paternoster, Saltzman, Chiricos, and Waldo 1983).

Although each of these relationships appears to be reciprocal, the predicted strengths of the associations are not of equal strength during the early adolescent period (see Figure 2). Beliefs that delinquent conduct is acceptable and positively valued may be emerging, but such beliefs are not fully articulated for 11- to 13-year-olds. Because of their emerging quality, they are viewed as more effect than cause, produced by delinquent behavior and associations with delinquent peers. As these values emerge, however, they have feedback effects, albeit relatively weak ones at these ages, on behavior and associations. That is, as the values become more fully articulated and delinquency becomes positively valued, it increases the likelihood of such behavior and further reinforces associations with like-minded peers.

Summary: When attention is focused on the interrelationships among associations with delinquent peers, delinquent values, and delinquent behavior, it appears that they are, in fact, reciprocally related. The world of human behavior is far more complex than a simple recursive one in which a temporal order can be imposed on interactional variables of this nature. Interactional theory sees these three concepts as embedded in a causal loop, each reinforcing the others over time.

Regardless of where the individual enters the loop, the following obtains: delinquency increases associations with delinquent peers and delinquent values; delinquent values increase delinquent behavior and associations with delinquent peers; and associations with delinquent peers increases delinquent behavior and delinquent values. The question now concerns the identification of factors that lead some youth, but not others, into this spiral of increasing delinquency.

Social Control Effects

As indicated at the outset of this essay, the premise of interactional theory is that the fundamental cause of delinquency is the attenuation of social controls over the person's conduct. Whenever bonds to the conventional world are substantially weakened, the individual is freed from moral constraints and is at risk for a wide array of deviant activities, including delinquency. The primary mechanisms that bind adolescents to the conventional world are attachment to parents, commitment to school, and belief in conventional values, and their role in the model can now be examined.

During the early adolescent years, the family is the most salient arena for social interaction and involvement and, because of this, attachment to parents has a stronger influence on other aspects of the youth's life at this stage than it does at later stages of development. With this in mind, attachment to parents[1] is predicted to affect four other variables. Since youths who are attached to their parents are sensitive to their wishes (Hirschi, 1969:16–19), and, since parents are almost universally supportive of the conventional world, these children are likely to be strongly committed to school and to espouse conventional values. In addition, youths who are attached to their parents, again because of their sensitivity to parental wishes, are unlikely to associate with delinquent peers or to engage in delinquent behavior.

In brief, parental influence is seen as central to controlling the behavior of youths at these relatively early ages. Parents who have a strong affective bond with their children, who communicate with them, who exercise appropriate parenting skills, and so forth, are likely to lead their children towards conventional actions and beliefs and away from delinquent friends and actions.

On the other hand, attachment to parents is not seen as an immutable trait, impervious to the effects of other variables. Indeed, associating with delinquent peers, not being committed to school, and engaging in delinquent behavior are so contradictory to parental expectations that they tend to diminish the level of attachment between parent and child. Adolescents who fail at school, who associate with delinquent peers, and who engage in delinquent conduct are, as a consequence, likely to jeopardize their affective bond with their parents, precisely because these behaviors suggest that the "person does not care about the wishes and expectations of other people . . ." (Hirschi, 1969:18), in this instance, his or her parents.

Turning next to belief in conventional values, this concept is involved in two different causal loops. First, it strongly affects commitment to school and in turn is affected by commitment to school. In essence, this loop posits a behavioral and attitudinal consistency in the conventional realm. Second, a weaker loop is posited between belief in conventional values and associations with delinquent peers. Youths who do not grant legitimacy to conventional values are more apt to associate with delinquent friends who share those views, and those friendships are likely to attenuate further their beliefs in conventional values. This reciprocal specification is supported by Burkett and Warren's findings concerning religious beliefs and peer associations (1987). Finally, youths who believe in conventional values are seen as somewhat less likely to engage in delinquent behavior.

Although belief in conventional values plays some role in the genesis of delinquency, its impact is not particularly strong. For example, it is not affected by delinquent behavior, nor is it related to delinquent values. This is primarily because belief in conventional values appears to be quite invariant; regardless of class of origin or delinquency status, for example, most people strongly assert conventional values (Short and Strodtbeck, 1965: Ch. 3). Nevertheless,

these beliefs do exert some influence in the model, especially with respect to reinforcing commitment to school.

Finally, the impact of commitment to school is considered. This variable is involved in reciprocal loops with both of the other bonding variables. Youngsters who are attached to their parents are likely to be committed to and succeed in school, and that success is likely to reinforce the close ties to their parents. Similarly, youths who believe in conventional values are likely to be committed to school, the primary arena in which they can act in accordance with those values, and, in turn, success in that arena is likely to reinforce the beliefs.

In addition to its relationships with the other control variables, commitment to school also has direct effects on two of the delinquency variables. Students who are committed to succeeding in school are unlikely to associate with delinquents or to engage in substantial amounts of serious, repetitive delinquent behavior. These youths have built up a stake in conformity and should be unwilling to jeopardize that investment by either engaging in delinquent behavior or by associating with those who do.

Low commitment to school is not seen, however, as leading directly to the formation of delinquent values. Its primary effect on delinquent values is indirect, via associations with delinquent peers and delinquent behavior (Conger, 1980:137). While school failure may lead to a reduced commitment to conventional values, it does not follow that it directly increases the acceptance of values that support delinquency.

Commitment to school, on the other hand, is affected by each of the delinquency variables in the model. Youths who accept values that are consistent with delinquent behavior, who associate with other delinquents, and who engage in delinquent behavior are simply unlikely candidates to maintain an active commitment to school and the conventional world that school symbolizes.

Summary: Attachment to parents, commitment to school, and belief in conventional values reduce delinquency by cementing the person to conventional institutions and people. When these elements of the bond to conventional society are strong, delinquency is unlikely, but when they are weak the individual is placed at much greater risk for delinquency. When viewed from an interactional perspective, two additional qualities of these concepts become increasingly evident.

First, attachment to parents, commitment to school, and belief in conventional values are not static attributes of the person, invariant over time. These concepts interact with one another during the developmental process. For some youths the levels of attachment, commitment, and belief increase as these elements reinforce one another, while for other youths the interlocking nature of these relationships suggests a greater and greater attenuation of the bond will develop over time.

Second, the bonding variables appear to be reciprocally linked to delinquency, exerting a causal impact on associations with delinquent peers and delinquent behavior; they also are causally effected by these variables. As the youth engages in more and more delinquent conduct and increasingly associates with delinquent peers, the level of his bond to the conventional world is further weakened. Thus, while the weakening of the bond to conventional society may be an initial cause of delinquency, delinquency eventually becomes its own indirect cause precisely because of its ability to weaken further the person's bonds to family, school, and conventional beliefs. The implications of this amplifying causal structure is examined below. First, however, the available support for reciprocal models is reviewed and the basic model is extended to later developmental stages.

Support for Reciprocal Structures

The previous section developed a theoretical rationale for moving from recursive to reciprocal causal structures of delinquency. Using an interactional perspective, delinquent behavior, especially sustained involvement with serious delinquent behavior, was viewed as part of an ongoing social process rather than simply a product of other social variables. The present section reviews sources of theoretical and empirical support for this perspective.

First, this model is logically consistent with the approaches of many other theoretical models; see, for example, those proposed by Hirschi (1969), Akers (1977), Elliott et al. (1979, 1985), Weis and Sedestrom (1981), and Snyder and Patterson (in press). Indeed, the present model can be viewed as a logical extension of those theories since it explicitly specifies reciprocal effects that have, until recently, remained largely implicit in criminological theory and research.

Second, as indicated above, recent panel studies that estimate reciprocal effects produce consistent support for this perspective. Whether concerned with unemployment and crime (Thornberry and Christenson, 1984), attachment to parents, commitment to school and delinquency (Liska and Reed, 1985), or religion, peers, and marijuana use (Burkett and Warren, 1987), each of these analyses suggest that there are substantial feedback effects involving delinquency and its presumed causes.

Third, using data from the National Youth Survey, Huizinga and Elliott (1986) report a number of significant reciprocal effects. Although they did not observe feedback effects from delinquent behavior to the conventional bonding variables posited by interactional theory, they do report reciprocal effects among the elements of the bond. They also report that delinquent behavior and associations with delinquent peers are mutually reinforcing (Huizinga and Elliott, 1986:12). Finally, they report that exposure to delinquent friends has significant feedback effects on a wide range of variables, including "internal deviant bonds, perceived sanctions, normlessness, prosocial aspirations, and involvement in prosocial roles" (Huizinga and Elliott, 1986:14).

Fourth, a large number of studies have found that delinquent behavior (including drug use) measured at one time has significant effects on the presumed "causes" of delinquency measured at a later time. Among the variables found to be affected by prior delinquency are educational and occupational attainment (Bachman, O'Malley, and Johnston, 1978: Kandel and Logan,

1984); dropping out of high school (Elliott and Voss, 1974; Bachman et al., 1978; Polk et al., 1981; Thornberry, Moore, and Christenson, 1985); unemployment (Bachman et al., 1978; Thornberry and Christenson, 1984); attachment to parents (Paternoster et al., 1983); commitment to school (Paternoster et al., 1983; Liska and Reed, 1985; Agnew, 1985); and belief in conventional values (Hindelang, 1974; Paternoster et al., 1983; Agnew, 1985). These empirical findings are quite consistent with theory that posits that delinquent behavior is not only produced by other social variables, but also exerts a significant causal influence on those variables.

DEVELOPMENTAL EXTENSIONS

The previous section developed a strategy for addressing one of the three major limitations of delinquency theories mentioned in the introduction—namely, their unidirectional causal structure. A second limitation is the nondevelopmental posture of most theories which tend to provide a cross-sectional picture of the factors associated with delinquency at one age, but which do not provide a rationale for understanding how delinquent behavior develops over time. The present section offers a developmental extension of the basic model.

Middle Adolescence

First, a model for middle adolescence, when the youths are approximately 15 or 16 years of age is presented (Figure 17.3). This period represents the highest rates of involvement in delinquency and is the reference period, either implicitly or explicitly, for most theories of delinquent involvement. Since the models for the early and middle adolescent periods have essentially the same structure and causal relationships (Figure 17.2 and 17.3), discussion focuses on the differences between them and does not repeat the rationale for individual causal effects.

Perhaps the most important difference concerns attachment to parents which is involved in relatively few strong relationships. By this point in the life cycle, the most salient variables involved in the production of delinquency are likely to be external to the home, associated with the youth's activities in school and peer networks. This specification is consistent with empirical results for subjects in this age range (Johnson, 1979:105; and Schoenberg, 1975, quoted in Johnson). Indeed, Johnson concludes that "an adolescent's public life has as much or more to do with his or her deviance or conformity than do 'under-the roof' experiences" (1979:116).

This is not to say that attachment to parents is irrelevant; such attachments are involved in enhancing commitment to school and belief in conventional values, and in preventing associations with delinquent peers. It is just that the overall strength of parental effects are weaker than at earlier ages when the salience of the family as a locus of interaction and control was greater.

The second major change concerns the increased importance of delinquent values as

FIGURE 17.3 A Reciprocal Model of Delinquent Involvement at Middle Adolescence[a]

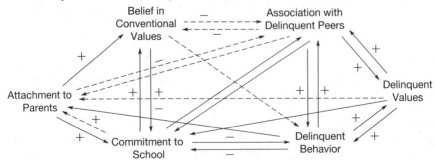

[a]Solid lines represent stronger effects; dashed lines represent weaker effects.

a causal factor. It is still embedded in the causal loop with the other two delinquency variables, but now it is as much cause as effect. Recall that at the younger ages delinquent values were seen as emerging, produced by associations with delinquent peers and delinquent behavior. Given their emergent nature, they were not seen as primary causes of other variables. At midadolescence, however, when delinquency is at its apex, these values are more fully articulated and have stronger effects on other variables. First, delinquent values are seen as major reinforcers of both delinquent associations and delinquent behavior. In general, espousing values supportive of delinquency tends to increase the potency of this causal loop. Second, since delinquent values are antithetical to the conventional settings of school and family, youths who espouse them are less likely to be committed to school and attached to parents. Consistent with the reduced saliency of family at these ages, the feedback effect to school is seen as stronger than the feedback effect to parents.

By and large, the other concepts in the model play the same role at these ages as they do at the earlier ones. Thus, the major change from early to middle adolescence concerns the changing saliency of some of the theoretical concepts. The family declines

in relative importance while the adolescent's own world of school and peers takes on increasing significance. While these changes occur, the overall structure of the theory remains constant. These interactive variables are still seen as mutually reinforcing over time.

Later Adolescence

Finally, the causes of delinquency during the transition from adolescence to adulthood, about ages 18 to 20, can be examined (Figure 17.4). At these ages one should more properly speak of crime than delinquency, but for consistency we will continue to use the term delinquency in the causal diagrams and employ the terms delinquency and crime interchangeably in the text.

Two new variables are added to the model to reflect the changing life circumstances at this stage of development. The more important of these is commitment to conventional activities which includes employment, attending college, and military service. Along with the transition to the world of work, there is a parallel transition from the family of origin to one's own family. Although this transition does not peak until the early 20s, for many people its influence is beginning at this stage. Included in this con-

FIGURE 17.4   A Reciprocal Model of Delinquent Involvement at Later Adolescence[a]

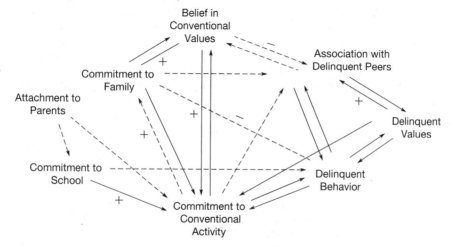

[a]Solid lines represent stronger effects; dashed lines represent weaker effects.

cept are marriage, plans for marriage, and plans for childrearing. These new variables largely replace attachment to parents and commitment to school in the theoretical scheme; they represent the major sources of bonds to conventional society for young adults.

Both attachment to parents and commitment to school remain in the model but take on the cast of exogenous variables. Attachment to parents has only a minor effect on commitment to school, and commitment to school is proposed to affect only commitment to conventional activities and, more weakly, delinquent behavior.

The other three variables considered in the previous models—association with delinquent peers, delinquent values, and delinquent behavior—are still hypothesized to be embedded in an amplifying causal loop. As indicated above, this loop is most likely to occur among adolescents who, at earlier ages, were freed from the controlling influence of parents and school. Moreover, via the feedback paths delinquent peers, delinquent values, and delinquent behavior further alienate the youth from parents and diminish commitment to school. Once this spiral begins, the probability of sustained delinquency increases.

This situation, if it continued uninterrupted, would yield higher and higher rates of crime as the subjects matured. Such an outcome is inconsistent with the desistance that has been observed during this age period (Wolfgang, Thornberry, and Figlio, 1987). Rates of delinquency and crime begin to subside by the late teenage years, a phenomenon often attributed to "maturational reform." Such an explanation, however, is tautological since it claims that crime stops when adolescents get older, because they get older. It is also uninformative since the concept of maturational reform is theoretically undefined.

A developmental approach, however, offers an explanation for desistance. As the developmental process unfolds, life circumstances change, developmental milestones are met (or, for some, missed), new social roles are created, and new networks of attachments and commitments emerge. The effects of these changes enter the processual model to explain new and often dramatically different behavioral patterns. In the present model, these changes are represented by commitment to conventional activity and commitment to family.

Commitment to conventional activity is influenced by a number of variables, including earlier attachment to parents, commitment to school, and belief in conventional values. And once the transition to the world of work is made, tremendous opportunities are afforded for new and different effects in the delinquency model. Becoming committed to conventional activities—work, college, military service, and so on—reduces the likelihood of delinquent behavior and associations with delinquent peers because it builds up a stake in conformity that is antithetical to delinquency.

Moreover, since the delinquency variables are still embedded in a causal loop, the effect of commitment to conventional activities tends to resonate throughout the system. But, because of the increased saliency of a new variable, commitment to conventional activities, the reinforcing loop is now set in motion to *reduce* rather than increase delinquent and criminal involvement.

The variable of commitment to family has similar, albeit weaker, effects since the transition to the family is only beginning at these ages. Nevertheless, commitment to family is proposed to reduce both delinquent associations and delinquent values and to increase commitment to conventional activity. In general, as the individual takes on the responsibilities of family, the bond to conventional society increases, placing additional constraints on behavior and precluding further delinquency.

These changes do not occur in all cases, however, nor should they be expected to since many delinquents continue on to careers in adult crime. In the Philadelphia cohort of 1945, 51% of the juvenile delinquents were also adult offenders, and the more serious and prolonged the delinquent careers were, the greater the odds of an adult career (Wolfgang et al., 1987; Ch. 4).

The continuation of criminal careers can also be explained by the nature of the reciprocal effects included in this model. In general, extensive involvement in delinquency at earlier ages feeds back upon and weakens attachment to parents and commitment to school (see Figures 17.2 and 17.3). These variables, as well as involvement in delinquency itself, weaken later commitment to family and to conventional activities (Figure 17.4). Thus, these new variables, commitment to conventional activities and to family, are affected by the person's situation at earlier stages and do not "automatically" alter the probability of continued criminal involvement. If the initial bonds are extremely weak, the chances of new bonding variables being established to break the cycle towards criminal careers are low and it is likely that criminal behavior will continue.

Behavioral Trajectories

The manner in which reciprocal effects and developmental changes are interwoven in the interactional model can be explicated by the concept of behavioral trajectories. At early adolescence, some youths are very weakly attached to their parents, very weakly committed to school, and do not grant legitimacy to conventional values. As indicated above, they are the most likely youngsters for high delinquency involvement. (The term delinquency involvement summarizes the causal loop containing delinquent behavior, delinquent values, and association with delinquent peers.) In turn, high delinquency involvement further attenuates the bonding to parent and to school. This early adolescent situation continues during middle adolescence and substantially reduces the chances of the person reestablishing (or perhaps establishing) bonds to conventional society during late adolescence.

In brief, a behavioral trajectory is established that predicts increasing involvement in delinquency and crime. The initially weak bonds lead to high delinquency involvement, the high delinquency involvement further weakens the conventional bonds, and in combination both of these effects make it extremely difficult to reestablish bonds to conventional society at later ages. As a result, all of the factors tend to reinforce one

another over time to produce an extremely high probability of continued deviance.

On the other hand, one can imagine many young adolescents who, at the outset, are strongly attached to their parents, highly committed to school, and believe in conventional values. The theoretical model predicts that this high level of bonding buffers them from the world of delinquency. Moreover, the reciprocal character of this loop establishes a behavioral trajectory for these youths that tends towards increasing conformity. Their initial strong conventional bonds reduce the chances of involvement in delinquency and thereby increase the chances of commitment to conventional activities and the like at later ages.

Thus, we can conceive of at least two types of adolescents with differing and diverging behavioral trajectories. In one trajectory, social bonds become progressively weaker and delinquent behavior progressively more likely, while in the other commitment to conformity becomes progressively stronger and delinquent behavior progressively less likely.

Of course, if there are these extremes, there are also intermediate cases. In many ways they are the most interesting since their eventual outcome is much more in doubt. For example, there are some youths who have a relatively high level of attachment to parents but low commitment to school (or vice versa). These adolescents are more likely candidates for delinquency involvement than are youths with both high attachment and commitment. But, should the delinquent involvement occur, its feedback effect on the bonding variables is less certain. While the delinquency may further reduce the already weak commitment to school, the strong attachment to parents may serve as a buffer to offset some of the negative feedback. Such a situation, in which the initial bonding variables are neither extremely high nor extremely low, allows for rather varied patterns of interactive effects as the developmental process unfolds. Moreover, the prediction of the eventual outcome for such youths awaits more direct empirical evidence establishing the relative strength of these competing effects.

The concept of behavioral trajectories raises an important theoretical issue. It suggests that the initial values of the process variables play a central role in the entire process since they set the basic path of the behavioral trajectories. Because of this, it is theoretically important to account for variation in those initial values. In the present paper the role of one general class of variables, position in the social structure, is used to illustrate this issue.

STRUCTURAL EFFECTS

Structural variables, including race, class, sex, and community of residence, refer to the person's location in the structure of social roles and statuses. The manner in which they are incorporated in the interactional model is illustrated here by examining only one of them, social class of origin.

Although social class is often measured continuously, a categorical approach is more consistent with the present model and with most theories of delinquency that incorporate class as a major explanatory variable—for example, strain and social disorganization theories. For our purposes, the most important categories are the lower class, the working lower class, and the middle class.

The lower class is composed of those who are chronically or sporadically unemployed, receive welfare, and subsist at or below the poverty level. They are similar to Johnson's "underclass" (1979). The working lower class is composed of those with more stable work patterns, training for semiskilled jobs, and incomes that allow for some economic stability. For these families, however, the hold on even a marginal level of occupational and economic security is always tenuous. Finally, the middle class refers to all families above these lower levels. Middle-class families have achieved some degree of economic success and stability and can reasonably expect to remain at that level or improve their standing over time.

The manner in which the social class of origin affects the interactional variables and the behavioral trajectories can be demonstrated by comparing the life expectancies of children from lower- and middle-class families. As compared to children from a middle-class background, children from a lower-class background are more apt to have (1) disrupted family processes and environments (Conger, McCarty, Wang, Lahey, and Kroop, 1984; Wahler, 1980); (2) poorer preparation for school (Cloward and Ohlin, 1960); (3) belief structures influenced by the traditions of the American lower class (Miller, 1958; Anderson, 1976); and (4) greater exposure to neighborhoods with high rates of crime (Shaw and McKay, 1942; Braithwaite, 1981). The direction of all these effects is such that we would expect children from lower-class families to be *initially* less bonded to conventional society and more exposed to delinquent values, friends, and behaviors.

As one moves towards the working lower class, both the likelihood and the potency of the factors just listed decrease. As a result, the initial values of the interactional variables improve but, because of the tenuous nature of economic and social stability for these families, both the bonding variables and delinquency variables are still apt to lead to considerable amounts of delinquent conduct. Finally, youths from middle-class families, given their greater stability and economic security, are likely to start with a stronger family structure, greater stakes in conformity, and higher chances of success, and all of these factors are likely to reduce the likelihood of initial delinquent involvement.

In brief, the initial values of the interactional variables are systematically related to the social class of origin. Moreover, since these variables are reciprocally related, it follows logically that social class is systematically related to the behavioral trajectories described above. Youngsters from the lowest classes have the highest probability of moving forward on a trajectory of increasing delinquency. Starting from a position of low bonding to conventional institutions and a high delinquency environment, the reciprocal nature of the interrelationships leads inexorably towards extremely high rates of delinquent and criminal involvement. Such a view is consistent with prevalence data which show that by age 18, 50%, and by age 30, 70% of low SES minority males have an official police record (Wolfgang et al., 1987).

On the other hand, the expected trajectory of middle-class youths suggests that they will move toward an essentially conforming life-style, in which their stakes in conformity increase and more and more preclude serious and prolonged involvement in delinquency. Finally, because the initial values of the interactional variables are mixed and indecisive for children from lower-working-class homes, their behavioral trajectories are much more volatile and the outcome much less certain.

Summary: Interactional theory asserts that both the initial values of the process variables and their development over time are systematically related to the social class of origin. Moreover, parallel arguments can be made for other structural variables, especially those associated with class, such as race, ethnicity, and the social disorganization of the neighborhood. Like class of origin, these variables are systematically related to variables such as commitment to school and involvement in delinquent behavior, and therefore, as a group, these structural variables set the stage on which the reciprocal effects develop across the life cycle.

CONCLUSION

The present article has developed an interactional theory of delinquent behavior. Unlike traditional theories of delinquency, interactional theory does not view delinquency merely as an outcome or consequence of a social process. On the contrary, it views delinquent behavior as an active part of the developmental process, interacting with other social factors over time to determine the person's ultimate behavioral repertoire.

The initial impetus towards delinquency comes from a weakening of the person's bond to conventional society, represented, during adolescence, by attachment to parents, commitment to school, and belief in conventional values. Whenever these three links to conformity are attenuated, there is a substantially increased potential for delinquent behavior.

For that potential to be converted to delinquency, especially prolonged serious delinquency, however, a social setting in which delinquency is learned and reinforced is required. This setting is represented by associations with delinquent peers and delinquent values. These two variables, along with delinquent behavior itself, form a mutually reinforcing causal loop that leads towards increasing delinquency involvement over time.

Moreover, this interactive process develops over the person's life cycle, and the saliency of the theoretical concepts vary as the person ages. During early adolescence, the family is the most influential factor in bonding the youth to conventional society and reducing delinquency. As the youth matures and moves through middle adolescence, the world of friends, school, and youth culture becomes the dominant influence over behavior. Finally, as the person enters adulthood, new variables, especially commitment to conventional activities and to family, offer a number of new avenues to reshape the person's bond to society and involvement with delinquency.

Finally, interactional theory posits that these process variables are systematically related to the person's position in the social structure. Class, minority-group status, and the social disorganization of the neighborhood of residence all affect the initial values of the interactive variables as well as the behavioral trajectories. Youths from the most socially disadvantaged backgrounds begin the process least bonded to conventional society and most exposed to the world of delinquency. Furthermore, the reciprocal nature of the process increases the chances that they will continue on to a career of serious criminal involvement. On the other hand, youths from middle-class families enter a trajectory which is strongly oriented toward conformity and away from delinquency.

But, regardless of the initial starting points or the eventual outcome, the essential point of an interactional theory is that the causal process is a dynamic one that develops over the person's life. And delinquent behavior is a vital part of that process; it is clearly affected by, but it also affects, the bonding and learning variables that have always played a prominent role in sociological explanations of delinquency.

EPILOGUE

The version of interactional theory presented here is an initial statement of this perspective and does not represent a complete model of all the factors that are associated with delinquency. For example, the role of other structural variables, especially race and sex, which are so strongly correlated with delinquency, has to be fully explicated to better understand the sources of both the delinquency and bonding variables. Similarly, greater attention needs to be paid to the influence of early childhood behaviors and family processes since it is increasingly clear that delinquency is part of a progressive sequence that begins at much earlier ages (Patterson and Dishion, 1985; Loeber and Stouthamer-Loeber, 1986).

In addition, other process variables similar to those incorporated in Figure 17.2 through 4 need to be considered. For example, the general issue of gang membership and co-offending should be examined in an interactional setting as should concepts such as self-concept and self-efficacy. Finally, developmental stages have been represented here by rough age categories, and they require more careful and precise definition in terms of physical maturation and psychological growth.

Despite these, and no doubt other, limitations, this article accurately represents the basic structure of an interactional theory of delinquency. It has identified the theory's core concepts and described the manner in which they are reciprocally related to account for the initiation of delinquency and its development over time. In the coming years, the theory described here will be developed theoretically and tested empirically.[2]

Notes

1. The term "attachment to parents" is used throughout the text, but it is clear that parent surrogates—for example foster parents or guardians—can also perform this function.

2. The Rochester Youth Development Study, supported by the Office of Juvenile Justice and Delinquency Prevention and directed with my colleagues Alan Lizotte, Margaret Farnworth,

and Susan Stern, is designed to examine the basic causes and correlates of delinquency from this perspective.

References

AGNEW, ROBERT
1985   Social control theory and delinquency: A longitudinal test. Criminology 23:47–62.

AKERS, RONALD
1977   Deviant Behavior: A Social Learning Perspective. Belmont: Wadsworth.

AKERS, RONALD L., MARVIN D. KROHN, LONN LANZA-KADUCE, AND MARCIA RADOSEVICH
1979   Social learning theory and deviant behavior. American Sociological Review 44:635–655.

ANDERSON, ELIJAH
1976   A Place on the Corner. Chicago: University of Chicago Press.

BACHMAN, JERALD G., PATRICK M. O'MALLEY, AND JOHN JOHNSTON
1987   Youth in Transition: Adolescence to Adulthood—Change and Stability in the Lives of Young Men. Ann Arbor: Institute for Social Research.

BRAITHWAITE, JOHN
1981   The myth of social class and criminality reconsidered. American Sociological Review 46:36–58.

BREHM, J.W. AND ARTHUR R. COHEN
1962   Explorations in Cognitive Dissonance. New York: Wiley.

BURKETT, STEVEN R. AND BRUCE O. WARREN
1987   Religiosity, peer influence, and adolescent marijuana use: A panel study of underlying causal structures. Criminology 25:109–131.

CLOWARD, RICHARD A. AND LLOYD E. OHLIN
1960   Delinquency and Opportunity: A Theory of Delinquent Gangs. Glencoe: Free Press.

CONGER, RAND D.
1980   Juvenile delinquency: Behavior restraint or behavior facilitation? In Travis Hirschi and Michael Gottfredson (eds.), Understanding Crime. Beverly Hills: Sage.

CONGER, RAND D., JOHN A. MCCARTY, RAYMOND K. WANG, BENJAMIN B. LAHEY, AND JOSEPH P. KROOP
1984   Perception of child, child-rearing values, and emotional distress as mediating links between environmental stressors and observed maternal behavior. Child Development 55:2,234–2,247.

CULLEN, FRANCIS T.
1984   Rethinking Crime and Deviance Theory: The Emergence of a Structuring Tradition, Totowa, NJ: Rowman and Allanheld.

ELLIOTT, DELBERT S.
1985   The assumption that theories can be combined with increased explanatory power: Theoretical integrations. In Robert F. Meier (ed.).

Theoretical Methods in Criminology. Beverly Hills: Sage.

ELLIOTT, DELBERT S., SUZANNE S. AGETON, AND RACHELLE J. CANTER
1979   An integrated theoretical perspective on delinquent behavior. Journal of Research on Crime and Delinquency 16:3–27.

ELLIOTT, DELBERT S., DAVID HUIZINGA, AND SUZANNE S. AGETON
1985   Explaining Delinquency and Drug Use. Beverly Hills: Sage.

ELLIOTT, DELBERT S. AND HARWIN L. VOSS
1974   Delinquency and Dropout. Lexington: Lexington Books.

FESTINGER, LEON
1957   A Theory of Cognitive Dissonance. Stanford: Stanford University Press.

GLUECK, SHELDON AND ELEANOR GLUECK
1950   Unraveling Juvenile Delinquency. Cambridge: Harvard University Press.

HANUSHEK, ERIC A. AND JOHN E. JACKSON
1977   Statistical Methods for Social Scientists. New York: Academic Press.

HEISE, DAVID R.
1975   Causal Analysis. New York: Wiley.

HINDELANG, MICHAEL J.
1974   Moral evaluations of illegal behaviors. Social Problems 21:370–384.

HINDELANG, MICHAEL J., TRAVIS HIRSCHI, AND JOSEPH G. WEIS
1981   Measuring Delinquency. Beverly Hills: Sage.

HIRSCHI, TRAVIS
1969   Causes of Delinquency. Berkeley: University of California Press.

HUIZINGA, DAVID AND DELBERT S. ELLIOTT
1986   The Denver High-Risk Delinquency Project. Proposal Submitted to the Office of Juvenile Justice and Delinquency Prevention.

JOHNSON, RICHARD E.
1979   Juvenile Delinquency and Its Origins. Cambridge: Cambridge University Press.

KANDEL, DENISE B. AND JOHN A. LOGAN
1984   Patterns of drug use from adolescence to young adulthood I. Periods of risk for initiation, continued risk and discontinuation. American Journal of Public Health 74:660–667.

KROHN, MARVIN D. AND JAMES MASSEY
1980   Social and delinquent behavior: An examination of the elements of the social bond. Sociological Quarterly 21, 529–543.

LAGRANGE, RANDY L. AND HELENE RASKIN WHITE
1985   Age differences in delinquency: A test of theory. Criminology 23:19–46.

LISKA, ALLEN AND MARK REED
1985   Ties to conventional institutions and delinquency. American Sociological Review 50:547–560.

LOEBER, ROLF AND MAGDA STOUTHAMER-LOEBER
1986   Family factors as correlates and predictors of juvenile conduct problems and delinquency. In

Norval Morris and Michael Tonry (eds.). Crime and Justice: An Annual Review of Research Chicago: University of Chicago Press.

MATSUEDA, ROSS
1982   Testing social control theory and differential association. American Sociological Review 47:489–504.

MILLER, WALTER B.
1958   Lower class culture as a generating milieu of gang delinquency. Journal of Social Issues 14:5–19.

PATERNOSTER, RAYMOND, LINDA E. SALTZMAN, GORDON P. WALDO, AND THEODORE G. CHIRICOS
1982   Perceived risk and deterrence: Methodological artifacts in perceptual deterrence research. Journal of Criminal Law and Criminology 73:1,238–1,258.

PATERNOSTER, RAYMOND, LINDA E. SALTZMAN, THEODORE G. CHIRICOS, AND GORDON P. WALDO
1983   Perceived risk and social control: Do sanctions really deter? Law and Society Review 17:457–479.

PATTERSON, GERALD R. AND THOMAS S. DISHION
1985   Contributions of families and peers to delinquency. Criminology 23:63–80.

POLK, KENNETH, CHRISTINE ADLER, GORDON BAZEMORE, GERALD BLAKE, SHEILA CORDRAY, GARRY COVENTRY, JAMES GALVIN, AND MARK TEMPLE
1981   Becoming Adult: An Analysis of Maturational Development from Age 16 to 30 of a Cohort of Young Men. Final Report of the Marion County Youth Study. Eugene: University of Oregon.

POOLE, ERIC D. AND ROBERT M. REGOLI
1979   Parental Support, delinquent friends and delinquency: A test of interactional effects. Journal of Criminal Law and Criminology 70:188–193.

SCHOENBERG, RONALD J.
1975   A Structural Model of Delinquency. Unpublished doctoral dissertation. Seattle: University of Washington.

SHAW, CLIFFORD R. AND HENRY D. MCKAY
1942   Juvenile Delinquency and Urban Areas. Chicago: University of Chicago Press.

SHORT, JAMES F. JR., AND FRED L. STRODTBECK
1965   Group Processes and Gang Delinquency. Chicago: University of Chicago Press.

SNYDER, J. AND GERALD PATTERSON
In Press Family interactions and delinquent behavior. Child Development.

THORNBERRY, TERENCE P.
1987   Reflections on the advantages and disadvantages of theoretical integration. Presented at the Albany Conference on Theoretical Integration in the Study of Crime and Deviance.

THORNBERRY, TERENCE P. AND R.L. CHRISTENSON
1984   Unemployment and criminal involvement: An investigation of reciprocal causal structures. American Sociological Review 49:398–411.

THORNBERRY, TERENCE P., MARGARET FARNWORTH, AND ALAN LIZOTTE
1986   A Panel Study of Reciprocal Causal Model of

Delinquency. Proposal submitted to the Office of Juvenile Justice and Delinquency Prevention.

THORNBERRY, TERENCE P., MELANIE MOORE, AND R.L. CHRISTENSON
1985   The effect of dropping out of high school on subsequent delinquent behavior. Criminology 23:3–18.

WAHLER, R.
1980   The insular mother: Her problems in parent-child treatment. Journal of Applied Behavior Analysis 13:207–219.

WEIS, JOSEPH G. AND JOHN SEDERSTROM
1981   The Prevention of Serious Delinquency: What to Do? Washington, D.C., U.S. Department of Justice.

WOLFGANG, MARVIN E., TERENCE P. THORNBERRY, AND ROBERT M. FIGLIO
1987   From Boy to Man—From Delinquency to Crime: Followup to the Philadelphia Birth Cohort of 1945. Chicago: University of Chicago Press.

QUESTIONS FOR DISCUSSION

1. Thornberry, in attempting to create an interactional theory of juvenile delinquency, suggests that there are three limitations of existing approaches that have sought to explain delinquency. Discuss these limitations.

2. Discuss the differences between recursive models of delinquency and reciprocal models of delinquency.

3. What are the major differences between the theoretical models for early, middle, and late adolescence? Which of these differences do you think are most important?

APPLICATIONS

1. According to Thornberry's model do you think the family or the school is more important in affecting a young person's propensity to become delinquent?

2. As an expert on juvenile delinquency, you have been asked to provide recommendations about how the family and schools could better involve themselves in the lives of young people and consequently reduce the delinquency problem. What would your recommendations be? Why?

KEY TERMS

affective   relating to or influencing feelings or emotions.

antithetical   being in direct or diametric opposition.

attenuation   lessening the amount of something or weakening it in relationship to something else.

causal loop   an act or event which is antecedently responsible for a subsequent effect, which then continues over time to reproduce the same or similar effect.

exogenous variables   those variables introduced or produced from outside a theoretical model that has already attempted to explain a phenomena.

impetus   a driving force; stimulation or encouragement resulting in increased activity.

reciprocal effects   when two or more variables are not mutually exclusive, but perpetually and mutually reinforce each other over time.

salient   something that projects outward and away from its surroundings; something that stands out or is striking.

social nexus   a social phenomena that has causal links or connections to other social phenomenon.

tenuous   having little substance or strength; as when a theory or assumption about human behavior is thought to be on "shaky ground."

12

Girls' Crime and Woman's Place: Toward a Feminist Model of Female Delinquency

Meda Chesney-Lind

Associate Professor of Women's Studies, Center for Youth Research at the University of Hawaii, Manoa

This article argues that existing delinquency theories are fundamentally inadequate to the task of explaining female delinquency and official reactions to girls' deviance. To establish this, the article first reviews the degree of the androcentric bias in the major theories of delinquent behavior. Then the need for a feminist model of female delinquency is explored by reviewing the available evidence on girls' offending. This review shows that the extensive focus on disadvantaged males in public settings has meant that girls' victimization and the relationship between that experience and girls' crime has been systematically ignored. Also missed has been the central role played by the juvenile justice system in the sexualization of female delinquency and the criminalization of girls' survival strategies. Finally, it will be suggested that the official actions of the juvenile justice system should be understood as major forces in women's oppression as they have historically served to reinforce the obedience of all young women to the demands of patriarchal authority no matter how abusive and arbitrary.

I ran away so many times. I tried anything man, and they wouldn't believe me. . . . As far as they are concerned they think I'm the problem. You know, runaway, bad label. (Statement of a 16-year-old girl who, after having been physically and sexually assaulted, started running away from home and was arrested as a "runaway" in Hawaii.)

"Girls' Crime and Woman's Place: Toward a Feminist Model of Female Delinquency," *Crime and Delinquency*, 35:1 (January 1989), pp. 5–29. Reprinted by permission of the publisher, Sage Publications. Inc.

You know, one of these days I'm going to have to kill myself before you guys are gonna listen to me. I can't stay at home. (Statement of a 16-year-old Tucson runaway with a long history of physical abuse [Davidson, 1982, p. 26].)

Who is the typical female delinquent? What causes her to get into trouble? What happens to her if she is caught? These are questions that few members of the general public could answer quickly. By contrast, almost every citizen can talk about "delinquency," by which they generally mean male delinquency, and can even generate some fairly specific complaints about, for example, the failure of the juvenile justice system to deal with such problems as "the alarming increase in the rate of serious juvenile crime" and the fact that the juvenile courts are too lenient on juveniles found guilty of these offenses (Opinion Research Corporation, 1982).

This situation should come as no surprise since even the academic study of delinquent behavior has, for all intents and purposes, been the study of male delinquency. "The delinquent is a rogue male" declared Albert Cohen (1955, p. 140) in his influential book on gang delinquency. More than a decade later, Travis Hirschi, in his equally important book entitled *The Causes of Delinquency*, relegated women to a footnote that suggested, somewhat apologetically, that "in the analysis that follows, the 'non-Negro' becomes 'white,' and the girls disappear."

This pattern of neglect is not all that unusual. All areas of social inquiry have been notoriously gender blind. What is perhaps less well understood is that theories developed to describe the misbehavior of working- or lower-class male youth fail to capture the full nature of delinquency in America; and, more to the point, are woefully inadequate when it comes to explaining female misbehavior and official reactions to girls' deviance.

To be specific, delinquent behavior involves a range of activities far broader than those committed by the stereotypical street gang. Moreover, many more young people than the small visible group of "troublemakers" that exist on every intermediate and high school campus commit some sort of juvenile offense and many of these youth have brushes with the law. One study revealed, for example, that 33% of all the boys and 14% of the girls born in 1958 had at least one contact with the police before reaching their eighteenth birthday (Tracy, Wolfgang, and Figlio, 1985, p. 5). Indeed, some forms of serious delinquent behavior, such as drug and alcohol abuse, are far more frequent than the stereotypical delinquent behavior of gang fighting and vandalism and appear to cut across class and gender lines.

Studies that solicit from youth themselves the volume of their delinquent behavior consistently confirm that large numbers of adolescents engage in at least some form of misbehavior that could result in their arrest. As a consequence, it is largely trivial misconduct, rather than the commission of serious crime, that shapes the actual nature of juvenile delinquency. One national study of youth aged 15–21, for example, noted that only 5% reported involvement in a serious assault, and only 6% reported having participated in a gang fight. In contrast, 81% admitted to having used alcohol, 44% admitted to having used marijuana, 37% admitted to having been publicly drunk, 42% admitted to having skipped classes (truancy), 44% admitted having had sexual intercourse, and 15% admitted to having stolen from the family (McGarrell and Flanagan, 1985, p. 363). Clearly, not all of these activities are as serious as the others. It is important to remem-

ber that young people can be arrested for all of these behaviors.

Indeed, one of the most important points to understand about the nature of delinquency, and particularly female delinquency, is that youth can be taken into custody for both criminal acts and a wide variety of what are often called "status offenses." These offenses, in contrast to criminal violations, permit the arrest of youth for a wide range of behaviors that are violations of parental authority: "running away from home," "being a person in need of supervision," "minor in need of supervision," being "incorrigible," "beyond control," truant, in need of "care and protection," and so on. Juvenile delinquents, then, are youths arrested for either criminal or noncriminal status offenses; and, as this discussion will establish, the role played by uniquely juvenile offenses is by no means insignificant, particularly when considering the character of female delinquency.

Examining the types of offenses for which youth are actually arrested, it is clear that again most are arrested for the less serious criminal acts and status offenses. Of the one and a half million youth arrested in 1983, for example, only 4.5% of these arrests were for such serious violent offenses as murder, rape, robbery, or aggravated assault (McGarrell and Flanagan, 1985, p. 479). In contrast, 21% were arrested for a single offense (larceny, theft) much of which, particularly for girls, is shoplifting (Sheldon and Horvath, 1986).

Table 1 presents the five most frequent offenses for which male and female youth are arrested and from this it can be seen that while trivial offenses dominate both male and female delinquency, trivial offenses, particularly status offenses, are more significant in the case of girls' arrests; for example the five offenses listed in Table 1 account for nearly three-quarters of female offenses and only slightly more than half of male offenses.

More to the point, it is clear that, though routinely neglected in most delinquency research, status offenses play a significant role in girls' official delinquency. Status offenses accounted for about 25.2% of all girls' arrests in 1986 (as compared to 26.9%

TABLE 1 Rank Order of Adolescent Male and Female Arrests for Specific Offenses, 1977 and 1986

Male				Female			
1977	% of Total Arrests	1986	% of Total Arrests	1977	% of Total Arrests	1986	% of Total Arrests
(1) Larceny-theft	18.4	(1) Larceny-theft	20.4	(1) Larceny-theft	27.0	(1) Larceny-theft	25.7
(2) Other offenses	14.5	(2) Other offenses	16.5	(2) Runaway	22.9	(2) Runaway	20.5
(3) Burglary	13.0	(3) Burglary	9.1	(3) Other offenses	14.2	(3) Other offenses	14.8
(4) Drug abuse violations	6.5	(4) Vandalism	7.0	(4) Liquor laws	5.5	(4) Liquor laws	8.4
(5) Vandalism	6.4	(5) Vandalism	6.3	(5) Curfew & loitering violations	4.0	(5) Curfew & loitering violations	4.7

	1977	1986	% N change		1977	1986	% N change
Arrests for serious violent offenses[a]	4.2%	4.7%	2.3	Arrests for serious violent offenses	1.8%	2.0%	+1.7
Arrests of all violent offenses[b]	7.6%	9.6%	+10.3	Arrests of all violent offenses	5.1%	7.1%	+26.0
Arrests for status offenses[c]	8.8%	8.3%	−17.8	Arrests for status offenses	26.9%	25.2%	−14.7

SOURCE: Compiled from Federal Bureau of Investigation (1987, p. 169).

a. Arrests for murder and nonnegligent manslaughter, robbery, forcible rape, and aggravated assault.
b. Also includes arrests for other assaults.
c. Arrests for curfew and loitering law violation and runaway.

in 1977) and only about 8.3% of boys' arrests (compared to 8.8% in 1977). These figures are somewhat surprising since dramatic declines in arrests of youth for these offenses might have been expected as a result of the passage of the Juvenile Justice and Delinquency Prevention Act in 1974, which, among other things, encouraged jurisdictions to divert and deinstitutionalize youth charged with noncriminal offenses. While the figures in Table 1 do show a decline in these arrests, virtually all of this decline occurred in the 1970s. Between 1982 and 1986 girls' curfew arrests increased by 5.1% and runaway arrests increased by a striking 24.5%. And the upward trend continues; arrests of girls for running away increased by 3% between 1985 and 1986 and arrests of girls for curfew violations increased by 12.4% (Federal Bureau of Investigation, 1987, p. 171).

Looking at girls who find their way into juvenile court populations, it is apparent that status offenses continue to play an important role in the character of girls' official delinquency. In total, 34% of the girls, but only 12% of the boys, were referred to court in 1983 for these offenses (Snyder and Finnegan, 1987, pp. 6–20). Stating these figures differently, they mean that while males constituted about 81% of all delinquency referrals, females constituted 46% of all status offenders in courts (Snyder and Finnegan, 1987, p. 20). Similar figures were reported for 1977 by Black and Smith (1981). Fifteen years earlier, about half of the girls and about 20% of the boys were referred to court for these offenses (Children's Bureau, 1965). These data do seem to signal a drop in female status offense referrals, though not as dramatic a decline as might have been expected.

For many years statistics showing large numbers of girls arrested and referred for status offenses were taken to be representative of the different types of male and female delinquency. However, self-report studies of male and female delinquency do not reflect the dramatic differences in misbehavior found in official statistics. Specifically, it appears that girls charged with these non-

TABLE 2 Comparison of Sex Differences In Self-Reported and Official Delinquency for Selected Offenses

	Self-Report[a] M/F Ratios (1976)	Official Statistics[b] M/F Arrest Ratio	
		1976	1986
Theft	3.5:1 (Felony Theft) 3.4:1 (Minor Theft)	2.5:1	2.7:1
Drug Violation	1:1 (Hard Drug Use)	5.1:1	6.0:1 (Drug Abuse Violation)
Vandalism	5.1:1	12.3:1	10.0:1
Disorderly Conduct	2.8:1	4.5:1	4.4:1
Serious Assault	3.5:1 (Felony Assault)	5.6:1	5.5:1 (Aggravated Assault)
Minor Assault	3.4:1	3.8:1	3.4:1
Status Offense	1.6:1	1.3:1	1.1:1 (Runaway, Curfew)

[a] Extracted from Rachelle Canter (1982, p. 383).
[b] Compiled from Federal Bureau of Investigation (1986, p. 173).

criminal status offenses have been and continue to be significantly over-represented in court populations.

Teilmann and Landry (1981) compared girls' contribution to arrests for runaway and incorrigibility with girls' self-reports of these two activities, and found a 10.4% overrepresentation of females among those arrested for runaway and a 30.9% overrepresentation in arrests for incorrigibility. From these data they concluded that girls are "arrested for status offenses at a higher rate than boys, when contrasted to their self-reported delinquency rates" (Teilmann and Landry, 1981, pp. 74–75). These findings were confirmed in another recent self-report study. Figueira-McDonough (1985, p. 277) analyzed the delinquent conduct of 2,000 youths and found "no evidence of greater involvement of females in status offenses." Similarly, Canter (1982) found in the National Youth Survey that there was no evidence of greater female involvement, compared to males, in any category of delinquent behavior. Indeed, in this sample, males were significantly more likely than females to report status offenses.

Utilizing Canter's national data on the extensiveness of girls self-reported delinquency and comparing these figures to official arrests of girls (see Table 2) reveals that girls are underrepresented in every arrest category with the exception of status offenses and larceny theft. These figures strongly suggest that official practices tend to exaggerate the role played by status offenses in girls' delinquency.

Delinquency theory, because it has virtually ignored female delinquency, failed to pursue anomalies such as these found in the few early studies examining gender differences in delinquent behavior. Indeed, most delinquency theories have ignored status offenses. As a consequence, there is considerable question as to whether existing theories that were admittedly developed to explain male delinquency can adequately explain female delinquency. Clearly, these theories were much influenced by the notion that class and protest masculinity were at the core of delinquency. Will the "add women and stir approach" be sufficient? Are these really theories of delinquent behavior as some (Simons, Miller, and Aigner, 1980) have argued?

This article will suggest that they are not. The extensive focus on male delinquency and the inattention the role played by patriarchal arrangements in the generation of adolescent delinquency and conformity has rendered the major delinquency theories fundamentally inadequate to the task of explaining female behavior. There is, in short, an urgent need to rethink current models in light of girls' situation in patriarchal society.

To understand why such work must occur, it is first necessary to explore briefly the dimensions of the androcentric bias found in the dominant and influential delinquency theories. Then the need for a feminist model of female delinquency will be explored by reviewing the available evidence on girls' offending. This discussion will also establish that the proposed overhaul of delinquency theory is not, as some might think, solely an academic exercise. Specifically, it is incorrect to assume that because girls are charged with less serious offenses, they actually have few problems and are treated gently when they are drawn into the juvenile justice system. Indeed, the extensive focus on disadvantaged males in public settings has meant that girls' victimization and the relationship between that experience and girls' crime has been systematically ignored. Also missed has been the central role played by the juvenile justice system in the sexualization of girls' delinquency and the criminalization of girls' survival strategies. Finally, it will be suggested that the official actions of the juvenile justice system should be understood as major forces in girls' oppression as they have historically served to reinforce the obedience of all young women to demands of patriarchal authority no matter how abusive and arbitrary.

The Romance of the Gang or the *West Side Story* Syndrome

From the start, the field of delinquency research focused on visible lower-class male delinquency, often justifying the neglect of girls in the most cavalier of terms. Take, for example, the extremely important and influential work of Clifford R. Shaw and Henry D. McKay who beginning in 1929, utilized an ecological approach to the study of juvenile delinquency. Their impressive work, particularly *Juvenile Delinquency in Urban Areas* (1942) and intensive biographical case studies such as Shaw's *Brothers in Crime* (1938) and *The Jackroller* (1930), set the stage for much of the subcultural research on gang delinquency. In their ecological work, however, Shaw and McKay analyzed only the official arrest data on male delinquents in Chicago and repeatedly referred to these rates as "delinquency rates" (though they occasionally made parenthetical reference to data on female delinquency) (see Shaw and McKay, 1942, p. 356). Similarly, their biographical work traced only male experiences with the law; in *Brothers in Crime*, for example, the delinquent and criminal careers of five brothers were followed for fifteen years. In none of these works was any justification given for the equation of male delinquency with delinquency.

Early fieldwork on delinquent gangs in Chicago set the stage for another style of delinquency research. Yet here too researchers were interested only in talking to and following the boys. Thrasher studied over a thousand juvenile gangs in Chicago during roughly the same period as Shaw and McKay's more quantitative work was being done. He spent approximately one page out of 600 on the five of six female gangs he encountered in his field observation of juvenile gangs. Thrasher (1927, p. 228) did mention, in passing, two factors he felt accounted for the lower number of girl gangs: "First, the social patterns for the behavior of girls, powerfully backed by the great weight of tradition and custom, are contrary to the gang and its activities; and secondly, girls, even in urban disorganized areas, are much more closely supervised and guarded than boys and usually well incorporated into the family groups or some other social structure."

Another major theoretical approach to delinquency focuses on the subculture of lower-class communities as a generating milieu for delinquent behavior. Here again, noted delinquency researchers concentrated either exclusively or nearly exclusively on male lower-class culture. For example, Cohen's work on the subculture of delinquent gangs, which was written nearly twenty years after Thrasher's, deliberately considers only boys' delinquency. His justification for the exclusion of the girls is quite illuminating:

> My skin has nothing of the quality of down or silk, there is nothing limpid or flute-like about my voice, I am a total loss with needle and thread, my posture and carriage are wholly lacking in grace. These imperfections cause me no distress—if anything, they are gratifying—because I conceive myself to be a man and want people to recognize me as a full-fledged, unequivocal representative of my sex. My wife, on the other hand, is not greatly embarrassed by her inability to tinker with or talk about the internal organs of a car, by her modest attainments in arithmetic or by her inability to lift heavy objects. Indeed, I am reliably informed that many women—I do not suggest that my wife is among them—often affect ignorance, frailty and emotional instability because to do otherwise would be out of keeping with a reputation for indubitable femininity. In short, people do not simply want to excel; they want to excel as a man or as a woman [Cohen, 1955, p. 138.]

From this Cohen (1955, p. 140) concludes that the delinquent response "however it may be condemned by others on moral grounds has least one virtue; it incontestably confirms, in the eyes of all concerned, his essential masculinity." Much the same line of argument appears in Miller's influential paper on the "focal concerns" of lower-class life with its emphasis on importance of trouble, toughness, excitement, and so on. These, the author concludes, predispose poor youth (particularly male youth) to criminal misconduct. However, Cohen's comments are notable in their candor and probably capture both the allure that male delinquency has had for at least some male theorists as well as the fact that sexism has rendered the female delinquent as irrelevant to their work.

Emphasis on blocked opportunities (sometimes the "strain" theories) emerged out of the work of Robert K. Merton (1938) who stressed the need to consider how some social structures exert a definite pressure upon certain persons in the society to engage in nonconformist rather than conformist conduct. His work influenced research largely

through the efforts of Cloward and Ohlin who discussed access to "legitimate" and "illegitimate" opportunities for male youth. No mention of female delinquency can be found in their *Delinquency and Opportunity* except that women are blamed for male delinquency. Here, the familiar notion is that boys, "engulfed by a feminine world and uncertain of their own identification . . . tend to 'protest' against femininity" (Cloward and Ohlin, 1960, p. 49). Early efforts by Ruth Morris to test this hypothesis utilizing different definitions of success based on the gender of respondents met with mixed success. Attempting to assess boys' perceptions about access to economic power status while for girls the variable concerned itself with the ability or inability of girls to maintain effective relationships, Morris was unable to find a clear relationship between "female" goals and delinquency (Morris, 1964).

The work of Edwin Sutherland emphasized the fact that criminal behavior was learned in intimate personal groups. His work, particularly the notion of differential association, which also influenced Cloward and Ohlin's work, was similarly male oriented as much of his work was affected by case studies he conducted of male criminals. Indeed, in describing his notion of how differential association works, he utilized male examples (e.g., "In an area where the delinquency rate is high a boy who is sociable, gregarious, active, and athletic is very likely to come in contact with the other boys, in the neighborhood, learn delinquent behavior from them, and become a gangster" [Sutherland, 1978, p. 131]). Finally, the work of Travis Hirschi on the social bonds that control delinquency ("social control theory") was, as was stated earlier, derived out of research on male delinquents (though he, at least, studied delinquent behavior as reported by youth themselves rather than studying only those who were arrested).

Such a persistent focus on social class and such an absence of interest in gender in delinquency is ironic for two reasons. As even the work of Hirschi demonstrated, and as later studies would validate, a clear relationship between social class position and delinquency is problematic, while it is clear that gender has a dramatic and consistent effect on delinquency causation (Hagan, Gillis, and Simpson, 1985). The second irony, and one that consistently eludes even contemporary delinquency theorists, is the fact that while the academics had little interest in female delinquents, the same could not be said for the juvenile justice system. Indeed, work on the early history of the separate system for youth, reveals that concerns about girls' immoral conduct were really at the center of what some have called the "childsaving movement" (Platt, 1969) that set up the juvenile justice system.

"The Best Place to Conquer Girls"

The movement to establish separate institutions for youthful offenders was part of the larger Progressive movement, which among other things was keenly concerned about prostitution and other "social evils" (white slavery and the like) (Schlossman and Wallach, 1978; Rafter, 1985, p. 54). Childsaving was also a celebration of women's domesticity, though ironically women were influential in the movement (Platt, 1969; Rafter, 1985). In a sense, privileged women found, in the moral purity crusades and the establishment of family courts, a safe outlet for their energies. As the legitimate guardians of the moral sphere, women were seen as uniquely suited to patrol the normative boundaries of the social order. Embracing rather than challenging these stereotypes, women carved out for themselves a role in the policing of women and girls (Feinman, 1980; Freedman, 1981; Messerschmidt, 1987). Ultimately, many of the early childsavers' activities revolved around the monitoring of young girls', particularly immigrant girls', behavior to prevent their straying from the path.

This state of affairs was the direct consequence of a disturbing coalition between some feminists and the more conservative social purity movement. Concerned about female victimization and distrustful of male (and to some degree female) sexuality, notable women leaders, including Susan B. Anthony, found common cause with the social purists around such issues as opposing the regulation of prostitution and raising the age of consent (see Messerschmidt, 1987). The consequences of such a partnership are an important lesson for contemporary feminist movements that are, to some extent, faced with the same possible coalitions.

Girls were the clear losers in this reform effort. Studies of early family court activity reveal that virtually all the girls who appeared in these courts were charged for immorality or waywardness (Chesney-Lind, 1971; Schlossman and Wallach, 1978; Shelden, 1981). More to the point, the sanctions for such misbehavior were extremely severe. For example, in Chicago (where the first family court was founded), one-half of the girl delinquents, but only one-fifth of the boy delinquents, were sent to reformatories between 1899–1909. In Milwaukee, twice as many girls as boys were committed to training schools (Schlossman and Wallach, 1978, p. 72); and in Memphis females were twice as likely as males to be committed to training schools (Shelden, 1981, p. 70).

In Honolulu, during the period 1929–1930, over half of the girls referred to court were charged with "immorality," which meant evidence of sexual intercourse. In addition, another 30% were charged with "waywardness." Evidence of immorality was vigorously pursued by both arresting officers and social workers through lengthy questioning of the girl and, if possible, males with whom she was suspected of having sex. Other evidence of "exposure" was provided by gynecological examinations that were routinely ordered in virtually all girls' cases. Doctors, who understood the purpose of such examinations, would routinely note the condition of the hymen: "admits intercourse hymen rupture," "no laceration," "hymen ruptured" are typical of the notations on the forms. Girls during this period were also twice as likely as males to be detained where they spent five times as long on the average as their male counterparts. They were also nearly three times more likely to be sentenced to the training school (Chesney-Lind, 1971). Indeed, girls were half of those committed to training schools in Honolulu well into the 1950s (Chesney-Lind, 1973).

Not surprisingly, large numbers of girls' reformatories and training schools were established during this period as well as places of "rescue and reform." For example, Schlossman and Wallach note that 23 facilities for girls were opened during the 1910–1920 decade (in contrast to the 1850–1910 period where the average was 5 reformatories per decade [Schlossman and Wallach, 1985, p. 70]), and these institutions did much to set the tone of official response to female delinquency. Obsessed with precocious female sexuality, the institutions set about to isolate the females from all contact with males while housing them in bucolic settings. The intention was to hold the girls until marriageable age and to occupy them in domestic pursuits during their sometimes lengthy incarceration.

The links between these attitudes and those of juvenile courts some decades later are, of course, arguable; but an examination of the record of the court does not inspire confidence. A few examples of the persistence of what might be called a double standard of juvenile justice will suffice here.

A study conducted in the early 1970s in a Connecticut training school revealed large numbers of girls incarcerated "for their own protection." Explaining this pattern, one judge explained, "Why most of the girls I commit are for status offenses, I figure if a girl is about to get pregnant, we'll keep her until she's sixteen and then ADC (Aid to Dependent Children) will pick her up" (Rogers, 1972). For more evidence of official concern with adolescent sexual misconduct, consider Linda Hancock's (1981) content analysis of police referrals in Australia. She noted that 40% of the referrals of girls to court made specific mention of sexual and moral conduct compared to only 5% of the referrals of boys. These sorts of results suggest that all youthful female misbehavior has traditionally been subject to surveillance for evidence of sexual misconduct.

Gelsthorpe's (1986) field research on an English police station also revealed how everyday police decision making resulted in disregard of complaints about male problem behavior in contrast to active concern about the "problem behavior" of girls. Notable, here, was the concern about the girls' sexual behavior. In one case, she describes police persistence in pursuing a "moral danger" order for a 14-year-old picked up in a truancy run. Over the objections of both the girl's parents and the Social Services Department and in the face of a written confirmation from a surgeon that the girl was still premenstrual, the officers pursued the application because, in one officer's words, "I know her sort . . . free and easy. I'm still suspicious that she might be pregnant. Anyway, if the doctor can't provide evidence we'll do her for being beyond the care and control of her parents, no one can dispute that. Running away is proof" (Gelsthorpe, 1986, p. 136). This sexualization of female deviance is highly significant and explains why criminal activities by girls (particularly in past years) were overlooked so long as they did not appear to signal defiance of parental control (see Smith, 1978).

In their historic obsession about precocious female sexuality, juvenile justice workers rarely reflected on the broader nature of female misbehavior or on the sources of this misbehavior. It was enough for them that girls' parents reported them out of control. Indeed, court personnel tended to "sexualize" virtually all female defiance that lent itself to that construction and ignore other misbehavior (Chesney-Lind, 1973, 1977; Smith, 1978). For their part, academic students of delinquency were so entranced with the notion of the delinquent as a romantic rogue male challenging a rigid and unequal class structure, that they spent little time on middle-class delinquency, trivial offenders, or status offenders. Yet it is clear that the vast bulk of delinquent behavior is of this type.

Some have argued that such an imbalance in theoretical work is appropriate as minor misconduct, while troublesome, is not a threat to the safety and well-being of the community. This argument might be persuasive if two additional points could be established. One, that some small number of youth "specialize" in serious criminal behavior while the rest commit only minor acts, and, two, that the juvenile court rapidly releases those youth that come into its purview for these minor offenses, thus reserving resources for the most serious youthful offenders.

The evidence is mixed on both of these points. Determined efforts to locate the "serious juvenile offender" have failed to locate a group of offenders who specialize only in serious violent offenses. For example, in a recent analysis of a national self-report data set, Elliott and his associates noted "there is little evidence for specialization in serious violent offending; to the contrary, serious violent offending appears to be embedded in a more general involvement in a wide range of serious and non-serious offenses" (Elliott, Huizinga, and Morse, 1987). Indeed, they went so far as to speculate that arrest histories that tend to highlight particular types of offenders reflect variations in police policy, practices, and processes of uncovering crime as well as underlying offending patterns.

More to the point, police and court personnel are, it turns out, far more interested in youth they charge with trivial or status offenses than anyone imagined. Efforts to deinstitutionalize "status offenders," for example, ran afoul of juvenile justice personnel who had little interest in releasing youth guilty of noncriminal offenses (Chesney-Lind, 1988). As has been established, much of this is a product of the system's history that encouraged court officers to involve themselves in the noncriminal behavior of youth in order to "save" them from a variety of social ills.

Indeed, parallels can be found between the earlier Progressive period and current national efforts to challenge the deinstitutionalization components of the Juvenile Justice and Delinquency Prevention Act of 1974. These come complete with their celebration of family values and concerns about youthful independence. One of the arguments against the act has been that it allegedly gave children the "freedom to run away" (Office of Juvenile Justice and Delinquency Prevention, 1985) and that it has hampered "reunions" of "missing" children with their parents (Office of Juvenile Justice, 1986). Suspicions about teen sexuality are reflected in excessive concern about the control of teen prostitution and child pornography.

Opponents have also attempted to justify continued intervention into the lives of status offenders by suggesting that without such

intervention, the youth would "escalate" to criminal behavior. Yet there is little evidence that status offenders escalate to criminal offenses, and the evidence is particularly weak when considering female delinquents (particularly white female delinquents) (Datesman and Aickin, 1984). Finally, if escalation is occurring, it is likely the product of the justice system's insistence on enforcing status offense laws, thereby forcing youth in crisis to live lives of escaped criminals.

The most influential delinquency theories, however, have largely ducked the issue of status and trivial offenses and, as a consequence, neglected the role played by the agencies of official control (police, probation officers, juvenile court judges, detention home workers, and training school personnel) in the shaping of the "delinquency problem." When confronting the less than distinct picture that emerges from the actual distribution of delinquent behavior, however, the conclusion that agents of social control have considerable discretion in labeling or choosing not to label particular behavior as "delinquent" is inescapable. This symbiotic relationship between delinquent behavior and the official response to that behavior is particularly critical when the question of female delinquency is considered.

Toward a Feminist Theory of Delinquency

To sketch out completely a feminist theory of delinquency is a task beyond the scope of this article. It may be sufficient, at this point, simply to identify a few of the most obvious problems with attempts to adapt male-oriented theory to explain female conformity and deviance. Most significant of these is the fact that all existing theories were developed with no concern about gender stratification.

Note that this is not simply an observation about the power of gender roles (though this power is undeniable). It is increasingly clear that gender stratification in patriarchal society is as powerful a system as is class. A feminist approach to delinquency means construction of explanations of female behavior that are sensitive to its patriarchal context. Feminist analysis of delinquency would also examine ways in which agencies of social control—the police, the courts, and the prisons—act in ways to reinforce woman's place in male society (Harris, 1977; Chesney-Lind, 1986). Efforts to construct a feminist model of delinquency must first and foremost be sensitive to the situations of girls. Failure to consider the existing empirical evidence on girls' lives and behavior can quickly lead to stereotypical thinking and theoretical dead ends.

An example of this sort of flawed theory building was the early fascination with the notion that the women's movement was causing an increase in women's crime; a notion that is now more or less discredited (Steffensmeier, 1980; Gora, 1982). A more recent example of the same sort of thinking can be found in recent work on the "power-control" model of delinquency (Hagan, Simpson, and Gillis, 1987). Here, the authors speculate that girls commit less delinquency in part because their behavior is more closely controlled by the patriarchal family. The authors' promising beginning quickly gets bogged down in a very limited definition of patriarchal control (focusing on parental supervision and variations in power within the family). Ultimately, the authors' narrow formulation of patriarchal control results in their arguing that mother's work force participation (particularly in high status occupations) leads to increases in daughters' delinquency since these girls find themselves in more "egalitarian families."

This is essentially a not-too-subtle variation on the earlier "liberation" hypothesis. Now, mother's liberation causes daughter's crime. Aside from the methodological problems with the study (e.g., the authors argue that female-headed households are equivalent to upper-status "egalitarian" families where both parents work, and they measure delinquency using a six-term scale that contains no status offense items), there is a more fundamental problem with the hypothesis. There is no evidence to suggest that as women's labor force participation accelerated and the number of female-headed households soared, aggregate female delinquency measured both by self-report and official statistics either declined or remained stable

(Ageton, 1983; Chilton and Datesman, 1987; Federal Bureau of Investigation, 1987).

By contrast, a feminist model of delinquency would focus more extensively on the few pieces of information about girls' actual lives and the role played by girls' problems, including those caused by racism and poverty, in their delinquency behavior. Fortunately, a considerable literature is now developing on girls' lives and much of it bears directly on girls' crime.

Criminalizing Girls' Survival

It has long been understood that a major reason for girls' presence in juvenile courts was the fact that their parents insisted on their arrest. In the early years, conflicts with parents were by far the most significant referral source; in Honolulu 44% of the girls who appeared in court in 1929 through 1930 were referred by parents.

Recent national data, while slightly less explicit, also show that girls are more likely to be referred to court by "sources other than law enforcement agencies" (which would include parents). In 1983, nearly a quarter (23%) of all girls but only 16% of boys charged with delinquent offenses were referred to court by non-law enforcement agencies. The pattern among youth referred for status offenses (for which girls are overrepresented) was even more pronounced. Well over half (56%) of the girls charged with these offenses and 45% of the boys were referred by sources other than law enforcement (Snyder and Finnegan, 1987, p. 21; see also Pope and Feyerherm, 1982).

The fact that parents are often committed to two standards of adolescent behavior is one explanation for such a disparity—and one that should not be discounted as a major source of tension even in modern families. Despite expectations to the contrary, gender-specific socialization patterns have not changed very much and this is especially true for parents' relationships with their daughters (Katz, 1979). It appears that even parents who oppose sexism in general feel "uncomfortable tampering with existing traditions" and "do not want to risk their children becoming misfits" (Katz, 1979, p. 24).

Clearly, parental attempts to adhere to and enforce these traditional notions will continue to be a source of conflict between girls and their elders. Another important explanation for girls' problems with their parents, which has received attention only in more recent years, is the problem of physical and sexual abuse. Looking specifically at the problem of childhood sexual abuse, it is increasingly clear that this form of abuse is a particular problem for girls.

Girls are, for example, much more likely to be the victims of child sexual abuse than are boys. Finkelhor and Baron estimate from a review of community studies that roughly 70% of the victims of sexual abuse are female (Finkelhor and Baron, 1986, p. 45). Girls' sexual abuse also tends to start earlier than boys (Finkelhor and Baron, 1986, p. 48); they are more likely than boys to be assaulted by a family member (often a stepfather) (DeJong, Hervada, and Emmett, 1983; Russell, 1986), and as a consequence, their abuse tends to last longer than male sexual abuse (DeJong, Hervada, and Emmett, 1983). All of these factors are associated with more severe trauma—causing dramatic short- and long-term effects in victims (Adams-Tucker, 1982). The effects noted by researchers in this area move from the more well known "fear, anxiety, depression, anger and hostility, and inappropriate sexual behavior" (Browne and Finkelhor, 1986, p. 69) to behaviors of greater familiarity to criminologists, including running away from home, difficulties in school, truancy, and early marriage (Browne and Finkelhor, 1986).

Herman's study of incest survivors in therapy found that they were more likely to have run away from home than a matched sample of women whose fathers were "seductive" (33% compared to 5%). Another study of women patients found that 50% of the victims of child sexual abuse, but only 20% of the nonvictim group, had left home before the age of 19 (Meiselman, 1978).

Not surprisingly, then, studies of girls on the streets or in court populations are showing high rates of both physical and sexual abuse. Silbert and Pines (1981, p. 409) found, for example, that 60% of the street prostitutes they interviewed had been sexually abused as juveniles. Girls at an Arkansas diagnostic unit and school who had been adjudicated for either status or delinquent offenses reported similarly high levels of sexual abuse as well as high levels of physical abuse; 53% indicated they had been sexually abused, 25% recalled scars, 38% recalled bleeding from abuse, and 51% recalled bruises (Mouzakitas, 1981).

A sample survey of girls in the juvenile justice system in Wisconsin (Phelps et al., 1982) revealed that 79% had been subjected to physical abuse that resulted in some form of injury, and 32% had been sexually abused by parents or other persons who were closely connected to their families. Moreover, 50% had been sexually assaulted ("raped" or forced to participate in sexual acts) (Phelps et al., 1982, p. 66). Even higher figures were reported by McCormack and her associates (McCormack, Janus, and Burgess, 1986) in their study of youth in a runaway shelter in Toronto. They found that 73% of the females and 38% of the males had been sexually abused. Finally, a study of youth charged with running away, truancy, or listed as missing persons in Arizona found that 55% were incest victims (Reich and Gutierres, 1979).

Many young women, then, are running away from profound sexual victimization at home, and once on the streets they are forced further into crime in order to survive. Interviews with girls who have run away from home show, very clearly, that they do not have a lot of attachment to their delinquent activities. In fact, they are angry about being labeled as delinquent, yet all engaged in illegal acts (Koroki and Chesney-Lind, 1985). The Wisconsin study found that 54% of the girls who ran away found it necessary to steal money, food, and clothing in order to survive. A few exchanged sexual contact for money, food, and/or shelter (Phelps et al., 1982, p. 67). In their study of runaway youth, McCormack, Janus, and Burgess (1986, pp. 392–393) found that sexually abused female runaways were significantly more likely than their nonabused counterparts to engage in delinquent or criminal activities such as substance abuse, petty theft, and prostitution. No such pattern was found among male runaways.

Research (Chesney-Lind and Rodriquez, 1983) on the backgrounds of adult women in prison underscores the important links between women's childhood victimizations and their later criminal careers. The interviews revealed that virtually all of this sample were the victims of physical and/or sexual abuse as youngsters; over 60% had been sexually abused and about half had been raped as young women. This situation prompted these women to run away from home (three-quarters had been arrested for status offenses) where once on the streets they began engaging in prostitution and other forms of petty property crime. They also begin what becomes a lifetime problem with drugs. As adults, the women continue in these activities since they possess truncated educational backgrounds and virtually no marketable occupational skills (see also Miller, 1986).

Confirmation of the consequences of childhood sexual and physical abuse on adult female criminal behavior has also recently come from a large quantitative study of 908 individuals with substantiated and validated histories of these victimizations. Widom (1988) found that abused or neglected females were twice as likely as a matched group of controls to have an adult record (16% compared to 7.5). The difference was also found among men, but it was not as dramatic (42% compared to 33%). Men with abuse backgrounds were also more likely to contribute to the "cycle of violence" with more arrests for violent offenses as adult offenders than the control group. In contrast, when women with abuse backgrounds did become involved with the criminal justice system, their arrests tended to involve property and order offenses (such as disorderly conduct, curfew, and loitering violations)(Widon, 1988, p. 17).

Given this information, a brief example of how a feminist perspective on the causes of female delinquency might look seems appropriate. First, like young men, girls are frequently the recipients of violence and sexual abuse. But unlike boys, girls' victimization and their response to that victimization is specifically shaped by their status as young women. Perhaps because of the gender and

sexual scripts found in patriarchal families, girls are much more likely than boys to be victims of family-related sexual abuse. Men, particularly men with traditional attitudes toward women, are likely to define their daughters or stepdaughters as their sexual property (Finkelhor, 1982). In a society that idealizes inequality in male/female relationships and venerates youth in women, girls are easily defined as sexually attractive by older men (Bell, 1984). In addition, girls' vulnerability to both physical and sexual abuse is heightened by norms that require that they stay at home where their victimizers have access to them.

Moreover, their victimizers (usually males) have the ability to invoke official agencies of social control in their efforts to keep young women at home and vulnerable. That is to say, abusers have traditionally been able to utilize the uncritical commitment of the juvenile justice system toward parental authority to force girls to obey them. Girls' complaints about abuse were, until recently, routinely ignored. For this reason, statutes that were originally placed in law to "protect" young people have, in the case of girls' delinquency, criminalized their survival strategies. As they run away from abusive homes, parents have been able to employ agencies to enforce their return. If they persisted in their refusal to stay in that home, however intolerable, they were incarcerated.

Young women, a large number of whom are on the run from homes characterized by sexual abuse and parental neglect, are forced by the very statutes designed to protect them into the lives of escaped convicts. Unable to enroll in school or take a job to support themselves because they fear detection, young female runaways are forced into the streets. Here they engage in panhandling, petty theft, and occasional prostitution in order to survive. Young women in conflict with their parents (often for very legitimate reasons) may actually be forced by present laws into petty criminal activity, prostitution, and drug use.

In addition, the fact that young girls (but not necessarily young boys) are defined as sexually desirable and, in fact, more desirable than their older sisters due to the double standard of aging, means that their lives on the streets (and their survival strategies) take on unique shape—one again shaped by patriarchal values. It is no accident that girls on the run from abusive homes, or on the streets because of profound poverty, get involved in criminal activities that exploit their sexual object status. American society has defined as desirable youthful, physically perfect women. This means that girls on the streets, who have little else of value to trade, are encouraged to utilize this "resource" (Campagna and Poffenberger, 1988). It also means that the criminal subculture views them from this perspective (Miller, 1986).

Female Delinquency, Patriarchal Authority, and Family Courts

The early insights into male delinquency were largely gleaned by intensive field observation of delinquent boys. Very little of this sort of work has been done in the case of girls' delinquency, though it is vital to an understanding of girls' definitions of their own situations, choices, and behavior (for exceptions to this see Campbell, 1984; Peacock, 1981; Miller, 1986; Rosenberg and Zimmerman, 1977). Time must be spent listening to girls. Fuller research on the settings, such as families and schools, that girls find themselves in and the impact of variations in those settings should also be undertaken (see Figueira-McDonough, 1986). A more complete understanding of how poverty and racism shape girls' lives is also vital (see Messerschmidt, 1986; Campbell, 1984). Finally, current qualitative research on the reaction of official agencies to girls' delinquency must be conducted. This latter task, admittedly more difficult, is particularly critical to the development of delinquency theory that is as sensitive to gender as it is to race and class.

It is clear that throughout most of the court's history, virtually all female delinquency has been placed within the larger context of girls' sexual behavior. One explanation for this pattern is that familial control over girls' sexual capital has historically been central to the maintenance of patriarchy (Lerner, 1986). The fact that young women

have relatively more of this capital has been one reason for the excessive concern that both families and official agencies of social control have expressed about youthful female defiance (otherwise much of the behavior of criminal justice personnel makes virtually no sense). Only if one considers the role of women's control over their sexuality at the point in their lives that their value to patriarchal society is so pronounced, does the historic pattern of jailing of huge numbers of girls guilty of minor misconduct make sense.

This framework also explains the enormous resistance that the movement to curb the juvenile justice system's authority over status offenders encountered. Supporters of the change were not really prepared for the political significance of giving youth the freedom to run. Horror stories told by the opponents of deinstitutionalization about victimized youth, youthful prostitution, and youthful involvement in pornography (Office of Juvenile Justice and Delinquency Prevention, 1985) all neglect the unpleasant reality that most of these behaviors were often in direct response to earlier victimization, frequently by parents, that officials had, for years, routinely ignored. What may be at stake in efforts to roll back deinstitutionalization efforts is not so much "protection" of youth as it is curbing the right of young women to defy patriarchy.

In sum, research in both the dynamics of girls' delinquency and official reactions to that behavior is essential to the developmental of theories of delinquency that are sensitive to its patriarchal as well as class and racial context.

References

ADAMS-TUCKER, CHRISTINE
1982   "Proximate Effects of Sexual Abuse in Childhood." *American Journal of Psychiatry* 193: 1252–1256.

AGETON, SUZANNE S.
1983   "The Dynamics of Female Delinquency, 1976–1980.," *Criminology* 21:555–584.

BELL, INGE POWELL
1984   "The Double Standard: Age." in *Women: A Feminist Perspective,* edited by Jo Freeman. Palo Alto, CA: Mayfield.

BLACK, T. EDWIN AND CHARLES P. SMITH
1981   *A Preliminary National Assessment of the Number and Characteristics of Juveniles Processed in the Juvenile Justice System.* Washington, DC: Government Printing Office.

BROWNE, ANGELA AND DAVID FINKELHOR
1986   "Impact of Child Sexual Abuse: A Review of Research," *Psychological Bulletin* 99:66–77.

CAMPAGNA, DANIEL S. AND DONALD I. POFFENBERGER
1988   *The Sexual Trafficking in Children,* Dover, DE; Auburn House.

CAMPBELL, ANN
1984   *The Girls in the Gang.* Oxford: Basil Blackwell.

CANTER, RACHELLE J.
1982   "Sex Differences in Self-Report Delinquency," *Criminology* 20:373–393.

CHESNEY-LIND, MEDA
1971   *Female Juvenile Delinquency in Hawaii,* Master's thesis, University of Hawaii.

———   1973. "Judicial Enforcement of the Female Sex Role," *Issues in Criminology* 3:51–71.

———   1978. "Young Women in the Arms of the Law," In *Women, Crime and the Criminal Justice System,* edited by Lee H. Bowker, Boston: Lexington.

———   1986. "Women and Crime: the Female Offender," *Signs* 12:78–96.

———   1988. "Girls and Deinstitutionalization: Is Juvenile Justice Still Sexist?" *Journal of Criminal Justice Abstracts* 20:144–165.

———   and Noelie Rodriquez 1983. "Women Under Lock and Key," *Prison Journal* 63:47–65.

CHILDREN'S BUREAU, DEPARTMENT OF HEALTH, EDUCATION AND WELFARE
1965   *1964 Statistics on Public Institutions for Delinquent Children.* Washington, DC; Government Printing Office.

CHILTON, ROLAND AND SUSAN K. DATESMAN
1987   "Gender, Race and Crime: An Analysis of Urban Arrest Trends, 1960–1980," *Gender and Society* 1:152–171.

CLOWARD, RICHARD A. AND LLOYD E. OHLIN
1960   *Delinquency and Opportunity,* New York: Free Press.

COHEN, ALBERT K.
1955   *Delinquent Boys: The Culture of the Gang,* New York: Free Press.

DATESMAN, SUSAN AND MIKEL AICKIN
1984   "Offense Specialization and Escalation Among Status Offenders," *Journal of Criminal Law and Criminology,* 75:1246–1275.

DAVIDSON, SUE, ED
1982   *Justice for Young Women.* Tucson, AZ; New Directions for Young Women.

DEJONG, ALLAN R., ARTURO R. HERVADA, AND GARY A. EMMETT
1983   "Epidemiologic Variations in Childhood Sexual Abuse," *Child Abuse and Neglect* 7:155–162.

ELLIOTT, DELBERT, DAVID HUIZINGA, AND BARBARA MORSE
1987   "A Career Analysis of Serious Violent Offenders," In *Violent Juvenile Crime: What Can We Do About It?* edited by Ira Schwartz, Minneapolis, MN: Hubert Humphrey Institute.

FEDERAL BUREAU OF INVESTIGATION
1987   *Crime in the United States 1986,* Washington DC; Government Printing Office.

FEINMAN, CLARICE
1980   *Women in the Criminal Justice System,* New York: Praeger.

FIGUEIRA-MCDONOUGH, JOSEFINA
1985   "Are Girls Different? Gender Discrepancies Between Delinquent Behavior and Control," *Child Welfare* 64:273–289.

———   1986 "School Context, Gender, and Delinquency," *Journal of Youth and Adolescence* 15:79–98.

FINKELHOR, DAVID
1982   "Sexual Abuse: A Sociological Perspective," *Child Abuse and Neglect* 6:95–102.

———   and Larry Baron. 1986. "Risk Factors for Child Sexual Abuse," *Journal of Interpersonal Violence* 1:43–71.

FREEDMAN, ESTELLE
1981   *Their Sisters' Keepers,* Ann Arbor; University of Michigan Press.

GELTSHORPE, LORAINE
1986   "Towards a Skeptical Look at Sexism," *International Journal of the Sociology of Law* 14:125–152.

GORA, JOANN
1982   *The New Female Criminal: Empirical Reality or Social Myth,* New York: Praeger.

HAGAN, JOHN, A. R. GILLIS, AND JOHN SIMPSON
1985   "The Class Structure of Gender and Delinquency: Toward a Power-Control Theory of Common Delinquent Behavior," *American Journal of Sociology* 90:1151–1178.

HAGAN, JOHN, JOHN SIMPSON, AND A. R. GILLIS
1987   "Class in the Household: A Power-Control Theory of Gender and Delinquency," *American Journal of Sociology* 92:788–816.

HANCOCK, LINDA
1981   "The Myth that Females are Treated More Leniently than Males in the Juvenile Justice System." *Australian and New Zealand Journal of Criminology* 16:4–14.

HARRIS, ANTHONY
1977   "Sex and Theories of Deviance," *American Sociological Review* 42:3–16.

HERMAN, JULIA L.
1981   *Father-Daughter Incest.* Cambridge, MA; Harvard University Press.

KATZ, PHYLLIS A.
1979   "The Development of Female Identity," In *Becoming Female: Perspectives on Development,* edited by Claire B. Kopp, New York: Plenum.

KOROKI, JAN AND MEDA CHESNEY-LIND
1985   *Everything Just Going Down the Drain.* Hawaii; Youth Development and Research Center.

LERNER, GERDA
1986   *The Creation of Patriarchy.* New York: Oxford.

MCCORMACK, ARLENE, MARK-DAVID JANUS, AND ANN WOLBERT BURGESS
1986   "Runaway Youths and Sexual Victimization: Gender Differences n an Adolescent Runaway Population," *Child Abuse and Neglect* 10:387–395.

MCGARRELL, EDMUND F. AND TIMOTHY J. FLANAGAN
1985   *Sourcebook of Criminal Justice Statistics–1984.* Washington, DC; Government Printing Office.

MEISELMAN, KAREN
1978   *Incest.* San Francisco: Jossey-Bass.

MERTON, ROBERT K.
1938   "Social Structure and Anomie." *American Sociological Review* 3(October):672–782.

MESSERSCHMIDT, JAMES
1986   *Capitalism, Patriarchy, and Crime: Toward a Socialist Feminist Criminology,* Totowa, NJ: Rowman & Littlefield.

———   1987. "Feminism, Criminology, and the Rise of the Female Sex Delinquent, 1880–1930," *Contemporary Crises* 11:243–263.

MILLER, ELEANOR
1986   *Street Woman,* Philadelphia: Temple University Press.

MILLER, WALTER B.
1958   "Lower Class Culture as the Generating Milieu of Gang Delinquency," *Journal of Social Issues* 14:5–19.

MORRIS, RUTH
1964   "Female Delinquency and Relational Problems," *Social Forces* 43:82–89.

MOUZAKITAS, C. M.
1981   "An Inquiry into the Problem of Child Abuse and Juvenile Delinquency," In *Exploring the Relationship Between Child Abuse and Delinquency,* edited by R. J. Hunner and Y. E. Walkers, Montclair, NJ: Allanheld, Osmun.

NATIONAL FEMALE ADVOCACY PROJECT
1981   *Young Women and the Justice System: Basic Facts and Issues.* Tucson, AZ; New Directions for Young Women.

OFFICE OF JUVENILE JUSTICE AND DELINQUENCY PREVENTION
1985   *Runaway Children and the Juvenile Justice and Delinquency Prevention Act: What is the Impact?* Washington, DC; Government Printing Office.

OPINION RESEARCH CORPORATION
1982   "Public Attitudes Toward Youth Crime: National Public Opinion Poll." Mimeographed. Minnesota; Hubert Humphrey Institute of Public Affairs, University of Minnesota.

PEACOCK, CAROL
1981   *Hand Me Down Dreams.* New York: Shocken.

PHELPS, R. J. ET AL.
1982   *Wisconsin Female Juvenile Offender Study Project Summary Report,* Wisconsin: Youth Policy and Law Center, Wisconsin Council of Juvenile Justice.

PLATT, ANTHONY M.
1969   *The Childsavers,* Chicago: University of Chicago Press.

POPE, CARL AND WILLIAM H. FEYERHERM
1982   "Gender Bias in Juvenile Court Dispositions," *Social Service Review* 6:1–17.

RAFTER, NICOLE HAHN
1985   *Partial Justice.* Boston: Northeastern University Press.

REICH, J. W. AND S. E. GUTIERRES
1979   "Escape/Aggression Incidence in Sexually Abused Juvenile Delinquents," *Criminal Justice and Behavior* 6:239–243.

ROGERS, KRISTINE
1972   "For Her Own Protection. . . . Conditions of Incarceration for Female Juvenile Offenders in the State of Connecticut," *Law and Society Review* (Winter):223–246.

ROSENBERG, DEBBY AND CAROLE ZIMMERMAN
1977   *Are My Dreams Too Much to Ask For?* Tucson, AZ.: New Directions for Young Women.

RUSSELL, DIANE E.
1986   *The Secret Trauma: Incest in the Lives of Girls and Women,* New York: Basic Books.

SCHLOSSMAN, STEVEN AND STEPHANIE WALLACH
1978   "The Crime of Precocious Sexuality: Female Juvenile Delinquency in the Progressive Era," *Harvard Educational Review* 48:65–94.

SHAW, CLIFFORD R.
1930   *The Jack-Roller,* Chicago: University of Chicago Press.

———   1938. *Brothers in Crime,* Chicago: University of Chicago Press.

———   and Henry D. McKay, 1942. *Juvenile Delinquency in Urban Areas,* Chicago: University of Chicago Press.

SHELDEN, RANDALL
1981   "Sex Discrimination in the Juvenile Justice System: Memphis, Tennessee, 1900–1917." *In Comparing Female and Male Offenders,* edited by Marguerite Q. Warren. Beverly Hills, CA: Sage.

———   and John Horvath, 1986. "Processing Offenders in a Juvenile Court: A Comparison of Males and Females." Paper presented at the annual meeting of the Western Society of Criminology, Newport Beach, CA, February 27–March 2.

SILBERT, MIMI AND AYALA M. PINES
1981   "Sexual Child Abuse as an Antecedent to Prostitution," *Child Abuse and Neglect* 5:407–411.

SIMONS, RONALD L., MARTIN G. MILLER, AND STEPHEN M. AIGNER
1980   "Contemporary Theories of Deviance and Female Delinquency: An Empirical Test," *Journal of Research in Crime and Delinquency* 17:42–57.

SMITH, LESLEY SHACKLADY
1978   "Sexist Assumptions and Female Delinquency," In *Women, Sexuality and Social Control,* edited by Carol Smart and Barry Smart, London: Routledge & Kegan Paul.

SNYDER, HOWARD N. AND TERRENCE A. FINNEGAN
1987   *Delinquency in the Untied States.* Washington, DC: Department of Justice.

STEFFENSMEIER, DARRELL J.
1980 "Sex Differences in Patterns of Adult Crime, 1965–1977," *Social Forces* 58:1080–1109.

SUTHERLAND, EDWIN
1978 "Differential Association." In *Children of Ishmael: Critical Perspectives on Juvenile Justice*, edited by Barry Krisberg and James Austin. Palo Alto, CA: Mayfield.

TEILMANN, KATHERINE S. AND PIERRE H. LANDRY, JR.
1981 "Gender Bias in Juvenile Justice." *Journal of Research in Crime and Delinquency* 18:47–80.

THRASHER, FREDERIC M.
1927 *The Gang.* Chicago: University of Chicago Press.

TRACY, PAUL E., MARVIN E. WOLFGANG, AND ROBERT M. FIGLIO
1985 *Delinquency in Two Birth Cohorts: Executive Summary.* Washington, DC: Department of Justice.

WIDOM, CATHY SPATZ
1988 "Child Abuse, Neglect, and Violent Criminal Behavior." Unpublished manuscript.

QUESTIONS FOR DISCUSSION

1. How does a feminist perspective on female delinquency differ from the traditional perspectives that typically focus on males? Why have traditional explanations been inadequate?

2. Discuss the patriarchal, class, and racial contexts of female delinquency.

3. According to the author, there is more childhood sexual and physical abuse among females. Why is this the case? How does this impact adolescent female delinquency?

APPLICATIONS

1. Is American society dominated by a patriarchal system? Cite examples from your own experience to support your response.

2. Stereotyping is a significant part of "genderizing" beliefs, attitudes, and behaviors about females and males. Construct a list of common stereotypes regarding females. Construct a similar list for males. Compare your lists to another class member's lists (preferably someone gender different than yourself). Discuss the similarities and differences. Do you foresee any of the stereotypes you have listed changing in the near future? Why?

KEY TERMS

androcentric dominated by or emphasizing a masculine interest or point of view.

egalitarian one who asserts or advocates the removal of inequalities among people.

patriarchal a characteristic of a social organization where men disproportionately control a large share of power; may refer to the head of a household or to beliefs and values that control institutions of government, industry, religion, and education.

status offense refers to an offense committed by a youth that if committed as an adult would not be illegal; illegal because of the status of being young.

stereotype a mental picture or attitude held by an individual or group, typically about another individual or group, which is an oversimplified opinion, a prejudiced appraisal, or a critical judgment.

symbiotic relationship a cooperative interaction between two individuals or groups.

venerate to honor or regard with reverence and/or acts of devotion.

13

Foundation for a General Strain Theory of Crime and Delinquency

Robert Agnew
Emory University

This paper presents a general strain theory of crime and delinquency that is capable of overcoming the criticisms of previous strain theories. In the first section, strain theory is distinguished from social control and differential association/social learning theory. In the second section, the three major types of strain are described: (1) strain as the actual or anticipated failure to achieve positively valued goals, (2) strain as the actual or anticipated removal of positively valued stimuli, and (3) strain as the actual or anticipated presentation of negatively valued stimuli. In the third section, guidelines for the measurement of strain are presented. And in the fourth section, the major adaptations to strain are described, and those factors influencing the choice of delinquent versus nondelinquent adaptations are discussed.

After dominating deviance research in the 1960s, strain theory came under heavy attack in the 1970s (Bernard, 1984; Cole, 1975), with several prominent researchers suggesting that the theory be abandoned (Hirschi, 1969; Kornhauser, 1978). Strain theory has survived those attacks, but its influence is much diminished (see Agnew, 1985a; Bernard, 1984; Farnworth and Leiber, 1989). In particular, variables derived from strain theory now play a very limited role in explanations of crime/delinquency. Several recent causal models of delinquency, in fact, either

"Foundation for a General Theory of Crime and Delinquency," *Criminology*, 30:1 (1992), pp. 47–87. Reprinted with permission of The American Society of Criminology.

entirely exclude strain variables or assign them a small role (e.g., Elliott et al., 1985; Johnson, 1979; Massey and Krohn, 1986; Thornberry, 1987; Tonry et al., 1991). Causal models of crime/delinquency are dominated, instead, by variables derived from differential association/social learning theory and social control theory.

This paper argues that strain theory has a central role to play in explanations of crime/delinquency, but that the theory has to be substantially revised to play this role. Most empirical studies of strain theory continue to rely on the strain models developed by Merton (1938), A. Cohen (1955), and Cloward and Ohlin (1960). In recent years, however, a wealth of research in several fields has questioned certain of the assumptions underlying those theories and pointed to new directions for the development of strain theory. Most notable in this area is the research on stress in medical sociology and psychology, on equity/justice in social psychology, and on aggression in psychology—particularly recent versions of frustration-aggression and social learning theory. Also important is recent research in such areas as the legitimation of stratification, the sociology of emotions, and the urban underclass. Certain researchers have drawn on segments of the above research to suggest new directions for strain theory (Agnew, 1985a; Bernard, 1987; Elliott et al., 1979; Greenberg, 1977), but the revisions suggested have not taken full advantage of this research and, at best, provide only incomplete models of strain and delinquency. (Note that most of the theoretical and empirical work on strain theory has focused on delinquency.) This paper draws on the above literatures, as well as the recent revisions in strain theory, to present the outlines of a general strain theory of crime/delinquency.

The theory is written at the social-psychological level: It focuses on the individual and his or her immediate social environment—although the macroimplications of the theory are explored at various points. The theory is also written with the empirical researcher in mind, and guidelines for testing the theory in adolescent populations are provided. The focus is on adolescents because most currently available data sets capable of testing the theory involve surveys of adolescents. This general theory, it will be argued, is capable of overcoming the theoretical and empirical criticisms of previous strain theories and of complementing the crime/delinquency theories that currently dominate the field.

The paper is in four sections. In the first section, there is a brief discussion of the fundamental traits that distinguish strain theory from the other two dominant theories of delinquency: social control and differential association/social learning theory (in the interest of brevity, the term *delinquency* is used rather than *crime and delinquency*). In the second section, the three major sources of strain are described. In the third section, guidelines for the measurement of strain are provided. And in the final section, the major adaptations to strain are listed and the factors influencing the choice of delinquent versus nondelinquent adaptations are discussed.

STRAIN THEORY AS DISTINGUISHED FROM CONTROL AND DIFFERENTIAL ASSOCIATION/SOCIAL LEARNING THEORY

Strain, social control, and differential association theory are all sociological theories: They explain delinquency in terms of the individual's social relationships. Strain theory is distinguished from social control and social learning theory in its specification of (1) the type of social relationship that leads to delin-

quency and (2) the motivation for delinquency. First, strain theory focuses explicitly on *negative relationships with others*: relationships in which the individual is not treated as he or she wants to be treated. Strain theory has typically focused on relationships in which others prevent the individual from achieving positively valued goals. Agnew (1985a), however, broadened the focus of strain theory to include relationships in which others present the individual with noxious or negative stimuli. Social control theory, by contrast, focuses on the *absence of significant relationships with conventional others and institutions*. In particular, delinquency is most likely when (1) the adolescent is not attached to parents, school, or other institutions; (2) parents and others fail to monitor and effectively sanction deviance; (3) the adolescent's actual or anticipated investment in conventional society is minimal; and (4) the adolescent has not internalized conventional beliefs. Social learning theory is distinguished from strain and control theory by its focus on *positive relationships with deviant others*. In particular, delinquency results from association with others who (1) differentially reinforce the adolescent's delinquency, (2) model delinquent behavior, and/or (3) transmit delinquent values.

Second, strain theory argues that adolescents are *pressured into delinquency by the negative affective states—most notably anger and related emotions—that often result from negative relationships* (see Kemper, 1978, and Morgan and Heise, 1988, for topologies of negative affective states). This negative affect creates pressure for corrective action and *may* lead adolescents to (1) make use of illegitimate channels of goal achievement, (2) attack or escape from the source of their adversity, and/or (3) manage their negative affect through the use of illicit drugs. Control theory, by contrast, denies that outside forces pressure the adolescent into delinquency. Rather, the absence of significant relationships with other individuals and groups *frees the adolescent to engage in delinquency*. The freed adolescent either drifts into delinquency or, in some versions of control theory, turns to delinquency in response to inner forces or situational inducements (see Hirschi, 1969:31–34). In differential association/social learning theory, the adolescent commits delinquent acts because group forces lead the adolescent to *view delinquency as a desirable or at least justifiable form of behavior* under certain circumstances.

Strain theory, then, is distinguished by its focus on negative relationships with others and its insistence that such relationships lead to delinquency through the negative affect—especially anger—they sometimes engender. Both dimensions are necessary to differentiate strain theory from control and differential association/social learning theory. In particular, social control and social learning theory sometimes examine negative relationships—although such relationships are not an explicit focus of these theories. Control theory, however, would argue that negative relationships lead to delinquency not because they cause negative affect, but because they lead to a reduction in social control. A control theorist, for example, would argue that physical abuse by parents leads to delinquency because it reduces attachment to parents and the effectiveness of parents as socializing agents. Likewise, differential association/social learning theorists sometimes examine negative relationships—even though theorists in this tradition emphasize that imitation, reinforcement, and the internalization of values are less likely in negative relationships. Social learning theorists, however, would argue that negative relationships—such as those involving physically abusive parents—lead to delinquency by providing models for imitation and implicitly teaching the child that violence and other forms of deviance are acceptable behavior.

Phrased in the above manner, it is easy to see that strain theory complements the other major theories of delinquency in a fundamental way. While these other theories focus on the absence of relationships or on positive relationships, strain theory is the only theory to focus explicitly on negative relationships. And while these other theories view delinquency as the result of drift or of desire, strain theory views it as the result of pressure.

THE MAJOR TYPES OF STRAIN

Negative relationships with others are, quite simply, relationships in which others are not treating the individual as he or she would like to be treated. The classic strain theories of Merton (1938), A. Cohen (1955), and Cloward and Ohlin (1960) focus on only one type of negative relationship: relationships in which others prevent the individual from achieving positively valued goals. In particular, they focus on the goal blockage experienced by lower-class individuals trying to achieve monetary success or middle-class status. More recent versions of strain theory have argued that adolescents are not only concerned about the future goals of monetary success/middle-class status, but are also concerned about the achievement of more immediate goals—such as good grades, popularity with the opposite sex, and doing well in athletics (Agnew, 1984; Elliott and Voss, 1974; Elliott et al., 1985; Empey, 1982; Greenberg, 1977; Quicker, 1974). The focus, however, is still on the achievement of positively valued goals. Most recently, Agnew (1985a) has argued that strain may result not only from the failure to achieve positively valued goals, but also from the inability to escape legally from painful situations. If one draws on the above theories—as well as the stress, equity/justice, and aggression literatures—one can begin to develop a more complete classification of the types of strain.

Three major types of strain are described—each referring to a different type of negative relationship with others. Other individuals may (1) prevent one from achieving positively valued goals, (2) remove or threaten to remove positively valued stimuli that one possesses, or (3) present or threaten to present one with noxious or negatively valued stimuli. These categories of strain are presented as ideal types. There is no expectation, for example, that a factor analysis of strainful events will reproduce these categories. These categories, rather, are presented so as to ensure that the full range of strainful events are considered in empirical research.

Strain as the Failure to Achieve Positively Valued Goals

At least three types of strain fall under this category. The first type encompasses most of the major strain theories in criminology, including the classic strain theories of Merton, A. Cohen, and Cloward and Ohlin, as well as those modern strain theories focusing on the achievement of immediate goals. The other two types of strain in this category are derived from the justice/equity literature and have not been examined in criminology.

Strain as the Disjunction Between Aspirations and Expectations/Actual Achievements

The classic strain theories of Merton, A. Cohen, and Cloward and Ohlin argue that the cultural system encourages everyone to pursue the ideal goals of monetary success and/or middle-class status. Lower-class individuals, however, are often prevented from achieving such goals through legitimate channels. In line with such theories, adolescent strain is typically measured in terms of the disjunction between *aspirations* (or ideal goals) and *expectations* (or expected levels of goal achievement). These theories, however, have been criticized for several reasons (see Agnew, 1986, 1991b; Clinard, 1964; Hirschi, 1969; Kornhauser, 1978; Liska, 1987; also see Bernard, 1984; Farnworth and Leiber, 1989). Among other things, it has been charged that these theories (1) are unable to explain the extensive nature of middle-class delinquency, (2) neglect goals other than monetary success/middle-class status, (3) neglect barriers to goal achievement other than social class, and (4) do not fully specify why only *some* strained individuals turn to delinquency. The most damaging criticism, however, stems from the limited empirical support provided by studies focusing on the disjunction between aspirations and expectations (see Kornhauser, 1978, as well the arguments of Bernard, 1984; Elliott et al., 1985; and Jensen, 1986).

As a consequence of these criticisms, several researchers have revised the above theories. The most popular revision argues that there is a youth subculture that emphasizes a variety of immediate goals. The achievement of these goals is further said to depend on a variety of factors besides social class: factors such as intelligence, physical attractiveness, personality, and athletic ability. As a result, many middle-class individuals find that they lack the traits or skills necessary to achieve their goals through legitimate channels. This version of strain theory, however, continues to argue that strain stems from the inability to achieve certain ideal goals emphasized by the (sub)cultural system. As a consequence, strain continues to be measured in terms of the disjunction between *aspirations* and *actual achievements* (since we are dealing with immediate rather than future goals, actual achievements rather than expected achievements may be examined).

It should be noted that empirical support for this revised version of strain theory is also weak (see Agnew, 1991b, for a summary). At a later point, several possible reasons for the weak empirical support of strain theories focusing on the disjunction between aspirations and expectations/achievements will be discussed. For now, the focus is on classifying the major types of strain.

Strain as the Disjunction between Expectations and Actual Achievements

As indicated above, strain theories in criminology focus on the inability to achieve *ideal* goals derived from the cultural system. This approach stands in contrast to certain of the research on justice in social psychology. Here the focus is on the disjunction between *expectations* and *actual achievements* (rewards), and it is commonly argued that such expectations are existentially based. In particular, it has been argued that such expectations derive from the individual's past experience and/or from comparisons with referential (or generalized) others who are similar to the individual (see Berger et al., 1972, 1983; Blau, 1964; Homans, 1961; Jasso and Rossi, 1977; Mickelson, 1990; Ross et al., 1971; Thibaut and Kelly, 1959). Much of the research in this area has focused on income expectations, although the above theories apply to expectations regarding all manner of positive stimuli. The justice literature argues that the failure to achieve such expectations may lead to such emotions as anger, resentment, rage, dissatisfaction, disappointment, and unhappiness—that is, all the emotions customarily associated with strain in criminology. Further, it is argued that individuals will be strongly motivated to reduce the gap between expectations and achievements—with deviance being commonly mentioned as one possible option. This literature has not devoted much empirical research to deviance, although limited data suggest that the expectations-achievement gap is related to anger/hostility (Ross et al, 1971).

This alternative conception of strain has been largely neglected in criminology. This is unfortunate because it has the potential to overcome certain of the problems of current strain theories. First, one would expect the disjunction between expectations and actual achievements to be more emotionally distressing than that between aspirations and achievements. Aspirations, by definition, are *ideal* goals. They have something of the utopian in them, and for that reason, the failure to achieve aspirations may not be taken seriously. The failure to achieve expected goals, however, is likely to be taken seriously since such goals are rooted in reality—the individual has previously experienced such goals or has seen similar others experience such goals. Second, this alternative conception of strain assigns a central role to the social comparison process. As A. Cohen (1965) argued in a follow-up to his strain theory, the neglect of social comparison is a major shortcoming of strain theory. The above theories describe one way in which social comparison is important: Social comparison plays a central role in the formation of individual goals (expectations in this case; also see Suls, 1977). Third, the assumption that goals are culturally based has sometimes proved problematic for strain theory (see Kornhauser, 1978). Among other things, it makes it difficult to integrate strain theory with social control and cultural deviance theory (see Hirschi, 1979). These latter theories assume that the individual is weakly tied to the cultural system or tied to alternative/oppositional subcultures. The argument that goals are existentially based, however, paves the way for integrations involving theory.[1]

Strain as the Disjunction between Just/Fair Outcomes and Actual Outcomes

The above models of strain assume that individual goals focus on the achievement of specific outcomes. Individual goals, for example, focus on the achievement of a certain amount of money or a certain grade-point average. A third conception of strain, also derived from the justice/equity literature, makes a rather different argument. It claims that individuals do not necessarily enter interactions with specific outcomes in mind. Rather, they enter interactions expecting that certain distributive justice rules will be followed, rules specifying how resources should be allocated. The rule that has received the most attention in the literature is that of equity. An equitable relationship is one in which the outcome/input ratios of the actors involved in an exchange/allocation relationship are equivalent (see Adams, 1963, 1965; Cook and Hegtvedt, 1983; Walster et al., 1978). Outcomes encompass a broad range of positive and negative consequences, while inputs encompass the individual's positive and negative contributions to the exchange. Individuals in a relationship will compare the ratio of their outcomes and inputs to the ratio(s) of specific others in the relationship. If the ratios are equal to one another, they feel that the outcomes are fair or just. This is true, according to equity theorists, even if the outcomes are low. If outcome/input ratios are not equal, actors will feel that the outcomes are unjust and they will experience distress as a result. Such distress is especially likely when individuals feel they have been underrewarded rather than overrewarded (Hegtvedt, 1990).

The equity literature has described the possible reactions to this distress, some of which involve deviance (see Adams, 1963, 1965; Austin, 1977; Walster et al., 1973, 1978; see Stephenson and White, 1968, for an attempt to recast A. Cohen's strain theory in terms of equity theory). In particular, inequity may lead to delinquency for several reasons—all having to do with the restoration of equity. Individuals in inequitable relationships may engage in delinquency in order to (1) increase their outcomes (e.g., by theft); (2) lower their inputs (e.g., truancy from school); (3) lower the outcomes of others (e.g., vandalism, theft, assault); and/or (4) increase the inputs of others (e.g., by being incorrigible or disorderly). In highly inequitable situations, individuals may leave the field (e.g., run away from home) or force others to leave the field.[2] There has not been any empirical research on the relationship between equity and delinquency, although much data suggest that inequity leads to anger and frustration. A few studies also suggest that insulting and vengeful behaviors may result from inequity (see Cook and Hegtvedt, 1991; Donnerstein and Hatfield, 1982; Hegtvedt, 1990; Mikula, 1986; Sprecher, 1986; Walster et al., 1973, 1978).

It is not difficult to measure equity. Walster et al. (1978:234–242) provide the most complete guide to measurement.[3] Sprecher (1986) illustrates how equity may be measured in social surveys; respondents are asked who contributes more to a particular relationship and/or who "gets the best deal" out of a relationship. A still simpler strategy might be to ask respondents how fair or just their interactions with others, such as parents or teachers, are. One would then predict that those involved in unfair relations will be more likely to engage in current and future delinquency.

The literature on equity builds on the strain theory literature in criminology in several ways. First, all of the strain literature assumes that individuals are pursuing some specific outcome, such as a certain amount of money or prestige. The equity literature points out that individuals do not necessarily enter into interactions with specific outcomes in mind, but rather with the expectation that a particular distributive justice rule will be followed. Their goal is that the interaction conform to the justice principle. This perspective, then, points to a new source of strain not considered in the criminology literature. Second, the strain literature in criminology focuses largely on the individual's outcomes. Individuals are assumed to be pursuing a specific goal, and strain is judged in terms of the disjunction between the goal and the actual outcome. The equity literature suggests that this may be an oversimplified conception and that the individual's *inputs* may also have to be considered. In particular, an equity theorist would argue that inputs will condition the individual's evaluation of outcomes. That is, individuals who view their inputs as limited will be more likely to accept limited outcomes as fair. Third, the equity literature also highlights

the importance of the social comparison process. In particular, the equity literature stresses that one's evaluation of outcomes is at least partly a function of the outcomes (and inputs) of those with whom one is involved in exchange/allocation relations. A given outcome, then, may be evaluated as fair or unfair depending on the outcomes (and inputs) of others in the exchange/allocation relation.

Summary: Strain as the Failure to Achieve Positively Valued Goals

Three types of strain in this category have been listed: strain as the disjunction between (1) aspirations and expectations/actual achievements, (2) expectations and actual achievements, and (3) just/fair outcomes and actual outcomes. Strain theory in criminology has focused on the first type of strain, arguing that it is most responsible for the delinquency in our society. Major research traditions in the justice/equity field, however, argue that anger and frustration derive primarily from the second two types of strain. To complicate matters further, one can list still additional types of strain in this category. Certain of the literature, for example, has talked of the disjunction between "satisfying outcomes" and reality, between "deserved" outcomes and reality, and between "tolerance levels" or minimally acceptable outcomes and reality. No study has examined all of these types of goals, but taken as a whole the data do suggest that there are often differences among aspirations (ideal outcomes), expectations (expected outcomes), "satisfying" outcomes, "deserved" outcomes, fair or just outcomes, and tolerance levels (Della Fave, 1974; Della Fave and Klobus, 1976; Martin, 1986; Martin and Murray, 1983; Messick and Sentis, 1983; Shepelak and Alwin, 1986). This paper has focused on the three types of strain listed above largely because they dominate the current literature.[4]

Given these multiple sources of strain, one might ask which is the most relevant to the explanation of delinquency. This is a difficult question to answer given current research. The most fruitful strategy at the present time may be to assume that all of the above sources are relevant—that there are several sources of frustration. Alwin (1987), Austin (1977), Crosby and Gonzalez-Intal (1984), Hegtvedt (1991b.), Messick and Sentis (1983), and Tornblum (1977) all argue or imply that people often employ a variety of standards to evaluate their situation. Strain theorists, then, might be best advised to employ measures that tap all of the above types of strain. One might, for example, focus on a broad range of positively valued goals and, for each goal, ask adolescents whether they are achieving their ideal outcomes (aspirations), expected outcomes, and just/fair outcomes. One would expect strain to be greatest when several standards were not being met, with perhaps greatest weight being given to expectations and just/fair outcomes.[5]

Strain as the Removal of Positively Valued Stimuli from the Individual

The psychological literature on aggression and the stress literature suggest that strain may involve more than the pursuit of positively valued goals. Certain of the aggression literature, in fact, has come to de-emphasize the pursuit of positively valued goals, pointing out that the blockage of goal-seeking behavior is a relatively weak predictor of aggression, particularly when the goal has never been experienced before (Bandura, 1973; Zillman, 1979). The stress literature has largely neglected the pursuit of positively valued goals as a source of stress. Rather, if one looks at the stressful life events examined in this literature, one finds a focus on (1) events involving the loss of positively valued stimuli and (2) events involving the presentation of noxious or negative stimuli (see Pearlin, 1983, for other topologies of stressful life events/conditions).[6] So, for example, one recent study of adolescent stress employs a life-events list that focuses on such items as the loss of a boyfriend/girlfriend, the death or serious illness of a friend, moving to a new school district, the divorce/separation of one's parents, suspension from school, and the presence of a variety of adverse conditions at work (see Williams and Uchiyama, 1989, for an overview of life-events scales for adolescents;

see Compas, 1987, and Compas and Phares, 1991, for overviews of research on adolescent stress).[7]

Drawing on the stress literature, then, one may state that a second type of strain or negative relationship involves the actual or anticipated removal (loss) of positively valued stimuli from the individual. As indicated above, numerous examples of such loss can be found in the inventories of stressful life events. The actual or anticipated loss of positively valued stimuli may lead to delinquency as the individual tries to prevent the loss of the positive stimuli, retrieve the lost stimuli or obtain substitute stimuli, seek revenge against those responsible for the loss, or manage the negative affect caused by the loss by taking illicit drugs. While there are no data bearing directly on this type of strain, experimental data indicate that aggression often occurs when positive reinforcement previously administered to an individual is withheld or reduced (Bandura, 1973; Van Houten, 1983). And as discussed below, inventories of stressful life events, which include the loss of positive stimuli, are related to delinquency.

Strain as the Presentation of Negative Stimuli

The literature on stress and the recent psychological literature on aggression also focus on the actual or anticipated presentation of negative or noxious stimuli.[8] Except for the work of Agnew (1985a), however, this category of strain has been neglected in criminology. And even Agnew does not focus on the presentation of noxious stimuli per se, but on the inability of adolescents to escape legally from noxious stimuli. Much data, however, suggest that the presentation of noxious stimuli may lead to aggression and other negative outcomes in certain conditions, even when legal escape from such stimuli is possible (Bandura, 1973; Zillman, 1979). Noxious stimuli may lead to delinquency as the adolescent tries to (1) escape from or avoid the negative stimuli; (2) terminate or alleviate the negative stimuli; (3) seek revenge against the source of the negative stimuli or related targets, although the evidence on displaced aggression is somewhat mixed (see Berkowitz, 1982; Bernard, 1990; Van Houten, 1983; Zillman, 1979); and/or (4) manage the resultant negative affect by taking illicit drugs.

A wide range of noxious stimuli have been examined in the literature, and experimental, survey, and participant observation studies have linked such stimuli to both general and specific measures of delinquency—with the experimental studies focusing on aggression. Delinquency/aggression, in particular, has been linked to such noxious stimuli as child abuse and neglect (Rivera and Widom, 1990), criminal victimization (Lauritsen et al., 1991), physical punishment (Straus, 1991), negative relations with parents (Healy and Bonner, 1969), negative relations with peers (Short and Strodtbeck, 1965), adverse or negative school experiences (Hawkins and Lishner, 1987), a wide range of stressful life events (Gersten et al., 1974; Kaplan et al., 1983; Linsky and Straus, 1986; Mawson, 1987; Novy and Donohue, 1985; Vaux and Ruggiero, 1983), verbal threats and insults, physical pain, unpleasant odors, disgusting scenes, noise, heat, air pollution, personal space violations, and high density (see Anderson and Anderson, 1984; Bandura, 1973, 1983; Berkowitz, 1982, 1986; Mueller, 1983). In one of the few studies in criminology to focus specifically on the presentation of negative stimuli, Agnew (1985a) found that delinquency was related to three scales measuring negative relations at home and school. The effect of the scales on delinquency was partially mediated through a measure of anger, and the effect held when measures of social control and deviant beliefs were controlled. And in a recent study employing longitudinal data, Agnew (1989) found evidence suggesting that the relationship between negative stimuli and delinquency was due to the *causal* effect of the negative stimuli on delinquency (rather than the effect of delinquency on the negative stimuli). Much evidence, then, suggests that the presentation of negative or noxious stimuli constitutes a third major source of strain.

Certain of the negative stimuli listed above, such as physical pain, heat, noise, and pollution, may be experienced as noxious largely for biological reasons (i.e., they may be unconditioned negative stimuli). Others may be conditioned negative stimuli, experienced as noxious largely because of their association with unconditioned negative stimuli (see Berkowitz, 1982). Whatever the case, it is assumed that such stimuli are experienced as noxious regardless of the goals that the individual is pursuing.

The Links Between Strain and Delinquency

Three sources of strain have been presented: strain as the actual or anticipated failure to achieve positively valued goals, strain as the actual or anticipated removal of positively valued stimuli, and strain as the actual or anticipated presentation of negative stimuli. While these types are theoretically distinct from one another, they may sometimes overlap in practice. So, for example, the insults of a teacher may be experienced as adverse because they (1) interfere with the adolescent's aspirations for academic success, (2) result in the violation of a distributive justice rule such as equity, and (3) are conditioned negative stimuli and so are experienced as noxious in and of themselves. Other examples of overlap can be given, and it may sometimes be difficult to disentangle the different types of strain in practice. Once again, however, these categories are ideal types and are presented only to ensure that all events with the potential for creating strain are considered in empirical research.

Each type of strain increases the likelihood that individuals will experience one or more of a range of negative emotions. Those emotions include disappointment, depression, and fear. Anger, however, is the most critical emotional reaction for the purposes of the general strain theory. Anger results when individuals blame their adversity on others, and anger is a key emotion because it increases the individual's level of felt injury, creates a desire for retaliation/revenge, energizes the individual for action, and lowers inhibitions, in part because individuals believe that others will feel their aggression is justified (see Averill, 1982; Berkowitz, 1982; Kemper, 1978; Kluegel and Smith, 1986: Ch. 10; Zillman, 1979). Anger, then, affects the individual in several ways that are conducive to delinquency. Anger is distinct from many of the types of negative affect in this respect, and this is the reason that anger occupies a special place in the general strain theory.[9] It is important to note, however, that delinquency may still occur in response to other types of negative affect—such as despair, although delinquency is less likely in such cases.[10] The experience of negative affect, especially anger, typically creates a desire to take corrective steps, with delinquency being one possible response. Delinquency may be a method for alleviating strain, that is, for achieving positively valued goals, for protecting or retrieving positive stimuli, or for terminating or escaping from negative stimuli. Delinquency may be used to seek revenge; data suggest that vengeful behavior often occurs even when there is no possibility of eliminating the adversity that stimulated it (Berkowitz, 1982). And delinquency may occur as adolescents try to manage their negative affect through illicit drug use (see Newcomb and Harlow, 1986). The general strain theory, then, has the potential to explain a broad range of delinquency, including theft, aggression, and drug use.

Each type of strain may create a *predisposition* for delinquency or function as a *situational event* that instigates a particular delinquent act. In the words of Hirschi and Gottredson (1986), then, the strain theory presented in this paper is a theory of both "criminality" and "crime" (or to use the words of Clarke and Cornish [1985], it is a theory of both "criminal involvement" and "criminal events"). Strain creates a predisposition for delinquency in those cases in which it is chronic or repetitive. Examples include a continuing gap between expectations and achievements and a continuing pattern of ridicule and insults from teachers. Adolescents subject to such strain are predisposed to delinquency because (1) nondelinquent strategies for coping with strain are likely to be taxed; (2) the threshold for adversity may be lowered by chronic strains (see Averill, 1982:289); (3) repeated or chronic strain may lead to a hostile attitude—a general dislike and suspicion of others and an associated tendency to respond in an aggressive manner (see Edmunds and Kendrick, 1980:21); and (4) chronic strains increase the likelihood that individuals will be high in negative affect/arousal at any given time (see Bandura, 1983; Bernard, 1990). A particular instance of strain may also function as the situational event that ignites a delinquent act, especially among adolescents predisposed to delinquency. Qualitative and survey data, in particular, suggest that particular instances of delinquency are often instigated by one of the three types of strain listed above (see Agnew, 1990; also see Averill, 1982, for data on the instigations to anger).

MEASURING STRAIN

As indicated above, strain theory in criminology is dominated by a focus on strain as goal blockage. Further, only one type of goal blockage is typically examined in the literature—the failure to achieve *aspirations*, especially aspirations for monetary success or middle-class status. The general strain theory is much broader than current strain theories, and measuring strain under this theory would require at least three sets of measures: those focusing on the failure to achieve positively valued goals, those focusing on the loss of positive stimuli, and those focusing on the presentation of negative stimuli. It is not possible to list the precise measures that should be employed in these areas, although the citations above contain many examples of the types of measures that might be used. Further, certain general guidelines for the measurement of strain can be offered. The guidelines below will also highlight the limitations of current strain measures and shed further light on why those measures are typically unrelated to delinquency.

Developing a Comprehensive List of Negative Relations

Strain refers to negative or adverse relations with others. Such relations are ultimately defined from the perspective of the individual. That is, in the final analysis adverse relations are whatever individuals say they are (see Berkowitz, 1982). This does not mean, however, that one must employ an idiosyncratic definition of adverse relations— defining adverse relations anew for each person one examines. Such a strategy would create serious problems for (1) the empirical study of delinquency, (2) the prediction and control of delinquency, and (3) efforts to develop the macroimplications of the general strain theory. Rather, one can employ a strategy similar to that followed by stress researchers.

First, one can draw on theory and research to specify those objective situations that might reasonably be expected to cause adversity among adolescents. This parallels stress research, which relies on inventories of stressful life events, and several standard inventories are in wide use. The items in such inventories are based, to varying degrees, on the perceptions and judgments of researchers, on previous theory and research, and on reports from samples of respondents (see Dohrenwend, 1974). In developing inventories of strainful events, criminologists must keep in mind the fact that there may be important group differences in the types of strain or negative relations most frequently encountered. A list of negative relations developed for one group, then, may overlook certain negative relations important for another group (see Dohrenwend, 1974). It may eventually be possible, however, to develop a comprehensive list of negative relations applicable to most samples of adolescents.

Second, criminologists must recognize that individuals and groups may experience the strainful events in such inventories differently (see Thoits, 1983). Limited data from the stress literature, for example, suggest that the impact of family stressors is greatest among young adolescents, peer stressors among middle adolescents, and academic stressors among old adolescents (Compas and Phares, 1991). Stress researchers have responded to such findings not by abandoning their inventories, but by investigating those factors that determine why one group or individual will experience a given event as stressful and another will not. And researchers have identified several sets of variables that influence the perception and experience of negative events (e.g., Compas and Phares, 1991; Pearlin, 1982; Pearlin and Schooler, 1978). Many of the variables are discussed in the next section, and they represent a major set of conditioning variables that criminologists should consider when examining the impact of strainful events on delinquency.

Examining the Cumulative Impact of Negative Relations

In most previous strain research in criminology, the impact of one type of negative relation on delinquency is examined with other negative relations ignored or held constant. So, for example, researchers will examine the impact of one type of goal blockage on delinquency, ignoring other types of goal blockage and other potential types of strain. This stands in sharp contrast to a central assumption in the stress literature, which is that stressful life events have a cumulative impact on the individual. Linsky and Straus (1986:17), for example, speak of the "accumulation theory," which asserts that "it is not so much the unique quality of any single event but the *cumulation* of several stressful events within a relatively short time span" that is consequential. As a result, it is standard practice in the stressful life-events literature to measure stress with a composite scale: a scale that typically sums the number of stressful life events experienced by the individual.

The precise nature of the cumulative effect, however, is unclear. As Thoits (1983:69) points out, stressful events may have an additive or interactive effect on outcome variables. The additive model assumes that each stressor has a fixed effect on delinquency, an effect independent of the level of the other stressors. Somewhat more plausible, perhaps, is the interactive model, which assumes that "a person who has experienced one event may react with even more distress to a second that follows soon after the first . . . two or more events . . . results in more distress than would be expected from the simple sum of their singular effects."

Whether the effect is additive or interactive, there is limited support for the idea that the level of stress/strain must pass a certain threshold before negative outcomes result (Linsky and Straus, 1986; Thoits, 1983). Below that level, stress/strain is unrelated to negative outcomes. Above that level, stress/strain has a positive effect on negative outcomes, perhaps an additive effect or perhaps an interactive effect.

Given these arguments, one should employ a composite index of strain in all analyses or examine the interactions between strain variables. Examining interactions can become very complex if there are more than a few indicators of strain, although it does allow one to examine the differential importance of various types of strain. If stressors have an interactive effect on delinquency, the interaction terms should be significant or the composite index should have a nonlinear effect on delinquency (see the discussion of interactions and nonlinear effects in Aiken and West, 1991). If the effect is additive, the interaction terms should be insignificant or the composite index should have a linear effect on delinquency (after the threshold level is reached). These issues have received only limited attention in the stress literature (see the review by Thoits, 1983), and they should certainly be explored when constructing measures of strain for the purpose of explaining delinquency. At a minimum, however, as comprehensive a list of negative events/conditions as possible should be examined.

There is also the issue of whether positive events/experiences should be examined. If prior stressors can aggravate the negative effect of subsequent stressors, perhaps positive events can mitigate the impact of stressors. Limited evidence from the stress literature suggests that lists of negative events predict better than lists examining the balance of negative and positive events (usually negative events minus positive events) (see Thoits, 1983:58–59; Williams and Uchiyama, 1989:101; see Gersten et al., 1974, for a possible exception). This topic, however, is certainly in need of more research. In addition to looking at the *difference* between desirable and undesirable events, researchers may also want to look at the *ratio* of undesirable to desirable events.

It should be noted that tests of strain theory in criminology typically examine the disjunction between aspirations and expectations for one or two goals and ignore all of the many other types of strain. The tests also typically assume that strain has a linear effect on delinquency, and they never examine positive as well as negative events. These facts may constitute additional reasons for the weak empirical support given to strain theory in criminology.

Examining the Magnitude, Recency, Duration, and Clustering of Adverse Events

Limited research from the stress and equity literatures suggest that adverse events are more influential to the extent that they are (1) greater in magnitude or size, (2) recent, (3) of long duration, and (4) clustered in time.

Magnitude

The magnitude of an event has different meanings depending on the type of strain being examined. With respect to goal blockage, magnitude refers to the size of the gap between one's goals and reality. With respect to the loss of positive stimuli, magnitude refers to the amount that was lost. And with respect to the presentation of noxious stimuli, magnitude refers to the amount of pain or discomfort *inflicted*.[11] In certain cases, magnitude may be measured in terms of a standard metric, such as dollars or volts delivered. In most cases, however, there is no standard metric available for measuring magnitude and one must rely on the perceptions of individuals (see Jasso, 1980, on quality versus quantity goods). To illustrate, researchers in the stress literature have asked judges to rate events according to the amount of readjustment they require or the threat they pose to the individual (see Thoits, 1983, for other weighting schemes). Such judgments are then averaged to form a magnitude score for each event. There is evidence, however, of subgroup differences in weights assigned (Thoits, 1983:53–55).

Magnitude ratings are then sometimes used to weight the events in composite scales. A common finding, however, is that lists of life events weighted by magnitude do *not* predict any better than unweighed lists (e.g., Gersten et al., 1974). This is due to the fact that the correlation between lists of weighted and unweighted events is typically so high (above .90) that the lists can be considered virtually identical (Thoits, 1983). Williams and Uchiyama (1989:99–100) explain this high correlation by arguing that severe life events, which are heavily weighted, have a low base rate in the population and so do not have a significant impact on scale scores. Studies that consider major and minor events separately tend to find that major events are in fact more consequential than minor events (Thoits, 1983:66).

It should be noted that the previous research on strain theory has paid only limited attention to the dimension of magnitude, even in those cases in which standard metrics for measuring magnitude were available. Samples, in fact, are often simply divided into strained and nonstrained groups, with little consideration of variations in the magnitude of strain.

Recency

Certain data suggest that recent events are more consequential than older events and that events older than three months have little effect (Avison and Turner, 1988). Those data focus on the impact of stress on depression, and so are not necessarily generalizable to the strain-delinquency relationship. Nevertheless, the data suggest that the recency of strain may be an important dimension to consider, and findings in this area might be of special use in designing longitudinal studies, in which the issue of the appropriate lag between cause and effect is central (although the subject of little research and theory).

Duration

Much theory and data from the equity and stress literatures suggest that events of long duration (chronic stressors) have a greater impact on a variety of negative psychological outcomes (Folger, 1986; Mark and Folger, 1984; Pearlin, 1982; Pearlin and Lieberman, 1979; Utne and Kidd, 1980). Some evidence, in fact, suggests that discrete events may be unimportant except to the extent that they affect chronic events (Cummings and El-Sheikh, 1991; Gersten et al., 1977; Pearlin, 1983). Certain researchers in the equity/justice literature have suggested that the expected duration of the event into the future should also be considered (Folger, 1986; Mark and Folger, 1984; Utne and Kidd, 1980; see especially the "likelihood of amelioration" concept).

Clustering

Data from the stress literature also suggest that events closely clustered in time have a greater effect on negative outcomes (Thoits, 1983). Such events, according to Thoits (1983), are more likely to overwhelm coping resources than events spread more evenly over time. Certain data, in particular, trace negative outcomes such as suicide and depression to a series of negative events clustered in the previous few weeks (Thoits, 1983).

ADAPTATIONS TO (COPING STRATEGIES FOR) STRAIN

The discussion thus far has focused on the types of strain that might promote delinquency. Virtually all strain theories, however, acknowledge that only *some* strained individuals turn to delinquency. Some effort has been made to identify those factors that determine whether one adapts to strain through delinquency. The most attention has been focused on the adolescent's commitment to legitimate means and association with other strained/delinquent individuals (see Agnew, 1991b).

The following discussion builds on this effort and is in two parts. First, the major adaptations to strain are described. This discussion points to a number of cognitive, emotional, and behavioral coping strategies that have not been considered in the criminology literature. Second, those factors that influence whether one adapts to strain using delinquent or nondelinquent means are described. This discussion also expands on the criminology literature to include several additional factors that affect the choice of adaptation.

Adaptations to Strain

What follows is a typology of the major cognitive, emotional, and behavioral adaptations to strain, including delinquency.

Cognitive Coping Strategies

Several literatures suggest that individuals sometimes cognitively reinterpret objective stressors in ways that minimize their subjective adversity. Three general strategies of cognitive coping are described below; each strategy has several forms. These strategies for coping with adversity may be summarized in the following phrases: "It's not important," "It's not that bad," and "I deserve it." This typology represents a synthesis of the coping strategies described in the stress, equity, stratification, and victimization literatures (Adams, 1963, 1965; Agnew, 1985b; Agnew and Jones, 1988; Averill, 1982; Della Fave, 1980; Donnerstein and Hatfield, 1982; Pearlin and Schooler, 1978; Walster et al., 1973, 1978). The stress literature, in particular, was especially useful. Stress has been found to have a consistent, although weak-to-moderate, main effect on outcome variables. Researchers have tried to explain this weak-to-moderate effect by arguing that the impact of stressors is conditioned by a number of variables, and much of the attention has been focused on coping strategies (see Compas and Phares, 1991; Thoits, 1984).

Ignore/Minimize the Importance of Adversity. The subjective impact of objective strain depends on the extent to which the strain is related to the central goals, values, and/or identities of the individual. As Pearlin and Schooler (1978:7) state, individuals may avoid subjective strain "to the extent that they are able to keep the most strainful experiences within the least valued areas of their life." Individuals, therefore, may minimize the strain they experience by reducing the absolute and/or relative importance assigned to goals/values and identities (see Agnew, 1983; Thoits, 1991a).

In particular, individuals may claim that a particular goal/value or identity is unimportant in an absolute sense. They may, for example, state that money or work is unimportant to them. This strategy is similar to Merton's adaptations of ritualism and retreatism, and it was emphasized by Hyman (1953). Individuals may also claim that a particular goal/value or identity is unimportant in a relative sense—relative to other goals/values or identities. They may, for example, state that money is less important than status or that work is less important than family and leisure activities.

The strategy of minimizing strain by reducing the absolute and/or relative emphasis placed on goals/values and identities has not been extensively examined in the strain literature. Certain evidence, however, suggests that it is commonly employed and may play a central role in accounting for the limited empirical support for strain theory. In particular, research on goals suggests that people pursue a wide variety of different goals and that they tend to place the greatest absolute and relative emphasis on those goals they are best able to achieve (Agnew, 1983; McClelland, 1990; Rosenberg, 1979:265–269; Wylie, 1979).

Maximize Positive Outcomes/Minimize Negative Outcomes. In the above adaptation, individuals acknowledge the existence of adversity but relegate such adversity to an unimportant area of their life. In a second adaptation, individuals attempt to deny the existence of adversity by maximizing their positive outcomes and/or minimizing their negative outcomes. This may be done in two ways: lowering the standards used to evaluate outcomes or distorting one's estimate of current and/or expected outcomes.

Lowering one's standards basically involves lowering one's goals or raising one's threshold for negative stimuli (see Suls, 1977). Such action, of course, makes one's current situation seem less adverse than it otherwise would be. Individuals may, for example, lower the amount of money they desire (which is distinct from lowering the importance attached to money). This strategy is also related to Merton's adaptations of ritualism and retreatism, and many of the critics of strain theory in criminology have focused on it. Hyman (1953) and others have argued that poor individuals in the United States are not strained because they have lowered their success goals—bringing their aspirations in line with reality. The data in this area are complex, but they suggest that this adaptation is employed by some—but not all—lower-class individuals (see Agnew, 1983, 1986; Agnew and Jones, 1988; see Cloward and Ohlin, 1960, and Empey, for data on "relative" aspirations).

In addition to lowering their standards, individuals may also cognitively distort their estimate of outcomes. As Agnew and Jones (1988) demonstrate, many individuals exaggerate their actual and expected levels of goal achievement. Individuals with poor grades, for example, often report that they are doing well in school. And individuals with little objective chance of attending college often report that they *expect* to attend college. (See Wylie, 1979, for additional data in this area.) In addition to exaggerating positive outcomes, individuals may also minimize negative outcomes—claiming that their losses are small and their noxious experiences are mild.

The self-concept literature discusses the many strategies individuals employ to accomplish such distortions (see Agnew and Jones, 1988; Rosenberg, 1979). Two common strategies, identified across several literatures, are worth noting. In "downward comparisons," individuals claim that their situation is less worse or at least no worse than that of similar others (e.g., Brickman and Bulman, 1977; Gruder, 1977; Pearlin and Schooler, 1978; Suls, 1977). This strategy is compatible with the equity literature, which suggests that one's evaluation of outcomes is conditioned by the outcomes of comparison others. Temporal comparisons may also be made, with individuals claiming that their situation is an improvement over the past. Recent research on the social comparison process suggests that individuals often deliberately make downward comparisons, especially when self-esteem is threatened (Gruder, 1977; Hegtvedt, 1991b; Suls, 1977). In a second strategy, "compensatory benefits," individuals cast "about for some positive attribute or circumstance within a troublesome situation . . . the person is aided in ignoring that which is noxious by anchoring his attention to what he considers the more worthwhile and rewarding aspects of experience" (Perlin

and Schooler, 1978:6–7). Crime victims, for example, often argue that their victimization benefited them in certain ways, such as causing them to grow as a person (Agnew, 1985b).

Accept Responsibility for Adversity. Third, individuals may *minimize* the subjective adversity of objective strain by convincing themselves that they *deserve* the adversity they have experienced. There are several possible reasons why *deserved* strain is less adverse than undeserved strain. Undeserved strain may violate the equity principle, challenge one's "belief in a just world" (see Lerner, 1977), and—if attributed to the malicious behavior of another—lead one to fear that it will be repeated in the future. Such reasons may help explain why individuals who make internal attributions for adversity are less distressed than others (Kluegel and Smith, 1986; Mirowsky and Ross, 1990).

Drawing on equity theory, one may argue that there are two basic strategies for convincing oneself that strain is deserved. First, individuals may cognitively minimize their positive inputs or maximize their negative inputs to a relationship. Inputs are conceived as contributions to the relationship and/or status characteristics believed to be relevant to the relationship (see Cook and Yamagishi, 1983). Second, individuals may maximize the positive inputs or minimize the negative inputs of others. Della Fave (1980) uses both of these strategies to explain the legitimation of inequality in the United States. Those at the bottom of the stratification system are said to minimize their own traits and exaggerate the positive traits and contributions of those above them. They therefore come to accept their limited outcomes as just (also see Kluegel and Smith, 1986; Shepelak, 1987).

Behavioral Coping Strategies

There are two major types of behavioral coping: those that seek to minimize or eliminate the source of strain and those that seek to satisfy the need for revenge.

Maximizing Positive Outcomes/Minimizing Negative Outcomes. Behavioral coping may assume several forms, paralleling each of the major types of strain. Individuals, then, may seek to achieve positively valued goals, protect or retrieve positively valued stimuli, or terminate or escape from negative stimuli. Their actions in these areas may involve conventional or delinquent behavior. Individuals seeking to escape from an adverse school environment, for example, may try to transfer to another school or they may illegally skip school. This rather broad adaptation encompasses Merton's adaptations of innovation and rebellion, as well as those coping strategies described in the equity literature as "maximizing one's outcomes," "minimizing one's inputs," and "maximizing the other's inputs."

Vengeful Behavior. Data indicate that when adversity is blamed on others it creates a desire for revenge that is distinct from the desire to end the adversity. A second method of behavioral coping, then, involves the taking of revenge. Vengeful behavior may also assume conventional or delinquent forms, although the potential for delinquency is obviously high. Such behavior may involve efforts to minimize the positive outcomes, increase the negative outcomes, and/or increase the inputs of others (as when adolescents cause teachers and parents to work harder through their incorrigible behavior).

Emotional Coping Strategies

Finally, individuals may cope by acting directly on the negative emotions that result from adversity. Rosenberg (1990), Thoits (1984, 1989, 1990, 1991b), and others list several strategies of emotional coping. They include the use of drugs such as stimulants and depressants, physical exercise and deep-breathing techniques, meditation, biofeedback and progressive relaxation, and the behavioral manipulation of expressive gestures through playacting or "expression work." In all of these examples, the focus is on alleviating negative emotions rather than cognitively reinterpreting or behaviorally altering the situation that produced those emotions. Many of the strategies are beyond the reach of most adolescents (Compas et al., 1988), and data indicate that adolescents often employ illicit drugs to cope with life's strains (Labouvie, 1986a, 1986b; Newcomb and Harlow, 1986). Emotional coping is especially likely when behavioral and cogni-

tive coping are unavailable or unsuccessful.

It should be noted that individuals may employ more than one of the above coping strategies (see Folkman, 1991). Also, still other coping strategies, such as distraction, could have been listed. It is assumed, however, that the above strategies constitute the primary responses to strain.

Predicting the Use of Delinquent versus Nondelinquent Adaptations

The above typology suggests that there are many ways to cope with strain—only some of which involve delinquency. And data from the stress literature suggest that individuals vary in the extent to which they use the different strategies (Compas et al., 1988; Menaghan, 1983; Pearlin and Schooler, 1978). These facts go a long way toward explaining the weak support for strain theory. With certain limited exceptions, the strategies are not taken into account in tests of strain theory.

The existence of the above coping strategies poses a serious problem for strain theory. If strain theory is to have any value, it must be able to explain the selection of delinquent versus nondelinquent adaptations. This issue has, of course, been raised before. Critics contend that Merton and other strain theorists fail to explain adequately why only *some* strained individuals turn to delinquency. This issue, however, is all the more pressing when one considers the full range of nondelinquent adaptations to strain listed above. It is therefore important to specify those factors that influence the choice of delinquent versus nondelinquent coping strategies.

The following discussion of influencing factors draws on the aggression, equity, and stress literatures (see especially Adams, 1965; Menaghan, 1982; Pearlin and Schooler, 1978; Walster et al., 1978). The aggression literature in psychology is especially useful. Adversity is said to produce a general state of arousal, which can facilitate a variety of behaviors. Whether this arousal results in aggression is said to be determined by a number of factors, many of which are noted below (see Bandura, 1973, 1983; Berkowitz,

1978, 1982). Those factors affect the choice of coping strategies by affecting (1) the constraints to nondelinquent and delinquent coping and (2) the disposition to engage in nondelinquent versus delinquent coping.

Constraints to Nondelinquent and Delinquent Coping

While there are many adaptations to objective strain, those adaptations are not equally available to everyone. Individuals are constrained in their choice of adaptations(s) by a variety of internal and external factors. The following is a partial list of such factors.

Initial Goals/Values/Identities of the Individual. If the objective strain affects goals/values/identities that are high in absolute and relative importance, and if the individual has few alternative goals/values/identities in which to seek refuge, it will be more difficult to relegate strain to an unimportant area of one's life (see Agnew, 1986; Thoits, 1991a). This is especially the case if the goals/values/identities receive strong social and cultural support (see below). As a result, strain will be more likely to lead to delinquency in such cases.

Individual Coping Resources. A wide range of traits can be listed in this area, including temperament, intelligence, creativity, problem-solving skills, interpersonal skills, self-efficacy, and self-esteem. These traits affect the selection of coping strategies by influencing the individual's sensitivity to objective strains and ability to engage in cognitive, emotional, and behavioral coping (Agnew, 1991a; Averill, 1982; Bernard, 1990; Compas, 1987; Edmunds and Kendrick, 1980; Slaby and Guerra, 1988; Tavris, 1984). Data, for example, suggest that individuals with high self-esteem are more resistant to stress (Averill, 1982; Compas, 1987; Kaplan, 1980; Pearlin and Schooler, 1978; Rosenberg, 1990; Thoits, 1983). Such individuals, therefore, should be less likely to respond to a given objective strain with delinquency. Individuals high in self-efficacy are more likely to feel that their strain can be alleviated by behavioral coping of a nondelinquent nature, and so they too should be less likely to respond to strain with delinquency (see Bandura, 1989, and Wang and Richarde, 1988, on self-efficacy; see Thoits, 1991b, on perceived control).

Conventional Social Support. Vaux (1988) provides an extended discussion of the different types of social support, their measurement, and their effect on outcome variables. Thoits (1984) argues that social support is important because it facilitates the major types of coping. The major types of social support, in fact, correspond to the major types of coping listed above. Thus, there is informational support, instrumental support, and emotional support (House, 1981). Adolescents with conventional social supports, then, should be better able to respond to objective strains in a nondelinquent manner.

Constraints to Delinquent Coping. The crime/delinquency literature has focused on certain variables that constrain delinquent coping. They include (1) the costs and benefits of engaging in delinquency in a particular situation (Clarke and Cornish, 1985), (2) the individual's level of social control (see Hirschi, 1969), and (3) the possession of those "illegitimate means" necessary for many delinquent acts (see Agnew, 1991a, for a full discussion).

Macro-Level Variables. The larger social environment may affect the probability of delinquent versus nondelinquent coping by affecting all the above factors. First, the social environment may affect coping by influencing the importance attached to selected goals/values/identities. For example, certain ethnographic accounts suggest that there is a strong social and cultural emphasis on the goals of money/status among certain segments of the urban poor. Many poor individuals, in particular, are in a situation in which (1) they face strong economic/status demands, (2) people around them stress the importance of money/status on a regular basis, and (3) few alternative goals are given cultural support (Anderson, 1978; MacLeod, 1987; Sullivan, 1989). As such, these individuals should face more difficulty in cognitively minimizing the importance of money and status.

Second, the larger social environment may affect the individual's sensitivity to particular strains by influencing the individual's beliefs regarding what is and is not adverse. The subculture of violence thesis, for example, is predicated on the assumption that young black males in urban slums are taught that a wide range of provocations and insults are highly adverse. Third, the social environment may influence the individual's ability to minimize cognitively the severity of objective strain. Individuals in some environments are regularly provided with external information about their accomplishments and failings (see Faunce, 1989), and their attempts at cognitively distorting such information are quickly challenged. Such a situation may exist among many adolescents and among those who inhabit the "street-corner world" of the urban poor. Adolescents and those on the street corner live in a very "public world"; one's accomplishments and failings typically occur before a large audience or they quickly become known to such an audience. Further, accounts suggest that this audience regularly reminds individuals of their accomplishments and failings and challenges attempts at cognitive distortion.

Fourth, certain social environments may make it difficult to engage in behavioral coping of a nondelinquent nature. Agnew (1985a) has argued that adolescents often find it difficult to escape legally from negative stimuli, especially negative stimuli encountered in the school, family, and neighborhood. Also, adolescents often lack the resources to negotiate successfully with adults, such as parents and teachers (although see Agnew, 1991a). Similar arguments might be made for the urban underclass. They often lack the resources to negotiate successfully with many others, and they often find it difficult to escape legally from adverse environments—by, for example, quitting their job (if they have a job) or moving to another neighborhood.

The larger social environment, then, may affect individual coping in a variety of ways. And certain groups, such as adolescents and the urban under-class, may face special constraints that make nondelinquent coping more difficult. This may explain the higher rate of deviance among these groups.

Factors Affecting the Disposition to Delinquency

The selection of delinquent versus nondelinquent coping strategies is not only dependent on the constraints to coping, but also on the adolescent's disposition to engage in delinquent versus nondelinquent coping. This disposition is a function of (1) certain temperamental variables (see Tonry et al., 1991), (2) the prior learning history of the adolescent, particularly the extent to which delinquency was reinforced in the past (Bandura, 1973; Berkowitz, 1982), (3) the adolescent's beliefs, particularly the rules defining the appropriate response to provocations (Bernard's, 1990, "regulative rules"), and (4) the adolescent's attributions regarding the causes of his or her adversity. Adolescents who attribute their adversity to others are much more likely to become angry, and as argued earlier, that anger creates a strong predisposition to delinquency. Data and theory from several areas, in fact, suggest that the experience of adversity is most likely to result in deviance when the adversity is blamed on another.[12] The attributions one makes are influenced by a variety of factors, as discussed in recent reviews by Averill (1982), Berwin (1988), R. Cohen (1982), Crittenden (1983, 1989), Kluegel and Smith (1986), and Utne and Kidd (1980). The possibility that there may be demographic and subgroup differences in the rules for assigning blame is of special interest (see Bernard, 1990; Crittenden, 1983, 1989).

A key variable affecting several of the above factors is association with delinquent peers. It has been argued that adolescents who associate with delinquent peers are more likely to be exposed to delinquent models and beliefs and to receive reinforcement for delinquency (see especially, Akers, 1985). It may also be the case that delinquent peers increase the likelihood that adolescents will attribute their adversity to others.

The individual's disposition to delinquency, then, may condition the impact of adversity on delinquency. At the same time, it is important to note that continued experience with adversity may create a disposition for delinquency. This argument has been made by Bernard (1990), Cloward and Ohlin (1960), A. Cohen (1955), Elliott et al. (1979), and others. In particular, it has been argued that under certain conditions the experience of adversity may lead to beliefs favorable to delinquency, lead adolescents to join or form delinquent peer groups, and lead adolescents to blame others for their misfortune.

Virtually all empirical research on strain theory in criminology has neglected the constraints to coping and the adolescent's disposition to delinquency. Researchers, in particular, have failed to examine whether the effect of adversity on delinquency is conditioned by factors such as self-efficacy and association with delinquent peers. This is likely a major reason for the weak empirical support for strain theory.

CONCLUSION

Much of the recent theoretical work in criminology has focused on the integration of different delinquency theories. This paper has taken an alternative track and, following Hirschi's (1979) advice, has focused on the refinement of a single theory. The general strain theory builds upon traditional strain theory in criminology in several ways. First, the general strain theory points to several new sources of strain. In particular, it focuses on three categories of strain or negative relationships with others: (1) the actual or anticipated failure to achieve positively valued goals, (2) the actual or anticipated removal of positively valued stimuli, and (3) the actual or anticipated presentation of negative stimuli. Most current strain theories in criminology only focus on strain as the failure to achieve positively valued goals, and even then the focus is only on the disjunction between aspirations and expectations/actual achievements. The disjunctions between expectations and achievements and just/fair outcomes and achievements are ignored. The general strain theory, then, significantly expands the focus of strain theory to include all types of negative relations between the individual and others.

Second, the general strain theory more precisely specifies the relationship between strain and delinquency, pointing out that strain is likely to have a cumulative effect on delinquency after a certain threshold level is reached. The theory also points to certain

relevant dimensions of strain that should be considered in empirical research, including the magnitude, recently, duration, and clustering of strainful events.

Third, the general strain theory provides a more comprehensive account of the cognitive, behavioral, and emotional adaptations to strain. This account sheds additional light on the reasons why many strained individuals do *not* turn to delinquency, and it may prove useful in devising strategies to prevent and control delinquency. Individuals, in particular, may be taught those nondelinquent coping strategies found to be most effective in preventing delinquency.

Fourth, the general strain theory more fully describes those factors affecting the choice of delinquent versus nondelinquent adaptations. The failure to consider such factors is a fundamental reason for the weak empirical support for strain theory.

Most of the above modifications in strain theory were suggested by research in several areas outside of traditional criminology, most notably the stress research in medical sociology and psychology, the equity/justice research in social psychology, and the aggression research in psychology. With certain exceptions, researchers in criminology have tended to cling to the early strain models of Merton (1938), A. Cohen (1955), and Cloward and Ohlin (1960) and to ignore the developments in related fields. And while these early strain models contain much of value and have had a major influence on the general strain theory in this paper, they do not fully exploit the potential of strain theory.

At the same time, it is important to note that the general strain theory is not presented here as a fully developed alternative to earlier theories. First, the macroimplications of the theory were only briefly discussed. It would not be difficult to extend the general strain theory to the macro level, however; researchers could focus on (1) the social determinants of adversity (for an example, see Bernard, 1990, on the urban underclass) and (2) the social determinants of those factors that condition the effect of adversity on delinquency. Second, the theory did not concern itself with the nonsocial determinants of strain, such as illness. It seems doubtful that adversity caused by nonsocial sources is a major source of delinquency because, among other things, it is unlikely to generate anger (see Averill, 1982). Nevertheless, nonsocial sources of adversity should be investigated. Third, the relationship between the general strain theory and other major theories of delinquency must be more fully explored. As hinted earlier, the relationship is rather complex. While the general strain theory is clearly distinct from control and differential association theory, strain may lead to low social control and association with delinquent others. Further, variables from the three theories may interact with one another in producing delinquency. Individuals with delinquent friends, for example, should be more likely to respond to strain with delinquency. The general strain theory then, is presented as a foundation on which to build.

It is not possible to test the general strain theory fully with currently available data sets, but it is possible to test core sections of the theory. Most data sets dealing with delinquency contain at least some measures of adversity and at least some measures of those factors said to condition the effect of adversity on delinquency. Given this fact, researchers could focus on the following core hypotheses derived from the theory:

First, adverse relations with others will have a positive effect on both general and specific measures of delinquency, with measures of social control and differential association held constant. This is especially true of adverse relations that are severe and that provide limited opportunities for nondelinquent coping. Prime examples, as discussed earlier, are adverse relations involving family, school, and neighborhood. It is hoped research will point to several measures of strain that are especially relevant to delinquency. Such measures can then be made a routine part of delinquency research, just as the elements of the social bond and measures of differential association are now routinely included in empirical studies.

Second, adverse relations will have a cumulative impact on delinquency after a certain threshold level is reached. Further, this cumulative impact will likely be interactive in nature; each additional increment in strain will have a greater impact than the one before.

Third, the impact of strain or adverse relations on delinquency will be conditioned by several variables, as listed above.

Strain theory is the only major theory to focus explicitly on negative relations with others and to argue that delinquency results from the negative affect caused by such relations. As such, it complements social control and differential association/social learning theory in a fundamental way. It is hoped that the general strain theory will revive interest in negative relations and cause criminologists to "bring the bad back in."

Notes

1. One need not assume that expectations are existentially based; they may derive from the cultural system as well. Likewise, one need not assume that aspirations derive from the cultural system. The focus in this paper is on *types* of strain rather than *sources* of strain, although a consideration of sources is crucial when the macroimplications of the theory are developed. Additional information on the sources of positively valued goals—including aspirations and expectations—can be found in Alves and Rossi, 1978; Cook and Messick, 1983; Hochschild, 1981; Jasso and Rossi, 1977; Martin and Murray, 1983; Messick and Sentis, 1983; Mickelson, 1990; and Shepelak and Alwin, 1986.

2. Theorists have recently argued that efforts to restore equity need not involve the specific others in the inequitable relationship. If one cannot restore equity with such specific others, there may be an effort to restore "equity with the world" (Austin, 1977; Stephenson and White, 1968; Walster et al., 1978.) That is, individuals who feel they have been inequitably treated may try to restore equity in the context of a totally different relationship. The adolescent who is inequitably treated by parents, for example, may respond by inequitably treating peers. The concept of "equity with the world" has not been the subject of much empirical research, but it is intriguing because it provides a novel explanation for displayed aggression. It has also been argued that individuals may be distressed not only by their own inequitable treatment, but also by the inequitable treatment of others (see Crosby and Gonzalez-Intal, 1984; Walster et al., 1978). We may have, then, a sort of vicarious strain, a type little investigated in the literature.

3. The equity literature has been criticized on a number of points, the most prominent being that there are a variety of distribution rules besides equity—such as equality and need (Deutsch, 1975; Folger,

1984; Mikula, 1980; Schwinger, 1980; Utne and Kidd, 1980). Much recent research has focused on the factors that determine the preference for one rule over another (Alves and Rossi, 1978; Cook and Hegtvedt, 1983; Deutsch, 1975; Hegtvedt, 1987, 1991a; Hochschild, 1981; Lerner, 1977; Leventhal, 1976; Leventhal et al., 1980; Schwinger, 1980; Walster et al., 1978). Also, the equity literature argues that individuals compare themselves with similar others with whom they are involved in exchange/allocation relations. However, it has been argued that individuals sometimes compare themselves with dissimilar others, make referential (generalized) rather than local (specific) comparisons, make internal rather than external comparisons, make group-to-group comparisons, or avoid social comparison altogether (see Berger et al., 1972; Hegtvedt, 1991b; Martin and Murray, 1983; see Hegtvedt, 1991b, and Suls and Wills, 1991, for a discussion of the factors affecting the choice of comparison objects). Finally, even if one knows what distribution rule individuals prefer and the types of social comparisons they make, it is still difficult to predict whether they will evaluate their interactions as equitable. Except in unambiguous situations of the type created in experiments, it is hard to predict what inputs and outcomes individuals will define as relevant, how they will weight those inputs and outcomes, and how they will evaluate themselves and others on those inputs and outcomes (Austin, 1977; Hegtvedt, 1991a; Messick and Sentis, 1979, 1983; Walster et al., 1973, 1978). Fortunately, however, the above three problems do not prohibit strain theory from taking advantage of certain of the insights from equity theory. While it is difficult to predict whether individuals will define their relationships as equitable, it is relatively easy to measure equity after the fact.

4. To add a still further complication, it has been suggested that anger may result from the violation of *procedural* as well as distributive justice rules (Folger, 1984, 1986; Lind and Tyler, 1988). Procedural justice does not focus on the fairness of outcomes, but rather on the fairness of the procedures by which individuals decide how to distribute resources. A central issue in procedural justice is whether all individuals have a "voice" in deciding how resources will be distributed. One might, then, ask adolescents about the fairness of the procedures used by parents, teachers, and others to make rules.

5. This strategy assumes that all standards are relevant in a given situation, which may not always be the case. In certain situations, for example, one may make local comparisons but not referential comparisons (see Brickman and Bulman, 1977; Crosby and Gonzales-Intal, 1984). In other situations, social comparison processes may not come into play at all; outcomes may be evaluated in terms of culturally derived standards (see Folger, 1986).

6. The stress literature has also focused on positive events, based on the assumption that such events might lead to stress by overloading the individual. Accumulating evidence, however, suggests that it is only undesirable events that lead to negative outcomes such as depression (e.g., Gersten et al., 1974; Kaplan et al., 1983; Pearlin et al., 1981; Thoits, 1983).

7. Certain individuals have criticized the stress literature for neglecting the failure of individuals to achieve positively valued goals. In particular, it has been charged that the stress literature has neglected "nonevents," or events that are desired or anticipated but do not occur (Dohrenwend and Dohrenwend, 1974; Thoits, 1983). One major distinction between the strain literature in criminology and the stress literature in medical sociology, in fact, is that the former has focused on "nonevents" while the latter has focused on "events."

8. Some researchers have argued that it is often difficult to distinguish the presentation of negative stimuli from the removal of positive stimuli (Michael, 1973; Van Houten, 1983; Zillman, 1979). Suppose, for example, that an adolescent argues with parents. Does this represent the presentation of negative stimuli, (the arguing) or the removal of positive stimuli (harmonious relations with one's parents)? The point is a valid one, yet the distinction between the two types of strain still seems useful since it helps ensure that all major types of strain are considered by researchers.

9. The focus on blame/anger represents a major distinction between the general strain theory and the stress literature. The stress literature simply focuses on adversity, regardless of whether it is blamed on another. This is perhaps appropriate because the major outcome variables of the stress literature are inner-directed states, like depression and poor health. When the focus shifts to outer-directed behavior, like much delinquency, a concern with blame/anger becomes important.

10. Delinquency may still occur in the absence of blame and anger (see Berkowitz, 1986; Zillman, 1979). Individuals who accept responsibility for their adversity are still subject to negative affect, such as depression, despair, and disappointment (see Kemper, 1978; Kluegel and Smith, 1986). As a result, such individuals will still feel pressure to take corrective action, although the absence of anger places them under less pressure and makes vengeful behavior much less likely. Such individuals, however, may engage in inner-directed delinquency, such as drug use, and if suitably disposed, they may turn to other forms of delinquency as well. Since these individuals lack the strong motivation for revenge and the lowered inhibitions that anger provides, it is assumed that they must have some minimal disposition for deviance before they respond to their adversity with outer-directed delinquency (see the discussion of the disposition to delinquency).

11. As Empey (1956) and others have pointed out, magnitude may also be measured in *relative* terms.

For example, suppose an individual earning $10,000 a year and an individual earning $100,000 both lose $100 in a burglary. In absolute terms, the magnitude of their loss is the same. Relative to their current income, however, the magnitude of their loss is quite different. In most cases, it would be difficult to develop precise measures of relative magnitude. Nevertheless, researchers should at the very least be sensitive to this issue when analyzing and interpreting data.

12. This is a major theme in the psychological research on aggression, in much of the recent research on equity, and in the emotions literature, and it is a central theme in Cloward and Ohlin's (1960) strain theory (e.g., Averill, 1982; Berkowitz, 1982; R. Cohen, 1982; Crosby and Gonzalez-Intal, 1984; Garrett and Libby, 1973; Kemper, 1978; Leventhal, 1976; Mark and Folger, 1984; Martin and Murray, 1984; Weiner, 1982; Zillman, 1979).

References

ADAMS, J. STACY
1963   Toward an understanding of inequity. Journal of Abnormal and Social Psychology 67:422–436.
1965   Inequity in social exchange. In Leonard Berkowitz (ed.), Advances in Experimental Social Psychology. New York: Academic Press.

AGNEW, ROBERT
1983   Social class and success goals: An examination of relative and absolute aspirations. Sociological Quarterly 24:435–452.
1984   Goal achievement and delinquency. Sociology and Social Research 68:435–451.
1985a   A revised strain theory of delinquency. Social Forces 64:151–167.
1985b   Neutralizing the impact of crime. Criminal Justice and Behavior 12:221–239.
1986   Challenging strain theory: An examination of goals and goal-blockage. Paper presented at the annual meeting of the American Society of Criminology, Atlanta.
1989   A longitudinal test of the revised strain theory. Journal of Quantitative Criminology 5:373–387.
1990   The origins of delinquent events: An examination of offender accounts. Journal of Research in Crime and Delinquency 27:267–294.
1991a   Adolescent resources and delinquency. Criminology 28:535–566.
1991b   Strain and subcultural crime theory. In Joseph Sheley (ed.), Criminology: A Contemporary Handbook. Belmont, Calif.: Wadsworth.

AGNEW, ROBERT AND DIANE JONES
1988   Adapting to deprivation: An examination of inflated educational expectations. Sociological Quarterly 29:315–337.

AIKEN, LEONA S. AND STEPHEN G. WEST
1991   Multiple Regression: Testing and Interpreting Interactions. Newbury Park, Calif.: Sage.

AKERS, RONALD L.
1985   Deviant Behavior: A Social Learning Approach. Belmont, Calif.: Wadsworth.

ALVES, WAYNE M. AND PETER H. ROSSI
1978   Who should get what? Fairness judgments of the distribution of earnings. American Journal of Sociology 84:541–564.

ALWIN, DUANE F.
1987   Distributive justice and satisfaction with material well-being. American Sociological Review 52:83–95.

ANDERSON, CRAIG A. AND DONA C. ANDERSON
1984   Ambient temperature and violent crime: Tests of the linear and curvilinear hypotheses. Journal of Personality and Social Psychology 46:91–97.

ANDERSON, ELIJAH
1978   A Place on the Corner. Chicago: University of Chicago Press.

AUSTIN, WILLIAM
1977   Equity theory and social comparison processes. In Jerry M. Suls and Richard L. Miller (eds.), Social Comparison Processes. New York: Hemisphere.

AVERILL, JAMES R.
1982   Anger and Aggression. New York: Springer-Verlag.

AVISON, WILLIAM R. AND R. JAY TURNER
1988   Stressful life events and depressive symptoms: Disaggregating the effects of acute stressors and chronic strains. Journal of Health and Social Behavior 29:253–264.

BANDURA, ALBERT
1973   Aggression: A Social Learning Analysis. Englewood Cliffs, N.J.: Prentice-Hall.
1983   Psychological mechanisms of aggression. In Russell G. Geen and Edward Donnerstein (eds.), Aggression: Theoretical and Empirical Reviews. New York: Academic Press.
1989   Human agency and social cognitive theory. American Psychologist 44:1175–1184.

BERGER, JOSEPH, MORRIS ZELDITCH, JR., BO ANDERSON, AND BERNARD COHEN
1972   Structural aspects of distributive justice: A status-value formulation. In Joseph Berger, Morris Zelditch, Jr., and Bo Anderson (eds.), Sociological Theories in Progress. New York: Houghton Mifflin.

BERGER, JOSEPH, M. HAMIT FISCK, ROBERT Z. NORMAN, AND DAVID G. WAGNER
1983   The formation of reward expectations in status situations. In David M. Messick and Karen S. Cook (eds.), Equity Theory: Psychological and Sociological Perspectives. New York: Praeger.

BERKOWITZ, LEONARD
1978   Whatever happened to the frustration-aggression hypothesis? American Behavioral Scientist 21:691–708.
1982   Aversive conditions as stimuli to aggression. In Leonard Berkowitz (ed.), Advances in Experimental Social Psychology. Vol. 15. New York: Academic Press.

1986   A Survey of Social Psychology. New York: Holt, Rinehart & Winston.

BERNARD, THOMAS J.
1984   Control criticisms of strain theories: An assessment of theoretical and empirical adequacy. Journal of Research in Crime and Delinquency 21:353–372.
1987   Testing structural strain theories. Journal of Research in Crime and Delinquency 24:262–280.
1990   Angry aggression among the "truly disadvantaged." Criminology 28:73–96.

BLAU, PETER
1964   Exchange and Power in Social Life. New York: John Wiley & Sons.

BREWIN, CHRIS R.
1988   Explanation and adaptation in adversity. In Shirley Fisher and James Reason (eds.), Handbook of Life Stress, Cognition and Health. Chichester, England: John Wiley & Sons.

BRICKMAN, PHILIP AND RONNIE JANOFF BULMAN
1977   Pleasure and pain in social comparison. In Jerry M. Suls and Richard L. Miller (eds.), Social Comparison Processes. New York: Hemishpere.

CLARKE, RONALD V., AND DEREK B. CORNISH
1985   Modeling offenders' decisions: A framework for research and policy. In Michael Tonry and Norval Morris (eds.), Crime and Justice: An Annual Review of Research. Vol. 6. Chicago: University of Chicago Press.

CLINARD, MARSHALL B.
1964   Anomie and Deviant Behavior. New York: Free Press.

CLOWARD, RICHARD A. AND LLOYD E. OHLIN
1960   Delinquency and Opportunity. New York: Free Press.

COHEN, ALBERT K.
1955   Delinquent Boys. New York: Free Press.
1965   The sociology of the deviant act: Anomie theory and beyond. American Sociological Review 30:5–14.

COHEN, RONALD L.
1982   Perceiving justice: An attributional perspective. In Jerald Greenberg and Ronald L. Cohen (eds.), Equity and Justice in Social Behavior. New York: Academic Press.

COLE, STEPHEN
1975   The growth of scientific knowledge: Theories of deviance as a case study. In Lewis A. Coser (ed.), The Idea of Social Structure: Papers in Honor of Robert K. Merton. New York: Harcourt Brace Jovanovich.

COMPAS, BRUCE E.
1987   Coping with stress during childhood and adolescence. Psychological Bulletin 101:393–403.

COMPAS, BRUCE E., VANESSA L. MALCARNE, AND KAREN M. FONDACARO
1988   Coping with stressful events in older children and young adolescents. Journal of Consulting and Clinical Psychology 56:405–411.

COMPAS, BRUCE E. AND VICKY PHARES
1991   Stress during childhood and adolescence: Sources of risk and vulnerability. In E. Mark Cummings, Anita L. Greene, and Katherine H. Karraker (eds.), Life-Span Developmental Psychology: Perspectives on Stress and Coping. Hillsdale, N.J.: Lawrence Erlbaum.

COOK, KAREN S., AND KAREN A. HEGTVEDT
1983   Distributive justice, equity, and equality. Annual Review of Sociology 9:217–241.
1991   Empirical evidence of the sense of justice. In Margaret Gruter, Roger D. Masters, Michael T. McGuire (eds.), The Sense of Justice: An Inquiry into the Biological Foundations of Law. New York: Greenwood Press.

COOK, KAREN S. AND DAVID MESSICK
1983   Psychological and sociological perspectives on distributive justice: Convergent, divergent, and parallel lines. In David M. Messick and Karen S. Cook (eds.), Equity Theory: Psychological and Sociological Perspectives. New York: Praeger.

COOK, KAREN S. AND TOSHIO YAMAGISHI
1983   Social determinants of equity judgments: The problem of multidimensional input. In David M. Messick and Karen S. Cook (eds.), Equity Theory: Psychological and Sociological Perspectives. New York: Praeger.

CRITTENDEN, KATHLEEN S.
1983   Sociological aspects of attribution. Annual Review of Sociology 9:425–446.
1989   Causal attribution in sociocultural context: Toward a self-presentational theory of attribution processes. Sociological Quarterly 30:1–14.

CROSBY, FAYE AND A. MIREN GONZALEZ-INTAL
1984   Relative deprivation and equity theories: Felt injustice and the undeserved benefits of others. In Robert Folger (ed.), The Sense on Injustice: Social Psychological Perspectives. New York: Plenum.

CUMMINGS, E. MARK AND MONA EL-SHEIKH
1991   Children's coping with angry environments: A process-oriented approach. In E. Mark Cummings, Anita L. Greene, and Katherine H. Karraker (eds.), Life-Span Developmental Psychology: Perspectives on Stress and Coping. Hillsdale, N.J.: Lawrence Erlbaum.

DELLA FAVE, L. RICHARD
1974   Success values: Are they universal or class-differentiated? American Journal of Sociology 80:153–169.
1980   The meek shall not inherit the earth: Self-evaluations and the legitimacy of stratification. American Sociological Review 45:955–971.

DELLA FAVE, L. RICHARD AND PATRICIA KLOBUS
1976   Success values and the value stretch: A biracial comparison. Sociological Quarterly 17:491–502.

DEUTSCH, MORTON
1975   Equity, equality, and need: What determines which value will be used as the basis of distributive justice. Journal of Social Issues 31:137–149.

DOHRENWEND, BARBARA SNELL AND BRUCE P. DOHRENWEND
1974   Overview and prospects for research on stressful life events. In Barbara Snell Dohrenwend and Bruce P. Dohrenwend (eds.), Stressful Life Events: Their Nature and Effects. New York: John Wiley & Sons.

DOHRENWEND, BRUCE P.
1974   Problems in defining and sampling the relevant population of stressful life events. In Barbara Snell Dohrenwend and Bruce P. Dohrenwend (eds.), Stressful Life Events: Their Nature and Effects. New York: John Wiley & Sons.

DONNERSTEIN, EDWARD AND ELAINE HATFIELD
1982   Aggression and equity. In Jerald Greenberg and Ronald L. Cohen (eds.), Equity and Justice in Social Behavior. New York: Academic Press.

EDMUNDS, G. AND D.C. KENDRICK
1980   The Measurement of Human Aggressiveness. New York: John Wiley & Sons.

ELLIOTT, DELBERT AND HARWIN VOSS
1974   Delinquency and Dropout. Lexington, Mass.: Lexington Books.

ELLIOTT, DELBERT, SUZANNE AGETON, AND RACHEL CANTER
1979   An integrated theoretical perspective on delinquent behavior. Journal of Research in Crime and Delinquency 16:3–27.

ELLIOTT, DELBERT, DAVID HUIZINGA, AND SUZANNE AGETON
1985   Explaining Delinquency and Drug Use. Beverly Hills, Calif.: Sage.

EMPEY, LAMAR
1956   Social class and occupational aspiration: A comparison of absolute and relative measurement. American Sociological Review 21:703–709.

1982   American Delinquency: Its Meaning and Construction. Homewood, Ill.: Dorsey.

FARNWORTH, MARGARET AND MICHAEL J. LEIBER
1989   Strain theory revisited: Economic goals, educational means, and delinquency. American Sociological Review 54:263–274.

FAUNCE, WILLIAM A.
1989   Occupational status-assignment systems: The effect of status on self-esteem. American Journal of Sociology 95:378–400.

FOLGER, ROBERT
1984   Emerging issues in the social psychology of justice. In Robert Folger (ed.), The Sense of Injustice: Social Psychological Perspectives. New York: Plenum.

1986   Rethinking equity theory: A referent cognitions model. In Hans Werner Bierhoff, Ronald L. Cohen, and Jerald Greenberg (eds.), Justice in Social Relations. New York: Plenum.

FOLKMAN, SUSAN
1991   Coping across the life-span: Theoretical issues. In E. Mark Cummings, Anita L. Greene, and Katherine H. Karraker (eds.), Life-Span Developmental Psychology: Perspectives on Stress and Coping. Hillsdale, N.J.: Lawrence Erlbaum.

GARRETT, JAMES AND WILLIAM L. LIBBY, JR.
1973   Role of intentionality in mediating responses to inequity in the dyad. Journal of Personality and Social Psychology 28:21–27.

GERSTEN, JOANNE C., THOMAS S. LANGER, JEANNE G. EISENBERG, AND LIDA OZEK
1974   Child behavior and life events: Undesirable change or change per se. In Barbara Snell Dohrenwend and Bruce P. Dohrenwend (eds.), Stressful Life Events: Their Nature and Effects. New York: John Wiley & Sons.

GERSTEN, JOANNE C., THOMAS S. LANGER, JEANNE G. EISENBERG, AND ORA SMITH-FAGON
1977   An evaluation of the etiological role of stressful life-change events in psychological disorders. Journal of Health and Social Behavior 18:228–244.

GREENBERG, DAVID F.
1977   Delinquency and the age structure of society. Contemporary Crises 1:189–223.

GRUDER, CHARLES L.
1977   Choice of comparison persons in evaluating oneself. In Jerry M. Suls and Richard L. Miller (eds.), Social Comparison Processes. New York: Hemisphere.

HAWKINS, J. DAVID AND DENISE M. LISHNER
1987   Schooling and delinquency. In Elmer H. Johnson (ed.), Handbook on Crime and Delinquency Prevention. New York: Greenwood.

HEALY, WILLIAM AND AUGUSTA F. BONNER
1969   New Light on Delinquency and Its Treatment. New Haven, Conn.: Yale University Press.

HEGTVEDT, KAREN A.
1987   When rewards are scarce: Equal or equitable distributions. Social Forces 66:183–207.

1990   The effect of relationship structure on emotional responses to inequity. Social Psychology Quarterly 53:214–228.

1991a   Justice processes. In Martha Foschi and Edward J. Lawler (eds.), Group Processes: Sociological Analyses. Chicago: Nelson-Hall.

1991b   Social comparison processes. In Edgar F. Borgotta and Marie E. Borgotta (eds.), Encyclopedia of Sociology. New York: Macmillan.

HIRSCHI, TRAVIS
1969   Causes of Delinquency. Berkeley: University of California Press.

1979   Separate and unequal is better. Journal of Research in Crime and Delinquency 16: 34–38.

HIRSCHI, TRAVIS AND MICHAEL GOTTFREDSON
1986   The distinction between crime and criminality. In Timothy F. Hartnagel and Robert A. Silverman (eds.), Critique and Explanation. New Brunswick, N.J.: Transaction Books.

HOCHSCHILD, JENNIFER L.
1981   What's Fair: American Beliefs about Distributive Justice. Cambridge, Mass,: Harvard University Press.

HOMANS, GEORGE C.
1961   Social Behavior: Its Elementary Forms. New York: Harcourt, Brace and World.

HOUSE, JAMES S.
1981   Work Stress and Social Support. Reading, Mass.: Addison-Wesley.

HYMAN, HERBERT
1953   The value systems of the different classes: A social- psychological contribution to the analysis of stratification. In Reinhard Bendix and Seymour Martin Lipset (eds.), Class, Status, and Power. New York: Free Press.

JASSO, GUILLERMINA
1980   A new theory of distributive justice. American Sociological Review 45:3–32.

JASSO, GUILLERMINA AND PETER H. ROSSI
1977   Distributive justice and earned income. American Sociological Review 42:639–651.

JENSEN, GARY
1986   Dis-integrating integrated theory: A critical analysis of attempts to save strain theory. Paper presented at the annual meeting of the American Society of Criminology, Atlanta.

JOHNSON, RICHARD E.
1979   Juvenile Delinquency and Its Origins. London: Cambridge University Press.

KAPLAN, HOWARD B.
1980   Deviant Behavior in Defense of Self. New York: Academic Press.

KAPLAN, HOWARD B., CYNTHIA ROBBINS, AND STEVEN S. MARTIN
1983   Toward the testing of a general theory of deviant behavior in longitudinal perspective: Patterns of psychopathology. In James R. Greenley and Robert G. Simmons (eds.), Research in Community and Mental Health. Greenwich, Conn.: Jai Press.

KEMPER, THEODORE D.
1978   A Social Interactional Theory of Emotions. New York: John Wiley & Sons.

KLUEGEL, JAMES R. AND ELIOT R. SMITH
1986   Beliefs about Inequality. New York: Aldine De Gruyter.

KORNHAUSER, RUTH ROSNER
1978   Social Sources of Delinquency. Chicago: University of Chicago Press.

LABOUVIE, ERICH W.
1986a   Alcohol and marijuana use in relation to adolescent stress. International Journal of the Addictions 21:333–345.
1986b   The coping function of adolescent alcohol and drug use. In Rainer K. Sibereisen, Klaus Eyfeth and George Rudinger (eds.), Development as Action in Context. New York: Springer.

LAURITSEN, JANET L., ROBERT J. SAMPSON, AND JOHN LAUB
1991   The link between offending and victimization among adolescents. Criminology 29:265–292.

LERNER, MELVIN J.
1977   The justice motive: Some hypotheses as to its origins and forms. Journal of Personality 45:1–52.

LEVENTHAL, GERALD S.
1976   The distribution of rewards and resources in groups and organizations. In Leonard Berkowitz and Elaine Walster (eds.), Advances in Experimental Social Psychology: Equity Theory: Toward a General Theory of Social Interaction. New York: Academic Press.

LEVENTHAL, GERALD S., JURGIS KARUZAJR, AND WILLIAM RICK FRY
1980   Beyond fairness: A theory of allocation preferences. In Gerald Mikula (ed.), Justice and Social Interaction. New York: Springer-Verlag.

LIND, E. ALLAN AND TOM R. TYLER
1988   The Social Psychology of Procedural Justice. New York: Plenum.

LINSKY, ARNOLD S. AND MURRAY A. STRAUS
1986   Social Stress in the United States. Dover, Mass.: Auburn House.

LISKA, ALLEN E.
1987   Perspectives on Deviance. Englewood Cliffs, N.J.: Prentice-Hall.

MCCLELLAND, KATHERINE
1990   The social management of ambition. Sociological Quarterly 31:225–251.

MACLEOD, JAY
1987   Ain't No Makin' It. Boulder, Colo.: Westview Press.

MARK, MELVIN M. AND ROBERT FOLGER
1984   Responses to relative deprivation: A conceptual framework. In Philip Shaver (ed.), Review of Personality and Social Psychology. Vol. 5. Beverly Hills, Calif.: Sage.

MARTIN, JOANNE
1986   When expectations and justice do not coincide: Blue collar visions of a just world. In Hans Weiner Bierhoff, Ronald L. Cohen, and Jerald Greenberg (eds.), Justice in Social Relations. New York: Plenum.

MARTIN, JOANNE AND ALAN MURRAY
1983   Distributive injustice and unfair exchange. In David M. Messick and Karen S. Cook (eds.), Equity Theory: Psychological and Social Perspectives. New York: Praeger.
1984   Catalysts for collective violence: The importance of a psychological approach. In Robert Folger (ed.), The Sense of Injustice: Social Psychological Perspectives. New York: Plenum.

MASSEY, JAMES L. AND MARVIN KROHN
1986   A longitudinal examination of an integrated social process model of deviant behavior. Social Forces 65:106–134.

MAWSON, ANTHONY R.
1987   Criminality: A Model of Stress-Induced Crime. New York: Praeger.

MENAGHAN, ELIZABETH
1982   Measuring coping effectiveness: A panel analysis of marital problems and coping efforts. Journal of Health and Social Behavior 23:220–234.
1983   Individual coping efforts: Moderators of the relationship between life stress and mental

health outcomes. In Howard B. Kaplan (ed.), Psychosocial Stress: Trends in Theory and Research. New York: Academic Press.

MERTON, ROBERT
1938   Social structure and anomie. American Sociological Review 3:672–682.

MESSICK, DAVID M. AND KEITH SENTIS
1979   Fairness and preference. Journal of Experimental Social Psychology 15:418–434.

1983   Fairness, preference, and fairness biases. In David M. Messick and Karen S. Cook (eds.), Equity Theory: Psychological and Sociological Perspectives. New York: Praeger.

MICHAEL, JACK
1973   Positive and negative reinforcement, a distinction that is no longer necessary; or a better way to talk about bad things. In Eugene Ramp and George Semb (eds.), Behavior Analysis: Areas of Research and Application. Englewood Cliffs, N.J.: Prentice-Hall.

MICKELSON, ROSLYN ARLIN
1990   The attitude-achievement paradox among black adolescents. Sociology of Education 63:44–61.

MIKULA, GEROLD
1980   Justice and Social Interaction. New York: Springer-Verlag.

1986   The experience of injustice: Toward a better understanding of its phenomenology. In Hans Werner Bierhoff, Ronald L. Cohen, and Jerald Greenberg (eds.), Justice in Social Relations. New York: Plenum.

MIROWSKY, JOHN AND CATHERINE E. ROSS
1990   The consolation-prize theory of alienation. American Journal of Sociology 95:1505–1535.

MORGAN, RICK L. AND DAVID HEISE
1988   Structure of emotions. Social Psychology Quarterly 51:19–31.

MUELLER, CHARLES W.
1983   Environmental stressors and aggressive behavior. In Russell G. Geen and Edward I. Donnerstein (eds.), Aggression: Theoretical and Empirical Reviews. Vol. 2. New York: Academic Press.

NEWCOMB, MICHAEL D. AND L.L. HARLOW
1986   Life events and substance use among adolescents: Mediating effects of perceived loss of control and meaninglessness in life. Journal of Personality and Social Psychology 51:564–577.

NOVY, DIANE M. AND STEPHEN DONOHUE
1985   The relationship between adolescent life stress events and delinquent conduct including conduct indicating a need for supervision. Adolescence 78:313–321.

PEARLIN, LEONARD I.
1982   The social contexts of stress. In Leo Goldberger and Shlomo Berznitz (eds.), Handbook of Stress. New York: Free Press.

1983   Role strains and personal stress. In Howard Kaplan (ed.), Psychosocial Stress: Trends in Theory and Research. New York: Academic Press.

PEARLIN, LEONARD I. AND CARMI SCHOOLER
1978   The structure of coping. Journal of Health and Social Behavior 19:2–21.

PEARLIN, LEONARD I. AND MORTON A. LIEBERMAN
1979   Social sources of emotional distress. In Robert G. Simmons (ed.), Research in Community and Mental Health. Vol. I. Greenwich, Conn.: Jai Press.

PEARLIN, LEONARD I., ELIZABETH G. MENAGHAN, MORTON A. LIEBERMAN, AND JOSEPH T. MULLAN
1981   The stress process. Journal of Health and Social Behavior 22:337–356.

QUICKER, JOHN
1974   The effect of goal discrepancy on delinquency. Social Problems 22:76–86.

RIVERA, BEVERLY AND CATHY SPATZ WIDOM
1990   Childhood victimization and violent offending. Violence and Victims 5:19–35.

ROSENBERG, MORRIS
1979   Conceiving the Self. New York: Basic.
1990   Reflexivity and emotions. Social Psychology Quarterly 53:3–12.

ROSS, MICHAEL, JOHN THIBAUT, AND SCOTT EVENBACK
1971   Some determinants of the intensity of social protest. Journal of Experimental Social Psychology 7:401–418.

SCHWINGER, THOMAS
1980   Just allocations of goods: Decisions among three principles. In Gerald Mikula (ed.), Justice and Social Interaction. New York: Springer-Verlag.

SHEPELAK, NORMA J.
1987   The role of self-explanations and self-evaluations in legitimating inequality. American Sociological Review 52:495–503.

SHEPELAK, NORMA J. AND DUANE ALWIN
1986   Beliefs about inequality and perceptions of distributive justice. American Sociological Review 51:30–46.

SHORT, JAMES F. AND FRED L. STRODTBECK
1965   Group Process and Gang Delinquency. Chicago: University of Chicago Press.

SLABY, RONALD G. AND NANCY G. GUERRA
1988   Cognitive mediators of aggression in adolescent offenders: 1. Developmental Psychology 24:580–588.

SPRECHER, SUSAN
1986   The relationship between inequity and emotions in close relationships. Social Psychology Quarterly 49:309–321.

STEPHENSON, G.M. AND J.H. WHITE
1968   An experimental study of some effects of injustice on children's moral behavior. Journal of Experimental Social Psychology 4:460–469.

STRAUS, MURRAY
1991   Discipline and deviance: Physical punishment of children and violence and other crimes in adulthood. Social Problems 38:133–154.

SULLIVAN, MERCER L.
1989   Getting Paid. Ithaca, N.Y.: Cornell University Press.

SULS, JERRY M.
1977   Social comparison theory and research. An overview from 1954. In Jerry M. Suls and Richard L. Miller (eds.), Social Comparison Processes. New York: Hemisphere.

SULS, JERRY M. AND THOMAS ASHBY WILLS
1991   Social Comparison: Contemporary Theory and Research. Hillsdale, N.J.: Lawrence Erlbaum.

TAVRIS, CAROL
1984   On the wisdom of counting to ten. In Philip Shaver (ed.), Review of Personality and Social Psychology: 5. Beverly Hills, Calif.: Sage.

THIBAUT, JOHN W. AND HAROLD H. KELLEY
1959   The Social Psychology of Groups. New York: John Wiley & Sons.

THOITS, PEGGY
1983   Dimensions of life events that influence psychological distress: An evaluation and synthesis of the literature. In Howard B. Kaplan (ed.), Psychosocial Stress: Trends in Theory and Research. New York: Academic Press.
1984   Coping, social support, and psychological outcomes: The central role of emotion. In Philip Shaver (ed.), Review of Personality and Social Psychology: 5. Beverly Hills, Calif.: Sage.
1989   The sociology of emotions. In W. Richard Scott and Judith Blake (eds.), Annual Review of Sociology. Vol. 15. Palo Alto, Calif.: Annual Reviews.
1990   Emotional deviance research. In Theodore D. Kemper (ed.), Research Agendas in the Sociology of Emotions. Albany: State University of New York Press.
1991a   On merging identity theory and stress research. Social Psychology Quarterly 54:101–112.
1991b   Patterns of coping with controllable and uncontrollable events. In E. Mark Cummings, Anita L. Greene, and Katherine H. Karraker (eds.), Life-Span Developmental Psychology: Perspectives on Stress and Coping. Hillsdale, N.J.: Lawrence Erlbaum.

THORNBERRY, TERENCE P.
1987   Toward an Interactional Theory of Delinquency. Criminology 25:863–891.

TONRY, MICHAEL, LLOYD E. OHLIN, AND DAVID P. FARRINGTON
1991   Human Development and Criminal Behavior. New York: Springer-Verlag.

TORNBLUM, KJELL Y.
1977   Distributive justice: Typology and propositions. Human Relations 30:1–24.

UTNE, MARY KRISTINE AND ROBERT KIDD
1980   Equity and attribution. In Gerald Mikula (ed.), Justice and Social Interaction. New York: Springer-Verlag.

VAN HOUTEN, RON
1983   Punishment: From the animal laboratory to the applied setting. In Saul Axelrod and Jack Apsche (eds.), The Effects of Punishment on Human Behavior. New York: Academic Press.

VAUX, ALAN
1988   Social support: Theory, Research, and Intervention. New York: Praeger.

VAUX, ALAN AND MARY RUGGIERO
1983   Stressful life change and delinquent behavior. American Journal of Community Psychology 11:169–183.

WALSTER, ELAINE, ELLEN BERSCHEID, AND G. WILLIAM WALSTER
1973   New directions in equity research. Journal of Personality and Social Psychology 25:151–176.

WALSTER, ELAINE, G. WILLIAM WALSTER, AND ELLEN BERSCHEID
1978   Equity: Theory and Research. Boston: Allyn & Bacon.

WANG, ALVIN Y. AND R. STEPHEN RICHARDE
1988   Global versus task-specific measures of self-efficacy. Psychological Record 38:533–541.

WEINER, BERNARD
1982   The emotional consequences of causal attributions. In Margaret S. Clark and Susan T. Fiske (eds.), Affect and Cognition: The Seventeenth Annual Carnegie Symposium on Cognition. Hillsdale, N.J.: Lawrence Erlbaum.

WILLIAMS, CAROLYN L. AND CRAIGE UCHIYAMA
1989   Assessment of life events during adolescence: The use of self-report inventories. Adolescence 24:95–118.

WYLIE, RUTH
1979   The Self-Concept. Vol. 2. Lincoln: University of Nebraska Press.

ZILLMAN, DOLF
1979   Hostility and Aggression. Hillsdale, N.J.: Lawrence Erlbaum.

QUESTIONS FOR DISCUSSION

1. Give a general explanation of strain theory. In what ways does strain theory differ from the following?
    a. control theory
    b. differential association

2. Discuss the three major types of strain.

3. How does the concept of equity effect the disjunction between just/fair outcomes and actual outcomes?

4. Discuss the following temporal components of stress and equity:
    a. magnitude
    b. recency
    c. duration
    d. clustering

5. Discuss three coping mechanisms that help a person adapt to stress/strain. How might we predict delinquent and non-delinquent outcomes?

APPLICATIONS

1. List ten situations or events that cause you stress or strain. Then, describe how you managed or attempted to lessen the stress for each of the ten items you have listed. Finally, explain how strain theory explains the adaptation or mechanism you used to reduce stress.

2. Using the list and explanations from the previous application, compare your adaptations to another class member's list. Do your adaptations and mechanisms match? How have you and the other class member used strain theory differently to explain stress reduction?

KEY TERMS

amelioration   refers to making something better or more tolerable.

equity theory   asserts that individuals engage in an interaction not with specific goals or outcomes in mind, but rather with an expectation of equality in what they give to and take from the relationship. An equitable relationship is one in which the outcome/input ratios of the actors involved in an exchange/allocation relationship are equivalent.

ethnographic   refers to systematic research about culture.

idiosyncratic   refers to a particularly peculiar characteristic of a human; an eccentricity or unusual temperament.

legitimation   refers to giving something a legal status or authorization; showing or affirming that something is justified.

mediation   intervening between conflicting individuals or groups to promote a settlement or compromise.

mitigate   causing something to become less severe or harsh; relieving or alleviating by intervention.

predisposition   having a preconceived suceptibility to an idea, an attitude, or a behavior.

self-efficacy   refers to an individual's ability or power to produce a desired effect; one's ability to control outcomes.

typology   an analysis or classification based on types or categories.

THE SOCIAL CONTEXT OF JUVENILE DELINQUENCY

*P*erhaps one of the greatest needs of every human being is to be accepted by others. The desire for acceptance shapes our personalities and influences the choices we make concerning the people with whom we associate. The social context of human behavior is of great importance to understanding ourselves and subsequently delinquency or any behaviors considered wrong by other groups or our own group members.

In our lifetime we belong to literally hundreds of groups, and throughout our lives we are continually influenced by others. Some of the most influential groups are small, intimate groups such as families or peers. The influence of the family on the young child's life and personality is so significant that virtually nothing else has a more lasting impact. The peer group and the need to be accepted by others are keys to understanding delinquency and youth culture. The articles in this section deal with the complicated social contexts in which delinquency is produced, experienced, and controlled.

Part III begins with "Family Dysfunction and Female Delinquency," by Jill Leslie Rosenbaum, who studied women raised in dysfunctional or abnormal households and their subsequent patterns of delinquency. Poor parent–child relationships, violence in the family, and substance abuse are correlates of the dysfunctional family. Rosenbaum claims that the women she studied were "double victims" because both their families and the criminal justice system victimized them.

David F. Greenberg, in "Delinquency and the Age Structure of Society," not only offers an analysis of age and delinquency but also discusses the crucial issue of adolescents being excluded from the world of adult work. Greenberg integrates several elements of the structural theories into his discussions, providing some very lucid insights.

William T. Pink's goal in "Schools, Youth, and Justice" is eventually to divert more juveniles away from the justice system by improving the effectiveness of all schools. The alarming increase in violence among youth, especially over the last thirty years, has brought new demands for safer school environments. This article offers some interesting facts and solutions in relation to schools and delinquency.

An empirical test of a Marxian-based theory that examines the relationship between gender and delinquency is presented by John Hagan, A. R. Gillis, and

John Simpson in "The Class Structure of Gender and Delinquency: Toward a Power-Control Theory of Common Delinquent Behavior." The authors conclude that the presence of power and the absence of control create conditions of freedom that often lead to the more common types of delinquency. The power-control explanation of family relations is especially intriguing.

The broken home has often been related to delinquency, and the debate over family structure and delinquency will no doubt continue. Richard E. Johnson, in "Family Structure and Delinquency: General Patterns and Gender Differences," claims that there is indeed a moderate relationship between structure and delinquency, especially self-reported official delinquency. He also helps to illuminate our understanding of the relationships between stepfather–son and father–daughter in an attempt to elaborate the issues of family structure and gender-based delinquency and the justice system's reactions to youths, especially females, living in absent-parent homes.

In many ways, the groups to which we belong are not family groups in a technical biological or adopted sense, yet they often appear as pseudo-families. Our friendship groups serve as some of the most influential and important social factors in our lives. Many adolescents serve as the semi-adult role models to children who are only a few years younger. For many of these children, a delinquent role model serves as their mentor into the adult world. The urban gang has become almost synonymous with violence, greed, and, to many, family. This is not to suggest that all groupings of adolescents are hell-bent on self or societal destruction, but rather to point out the complex nature and structure of youth misbehavior in relation to the larger societal evolution. As a whole, American society has changed so dramatically over the last century that no social institution, from family to government, even remotely resembles the rather simple structures of a hundred years ago.

The four remaining articles in Part III address many of the significant issues in delinquency against the backdrop of the emergence of youth culture. We begin with Jeffery Fagan's "The Social Organization of Drug Use and Drug Dealing among Urban Gangs," which describes types of gangs and their organizational structures, and points out that most violence between gangs is fueled by the historical issues of territory and status, not by disputes involving drugs or drug sales. The marginalization of many gangs may reflect the marginalization of the larger neighborhood in which they operate.

Another excellent article, "Girls, Guys and Gangs: The Changing Social Context of Female Delinquency," is presented by Peggy C. Giordano. She dismantles the longstanding assertion that female delinquency represents personal maladjustments and points to the group context of all delinquency. Like boys in these subcultural groups, girls are also influenced by their same-sex peers and often commit delinquent acts by modeling themselves after other girls in the gang.

The subcultural world of teenage prostitution is examined by Terry Williams and William Kornblum in "Players and Ho's." The backgrounds, attitudes, and prospects for the future of both pimps and prostitutes make this a lively but complicated piece of research. An entirely different, confusing, and frightening subculture unfolds to expose the wasted human potential that is often the by-product of the larger social context.

Our final selection, "The Appearance of Youthful Subculture: A Theoretical Perspective on Deviance," by Lynne Richards, suggests that all human behavior is directed toward the positive interpretation of self and self-esteem. This appearance underlies, she claims, many of the processes at work in producing and maintaining youthful subcultures. The dramatic status changes for youth and the corresponding societal reactions have created spectacular examples of subcultural identities, clothing, language, and foundations for change in the larger society.

14

Family Dysfunction and Female Delinquency

Jill Leslie Rosenbaum

This article examines the family backgrounds of a group of women who, as adolescents in the early 1960s, were committed to the California Youth Authority predominantly for status offenses and continued their criminal behavior into adulthood. Particular attention is paid to various measures of dysfunction, including family violence, parent-child conflict, family size, structure, and stability. Little variation existed within the various independent measures; all of the women came from dysfunctional homes. The manner in which these young women were dealt with by the Youth Authority is examined within the context of the cultural attitudes of that particular time.

Much is expected of the American family. Thus it is not surprising that various aspects of family life and relationships have been viewed as the source of delinquency, including parental absence, family size, birth order, and quality of parent-child interaction. Glueck and Glueck (1950) found that paternal discipline, maternal supervision, affection of both parents, and family cohesiveness were more important than father's presence and family size. While there are numerous criticisms of their research, the Gluecks' established the importance of understanding the family's impact on delinquent behavior.

"Family Dysfunction and Female Delinquency," *Crime and Delinquency*, 35:1 (January 1989), pp. 31–44. Reprinted by permission of the publisher, Sage Publications, Inc.

Aside from the Gluecks' research, three other longitudinal studies indicate the influence of the family on adult criminality. In her thirty-year follow-up study of men who, as youth, had participated in the Cambridge-Somerville delinquency prevention project, Joan McCord (1979) showed the impact on adult criminality of childhood family dimensions. Robins (1966) also found family variables to be an important factor in later adult behavior in her follow-up of youth referred to a child guidance clinic between 1922 and 1932. In their retrospective study of delinquents, Osborn and West (1978) found that those with the most serious records came from large, low-income families and had criminal parents.

A great deal of attention has been paid to the absence of at least one parent. At best, however, there is a weak association between broken homes and delinquent behavior (e.g., Gove and Crutchfield, 1982; Rosen and Neilson, 1982; Wilkinson, 1974). Rosen (1985) suggests, "Although it may be possible to dismiss the broken home as the single major factor in delinquency causation, it still may be significant when combined with other factors."

Some have argued that large families are conducive to delinquent behavior (Nye, 1958; Rosen, 1985; Fischer, 1984). The higher rate of delinquent behavior in large families may result from parents having less time and energy per child and thus less attachment to their children than parents with fewer children (Hirschi, 1983).

Research consistently has shown that those youth whose bond to their parents is weak are more likely to be delinquent. According to Hirschi (1969), youth who are more attached to their parents have greater direct and indirect controls placed on their behavior. The parental attachment factor explains delinquency better than any other factor (Nye, 1958; Gold, 1963; Hindelang, 1973; Gove and Crutchfield, 1982; Rosenbaum, 1987).

Morris (1964) and Gold (1970) have suggested that female delinquency is more likely than male delinquency to reflect problems at home. Therefore, it may be that women who end up in state facilities tend to come from the most troubled families. Indeed, it may be that their homes are more troubled than those of their male counterparts. Moreover, society's attitudes toward females and their particular needs may have a great deal to do with the fate of delinquent and runaway girls.

In contrast to previous research that has dealt mostly with male delinquents, this study examined the impact of the family on a group of delinquent females. Utilizing case files beginning with first arrest and concluding with discharge from the California Youth Authority, delinquent women and potential dysfunction in their families were explored. In doing so, such variables as family size and structure, family criminality, mental health and alcohol problems, family conflict, and family violence were examined.

DATA AND METHODS

The Sample

In 1980, records were requested on 240 women who had been committed to the California Youth Authority (CYA), the state agency for juvenile offenders. All of these girls had, as juveniles, taken part in a CYA experimental program in the early 1960s, the Community Treatment Project (CTP). This program began in 1961 as a combined experimental and demonstration project to assess the effect of keeping delinquent youth in the community under intensive supervision (Lerman, 1975). One of the assumptions behind

this program was that troubled youth should remain in the community in order to cope better with both family tensions and community pressures. It was believed that these youth would confront problems and work toward solutions more effectively within the community than within the confines of an institution (Adams and Grant, 1961). All of the individuals taking part in this program spent at least thirty days in a state facility; however, many of them spent the majority of their CYA commitment in the community.

The records requested included adult arrest records and CYA files of all women committed to the CYA from the San Francisco and Sacramento Valley areas during the early sixties. Records were returned from California Identification and Investigation (C.I.&I.) on 159 of these women. In total, 59 of the 240 cases were unavailable because the juvenile records had been purged, and 22 others could not be located. Comparisons of the missing cases were those available indicated minor differences. The only variable showing a significant difference was race (fewer minority women had their records purged). Although we assumed that those with purged records had fewer arrests than those on whom we had complete records, a five-year follow-up by the CYA indicated that most of the purged group had at least one postrelease arrest.

The ethnic makeup of the final sample of 159 was 51% white, 30% black, 9% Latino, and the remaining 10% were Asian or Native American. Two-thirds of the girls had been committed to the Youth Authority only for status offenses, mostly for running away.

Method

All C.I.&I. arrest data were coded by two independent coders who were in agreement 92% of the time. Upon completion three independent coders reviewed the Youth Authority records that included home investigation reports, information gathered at intake reception centers, parole reports, and discharge summaries. The reports consisted of all of the written comments of those individuals who worked with the CYA wards during their commitment to the Youth Authority. These individuals included parole agents, social workers, teachers, and CYA chaplains. From these reports, family background data were coded. The interrater reliability was 88%.

In coding arrests, arrest incidents were used rather than charges. Only the most serious charge at each incident was coded regardless of whether the charges were altered at a later date or whether the women were actually convicted of another offense. Thus the data may underestimate the number of criminal acts committed by these women. Blumstein and Cohen (1979) have argued that, because of plea bargaining and other reasons for altering or dismissing charges, initial arrest charges probably are better indicators of actual behavior than convictions.

FINDINGS

Preliminary analysis of the adult arrest records indicated that all but 6 of the 159 (96%) were arrested as adults. Most of the women (70%) had at least four arrests after their release from the CYA and nearly all (82%) had been convicted of at least one moderately serious crime (not included were such offenses as prostitution, possession of any drug, and theft of less than $100; Warren and Rosenbaum, 1986). Although women are considered to be less threatening to society than men, only a small percentage of all arrests were the "stereotypic" female crimes of prostitution and drug offenses (Rosenbaum, 1988).

Originally we had hypothesized that those with less serious records would have come from the most functional families. However, there was very little variation within the numerous family structure and family problem variables included in these data. All of the girls came from extremely troubled homes.

It became clear, in fact, that we have no cause to be surprised that these women became serious offenders. Indeed it would have been surprising had they not. As indicated by the results to be presented, these women came from families where conformity

to societal expectations was the exception rather than the rule.

Family Structure

Although there is little consensus on this issue, recent research by Van Vooris et al. (1988) indicates that a relationship between status offenses and broken homes and status offenses and single-parent families does exist. Consistent with these data, very few of these girls came from intact families (7%). At the time of their commitment to the CYA, 25% were living in two-adult homes; however, some of these were foster homes, others were the homes of relatives. For example, one girl was living with her grandparents who were both 81 years old. Still others were living with their mother and one of a number of stepfathers or boyfriends. One out of ten of the girls had been deserted by both parents. The remainder of the sample were living in single-parent homes.

By the time these girls were 16, their mothers had been married an average of four times. One mother had married three times in the previous seven years. Another had been married five times since the birth of her daughter (four divorces and one death), and was planning to marry for a sixth time. Still another example was a woman who had married a number of times with some of the marriages overlapping. This woman was married to a man in northern California, but thought she still might be married to a previous husband who was currently living in Mexico. He had left for Mexico and never returned; the woman thought that this was because he already was married when they had married.

Family Size

Family size has been cited as a factor in delinquency causation (Hirschi, 1969). In this study three girls were only children, while another six had one sibling. But, the average was 4.3 children per family. Not surprisingly, given the number of multiple marriages, children in a "family" often were fathered by a variety of men. For example, one girl had four siblings, each fathered by a different man. Another ward's mother had nine children with all but two fathered by different men. Still another was one of eight children by at least three different fathers, with the mother unsure who fathered the ward and her younger sister. Yet for this group of girls the actual size of the family appears to be less important than the way it functioned.

Family Criminality

A minority (24%) of the girls came from families where no other criminality was present. In total, 76% of the wards had at least one other family member with a criminal record. Often several family members had records. Similar numbers of the known birth fathers and mothers had served time in state prison (30% and 32%, respectively). Case files frequently indicated that the girls' brothers and/or sisters were in placement at a Youth Authority facility, while others were in jail or prison.

Parental criminal activity ranged from fairly minor offenses to serious violent crimes. Of the mothers, 51% had felony arrest records. Many were for such offenses as narcotics violations and welfare-related offenses. The fathers tended to have difficulty with alcohol, which often led to assaults and other criminal behavior. One father had an arrest record that included sodomy, assault, burglaries, and forgeries. The day after he was released from San Quentin he was arrested for another burglary and forgery. One of the other wards was not on speaking terms with anyone in her family, except a brother who was serving time in San Quentin.

Family Violence

Farber and Kinast (1984, p. 298) found in their study of runaways that "an astounding amount of violence was directed toward youth who ran away." Although much data on family violence are missing, it is evident that violence was present in many of these homes. Records failed to mention spousal violence unless specific charges were filed. However, a number of the known fathers had spent time in jail for "fighting with wife." One father in particular had been committed to DeWitt State Hospital following a fight with his wife over the presence of the wife's boyfriend. Another beat the mother of one ward numerous times because she had listed her husband as the girl's father even though she knew another man had sired the child. One particular file notes that "the girl had strong memories of watching or hearing her mother being choked by the father and also of being locked in the closet for long periods of time." Still another indicated that the father of a ward had died from stab wounds inflicted by the mother. Although this woman was charged with murder, she was never convicted and continued to have custody of the children.

In total, 37% of the mothers had been charged with child abuse and/or neglect. One mother whose new boyfriend did not like children packed their belongings and locked them out of the house. Another left four children between the ages of 6 and 15 alone without money for a month while she went to Hawaii to "rejuvenate herself." Some mothers had abuse and/or neglect charges filed within the first six months of the girl's life. One woman was arrested when her daughter was 2 weeks old for child neglect; and, according to the social worker, "by the time the girl was sent to the CYA, her mother had the longest record of abuse and neglect charges one could imagine." In yet another family, "the ward's parents never cared for the children and were continuously sentenced to the county jail. After the parents' third arrest, the four children were placed in the home of their grandmother, who herself had served time in jail in the past for neglecting her children."

Family Conflict

At least a weak relationship between family conflict and delinquent behavior has been found in a number of studies (see McCord and McCord, 1959; Gove and Crutchfield, 1982; Canter, 1982; Cernkovich and Giordano, 1987). In the two-parent families examined in this study a great deal of conflict was present. Of these parents, 71% fought regularly about the children. Since there were often his, hers, and theirs present, the sources of conflict tended to result from one set of children having a bad influence on the others, the type of punishment invoked, or one particular child receiving too much attention. Conflict in the home was not limited to the children, for conflict over the use of alcohol was present in 81% of the homes. Case files indicate that 34% of the fathers were known alcoholics as were 31% of the mothers. Furthermore, many of the parents had histories of mental illness. In total, 29% of the fathers and 27% of the mothers had been diagnosed as neurotic or psychotic. A caseworker described one of these families in the following way: "The father appears to be an ineffectual, highly neurotic person who is maintaining a very sick relationship with an alcoholic woman." The case files indicate that this case was not atypical.

Parent-Child Relationships

A poor relationship between parent and child is highly influential in the child's subsequent delinquency (see Patterson, 1982; Hirschi, 1969; Nye, 1958; Gove and Crutchfield, 1982; Rosenbaum, 1987; Van Vooris et al., 1988). Not only did these girls probably suffer from their parents' broken marriages and multiple relationships, alcoholism, and mental illness, but they typically lacked the nurturing youth require. Many of the girls received very little positive feedback from parents in the home. Of the fathers who were present, 53% were viewed by the parole officers as rejecting of the girl, as were 47% of the mothers. Rejection came in many forms. One father was so angry that his child was a girl that he made her dress in boy's clothing and cut her hair extremely short. Another father wanted nothing to do with his daughter until she conformed to his rules; he requested that she be "locked in a room until she conformed to his rules or until she was twenty-one—whichever comes first." One ward said of her parents: "My mother is cruel and has never shown any love for me and my father has always been ashamed of me." That these girls chose to run away from such homes is not surprising.

Research on parental supervision and delinquency has indicated that a relationship between the two exists (Nye, 1958; Hirschi, 1969; Hindelang, 1973; Bahr, 1979; Wells and Rankin, 1988). Of the 159 homes studied, consistent supervision of the youth was present in a minority of the homes (22%). The mothers appeared to be not only neglectful, but 96% were described as passive and 67% as irresponsible. One typical mother was described as "an hysterical and frantic woman whose supervision and discipline fluctuate from lax to severe."

Generational Cycles

The mothers of the CYA wards tended to marry young, with 44% having had the ward by the time she was 18 though only 32% of the girls were oldest children. The mothers' psychological and financial resources were obviously limited and the added burden of children appeared to increase the strain.

These daughters tended to follow in their mothers' footsteps and begin bearing children at an early age. By the time they were discharged from the Youth Authority over half (56%) of the wards had children. Some had more than one. One girl had two children before the age of 16 and a third while committed to the CYA. Parents often encouraged this behavior. One mother explained to her daughter's parole officer that she was happy to hear that her 15-year-old daughter was pregnant—"that is what women are supposed to do." Another ward wanted to place her yet unborn child up for adoption, but her parents refused to grant permission.

The men in the wards' lives bore a striking resemblance to the men chosen by their mothers. Many were significantly older than the girls and had criminal records. One 16-year-old girl had married her 34-year-old pimp, who had a number of arrests and convictions for drug offenses. Another 16-year-old's boyfriend was 22, twice married, with seven children, two by the wives and five by five separate girlfriends. This man also had a record for stabbing his mother and beating one wife. Still others were residing with men who were physically abusive toward both them and their children.

The wards' mothers did not have the supports or resources needed to cope with their environments. They often were socially isolated and distrusted those attempting to help. They viewed welfare workers as individuals trying to take away funds, and social workers as trying to take away their children. These attitudes and fears began long before the wards were born, perhaps even before their mothers were born. The mothers of the CTP girls did not know how to be mothers, for they were often children themselves when their children were born, and lacked the emotional resources to instill a sense of trust and security necessary for self-esteem and growth. Over time, just trying to survive depleted whatever emotional resources they might once have had.

The mothers were passive by nature and, because their lives consisted of a series of crises, they were inconsistent authority figures. Rules were made one day and forgotten the next because of financial difficulties, conflicts with the men in their life, and problems with other children.

DISCUSSION

The preceding analysis indicated that there was virtually no variability on the various measures of family dysfunction. Although some variation existed with respect to the number of actual arrests, more than 90% of the women had arrests after their release from the CYA. Statistical analysis of the various family dysfunction measures and arrest data was relatively useless because of the overwhelming concordance of the dysfunctions and subsequent delinquent behavior.

Homer (1973) categorizes runaways into two types, youth who are "running from" and those that are "running to." The CTP girls who ran generally fit the "running from" category. Individuals who fall into this category are generally weak, not trusting of others, and lack warmth and nurturing during childhood. It is possible that running away and the subsequent delinquent behavior may have been a plea for the love they lacked. Since the records indicate that these girls often returned home on their own accord, it

may be that they were hoping that, upon their return, they would find the mothering and protection they so desperately sought. Unfortunately, their mothers were unable to give these girls the nurturing they desired, for they had not been adequately nurtured themselves. Instead these mothers often turned to their daughters for nurturing, thus reversing roles and having the daughter mother her own mother.

After close examination of the files, it appears that not only were these women victims, they were double victims: victims of their families and victims of the criminal justice system as well. Most of these girls were sentenced to the CYA for status offenses (mostly running away). That they chose to run away from home is not surprising given the data on their home life. The numerous attempts to run away also may have been futile efforts to break the generational cycle of despair. In this respect it is important to remember that prior to 1978, girls who ran away from home received severe court sanctions. They were more likely to be held in detention than were female delinquents and male runaways (Mann, 1979).

Society's belief in the family unit and the notion that young girls need their mother may have been the major contributing forces behind their later, more serious criminal behavior. Not only did the criminal justice system continue to return these girls to their mothers after they ran away, but even after they had been made wards of the court, they were returned home once again. These were often homes like one described by a social worker as "an animal-like environment." One girl was returned to her family, even though they sometimes lived in an abandoned car. Still another was returned home, although her parole officer stated, "both her parents seem to be ineffectual, highly disturbed people, who have as a result damaged all their children." Despite these instances (which were typical), the CTP believed that youth were better off in their homes and tried to return as many as possible. This was such a high priority that one ward was returned to her home upon the mother's release from prison for throwing lye in her lover's face, because her parole officer believed "the girl had not been too damaged." No doubt, these adolescent girls' attitudes and ideas about the world were largely shaped by their mothers, who were often alcoholic or diagnosed as psychotic/neurotic, who averaged four marriages, and who frequently provided role models for criminal careers. In light of these findings, it is not surprising that these young runaways became serious adult offenders.

The early CYA records indicate that many of these runaways were sent to the Youth Authority for lack of any alternative placements. With fathers whose whereabouts were unknown and mothers who were often in jail, prison, or mental health facilities, the Youth Authority may have been the only available option. Many of the girls lacked supervision from an early age. When they ran away or were removed from the home due to child abuse/neglect or other charges, the youth often found themselves in foster homes. In fact, at one time or another during their CYA commitment 67% were removed from the home and placed in group and foster homes (Turner, 1969). In these homes the girls experienced sharp changes, particularly in rules and discipline, for which they were ill prepared. As a result, there were numerous complaints to officials and/or runaways in the first few months of foster care. This is not surprising since, according to Russell (1981, p. 65), "Family disruptions which necessitate the placing of children away from the home produce many disorganizing emotional conflicts which can render their adjustment in any new living situation problematical and can predispose them to running away." However, many of the adolescents were deemed foster home failures and thus were sent to the CYA.

It is important that we remember what is missing from the early CYA files. For instance, we know of family violence only when official action was taken. Yet it is evident, if we look closely, that in a number of families there was significant violence and some instances of incest. But in the early sixties criminal justice agencies and the community were not as aware of the extent and nature of family violence and child sexual abuse. Thus, while we know that these families were dysfunctional, the full extent of the difficulties faced cannot be known from the case files.

The rationale for the CTP program was to keep many of these girls in the community in order to "work out" difficulties in their homes and the community in the hope that this would further reduce their criminality. The program did not succeed in keeping these women from further involvement in the criminal justice system, as originally hoped (Palmer, 1974; Lerman, 1975; Warren and Rosenbaum, 1986). The failure of CTP may be due to the fact that the deep-seated nature and long term implications of their family problems were not understood. This may have been the result of both the cultural attitudes at the time and the fact that the wide array of family therapy available today was not available to the CTP practitioners during the 1960s.

Labeling theorists could easily look only at the arrest data and claim that the system was at fault, that left alone these girls would have matured and their criminality was simply childhood excitement. However, when one delves into the backgrounds of these offenders the picture becomes clouded. While some of these girls may have fared much better had they not become involved with the system, many would have had ongoing difficulties with the criminal justice system; some, perhaps, may have had even more serious records. To argue that the system was at fault would appear to be a simplistic claim. It is impossible to disentangle the system effects and the family effects on the adult criminal behavior of these girls. Finally, it is clear that the options available for dealing with runaways were severely limited.

In retrospect, the initial findings of persistence in offending and increased severity no longer appear surprising. Furthermore, family structure, family instability, and family mental health do not explain the difference in the severity of the adult criminal records, in that all of the women came from very dysfunctional homes. Although we were unable to predict types of later criminality as was done in a follow-up of males (McCord, 1979), this analysis does give some insight into the reasons for CYA commitment and the families in which these girls were raised.

It may be that females have more difficulty than males in handling the stress of dysfunctional homes, which may account for their higher runaway rate. It is also possible that young women are more likely to become double victims than young men. The high rate of return to dysfunctional homes reflects society's, and thus the CTP's, belief that girls need their mothers, regardless of the mother's stability. Further research on both male and female delinquents is necessary in order to understand the possible differences in their family backgrounds, as well as the potential for double victimization.

References

ADAMS, S. AND M. Q. GRANT
1961   *A Demonstration Project: An Evaluation of Community Located Treatment for Delinquents.* Sacramento: California Youth Authority.

BAHR, S.
1979   "Family Determinants and Effects of Deviance." In *Contemporary Theories About the Family,* edited by W. Burr, R. Hill, F. Nye, and I. Reiss. New York: Free Press.

BLUMSTEIN, A. AND J. COHEN
1979   "Estimation of Individual Crime Rates from Arrest Records." *Journal of Criminal Law and Criminology* 70(4):561–585.

CANTER, R.
1982   "Family Correlates of Male and Female Delinquency." *Criminology* 20:149–167.

CERNKOVICH, S. AND P. GIORDANO
1987   "Family Relationships and Delinquency." *Criminology* 25:295–319.

FARBER, E. AND C. KNAST
1984   "Violence in Families of Adolescent Runaways." *Child Abuse and Neglect* 8:295–299.

FISCHER, D. G.
1984   "Family Size and Delinquency." *Perceptual and Motor Skills* 58:527–534.

GLUECK, S. AND B. GLUECK
1950   *Unraveling Juvenile Delinquency.* Cambridge, MA: Harvard University Press.

GOLD, MARTIN
1963   *Status Forces in Delinquent Boys.* Ann Arbor, MI: Institute for Social Research.
1970   *Delinquency in an American City.* Monterey, CA: Brooks/Cole.

GOVE, W. AND R. CRUTCHFIELD
1982   "The Family and Juvenile Delinquency." *Sociological Quarterly* 23:301–319.

HINDELANG, M. J.
1973   "Causes of Delinquency: A Partial Explication and Extension." *Social Problems* 20:471–487.

HIRSCHI, T.
1969   *Causes of Delinquency.* Berkeley: University of California Press.
1983   "Crime and Family Policy." In *Juvenile Delinquency: A Justice Perspective,* edited by R. Weisheit and R. Culbertson. Prospect Heights, IL: Waveland.

HOMER, L.
1973   "Community-Based Resources for Runaway Girls." *Social Casework* 54(October):473–479.

LERMAN, P.
1975   *Community Treatment and Social Control: A Critical Analysis of Juvenile Correctional Policy.* Chicago: University of Chicago Press.

MCCORD, J.
1979   "Some Child-Rearing Antecedents of Criminal Behavior in Adult Men." *Journal of Personality and Social Psychology,* 37:1477–1486.

MCCORD, W. AND J. MCCORD
1959   *Origins of Crime.* New York: Columbia University Press.

MANN, C. R.
1979   "The Differential Treatment Between Runaway Boys and Girls in Juvenile Court." *Juvenile and Family Court Journal* 30(2):37–48.

MORRIS, RUTH
1964   "Female Delinquency and Relational Problems." *Social Forces* 43:82–89.

NYE, F.
1958   *Family Relationships and Delinquent Behavior.* New York: John Wiley.

OSBORN, S. AND D. WEST
1978   "The Effectiveness of Various Predictors of Criminal Careers." *Journal of Adolescence* 1:101–117.

PALMER, T.
1974   *Correctional Intervention and Research.* Lexington, MA: D.C. Heath.

PATTERSON, G.
1982   *Coercive Family Process.* Eugene, OR: Castalia.

ROBINS, L.
1966   *Deviant Children Grown Up.* Baltimore: Williams & Wilkins.

ROSEN, L.
1985   "Family and Delinquency: Structure or Function?" *Criminology* 23:553–573.
———   and K. Neilson. 1982 "Broken Homes." In *Contemporary Criminology,* edited by L. Savitz and N. Johnston. New York: John Wiley.

ROSENBAUM, J.
1987   "Social Control, Gender and Delinquency: An Analysis of Drug, Property and Violent Offending." *Justice Quarterly* 4(1):117–132.
1988   "Age, Race and Female Offending." *Journal of Contemporary Criminal Justice* 4(3).

RUSSELL, D.
1981   "On Running Away." In *Self-Destructive Behavior in Children and Adolescents,* edited by C. Wells and I. Stuart. New York: Van Nostrand Reinhold.

TURNER, ESTELLE
1969   *A Girls' Group Home: An Approach to Treating Delinquent Girls in the Community.* Sacramento: California Youth Authority.

VAN VOORIS, P., F. CULLEN, R. MATHERS, AND C. GARNER
1988   "The Impact of Family Structure and Quality on Delinquency: A Comparative Assessment of Structural and Functional Factors." *Criminology* 26(2):235–261.

WARREN, M. Q. AND J. ROSENBAUM
1986   "Criminal Careers of Female Offenders." *Criminal Justice and Behavior* 13(4):393–418.

WEBB, D.
1984   "More on Gender and Justice." *Sociology* 18(3):367–381.

WELLS, L. AND J. RANKIN
1988   "Direct Parental Controls and Delinquency." *Criminology* 26:263–285.

WEST, D. AND D. FARRINGTON
1973   *Who Becomes Delinquent?* London: Heinemann.

WILKINSON, K.
1974   "The Broken Family and Juvenile Delinquency: Scientific Explanation or Ideology?" *Social Problems* 21:726–739.

QUESTIONS FOR DISCUSSION

1. Rosenbaum's study of women committed to the California Youth Authority (CYA) hypothesized that less serious offenders would have come from the most functional families as compared to the more serious offenders. Was this supported by her findings?

2. List and describe the seven variables discussed by Rosenbaum in her research.

3. According to Rosenbaum, why does "double victimization" occur with women and not men?

APPLICATIONS

1. Identify a family you believe to be dysfunctional. How are the children, particularly the young women, affected by this condition? What characteristics can you identify in this family that are also reported by Rosenbaum?

2. Often we speak of functional and dysfunctional families. Most of the emphasis, however, is placed on dysfunctional families, as in the article you have just finished reading. What comes to mind when you think of a "functional" family? Discuss with your classmates what you believe characterizes a functional family. How does your characterization differ from others in your class?

KEY TERMS

concordance   when something is in agreement or accord with something else.

dysfunctional   refers to impaired or abnormal functioning.

ineffectual   when something does not produce the proper or intended effect.

neurotic   one who is affected with a mental and emotional disorder of the personality; usually accompanied by various physical and mental disturbances like anxieties, phobias, or other visceral symptoms.

psychotic   one who suffers a fundamental mental derangement characterized by a defective or lost contact with reality; schizophrenic, multiple personalities, delusions of grandeur.

significant difference   a statistical term referring to something that is not only different but also statistically different enough that the difference cannot be explained by coincidence or chance factors.

sodomy   sexual relations or copulation with a member of the same sex or with an animal.

15

Delinquency and the Age Structure of Society

David F. Greenberg

An extraordinary amount of crime in America is the accomplishment of young people, . . . [although] delinquents commonly abandon crime in late adolescence, . . . [and] arrest rates for vandalism and [nonviolent] property crimes . . . decline with age . . . [more] rapidly . . . than . . . arrest rates for narcotics violations and [violent] offenses . . .[1] This pattern is a fairly recent development. The peak ages for involvement in crime seem to have been higher in nineteenth-century America than they are today. Other industrialized capitalist nations, such as England, seem to have undergone a similar shift in the age distribution of involvement in crime. By contrast, comparatively few crimes are committed by young people in the less industrialized nations of the modern world.[2]

The increasingly disproportionate involvement of juveniles in major crime categories is not readily explained by current sociological theories of delinquency, but it can be readily understood as a consequence of the historically changing position of juveniles in industrial societies. This changing position has its origin, at least in Europe and the United States, in the long-term tendencies of a capitalist economic system.

"Delinquency and the Age Structure of Society," *Contemporary Crises: Crime, Law, and Social Policy,* 1 (1977), pp. 189–223. Reprinted by permission of Kluwer Academic Publishing Group.

Delinquency Theory and the Age Distribution of Crime

Since neither the very young nor the very old have the prowess and agility required for some types of crime, we might expect crime rates to rise and then fall with age. But the sharp decline in involvement in late adolescence cannot be explained in these terms alone. If age is relevant to criminality, the link should lie primarily in its social significance. Yet contemporary sociological theories of delinquency shed little light on the relationship between crime and age. If, for example, lower class male gang delinquency is simply a manifestation of a lower class subculture, as Miller (1958) has maintained, it would be mysterious why 21-year-olds act in conformity with the norms of their subculture so much *less* often than their siblings just a few years younger—unless the norms themselves were age-specific. While age-specific expectations may contribute to desistance from some forms of delinquent play, such as vandalism and throwing snowballs at cars, as Clark and Haurek (1966) suggest, there is no social class in which felony theft and violence receive general *approval* for persons of any age. Moreover, adult residents of high crime areas often live in fear of being attacked by teenagers, suggesting that if delinquency is subcultural, community does not form the basis of the subculture.

The difficulty of accounting for "maturational reform" within the framework of the motivational theories of Cloward and Ohlin (1960) and Cohen (1955) has already been noted by Matza (1964:24–27). In both theories, male delinquents cope with the problems arising from lower class status by entering into and internalizing the norms of a subculture which repudiates conventional rules of conduct and *requires* participation in crime. As with other subcultural theories, it is not at all clear why most subculture carriers abandon activities that are so highly prized within the subculture with such haste.

This desistance is especially perplexing in anomie or opportunity theories (Merton, 1957; Cloward and Ohlin, 1960) because the problem assumed to cause delinquency, namely the anticipation of failure in achieving socially inculcated success goals through legitimate means, does not disappear at the end of adolescence. At the onset of adulthood, few lower and working class youths are close to conventionally defined "success," and their realization that opportunities for upward mobility are drastically limited can only be more acute. Students can perhaps entertain fantasies about their future prospects, but graduates or dropouts must come to terms with their chances.

Cloward and Ohlin do note that many delinquents desist, but explain this in ad hoc terms unrelated to the main body of their theory. Writing of neighborhoods where violence is common, they assert:

> As adolescents near adulthood, excellence in the manipulation of violence no longer brings status. Quite the contrary, it generally evokes extremely negative sanctions. What was defined as permissible or tolerable behavior during adolescence tends to be sharply proscribed in adulthood. New expectations are imposed, expectations of "growing up," of taking on adult responsibilities in the economic, familial, and community spheres. The effectiveness with which these definitions are imposed is attested by the tendency among fighting gangs to decide that conflict is, in the final analysis, simply "kid stuff.". . . In other words, powerful community expectations emerge which have the consequence of closing off access to previously useful means of overcoming status deprivation (Cloward and Ohlin, 1960:185).

In view of Cloward and Ohlin's characterization of neighborhoods where gang violence is prevalent as so disorganized that no informal social controls limiting violence can be exercised (1960:174–75), one can only wonder whose age-specific expectations are being described. Cloward and Ohlin do not say. This explanation, for which Cloward and Ohlin produce no supporting evidence, is inconsistent with their own larger theory of delinquent subcultures. In addition, it seems inconsistent with the *slowness* of the decline in the violence offense categories.

In a departure from the emphasis placed on social class membership in most motivational theories of delinquency, Bloch and Niederhoffer (1958) interpret such forms of delinquency as adolescent drinking, sexual experimentation, and "wild automobile rides" as responses to the age status problems of adolescence. Denied the prerogatives of adulthood, but encouraged to aspire to adulthood and told to "act like adults," teenagers find in these activities a symbolic substitute which presumably is abandoned as soon as the genuine article is available. As an explanation for joy-riding and some status offenses, this explanation has manifest plausibility. For other categories it is more problematic, since it assumes that delinquents interpret activities engaged in largely by adolescents as evidence of adult stature. When Bloch and Niederhoffer turn to more serious teenage crime, their explanations are vague and difficult to interpret, but in any event seem to depend less on the structural position of the juvenile.

In *Delinquency and Drift*, Matza (1964) provides an alternative approach to the explanation of desistance. His assumption that many delinquents fully embrace neither delinquent nor conventional norms and values, but instead allow themselves to be easily influenced without deep commitment, makes desistance possible when the delinquent discovers that his companions are no more committed to delinquency than he is. This discovery is facilitated by a reduction in masculinity anxiety that accompanies the attainment of adulthood. There are valuable insights in this account, but unresolved questions as well. Insofar as the discovery of a shared misunderstanding depends on chance events, as Matza suggests (1964:54–58), *systematic* differences in desistance remain unexplained. Why does desistance from violence offenses occur later and more slowly than for theft offenses? Why are some juveniles so much more extensively involved in delinquency than others? Matza's remarkable presentation of the subjective elements in delinquency must be supplemented by an analysis of the objective, structural elements in causation, if such questions are to be answered.

That is the approach I will take. I will present an analysis of the position of juveniles in American society and elaborate the implications of that position for juvenile involvement in crime. The explanation of high levels of juvenile involvement in crime will have two major components. The first, a theory of motivation, locates sources of motivation toward criminal involvement in the structural position of juveniles in American society. The second, derived from control theory, suggests that the willingness to act on the basis of criminal motivation is distributed unequally among age groups because the cost of being apprehended are different for persons of different ages. Although some of the theoretical ideas (e.g., control theory) on which I will be drawing have already appeared in the delinquency literature, each by itself is inadequate as a full theory of delinquency. When put together with some new ideas, however, a very plausible account of age and other systematic sources of variation in delinquent involvement emerges.

Anomie and the Juvenile Labor Market

Robert Merton's discussion of anomie has provided a framework for a large volume of research on the etiology of crime. Although Merton observed that a disjunction between socially inculcated goals and legitimate means for attaining them would produce a strain toward deviance, *whatever the goal* (Merton, 1957:166), specific application of the perspective to delinquency has been restricted to an assessment of the contribution to delinquency causation of the one cultural goal Merton considered in depth, namely occupational success. Cloward and Ohlin for example, attribute lower class male delinquency to the anticipation of failure in achieving occupational goals as adults. These youths' involvement in theft is interpreted as a strategy for gaining admission to professional theft and organized crime circles, that is, a way of obtaining the tutelage and organizational affiliations necessary for the successful pursuit of *career* crime, rather than for immediate financial return. Crime is thus seen as a means toward the attainment of *future* goals rather than *present* goals.

The assumption that delinquency is instrumentally related to the attainment of adult goals is plausible only for limited categories of delinquency, however; e.g., students who cheat on exams in the face of keen competition for admission to college or graduate school, and youths who save what they earn as pimps or drug merchants to capitalize investment in conventional business enterprises. For other forms of delinquency this assumption is less tenable. Delinquents would have to be stupid indeed to suppose that shoplifting, joy-riding, burglary, robbery or drug use could bring the prestige or pecuniary rewards associated with high status lawful occupation. Nor is there evidence that most delinquents seek careers in professional theft or organized crime. In the face of Cohen's characterization of delinquents as short-run hedonists (1955:25), and the difficulty parents and teachers encounter in attempting to engage delinquent youths in activities which could improve chances of occupational success (like school homework), the future orientation assumed in opportunity theory is especially farfetched.

The potential explanatory power of anomie theory, is, however, not exhausted by Cloward and Ohlin's formulation, because delinquency can be a response to a discrepancy between aspirations and expectations for the attainment of goals other than occupational ones. Most people have a multiplicity of goals, and only some of them are occupational. As the salience of different life goals can vary with stages of the life cycle, our understanding of delinquency may be advanced more by examining those goals given a high priority by adolescents than by considering the importance attached to different goals in American culture generally.

The transition from childhood to adolescence is marked by a heightened sensitivity to the expectations of peers and a reduced concern with fulfilling parental expectations (Blos, 1941; Bowerman and Kinch, 1959; Tuma and Livson, 1960; Conger, 1973:282–92). Popularity with peers becomes highly valued, and exclusion from the most popular cliques leads to acute psychological distress.

Adolescent peer groups and orientation to the expectations of peers are found in many societies (Eisenstadt, 1956; Bloch and Neiderhoffer, 1958); but the natural tendency of those who share common experiences and problems to prefer one another's company is accentuated in American society by the importance that parents and school attach to popularity and to developing social skills assumed to be necessary for later occupational success (Mussen et al., 1969). In addition, the exclusion of young people from adult work and leisure activity forces adolescents into virtually exclusive association with one another, cutting them off from alternative sources of validation for the self (as well as reducing the degree of adult supervision). A long-run trend toward increased age segregation created by changing patterns of work and education has increased the vulnerability of teenagers to the expectations and evaluations of their peers (Panel on Youth, 1974).

This dependence on peers for approval is not itself criminogenic. In many tribal societies, age-homogeneous bands of youths are functionally integrated into the economic and social life of the tribe and are not considered deviant (Mead, 1939; Eisenstadt, 1956:56–92). In America, too, many teenage clubs and cliques are not delinquent. Participation in teenage social life, however, requires resources. In addition to personal assets and skills (having an attractive appearance and "good personality," being a skilled conversationalist, being able to memorize song lyrics and learn dance steps, and in some circles, being able to fight), money is needed for buying clothes, cosmetics, cigarettes, alcoholic beverages, narcotics, phonograph records, transistor radios, gasoline for cars and motorcycles, tickets to films and concerts, meals in restaurants, and for gambling. The progressive detachment of teenage social life from that of the family and the emergence of advertising directed toward a teenage market (this being a creation of post-war affluence and the "baby boom") have increased the importance of these goods to teenagers and hence have inflated the costs of their social activities.

When parents are unable or unwilling to subsidize their children's social life at the level required by local convention, when children want to prevent their parents from learning of their expenditures, or when they are reluctant to incur the obligations created by taking money from their parents, alternative sources of funds must be sought. Full or part-time employment once constituted such an alternative, but the long-run, persistent decline in teenage employment and labor force participation has progressively eliminated this alternative. During the period from 1870 to 1920, many states passed laws restricting child labor and establishing compulsory education. Therefore, despite a quadrupling of the "gainfully employed" population from 1870 to 1930, the number of gainfully employed workers in the 10- to 15-year-old age bracket *declined*. The Great Depression resulted in a further contraction of the teenage labor force and increased the school-leaving age (Panel on Youth, 1974:36–38). In 1940 the U.S. government finally stopped counting all persons over the age of 10 as part of the labor force (Tomson and Fiedler, 1975)!

In recent years, teenage labor market deterioration has been experienced mainly by black teenagers. From 1950 to 1973, black teenage labor force participation declined from 67.8% to 34.7%, while white teenage labor force participation remained stable at about 63%. The current recession has increased teenage unemployment in the 16- to 19-year-old age bracket to about 20%, with the rate for black teenagers being twice as high.

This process has left teenagers less and less capable of financing an increasingly costly social life whose importance is enhanced as the age segregation of society grows. Adolescent theft then occurs as a response to the disjunction between the desire to participate in social activities with peers and the absence of legitimate sources of funds needed to finance this participation.

Qualitative evidence supporting this explanation of adolescent theft is found in those delinquency studies that describe the social life of delinquent groups. Sherif and Sherif noted in their study of adolescent groups that theft was often instrumentally related to the group's leisure-time social activities:

> In several groups . . . stealing was not the incidental activity that it was in others. It was regarded as an acceptable and necessary means of getting needed possessions, or, more usually, cash. Members of the aforementioned groups frequently engaged in theft when they were broke, usually selling articles other than clothing, and *often using the money for group entertainment and treats* (1964:174).

Similarly, Werthman (1967) reports that among San Francisco delinquents,

> shoplifting . . . was viewed as a more instrumental activity, as was the practice of stealing coin changers from temporarily evacuated buses parked in a nearby public depot. In the case of shoplifting, most of the boys wanted and wore the various items of clothing they stole; and when buses were robbed, either the money was divided among the boys, or it was used to buy supplies for a party being given by the club.

Studies of urban delinquent gangs or individuals in England (Fyvel, 1962; Parker, 1974), Israel and Sweden (Toby, 1967), Taiwan (Lin, 1959), Holland (Bauer, 1964), and Argentina (DeFleur, 1970) present the same uniform picture: unemployed or employed-but-poorly-paid male youths steal to support their leisure-time, group-centered social activities. Only to a very limited extent are the proceeds of theft used for biological survival (e.g., food).

Where parents subsidize their children adequately, the incentive to steal is obviously reduced. Because the cost of social life can increase with class position, a strong correlation between social class membership and involvement in theft is not necessarily predicted. Insofar as self-reporting studies suggest that the correlation between participation in nonviolent forms of property acquisition and parental socioeconomic status is not very high, this may be a strong point for my theory. By contrast, the theories of Cohen, Miller, and Cloward and Ohlin all clash with the self-reporting studies.

In view of recent suggestions that increases in female crime and delinquency are linked with changing gender roles (of which the women's liberation movement is taken either as a cause or a manifestation), it is of interest to note that the explanation of adolescent theft presented here is applicable to boys and girls, and in particular, allows for female delinquency in support of *traditional* gender roles related to peer involvement in crime. The recent increases in female crime have occurred largely in those forms of theft where female involvement has traditionally been high, such as larceny (Simon, 1975), and are thus more plausibly attributed to the same deteriorating economic position that males confront than to changes in gender role.

As teenagers get older, their vulnerability to the expectations of peers is reduced by institutional involvements that provide alternative sources of self-esteem; moreover, opportunities for acquiring money legitimately expand. Both processes reduce the motivation to engage in acquisitive forms of delinquent behavior. Consequently, involvement in theft should fall off rapidly with age, and it does.

Delinquency and the School

To explain juvenile theft in terms of structural obstacles to legitimate sources of money at a time when peer-oriented leisure activities require it is implicitly to assume that money and goods are stolen because they are useful. Acts of vandalism, thefts in which stolen objects are abandoned or destroyed, and interpersonal violence not necessary to accomplish a theft cannot be explained in this way. These are the activities that led Albert Cohen to maintain that much delinquency is "malicious" and "non-utilitarian" (1955:25) and to argue that the content of the delinquent subculture arose in the lower class male's reaction to failure in schools run according to middle class standards.

Although Cohen can be criticized for not indicating the criteria used for assessing rationality—indeed, for failure to find out from delinquents themselves what they perceived the goals of their destructive acts to be—and though details of Cohen's theory (to be noted below) appear to be inaccurate, his observation that delinquency may be a response to school problems need not be abandoned. Indeed, the literature proposing a connection between one or another aspect of school and delinquency is voluminous (see for example, Polk and Schafer, 1972). I believe that two features of the school experience, its denial of student autonomy, and its subjection of some students to the embarrassment of public degradation, are especially important in causing "non-utilitarian" delinquency.

In all spheres of life outside the school, and particularly within the family, children more or less steadily acquire larger measures of personal autonomy as they mature. Over time, the "democratization" of the family has reduced the age at which given levels of autonomy are acquired. The gradual extension of freedom that normally takes place in the family (not without struggle!) is not accompanied by parallel deregulation at school. Authoritarian styles of teaching, and rules concerning such matters as smoking, hair styles, manner of dress, going to the bathroom, and attendance, come into conflict with expectations students derive from the relaxation of controls in the family.[3] The delegitimation of hierarchical authority structures brought about by the radical movements of the 1960s has sharpened student awareness of this contradiction.

The symbolic significance attached to autonomy exacerbates the inherently onerous burden of school restrictions. Parents and other adults invest age-specific rights and expectations with moral significance by disapproving "childish" behavior and by using privileges to reward behavior they label "mature." Because of this association, the deprivation of autonomy is experienced as "being treated like a baby," that is, as a member of a disvalued age-status.

All students are exposed to these restrictions, and to some degree, all probably resent them. For students who are at least moderately successful at their schoolwork, who excel at sports, participate in extracurricular school activities, or are members of popular cliques, this resentment is likely to be more than compensated for by rewards associated with school attendance. These students tend to conform to school regulations most of the time, rarely collide with school officials, and are unlikely to feel overtly hostile to school or teachers. Students who are unpopular, and whose academic record, whether from inability or disinterest, is poor, receive no comparable compensation. For them, school can only be a frustrating experience: it brings no current gratification and no promise of future payoff. Why then should they put up with these restrictions? These students often get into trouble, and feel intense hostility to the school.

Social class differences must of course be taken into account. Preadolescent and early adolescent middle and upper class children are supervised more closely than their working class counterparts, and thus come to expect and accept adult authority, while working class youths, who enter an unsupervised street life among peers at an early age, have more autonomy to protect, and guard their prerogatives jealously (Psathas, 1957; Kobrin, 1962; Werthman, 1967; Rainwater, 1970:211–34; Ladner, 1971:61–63). To the extent that they see in the school's denial of their autonomy, preparation for a future in occupations that also deny autonomy, and see in their parents' lives the psychic costs of that denial, they may be more prone to rebel than middle class students, who can generally anticipate entering jobs that allow more discretion and autonomy.

Middle class youths also have more to gain by accepting adult authority than their working class counterparts. Comparatively affluent parents can control their children better because they have more resources they can withhold and are in a better position to secure advantages for their children. Children who believe that their future chances depend on school success are likely to conform even if they resent the school's attempt to regulate their lives. On the other hand, where returns on school success are reduced by class or racial discrimination (or the belief that these will be obstacles, even if the belief is counter to fact), the school loses this source of social control. For similar reasons, it loses control over upper class children, since their inherited class position frees them from the necessity of doing well in school to guarantee their future economic status.

Only a few decades ago, few working class youths—or school failures with middle class family backgrounds—would have been exposed to a contradiction between their expectations of autonomy and the school's attempts to control them, because a high proportion of students, especially working class students, left school at an early age. However, compulsory school attendance, low wages and high unemployment rates for teenagers, along with increased educational requirements for entry-level jobs, have greatly reduced dropout rates. Thus in 1920, 16.8% of the 17-year-old population were high school graduates; and in 1956, 62.3% (Toby, 1967). In consequence, a greater proportion of students, especially those who benefit least from school, is exposed to this contradiction.[4]

Common psychological responses to the irritation of the school's denial of autonomy range from affective disengagement ("tuning out" the teacher) to smoldering resentment, and at the behavioral level responses range from truancy to self-assertion through the flouting of rules. Such activities as getting drunk, using drugs, joy riding, truanting, and adopting eccentric styles of dress, apart from any intrinsic gratification these activities may provide, can be seen as forms of what Gouldner has called "conflictual validation of the self" (1970:221–22). By helping students establish independence from authority (school, parents, etc.), these activities contribute to self-regard. Their attraction lies in their being forbidden.

As a status system, the school makes further contributions to the causation of delinquency. Almost by definition, status systems embody invidious distinctions. Where standards of evaluation are shared, and position is believed to reflect personal merit, occupants of lower statuses are likely to suffer blows to their self-esteem (Cohen, 1955:112–13; Sennett and Cobb, 1972). The problem is somewhat alleviated by a strong tendency to restrict intimate association to persons of similar status. If one's associates are at roughly the same level as oneself, they provide the standards for self-evaluation (Hyman, 1968). In addition, "democratic" norms of modesty discourage the flaunting of success and boasting of personal merit, thereby insulating the less successful from an implied attribution of their failures to their own deficiencies.

These niceties are not, however, universal in applicability. In our society, certification as a full-fledged social member is provided those whose commitment to the value of work and family is documented by spouse, home, car and job (for women, children have traditionally substituted for job). Institutional affiliations are thus taken as a mark of virtue, or positive stigma. Those who meet these social criteria are accorded standards of respect in face-to-face interaction not similarly accorded members of unworthy or suspect categories (e.g., prison and psychiatric hospital inmates, skid row bums, the mentally retarded). In particular, these full-fledged members of society are permitted to sustain self-presentations as dignified, worthy persons, regardless of what may be thought or said of them in private.

Students, especially failing students, and those with lower class or minority origins, are accorded no comparable degree of respect. As they lack the appropriate institutional affiliations, their moral commitment to the dominant institutions of society is suspect. In this sense, they are social strangers; we don't quite know what we can expect from them. They are, moreover, relatively powerless. In consequence, they are exposed to evaluations from which adults are ordinarily shielded. School personnel continuously communicate their evaluations of students through grades, honor rolls, track positions, privileges, and praise for academic achievement and proper deportment. On occasion, the negative evaluation of students conveyed by the school's ranking systems is supplemented by explicit criticism and denunciation on the part of teachers who act as if the academic performance of failing students could be elevated by telling them they are stupid, or lazy, or both. Only the most extreme failures in the adult world are subjected to degradation ceremonies of this kind.

Cohen (1955) has argued that working class youths faced with this situation protect their self-esteem by rejecting conventional norms and values. Seeking out one another for mutual support, they create a delinquent subculture of opposition to middle class norms in which they can achieve status. This subculture is seen as supporting the non-utilitarian acts of destructiveness that alleviate frustration. There is little difficulty in finding evidence of adolescent destructiveness, but the choice of target may be more rational (or less non-utilitarian) than Cohen allows. If the school is a major source of the juvenile's frustration, then the large and growing volume of school vandalism and assaults on teachers may, in the perpetrator's own frame of reference, not be irrational at all, even though it may be targeted on those who themselves are not necessarily to blame for what the school does. Other targets may be chosen because of their symbolic value, such as members of a despised racial group or class stratum, or adults, who represent repressive authority. Even random violence, though comparatively rare, can be a way of experiencing the potency and autonomy that institutions—the school among them—fail to provide (Silberman, 1978).

Self-reporting studies of delinquency indicate the association between class and most forms of delinquency to be weaker than Cohen supposed. School failure, though class-linked, is not the monopoly of any class, and the self-esteem problems of middle class youths who fail are not necessarily any less than those of working class schoolmates; indeed since parental expectation for academic achievement may be higher in middle class families, and since school failure may augur downward mobility, their problems could conceivably be worse. If delinquency restores self-esteem lost through school failure, it may serve this function for students of all class backgrounds.

The impact of school degradation ceremonies is not limited to their effect on student's self-esteem. When a student is humiliated by a teacher the student's attempt to present a favorable self to schoolmates is undercut. Even students whose prior psychological disengagement from the value system of the school leaves their self-esteem untouched by a teacher's disparagement may react with anger at being embarrassed before peers. It is the situation of being in the company of others whose approval is needed for self-esteem that makes it difficult for teenagers to ignore humiliation that older individuals, with alternative sources of self-esteem, could readily ignore.

Visible displays of independence from, or rejections of, authority can be understood as attempts to reestablish moral character in the face of affronts. This can be accomplished by direct attacks on teachers or school, or through daring illegal performances elsewhere. These responses may or may not reflect anger at treatment perceived to be unjust, may or may not defend the student against threats to self-esteem, may or may not reflect a repudiation of conventional conduct norms. What is crucial is that these activities *demonstrate* retaliation for injury and the rejection of official values to an audience of peers whose own resentment of constituted authority causes it to be appreciative of rebels whom it would not necessarily dare to imitate. Secret delinquency and acts that entailed no risk would not serve this function.

Field research on the interaction between teachers and delinquent students (Werthman, 1967), and the responses of delinquent youths to challenges to their honor (Short and Strodtbeck, 1965; Horowitz and Schwartz, 1974), support this dramaturgical interpretation of delinquency. Most gang violence seems not to erupt spontaneously out of anger, but is chosen and manipulated for its ability to impress others. Non-utilitarian forms of theft, property destruction and violence may well be understood as quite utilitarian if their purpose is the establishment or preservation of the claim to be a certain sort of person, rather than the acquisition of property.

Goffman (1974) has called attention to

the common features of other, mainly non-criminal activities in which participants establish moral character through risk-taking. Such activities as dueling, bull fighting, sky diving, mountain climbing, big game hunting, and gambling for high stakes are undertaken for the opportunity they provide to carve out a valued social identity by exhibiting courage, daring, pluck and composure.

These qualities are those the industrial system (factory and school) tend to disvalue or ignore: the concept of seeking out risks and "showing off" is antithetical to the traditional ethos of capitalism, where the emphasis has been placed on minimizing risk, using time productively, and suppressing the self to demonstrate moral character. Consequently, those who seek prestige through risk-taking traditionally come from classes not subject to the discipline and self-denial of industrial production, e.g., the European nobility, bohemian populations, and the unemployed poor.

More recently, as production has come to require less sacrifice and self-denial from large sectors of the work force, and to require the steady expansion of stimulated consumption for its growth, the more affluent sectors of the labor force are increasingly encouraged to seek an escape from the routine of daily life through mild forms of risk-taking (e.g., gambling and skiing) as well as through the leisure use of drugs and sex.

The similarity between the subculture of delinquency and that of the leisurely affluent, noted by Matza and Sykes (1961), makes sense in view of the position of the delinquent vis à vis the school. Like the factory, the school frequently requires monotonous and meaningless work. Regimentation is the rule. Expressions of originality and spontaneity are not only discouraged, but may be punished. Sociability among students is prohibited by the discipline of the classroom. Students who reap no present rewards from their schoolwork or who anticipate only the most limited occupational returns as a compensation for their adherence to the onerousness of school discipline are free to cultivate the self-expressive traits which the school fails to reward, because they will lose nothing that is important to them by doing so. As Downes (1966) points out, they may come to regard adults who work as defeated and lifeless because of their subordination to a routine that necessitates self-suppression, and hence try to avoid work because of the cost in self-alienation.

Traditionally this has been especially true of students with lower class backgrounds; however, when the political and economic institutions of sectors of society lose their legitimacy, students of other classes may find the prospect of entering conventional careers in those sectors so repugnant that they lose the motivation to achieve in school, and also cultivate lifestyles based on self-expression or politically motivated risk-taking. The bright hippies and radicals from white middle class backgrounds in the late 1960s are a case in point.

The similarity between delinquent and non-criminal recreational risk-taking warns us that the pursuit of status through risk-taking does not *necessarily* arise from problems in self-esteem. Once a status system rewarding delinquent activity exists, students may act with reference to it in order to *increase* prestige in the group, not only to prevent prestige from falling. Thus teachers may be provoked (Werthman, 1967), gang rivals taunted, and daring thefts and assaults perpetrated, even in the absence of humiliation.

When students drop out or graduate from high school, they enter a world that, while sometimes inhospitable, does not restrict their autonomy and assault their dignity in the same way the school does. The need to engage in crime to establish a sense of an autonomous self and to preserve moral character through risk-taking is thus reduced. In addition, the sympathetic audience of other students of the same age is taken away. Thus school-leaving eliminates major sources of motivation toward delinquency. Indeed, American studies indicate that the self-esteem of dropouts rises after they leave school (Bachman et al., 1972) and that dropping out produces an immediate decline in delinquency involvement (Mukherjee, 1971; Elliot and Voss, 1974). In England, when the school-leaving age was raised by one year, the peak age for delinquency rose simultaneously by one year

(McClean and Wood, 1969). These findings are especially ironic, in that nineteenth-century reformers touted the extension of public schooling as a way of reducing delinquency; and present-day delinquency prevention programs have involved campaigns to keep delinquents in school.[5]

Masculine Status Anxiety and Delinquency

Many observers have remarked on the disproportionate involvement of males in delinquency, and the exaggerated masculine posturing that characterizes their involvement, particularly where violence offenses are concerned. This behavior pattern has been explained as a "masculine protest" against maternal domination and identification, especially in the female-based households of the lower class (Parsons, 1947; Cohen, 1955:162–69; Miller, 1958). In such households, the argument goes, boys will tend to identify with the mother, and hence will experience uncertainty and anxiety in later years in connection with their identification as a male. To allay this anxiety, they reject the "good" values of the mother and engage in "masculine" forms of delinquency.

Application of the theory to delinquency in the United States has not been entirely successful. Male delinquency does appear to be associated with what has been interpreted as anxiety over masculinity, but it is independent of whether the household in which the child is raised lacks an adult male (Monahan, 1957; Tennyson, 1967; Rosen, 1969). This finding points to the need for a revision in the argument.

Hannerz (1969) has pointed out that children raised in homes without fathers may still have alternative male role models. Indeed, children raised in a community where adult male unemployment rates are high may spend more of their time in the company of adult males who could serve as role models than their middle class peers. Males who are not in doubt about their identity as males may nevertheless feel anxiety in connection with anticipated or actual inability to fulfill traditional sex role expectations concerning work and support of family. This

masculine *status* anxiety can be generated by a father who is present but ineffectual, and by living in a neighborhood where, for social-structural reasons, many men are unemployed—regardless of whether one's own father is present in the household.

Men who experience such anxiety because they are prevented from fulfilling conventional male role expectations may attempt to alleviate their anxiety by exaggerating those traditionally male traits that *can* be expressed. Attempts to dominate women (including rape) and patterns of interpersonal violence can be seen in these terms. In other words, crime can be a response to masculine status anxiety no less than to anxiety over male identity; it can provide a sense of potency that is expected and desired but not achieved in other spheres of life.

In this interpretation, a compulsive concern with toughness and masculinity arises not from a hermetically sealed lower-class subculture "with an integrity of its own" nor from the psychodynamics of a female-headed household (Miller, 1958), but as a response to a contradiction between structural economic-political constraints on male status attainment and the cultural expectations for men that permeate American society. The role of the subculture Miller describes is to make available the behavioral adaptations that previous generations have developed in response to this contradiction.

If I am correct in assuming that delinquents in the last years of elementary school and early years of high school are not excessively preoccupied with their occupational prospects, but become more concerned with their futures toward the end of high school, then masculine anxiety during these early years must stem from other sources. One plausible source lies in the contradiction between the school's expectations of docility and submission to authority, and more widely communicated social expectations of masculinity. While the school represses both boys and girls, the message that girls get is consistent with society's message; the message boys receive is contradictory. This difference would help to explain sex differences in delinquency in early adolescence. Most of the male behavior that can be explained plausibly in this way—smoking, sexual conquest, joy-riding, vandalism, fighting—is fairly trivial, and either becomes legal in mid to late adolescence or abates rapidly. Anxiety over inability to fulfill traditional male occupational roles would be expected to show up late in adolescence.

One would expect masculine status anxiety to appear with greatest intensity and to decline most slowly in those segments of the population in which adult male unemployment is exceptionally high. This conforms to the general pattern of arrests for violent offenses such as homicide, forcible rape and assaults—offenses often unconnected with the pursuit of material gain, and hence most plausibly interpreted as a response to masculine status anxiety. Rates of arrest for these offenses peak in the immediate post–high school age brackets (several years later than for the property offenses) and the decline is slower than for property offenses. Moreover, blacks are overrepresented in violence offense arrests to a much greater degree than in arrests for property offenses.

Cost of Delinquency

So far, some possible sources of age-linked variation in motivation to participate in criminal activity have been identified, but this is only half the story, for one may wish to engage in some form of behavior but nevertheless decide not to do so because its potential costs are deemed unacceptably high. Costs can be a consequence of delinquency, and must be taken into account. Control theorists have begun to do so (Briar and Piliavin, 1965; Hirschi, 1969; Piliavin et al. 1969).

In early adolescence the potential costs of all but the most serious forms of delinquency are relatively slight. Parents and teachers are generally willing to write off a certain amount of misbehavior as "childish mischief," while enormous caseloads have forced juvenile courts in large cities to adopt a policy that comes very close to what Schur (1973) has called "radical nonintervention." Given the slight risk of apprehension for any single delinquent act, the prevalence of motivations to violate the law, and the low cost of lesser violations, we should expect minor infractions to be common among juveniles, and the self-reporting studies generally suggest that they are. As teenagers get older, the potential costs of apprehension increase: victims may be more prone to file a complaint, and police to make an arrest. Juvenile court judges are more likely to take a serious view of an older offender, especially one with a prior record. Older offenders risk prosecution in criminal court, where penalties tend to be harsher, and where an official record will have more serious consequences for later job opportunities.

Delinquents are acutely sensitive to these considerations. According to several youthful offenders testifying before the New York State Select Committee at a hearing on assault and robbery against the elderly, "If you're 15 and under you won't go to jail. . . . That's why when we do a 'Rush and Crib'— which means you rush the victim and push him or her into their apartment, you let the youngest member do any beatings. See, we know if they arrest him, he'll be back on the street in no time" (Williams, 1976). Thus the leniency of the juvenile court contributes to high levels of juvenile crime.

Just as the costs of crime are escalating, new opportunities in the form of jobs, marriage, or enlistment in the armed forces create stakes in conformity and, as Matza points out (1964:55), may also relieve problems of masculine status anxiety. Toward the end of high school, when student concern about the future increases, the anticipation of new opportunities is manifested in desistance from delinquency and avoidance of those who do not similarly desist. Consistent with this interpretation is the fact that in both England and the United States, the peak year for delinquent involvement is the year *before* school-leaving.

Those whose opportunities for lucrative employment are limited by obstacles associated with racial and/or class membership, however, will have far less reason to desist from illegal activity than those whose careers are not similarly blocked. The jobs available to young members of the lower strata of the working class tend to be limited, tedious, and low paying. Marriage may appear less appealing to young men whose limited prospects promise inability to fulfill traditional male expectations as breadwinner. Even an army career may be precluded by an arrest record, low intelligence test scores, physical disability, or illiteracy. Thus the legitimate opportunity structure, even if relatively useless for understanding entrance into delinquency, may still be helpful in understanding patterns of desistance.

The same may be said of the illegal opportunity structure. Those few delinquents who are recruited into organized crime or professional theft face larger rewards and less risk of serious penalty than those not so recruited, and their personal relationships with partners may be more satisfying. They should be less likely to desist from crime, but their offense patterns can be expected to change.

This reasoning suggests that the association between criminal involvement on the one hand and race and class on the other should be stronger for adults than for juveniles. If this is so, arrest rates in a given offense category should decline more rapidly for whites and youths with middle class backgrounds than for blacks and youths with working class and lower class backgrounds, and they do (Wolfgang et al., 1972).

Delinquency and the Social Construction of the Juvenile

Among the structural sources of adolescent crime identified here, the exclusion of juveniles from the world of adult work plays a crucial role. It is this exclusion that simultaneously exaggerates teenagers' dependence on peers for approval and eliminates the possibility of their obtaining funds to support their intensive, leisure-time social activities. The disrespectful treatment students receive in school depends on their low social status, which in turn reflects their lack of employment and income. In late adolescence and early adulthood, their fear that this lack of employment will persist into adulthood evokes anxiety over achievement of traditional male gender role expectations, especially among males in the lower levels of the working class, thus contributing to a high level of violence.

Institutionalized leniency to juvenile offenders, which reduces the potential costs of delinquency, stems from the belief that teenagers are not as responsible for their actions as adults. The conception of juveniles as impulsive and irresponsible gained currency around the turn of the century, when organized labor and Progressive reformers campaigned for child labor laws to save jobs for adults, a goal given high priority after the Depression of 1893. This conception was, in a sense, self-fulfilling. Freed from ties to conventional institutions, teenagers *have* become more impulsive and irresponsible.

The exclusion of teenagers from serious work is not characteristic of all societies. Peasant and tribal societies could not afford to keep their young idle as long as we do. In such societies, juvenile crime rates were low. Under feudalism, too, children participated in farming and handicraft production as part of the family unit beginning at a very early age.

In depriving masses of serfs and tenant farmers of access to the means of production (land), European capitalism in its early stages of development generated a great deal of crime, but in a manner that cut across age boundaries. Little of the literature on crime in Elizabethan and Tudor England singles out juveniles as a special category.

The industrial revolution in the first half of the nineteenth century similarly brought with it a great deal of misery, but its effect on crime was not restricted to juveniles. Children of the working class in that period held jobs at an early age and in some sectors of the economy were given preference. Only middle and upper class children were exempt from the need to work, and they were supervised much more closely than they are nowadays. As far as can be judged, juvenile crime in that period was a much smaller fraction of the total than at present, and was more confined to the lower classes than it is now.

In modern capitalist societies, children of all classes share, for a limited period, a common relationship to the means of production (namely exclusion) which is distinct from that of most adults, and they respond to their common structural position in fairly similar ways. Although there are class differences in the extent and nature of delinquency, especially violent delinquency, they are less pronounced than for adults, for whom occupational differentiation is much sharper.

The deteriorating position of juveniles in the labor market in recent years has been ascribed to a variety of causes, among them the inclusion of juveniles under minimum wage laws; changes in the structure of the economy (less farm employment); teenage preference for part-time work (to permit longer periods of education), which makes teenage labor less attractive to employers; and the explosion in the teenage labor supply, created by the baby boom, at a time when women were entering the labor market in substantial numbers (Kalacheck, 1973). Whatever contribution these circumstances may have made to shifting teenage employment patterns in the short run, the exclusion of juveniles from the labor market has been going on for more than a century, and may more plausibly be explained in terms of the failure of the oligopoly-capitalist economy to generate sufficient demand for labor than to these recent developments (Carson, 1972; Bowers, 1975).[6]

In both the United States and England, the prolongation of education has historically been associated with the contraction of the labor market, casting doubt on the view that more education is something that the general population has wanted for its own sake. Had this been true, the school-leaving age would have jumped upward in periods of prosperity, when a larger proportion of the population could afford more education, not during depressions. Moreover, the functionalist argument that increased education is necessary as technology becomes more complex would apply at best to a small minority of students, and rests on the dubious assumption that full-time schooling is pedagogically superior to alternative modes of organizing the education of adolescents.

The present social organization of education, which I have argued contributes to delinquency, has also been plausibly attributed to the functional requirement of a capitalist economy for a docile, disciplined and stratified labor force, as well as to the need to keep juveniles out of the labor market. Thus the high and increasing level of juvenile crime we are seeing in present-day United States and in other Western countries originates in the structural position of juveniles in an advanced capitalist economy.

Delinquency is not, however, a problem of capitalism alone. Although there are many differences between crime patterns in the United States and the Soviet Union, the limited information available indicates that delinquency in the Soviet Union is often associated with leisure-time consumption activities on the part of youths who are academic failures, and who either are not working or studying, or are working at or preparing for unrewarding jobs (Connor, 1970; Polk, 1972, This suggests that some of the processes described here may be at work in the Soviet Union. Since Soviet society is based on hierarchical domination and requires a docile, disciplined and stratified labor force, this parallel is not surprising. Yet it must not be forgotten that the parallel is only partial. The Soviet economy, for example, does not generate unemployment the way the capitalist economies of the West do. Insofar as can be learned from Soviet sources, juvenile delinquency has declined in recent decades, whereas it has increased rapidly in most of the capitalist nations.

Discussion

For decades, criminologists have proposed such reforms as eliminating poverty and racial discrimination to solve the crime problem (see Silberman, 1978, for the latest of this genre). None of them seriously addresses how the serious obstacles to achieving this task are to be overcome within the framework of a capitalist society. To suppose that the writing of an article or a book calling for an end to poverty and racism will actually contribute to ending poverty and racism is to betray a whimsical bit of utopianism. Marxist theorists tend to see these problems as largely produced by a class society, and insoluble within it. Efforts to tackle these problems may certainly be worthwhile, but not because they can be expected to achieve full success.

My analysis of delinquency suggests that most proposed "solutions" to the delinquency problem would have limited impact. Thoroughly integrating teenagers into the labor force, on at least a part-time basis, would go far toward reducing delinquency. But the jobs for adolescents are not there; and the drastic restructuring of education that would be required is hardly to be expected in the forseeable future.

If young people had a good understanding of the structural sources of their frustration and oppression, their response might well be different. Instead of individualistic and predatory adaptations, we might see collective, politicized, and non-predatory challenges to their exclusion. It seems unlikely that such a radical transformation in consciousness would develop spontaneously, but in the context of a mass socialist movement, it could well occur.

Notes

1. Arrest rates broken down by age can be found in any recent edition of the FBI's *Uniform Crime Reports*.

2. See, for example, Christiansen (1960), Toby (1967), DeFleur (1970), and Christie (1978).

3. These expectations are derived from young peoples' knowledge of family arrangements in our society generally, not from their own family circumstances alone. When controls in their own family are not relaxed, this can provide an additional source of conflict.

4. The emphasis given to school problems as a cause of delinquency in the criminological literature of the 1950s and 1960s was probably due at least in part to there being more delinquents *in* school then than in earlier decades.

5. Although this evidence confirms that the school does contribute to delinquency, it is hardly necessary. In Argentina, patterns of delinquency are fairly similar to those in the U.S., even though the school-leaving age for working class children is 10, and delinquents report favorable attitudes toward school (DeFleur, 1970). In the United States, unsatisfactory school experiences simply add to the economic motivations created by the exclusion of juveniles from the labor market.

6. The theory of supply and demand in economics demonstrates that with a given demand for a product, profits will be maximized at a lower level of production if the producing firm is a monopoly than if it is faced with competition.

Thus the demand for labor has declined relative to the volume of production as American business has become more concentrated in a small number of giant corporations. The replacement of workers by machinery further reduces employment. Monopolization speeds up this process because large firms can more easily afford large investments in machinery. Large corporations can also relocate in other parts of the country or overseas to reduce costs of production, generating unemployment where disinvestment occurs. Since the labor market is not fully competitive, wages do not fall to a level that would permit full employment; such factors as minimum wage laws, labor unions, welfare for the unemployed, and illegal income all help to maintain wages above the competitive level.

References

BACHMAN, J.G., S. GREEN AND I. WIRTANEN
1972   *Dropping Out: Problem or Symptom*. Ann Arbor: Institute for Social Research.

BAUER, E.J.
1964   "The Trend of Juvenile Offenses in the Netherlands and the United States." *Journal of Criminal Law, Criminology and Police Science* 55:359–69.

BLOCH, H.A., AND A. NIEDERHOFFER
1958   *The Gang*. New York: Philosophical Society.

BLOS, P.
1941   *The Adolescent Personality: A Study of Individual Behavior*. New York: Appleton.

BOWERMAN, C.E., AND J.W. KINCH
1959   "Changes in Family and Peer Orientation of Children between the Fourth and Tenth Grades." *Social Forces* 37:206.

BOWERS, N.
1975   "Youth and the Crisis of Monopoly Capitalism." In *Radical Perspectives on the Economic Crisis in Monopoly Capitalism*. New York: Union of Radical Political Economics.

BRIAR, S., AND I. PILIAVIN
1965   "Delinquency, Situational Inducements, and Commitment to Conformity." *Social Problems* 13:35–45.

CARSON, R.B.
1972   "Youthful Labor Surplus in Disaccumulationist Capitalism." *Socialist Revolution* 9:15–44.

CHRISTIANSEN, K.
1960   "Industrialization and Urbanization in Relation to Crime and Juvenile Delinquency." *International Review of Criminal Policy* 16:3.

CHRISTIE, N.
1978   "Youth as a Crime-Generating Phenomenon." In Barry Krisberg and James Austin (eds.), *The Children of Ishmael*. Palo Alto, Calif.: Mayfield.

CLARK, J.P., AND E.W. HAUREK
1966   "Age and Sex Roles of Adolescents and Their Involvement in Misconduct: A Reappraisal." *Sociology and Social Research* 50:495–503.

CLOWARD, R., AND L. OHLIN
1960　*Delinquency and Opportunity.* New York: Free Press.

COHEN, A.
1955　*Delinquent Boys.* New York: Free Press.

CONGER, J.J.
1973　"A World They Never Knew: The Family and Social Change." *Daedalus* 100:1105–38.

CONNOR, W.
1970　*Deviance in Soviet Society.* New York: Columbia University Press.

DEFLEUR, L.
1970　*Delinquency in Argentina.* Pullman: Washington State University Press.

DOWNES, D.M.
1966　*The Delinquent Solution: A Study in Subcultural Theory.* New York: Free Press.

EISENSTADT, S.N.
1956　*From Generation to Generation: Age Groups and Social Structures.* New York: Free Press.

ELLIOTT, D.S., AND H.L. VOSS
1974　*Delinquency and Dropout.* Lexington: D.C. Health.

FYVEL, T.R.
1962　*Troublemakers.* New York: Schocken Books.

GOFFMAN, E.
1974　"Where the Action Is." In *Interaction Ritual.* Garden City: Anchor Books.

GOULDNER, A.
1970　*The Coming Crisis in Western Sociology.* New York: Basic Books.

HANNERZ, U.
1969　*Soulside: Inquiries into Ghetto Culture.* New York: Columbia University Press.

HIRSCHI, T.
1969　*The Causes of Delinquency.* Berkeley: University of California Press.

HOROWITZ, R., AND G. SCHWARTZ
1974　"Honor, Normative Ambiguity and Gang Violence." *American Sociological Review* 39:238–51.

HYMAN, H.H.
1968　"The Psychology of Status." In H.H. Hyman and E. Singer (eds.). *Readings in Reference Group Theory and Research.* New York: Free Press.

KALACHECK, E.
1973　"The Changing Economic Status of the Young." *Journal of Youth and Adolescence* 2:125–32.

KOBRIN, S.
1962　"The Impact of Cultural Factors in Selected Problems of Adolescent Development in the Middle and Lower Class." *American Journal of Orthopsychiatry* 33:387–90.

LADNER, J.
1971　*Tomorrow's Tomorrow: The Black Woman.* Garden City: Doubleday.

LIN, T.
1959　"Two Types of Delinquent Youth in Chinese Society." In Martin K. Opler (ed.), *Culture and Mental Health.* New York: Macmillan.

MCCLEAN, J.D., AND J.C. WOOD
1969　*Criminal Justice and Treatment of Offenders.* London: Sweet and Maxwell.

MATZA, D.
1964　*Delinquency and Drift.* New York: Wiley.
———　and G. Sykes 1961 "Juvenile Delinquency and Subterranean Values." *American Sociological Review* 26:712–19.

MEAD, M.
1939　*From the South Seas: Part III. Sex and Temperament in Three Primitive Societies.* New York: Morrow.

MERTON, R.K.
1957　*Social Theory and Social Structure,* rev. ed. New York: Free Press.

MILLER, W.B.
1958　"Lower Class Subculture as a Generating Milieu of Gang Delinquency." *Journal of Social Issues* 14:5–19.

MONAHAN, T.P.
1957　"Family Status and the Delinquent: A Reappraisal and Some New Findings." *Social Forces* 35:251–58.

MUKHERJEE, S.K.
1971　*A Typological Study of School Status and Delinquency.* Ann Arbor, Mich.: University Microfilms.

MUSSEN, P.H., J.J. CONGER AND J. KAGAN
1969　*Child Development and Personality.* New York: Harper and Row.

PANEL ON YOUTH OF THE PRESIDENT'S SCIENCE ADVISORY COMMITTEE
1974　*Youth: Transition to Adulthood.* Chicago: University of Chicago Press.

PARKER, H.H.
1974　*View from the Boys.* North Pomfret, Vt.: David and Charles.

PARSONS, T.
1947　"Certain Primary Sources and Patterns of Aggression in the Social Structure of the Western World." *Psychiatry* 10:167–81.

PILIAVIN, I.M., A.C. VADUM AND J.A. HARDYCK
1969　"Delinquency, Personal Costs and Parental Treatment: A Test of a Reward-Cost Model of Juvenile Criminality." *Journal of Criminal Law, Criminology and Police Science* 60:165–72.

POLK, K.
1972　"Social Class and the Bureaucratic Response to Youthful Deviance." Paper presented to the American Sociological Association.

POLK, K., AND W.E. SCHAFER
1972　*Schools and Delinquency.* Englewood Cliffs, N.J.: Prentice-Hall.

PSATHAS, G.
1957　"Ethnicity, Social Class, and Adolescent Independence from Parental Control." *American Sociological Review* 22:415–23.

RAINWATER, L.
1970 *Behind Ghetto Walls.* Chicago: Aldine.

ROSEN, L.
1969 "Matriarch and Lower Class Negro Male Delinquency." *Social Problems* 17:175–89.

SCHUR, E.M.
1973   *Radical Non-Intervention: Rethinking the Delinquency Problem.* Englewood Cliffs, N.J.: Prentice-Hall.

SENNETT, R., AND J. COBB
1972   *The Hidden Injuries of Class.* New York: A. Knopf.

SHERIF, M., AND C.W. SHERIF
1964   *Reference Groups: Exploration into Conformity and Deviation of Adolescents.* New York: Harper and Row.

SHORT, J.F., AND F.L., STRODTBECK
1965   *Group Process and Gang Delinquency.* Chicago: University of Chicago Press.

SILBERMAN, C.
1978   *Criminal Violence, Criminal Justice.* New York: Random House.

SIMON, R.J.
1975   *Women and Crime.* Lexington, Mass.: Lexington Books.

TENNYSON, R.A.
1967   "Family Structure and Delinquent Behavior." In M.W. Klein (ed.), *Juvenile Gangs in Context.* Englewood Cliffs, N.J.: Prentice-Hall.

TOBY, J.
1967   "Affluence and Adolescent Crime." In *Task Force Report: Juvenile Delinquency and Youth Crime,* pp. 132–44. Washington, D.C.: Government Printing Office.

TOMSON, B., AND E.R. FIEDLER
1975   "Gangs: A Response to the Urban World," Part II. In D.S. Cartwright, Barbara Tomson, and Herschey Schwartz (eds.), *Gang Delinquency.* Monterey, Calif.: Brooks/Cole.

TUMA, E., AND N. LIVSON
1960   "Family Socioeconomic Status and Attitudes toward Authority." *Child Development* 31.

WERTHMAN, C.
1967   "The Function of Social Definitions in the Development of Delinquent Careers," pp. 155–70. In *Task Force Report: Juvenile Delinquency.* Washington, D.C.: Government Printing Office.

WILLIAMS, L.
1976   "Three Youths Call Mugging the Elderly Profitable and Safe." *New York Times,* December 8, p. B2.

WOLFGANG, M.E., R.M. FIGLIO AND T. SELLIN
1972   *Delinquency in a Birth Cohort.* Chicago: University of Chicago Press.

QUESTIONS FOR DISCUSSION

1. Discuss how juveniles are affected by the financial costs of their social lives and the labor market.

2. How do typical schooling practices actually contribute to delinquency?

3. What is meant by "masculine status anxiety"?

4. In what ways do the status of age and a capitalist economy contribute to delinquency?

APPLICATIONS

1. Were you employed during your years in high school?
   a. If "yes," why did you work? Were you able to engage in other activities as a result of working? Do you think working kept you out of "trouble"?
   b. If "no," why didn't you work? Do you think that as a result of not working you got into more "trouble" than someone who worked? Explain.

2. Based on your experience, through twelve years of public school, do you think that the way in which schools are conducted contributes to delinquency? Why? How would you change the school system in your community?

KEY TERMS

dramaturgical   refers to an individual presenting him or herself to others in a manner analogous to a stage actor's presentation to an audience. This social "presentation of self" may be authentic or unauthentic depending on such things as the audience, the role expectation, or how the actor chooses to manipulate other social actors.

ethos of capitalism   the guiding beliefs or principles of an economy based on the accumulation of capital and profit.

genre   a category of something that is characterized by a particular style, form, or content.

pecuniary rewards rewards that consist of payment with money.

pedagogical relating to or befitting education or teaching; refers to how and in what order educational materials are disseminated by an instructor.

plausibility when something appears worthy of belief or an assertion that is logically constructed.

prerogative an exclusive right, privilege, or power.

repugnant when something is distasteful or adverse; inconsistent or incompatible.

16

Schools, Youth, and Justice

William T. Pink

This article posits that using the literature on school effectiveness as a basis for creating effective schools, holds the most promise for developing an efficient and cost-effective delinquency prevention strategy. It is argued that typical organizational and instructional practices of schools, maintain a two-trajectory system of education that ill-prepares low trajectory youth for success in school and the out-of-school world, and thus creates the conditions that generate troublesome and delinquent behavior. A detailed strategy for creating effective schools is presented that is grounded in the notion of using collaborative group decision making to develop specific plans for local school improvement. It is argued that effective schools, orchestrated with changes in the occupational arena, will reduce the flow of juveniles into the justice system.

Those who cannot remember the past are condemned to repeat it.

—Santayana

Much has been written about the phenomenon called juvenile delinquency. It is a problem that is persistent in the face of a variety of strategies designed to realize its eradication. It is not a problem unique to American society. While the type and number of offenses may vary, no society has found a "cure." Thus, developing state and federal policy in the field of juvenile justice is

"Schools, Youth, and Justice," *Crime and Delinquency*, 30 (July 1984), pp. 439–461. Reprinted by permission of Sage Publications, Inc.

fraught with problems (such as, how should the police respond to first time status offenders, what "treatment" options should be used by the juvenile court when processing youths who have committed serious property offenses, or what prevention strategy deserves funding for experimentation). About the only thing agreed on by those working in the field is that there appear to be no easy quick-fix solutions.

While much data exists about the types of offenses committed, the distribution of offenses by race, class, sex, and geography, and the relative effectiveness of different "treatments," decisions, and policy, and most especially changes to existing policy, these are more often based on political expediency and cost factors than on sound evidence and reasoning. Further confounding this decision-making process is the fact that policy is frequently made without any serious exploration of the contextual realities facing juveniles in both the school and occupational arenas, and without the benefit of valid data about the comparative effectiveness of different "treatments" on randomly assigned youth (see Pink, 1982a).

There have been a number of theories proposed to explain the etiology of delinquency. Some have been empirically tested, at least in part. As yet, however, no single theory has been entirely successful in describing the reason young people engage in delinquent acts and/or in describing a "treatment" that would eliminate or significantly reduce recidivism. These theories of delinquency fall into one of three categories: First, theories that attempt to describe the conditions, personal and/or situational, that cause young people to become involved in delinquent acts. The outcome is prevention strategies; Second, theories that attempt to describe the conditions, either personal and/or situational, that cause young people to continue committing delinquent acts. The outcome is remediation strategies; Third, theories that attempt to describe the conditions, either personal and/or situational, that cause young people to commit and continue committing delinquent acts. The outcome is a set of related strategies that focus on both prevention and remediation.

In the majority of cases, interventions have been based on these competing theories of delinquency. It is self-evident that these interventions bring with them varying limitations. Intervention aimed at prevention may well reduce the numbers of youths reaching the juvenile court, but it does nothing to help those that do reach the court. Intervention aimed at remediation may well help those reaching the court, but does nothing to stem the tide arriving at the court steps. Thus it would seem that a strategy that focuses on both prevention and remediation is the only defensible course of action.

Given the magnitude of the task to develop a theory of delinquency and a set of prevention and remediation interventions, to say nothing of the space limitations of a journal article, the present focus will be narrowed to the issue of prevention. The article does, however, talk to the issue of remediation when developing the framework for thinking about the critical factors driving youths into delinquent involvements.

In developing a position that calls for us to rethink prevention strategies, five points need to be advanced at the outset. First, the schooling experience is the critical factor in the development of adolescent identity and careers. Second, intervention in schools offers the best opportunity to develop effective prevention. Third, recent research on school improvement and effectiveness suggests both a content and process for such intervention. Fourth, the articulation between schooling and early occupational careers must be made more explicit. Fifth, the juvenile justice system must work in concert with school districts and other community service agencies to orchestrate change in school, social, and occupational arenas to maximize the success experiences for all youths. In short, it is argued that manageable and cost-effective reforms in the schooling and occupational arenas can be effective in directing youths away from delinquent involvements and into pro-social and productive activities.

TOWARD A THEORY OF DELINQUENCY

Historically, theories of delinquency have been class based. They have emphasized the personal limitations of individuals, or classes of individuals, and the relationship between these individuals and the social structure of society. Researchers such as Cloward and Ohlin (1960), Cohen (1955), and Miller (1958) have argued that working-class boys have difficulty accessing the opportunity structure of society. The school is seen as an important arena for gaining conventional status and success. Boys failing to gain such conventional status and success seek other ways to enjoy status and success. The result is delinquent behavior. Both Cohen (1955) and Merton (1968) argue that all people aspire to the attainment of commonly defined (success) goals. Merton argues that people strive to achieve these goals by using institutionally prescribed means, but that these means are inversely related to social class position. For Merton, such barriers lead some to the use of illegitimate channels to achieve these stated goals. Cohen extends this line of reasoning to state that the focus of this blocked goal attainment for lower-class youths is the school. In short, these class-based theories suggest that either personal or class-related limitations, together with differential access to the opportunity structure of society, both cause and maintain a subculture of delinquency.

Recent evidence about the scope of delinquency has indicated that it can no longer be accurately characterized as a working-class activity. Consequently, more contemporary theories have attempted to reconceptualize why youths engage in delinquent acts. Theories and perspectives variously named Strain, Control, Interactional, and Labeling have appeared in the literature. Central to most of these explanations is the notion that some youths are less bound to, or committed to, the traditional values and institutions of society than are their peers; this may be caused by a lack of success, or too few binding structures, or a combination of stigmatizing labels and the negative impact of associating with delinquent peers. Regardless of the theory, this group of youths is seen as vulnerable and therefore more likely to engage in delinquent activity. Such youths tend to be identified both by the school and justice system and targeted for "treatment." As a result of this process of identification, these youths are frequently separated from their less deviant peers. It is argued that they become typed or labeled as deviant, and that the "treatment" that was designed to help them frequently becomes part of the problem, in that it serves to maintain a deviant identity. Lemert (1967) called this process Secondary Deviance. Again, the school is seen as an important arena for the development of this differential attachment or commitment to conventional values and behavior.

In attempting to reconceptualize the causes of delinquency, Hirschi (1969:132) has argued that "the causal chain runs from academic incompetence to poor school performance to disliking of school to rejection of the school authority to the commission of delinquent acts." While others would want to add that this supports a class position, since lower-class youths generally do poorer in school than do middle-class youths, we cannot assume that academic incompetence (however measured) is a direct outcome of social class origin. Moreover, Hirschi's data do not support such an interpretation. A more refined position regarding the movement of youths from class origins to class destination posits that early in a student's school career, decisions are made about ability and educability that mesh with commonplace organizational practices of schools, that is, ability grouping, tracking, and special education remediation, that in turn serve, over time, to solidify both in-school and out-of-school identities for students that finally govern options in both career and life choices (Kelly, 1978; Pink, 1978 and 1982; Pink and Noblit, 1977; Polk and Schafer, 1972). What this position suggests is that students, regardless of ascriptive characteristics such as I.Q., class, race, and sex, are more likely to become involved in delinquent activity if they have a school career that involves placement in low status or low academic groups, together with treatment by the school that indicates restricted rather than unrestricted career and life choices. While it is evident that disproportionate numbers of working-class, low measured I.Q., minority, and male students have this experience in schools, this should not be seen as support for the position that it is *these* characteristics that "cause" delinquent involvements. Sufficient evidence exists to demonstrate that when controlling these variables, the relationship between the school experience and delinquency remains strong (Hargreaves, 1967; Ogbu, 1974; Rist, 1970; Schafer and Olexa, 1971).

SCHOOLS AND DELINQUENCY REVISITED: THE DEVELOPMENT OF STUDENT IDENTITY

Students attending school are routinely compared with each other using a common yardstick, usually scores in a standardized achievement test. Frequently, schools also make placement and personal decisions about students based on factors such as personal appearance, language facility, and previous teacher comments (Cicourel and Kitsuse, 1963; Goodlad, 1984; Pink and Sweeney, 1978; Rist, 1970 and 1978). The net result is that students are placed into one of two pathways or educational strands that have not only immediate significance on what students will do and be expected to do in school but also, of more long range importance, for what students will be able to do when they leave school. Simplistically, the two pathways can be characterized as academic/success/high status/college preparatory/professional occupation in orientation and nonacademic/failure/low status/non-college/low skill occupation in orientation.

This distinction can possibly best be understood by viewing schools as a means for providing each student cultural capital that allows him or her to thrive and prosper in the postschool world. The greater the capital, the greater the likelihood of enjoying prosperity. Students in the low trajectory, however, enjoy limited opportunity to gain sufficient capital for such prosperity. That is to say, the school is organized in such a way that prevents low trajectory students from getting the same educational opportunities as their high trajectory peers, which in turn translate into limited options in the occupational arena (see Apple, 1982; Berg, 1971; Bourdieu and Passerson, 1977; Bowles and Gintis, 1976; Young and Whitty, 1977).

This categorization of students into these two trajectories may begin very informally in the elementary school, via such practices as ability grouping within the heterogeneous classroom and singling out students for Chapter I remediation. It becomes more formalized through the junior high school and high school years, via practices such as tracking students into differentially paced class sections, and/or differentiated curricular strands (such as, college prep, commercial, basic, remedial). While these practices may not be seen by students, teachers, and parents as a formal district-wide mechanism for classifying students, nevertheless they function in a very systematic way to separate students into these two distinct pathways or trajectories. This pattern may be even less visible and understood in urban districts where entire schools may be organized in such a way as to provide students *only* the nonacademic/failure/low status/noncollege/low skill occupational pathway. This may explain, in part, why delinquent involvement is highest in urban districts with a high concentration of minority students.

What is revealed by such a systematic analysis of the link between students' status origins, schooling experiences, and occupational/life options is that the school is the major arena in which students forge their identities. More precisely, it is the school that is the major force in manipulating or shaping student identity. The kind of person a student becomes, including the range of skills

he or she acquires, is in great part a direct function of the type of learning environment created by the school. Consequently, it can be reasoned that students enjoying success in school, that is, the high trajectory students, are likely to be committed to the goals of the institution and unlikely to be engaging in delinquent activity. By contrast, students enjoying little success in school, that is, the low trajectory students, are unlikely to be committed to the goals of the institution, but likely to be engaged in delinquent activity. These students have little to lose by engaging in delinquent activity. Interestingly, a range of data support such an interpretation of student behavior (Kelly and Pink, 1973; Ogbu, 1974; Polk, 1969; Toby and Toby, 1962).

What is it about schooling that is so influential in shaping student identity? How do decision about educability made early in a student's school career relate to options in the postschool career? What is the relationship between placement in an academic track, the kind of schooling experience enjoyed, and occupational choice? While there appear to be a number of interrelated factors that shape the answers to these questions, they can be organized under three headings: (a) Developing Skills, (b) Developing Competence, and (c) Developing Status.

Developing Skills

The school is the central institution for dispensing the skills prized in contemporary society. Mastering these valued skills, such as reading, writing, and conceptual thinking, serves as a ticket for subsequent entry into a wide number of educational, occupational, and social arenas. Placement in the high trajectory or pathway signals to teachers, student, and parents that it is an expectation that the student can achieve high quality work and thus can legitimately aspire to success in postschool arenas. Conversely, placement in the low trajectory signals to all low expectations for both school and postschool success.

Evidence would indicate that students assigned to low ability groups or tracks and expected to be inferior in performance and behavior to their peers assigned to high ability groups or tracks, infrequently develop the level of skill of their better situated peers. To the extent that this pattern is set in place in the early elementary years determines that it is here where intervention in the form of educational reform should begin. Targeting intervention in later years may be too late. Is this differential school performance a function of social class, race, or I.Q. differences? Research evidence suggests it is not. Studies controlling these and other sociopsychological factors show that students in the low trajectory consistently perform poorly, academically and behaviorally, compared to their high trajectory peers (Hargreaves, 1967; Jones et al., 1972; Rosenbaum, 1976; Rutter et al., 1979; Willis, 1977). Evidence would suggest that the learning environment experienced by low trajectory students in school is qualitatively different from that experienced by high trajectory students. Factors such as teacher expectations for work load and behavior, the amount of academic learning time accumulated per day, frequent diagnosis of individual learning difficulties, and the number and intensity of teacher interactions involving both school related and personal matters, all significantly differentiate the schooling experience of high and low trajectory students. The fact is that students placed in the high trajectory setting have greater opportunities to learn skills and be successful within the school setting than students placed in a low trajectory setting. Where skills are important marketable attributes, it is clear that the way schools are commonly organized and managed systematically prevents a sizable proportion of the student body from acquiring these skills. Mastering a skill such as reading early in the school career is important for both learning *all* other subjects in the school setting and being able to learn independently in the out-of-school setting. Moreover, a failure to read gains in importance the longer it remains unremediated. Graduating from school with less than a ninth-grade reading level becomes a serious handicap within the occupational arena. It is through this manipulation of the skills acquired by students that schools play such a central role in defining student identity. Moreover, by withholding essential skills from students, the school becomes a primary instrument in creating vulnerability to delinquent involvement.

Developing Competence

The school provides the major arena in which students can demonstrate competence. Inasmuch as the school defines the criteria for both competence and incompetence, explicitly by teaching and enforcing rules of learning, inquiry, and conduct, implicitly by the expectations of staff for differential achievement and behavior, and placing students into the high or low trajectories (such placement carrying with it both formal and informal messages about the educability of students located in different trajectories), then adolescent competence is defined largely by the academic label carried by the student. In short, schools define a competent youth as one who does well academically, conforms to the rules of the building, and shows the proper deference to adults. By contrast, an incompetent youth is one who demonstrates academic and behavior problems. Even nonacademic extracurricular activities such as sports, debate, or drama, activities that provide a second avenue for demonstrating competence, usually carry the prerequisite of maintaining passing grades. Thus students having academic difficulties, this is, students in the low trajectory, are not only constantly reminded of their inferiority to their more successful peers, but also denied opportunities to develop such competence.

From this analysis of the way the organization of schooling functions to manipulate the students' sense of competence, it is easy to see why low trajectory students may develop low commitment to the school and its value system, have a low sense of competence or self-worth within the school arena, and thus become disproportionately involved in troublesome and/or delinquent behavior. For them, school has little meaning or relevance for either their immediate or more long range lives. While many students do not come to understand the significance of their school career until after they have entered high school, nevertheless, the evidence suggests that beginning in the early elementary grades, the troublesome students come disproportionately from the low trajectory group.

The full meaning of this manipulation of the students' sense of competence is made explicit when we look at the institutionalization of these two trajectories from elementary through junior high to high school. As emphasized above, students showing initial academic difficulty and placed in low trajectory ability groups or tracks, are unlikely *ever* to catch up to their peers who are placed in the high trajectory. This is in part a function of the learning environment of the remediation program offered to low achievers. It is also a function of the perceived difference between the two trajectories. Simply stated, the problem is that assignment to a low trajectory is not part of a competent student's biography, and assignment there frequently brings the student into contact with a different and more restrictive set of rules and expectations that function to increase the probability of being further labeled as incompetent and a troublemaker. This, over time, so fills out the biography with information about negative labels and stigmatizing behaviors that students find it difficult to escape even when moving from school to school. The result is that students having difficulty in school infrequently develop a sense of competence within the school arena.

Developing Status

By controlling access to the skills acquired by students, together with the sense of competence students develop as an outgrowth of this skills acquisition, the school functions as the major arena in which students gain status. Who you are in the school setting, and to a large degree who you are in the out-of-school setting, is defined by the value structure of the school. The school values and rewards academic competence by conferring high status on students demonstrating such competence. It also rewards, via status, acceptable social and physical competence—again, a minimum level of academic competence must be maintained to remain eligible for such status. It is no accident, therefore, that subcultures found in schools

are based in large part on the distinctions inherent in the two trajectory system: high status and rewards being differentially enjoyed by high trajectory students when contrasted with their low trajectory peers (see Coleman, 1961; Gordon, 1957; Hargreaves, 1967; Polk and Pink, 1971). Again, it seems reasonable to argue that students without status in an institution that is the major dispenser of both formal and informal adolescent status may, without encouragement to do otherwise, develop a low commitment to the rules and goals of that institution. Moreover, it seems reasonable to argue that low trajectory students, devoid of status *and* a way to improve their status, will demonstrate their low stake in schooling by continuing to do poorly academically and by engaging in troublesome and delinquent behavior (Ogbu, 1974; Pearl, 1972; Pink, 1982b; Schafer and Olexa, 1971; Willis, 1977).

DELINQUENCY PREVENTION THROUGH SCHOOL IMPROVEMENT

Historically, schools have not enjoyed much support as an avenue for delinquency prevention. This may have been a mistake. Popular theories of delinquency have placed the motivation for delinquent involvement with psychogenic and/or social distinctions: factors clearly outside the control of schools (Aichhord, 1955; Burt, 1938; Cohen, 1955; Grossbard, 1962; Hathaway and Monaches, 1953; Merton, 1968; Reiss, 1952; Toby, 1957). Moreover, much large-scale educational research about the impact of schools on the cognitive and social development of students has reported that the school has little importance when compared with family characteristics (see Coleman et al., 1966; Jencks et al., 1972; Rehberg and Rosenthall, 1978). While the school may have been seen as unimportant, schooling has enjoyed a more central role.

The recently developed concepts of normalization and deinstitutionalization, that is, removing status offenses from the statutes, and seeking community-based diversion options rather than committing "low-risk" youths to correctional institutions, have recognized the importance of delinquent youths continuing their education *with* nondelinquent youth. Unfortunately, youth participating in such diversion options have frequently found themselves placed back in the same low trajectory educational settings that originally contributed to their delinquent involvement. Returning students to an unchanged school setting with the expectation that things might go better the second time around, is not a defensible remediation strategy.[1] Thus, while education has been seen as important, the process and structure of education has yet to be seen as equally important. Predictably, as the results of past diversion efforts focused on the school have been less than commendable, policymakers have tended to look elsewhere for prevention/ remediation strategies.

Alternative Schools as Prevention

The alternative school is one strategy that recognizes the importance of changing the process of delivering education to low trajectory students. However, in the majority of school districts attempting such a strategy, alternative schools usually become "dumping grounds" for troublesome youths in the district. To date, the major concern has been how to remove troublesome students from their regular school. Less effort has been expended in thinking through the content of an alternative education for the student.[2] Thus, the educational setting of alternative schools differs little from that experienced in the schools from which the students were transferred: as a consequence, such students infrequently overcome the learning deficits that initially caused them to be placed in the low trajectory group. Not only is such an alternative school perceived as inferior to regular schools, but by association, are those students who attend. In short, a most promising institutional response to low achievement and troublesome behavior is frequently so conceptually flawed that it becomes part of the problem, not the solution, to low achievement and antisocial behavior. We should also note that alternative schools are found almost exclusively at the high school level. Problems for elementary or junior high stu-

dents are thus completely unaddressed by this intervention.[3]

All is not lost, as there are some beacons of hope on the educational terrain. Gold and Mann (1983:306), for example, have reported on a study of experimental alternative schools that comes close to testing the notion that changing the educational setting in fundamental ways will reduce delinquent involvements. The authors were interested in locating a certain type of alternative school to test the notion that failure in school leads to low self-esteem that leads, in turn, to efforts to counteract it—such responses could range all the way from alienation and withdrawal to rebelliousness and delinquent acts:

> The alternative school programs made special efforts (1) to provide their students, who had had histories of scholastic failure, with experiences of success, largely through individualized instruction and evaluation: and (2) to provide social support from warm, accepting teachers. According to the theory, scholastic success and social support were hypothesized to raise the students' self-esteem and strengthen the social bonds that integrate students' self-esteem and strengthen the social bonds that integrate students with their schools. Thus, the provocation to be delinquent would be reduced, the social constraints against delinquency would be strengthened, and consequently disruptive and delinquent behavior would decline.

While this study lacked random assignment to treatments and a mixing of "problem" with "normal" students, the findings nevertheless are supportive of the notion that a restructured learning setting can improve academic achievement and reduce delinquent involvement. The study is important because it demonstrates that relatively minor modifications in the schooling experience, independent of factors such as family, I.Q. and social class, can impact student achievement, self-esteem, and delinquent involvement.

The schools in the Gold and Mann study attempted to change both how the curriculum was taught as well as the setting in which it was taught. The authors report significant changes in delinquent involvements. What these three schools failed to do was successfully reintegrate the students with their high trajectory peers and work to reduce the barriers to successful movement from school to occupations. That is, the prevention intervention did not result in making its graduates competitive with the average graduate of the high trajectory who was enrolled in the conventional school. The danger here is that a separatist program for troublesome youths can become a spoiled image program. If only "bad" students are enrolled, then stigma attaches to both the program *and* all those who attend. A second danger is that a credential earned from such a program can be viewed as inferior to a credential earned at a "conventional" school. This is important because the credential becomes a part of the permanent record of the student and thus becomes a factor in *every* transaction in the occupational arena (such as, a GED versus a conventional diploma). A better intervention strategy is one that keeps all types of students enrolled in the program, thus opening occupational options rather than closing them off. While the outcome of this separatist strategy can be seen as a limitation of the intervention, it should not be a surprise. Until very recently, the literature on schooling effects offered few suggestions about alternative strategies for low trajectory youths. However, some recent research about both the content and the process of school improvement is beginning to provide an outline of how this might be accomplished. The significance of this new research is that it suggests that the typical low trajectory student *can* learn and be successful if schools are structured and teach in certain ways.

Creating Effective Schools

The pioneer work of researchers such as Brookover and his associates (1978 and 1979) and Edmonds (1979), has led to a body of research and writing known as The Effective Schools literature. Contrary to the widely disseminated findings of the large-scale surveys previously reported by Coleman (1966) and Jencks et al. (1972), the effective schools literature suggests that there are specific characteristics of schools that, if present,

make schooling effective. Edmonds (1979: 16) defines effective schools as those that "bring children of the poor to those minimal masteries of basic school skills that now describe minimally successful pupil performance for the children of the middle class." This initial work has served to popularize five components of effective schools: strong administrative leadership, high expectations for student achievement, an orderly atmosphere conducive to learning, an emphasis on basic skill acquisition, and frequent monitoring of pupil progress. The result has been that many districts have begun effective school projects and/or targeted district-wide staff development at the five specific characteristics. The premise has been, if some schools why not all schools? Sadly, as with some other promising interventions, most school districts have acted without understanding the substance of the five characteristics, the relationship between the characteristics, or the most effective ways to implement the characteristics at the individual school level. Moreover, districts have tended to use *only* this literature to shape their intervention. Thus, in the majority of cases, school effectiveness is defined narrowly as student achievement in reading and mathematics, and the major avenue to achieve this is utilizing the five components enumerated by Edmonds. Consequently, the results of effective school interventions in cities such as St. Louis, Milwaukee, and New York have been less than spectacular.

These mixed results should not be surprising since the effective schools literature on which interventions are based is at best incomplete. Several researchers (MacKenzie, 1983; Pink, 1983 and 1984; Purkey and Smith, 1983; and Rowan et al., 1983) have detailed a series of limitations with the literature that indicates why it *cannot* be seen as a blueprint for school improvement. In particular, they note (a) that the data are predominantly correlational rather than longitudinal, (b) that there is little agreement concerning the definition of an effective school, or of the five components, (c) that it is not clear if and how the components are nested together, (d) that it is not clear if the components are in any priority order, or enjoy any strengths relative to each other, (e) that the literature does not specify how the effective school characteristics were originally created in the school studied, *or* how they are currently maintained, and (f) that it is not clear how best to transport the five characteristics from school to school. Pink (1983) also emphasizes that this literature does not discuss the best classroom instructional arrangements to facilitate learning for the low trajectory students. What is needed, as Pink (1983) and Purkey and Smith (1983) argue, is a synthesis of research on school improvement. Such a synthesis would draw from diverse literature (such as, school effects, school change, school organization, classroom instruction, participation, and staff development) and would begin to *detail* the characteristics of effective schools (such as, what does a principal do in asserting strong leadership? What organizational arrangements contribute to an orderly school atmosphere? What instructional strategies are most effective for high and low trajectory students?). Such a synthesis is in its infancy. As it develops, it will reveal gaps in our knowledge where additional research is needed.

Despite these limitations that seriously hamper schools using *only* the effective schools literature to inform efforts at school improvement, there are some extremely promising outcomes from this broad interest in creating effective schools that speak directly to delinquency prevention. First, it has helped to restore faith in the schools as a means to improve student achievement and behavior. Second, it has focused attention on the need to change school practices to improve the learning of low trajectory youth. Third, it has provided a framework within which to conceptualize both the assessment of current practices and their subsequent refinement. Fourth, it has provided a language and a set of ideas that parents can use to gain access to the debate about the goals, objectives, and outcomes of schooling. Fifth, it has provided a focus to draw together relatively diverse research about schools and school effectiveness (such as, literature on classroom effectiveness, expectations, school organization, staff development, and school change).

The promise of the school effectiveness movement is that it might well produce some systematic knowledge about how best to teach and organize for students who arrive at school with very different interests, experiences, and levels of skills. This has a great deal to do with delinquency prevention.

Effective Schools as Prevention

The position developed so far is that the creation of effective schools is a potentially effective delinquency prevention strategy. Moreover, the fact that previous attempts to improve the education of delinquent or pre-delinquent youths have proved to be poor preventive strategies, does not diminish the potential of *this* strategy. The previous school-based intervention strategies were ineffective because they did not take into account the relationship among the students' location in the two trajectory system, differential opportunities for learning, and available career options. The difficulties with using only the effective schools literature to create effective schools notwithstanding, it is argued that by dismantling the two trajectory system, and providing varied and equitable opportunities for *all* youths to develop skills, competence, and status, then *all* students will enjoy more positive and successful experiences than negative and unsuccessful experiences during these critical formative years. As a consequence of making schooling more meaningful and rewarding students would have more to gain by engaging in prosocial rather than delinquent behavior. Obviously, the next level of concern is aligning the occupational arena with the product of the newly created effective school: it is essential that the promise of success offered to low trajectory youths through the creation of an effective school be realized through wide, rather than restricted, career options. The ability to translate the skills, competence, and status gained in school into mobility and success within the occupational arena is a key factor in the conceptualization of schooling as an effective delinquency prevention strategy. Without such a correspondence, school will continue to be unimportant in the lives of youths. The result will be a continuing flow of youths into the justice system.

While it is important to recognize the urgent need to reshape the occupational arena, it is clearly beyond the scope of this article to detail a plan for such a reorganization. It is possible, however, to detail a six-point, low cost strategy for creating effective schools. It must be emphasized that this strategy draws on findings from several sets of literature in addition to the effective schools research, that is, school change, classroom and school organization, classroom instruction, participation, and staff development.

1. Each school district should create a climate that encourages and supports innovation and change based on research evidence about effective instructional and organizational practices. The recent series of reports focusing on the current status of public education can provide the platform for such reforms. Public interest is currently high with respect to school improvement.

   With this climate of support for change, emphasis should be placed on the development of school specific programs based on student needs, and a method of delivering that program that is grounded in the research on effective instructional and organizational practice. This plan should detail school activities for an academic year and should be evaluated annually. The key to success here is that this planning process involve both the staff and community (including students and parents) in collaborative planning and decision making. As collegial relationships are built, and common goals and expectations developed, then a greater sense of partnership can be forged between the school and the community it serves.

2. Each school should develop a specific plan that details both the content and the process of the following six components identified as key in the school improvement literature:

   a. Instruction: How will teachers teach in this school? What shared assumptions, beliefs, or norms are held about the act of teaching? Will homework be assigned? How much homework, and how is it coordinated between subjects? How do we handle discipline? How is grouping to be managed? How will students not mastering the required material be retaught? What teaching styles are appropriate for the range of students in the school? How can we decrease classroom interruptions and increase academic learning time for all students? How can student achievement be monitored? How will teacher fidelity to agreed upon instructional strategies be monitored? What organizational changes must be made to ensure that *all* students learn the basic curriculum?

   b. Expectations: How will high expectations for student learning be projected by staff and administration? What teacher behaviors contribute to maximizing student achievement? How can teachers monitor and provide feedback to each other about their teaching? How can parents be involved in projecting expectations for success to students?

   c. Curriculum Alignment: How can objectives and assessment be matched with instruction? What skills should be taught in what sequence to students? How are resources used to focus on skills identified as essential? What assessment methods should be used to check for mastery? How can skills be broken down into smaller units for testing for mastery? What organizational arrangements, such as grade level meetings, will facilitate coordination of curriculum alignment activities?

   d. Climate: How can the learning environment of schools be improved? How can student excellence be acknowledged? How can orderly and attractive schools be created and maintained over time? What practices foster high student and faculty morale?

   e. Leadership: What is the appropriate role of the school administration in creating and maintaining an effective school? What are faculty perceptions of the administration style? How can school administrators best facilitate instructional improvement? What leadership roles can faculty play in school improvement? How can school administrators develop and use collaborative planning and shared decision making to improve schools? How can administrators best utilize the strengths of faculty in facilitating school improvement?

f. Parent/Community Involvement: What roles can parents and community play to aid with school improvement efforts? What organizational changes can be made to involve parents and community in collaborative decision making?

These components are important elements in schools found to be effective in improving student achievement and reducing troublesome and delinquent behavior: they should be the focus of local school improvement efforts. In answering specific questions such as these, the plan will make the goals and objectives of schooling clear. It is also important to focus the improvement on all six components. The plan should detail how the various activities proposed will be evaluated, as well as what staff development activities will be required to assist faculty, administration, and community to implement these activities. The emphasis here is on the benefit derived from involving *all* those involved in the educative process, *including* students at the junior and senior high levels, in working through not only the goal setting but also the form and substance of the school improvement plan.[4] The result of this planning process will be more than public knowledge of what schools are trying to do. The process also sensitizes schools to the needs and aspirations of the community. Throughout this planning process, it is essential that the participants have access to current knowledge about the best practices in each component as they develop school improvement plans.

3. Local school districts must provide the support needed to actualize school improvement plans: one important support is guaranteeing the stability of faculty

and administration for a three- to five-year period. This involves commitment from school superintendents to a considerable measure of autonomy for schools in their district, as well as the availability of technical and content knowledgeable staff. Discretionary funds should be made available to schools to customize programs to the objectives developed in their improvement plan. Without this level of endorsement and support, as contrasted with a district-wide mandate that certain things "will be done" (such as, the designation by the central office that certain schools will be part of an effective schools project), the potential for such school based planning is minimized.

4. School districts must develop ways of rewarding faculty for giving time and energy to school improvement activities. This might take the form of providing time during the school day and/or additional salary to engage in planning. Without a system to recognize and reward teachers for important contributions to school improvement, the process is likely to be given a low priority and result in inconsequential school improvement plans.

5. Each school district must develop an ongoing staff development plan for teachers and administrators that emphasizes improving knowledge and understanding about effective instruction and organization. It is essential, for example, that school improvement plans contain ways to restructure the learning experience for low trajectory youths by incorporating the most effective instructional techniques (such as, mastery learning, direct teaching, student team games). Thus, the staff development effort *must* be able to deliver assistance and training in areas slated for improvement in the plans. The staff development should enable teachers and administrators to gain new knowledge and skills, practice these new skills, and receive continuous feedback and coaching concerning this practice. It should also create opportunities for both to work cooperatively in

making instructional decisions that are based on sound research evidence. It is imperative that staff development be continuous throughout the school year, and that time be provided for these activities during the school day. Evidence suggests that the typical one-shot in service format is ineffective with respect to bringing about a change in behavior. Without time to plan for change, little change occurs.

6. In order to bring practice at the local school level into line with what is known from research to be effective, staff development activities must be tied to teacher and administrator evaluation. Ongoing monitoring of the school improvement plan is essential. In short, teachers and administrators should be hired and fired on their ability, *after* intensive staff development involving knowledge dissemination, practice, coaching, and feedback to model effective instructional and organizational practices has taken place.

In summary, it has been argued that effective schools, schools that improve the achievement of all students and reduce the incidence of delinquent involvements, *can* be created by (a) synthesizing knowledge about successful instructional and organizational practices, (b) incorporating such practices into specific educational improvement action plans, (c) providing staff development for faculty and administrators concerning the implementation of these practices, (d) monitoring the implementation and outcomes of these practices, and (e) annually modifying school improvement plans to reflect what has been learned during the previous year. In this way, all students attending schools will have the opportunity to succeed and maintain a range of options for postschool careers.[5] The result should be significantly fewer youths entering the juvenile justice system.[6] The next test becomes whether the occupational arena can be restructured to accommodate in an equitable way, well-prepared students from different class, race, and ethnic backgrounds in significantly greater numbers than ever before.

Notes

1. Other strategies such as in-school suspension rooms, or special classes for the severe underachiever are frequently used. They are usually ineffective as both a remediation for low achievers and antisocial behavior. This lack of success can be attributed in great part to the fact that little attempt is made to change the learning environment and teach these students using different instructional strategies (See Chobot and Garibaldi, 1982; Deal and Nolan, 1978; Newman, 1981).

2. Newman (1981), for example, argues that alternatives should be evaluated on criteria such as: voluntary choice, clear and consistent goals, small size, participation, extended and cooperative roles, and integrated work. His analysis reveals that few schools respond to low achieving and/or troublesome youths by implementing these principles for reducing student alienation.

3. There is a lesson here to be learned from public health, where approximately 90% of monies are targeted at prevention, and the remaining 10% at remediation. Preventing the learning and development problems that contribute to driving students into delinquent involvements should be the main focus of delinquency prevention. Focusing on the junior and senior high school student may be too late if we want to impact learning and development difficulties that often originate with the type of schooling experiences existing in kindergarten classrooms. It is the elementary school that should be the *prime* focus in delinquency.

4. It cannot be overemphasized that successful implementation of an effective school plan depends on the faculty, administration, and community seeing the value of the changes and "buying into" the change strategies. It is not a question of "can the effective practices be implemented in the average school," but rather, "is the school and its community willing to invest in bringing these practices into their school?" Cost is not a critical factor. Most of the practices require a change in thinking and organizing for instruction, rather than large injections of additional monies. Mandating change is clearly a questionable tactic. Ownership of the improvement plan appears to be the key to successful implementation of the change strategy. The major focus is on improving instruction and organization of schools by using the research on effective practice, and *not* on the significantly more costly factors such as lengthening the school day and year, merit pay for teachers, reducing class size, and reducing the number of classes taught each day, that are being promoted in many recent national commissions and reports.

5. Two important ideas are implicit in this conception of an effective school. First, that schools can teach with equal facility students at either end of the learning continuum. Here, students achieving below grade level will learn at rates equal to or greater than students achieving at or above grade level. Second,

that all students can learn in the *same* school. This latter idea is important because it brings into question the commonplace practice of isolating academically deficient and/or troublesome students into separate classrooms or buildings.

6. The justice system can contribute to this process by engaging in activities such as (a) funding research on effective instructional and organizational practices, (b) sitting on school improvement planning teams, (c) collaborating on the articulation of schooling with work experience, (d) providing information to students on issues such as drug and alcohol dependence, and (e) facilitating the integration of youths with community agencies.

References

A NATION AT RISK: THE IMPERATIVE FOR EDUCATIONAL REFORM
1983   Washington, D.C.: Government Printing Office.

AICHORD, A.
1955   *Wayward Youth.* New York: Meridian Books.

APPLE, M.W.
1982   "Reproduction and contradiction in education," in M.W. Apple (ed.) *Cultural and Economic Reproduction in Education.* London: Routledge and Kegan Paul.

BERG, I.
1971   *Education and Jobs.* Boston: Beacon Press.

BOURDIEU, P. AND J.C. PASSERON
1977   Reproduction in Education, Society and Culture. London: Sage.

BOWLES, S. AND H. CINTIS
1976   Schooling in Capitalist America. New York: *Basic Books.*

BROOKOVER, W.B., ET AL.
1978   "Elementary school social climate and school achievement." *Amer. Educational Research J.* 15:552–565. (1979). School Social Systems and Student Achievement: Schools Can Make a Difference. New York: *Praeger.*

BURT, C.
1938   The Young Delinquent. England: *Univ. of London Press.*

CHOBOT, R.B. AND A. GARIBALDI
1982   "In school alternatives to suspension: a description of ten school districts' progress." Urban Rev. 14:317–336.

CICOUREL, A. AND J. KITSUSE
1963   The Educational Decision Makers. New York: *Free Press.*

CLOWARD, R.A. AND L.E. OHLIN
1960   Delinquency and Opportunity: A Theory of Delinquent Gangs. New York: *Free Press.*

COHEN, A.
1955   Delinquent Boys. Glencoe, IL: *Free Press.*

COLEMAN, J.S.
1961   The Adolescent Society. New York: *Free Press.*

COLEMAN, J.S., ET AL.
1966   Equality of Educational Opportunity. Washington, DC: Government Printing Office.

DEAL, T. AND R. NOLAN
1978   Alternative Schools. Chicago: Nelson Hall.

EDMONDS, R.
1970   "Effective schools for the urban poor." *Educational Leadership* 37:15–29.

GOLD, M. AND D. MANN
1983   "Alternative schools for troublesome youth." *Urban Rev.* 14:305–316.

GOODLAD, J.
1984   A Place Called School. New York: McGraw-Hill.

GORDON, C.W.
1957   The Social System of the High School. Glencoe, IL: *Free Press.*

GROSSBARD, A.
1962   "Ego deficiency in delinquents." *Social Casework* (April): 71–78.

HARGREAVES, D.H.
1967   Social Relations in a Secondary School. New York: *Humanities Press.*

HATHAWAY, S. AND E.D. MONACHES (EDS.)
1953   Analyzing and Predicting Juvenile Delinquency with the Minnesota Multiphasic Personality Inventory. Minneapolis: *Univ. of Minnesota Press.*

HERSCHI, T.
1969   Causes of Delinquency. Berkeley: *Univ. of California Press.*

JENCKS, C., ET AL.
1972   Inequality: A Reassessment of the Effects of Family and Schooling in America. New York: *Basic Books.*

JONES, J., ET AL.
1972   "Increasing the gap." *Education and Urban Society* 4:339–349.

KELLY, D.H.
1978   How the School Manufactures Misfits. South Pasadena: *Newcal Publications.*

KELLY, D.H. AND W.T. PINK
1973   "School commitment, youth rebellion and delinquency." *Criminology* (February): 473–485.

LEMERT, E.M.
1967   Human Deviance, Social Problems and Social Control. Englewood Cliffs, NJ: Prentice Hall.

MACKENZIE, D.E.
1983   "Research for school improvement: an appraisal of some recent trends." *Educational Researcher* 12:5–17.

MERTON, R.K.
1968   Social Theory and Social Structure. New York: *Free Press.*

MILLER, W.B.
1958   "Lower class culture as a generating milieu of gang delinquency." J. of Social Issues XIV: 5–19.

NEWMAN, F.M.
1981   "Reducing alienation in high schools: implications of theory." Harvard Educational Rev. 51:546–564.

OGBU, J.
1974   The Next Generation. New York: Academic Press. (1978). Minority Education and Caste: The American System in Cross-Cultural Perspective. New York: *Academic Press.*

PEARL, A.
1972   The Atrocity of Education. St. Louis: New Critics Press.

PINK, W.T.
1978   "Rebellion and success in the high school." *Contemporary Education* 49: 78–84. (1982a). "Academic failure, student social conflict and delinquent behavior." *Urban Rev.* 14:141–180. (1982b). "The school principal and school climate: effects on disruption and academic performance," in G. Noblit and B. Johnson (eds.) The Principal and School Desegregation: An Anthology of Interpretive Studies. Springfield, IL: Charles C. Thomas. (1983). "Translating the literature on effective schools into practice: some words of caution." Presented at the AESA meetings, November, Milwaukee, Wisconsin. (1984). "Creating effective schools: problems in translating the literature into practice." *Educational Forum.*

PINK, W.T. AND G.W. NOBLIT
1977   "The consequences of labeling in early adult careers." *Education* 98:32–40.

PINK, W.T. AND M. SWEENEY
1978   "Teacher nomination, deviant career lines and the management of stigma in the junior high school." *Urban Education XIII:* 361–380.

POLK, K.
1969   "Class, strain and rebellion among adolescents." *Social Problems* 17:214–223.

POLK, K. AND W.T. PINK
1971   "Youth culture and the school: a replication." *British J. of Sociology* (June): 160–171.

POLK, K. AND W. SCHAFER (EDS.)
1972   Schools and Delinquency. Englewood Cliffs: Prentice Hall.

PURKEY, S.C. AND M.S. SMITH
1983   "Effective schools: a review." *Elementary School J.* 83:427–452.

TEHBERG, R. AND E. ROSENTHALL
1978   Class and Merit in the American High School. New York: *Longman.*

REISS, A.J., JR.
1952   "Social correlates of psychological types of delinquency." *Amer. Soc. Rev.* (December): 710–718.

RIST, R.
1970   "Social class and teacher expectation." *Harvard Educational Rev.* 49:411–451. (1978). The Invisible Children: Social Integration in American Society. Cambridge: *Harvard Univ. Press.*

ROSENBAUM, J.E.
1976   Making Inequality. New York: John Wiley.

ROWAN, B., ET AL.
1983   "Research on effective schools: a cautionary note." *Educational Researcher* 12:24–31.

RUTTER, M., ET AL.
1979   Fifteen Thousand Hours. Cambridge: *Harvard Univ. Press.*

SCHAFER, W. AND C. OLEXA
1971   Tracking and Opportunity, Scranton, PA: Chandler.

TOBY, J.
1957   "The differential impact of family disorganization." *Amer. Soc. Rev.* (October): 505–512.

TOBY, J. AND M. TOBY
1962   "Low school status as a predisposing factor in sub-cultured delinquency." New Brunswick: *Rutgers University (mimeo).*

WILLIS, P.E.
1977   Learning to Labour. Farnsborough, England: *Saxon House.*

YOUNG, J. AND G. WHITTY (EDS.)
1977   Society, State and Schooling. Guildford, England: *Falmer Press.*

QUESTIONS FOR DISCUSSION

1. According to Pink, in what ways does school influence and shape student identity?

2. What are the major differences between high and low trajectory students?

3. Describe how the school becomes a "major arena" for acquiring status.

4. List and describe Pink's six points for creating effective schools.

APPLICATIONS

1. From your standpoint, how should we specifically improve public schools in the following areas?
   a. instruction
   b. curriculum, course offerings
   c. classroom and school environment

2. You have been given the task, as an expert, to make recommendations about how the schools and parents could improve their relationships and effectively address problems of low trajectory students. What would your recommendations be?

KEY TERMS

collaborative refers to working jointly or together with others on a mutually defined project or goal.

conceptualization the process of forming a thought or an idea based on the observation of particular events that have an apparent relationship.

correlational data data produced by observing and analyzing the relationship between two or more variables measured at one point in time. Correlation suggests that the variables are co-related but does not assume a causal relationship.

discretionary refers to an individual's or group's power of decision making or latitude in making choices.

longitudinal data data produced by observing and analyzing the relationship between two or more variables over a period of time.

Analysis may include determining causal links and elements of change in the measured variables for any given points over time.

political expediency when something is done solely for a political goal or end; a politician may use rhetoric or act in a particular way not because he or she is effectively addressing an issue, but because to do so garners public support and improves re-election chances.

remediation the act or process of providing a remedy or a solution to a problem.

synthesis the combining of typically diverse objects, items, substances, or ideas into a coherent whole.

trajectory a path, progression, or line of development.

17

The Class Structure of Gender and Delinquency: Toward a Power-Control Theory of Common Delinquent Behavior

John Hagan

A. R. Gillis

John Simpson
University of Toronto

Though seldom considered together, class and gender are among the most frequently analyzed correlates of delinquency today. This paper formulates and tests a neo-Marxian, class-based, power-control theory of gender and delinquency. Using this theory and a prediction made by Bonger more than a half-century ago, the article demonstrates that the relationship between gender and common forms of delinquency declines with each step down the class structure. Furthermore, where this relationship is strongest, it can be statistically removed by taking theoretically predicted variables into account. A power-control theory does much to specify and explain the class structure of gender and delinquency, and in doing so it demonstrates the social bases of this relationship.

Class and gender are among the most frequently analyzed correlates of delinquency today. Gender is a strong and consistent correlate (e.g., see Simon 1975; Harris 1977), whereas class is weak and uncertain (Hinde-

lang, Hirschi, and Weis 1981). The situation is an embarrassment to sociological theories of delinquency. Although most such theories attach great importance to class, there is doubt about the correlation on which they rest. Furthermore, although it is generally assumed that the effect of gender is socially based, there is no clear evidence that the gender-delinquency relationship can be removed when social variables are taken into account. Class apparently accounts for too little delinquency (Hirschi 1972); gender stubbornly accounts for too much (Steffensmier 1980). Curiously, the issues of class and gender have not been joined in delinquency research. We believe that this is a crucial omission, for a combined consideration of class structure and gender is the key to a sociological understanding of the effect of gender on delinquency.

The failure to link class and gender in delinquency research betrays a neglect of classical criminological theory. The father figure of Marxian criminology, William Bonger, offered one of the first statistical demonstrations of the strong correlation between gender and criminality. He then pointed specifically to the importance of

"The Class Structure of Gender and Delinquency: Toward a Power-Control Theory of Common Delinquent Behavior," *American Journal of Sociology*, 80:6 (1985), pp. 1151–1158. Reprinted by permission of the author and publisher.

class structure for a theoretical understanding of the social basis of this relationship: "A very conclusive proof of the thesis that the social position of woman is what explains her lower criminality, is as follows. The difference in the manner of life of the two sexes decreases as we descend the social scale. If the social position of woman is then an important determinant of her lower criminality, the figures ought to show that the criminality of men differs more from that of women in the well-to-do classes than in classes less privileged" (1916, p. 477).

Of course, Bonger had neither the data nor the analytic techniques to test adequately his prediction of the interactive effect of class and gender on delinquency. Today we do; but such testing requires that we first think carefully about several issues of theory and measurement.

THE STUDY OF CLASS AND DELINQUENCY

Two fascinating empirical regularities involve the level of agreement that survey respondents demonstrate in ranking the prestige of occupations and the seriousness of crimes (Rossi et al. 1974, p. 224). These regularities may explain why sociologists who have sought to link class with delinquent behavior have substituted the measurement of socioeconomic status for the operationalization of class and have worried so much about the seriousness of the illegal acts they have studied. By carefully measuring socioeconomic status and/or focusing on serious offenses, they may have hoped to salvage the theoretically expected class-delinquency relationship. The magnitude of the results is a questionable match for the efforts expended: when found, the relationship is modest (Elliot and Ageton 1980; Thornberry and Farnsworth 1982), uncertain (Braithwaite 1981), and possibly in decline (Tittle, Villemez, and Smith 1978).

The paucity of prior results alone might encourage a rethinking of the class-delinquency issue, but there are also theoretical and methodological reasons to pursue alternative formulations. To begin, the substitution of socioeconomic status for class is inappropri-

ate. Such measures are a Weberian offshoot of the Marxian conceptualization of class (Bendix 1974). An attractive feature of these measures is that they provide precise, continuous scores that can be used to rank individuals in terms of status. Delinquency theories, however, rarely focus on such fine gradations of status. Hirschi makes this point with regard to the lower end of the class structure, noting that "the *class* model implicit in most theories of delinquency is a peculiarly top-heavy, two-class model made up of the overwhelming majority of respectable people on the one hand and the lumpenproletariat on the other" (1969, p. 71). Conflict and Marxian theories extend attention to the top of the class structure. Still, there is no theoretically informed basis for dividing gradational status measures into discrete class groupings. Alternatively, neo-Marxian scholars have developed survey measures that operationalize the classes in relational, that is, structural, rather than gradational terms (e.g., Wright 1980, p. 198). Within this framework, classes are conceived as not merely "above" or "below" one another. Instead, they are defined in terms of their social relation to one another, with each class located in a discrete structural position within the social organization of the relations of production.

This kind of relational class measure seems especially well suited to the juncture we have reached in the empirical study of class and delinquency. Gradational status measures have led researchers to look for an unconditional linear relationship between class and delinquency. But the effect of class on delinquency may be conditioned, indeed suppressed, by other variables (Hirschi 1969, p. 73). Or, to put the matter the other way around, as in the discussion of Bonger above, class may condition the influence of other important variables (e.g., gender) on delinquency. Gradational measures of status do not lend themselves to the exploration of these kinds of discrete conditional relationships.

The measurement of delinquency is an equally important issue. Self-report surveys were an important innovation in the measurement of delinquency. They made it possible to collect extensive information on suspected causes of delinquency, along with first-person reports of delinquent behavior. Early self-report surveys concentrated on minor but frequent forms of juvenile misconduct that were only weakly, if at all, related to socioeconomic status. Recent surveys have concentrated on measures of more serious delinquency. The move to more serious self-report items has important methodological and theoretical implications. Methodologically, as Hindelang et al. (1979) note, very serious forms of delinquency (such as murder, forcible rape, and armed robbery) are sufficiently rare to make survey designs problematic. Equally important, however, is that fact that conflict, Marxian, and other theories of crime regard conceptions of seriousness as a matter to be explained rather than assumed (e.g., Black 1979). The recent emphasis on "serious" forms of delinquency may therefore mistake an issue of theory for an issue of method. Certainly, it is a mistake to equate what is serious with what is important. Consider the following:

Theories of adult criminality are often extensions of theories of delinquency. This is partly because of the large theoretical importance attached to childhood and adolescent socialization experiences, but also because adolescents are more easily studied. We have few etiological theories of white-collar crime (Wheeler 1976; Hagan, Nagel, and Albonetti 1980) and no theories of white-collar delinquency. If we restrict our attention to very serious forms of delinquency, there will be little on which to build such theories: the theoretical problem of white-collar delinquency will have been defined away by our measures. Because there will also be very few serious female delinquents, it may be similarly difficult to study gender and delinquency. We are arguing, then, for the moderation of a trend, for the study of more common as well as more serious forms of delinquency. Hindelang et al. defend this position well when they note that "self-report measures of delinquency must reflect the definition of delinquency implicit in the theory at issue. . . . Restricting research to a single measuring device would inhibit the growth of new theories and would lock the field into a rigid pattern of social reporting or account-

ing" (1981, pp. 88–89). We now turn to the theory of delinquency we wish to address.

TOWARD A POWER-CONTROL THEORY OF COMMON DELINQUENT BEHAVIOR

Two concepts organize the classical theories of delinquency: power and control. The empirical distinction between these concepts is partly one of level of analysis. Power theories tend to be macrostructural and control theories microstructural, but they share a structural interest in relations of dominance. Power theories focus on relations of dominance that derive from control over the means of production; control theories focus on relations of dominance established within the family. In this article we join parts of these two theoretical traditions to form a power-control theory of common delinquent behavior.

Our discussion will focus on what we have noted to be one of the strongest and most consistent correlations in delinquency research: that between gender and delinquency. Power-control theory specifies where this correlation is strongest and most difficult to remove, as well as where it is weakest and most easily explained. Relations of dominance emphasized in the power tradition, and defined in terms of class, are used to specify the conditions under which the gender-delinquency relationship rises and falls. Relations of dominance emphasized in the control tradition and explored in terms of the family are used to explain gender-delinquency relationships within specific classes.

Both the power and control traditions lead us to consider the conditions under which adolescents are free to deviate from social norms. Both the presence of power and the absence of control contribute to these conditions. It is assumed that freedom to deviate is directly related to class position, that males are freer to deviate than are females, and that males are freest to deviate in the higher classes. Note that this set of assumptions forms a basis for a prediction such as Bonger's: The relationship between gender and delinquency will increase with movement up the class structure, and it will decrease with movement down.

Our reversal of the theoretically expected, negative class-delinquency relationship is unconventional, but not unprecedented. Indeed, the proposed positive relationship is as durable as the observation that power corrupts and has found one place in sociological theory through Sorokin and Lunden's (1959) *Power and Morality*. They propose that power has an "intoxifying" effect, such that holders of power come to see themselves as above (i.e., free of) the moral and legal precepts that control ordinary persons. The expected result is that "the moral behavior of ruling groups tends to be more criminal and submoral than that of the ruled strata of the same society" (1959, p. 37). Because "ruling groups" have not been meaningfully distinguished in self-report research, this proposition remains untested for delinquents as well as adults. Instead, it thrives on stories of "rich kids" and tales such as those about the young Kennedys (Collier and Horowitz 1984).

A similar theme was suggested in Veblen's *The Theory of the Leisure Class*. In a passage that stimulated Matza and Sykes's (1961) theory of subterranean values, Veblen wrote that "the ideal pecuniary man is like the ideal delinquent in his unscrupulous conversion of goods and persons to his own ends, and in a callous disregard of [i.e., freedom from] the feelings and wishes of others or the remoter effects of his actions" (1934, p. 237). Matza and Sykes argue that this similarity reflects a dispersion of leisure class values—the search for adventure, excitement, and thrills, or what we call a "taste for risk"—throughout society, causing delinquency at all class levels. They call special attention to common forms of "white collar delinquency" (p. 718) but stop short of asserting a positive class-delinquency relationship. The dispersion they emphasize has a democratizing, and therefore diminishing, effect. Still, a small positive relationship between class position and common forms of delinquency is fully consistent with Matza and Sykes's theory: the dispersion they propose is downward through the class structure. A power-control theory of delinquent behavior proposes a

class-delinquency relationship of similar size and direction.

If it is indeed relational position in the social structure, rather than type of individual, that explains delinquent behavior, it should be possible to specify and explain the gender-delinquency correlation by taking relational position fully into account. In the data analysis that follows, we consider these two kinds of relations of dominance: the controls exercised or experienced by the head of household in relation to others in the workplace and the controls exercised by parents in relation to their children. We have already discussed the role of class relations in specifying the gender-delinquency relationship. We turn now to the role of familial controls in transmitting the effects of gender on delinquency within class categories.

A fundamental instrument-object relationship structures family-based relations of dominance (Hagan, Simpson, and Gillis 1979). The two sides of this relationship are that mothers more than fathers are the instruments of familial controls and that daughters more than sons are the objects of familial controls. This relationship is the core of what Rosabeth Kanter (1974) calls the "intimate oppression" of informal social control. This is the kind of relationship that a Marxist-feminist theory suggests is central to the "reproduction of order." There is evidence (Cummings 1977) that such an instrument-object cycle even persists among working women who come to believe in "Horatia Alger as a feminist role model"—a woman who makes time to be both the primary socializer of her children *and* the architect of a career. In other words, even among more liberated women, the instrument-object relationship may be perpetuated. How, then, does this relationship mediate the effects of gender on delinquency?

The answer to this question ties family relations of dominance to issues of deterrence and legal sanctions. Gibbs provocatively observes, "The secret scandal of the Marxist theory of criminal law is that it tacitly attributes validity to the deterrence doctrine" (1978, p. 106). Gibbs makes his point by posing a rhetorical question: "How can legal punishment be used as a repressive instrument by a dominant class if the threat of punishment does not deter?" A power-control theory of delinquent behavior asserts that threat of punishment, or at least the perception of such a threat, does deter delinquency. This much is not new. What is new is our argument that the bases of this repressive effect are the relations of dominance established in the family. That is, adolescents, especially female adolescents, are taught to avoid risks generally and the risk of legal sanctions specifically. The testable implications of this part of a power-control theory of delinquency are that females will be deterred more by the threat of legal sanctions than males and that this effect will be produced more through maternal than paternal controls. The causal model of gender and delinquency that we have described is summarized in Figure 1. The class categories within which this model will be explored are set out in Table 1 (discussed in greater detail below).

The class structure of the gender-delinquency relationship should be reemphasized. What a power-control theory of common delinquent behavior is saying is that in all classes males are freer to be delinquent than females but that it is in the most powerful classes that males are freest to be delinquent. The presence of power and the absence of control play a joint role in specifying and mediating this gender-delinquency relationship.

THE DATA

Before we introduce measures of theoretical concepts, it is necessary to describe our data, which come from a survey conducted in the Toronto metropolitan area. Past surveys have not included the employment information necessary to form the relational class measures that are central to a power-control theory of delinquent behavior. This is understandable, in that adolescents might not have been assumed to have accurate knowledge of the necessary information. Parents of students included in our survey were followed up by telephone, and we collected from them the information needed for our measure of class position, which is discussed in detail below. Our survey brings together this indicator of class position with measures of other etiological variables for the first time in a single study.

The survey was conducted during the first four months of 1979. The population consisted of the students and parents from seven secondary schools serving widely varied neighborhoods. The sampling frame consisted of school board lists of the names and addresses of students, from which a stratified random sample was drawn. Addresses with apartment and unit numbers were used to distinguish respondents living in multiple-family and single detached housing, allowing us to select equal numbers of respondents from each type of residence. Our purpose was to assure that our sample varied widely in class composition (see also Simpson and Hagan 1983).

We paid each student $5.00 to participate at school in the survey. By paying the students and assuring them of the confidentiality of their responses, we communicated the seriousness of the study. We believe that this increased the quality as well as the quantity of participation. The questionnaire was

FIGURE 1　Causal Model of Gender and Delinquency

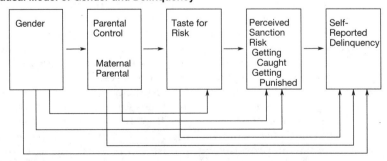

TABLE 1   Criteria for Class Categories

Class	Control over Means of Production	Control over Work of Others	Relation to Labor Power	Distribution
Employers	Owner	Controls employees	Buys labor	8.95% (41)
Managers	Nonowner	Controls subordinates	Sells labor	43.89% (201)
Workers	Nonowner	No control of others	Sells labor	37.99% (174)
Surplus population	Nonowner	No control of others	Unable to sell labor	9.17% (42)

NOTE.—*N*'s in parentheses.

administered to groups of students and the response rate was 72%. One of the investigators read the questionnaire aloud, with respondents following along and filling out their own questionnaires. We used this procedure to increase comprehension and the reliability of responses. Parents subsequently were contacted by telephone to obtain the employment data that we discuss next. Analyses reported in this paper involve 458 adolescents. For all of them, a head of household was known to be either employed or unemployed (not retired, a student, or a housewife). Additional occupational information was available concerning employed heads of household. Within-class means and standard deviations for variables described below are presented in the Appendix.

A NEO-MARXIAN MEASURE OF CLASS

Although the concept of class is central to Marxian and conflict theories of crime (Colvin and Pauly 1983; Spitzer 1975; Greenberg 1977; Chambliss and Seidman 1971; Quinney 1977; Taylor, Walton, and Young 1973), this concept has never before been operationalized in self-report research (cf. Hagan and Albonetti 1982). Our approach to the measurement of class is informed by Marxian ideas. Most important, we proceed from the assumption that classes are to be measured in relational rather than gradational terms. We use three conceptual criteria to distinguish four class positions. The three criteria consider control over the

means of production, control over the work of others, and relationship to labor power. The four class positions include employers, managers, workers, and unemployed workers, whom, following Marx, we call the surplus population. The relationships between the conceptual criteria and class categories are presented in Table 1. Respondents are located in class categories on the basis of four survey questions:

1. "Is the head of your household currently working full-time?"

2. "Does the head of your household currently work for him/herself or for someone else?"

3. "Are there any people who work for him or her or are paid by him or her?"

4. "Does the head of your household supervise anybody as part of his or her job?"

Employers are first of all *owners* of the means of production. This criterion is reflected in the second item above: those who work for themselves own some means of production. Second, employers are *in control of employees.* An affirmative response to question 3 above captures this second dimension. This second criterion is important as a means of eliminating from the employer class persons who are self-employed but employ no others, that is, members of the petty bourgeoisie. (We do not consider the latter class in our analysis because Marxists typically argue that "the petty bourgeoisie represent a remnant from an earlier era of capitalist development and, as a class, . . . is progressively becoming less important" [Wright and Perrone 1977, p. 43].) Third, employers are *buyers of labor power.* This criterion is satisfied by affirmative responses to questions 1 and 2 on current work status. Defined in this way, employers constitute 8.95% of our sample. We refer to the occupants of this class position as "employers" rather than "capitalists" because most in this category employ fewer than 10 workers (Wright 1978, p. 1370). Ideally, we would distinguish between small employers and actual capitalists. As Wright et al. (1982, p. 712) have recently noted, however, to do so is to restrict empirical analyses to an extraordinarily small part of the population that is difficult to reach with a survey design. Our strategy follows Wright in merging small with large employers into a more diffuse "employer" class-category. Our employer class is within about 1% of the estimate given for such a class in Wright's work (see Wright 1978; Wright and Perrone 1977; Wright et al. 1982).

Our second class-category consists of managers. Members are identified first as *nonowners* by a negative answer to the question about self-employment. They are also identified as being *in control of subordinates* by an affirmative answer to the fourth question. Finally, managers are *sellers of labor.* Heads of household are classified thus on the basis of a positive answer to the first question, about current work status, and a negative answer to the second question, about self-employment. Defined in this way, the managerial class constitutes 43.89% of our sample. This figure corresponds closely to the "minimum" estimate given to a combined grouping of managers and supervisors in Wright's most recent American survey (Wright et al. 1982), a grouping that corresponds to what we are calling the managerial class. This grouping can be reduced by adding considerations of sanction or task authority and hierarchy to the criteria applied. As noted in an earlier section, however, delinquency theory has focused on the top and bottom of the class structure, and we have therefore not introduced this detail into the middle levels of our class analysis.

Our third class-category is made up of workers. Members of this class are obviously *nonowners* of the means of production; this fact is captured by the self-employment item. Also, they exercise *no control over the work of others.* Negative answers to questions 3 and 4 place heads of households in this category. Finally, they are *sellers of labor;* this criterion is satisfied by the foregoing information and a positive answer to the question about current work status. Defined in this way, the working class constitutes 37.99% of our sample. Wright et al. observe, "If . . . we exclude from the working class those who indicate in their questionnaires that they in any way supervise other people or that they have even very modest levels of autonomy, the size of the working class is reduced to 35 percent" and that "what these figures suggest is that 35 percent of all positions are unambiguously working class . . ." (1982, p. 718). Alternative criteria increase the size of the working class and decrease the size of the managerial class. If our criteria are in error, it is probably in the direction of protecting the integrity of the working-class category.

The last category in our classification consists of unemployed workers, whom we call the surplus population. Although Marxian criminologists have emphasized the importance of this class (Colvin and Pauly 1983; Spitzer 1975; Clelland and Carter 1979), recent Marxian operationalizations of the class structure (e.g., Wright 1978; Wright and Perrone 1977; Robinson and Kelly 1979; Wright et al. 1982) have not included it. This is ironic because Marx attached great importance to this "surplus population" in developing his "general law of capitalist accumulation" (1912, p. 7). Because delinquency theories in general, and Marxian theories of crime in particular, attach great significance to the bottom of the class structure, we include the surplus population in our operationalization. The surplus population are *nonowners* of the means of production, as indicated by negative responses to the self-employment question; they have *no control over other workers,* as indicated by responses to questions 3 and 4; and they are *unable to sell their labor,* as indicated by their responses to the question on current work status. Defined in this way, the surplus population constitutes 9.17% of our sample, a figure that corresponds well to current unemployment statistics.

Overall, our measure appears to represent the class structure well. It may slightly underrepresent the working class and slightly overrepresent the managerial class, but even so, the representation of these classes is within the range of reasonable estimates established by Wright's (1982) American survey. At minimum, we have achieved our goal of securing a sample of broad class composition. For purposes of comparison, we also include in our analyses Duncan's (1961) American socioeconomic index of occupations and Blishen's (1961) Canadian occupational class scale. These belong to the type of gradational status measures used in conventional self-report surveys.

A THEORETICALLY RELEVANT SCALE OF DELINQUENCY

The theory we have proposed assumes that the presence of power and the absence of control exercise their influence, at least in part, through a cognitive process in which actors evaluate courses of action. We have therefore included variables representing actors' socially acquired tastes for risk and their perceptions of the risks of getting caught and punished, for delinquent behavior, as crucial mediating factors in the causal model depicted in figure 1. These variables represent cognitive states. For them to be operative, there must be some calculation that leads to the delinquent behavior considered. Our premise is that this will be truer of minor forms of theft and aggression than it will be of more serious criminal behavior, particularly the crimes of violence emphasized in indices of "serious" crime and delinquency. Ours is a theory of common delinquent behavior.

Past studies of common delinquency have included "many items that are not sufficiently specified to justify the assumption that the reported behavior would be reasonably definable as delinquent" (Hindelang et al. 1981, p. 45). We have addressed this problem by using an adapted version of Hirschi's (1969) self-report delinquency scale. Our only alteration was to restrict the period of coverage to the preceding year, a decision encouraged by Hirschi's subsequent analysis (see 1969, p. 62), by rephrasing the items and using the following as response categories: never, once, two to three times, often, and many times. The six-item scale asked how often in the last year the respondents had: taken things (worth less than $2.00, between $2.00 and $50, over $50) that did not belong to them; taken a car for a ride without the owner's permission; intentionally banged up something that did not belong to them; and, excluding fights with a brother or sister, intentionally beaten up or hurt anyone. Hirschi contrasts this scale with others, noting that "items included in our scale have logical validity, since they measure petty theft and grand larceny, auto theft, vandalism (malicious mischief), and battery—all offenses that are commonly thought to result in punishment by agents of the larger society, if detected" (1969, pp. 55–56).

Some argue that common delinquencies are not reported as accurately as serious ones (Kleck 1982). The recent work on Hindelang, Hirschi, and Weis suggests that the reverse is true, "apparently because the latter are typically more complex and ambiguous than the former" (Hirschi et al. 1982, p. 434). A second concern involves class bias in recall. Hindelang et al. find no evidence of class bias and instead conclude that "self-report delinquency measures are as valid among lower-class as among middle-class white males" (1981, p. 196). If there were class bias, recent theorizing suggests that it would make self-reports of common delinquency a conservative test of a positive class-delinquency relationship, because "middle- and upper-class people have more to lose by self-disclosure and therefore would have more incentive to lie" (Tittle, Villemez, and Smith 1982, p. 437; see also Hirschi 1969, p. 60). Scores on the six items are added together to form the delinquency scale used below. The α reliability coefficient is .78.

Measurement of Intervening Variables

Three kinds of intervening variables are included in our causal model of gender and delinquency: parental controls, taste for risk, and perceived sanction risk. Our measures of parental controls are drawn from the work of Hirschi, who regards them as indicators of "attachment" (1969, pp. 88–89). The four questions ask, "Does your (father) (mother) know (where you are) (who you are with) when you are away from home?" The response categories—"always," "usually," "sometimes," and "never"—are used to form separate two-item additive measures of maternal ($\alpha = .66$) and paternal ($\alpha = .78$) controls. We use these items in conjunction with sex of respondent to explore the instrument-object relationship between mothers and daughters postulated above. We believe that these measures reflect the means by which important gender relations are established, with implications for intervening attitudes and consequent actions, including delinquent behavior.

Among the attitudes that we expect to be influenced by the instrument-object relationship we have emphasized is a socially acquired taste for risk ($\alpha = .67$). This is measured by adding Likert-scaled responses to two statements: "I like to take risks" and "The things I like to do best are dangerous." Power-control theory predicts that taste for risk is sexually stratified, with males more than females taught to value risk taking. In turn, the taste for risk is expected to sexually stratify perceived risks of getting caught and punished for delinquent behavior.

There is now solid evidence that perceived risks of sanctioning deter delinquent behavior (e.g., Jensen, Erickson, and Gibbs 1978; Erickson, Gibbs, and Jensen 1977). Our causal model predicts that a higher taste for risk leads to a lower perceived risk of sanctioning; in other words, taste for risk and perception of risk are inversely related. Perceived risks of getting caught and punished are measured separately. The three "risk of getting caught" items are derived from the work of Jensen et al. (1978) and involve estimations of the likelihood of getting caught for specific delinquent acts. Respondents were asked: "Could you (break into a place) (steal from a store) (write graffiti) and not get caught?" Likert responses ranging from "definitely yes" to "definitely no" were summed to scale per-

ceived risks of getting caught ($\alpha = .76$). Perceived risk of punishment was measured by asking respondents to agree or disagree in Likert fashion to more generally formulated statements such as, "If you break the law, you will wind up being (charged by police) (sent to court) (sent to an institution)." Scores on these items were summed to scale perceived risks of punishment ($\alpha = .74$). Our interest is in the deterrent/repressive effects of these perceptions and their mediating role in explaining the gender-delinquency relationship within the class categories whose effects we consider next.

Equations

In the first part of our analysis we estimate the following equations:

self-reported delinquency = $a + b_1$
American SES,   (1)
self-reported delinquency = $a + b_1$
Canadian SES,   (2)
self-reported delinquency = $a + b_1$
Marxian four-class measure,   (3)
and
self-reported delinquency = $a + b_1$
Marxian two-class measure   (4)
$+ b_2$ gender.

This set of equations is estimated for each of the six self-report delinquency items and then the scale (see Table 2). The first two equations replicate traditional analyses of socioeconomic status and delinquency. The third substitutes a neo-Marxian four-class measure for socioeconomic status. Our fourth equation regresses self-reported delinquency on a more traditional, Marxian two-class measure that merges the surplus population, workers, and managers into a single working class, which is contrasted with employers. This equation also includes gender. Both the Marxian two-class measure and gender are dummy variables, with employers and men each coded one and workers and women coded zero. Gender is unrelated to class or SES, so inclusion of gender in the first three equations would provide no additional information. As we will see, the first three equations are of interest for comparative purposes only.

TABLE 2 Regressions of Self-reported Delinquency Items on Class and Gender Measures

Variable	Theft under $2	Theft $2–$50	Theft $50 +	Car Theft	Vandalism	Fighting	Delinquency Scale	N
Equation (1): American SES: b	.00	.00	.00	.00	.00	.00	.00	
β	.03	.03	−.04	.06	.00	−.02	.02	411
	(.00)	(.00)	(.00)	(.00)	(.00)	(.00)	(.00)	
Constant	1.92	1.37	1.18	1.19	1.65	1.75	9.06	
Equation (2): Canadian SES: b	.00	.00	.00	.00	.00	.00	.00	
β	−.01	.01	−.01	.05	-.04	.00	.00	432
	(.00)	(.00)	(.00)	(.00)	(.00)	(.00)	(.01)	
Constant	2.02	1.43	1.13	1.25	1.71	1.70	9.27	
Equation (3): Marxian four-class model: b	.06	.04	.04	.06	.03	.11*	.22	
β	.04	.04	.06	.06	.02	.08	.05	458
	(.07)	(.05)	(.03)	(.05)	(.06)	(.06)	(.22)	
Constant	2.16	1.55	1.03	1.48	1.56	1.97	9.75	
Equation (4): Marxian two-class model: b	.40*	.38***	.14*	.28**	−.06	.30**	1.43**	
β	.10	.12	.08	.10	−.02	.08	.11	458
	(.18)	(.14)	(.08)	(.13)	(.15)	(.15)	(.57)	
Gender: b	.37****	.27****	.13***	.41****	.41****	.69****	2.28****	
β	.16	.15	.13	.25	.22	.35	.31	
	(.11)	(.08)	(.05)	(.07)	(.09)	(.09)	(.33)	
Constant	1.78	1.26	1.04	1.09	1.42	1.31	7.90	

NOTE—Standard errors in parentheses.
* Significant at .10 level.
** Significant at .05 level.
*** Significant at .01 level.
**** Significant at .001 level.

So far we have considered only the main effects of class and gender on self-reported delinquency; these effects represent only a small part of our theoretical interests. The remainder of our analysis explores the interaction of class and gender on the delinquency scale by estimating within the four neo-Marxian classes the effects of gender on delinquency. The causal model of gender and delinquency presented in figure 1 forms the basis for this analysis. We explore this model with a set of reduced-form and structural equations estimated within each class. Tables 3–6 present the reduced-form and structural coefficients for the four classes. The equations are:

$$\text{self-reported delinquency scale} = a + b_1 \text{ gender}, \quad (5)$$

$$\text{self-reported delinquency scale} = a + b_1 \text{ gender} + b_2 \text{ maternal controls} + \beta_3 \text{ paternal controls} \quad (6)$$

$$\text{self-reported delinquency scale} = a + b_1 \text{ gender} + b_2 \text{ maternal controls} + b_3 \text{ paternal controls} + b_4 \text{ taste for risk.} \quad (7)$$

and

$$\text{self-reported delinquency scale} = a + b_1 \text{ gender} + b_2 \text{ maternal controls} + b_3 \text{ paternal controls} + b_4 \text{ taste for risk} + b_5 \text{ risk of getting caught} + b_6 \text{ risk of getting punished.} \quad (8)$$

The first columns of tables 3–6 present the regression of delinquency on gender (eq. [5]), providing a measure of the total effect of gender within the specified classes. The second column adds the two sources of parental influence, maternal and paternal controls (eq. [6]). The third column adds taste for risk (eq. [7]). The last column adds the perceived risks of getting caught and getting punished (eq. [8]). The differences in the coefficients in any two adjacent columns represent the indirect effects of variables in the prior column by way of variables added in the subsequent column. Coefficients in the fourth column are the direct effects of the variables (Alwin and Hauser 1975). Comparison of the gender coefficients in the first column of each table will allow us to test the declining effect of

TABLE 3   Regressions of Self-reported Delinquency on Independent Variables in Reduced Form and Structural Equations within Employer Class

Independent Variable	Equations			
	(5)	*(6)*	*(7)*	*(8)*
Gender: *b*	4.08***	2.44*	2.44*	1.88
β	.41	.25	.25	.19
	(1.45)	(1.31)	(1.25)	(1.27)
Constant	8.40			
Parental controls:				
Maternal: *b*		−1.17**	−.66	−.25
β		−.36	−.20	−.08
	(.49)	(.52)	(.53)	
Paternal: *b*		−.72	−.75*	−.57
β		−.24	−.25	−.19
	(.46)	(.43)	(.44)	
Constant		19.02		
Taste for risk: *b*			.75**	.77**
β			.31	.32
		(.34)	(.33)	
Constant			11.58	
Perception of risk:				
Getting caught: *b*				−.11
β				−.07
				(.28)
Getting punished: *b*				−.53*
β				−.28
			(.30)	
Constant				13.72
Indirect effect	—	.16	.00	.06
% of total effect	—	39	0	15

NOTE—Standard errors in parentheses.
* Significant at .10 level.
** Significant at .05 level.
*** Significant at .01 level.

gender on delinquency predicted by Bonger to occur with each step down the class structure. Consideration of the effects estimated in the remaining columns will allow us to determine whether gender exercises its influence within classes in the way our causal model and earlier theoretical discussion predict.

RESULTS

The regression coefficients that result from estimating equations (1)–(4) are presented in Table 2. Recall that the main effects estimated in this table are not our pri-

mary interest; our focus is the interaction of class and gender on delinquency, which we consider below. Because this research explores a new theoretical perspective, we use a .10 criterion of significance.

As in most prior studies focusing on common forms of self-reported delinquency, whether an American (Duncan 1961) or Canadian (Blishen 1961) status measure is used, there is no evidence of a significant relationship between socioeconomic status and common delinquency. The standardized coefficients for equations (1) and (2) hover around zero and depart in either direction about equally often, without ever reaching statistical significance. When a neo-Marxian

TABLE 4 Regressions of Self-reported Delinquency on Independent Variables in Reduced Form and Structural Equations within Managerial Class

Independent Variable	Equations			
	(5)	(6)	(7)	(8)
Gender: b	2.29****	1.78****	1.49****	1.41****
β	.34	.26	.22	.21
	(.45)	(.44)	(.42)	(.42)
Constant	7.87			
Parental controls:				
Maternal: b		−.54***	−.38**	−.30
β		−.23	−.16	−.13
		(.19)	(.18)	(.19)
Paternal: b		−.28	−.15	−.14
β		−.13	−.07	−.06
		(.17)	(.16)	(.16)
Constant		12.57		
Taste for risk: b			.64****	.60****
β			.35	.33
			(.12)	(.12)
Constant			7.10	
Perception of risk:				
Getting caught: b				−.15*
β				−.11
				(.09)
Getting punished: b				−.01
β				−.02
				(.09)
Constant				8.44
Indirect effect	—	.08	.02	.01
% of total effect	—	23	6	3

NOTE—Standard errors in parentheses.
* Significant at .10 level.
** Significant at .05 level.
*** Significant at .01 level.
**** Significant at .001 level.

four-class measure is substituted for socioeconomic status in equation (3), the coefficients become more consistently positive. But only the coefficient for fighting is significant ($P < .10$), and it is weak ($β = .08$). When a more traditionally Marxian two-class measure is introduced in equation (4), a more consistent pattern of significance and slightly greater strength emerges. Five of the six item coefficients (the three levels of theft, car theft, and fighting) and the combined scale are significant and positive in direction. This means that children of the employer class are slightly more likely than those of other classes to engage in these common forms of delinquency. The standardized coefficient for the scale is .11, with children of the

employer class scoring on average 1.43 points higher than children of other classes ($P < .05$) on the delinquency scale.

Equation (4) also includes gender, the effect of which is stronger than class for every item and the scale. On average, males score 2.28 points higher on the delinquency scale than females ($β = .31$, $P < .001$). The strongest gender effects are for taking cars ($β = .25$, $P < .001$) and fighting ($β = .35$, $P < .001$). All seven gender coefficients are significant, and the strength of the relationships is consistent with those found in previous American and Canadian studies (see Linden and Fillmore 1980).

The foregoing main effects of class and gender are consistent with the power-control

TABLE 5 Regressions of Self-reported Delinquency on Independent Variables in Reduced Form and Structural Equations within Working Class

Independent Variable	Equations			
	(5)	(6)	(7)	(8)
Gender: b	2.05****	1.33**	1.20***	1.35***
β	.29	.19	.17	.19
	(.51)	(.52)	(.46)	(.45)
Constant	7.93			
Parental controls:				
Maternal: b		−.81****	−.32	−.32*
β		−.33	−.13	−.13
		(.22)	(.21)	(.21)
Paternal: b		.07	−.03	.02
β		.03	.00	.01
		(.21)	(.18)	(.18)
Constant		12.55		
Taste for risk: b			.89****	.63****
β			.48	.34
			(.12)	(.15)
Constant			4.67	
Perception of risk:				
Getting caught: b				−.06
β				−.04
				(.10)
Getting punished: b				−.30***
β				−.23
				(.09)
Constant				10.23
Indirect effect	—	.10	.02	−.02
% of total effect	—	34	7	—

NOTE—Standard errors in parentheses.
* Significant at .10 level.
** Significant at .05 level.
*** Significant at .10 level.
**** Significant at .001 level.

theory we have proposed. The relative power that derives from being male and located in the employer class produces the expected effects in terms of somewhat higher rates of common delinquency. The more challenging prediction of the theory is that class and gender interact in such a way that males from the employer class are the most likely to be delinquent. We have argued that it is these respondents who are in the highest positions of power and therefore are most free to deviate. As we will see, the interaction that tests this set of assumptions is indeed significant. Of course, this interaction can be examined in two ways; how gender conditions the effect of class on delinquency or how class conditions the effect of gender on delinquency. We will emphasize the latter because this is the way that Bonger sets up the problem and the way in which we have developed our theory. Nonetheless, before proceeding to these results, we can first summarize the way in which gender conditions the effect of class: males from the employer class score on average 2.39 points higher than males from other classes on the delinquency scale ($\beta = .16$, $P < .001$), whereas females from the employer class score on average only .41 points higher than females from other classes on this scale ($\beta = .04$, $P > .10$). A between-class t-test for these coefficients indicates the statistical significance of this difference ($t = 2.22$, $P <$

TABLE 6 Regressions of Self-reported Delinquency on Independent Variables in Reduced Form and Structural Equations within Surplus Population

Independent Variable	Equations			
	(5)	(6)	(7)	(8)
Gender: b	1.42	−.03	−.25	−.61
β	.17	.00	−.03	−.07
	(1.28)	(1.18)	(1.02)	(.98)
Constant	8.81			
Parental controls:				
Maternal: b		−1.39**	−1.01***	−.58
β		−.55	−.40	−.23
		(.46)	(.41)	(.43)
Paternal: b		−.12	−.38	−.39
β		−.04	−.15	−.15
		(.46)	(.40)	(.39)
Constant		17.32		
Taste for risk: b			1.05****	1.06****
β			.45	.45
			(.28)	(.27)
Constant			10.38	
Perception of risk:				
Getting caught: b				−.47**
β				−.34
				(.20)
Getting punished: b				.04
β				.03
				(.16)
Constant				12.08
Indirect effect	—	.17	−.03	−.04
% of total effect	—	100.0	—	—

NOTE—Standard errors in parentheses.
* Significant at .10 level.
** Significant at .05 level.
*** Significant at .01 level.
**** Significant at .001 level.

.05). Gender modifies and suppresses the effect of class on delinquency in the expected way.

Bonger, however, implicitly proposed an even more stringent test of interaction: He argued that the effect of gender on delinquency would decline with each step down the class structure. We have identified four classes that are consistent with Bonger's Marxian perspective. By comparing the results of estimating equation (5) in each of the four classes, that is, the coefficients in column 1 of tables 3–6, we are provided with a test of his thesis. The results follow the steplike sequence predicted: on average, males score 4.08 points higher than females on the delinquency scale

in the employer class ($\beta = .41$, $P < .01$), 2.29 points higher than females in the managerial class ($\beta = .34$, $P < .001$), 2.05 points higher in the working class ($\beta = .29$, $P < .001$) and only 1.42 points higher in the surplus population ($\beta = .17$, $P > .10$). Note that the gender coefficient in the surplus population is reduced to insignificance. These results strongly support Bonger's argument that the effect of gender can be shown to be a product of social position by specifying where in the social structure the relationship is observed.

Table 7 shows the results of *t*-tests for the interclass comparison of gender coefficients. The first row corresponds to the estimated equations that we have considered within

TABLE 7 Comparison of Class Category Gender Coefficients

Equation	Employers/ Managers	Employers/ Workers	Employers/ Surplus	Surplus/ Workers	Surplus/ Managers
(5):					
Difference	1.79	2.03	2.66	.63	.87
t-value	2.29**	2.45**	2.27**	.78	1.13
(6):					
Difference	.66	1.11	2.47	1.36	1.81
t-value	.87	1.37	2.21**	1.70*	2.41**
(7):					
Difference	.95	1.24	2.69	1.45	1.74
t-value	1.28	1.61	2.54**	1.93*	2.42**
(8):					
Difference	.47	.53	2.49	1.96	2.02
t-value	.44	.69`	2.37**	2.65*	2.85***

* Significant at .10 level.
** Significant at .05 level.
*** Significant at .01 level.

each class to this point. These significance tests confirm what is apparent from the gender coefficients: it is within the employer class that the effect of gender differs most from the rest, because this coefficient is significantly different from that of gender in each of the other three classes. A power-control theory of delinquent behavior now tries to address whether we can further specify how this occurs. The premise of the theory is that the presence of power and the absence of control give freedom to deviate that results among adolescents, especially employer class males, in common forms of delinquency. Equations (6)–(8) test this premise by bringing into our analysis the three remaining concepts emphasized in our theory: parental controls, taste for risk, and perception of sanction risk.

Equation (6) introduces parental controls, maternal and paternal, into our analysis. Within each class, consideration of parental controls substantially reduces the effect of gender on delinquency (tables 3–6). On average, males are now 2.44 points higher than females on the delinquency scale in the employer class ($\beta = .25$, $P < .10$), score 1.78 points higher than females in the managerial class ($\beta = .26$, $P < .001$), 1.33 points higher in the working class ($\beta = .19$, $P < .05$), and no higher in the surplus population ($b = -.03$, $\beta = .00$, $P > .10$). Note that the gender coefficient in the surplus popula-

tion is now not only nonsignificant but nonexistent. In the higher classes the gender coefficients are reduced in size but are still individually significant. However, the interclass comparisons in table 7 reveal that the gender coefficient in the employer class is no longer significantly different from that of gender in the managerial or working class. Consequently, differences in parental control account for the higher delinquency of males in the employer class than in the managerial or working class; the former apparently are left freer by their parents to pursue common forms of delinquency, and they do so. In all three of the higher classes, however, males are still more delinquent than females, even when parental controls are taken into account. This is not the case in the surplus population: when parental controls are taken into account here, there is no evidence of any gender-delinquency relationship. Overall, these results confirm that freedom from parental controls has much to do with differences within and between classes in the effect of gender on delinquency. These are the most powerful intervening variables in our analysis. We now examine why this is so.

The power-control theory of delinquent behavior postulates an instrument-object relationship between mothers and daughters as a key factor in explaining gender differences in delinquency. The instrumental role assigned to mothers is clear in our data.

Within each class, the effect of maternal control in equation (6) is statistically significant, whereas the maternal control in equation (6) is statistically significant, whereas the effect of paternal control is not. In other words, mothers are more instrumental than fathers in controlling their children. That daughters more than sons are the objects of this control is reflected in the substantial reduction in the effect of gender on delinquency that results from introducing maternal control into equation (6). Paternal control comes very close to exercising significant effects in the employer ($b = -.72$, $P < .20$) and managerial ($b = -.28$, $P < .20$) classes, and this effect is largest in the employer class. Nonetheless, in these classes as in the others, the instrument-object roles assigned to mothers and daughters is clearly demonstrated. The other side of this relationship is the freedom to deviate that it grants to adolescent males, particularly in the employer class.

We turn next to the sexually stratified attitudes and perceptions that are postulated in our model to result from the instrument-object relationship we have identified. The first of these, taste for risk, is introduced in equation (7). This variable has a relatively strong ($\beta = .31$ to $.48$) and significant effect on delinquent behavior in all four classes (tables 3–6). The important mediating effect of this variable in explaining delinquency is also reflected in the fact that it substantially reduces the effect of maternal controls in all four classes. Nevertheless, although this variable reduces the effect of gender on delinquency in the managerial and working class (as noted above, there is no remaining significant effect in the surplus population), it has absolutely no mediating role in the employer class. The gender coefficients for the employer class in equations (6) and (7) are identical (2.44). The potential importance of this finding is discussed further below.

The last intervening variables introduced into equation (8) involve perceptions of sanction risk. These variables reverse the pattern for taste for risk: only in the employer class do perceptions of sanction risk substantially reduce the effect of gender on delinquency ($b = 1.88$, $\beta = .19$); this effect is no longer statistically significant. More specifi-

cally, it is the perceived risk of getting punished ($\beta = -.53$, $b = -.28$, $P < .10$) that finally reduces the effect of gender to nonsignificance in this class. Males are apparently more delinquent than females in the employer class because they are less controlled by their mothers and less likely to perceive the risks of getting punished as threatening. Under these conditions, males in the employer class are the most delinquent respondents in our sample.

Finally, we call attention to the bottom row of table 7. This row presents the interclass significance tests for the gender coefficients in equation (8), which includes all the variables in our model. When the zero-order gender coefficients were compared between classes in row 1, the employer class coefficient was significantly different from all others. Now the surplus population stands out. That is, with parental controls and the risk variables taken into account in equation (8), there are no significant differences in the size of the gender effects between the upper three classes. But controlling for these variables in the surplus population results in a reversal of sign for gender ($b = -.61$). Although this effect individually is not statistically significant, it is significantly different from the gender effects in the other three classes. In this sense, at least, the effect of gender remains unique in the surplus population.

DISCUSSION AND CONCLUSIONS

Ours is not the first theory of delinquent behavior to be informed by Marxian ideas (see Spitzer 1975; Greenberg 1977; Colvin and Pauly 1983). It is, however, the first such formulation to be empirically tested; and it is the first Marxian-based theory to address one of the most important relationships in delinquency research: that between gender and delinquency. We have demonstrated, using a power-control theory of delinquency and a prediction made by Bonger more than a half-century ago, that the relationship between gender and common forms of delinquency declines with each step down the class structure. Furthermore, where this relationship is strongest, it can be statistically removed by taking theoretically predicted variables into account. A power-control theory does much to specify and explain the class structure of gender and delinquency, and in doing so it demonstrates the social bases of this relationship.

The core assumption of our theory is that the presence of power and the absence of control create conditions of freedom that permit common forms of delinquency. It is important to emphasize that this formulation is different from existing Marxian theories of delinquency. This theoretical difference may derive from the different phenomena selected for explanatory attention. Recently, Marxian theorists have followed delinquency researchers in focusing on serious forms of delinquency. For example, Colvin and Pauly announce in the first sentence of their statement of a "structural-Marxist theory of delinquency production" that their interest is in "serious patterned delinquent behavior, defined as repeated engagement of a juvenile in the FBI's Part One Index crimes" (1983, p. 513).

We have noted previously that persons high in the class structure rarely commit such offenses even once, much less repeatedly. This is, of course, the class premise of a Marxian theory of serious delinquency. The theoretical question is, What is it about conditions at the bottom of the class structure that pressures persons to commit such acts?

Our focus, however, has been on common forms of delinquency. We see no reason to assume that class, measured in Marxian terms, is related to common forms of delinquency in the same way that it is to serious delinquency. Indeed, we have argued that positions of power, defined in terms of class and gender, are conducive to higher rates of common delinquency. The theoretical question we ask is, What is it about conditions at the *top* of the social structure that *allows* persons to commit such acts?

The first kind of theory assumes that people are driven to delinquency: the second, that they are more delinquent because they are free to be so (see Hirschi 1969, chap. 1). That one theory receives empirical support need not mean that the other is wrong. The two kinds of delinquency may demand different explanations.

It is important to clarify further why we have focused on common forms of delinquency. Hindelang et al. have estimated that the annual prevalence of serious delinquency in the population is less than 2%–3% (1979, p. 1010). Given the small class fractions that interest Marxian scholars (the surplus population is smaller than 10% and the capitalist class smaller still) and the infrequency of such delinquencies, it will be extremely difficult to test Marxian theories of serious delinquency. The skewness of the two distributions will require either exceptionally large samples or samples that are heavily stratified on the basis of known correlates of serious delinquency (e.g., known court records). The former approach will require financing on a grander scale than contemporary victimization surveys (which involve more than 100,000 screening interviews); the latter approach raises serious problems of generalization, involving a use of official data sources that has thus far proved anathema to radical criminologists. On the basis of this knowledge, we fear that empirical tests of Marxian theories of serious delinquency are unlikely to emerge soon.

Meanwhile, there is much to be learned by both Marxists and non-Marxists about the class structure of gender and more common forms of delinquency. For example, our data are in some ways quite congenial to a conventional functionalist understanding of stratification and its consequences. Consider our findings regarding one variable, "taste for risk." This variable plays a significant role in mediating the gender-delinquency relationship in the managerial and working class but not in the employer class. To the extent that risk taking is valued, at least among men in Western capitalist societies, the former findings are consistent with traditional understandings of the role of socialization in fostering attitudes that are conducive to upward mobility. Delinquency can be understood here as an unintended consequence. Nonetheless, at the top of the class structure, males in the employer class are more delinquent than females, not because they have a higher taste for risk but simply because they are less controlled by their parents and believe that they are less likely to be pun-

APPENDIX

Means and Standard Deviations of Variables Used in Regression Equations

	Full Sample	Employers	Professional Managerial Class	Workers	Surplus Population
Gender	.52	.51	.52	.53	.50
	(.50)	(.51)	(.50)	(.50)	(.51)
Paternal control:					
Maternal	5.64	5.59	5.71	5.67	5.24
	(1.45)	(1.53)	(1.42)	(1.41)	(1.65)
Paternal	4.79	4.51	4.82	4.94	4.31
	(1.52)	(1.66)	(1.53)	(1.45)	(1.57)
Taste for risk	6.31	6.22	6.35	6.39	5.91
	(1.88)	(2.06)	(1.84)	(1.92)	(1.76)
Perceived sanction risk:					
Getting caught	8.79	8.46	8.73	8.97	8.69
	(2.64)	(3.08)	(2.46)	(2.67)	(2.98)
Getting punished	8.09	7.73	8.02	8.25	8.14
	(2.55)	(2.63)	(2.31)	(2.65)	(3.10)
Self-reported delinquency	9.21	10.49	9.06	9.01	9.52
	(3.63)	(5.02)	(3.38)	(3.53)	(4.15)

NOTE—SDs in parentheses.

ished for their delinquencies. This is the stuff from which more critical theories are made.

Our findings therefore are not all of a piece. They do affirm one simple conclusion, however: Marxists and non-Marxists alike will benefit from operationalizing the concepts of class, gender, and delinquency as we have done in this paper. Indeed, our findings indicate that to do otherwise is to obscure the class structure of gender and common forms of delinquency.

Refrences

ALWIN, DUANE, AND ROBERT HAUSER
1975 "The Decomposition of Effects in Path Analysis." *American Sociological Review* 40:37–47.

BENDIX, REINHARD
1974 "Inequality and Social Structure: A Comparison of Marx and Weber." *American Sociological Review* 9:149–61.

BLACK, DONALD
1979 "Common Sense in the Sociology of Law." *American Sociological Review* 44:18–26.

BLISHEN, B.
1961 "The Construction and Use of an Occupational Class Scale." In *Canadian Society*, edited by B. Blishen et al. Toronto: macmillan.

BONGER, WILLIAM
1916 *Crime and Economic Conditions.* Book 2. Boston: Little, Brown.

BRAITHWAITE, JOHN
1981 "The Myth of Social Class and Criminality Reconsidered." *American Sociological Review* 46:36–57.

CHAMBLISS, WILLIAM, AND ROBERT SEIDMAN
1971 *Law, Order and Power.* Reading, Mass.: Addison-Wesley.

CLELLAND, DONALD, AND TIMOTHY CARTER
1980 "The New Myth of Class and Crime." *Criminology* 18:319–36.

COLLIER, PETER, AND DAVID HOROWITZ
1984 *Kennedys: An American Drama.* New York: Summit.

COLVIN, MARK, AND JOHN PAULY
1983 "A Critique of Criminology: Toward an Integrated Structural-Marxist Theory of Delinquency Production." *American Journal of Sociology* 89:513–52.

CUMMINGS, L. D.
1977 "Value Stretch in Definitions of Career among College Women: Horatio Alger as Feminist Model." *Social Problems* 25:65–74.

DUNCAN, O. D.
1961 "A Socioeconomic Index for All Occupations." In *Occupations and Social Status*, edited by Albert Reiss. New York: Free Press.

ELLIOT, DELBERT, AND SWAN AGETON
1980 "Reconciling Race and Class Differences in Self-Reported and Official Estimates of Delinquency." *American Sociological Review* 45:95–110.

ERICKSON, M. L., J. P. GIBBS, AND G. F. JENSEN
1977   "Deterrence and the Perceived Certainty of Legal Punishment." *American Sociological Review* 42:305–17.

GIBBS, JACK
1978   "Deterrence, Penal Policy and the Sociology of Law." In *Research in Law and Sociology*, edited by Rita Simon. Greenwich, Conn.: JAI.

GREENBERG, DAVID
1977   "Delinquency and the Age Structure of Society." *Contemporary Crises* 1:189–223.

HAGAN, JOHN, AND CELESTA ALBONETTI
1982   "Race, Class and the Perception of Criminal Injustice in America." *American Journal of Sociology* 88:329–55.

HAGAN, JOHN, ILENE NAGEL, AND CELESTA ALBONETTI
1980   "The Differential Sentencing of White Collar Offenders in Ten Federal District Courts." *American Sociological Review* 45:802–20.

HAGAN, JOHN, JOHN SIMPSON, AND A. R. GILLIS
1979   "The Sexual Stratification of Social Control." *British Journal of Sociology* 30:25–38.

HARRIS, ANTHONY
1977   "Sex and Theories of Deviance: Toward a Functional Theory of Deviant Type-Scripts." *American Sociological Review* 42:3–15.

HINDELANG, MICHAEL, TRAVIS HIRSCHI, AND JOSEPH WEIS
1979   "Correlates of Delinquency: The Illusion of Discrepancy between Self-Report and Official Measures." *American Sociological Review* 44:995–1014.

———. 1981. *Measuring Delinquency*. Beverly Hills, Calif.: Sage.

HIRSCHI, TRAVIS
1969   *Causes of Delinquency*. Berkeley and Los Angeles: University of California Press.

———. 1972. "Social Class and Crime." In *Issues in Social Inequality*, edited by D. Theilbar and S. Feldman. Boston: Little, Brown.

HIRSCHI, TRAVIS, MICHAEL HINDELANG, AND JOSEPH WEIS
1982   "Reply to 'On the Use of Self-Report Data to Determine the Class Distribution of Criminal and Delinquent Behavior.'" *American Sociological Review* 47:433–35.

JENSEN, G. F., M. L. ERICKSON, AND J. P. GIBBS
1978.   "Perceived Risk of Punishment and Self-reported Delinquency." *Social Forces* 57:57–78.

KANTER, ROSABETH
1974   "Intimate Repression." *Sociological Quarterly* 15 (2): 320–24.

KLECK, GARY
1982   "On the Use of Self-Report Data to Determine the Class Distribution of Criminal and Delinquent Behavior." *American Sociological Review* 47:427–33.

LINDEN, RICK, AND CATHY FILLMORE
1980   "A Comparative Study of Delinquency Involvement." In *Crime in Canadian Society*, edited by R. Silverman and J. Teevan. Toronto: Butterworths.

MARX, KARL
1912   *Capital*. Vol. 1. Chicago: Kerr.

MATZA, DAVID, AND GRESHAM SYKES
1961   "Juvenile Delinquency and Subterranean Values." *American Sociological Review* 26:712–17.

QUINNEY, RICHARD
1977   *Class, State and Crime*. New York: Longman.

ROBINSON, ROBERT, AND JONATHAN KELLY
1979   "Class as Conceived by Marx and Dahrendorf." *American Sociological Review* 44:38–58.

ROSSI, P., E. WAITE, C. BASE, AND R. BERK
1974.   "The Seriousness of Crime: Normative Structure and Individual Differences." *American Sociological Review* 39:224–37.

SIMON, RITA
1975   *Women and Crime*. New York: Lexington.

SIMPSON, JOHN, AND JOHN HAGAN
1983   "Evaluation of a Vandalism Prevention Project." Report to the Research Division. Ottawa: Ministry of the Solicitor General of Canada.

SOROKIN, PITIRIM, AND WALTER LUNDEN
1959   *Power and Morality*. Boston: Sargent.

SPITZER, STEVEN
1975   "Toward a Marxian Theory of Deviance." *Social Problems* 22:638–51.

STEFFENSMIER, D.
1980   "Sex Differences in Patterns of Adult Crimes, 1965–77: A Review and Assessment." *Social Forces* 58:1080–1108.

TAYLOR, IAN, PAUL WALTON, AND JOCK YOUNG
1973   *The New Criminology*. London: Routledge & Kegan Paul.

THORNBERRY, TERRENCE, AND MARGARET FARNSWORTH
1982   "Social Correlates of Criminal Involvement: Further Evidence on the Relationship between Social Status and Criminal Behavior." *American Sociological Review* 47:505–17.

TITTLE, CHARLES, WAYNE VILLEMEZ, AND DOUGLAS SMITH
1978   "The Myth of Social Class and Criminality: An Empirical Assessment of the Empirical Evidence." *American Sociological Review* 43:643–56.

———. 1982. "One Step Forward, Two Steps Back: More on the Class/Criminality Controversy." *American Sociological Review* 47:435–37.

VEBLEN, THORSTEIN
1934   *The Theory of the Leisure Class*. New York: Mentor.

WHEELER, STANTON
1976   "Trends and Problems in the Sociological Study of Crime." *Social Problems* 23:525–33.

WRIGHT, ERIK OLIN
1978   "Race, Class and Income Inequality." *American Journal of Sociology* 83:1368–97.

———. 1980. "Varieties of Marxist Conceptions of Class Structure." *Politics and Society* 9:299–322.

WRIGHT, ERIK OLIN, AND LUCA PERRONE
1977   "Marxist Class Categories and Income Inequality." *American Sociological Review* 42:32–55.

WRIGHT, ERIK OLIN, CYNTHIA COSTELLO, DAVID HACHEN, AND JOEY SPRAGUE
1982   "The American Class Structure." *American Sociological Review* 47:709–26.

QUESTIONS FOR DISCUSSION

1. The authors suggest that gender and class have not been joined in delinquency research in the past. Why is this, according to the authors, a serious omission?

2. What is the difference between defining *class* in gradational rather than structural terms?

3. How does power-control theory attempt to explain familial relations?

4. What distinguishes a Neo-Marxian explanation of crime from individual and sociocultural explanations?

5. Did this research support the notion that the relationship between gender and common forms of delinquency declines with each step down the class structure?

APPLICATIONS

1. Consider two adolescents from differing class backgrounds. The first youth is from the lower class with limited economic power, and the second youth is from the upper middle class or upper class, where economic power and access to resources are great. Both youths have been apprehended by the police for stealing compact discs from a local music store. In what ways might each youth's motivation to steal be different?

2. Based on the article you have just read, explain how a stable family and economic considerations affect delinquency.

KEY TERMS

bourgeois a French word used in Marxian theory to describe the social middle class; those who have an interest in material wealth and who are dominated by commercial and industrial interests.

coefficient a number that serves as some measure of an attribute or variable.

deterrence the inhibition of criminal behavior by fear; usually involves the threat of punishment, incarceration, or execution.

intervening variable a variable that may intercede in a presumed causal relationship such that rather than a cause directly producing an effect, the cause produces some other variable which then produces the effect.

Likert scale a common scale used in questionnaires; Likert items are those using such response categories as *strongly agree, agree, disagree,* and *strongly disagree.*

obscure to conceal, hide, or cover; to make something unclear.

operationalize to develop concrete definitions by which observations are to be categorized and subsequently measured.

paucity refers to the smallness of quantity or numbers; a scarcity or lack of something.

proletariat a French word often used in Marxian theory to refer to the lowest social or economic class of a community.

regression analysis a form of data analysis where the relationships between variables are presented in the form of an equation such that future values of the variables can be mathematically predicted using known variables in the present.

skewness used in statistical terminology to indicate that a normal population curve is not symmetrical such that the peak of the curve has developed to the right or left of the arithmetic average or mean.

stratified random sample a sample not drawn merely in a random fashion from a population but drawn from homogeneous subsets of the population.

unscrupulous acting with disregard for what is considered right, proper, or fair.

18

Family Structure and Delinquency: General Patterns and Gender Differences

Richard E. Johnson
Brigham Young University

In a sample of over 700 high-school sophomores, a five-category measure of family structure is found to be not related to either frequency or seriousness of self-reported illegal behavior, except for unusually high delinquent behavior by boys from mother/stepfather homes. On the other hand, family structure does show an overall association with self-reported trouble with police, school, and juvenile court officials. Specifically, while boys (not girls) with stepfathers admit the most delinquent acts, controlling for the amount of admitted delinquency shows that officials are more likely to respond to the misbehavior of children (especially girls) from mother-only families. None of these findings are accounted for by race, social class, the quality of parent-child relationships, or the quality of school experiences.

The "broken" home has for many years been thought to be a major factor in the causation of juvenile delinquency. In support of this view, studies have consistently found that adolescents who are processed through the juvenile justice system are disproportionately likely to come from broken homes (Glueck and Glueck, 1950; California Youth Authority, 1971; Chilton and Markle, 1972; Smith and Walters, 1978). Findings from self-report studies of delinquent behavior, however, complicate the issue. Self-report studies have

found little or no overall relationship between family intactness and reported delinquent behavior, even though some of the slight differences are statistically significant (Nye, 1958; Dentler and Monroe, 1961; Hirschi, 1969; Gold, 1970; Austin, 1978; Hennessey, Richards, and Berk, 1978; Wadsworth, 1979; Canter, 1982).

In part because of the self-report findings, the typical conclusion is that the quality of the parent-child relationship (often termed the strength of the parent-child attachment), rather than the intactness of the family, matters most in determining the actual behavior of the children (McCord, 1982). The persistent correlation between official delinquency and family intactness is commonly explained as an indication of the paternalistic, self-fulfilling, and/or biased response of the juvenile justice system to children from broken homes. Still, some authors continue to focus on the broken home—especially the father-absent home—as a key determinant of actual misconduct (Biller, 1971, 1974; Stern, Northman, and Van Slyck, 1984; Dornbusch, Carlsmith, Bushwall, Ritter, Leiderman, Hastorf, and Gross, 1985).

While family structure and quality of parent-child ties are often examined as separate and competing possible causes of delinquency, researchers generally overlook the interrelationships among these and other variables thought to be factors in the etiology of delinquent behavior in their own right. The fact is that a correlation between family

"Family Structure and Delinquency: General Patterns and Gender Differences," *Criminology*, 24:1 (1989), pp. 65–84. Reprinted by permission of The American Society of Criminology.

intactness and delinquent behavior, for example, could be explained by any number of different processes. The most commonly suggested process is that a family breakup reduces the quality of parent-child relationships, which in turn increases the likelihood of delinquent behavior. The parent-child relationship can be damaged simply by the physical separation created by a family breakup, or the child may distance himself or herself psychologically from parents who are resented for their roles in disrupting the family. Additionally, there is evidence that suggests that coming from a broken home creates difficulties for the child at school (Zakariya, 1982), presumably due in part to the child's reduced ability to concentrate on schoolwork when troubled by the situation at home, or due in part to a single parent's lack of time and/or energy to assist and support the child with homework. Each of these possible consequences of family breakup, in turn, may independently produce delinquent behavior. In short, there certainly are theoretical grounds for believing in a causal link between family breakup and delinquent behavior.

Even if broken homes fail to increase the actual amount of delinquent behavior, agents of society may respond differently to children from intact and broken homes. Thus, official delinquency and self-reported delinquent behavior need not be related to family structure in the same way. Depending on the choice of measuring device for "delinquency," substantive conclusions could vary. Similarly, the manner in which family structure is measured might also influence the nature of the substantive conclusions. The traditional broken-versus-intact dichotomy is probably too crude for most research questions.

In light of the above discussion, the present study addresses the following questions: (1) Is there in fact an association between family structure and delinquency? (2) Does the answer to the first question depend on which indicators of delinquency are used? (3) How do plausible intervening variables, such as the quality of parent-child ties and the quality of one's school experiences, affect the overall picture?

Data and Methods

The data were gathered by administering an anonymous questionnaire to 734 high-school sophomores in a large American city in the spring of 1975. All in attendance on a given day at three high schools completed the questionnaire in a classroom setting within a one-hour school period. The omission of school absentees probably reduces the variation in some of the variables of interest (for example, school and delinquency measures), which would bias estimates of the true levels of these variables in a larger population. But such estimates are not the purpose of the present paper. For the present purpose, the only effect of any sampling-imposed variance reductions is likely to be a slight attenuation of the strengths of the relationships from those one would find in a broader sample. There is no reason to believe that sampling procedures will introduce any distortion into the pattern of relationships among the variables. Further research must determine the generalizability of the present findings to distinctively different samples.

The schools served a variety of socioeconomic and racial groups, with the exception of hardcore slums or exclusively wealthy areas. The sample contains approximately equal numbers of males and females and has a racial/ethnic composition of 71% white, 16% Asian, 8% black, and 5% other. The sample does not statistically represent any particular population, but it approximates the situation of the vast majority of nonrural American youth. (Further details of the sampling procedures are available in Johnson, 1979).

The family structure variable is measured by a five-category typology of family structure. Each home is classified according to what combination of parents resides in the home: real father/real mother (n = 454), real father/stepmother (n = 22), real father only (n = 14), real mother/stepfather (n = 67), and real mother only (n = 115). A total of 62 of the 734 respondents were excluded from the analysis due to nonresponse or to unclassifiable family structures, such as living with nonparent relatives. This type of detailed measurement of family structure will allow for much more useful analyses than would the lumping together of all homes into either intact or broken categories. Unfortunately, further details such as the reason for the absence of a parent (death versus divorce) or the length of absence are not available.

Delinquency is measured in two distinct ways in order to highlight the difference between misconduct and official response to that misconduct. First, self-reported delinquent behavior consists of the number of times that the student reported having committed acts within specific categories of theft, vandalism, and assault during the past year. The measure specifically excludes juvenile status offenses. Second, self-reported official trouble counts the number of school suspensions, nontraffic police apprehensions, and juvenile court appearances that the student reported having experienced. These diverse types of official intervention are combined into a single measure to assure sufficient variation for statistical procedures and because the focus of the discussion is on the general likelihood of official intervention. Specific questionnaire items for these and the other variables, and their scoring, are provided in the appendix. While these two measures of delinquency are certainly not mutually exclusive (some acts might result in official trouble), they are still conceptually separable. And they are only moderately correlated in the present sample (r = .30, significance < .001).

The quality of the parent-child relationship is measured by a combination of 18 items (nine for each parent) tapping the subject's perceptions of his or her parent's love and concern for him and his reported degree of emotional and behavioral attachment to his parent. More specifically, the items deal with how much the student feels trusted and respected by each parent; how much anger and resentment he feels toward each parent; and the extent to which he feels close to, confides in, spends free time with, and wants to maintain future ties with, each parent. All items were asked separately for father and mother. The single highest quality of mother or father bond, rather than the sum, is used as the measure of the quality of

the parent-child relationship. This technique has been shown to be theoretically sound, and to make little difference in results compared to the use of additive scales (Hirschi, 1969: 100, ff.; Johnson, 1979: 76, ff.).

Quality of school experiences is an 11-item index combining reported success in school and reported attachment to school and teachers. Specific items measure grades and the importance of grades, difficulty with schoolwork, perceived teacher expectations, level of feeling like a success in school, attitudes toward homework and the importance of education, time and effort spent on schoolwork, and how much the student cares about what the teacher thinks of him.

The common control variables of age and social class are not entered in the following analyses because they were found to be unrelated to family structure, self-reported delinquent behavior, and self-reported official trouble in the present sample. Race will be entered as a relevant control in selected analyses, as it is correlated with some of the variables in question. Separate analyses for males and females will be conducted so as not to mask important interactions.

Findings

Whether there is a relationship between family structure and delinquency depends on which measure of delinquency is employed. Table 1 shows the results, for males and females separately, of a one-way analysis of variance between type of home and self-reported delinquent behavior. Table 2 shows parallel results for type of home and self-reported official trouble. Overall, Table 1 shows that home type has virtually no relationship with self-reported delinquent behavior. On the other hand, the findings in Table 2 confirm the belief that home type is moderately but significantly related to self-reported official trouble. The eta of .31 for females in Table 2, for example, is directly analogous to a Pearson's r, so that the eta-squared of .10 can be interpreted as the proportion of the variation in females' self-reported official trouble that is explained by type of home. And while Table 2 combines three types of official trouble, it is important to note that

TABLE 1 The Relationship between Family Structure and Self-Reported Delinquent Behavior among Males and Females

	Natural Father/ Natural Mother	Natural Father/ Step- Mother	Natural Father/ No Mother	Step- Father/ Natural Mother	No Father/ Natural Mother
Males					
Mean = 6.4	6.1	3.8	3.2	11.7	6.1
(n = 331)	(n = 233)	(n = 9)	(n = 9)	(n = 26)	(n = 54)
F = 1.592					
Significance = 0.176					
eta = .14, eta^2 = .02					
Females					
Mean = 2.5	2.5	2.3	0.0	2.6	2.8
(n = 319)	(n = 209)	(n = 11)	(n = 5)	(n = 39)	(n = 55)
F = 0.190					
Significance = 0.943					
eta = 0.5, eta^2 = .00					

Mean number of delinquent acts

the author found the same overall pattern described above when school suspensions, police apprehensions, and juvenile court appearances were considered separately as the dependent variable.

The overall results in both tables are similar for males and females, with the only difference being that the absolute levels of both measures of delinquency are consistently higher for males. In general, these gender similarities concur with recent evidence which indicates that the relevance of the broken home to delinquency does not differ significantly for males and females (Koziey and Davies, 1982; Canter, 1982; Rosen and Nielson, 1982; Dornbusch et al., 1985).

In the present sample, race is related to both family structure and self-reported official trouble, but is unrelated to self-reported delinquent behavior. Specifically, blacks are more likely than whites to come from broken homes and to report official trouble, while Asians are less likely than whites to come from broken homes and report official trouble. Under such circumstances, it is possible that the relationship between family structure and self-reported official trouble is spurious due to race.

Ideally, tables parallel to Tables 1 and 2 would be presented for the separate racial

groups. Unfortunately, the sizes of such subsamples become too small for analysis of variance to be meaningful. For example, there is only one black in a father-only family, one black in a father/stepmother family, and three Asians in mother/stepfather families among the 734 respondents. Of course, the subsample sizes are diminished even further when race/sex combinations are analyzed. The net result is that among the blacks (n = 60) or Asians (n = 114), all differences in either measure of delinquency among the home types must be viewed as nonsignificant, or possibly due to chance, if the results are intended to apply to some larger population from which the sample was hypothetically randomly selected.

There is clear evidence, however, that the general pattern shown in Tables 1 and 2 is not due to race and is not race-specific. Within every racial group and every race/sex subgroup (analysis not shown here), the overall relationship between family structure and self-reported official trouble is stronger (measured by eta) and less likely to be a product of sampling error (more significant) than the relationship between family structure and self-reported law violation. Among the larger number of white respondents, the results match the total sample results in sta-

TABLE 2 The Relationship between Family Structure and Self-Reported Official Trouble among Males and Females

	Natural Father/ Natural Mother	Natural Father/ Step- Mother	Natural Father/ No Mother	Step- Father/ Natural Mother	No Father/ Natural Mother
Males					
Mean = 1.1 (n = 343) F = 6.022 Significance = 0.000 eta = .26, eta^2 = .07	0.8 (n = 238)	1.1 (n = 11)	0.7 (n = 9)	2.2 (n = 27)	1.5 (n = 58)
Females					
Mean = 0.6 (n = 323) F = 8.470 Significance = 0.000 eta = .31, eta^2 = .10	0.4 (n = 211)	0.5 (n = 11)	1.0 (n = 5)	0.5 (n = 40)	1.3 (n = 56)

Mean number of official troubles

tistical significance as well as general pattern. For the cases in the present sample, it is simply a fact that the overall results hold for all race and sex categories.

In addition to family structure's overall relationships with the two measures of delinquency, some interesting differences appear in Tables 1 and 2 among the various types of "broken" homes. With attention focused on specific home types, more gender differences appear and will be analyzed. However, small subsample sizes once again preclude a detailed look at race differences and race/sex interactions. The patterns of mean delinquency scores (using either measure of delinquency) do vary across the types of family structure among the sometimes extremely small race/sex subgroups (not shown), but they do so haphazardly in ways that are not suggestive of any consistent effect of race, gender, or interaction of the two.

The results in Table 1 indicate that actual law violation varies only slightly among girls from different family structures (the 0.0 for the father-only group is based on only five cases). But within the overall nonsignificant pattern of differences for the boys, there is an exceedingly high number of illegal acts (11.7 per boy per year) reported by males (n = 26) from families with mothers and step-

fathers. This amount of delinquent behavior stands out as significantly different (substantively and statistically) from the number of law violations among the boys from the other types of homes.

These results are similar to those of Hirschi (1969), Gold (1970), and Dornbusch et al. (1985) and suggest that it may not be the presence or absence of a good or normal parent-child relationship that matters. Rather, the presence of an "outsider" with the potential thus created for resentment or alienation could be a more salient factor in influencing adolescent misconduct, especially for boys with stepfathers. In other words, along the continuum of "quality of parent-child relationship," variations near the positive end or near the neutral center may not matter much in producing delinquency. But having a literally very negative or antagonistic relationship could still be very relevant. The statistical relationship between parent-child ties and delinquency would then be nonlinear, with effects on delinquency arising only from extremely negative parent-child relationships. Consequently, certain kinds of "mended" families, if they produce alienation or resentment, may be more delinquency-producing than are "broken" families per se.

Turning to reports of official trouble, Table 2 shows that both sons and daughters from intact families (column one) report lower amounts of official trouble than would be expected from their approximately "average" amounts of self-reported law violations shown in Table 1. On the other hand, the opposite seems to be true for boys and especially girls in homes with no fathers (column five). Their rates of official trouble seem to be too high for their near-average amounts of law violation. At first glance, it appears that fatherless children act in ways that are of more concern to authorities, or that authorities are overresponding to the illegal acts of children from this type of broken home. Finally, the high amount of self-reported official trouble for boys with stepfathers seems to be warranted by virtue of their extensive delinquent behavior reported in Table 1.

These patterns are more readily examined if the amount of illegal behavior is controlled for by computing a ratio for each type of family structure which shows the mean number of self-reported illegal acts (from Table 1) divided by the mean number of times that same category of students reports getting into official trouble (from Table 2). For example, the grand mean in Table 1 is 4.46 illegal acts and the grand mean in Table 2 is 0.83 times in official trouble. For the total sample, then, the acts-per-official-trouble ratio in 5.37 (4.46 divided by 0.83), indicating that for every official intervention (from police, school authorities, and the juvenile court) which the students report, those same students admit committing 5.37 acts of theft, vandalism, or violence. The higher the ratio, the more the adolescents are "getting away" with certain kinds of illegal behavior.

This acts-per-official-trouble ratio is not intended to measure the probability of getting into official trouble when breaking certain laws or to estimate punishment efficiency. The measures of self-reported actions and self-reported official trouble are not parallel enough for such uses. The measure of self-reported official trouble is not limited to just past year acts of theft, vandalism, and violence. The variation in such a measure for this sample would be too limited. Instead, the purpose here is to compare the official

trouble experiences of children from different family structures while controlling for their differences in three major categories of criminal behavior. The limitations of the ratio measure apply evenly across all family structure categories.

At this point, it seems safest and wisest to restrict this portion of the analysis to just the white adolescents. In examining the possibility of differential response by authorities to similar behavior by different categories of youth, the problem of the results being confounded by possible racial discrimination is obvious. With small numbers of Asians and blacks in many family structure categories, statistical controls for race are not possible. The only alternative is to examine whites only.

Table 3 reports the acts-per-official-trouble ratios for the white males and white females from the five types of families. The combined ratio is 5.27, which compares very closely with the 5.37 ratio for all races combined, indicating very little racial effect on the ratio of official interventions to delinquent acts. The numbers of cases in the father/stepmother and father-only categories are too small to allow for drawing conclusions about those family structures. All that can be said here is that the data are suggestive that children from those types of broken homes appear to be somewhat less likely to get away with (or more likely to experience official intervention for) their illegal acts than are children from intact families. The patterns are strikingly similar for males and females.

The patterns of acts-per-official trouble across the remaining home types are likewise very similar for boys and girls. In spite of the fact that the boys admit a mean number of illegal acts that is two and one half times the mean for the girls (from Table 1), the sexes have almost identical rates of official trouble when the number of acts is controlled. The boys admit slightly over five (5.44) acts per official response, while the girls admit slightly under five (4.90). Furthermore, the gender similarities remain when family structure is specified. Even the highly delinquent boys with stepfathers do not show an unusual acts-per-official-trouble ratio. For boys, and even more so for girls, the most impressive change in the acts-per-official-trouble ratio occurs as

TABLE 3 The Relationship between Family Structure and the Ratio of the Group's Mean Number of Delinquent Acts Divided by the Group's Mean Number of Official Troubles, among White Males and Females

	Natural Father/ Natural Mother	Natural Father/ Step- Mother	Natural Father/ No Mother	Step- Father/ Natural Mother	No Father/ Natural Mother
Males					
Ratio = 5.44 (n = 244)	5.81 (n = 175)	3.46 (n = 9)	1.00 (n = 3)	6.28 (n = 20)	4.02 (n = 37)
Females					
Ratio = 4.90 (n = 221)	7.88 (n = 133)	4.40 (n = 8)	0.00 (n = 5)	5.19 (n = 35)	2.78 (n = 40)

Acts-per-trouble ratio

a decline in the ratio in families headed by a single mother. Family structure is clearly more relevant than gender in affecting the propensity of officials to respond to the law violations of these adolescents, with children from mother-only families being especially likely to get into official trouble.

As an additional check on this finding, a dummy variable was created to compare the mother-only (scored 1) and the intact-family (scored 0) respondents. The correlation (Pearson's r) between the mother-only/intact-family dummy variable and official trouble is .23 (significance = .000) among the girls and .02 (significance = .375) among the boys. With police, school, and court trouble considered separately, all three are significantly related to mother-only family structure among the girls, and not one is significantly related among the boys. In all likelihood, then, a meaningful relationship between mother-only family structure and official trouble exists primarily among female adolescents. The significant correlation among the girls (r = .23) remains almost unaffected when self-reported delinquent behavior is controlled (partial r = .21, significance = .000). These results suggest that the police and school and court authorities, considered separately or together, find it easier or more appropriate to officially respond to the behavior of daughters of single mothers than to the behavior of females in intact families, given equal numbers of self-reported criminal violations.

But is the number of criminal violations too crude a measure to detect how delinquent the respondents are? Perhaps the females from single-mother homes are committing more serious offenses and are therefore rightfully in more trouble with officials, rather than receiving differential treatment for similar offenses. To check this possibility, the self-reported delinquent behavior scale (in the appendix) was modified to reflect the seriousness of one's illegal behavior. In the seriousness scoring, theft of items valued at less than five dollars is excluded, along with theft of a car belonging to a friend or relative. Medium theft and medium property destruction (5 to 50 dollars) are weighted by a factor of one; large theft and destruction (more than 50 dollars), "real" car theft, and simple assault are weighted by two; and personal attacks with weapons and a willingness to seriously injure the victim are multiplied by three. The weighted scores are then summed to form a scale with possible scores ranging from 0 to 260. There is an actual range of 0 to 113 in the sample, with 64% of the respondents scoring zero, or having no serious self-reported law violation.

The conclusions remain unchanged when seriousness of self-reported delinquent behavior is substituted for frequency. Among white females, there are no significant differences in the seriousness of self-reported law violations across the five family structures (F = .213, p = .931). Among the white males, there is overall statistical significance (F = 2.914, p = .022), but it is due to high seriousness among the sons of mothers and stepfathers (as with the frequency data in Table 1). There is no evidence that either the males or females in mother-only homes are disproportionately involved in serious delinquent behavior. And controlling for seriousness of self-reported delinquent behavior does not reduce the correlation (r = .23) among the females between official trouble and coming from a single-mother family.

To this point, then, the evidence supports two conclusions: (1) In terms of frequency or seriousness of actual behavior, it is males in mother/stepfather homes who are especially delinquent, and (2) officials are more inclined to intervene in the lives of girls from single-mother families than they are to intervene in the lives of girls from intact families, even controlling for the frequency and the seriousness of self-reported criminal behavior.

The roles of possible intervening variables should be checked before conclusions are drawn about the likely reasons for these findings. Perhaps delinquent behavior, or even the response of an official to perceived delinquent behavior, is not so much a product of a broken home per se as it is a product of a poor parent-child relationship or of having negative school experiences. Each of these conditions, in turn, could simply occur disproportionately in certain types of broken homes.

Let us look first at the higher self-reported delinquent behavior of the males with stepfathers. How much of a correlation is there between this type of family structure and delinquent behavior, and can it be attributed to poorer relationships between parents and sons that might understandably occur in such "mended" families? Or has sampling provided a relatively small number of males in this family structure category (n = 20 when restricted to whites) who happen to have had negative school experiences and are more delinquent for that reason?

To answer these questions, a dummy variable was created to distinguish the white males with stepfathers from the white males from intact families, scored 0 for intact and 1 for stepfather. The correlation (Pearson's r)

among the boys between this dummy variable and self-reported delinquent behavior is .21 (n = 260, significance = .000). However, there are no significant correlations between the stepfather/intact-family dummy variable and either the quality of the parent-child relationship or the quality of school experiences. The original correlation of .21 between delinquent behavior and stepfather-versus-intact is not reduced when controlling for parent-child ties (partial r = .23) for school experiences (partial r = .22), or for both together (partial r = .22).

In short, the white males with stepfathers self-report significantly more delinquent behavior than the white males from intact homes, but it is not because of differences in school experiences or differences in positive attachment to a parent. There remains the possibility, however, that "negative attachment" to one's stepfather is perhaps the more relevant end of the parental attachment continuum. An "antifather" index was created (shown in the appendix) to tap positive responses from the student to questions about feelings of anger or rebellion toward one's acting father, or feelings of being ridiculed by one's acting father. The stepfather/intact dummy variable correlates with the antifather measure at r = .15 (significance = .01), indicating more negative father feelings by the boys with stepfathers. However, the original correlation (r = .21) between stepfather-versus-intact and self-reported delinquency is only slightly reduced when antifather feelings are controlled (partial r = .19, significance = .002). In sum, the link between a family structure of mother and stepfather and self-reported delinquent behavior (for boys only) remains largely unaffected by the introduction of several control variables.

What about the greater amounts of self-reported "official delinquency" by girls from mother-only homes? Is there bias on the part of officials, or is there understandable intervention based on poorer parent-child relationships or poorer school performances that occur disproportionately among girls in single-mother families? Once again, the analysis here is restricted to whites to obtain adequate sample sizes and avoid possible confounding of the results with racial differences. However, all of the general patterns reported for whites are paralleled when nonwhites are included in the computations.

Compared to girls from intact families, mother-only girls do not report any differences in the overall quality of their parent-child relationships (r = .06, significance = .17, using the dummy variable for family structure with 1 being mother-only and 0 being intact family). Neither are there significant differences in specifically antimother or antifather feelings between intact-family and mother-only white females. There is, often by definition, a lower amount of positive attachment to fathers in mother-only homes, but controlling for that variable does not explain away any of the correlation between mother-only family structure and official trouble among the females. In fact, the original correlation between mother-only family structure and official trouble is unaffected by controls for all measures of parent-child ties, taken singly or in combination.

There is a moderately strong negative correlation (r = −.33, significance = .000) among the white females between school experiences and self-reported official trouble. Lower levels of success in, enjoyment of, and involvement in school work and activities predict more official trouble. It is possible that the mother-only girls just happen to have disproportionately fewer positive school experiences, or that a mother-only family structure contributes to negative school experiences, and that the more directly relevant factor in producing official trouble is really the school experience.

In the present sample of white females, however, there is only a weak correlation (r = −14, significance = .017) between mother-only (versus intact) family structure and quality of school experiences. And controlling for quality of school experiences fails to reduce the original correlation (r = .23) between mother-only family structure and official trouble (partial r = .24). Thus, the data indicate that while mother-only family structure may have a slight negative effect on the school experiences of daughters, such a process fails to explain the persisting relationship between mother-only structure and self-reported official trouble.

It appears that no variables under consideration here can be called upon to reduce or explain the correlation between mother-only family structure and self-reported official trouble among white females. (One should remember that there is no such correlation among white males.) Even when quality of school experiences and quality of parent-child relationships are controlled simultaneously, the original association is not reduced at all.

Summary and Discussion

Taken as a whole, the data presented here support the claim that family structure is moderately related to delinquency, but with several qualifications. The first major point to be made is that measurement does make a difference. The findings lend credence to the conclusions of both self-report and official delinquency studies. The general pattern in these data is that family structure predicts self-reported official trouble better than it predicts self-reported theft, vandalism, and violence. Family structure is clearly related to self-reported official trouble in this study, so it is no surprise that it has been found by others to be related to actual records of official trouble. Similarly, the present lack of a general relationship between the family structure and self-reported law violation is consistent with other self-report findings. Perhaps Rosen and Neilson (1982) are correct in their conclusion that the broken home is not a significant factor in the development of delinquent tendencies.

Before discounting the role of the broken home in possibly leading to actual misconduct, however, further attention should be directed toward the issue raised here regarding stepfathers and sons. Although the subsample size (n = 26) is inadequate for firm conclusions, the boys with stepfathers reported many more law violations than any other groups of adolescents. Dornbusch et al. (1985) report a similar sex-specific stepfather effect using several different indicators of adolescent deviance. This might indicate that the quality of the parent-child relationship may indeed intervene between family structure and delinquent behavior, but in an unusual way. It may be that the control theory image of a delinquency-preventing positive attachment to parents (the kind measured in this study and virtually all self-report studies) is not terribly relevant. Instead, there may be some level of a "negative attachment" of tension or conflict between parent and child that, when exceeded, becomes a force leading to misconduct. And this condition could indeed be more prevalent in stepfather-son relationships.

An admittedly rough "antifather" measure employed here was devised after the fact and did correlate mildly with having a stepfather ($r = .15$), but there is no compelling evidence for or against the "negative attachment to stepfather" argument in the present data set. Future research, based on larger samples of boys with stepfathers and using measures specifically designed to tap the relevant variables, should pursue a test of the notion that boys with stepfathers may be especially delinquent, and that their delinquency may in part be a reaction to feelings of antagonism toward either the present stepfather and/or the absent father.

Turning to reports of trouble with police, juvenile court, and school officials, the daughters of single mothers and the sons of mother/stepfather combinations report significantly more such contacts. This comes as no surprise for the mother/stepfather boys, because they also report more misconduct. But the reason for the higher level of self-reported official trouble among mother-only females remains unclear. It does not seem to be due to more law violation, more serious law violation, the quality of parent-child ties, or the quality of school experiences. Rather, there must be some other reason that the presence of a father in the home makes a significant difference in preventing a female adolescent from getting into official trouble, even though the father's presence has little or no effect on the amount or seriousness of self-reported law violation. It is very tempting to conclude that the official system is indeed responding differently to similar behavior by adolescents from different types of families—families which do not otherwise differ in expected ways along several dimensions presumed to relate to delinquent behavior.

The weight of the evidence is consistent with the view that school and justice officials discriminate on the basis of family structure alone. Presumably, these officials perceive the daughters of single mothers to be in greater need of their intervention, or perhaps the single mother is not powerful enough to prevent unwanted intervention into the lives of her children. Of course, the present evidence for such an interpretation is only indirect. There could be many other reasons for the disproportionate intervention by officials into the lives of mother-only young women. For example, the demeanor of the adolescent when confronted by an official could surely have as much to do with the official's response as does the nature of the illegal behavior (Piliavin and Briar, 1964). Or the daughters of single mothers could be disproportionately involved in status offense behavior, to which school and legal authority also respond. There is no reason why daughters of single mothers would be expected to exhibit less respectful demeanor or greater numbers of status offenses (especially since they do not appear to exhibit more misconduct by other measures), but the point is that this and other possible explanations cannot be ruled out without data to directly test them.

As is the usual case in delinquency research, none of the correlations reported here are extremely high. If delinquency is to be understood, one certainly needs to look beyond family variables alone. Of course, longitudinal data would also allow a closer examination of causal processes beyond what can be inferred here from cross-sectional data and logic. It would likewise be helpful to sort out families disrupted by divorce from those disrupted by parental death, to control for the length of time the family has had its present structure, and to check the constancy of the findings since 1975. Finally, precisely parallel offense-specific measures of self-report and official delinquency, including a wider variety of criminal and status offenses, would certainly be useful. As usual, however, most of these suggestions call for very large data sets, very expensive study designs, or the loss of respondent anonymity.

The findings reported here should provoke further research that is less exploratory and overcomes some of the practical limitations of the present study. Family structure, independent of the effects of the quality of parent-child relationships, predicts certain measures of delinquency for certain categories of adolescents. For boys, there seems to be a real delinquent behavior-producing influence of having a stepfather in the home, but other than that, family structure is quite independent of self-reported delinquent behavior. Yet there remains an overall association between family structure and self-reported official trouble. For girls, family structure appears to make little or no difference in self-reported criminal behavior. In spite of that, girls in mother-only families are disproportionately likely to be suspended from school, picked up by the police, and sent to juvenile court. In their case, the broken home may be producing official delinquents without producing more delinquent behavior.

Appendix:

Measurement of the Variables (with Scoring in Parentheses), Index Scores as Simple Sums unless Otherwise Specified

Family Structure

This is a nominal variable with no numerical scoring. Questionnaire items included the following (with parallel items for mother):

1. Who is now acting as "father" for you?
   a. Real father
   b. Stepfather
   c. Foster father
   d. Grandfather
   e. Other relative
   f. Other unrelated adult male
   g. No one
2. Is your "father" (or adult male guardian) that you just described living at home with you?
   a. Yes
   b. Sometimes
   c. No
   d. I have no father

Students responding "real father; yes at home" and "real mother; yes at home" to these questions were classified as natural father/natural mother (intact) family struc-

ture. Natural father/stepmother structure was obtained by responding "real father; yes at home" and "stepmother; yes at home." A structure of natural father/no mother was assigned to responses of "real father; yes at home" and no mother or stepmother in the home. Stepfather/natural mother structure required "stepfather; yes at home" and "real mother; yes at home" responses. And those responding that they had no father or stepfather in the home, along with "real mother; yes at home," were classified as no father/real mother.

Self-Reported Delinquent Behavior (0–160)

For each item, responses of 0 to 10 are scored with the actual number. Responses of eleven or more were scored as 20.

1. In the past year have you taken things of small value (worth less than $5) that did not belong to you?
2. In the past year have you taken things of some value (worth between $5 and $50) that did not belong to you?
3. In the past year have you taken things of large value (worth more than $50) that did not belong to you?
4. In the past year have you taken a car for a ride without the owner's permission?
5. In the past year have you banged up or destroyed things of some value (worth between $50) that did not to you on purpose?
6. In the past year have you banged up or destroyed things of large value (worth more than $50) that did not belong belong to you on purpose?
7. Not counting fights you may have had with your brother or sister, have you beaten up or hurt anyone on purpose in the past year?
8. In the past year have you attacked someone with a weapon other than your fists, willing to injure the person seriously if it came to that?

Self-Reported Official Trouble (0–9)

1. Have you ever been suspended from school?
2. Not counting traffic tickets, have you ever been picked up by the police?

3. Have you ever had to go to juvenile court for something you did?
   (0) Never
   (1) Once
   (2) Twice
   (3) Three or more times

Parent-Child Relationship (0–19)

For every item below regarding father, there was a parallel questionnaire item regarding mother. The score on this variable is the larger of either the sum of the father items or the sum of the mother items.

1. Do you care what your father thinks of you?
   (3) Very much
   (2) Somewhat
   (1) Hardly
   (0) Not at all

	Always	Usually	Sometimes	Seldom	Never
2. It has been hard for me to please my father.

	(0)	(0)	(0)	(1)	(2)
3. My father has made fun of or ridiculed my ideas.

	(0)	(0)	(0)	(1)	(2)
4. My father has trusted me.

	(2)	(1)	(0)	(0)	(0)
5. My father has seemed to wish I were a different type of person.

	(0)	(0)	(0)	(1)	(2)
6. When I have problems I confide in my father.

	(2)	(1)	(0)	(0)	(0)
7. When I have free time I spend it with my father.

	(2)	(1)	(0)	(0)	(0)

	Strongly Agree	Agree	Undecided	Disagree	Strongly Disagree
8. I'm closer to my father than are most people my age.

	(2)	(1)	(0)	(0)	(0)
9. As an adult, I want to live near where my father will be living.

	(2)	(1)	(0)	(0)	(0)

Quality of School Experiences (0–22)

1. I've had more difficulty doing well in school than most people my age.

2. Homework is a waste of time.
   (0) Strongly agree, agree, or undecided
   (1) Disagree
   (2) Strongly disagree
3. I try hard in school.
4. Education is so important that it's worth it to put up with things about school that I don't like.
   (2) Strongly agree
   (1) Agree
   (0) Undecided, disagree, strongly disagree
5. What kind of work have teachers expected from you?
   (2) Excellent work
   (1) Good work
   (0) Average work, Fair work, Poor work, No kind of work in particular
6. What has been your most common grade in school?
   (2) A
   (1) B
   (0) C, D, We don't get letter grades.
7. Do you feel like you've been a success in school?
8. Do you finish your homework?
   (0) Never, Seldom, Sometimes
   (1) Usually
   (2) Always
9. Do you like school in general?
10. Do you care what teachers think of you?
    (2) Very much
    (1) Somewhat
    (0) Hardly, Not at all
11. How important are grades to you personally?
    (2) Very important
    (1) Somewhat important
    (0) Hardly important, Not at all important

Anti-Father (0–4)

1. I feel angry or rebellious toward my father [or stepfather].
2. My father [or stepfather] has ridiculed or made fun of my ideas.
   (2) Always
   (1) Usually
   (0) Sometimes, Seldom, Never

References

AUSTIN, ROY L.
1978   Race, father-absence, and female delinquency. Criminology 15: 487–504.

BILLER, HENRY
1971   Father, Child and Sex Role. Lexington, MA: Heath Lexington.
1974   Paternal Deprivation. Lexington, MA: Heath Lexington.

CALIFORNIA YOUTH AUTHORITY
1971   Statistical Report. Sacramento: California Department of Youth Authority.

CANTER, RACHELLE J.
1982   Family correlates of male and female delinquency. Criminology 20: 149–168.

CHILTON, ROLAND J. AND GERALD E. MARKLE
1972   Family disruption, delinquent conduct and the effect of subclassification. American Sociological Review 37: 93–99.

DENTLER, ROBERT A. AND LAWRENCE J. MONROE
1961   Social correlates of early adolescent theft. American Sociological Review 26: 733–743.

DORNBUSCH, SANFORD M., J. MERRILL CARLSMITH, STEVEN J. BUSHWALL, PHILIP L. RITTER, HERBERT LEIDERMAN, ALBERT H. HASTORF, AND RUTH T. GROSS
1985   Single parents, extended households, and the control of adolescents. Child Development 56: 326–341.

GLUECK, SHELDON AND ELEANOR GLUECK
1950   Unraveling Juvenile Delinquency. Cambridge: Harvard University Press.

GOLD, MARTIN
1970   Delinquent Behavior in an American City. Monterey, CA: Brooks/Cole.

HENNESSEY, MICHAEL, PAMELA J. RICHARDS, AND RICHARD A. BERK
1978   Broken homes and middle-class delinquency. Criminology 15: 505–528.

HIRSCHI, TRAVIS
1969   Causes of Delinquency. Berkeley: University of California Press.

JOHNSON, RICHARD E.
1979   Juvenile Delinquency and its Origins. Cambridge: Cambridge University Press.

KOZIEY, PAUL W. AND LEIGH DAVIES
1982   Broken homes: Impact on adolescents. The Alberta Journal of Educational Research 28: 95–99.

MCCORD, JOAN
1982   A longitudinal view of the relationship between parental absence and crime. In John Gunn and David P. Farrington (eds.), Abnormal Offenders, Delinquency, and the Criminal Justice System. New York: Wiley.

NYE, F. IVAN
1958   Family Relationships and Delinquent Behavior. New York: Wiley.

PILIAVIN, IRVING AND SCOTT BRIAR
1964   Police encounters with juveniles. American Journal of Sociology 70: 206–214.

ROSEN, LAWRENCE AND KATHLEEN NEILSON
1982   Broken homes. In Leonard D. Savitz and Norman Johnston (eds.), Contemporary Criminology. New York: Wiley.

SMITH, RICHARD M. AND JAMES WALTERS
1978   Delinquent and non-delinquent males' perceptions of their fathers. Adolescence 13: 21–28.

STERN, MARILYN, JOHN E. NORTHMAN, AND MICHAEL R. VAN SLYCK
1984   Father absence and adolescent "problem behaviors": Alcohol consumption, drug use and sexual activity. Adolescence 19: 301–312.

WADSWORTH, MICHAEL
1979   Roots of Delinquency. New York: Barnes and Noble.

ZAKARIYA, SALLY BANKS
1982   Another look at the children of divorce. Principal 62: 34–38.

QUESTIONS FOR DISCUSSION

1. What role does family structure play in self-reported "trouble with the law"?

2. Johnson asserts that schools and justice officials discriminate on the basis of family structure alone; that is, daughters of single mothers are in greater need of intervention. Provide reasons why this may be true.

3. How is the higher level of self-reported delinquency by males with stepfathers explained by Johnson?

APPLICATIONS

1. Think of any friends or peers that you may have had in high school who came from intact family structures and from family structures that were broken. Can you recall any difference in the way your friends from the two types of families behaved? Did the friends from broken family structures get into more trouble at school or with the law? If so, what kinds of trouble?

2. Based on your experience, how were young women and young men treated differently by school officials, parents, and the police?

KEY TERMS

alienation   refers to being estranged or separated from society or family in terms of values, norms, beliefs, or behaviors.

antagonistic   characterizes one who contends or opposes other ideas, people, or institutions.

credence   when something has credibility or can be reasonably accepted as true or real.

demeanor   one's behavior toward others; a person's demonstrated or exhibited behavior.

dependent variable   a variable that is assumed to depend on or be caused by an independent variable.

dichotomy   a division of two mutually exclusive or seemingly contradictory concepts or groups into diametrically opposed categories for the purpose of analysis.

dummy variable   refers to a qualitative variable; demographic questions are often coded for analysis as dummy variables (i.e., gender, religion, marital status).

haphazard   a characteristic of something that happens by chance or at random; may lack planning, order, or direction.

independent variable   a variable presumed to cause a dependent variable; a variable whose values are not problematic or the focus of analysis, but rather a given.

paternalistic   when one of supposed authority supplies needs or attempts to regulate the conduct of those under his control.

19

The Social Organization of Drug Use and Drug Dealing among Urban Gangs

Jeffrey Fagan
Rutgers University

Youth gangs are a major part of the urban land-scape. Gang members always have been involved in collective and individual violence and, in recent years, in drug use and drug dealing. Involvement in drug dealing recently has been associated with increased violence among gangs. However, variation in organizational and social processes within gangs suggests that there also will be variation in drug-crime relationships among gang members. Analyses of the drug-crime relationships were conducted from interviews with 151 gang members in three cities. Four types of gangs were identified, and similar gang types were observed in the three cities. All gang types had high involvement in drug use, but drug dealing varied. The severity of collective gang crime was associated with the prevalence of drug use within a gang. Drug dealing occurred among gangs with both high and low involvement in violence and other crimes. Involvement in cocaine, opiates, and PCP occurred among both violent and nonviolent gangs, as well as among gangs with different involvement in drug dealing. The results suggest that the drug-crime relationship is skewed and spurious for gang members, similar to relationships among nongang inner-city adolescents. Members of violent gangs more often reported the existence of several features of social organization and cohesion in their gangs, independent of gang involvement in drug use and dealing. Similar to other urban adolescents, for gang members violence is not an inevitable consequence of involvement in drug use or dealing.

"The Social Organization of Drug Use and Drug Dealing Among Urban Gangs," *Criminology*, 27:1 (1989), pp. 633–669. Reprinted by permission of The American Society of Criminology.

INTRODUCTION

Youth gangs have been part of the American urban landscape for nearly two centuries (Spergel, 1989). In the modern era, Thrasher's (1927) classic study found more than 1,300 gangs in Chicago alone in the 1920s and noted the consistency of gang formation and social processes in a spectrum of predominantly European immigrant groups. Chicano and Mexican gangs have persisted in most Latino communities in California since the large waves of immigration began after the Mexican revolution (Moore, 1978). Gang formations have continued to be cultural institutions in Latino communities in the United States, from the Pachucos of the World War II era, who were involved in the infamous "Zoot Suit" riots, to the Vato Locos, who inhabit the street corners of East Los Angeles and several other southwestern cities. Gangs have also long established their presence in African-American communities in many large eastern and midwestern cities (Suttles, 1968).

The terms "gang" and "violence" often appear together in both the popular and social scientific literature. Gang research has emphasized violence by gang members, despite empirical evidence that violence is prevalent but infrequent among gang members and has different origins and subjective meanings across social and situational contexts (Hagedorn, 1988; Horowitz, 1983; Klein and Maxson, 1989; Vigil, 1988). Yablonsky (1963) found violence to be the driving organizational force and normative behavioral fabric for street gangs. Miller (1975), however, found that although violence did occur among gangs, it was perhaps the least prevalent of all major gang-specific behaviors; gang members actually tried to avoid violence and engaged in ritualistic forms of violent interactions that minimized injury. Keiser's (1969) ethnographic research on the Vice Lords of Chicago reports that "gang-bangs" or street fights between gangs were the most infrequent occurrence of Vice Lord gang life. More recently, Moore (1978) in East Los Angeles and Horowitz (1987) in Chicago found that violence among Latino gangs served a variety of specific functions, ranging from organizational maintenance to social control.

In this decade, adolescent violence has been associated with drug use and drug selling (Elliott and Huizinga, 1984; Wish and Johnson, 1986). Although the relationship among drug use, drug selling, and serious youth crime is consistently strong, gangs are diverse, complex, and shifting organizations whose members participate variably in crime, drug use, and drug dealing (Hagedorn, 1988; Klein and Maxson, 1989; Spergel, 1989). Accordingly, this study examines the extent and nature of the interaction of drug use, dealing, and violence among gang members in urban areas characterized by the social disorganization cited in early gang research (e.g., Shaw and McKay, 1943) and in more recent studies of violence by adolescents (Laub, 1983; Shannon, 1984) and gang members (Curry and Spergel, 1988).

Drug Involvement of Gang Members

There is great diversity among gangs and gang members in the nature of their affiliation, social organization, and involvement in delinquency and violence (Bookin-Weiner and Horowitz, 1983; Dolan and Finney, 1984; Klein and Maxson, 1989; Spergel, 1984). Drug use is also a diverse phenomenon in

gangs, as is the relation of drug use to gang violence (Stumphauzer et al., 1981). Although much gang violence is unrelated to drug involvement, there is evidence that the rates and severity of substance use and involvement in drug trafficking may be higher in gangs than among other urban youths.

Drug Selling

Whether to finance personal drug use, as an avenue to gang affiliation or social status, or as a means of income, the lure of drug sales for inner-city youths is apparent. Dolan and Finney (1984), Moore (1978), and Spergel (1984), among others, suggest that gang members may be involved more often in drug trafficking than other adolescents (cf., Klein et al., 1988). Until this decade, most gang studies suggested that gang involvement in drug trafficking was minor and confined generally to "soft" drugs, such as marijuana. Notable exceptions were Spergel (1966) and Moore (1978), who found close connections between gang membership and both drug use and selling.

Recent evidence suggests that gang members may have greater involvement in drug distribution, particularly of "hard" drugs, than other youths. Analyses of gang involvement in rock cocaine trafficking (Klein et al., 1988) suggest that gangs in Los Angeles frequently are involved in drug selling. They also report, however, that gang members may be less involved in cocaine trafficking and its growth than nongang members in Los Angeles during 1983–1985, the period when rock cocaine emerged in that city.

Mieczkowksi (1986) reports the use of violence among organizations of adolescent heroin sellers in Detroit, and Cooper (1987) describes Detroit youth gangs organized around crack cocaine distribution. In several Chicago neighborhoods, gangs control drug sales to juveniles (Recktenwald and Sheppard, 1984; Spergel, 1984). Dolan and Finney (1984) show the economic lure of drug sales for gang members, relative to other economic opportunities. Klein (1985) suggests that the sudden emergence of rock or crack cocaine provided unique economic opportunities, of which Los Angeles gangs quickly took advantage.

Drug selling offers several roles for gang members. Moore (1978) shows how minor roles in drug selling were entry-level jobs for adolescents at the early stages of gang affiliation. Older gang members have more "important" roles in directing drug trafficking activities. For others, drug involvement may be both a job and a form of social "glue" that binds them to the gang in the pursuit of drugs and the money to finance drug use. Drug distribution may also provide economic support for other gang activities and income for individual gang members.

Drug Use among Gang Members

Until recently, little distinction has been made regarding patterns of drug use among gangs and the relationship among drug use, gang cohesion, and gang activities. Stumphauzer et al. (1981) note that patterns of drug use varied within and among Los Angeles gangs. Dolan and Finney (1984) and Campbell (1984) illustrate the commonplace role of drug use in gang life among both male and female youths. Vigil (1988) describes a variety of meanings and functions of drug use among Chicano gang members in East Los Angeles, from social "lubricant" during times of collective relaxation to facilitator of ritual behaviors, such as *locura* (exaggerated and spontaneous) acts of aggression or violence. In these contexts, drug use provides a means to social status and acceptance, as well as mutual reinforcement, and it is a natural social process of gang life.[1]

Feldman et al., (1985) observed three distinct styles of drug involvement and its relationship to violence among Latino gangs in San Francisco. The styles were determined in part by the role and meaning of drug use in gang social processes. The *fighting* gangs consisted of young men who were antagonistic toward other gangs. They aggressively responded to any perceived move into their turf by other gangs or any outsider. Drug use and selling were evident among these gangs, but they were only situationally related to their violence through territoriality. Violence occurred in many contexts unrelated to drug use or selling, and it was an important part of the social process of gang affiliation. The *entrepreneurial* gangs consisted of youths who

were concerned with attaining social status by means of money and the things money can buy. They very often were active in small-scale illegal sales of marijuana, oral amphetamines, and PCP. Fighting and violence were part of this style, but again they were situationally motivated by concerns over money and/or drugs. The last style was evident in gangs whose activities were *social* and recreational and gave little or no evidence of fighting or violence.

Drug use is not allowed in some youth gangs regardless of the gang's involvement in drug selling. Chin (1986) found that drug use was rejected entirely by nearly all Chinese gangs in New York City, despite their active involvement in heroin distribution. They used violence to protect their business territories from encroachment by other gangs and to coerce their victims to participate in the gang's ventures. These gangs were hierarchically organized, had strict codes, and meted out violent consequences for rule violations by members. Cooper (1987) described organizations of adolescent crack sellers in Detroit that prohibited drug use among their members. Leaders in these groups were wary of both threats to efficiency and security if street-level sellers were high and the potential for cooptation of their business goals if one of their members became a consumer of their goods. The gangs were organized around income, and they saw drug use as detracting from the selling skills and productivity of the members. Expulsion from the gang resulted from breaking this rule, but other violent reprisals also were possible.

Mieczkowski (1986) studied street-level adolescent drug runners in heroin-dealing organizations, also in Detroit, and found a rejection of heroin use by members of the runner organizations. These groups, however, accepted recreational use of other drugs by members, primarily marijuana and cocaine in social situations not involved with dealing. They particularly found danger in being high on any drug while on the job, and superiors in these organizations enforced the prohibition against heroin use while working by denying runners their consignment and thereby shutting off their source of income.

Violence was occasionally used by superiors (crew bosses) to enforce discipline. Sellers looked down on their heroin-using customers, despite having tried it themselves at some point in their lives. Their own experience with heroin in part explains their general disapproval of heroin use.

Role of Social Organization

The discovery of diverse patterns of criminality and drug involvement among gang members and gangs suggests that there are factors in the social organization of gangs and processes of affiliation or cohesion that either encourage or discourage these patterns. Such diversity also exists among general adolescent populations (Fagan et al., in press; Schwendinger and Schwendinger, 1985; White et al., 1987), which suggests that gangs reflect patterns of affiliation and collective behavior that are similar to those of other adolescent subcultures. Accordingly, violence, which historically has been taken as a defining feature of gangs, and drug involvement may more accurately be conceptualized as contingent behaviors among adolescents. Such contingencies rarely have received theoretical or empirical attention in prior research.

Little research has examined whether diverse patterns of drug involvement among gangs are influenced by the social organization of gangs, their processes of affiliation, and their strategies for maintaining behavioral norms. That gangs have specific social structures that vary by gang and locale has been well validated (see Klein and Maxson, 1989, for a review of this literature). This diversity extends also to the coexistence of conventional and deviant values (Keiser, 1969). The ethnographic literature on gang involvement strongly suggests that gangs have a natural social structure, are well stratified, and appear to undergo developmental sequences not unlike other social groups or organizations (Hagedorn, 1988; Horowitz, 1983; Moore, 1978; Vigil, 1988). Moreover, the reasons for gang affiliation are quite varied, ranging from social status, to protection from other gangs, to economic opportunity (Anderson and Rodriguez, 1984; Erlanger, 1979). These motivations, in turn, may lead to quite different levels of involvement in drug use or sales and other criminal activities.

Methodological Issues

The study of drug use and selling among gangs is complicated by several methodological concerns. First, research on gangs reflects a lack of consensus on the basic definitions and characteristics of gangs. Definitions of gangs in the 1950s and 1960s reflected etiological interests as well as the attributes of the social areas where gangs were most visible. Klein (1971) found gang membership to be a transitory phenomenon that atrophied as gang members approached adulthood, though the upper end of the age range may have increased in recent years (Klein and Maxson, 1989). Moore's (1978) study of Mexican-American communities in East Los Angeles found that gang membership and identity often extend well into adulthood. In her study, gang activities continued in prisons and through illicit drug trade long after members fade from view as street corner youths. But the length of affiliation with gangs is likely to reflect the motivation for the initial affiliation, the cohesiveness of the particular gang, and specific social or personal circumstances that may influence an individual's life-style decisions during the transition to adulthood. Klein and Maxson (1989) suggest that the definition of gangs has evolved in concert with changes in social policy on how to control gangs, specifically their violent behaviors and, more recently, drug involvement.

Second, the definition of "gang crime" also varies across jurisdictions, depending on the interests of the definer. The determination of a "gang-related offense" is a subjective process and likely to vary by city, agency, and researcher (Klein and Maxson, 1989). The distinctions between youth groups and gangs have varied over the years, as have the distinctions between gang crimes and nongang delinquent acts. Law enforcement agencies disagree, for example, on whether any crime committed by a known gang member should be labeled as a gang crime regardless of the specific context or meaning of the event. Spergel (1989) cites extraordinary variability in gang-related homicides in Chicago and Los Angeles, which he suggests, is attributable to the differences in criteria for labeling an event as "gang-related." Obviously, such definitional issues will bear on methodological decisions in gang research, empirical knowledge of gangs, and theory development.

Third, the concentration of large numbers of gangs in urban areas such as Los Angeles and Chicago presents sampling problems that raise questions of external validity. The traditional gang, with its unstable membership, shifting leadership, and fluid norms, also presents sampling difficulties. Short and Strodtbeck (1965) concluded that it is difficult if not impossible to develop probability samples of gangs and gang members due to the constant changes in gang membership and identity.

Gang research generally has relied on either ethnographic studies of gangs or analyses of official records from law enforcement and other social agencies on gangs, gang activity, and gang members. Few efforts have been made to study gang members systematically using survey methods with random or theoretical samples. Researchers confront a number of problems. Gang members span a broad age range. Initiates and "juniors" often are early adolescents. "Veteranos" and "OGs" (old guys) continue their gang involvement until 30 to 40 years of age, although their gang participation may be infrequent and marginal. Uncovering features of gang life also poses difficulties. Members tend to conceal their own activities or not be aware of the activities of others. To overcome suspicion about researchers and problems of gaining access to the concealed aspects of gang life, ethnographic research has been the dominant mode of gang research.

The measurement and theoretical advances of the past decade in delinquency research (Elliott et al., 1985; Hindelang et al., 1981) have not been applied to gang research. Klein and Maxson (1989), among others, noted the paradigm shift in the past decade from etiological research on gang formation and behaviors to crime control and suppression, and blamed it for the limited advances in theory and knowledge about

gangs since the work of the late 1970s. Major consequences have been the inability to answer important and basic questions on gang formation and to compare gang and nongang youths, gangs of different behavioral orientations, and the variation in gang processes and behaviors in different social contexts.

Purpose of Study

This study examines patterns of individual and collective crime, drug use, and drug dealing among gangs and gang members in three cities. First, variations among gangs in their patterns of drug involvement and other criminal activity are determined empirically from samples of gang members in specific neighborhoods in each city. Second, whether social organizational features and subcultural processes within gangs mediate these patterns is analyzed from gang members' self reports on gang structures and processes.

The relationship between drug use and youth crime is well established in research on adolescents (Elliott et al., 1985; Fagan et al., in press; White et al., 1987) and young adults (Chaiken and Chaiken, 1989; Gandossy et al., 1980). Goldstein (1985) has described the different ways that drug involvement contributes to violence. Among gang members, there is a positive correlation between group crimes and violence (Klein and Maxson, 1989; Piper, 1985; Tracy and Piper, 1984). There also appear to be discrete patterns within gangs on these behaviors (Dolan and Finney, 1984; Feldman et al., 1985). In addition, Fagan et al. (in press) shows that drug use occurs among both violent delinquents and nondelinquent youths, and that violence occurs with and without drug involvement. Accordingly, it seems that while drug involvement contributes to patterns of violence, the relationship is contingent on unique factors in what appear to be parallel but independent subcultures.

The diversity of gang structures and criminal activities observed in earlier studies suggests that drug involvement will vary in its contribution to other criminal activity, particularly violence. Whether organizational features of gangs influence their drug involvement has not been studied. The extent to which violence and drug use among gang members and gangs are spuriously related or reflect variation in gang structures or their subcultures, has also been neglected in theory and empirical research. Gang research, however, has illustrated the relationship between gang violence and social organizational factors, such as cohesion and hierarchy. This suggests that distinct subcultural processes or differences in the social organization of youth networks may mediate the occurrence and severity of these behaviors within discrete social networks of youths (Schwendinger and Schwendinger, 1985).

The interactions among drug involvement, violence, other gang and nongang crimes, and the social organization of gangs are examined in this study. If drug use is spuriously associated with violence among inner-city adolescents, then variation also may be expected in drug-crime relationships among gang members.[2] That is, crime and violence among gangs should occur independently of substance use.[3] Drug selling and violence, however, are positively associated among adolescents, as are serious drug use (of cocaine, heroin, and PCP) and violence. Since violence among gangs is associated with gang structure and cohesive social processes, then serious drug involvement among gangs should occur for those gangs with more formal structures and social processes.

METHODS

Samples

Surveys were conducted in 1984 and 1985 in three-inner city, "high-crime" neighborhoods in A- and B-level SMSAs: South Central Los Angeles, the University Heights section of San Diego, and the neighborhoods on the west side of Chicago.[4] By limiting the study to inner-city areas, gang behaviors and processes could be examined in areas with high concentrations of the ecological correlates of violence and other crimes (Sampson, 1986). Gang problems in all three cities have been extensively documented (Maxson and

Klein, 1983; Pennell and Curtis, 1982; Spergel, 1984).

Respondents ranged in age from 13 to 20 years, were predominantly from minority groups, and were male. The final sample included 151 gang members, spread evenly among the three sites. The sampling procedure employed purposive "snowball" samples of gang members (Biernacki and Waldorf, 1981). This is an optimal choice, given the difficulty of identifying a gang universe from which to sample randomly (Short and Strodtbeck, 1965). This strategy was chosen instead of sampling from law enforcement rosters of known gang members because of the potential variability across cities in the definition of gang member and gang crime (Klein and Maxson, 1989; Spergel, 1989). The snowball strategy provided flexibility in targeting, locating, and recruiting members of all known or emerging gangs. Moreover, because the snowball process involves respondents nominating other respondents and identifying other possible chains of respondents, the likelihood of excluding specific gangs is minimized.

Gang members were recruited through intermediaries chosen from neighborhood-based organizations and agencies in each study neighborhood. Intermediaries included gang intervention programs, social service organizations, and neighborhood advocacy groups. The organizations were chosen because of their detailed knowledge of local gang scenes, their neutrality with respect to intra-gang conflicts or conflicts with law enforcement, and their access to a variety of gang members with different types of gang affiliation and activity. Their knowledge of local gang networks also minimized omission of unknown networks of gangs in their areas.

The management of chains was a critical task to ensure that all known gang networks were included, that no specific gang was over-represented, and that unknown networks were not excluded from the samples, and to incorporate any new (unanticipated) gangs that were discovered during the nomination part of the interview. Decisions on management of the chains were made by research staff in consultation with staff from the intermediary organizations. The sample of gangs represented by respondents were reviewed periodically with staff from the intermediary organizations to determine whether members of all gangs active in the neighborhood were included in the sample. One limitation of the data was the reliance on only one source to validate the representativeness of the sample of neighborhood gangs. Moreover, though representative of the study neighborhoods, the gang samples may not be representative of gangs active throughout each city.

Two recruitment processes were used. First, gang members were asked by intermediaries to refer others within their gang or gangs they knew but with whom they were not actively in conflict. A short screening interview, administered by volunteers from the intermediary organizations, determined their eligibility. Second, referrals were solicited from social agencies that routinely deal with gang members. The intermediary agencies and the neighborhood volunteers were known to and involved with gang members in several ways: mediators of gang disputes, counselors for school or family problems, organizers of neighborhood recreational activities, or monitors at school events. Volunteers worked in these organizations only if they had no personal ties to or experiences with (e.g., victimization) gangs or gang members.

The use of the gang chains also permitted stratification by age, an important factor given the correlation of age with specific roles within gangs (Klein and Maxson, 1989). Because of the hierarchical structure of the gangs in these areas, a variation of the typical chain referral procedure was used.[5] Gang members were solicited as groups. Accordingly, in approaching gang members, they were asked to suggest members of different ages and with different roles in the gang (e.g., "juniors" or "wannabes," "people who make or enforce the rules," and older gang members).

Gangs and gang members met the definition used by Klein (1971:13):

> we shall use the term [street gang] to refer to any denotable . . . group [of adolescents or young adults] who (a) are generally perceived as a distinct aggregation by others in the neighborhood, (b) recognize themselves as a denotable group (almost invariably

with a group name), and (c) have been involved in a sufficient number of [illegal] incidents to call forth a consistent negative response from neighborhood residents and/or enforcement agencies.

This definition restricted the eligible gangs and members to those involved in illegal activities. Although most gang members and even members of streetcorner groups or youth groups are involved in at least some minor delinquency (including drug use), this definition excludes the unknown percentage of youth groups or gangs who do not commit illegal acts. Accordingly, the Guardian Angels, an anticrime gang, would not meet this definition, nor would a Chinese secret society (Chin, 1986).

Survey Procedures

The surveys were conducted in groups of 10 in the facilities of the intermediary organizations; several sessions were scheduled to accommodate working youths and those with other commitments. To avoid repeats, volunteer proctors from the intermediary agencies who were familiar with neighborhood youths monitored attendance and selected out repeaters. Together with the researchers, they kept anonymous records of the number of participants from each gang in the sample. Care was taken to avoid inadvertent contact between rival gangs, mainly through scheduling and using a facility on "neutral" turf for all contacts.

In each case, the surveys were described as voluntary and anonymous. Neither names nor identifiers were requested anywhere on the survey forms. Participants received a stipend for their participation (e.g., coupons from local record stores, T-shirts, or caps), which were handed out at the completion of the session.

Survey items were read aloud by research staff while respondents followed along on the survey form. The proctors also held up large displays of the response sets for sequences of items (e.g., delinquency or drug use items). In addition, two or three volunteers from local neighborhood organizations were stationed in the rear of the rooms to answer respondents' questions and provide other assistance as needed. Care was taken these volunteers neither knew nor recognized the gang members. The volunteers were selected to be older than the gang members (usually, about 25 years of age) and were residents of the neighborhood.[6] Both male and female volunteers were used.

Measures and Constructs

The survey included demographic items, self-reported delinquency and drug use/sales measures, and items on respondents' perceptions of whether members of their gang participated in various types of gang activities (both legal and illegal), involvement in school or work, family life, and family approval of, or participation in the gangs. Other items asked about gang structures and roles, gang activities and organization (e.g., recruitment, enforcement of gang discipline), other gangs in the area (e.g., colors, turf, conflicts, activities), and items on gang relations with law enforcement and other social agencies.

Self-reported delinquency (SRD) and gang delinquency items included questions on specific acts that reflected "high consensus" deviance (Thio, 1983), primarily acts that harm, injure, or do damage. A 27-item index included behaviors that, with the exception of homicide and sexual assault, included all Uniform Crime Report (UCR) Part I offenses and many Part II offenses. The categorical response set for self-reports ranged from "never" to "several times a year" for the past year. Similar to other studies (e.g., Elliott et al., 1985), the recall period was 12 months, from "Christmas a year ago to this past Christmas." Such anchoring techniques enable respondents to reconstruct behaviors. For reports of gang activities, responses asked only for how many members of the gang were involved (from "none" to "all or nearly all"). Indices were constructed from aggregations of homogeneous behaviors to be consistent with UCR categories, using a procedure similar to that used by Elliott and Huizinga (1984). Indices were derived by summing the reported incidence or prevalence scores for nonoverlapping items within scales. The items and index construction are shown in the appendix.

The questions for alcohol and drug use followed the same format and response sets

as the SRD items. Drug sales was included as a SRD item. Questions about personal use of substances were included in separate items. Two alcohol items (beer or wine; whiskey, gin, vodka, or other liquor) and seven illicit drug (marijuana, cocaine, heroin or opiates, hallucinogens, amphetamines or "speed," barbiturates or "downers," and inhalants or "glue sniffing") items were included. Individual substances were used to capture what ethnographic data suggest are distinct drug use patterns by youth network and locale (Feldman et al., 1979).

Gang structure and process measures covered recruitment and initiation processes, enforcement of gang hierarchy and leadership forms, and the range of legitimate and illegitimate activities by gang types. "Natural social controls" within gangs also were covered, including various forms of leadership, assessments of their strength (from the unanimity of gang members' responses), and the diversity versus concentration of leadership.

Overall, the SRD measures have strong explanatory power in both cross-sectional and longitudinal studies of serious delinquency and under a variety of sampling conditions, including samples of institutionalized male delinquents and general populations of male adolescents from six inner-city neighborhoods (Fagan et al., 1986). Fagan et al. (1987) validated the SRD items using both male and female adolescents in the same inner-city neighborhoods using both demographic and theoretical variables. Reliability analyses included calculation of consistency measures (Cronbach's alpha) for each SRD index, and again for site-specific calculations. In general, reliabilities were at least adequate (alpha = .70) or excellent (alpha = .90) for the gang samples, both within and across cities.

RESULTS

Incidence and Prevalence of Delinquency and Drug Use by Gang Members

Table 1 summarizes the self-reports by gang members of their involvement in each type of behavior in the prior year and their

TABLE 1 Prevalence and Frequency of Collective and Individual Behaviors of Gang Members in Prior Year (N = 151)

Self-reported Offense-specific Behaviors	Gang Acts, Prevalence*	Individual Acts		
		At Least Once	Regular: Three or More Times	Frequent: Twelve or More Times
Felony Assault	55.6%	53.0%	27.8%	14.8%
Minor Assault	45.7	45.5	16.9	8.9
Robbery	59.6	57.8	35.8	22.0
Felony Theft	67.5	64.2	37.6	22.0
Minor Theft	58.3	56.4	35.4	23.6
Vandalism	55.0	59.8	34.0	19.7
Illegal Services	53.0	48.3	27.6	15.5
Weapons	53.6	58.6	34.4	18.9
Extortion	57.6	67.5	36.0	21.1
Drug Sales	62.9	51.3	23.8	14.1
Alcohol	72.8	79.2	50.4	40.8
Marijuana	67.5	73.6	44.8	33.6
PCP, Psychedelics	53.6	51.4	32.7	22.4
Speed, Barbiturates	51.0	48.1	26.9	17.3
Cocaine	53.6	48.2	35.0	13.4
Heroin, Other Opiates	41.7	40.8	16.5	12.6

* Percentage of respondents reporting that "a few" or more gang members were involved in that behavior in the prior year.

reports of the behaviors of others members of their gang. The table shows the percentage of gangs involved in each behavior during the prior year, based on reports by individual gang members about their gangs. Two measures of individual acts by gang members are reported: the percentage of gang members reporting at least one act in the prior year (prevalence) and the frequency of those behaviors among individual gang members reporting at least one act. For gang members reporting at least 1 act, the percentages of those reporting 3 or more such acts and 12 or more such acts (at least 1 act per month) are shown. Because gang members were carefully sampled to avoid overrepresentation by members of any individual gang, redundancy was minimized.[7]

Prevalence

Collective and individual involvement in drug use and nondrug crimes was high. There is general concordance in respondents' reports of the prevalence of gang involvement in each crime type and their own involvement. Both violent and nonviolent crimes are common behaviors within gangs and among their members in these

cities, similar to patterns found by Tracy and Piper (1984) among male gang members in Philadelphia. Felony theft (theft of property or goods worth more than $100) was the most prevalent crime type for collective behaviors, more prevalent than minor theft.[8] Extortion was the most prevalent individual act. Drug selling also was prevalent as a collective behavior of the gangs, but it was not as prevalent among their members. Alcohol and marijuana were the most prevalent drugs used, both collectively and individually. The prevalence estimates for other drugs also are quite high. Heroin use, generally infrequent among adolescents (Johnson et al., 1985), was used in over 40% of the gangs and by a similar percentage of gang members.

The individual prevalence rates for both drug use and delinquency were higher for gang youths than for general adolescent populations in inner cities. Fagan et al. (1986) analyzed self-reports from a general adolescent sample from six inner-city neighborhoods. They reported that 23.6% of the male adolescents were involved in felony theft, and 13.9% were involved in robbery in the prior year.[9] The prevalence of felony robbery, felony theft, marijuana use, and drug sales among individual gang members in this study generally are closer to prevalence rates for institutionalized juvenile offenders than for other inner-city male adolescents (Cernkovich et al., 1986; Fagan et al., 1986). Among the institutionalized delinquents in the Fagan et al. (1986) sample, for example, 82% were involved in felony theft and 58% in robbery.

Frequency

For individual gang acts, the percentage reporting "regular" (three or more acts in the prior year) and "frequent" (12 or more acts) involvement was calculated from the percentage of those reporting at least one act. Fewer gang members reported regular and frequent individual acts than reported any involvement. A small percentage of gang members were involved frequently for most criminal acts, a widely observed epidemiological pattern in delinquency research (e.g., Elliott and Huizinga, 1984; Wolfgang et al., 1972). For most drug use and nondrug crime categories, regular involvement was reported by many of those reporting any involvement, and frequent involvement was reported by many of those reporting regular involvement. However, for alcohol and marijuana use, there were only small differences in the number of respondents reporting regular and frequent involvement.

Among violent offenses, fewer gang members reported frequent felony and minor assault than any other (nondrug) delinquent behaviors. Robbery was one of the most frequent acts; 22% reported 12 or more robberies in the prior year. Robbery, felony theft, minor theft, and extortion were the most frequent self-reported individual acts. Also, the fewest respondents reported both regular and frequent minor assaults and drug sales, although they appear to be both more frequent and more prevalent among gang members than other adolescent groups (Elliott and Huizinga, 1984; Fagan et al., in press). For drug use, the percentages of respondents reporting frequent marijuana and alcohol use were highest. Among all behaviors, the disparity between regular and frequent use was least for these two categories. Cocaine and heroin use were reported by the smallest number of

gang members in all frequency categories, though the percentages in each category still exceed those in most general adolescent population estimates (see Elliott and Huizinga, 1984; Fagan et al., in press).

Overall, violent acts (other than robbery) and drug sales were the individual behaviors least often reported as frequent by gang members. The involvement of a relatively small percentage of gang members in frequent violence, together with their more frequent participation in nonviolent crime, suggest that gang violence still is a relatively infrequent behavior for gang members compared with nonviolent behaviors. The prevalence of frequent violence among gang members in the sample, however, is still higher than among other adolescents.

Finally, Table 1 affords a comparison of frequent crime participation between gang members and nongang youths. There are nearly twice as many "frequent" violent offenders among the gang members in this study compared with males in other adolescent samples (e.g., Wolfgang et al., 1972). Tracy (1979) found similar differences between gang and nongang members among males in Philadelphia. The percentage involved in frequent serious violent or property delinquent acts in this study is higher than in both the National Youth Survey (Elliott and Huizinga, 1984) and general inner-city adolescent samples (Fagan et al., 1987). Using similar item and index construction, those studies found that less than 9% reported three or more serious or violent behaviors in the prior year. For virtually all crime types and drug categories, frequent participation by gang members in this study exceeds self-reports of involvement in similar behaviors among nongang youths. The number of gang members reporting frequent participation was higher than for institutionalized male delinquents in virtually all drug and nondrug behavior categories (Cernkovich et al., 1986; Fagan et al., 1986).

Typologies of Drug Involvement among Gangs

Typologies were developed to classify gangs on their patterns of drug use, selling, and other criminal behaviors. Groups were constructed from gang members' reports on whether members of their gang were involved in each of the drug use and delinquency behaviors in the indices in Table 1. The groups reflect differences between gangs in the joint distributions of drug use, drug selling, and nondrug crimes, but they should be interpreted only as illustrative of the patterns and not reified as existing types of gangs. Also, the procedure of obtaining reports by gang members about others in their gang raises validity concerns. Gang violence, for example, often occurs as group offenses, which leads to exaggerations of the extent of collective gang involvement (see Reiss, 1986, on group offending). Also, gang members may not be well informed about the behaviors of others in the gang (Klein and Maxson, 1989).

There are two choices for identifying dimensions for typology development: either accept the original behavioral measures or use transformed scores. The latter promises to reconcile anomalies within the raw data and root out sampling artifacts. But transformations, such as log linear models or factor analytic procedures, have their own implicit biases and assumptions, which may introduce new meaning into the distributions.[10] Thus, the raw scores were used here to avoid biases inherent in the transformation procedures. This selection seemed appropriate given the categorical response sets and the unique sample construction procedures.

Typology development was based on the 11 offense-specific indices and the 10 drug-use items in the appendix. An iterative partitioning method was used to identify patterns of drug use, drug sales, and criminality of the gangs as reported by their gang members. Squared Euclidean distance (Ward's centroid method) was used as the similarity measure (Aldenfelder and Blashfield, 1984). A k-means pass was used as the method to assign cases to clusters. The result was a non-hierarchical cluster analytic solution that optimizes the minimum variance within clusters. This approach to grouping subjects uses their relative proximity in a specified dimensional space. The nonhierarchical centroid methods is less useful than the hierarchical

models as a heuristic tool because it displays neither agglomerative nor diversive linkages (e.g., dendograms). This weakness was addressed by running sequential solutions that specify cluster sizes of from three to seven. Comparisons of each successive iteration approximated a divisive hierarchical analysis.

The four-cluster solution was selected based on the shifts in cluster membership in successive iterations and on the conceptual integrity (i.e., face validity) of the solution. The validation procedures relied on interpretation plus the face validity and internal consistency of the aggregate behavioral characteristics of each group and the overall sample classification. This is a purely classificatory procedure, with no questions of statistical significance in the derivation procedure. The clusters are a heuristic tool that is instructive for partitioning the gangs into groups for descriptive purposes, but they should be regarded cautiously as distinct types of gangs.

Table 2 shows cluster membership and the mean prevalence score for each of the cluster dimensions. Each offense-specific index includes several items, so that index scores varied by the number of behaviors that members reported for their gang.[11] Analysis-of-variance tests for all index scores were significant (p = .001). Table 3 summarizes the results and shows the relative degrees of gang involvement for each dimension of gang behavior. The descriptions below include the percentage of gangs in each type (based on individual gang members' reports about collective acts of their gang).

- Type 1 (28 percent) is involved in few delinquent activities and little drug use other than alcohol and marijuana use. These gangs also have low involvement in drug sales (most likely to finance their own drug use). This is basically a social group whose patterns of use reflect general adolescent experimentation in drug use and delinquency. This type of gang appears to be a "social gang."

- Type 2 (7 percent) gangs have few members involved in nondrug criminal behaviors, but relatively high prevalence of several types of drug use, drug sales, and

TABLE 2 Gang Drug and Crime Behaviors, by Type of Gang

	Gang Type			
Gang Behaviors	1	2	3	4
(N)	(43)	(10)	(56)	(42)
Felony Assault	.09	.00	1.36	1.48
Minor Assault	.00	.00	.63	.81
Robbery	.05	.00	2.02	2.38
Felony Theft	.09	.00	4.00	4.40
Minor Theft	.00	.00	1.73	2.31
Vandalism	.00	1.50	1.18	1.48
Illegal Services	.07	.00	.75	.88
Weapons	.02	.00	1.93	2.52
Extortion	.02	.00	.77	.86
Drug Sales	.16	1.50	1.07	1.67
Alcohol	.44	1.50	1.55	1.67
Marijuana	.23	.80	.84	.88
Cocaine	.02	.70	.66	.86
Heroin	.00	1.50	.34	1.36
PCP, Psychedelics	.09	2.10	.64	2.45
Speed, Barbiturates	.09	2.60	.57	2.60

NOTE: Scale scores are mean prevalence scores for ordinal measures of gang members' participation in each behavior in the prior year. ANOVA tests for gang-type differences were significant ($P < .000$) for all scales.

TABLE 3 Drug and Alcohol Use, Drug Dealing, and Other Behaviors, by Type of Gang (Summary)

	Gang Type			
Behaviors	1	2	3	4
(N)	(43)	(10)	(56)	(42)
Violent Crime	Low	Low	High	High
Felony Property Crime	Low	Low	High	High
Other Property Crime	Low	High	High	High
Weapons	Low	Low	High	High
Drug Sales	Low	High	Medium	High
Alcohol	Low	High	High	High
Marijuana	Low	High	High	High
Cocaine, Heroin, PCP	Low	High	Medium	High

one type of delinquency—vandalism. Their drug sales, in the absence of other forms of crime, are likely to be supportive of their own drug use. Their extensive involvement in drug use suggests that their affiliation may be based on mutually supportive patterns of drug use and dealing to support group and individual drug use. This type seems to be a "party gang" that otherwise manifests several of the subcultural and organizational features of gangs.

• Type 3 (37 percent) gangs appear to include serious delinquents who have extensive involvement in several types of delinquent acts, both serious and nonserious, and both violent and property offenses. This type of gang's involvement in drug sales, however, is far lower than for the "party gangs," as is their use of serious substances (cocaine, heroin, amphetamines, and PCP). The absence of extensive involvement in serious drug use and drug sales suggests that drugs play a secondary role in their criminal activities and that drug use is most likely recreational or social in nature (Fields, 1985). This group resembles serious delinquents identified in other studies of inner-city adolescents, and the members can be appropriately called "serious delinquents."

• Type 4 (28 percent) gangs differ from the third group only in their extensive involvement in serious drug use and higher rates of drug sales. We might speculate that their criminality and drug sales are linked and that rather than social drug use, their drug use and selling reflect a systemic relationship with other criminal acts. As shown below, this is a highly cohesive and organized type, and it is probably at the highest risk for becoming a more formal criminal organization. At this stage, they appear to be more of an incipient, or nascent "organization."

The typology suggests that the complex relationship between substance use and dealing and delinquency observed among inner-city adolescents (Fagan et al., in press) also applies to gang members. Use of cocaine, PCP, and other serious drugs appears to be a routine feature of gang life only for gangs who otherwise are involved marginally in nondrug crimes. Drug selling is evident among both violent and nonviolent gangs, but it is not evident among one gang type that reports frequent violence. However, involvement in serious drug use occurs together with higher rates of drug selling in another gang type.

The high prevalence of drug use among "social" gangs and of drug use and selling among "party" gangs suggests that drug involvement is not inextricably linked to violence. Table 3 shows a high prevalence of violence among gangs with both high and moderate involvement in drug selling and also with low-to-moderate involvement in serious substances. One must look to factors other than drug involvement to explain violence among gang members. On the other hand, Table 2 implies that a strong relationship exists among violence, serious crime, frequent intoxication, and drug dealing among gang members, just as there is among other inner-city adolescents. The relationship among gang violence, nonviolent crimes, drug selling, and drug use is complex. Violence occurs in gangs with distinct drug use patterns, but rarely among gangs that also are not involved with drug use and drug selling.

Variation in gang violence by city is well established (Spergel, 1989). Whether this represents variation in ecological and community stability factors, historical processes of gang formation, police responses, ethnic differences and acculturation processes, or other factors is unknown. It is possible that the gang types simply represent city differences or ethnic variation within the sample. Accordingly, gang types were compared by city to determine if patterns reflected specific patterns within cities or valid representations of natural variation among gangs in different ecological settings.

Differences were evident, though not statistically significant ($p = .078$), by city (Table 4). In Los Angeles, there was a higher percentage of "social" gangs and a lower percentage of "organizations" than in the other two cities. Recent evidence on gang violence in Los Angeles suggests that Los Angeles gang members in this study underreported gang involvement in violence (Baker, 1988;

TABLE 4 Distribution of Gang Types, by City

City	Gang Type			
	1	2	3	4
Chicago	22.0%	4.0%	36.0%	38.0%
Los Angeles	38.0	12.0	36.0	14.0
San Diego	25.5	3.9	39.2	31.4
N	43	10	56	42
Percent	28.5	6.6	37.1	27.8

Chi-square = 11.38 $p = .078$

Klein et al., 1988). Their responses may reflect the complex role of the intermediary group with gangs, the local schools, and the police, or simply denial by gang members of their violence. Nevertheless, the consistency between Chicago and San Diego, together with the minor differences in Los Angeles for all but type 1, supports the generalizability of the gang types across disparate urban settings. Also, ethnic differences seem to be unrelated to gang type. Respondents in Los Angeles and Chicago primarily were African-American gang members, while respondents in San Diego included both Chicano and Asian gangs. The similarity in distributions among cities suggests that there may exist differences within ethnic groups in gang types. Conclusive evidence of such variations requires more systematic study across ethnic groups.

Core and Marginal Involvement in Gang Delinquency and Drug Use

Members of gangs vary by role, reason for affiliation, and extent of participation in delinquent activities. Gang membership and roles also shift over time, as members move in and out of various roles. Membership tenure varies, as does the length of time for members to move up from less important to more visible roles. Dropping back from leadership also is not uncommon (Moore, 1978; Vigil, 1988). Roles within gangs also may vary according to the nature of the activity—leaders for drug selling may differ from leaders or soldiers in "gangbanging." Spergel (1989) refers to gang members with different leadership roles as "floaters." Despite the diversity and fluidity of gang affiliation and roles, there is consensus that core members are involved in a wider range of delinquent acts than fringe or situational members. Research on gangs has not examined the complicating role of involvement in drug use or sales, however.

Table 5 shows the percentage of respondents within gang types who reported "regular" substance use or delinquency in the past year—that is, those who reported more than "a few" (three or more) occasions in that time.[12] The behavior categories are the same ones used to construct the gang typology. Comparisons across gang types for all variables were significant. The results show that regular participation by individuals increased with the seriousness of collective gang acts. That is, a higher percentage of members in

TABLE 5 "Regular" Self-reported Substance Use and Other Delinquency, by Type of Gang

Self-reported Behaviors	Gang Type				Significance, p (Chi-square)
	1	2	3	4	
Felony Assault	12.0	33.3	28.9	35.9	.04
Minor Assault	4.4	33.3	15.6	27.5	.001
Robbery	4.3	50.0	40.9	47.2	.001
Felony Theft	4.6	16.7	48.9	47.2	.001
Minor Theft	10.1	16.7	37.7	51.4	.000
Vandalism	8.7	16.7	37.6	47.4	.004
Illegal Services	4.4	28.6	29.8	38.4	.004
Weapons	8.0	33.3	41.3	43.6	.002
Extortion	12.5	33.3	38.6	47.5	.004
Drug Sales	16.0	16.7	26.7	37.1	.056
Alcohol	29.6	14.3	58.9	60.0	.000
Marijuana	26.0	14.3	54.9	50.0	.026
PCP, Psychedelics	12.0	16.7	29.0	52.7	.000
Speed, Barbiturates	4.1	0	30.8	42.8	.000
Cocaine	4.1	0	22.7	44.7	.000
Heroin, Other Opiates	4.4	0	12.8	31.4	.000

NOTE: "Regular" use means respondents reported using "a few times" or more often in the prior year.

seriously delinquent gangs (types 3 and 4) reported regular or frequent participation (more than three times in the prior year) than in the other gang types. There are exceptions, though. The percentage of "party" gang members reporting regular assault and robbery was similar to reports from members of "serious delinquents" or the "organizations." Also, fewer members of "party gangs" reported regular involvement in drug use than in the "social gangs." The small number describing their gang as "party gangs" (10 gang members) leaves this group more vulnerable to sampling error than the others. Whether this is an artifact of the gang members selected or an anomaly of the design is not clear.

Nevertheless, there is variation in the extent and nature of individual participation in delinquency and drug use—that is, marginal or infrequent involvement in serious delinquent acts exists within gangs together with core or frequent involvement in those acts. For all gang types and nondrug crimes, fewer than half of the respondents reported more than three acts in the prior year. Gang members also do not appear to specialize. For the more serious gang types, the percentage of members reporting regular violence was only slightly lower than the percentage reporting regular property crimes. The similarities suggest a diverse pattern of behaviors among gang members within each type. Only for alcohol and marijuana use do a majority of respondents within the two most serious gang types report regular use. This further illustrates that drug use is intrinsic to gang life among more violent gangs. Finally, these trends did not vary among gang leaders. There were no significant differences between self-reported leaders and others in their self-reported regular involvement in drug use or delinquency.

The participation of members of "social gangs" in a range of delinquent acts also illustrates diversity within gangs. Fewer than 1 in 10 respondents in the "social gangs" reported regular individual involvement in most types of crime. These reports were consistent with their reports of collective gang involvement. It is uncertain, however, whether their delinquency occurred as part of a gang act or independently.

Social Organization

In several studies (Dolan and Finney, 1984; Feldman et al., 1985; Hagedorn, 1988; Moore, 1978; Vigil, 1988), drug use and dealing were found to be endemic to gangs. Those studies also reveal covariation between the extent or severity of gang crime and drug involvement, however. Economic opportunity, normative adolescent experimentation and developmental progressions, presumed causal linkages with criminality, and specific gang and ethnic traditions are competing explanations for drug involvement by gangs. Little effort has been made to explain variation among gangs on drug use, and virtually no studies link gang social processes or structure to drug involvement or joint drug-crime behaviors. Accordingly, the analysis turns to the relationship between the social organization and processes of gangs and the severity of gang violence, other delinquency, and drug use.

A range of structural and process dimensions were compared by gang type. Formal structure included the presence of established leaders, rules or codes, formal roles, age stratification for roles, and role for girls. The "serious delinquents" and "organizations" had the highest degree of formal structure (Table 6).[13] A higher percentage of "social" and "party" gangs reported frequent meetings. Since "meetings" possibly was interpreted as meaning both hanging out and more organized discussion of activities, these differences have mixed meaning with respect to social processes among gang members. Members of "social gangs" more often reported that initiation occurred before 13 years of age. There were no significant differences for gang identifiers (i.e., symbols, etc.).

Reports of specific roles for girls in the gang may indicate a formal structure among more active delinquent gangs. Prior studies (Campbell, 1984; Dolan and Finney, 1984; Thrasher, 1927) have identified roles for girls in gangs that confer status and offer excitement, such as provocation of fights, infiltration and spying on rival gangs, carrying messages, and carrying weapons. The latter occurs both for strategic and protective reasons, such as to avoid arrest of male gang

TABLE 6   Social Organization and Conventional Values, by Gang Types

	Gang Type				
	1	2	3	4	Significance, p (Chi-square)
Social Organization					
You can join before you are 13	65.9%	20.0%	38.9%	41.1%	.02
There are initiation rites	54.8	30.0	65.5	59.0	.20
The gang has established leaders	23.7	10.0	47.9	52.8	.01
The gang has regular meetings	64.9	75.0	40.8	51.3	.03
The gang has specific rules or codes	31.6	20.0	63.8	61.5	.000
Gang members have specific roles	33.3	20.0	52.9	65.0	.001
There are roles for each age group	27.8	20.0	52.8	40.5	.057
The gang has symbols and colors	66.7	100	88.9	79.2	.42
There are specific roles for girls	25.7	11.1	62.3	54.1	.001
Conventional Values*					
School is important to me	46.5	22.2	67.3	38.1	.051
School is important to the gang	58.1	44.4	81.8	63.4	.061
Work is important to me	52.5	14.3	72.0	57.1	.13
Work is important to the gang	20.5	0	34.0	15.2	.15
I have worked in the past 6 months	40.5	0	42.9	41.0	.18
I want to work	87.9	55.6	88.9	88.2	.059
Parents influence gang members	24.3	0	7.5	12.8	.10
Parents supervise me	53.5	40.0	25.0	28.6	.05
Parents are involved with gang	13.5	0	9.8	13.5	.72

* Percentage reporting "somewhat" or "very much."

members. Campbell (1984) reports that girls often are involved actively in drug use and sales by the gang. Girls are a distinct minority within gangs, however, and research has not been conclusive on the formality of female gang structures or whether their participation in gang processes and behaviors is auxiliary or integral to the gang's primary activities. The reports of specific roles for girls in the "serious delinquents" and "organizations" suggest that female roles may be more formal and integrated among more active and violent gangs and auxiliary among less cohesive and noncriminal gangs.

Reports of gang organization and social processes occurred more often among members of "serious delinquents" and "organizations." There were few differences between "serious delinquents" and "organizations" in reports of leadership, rules or codes of behavior, and specific roles within gangs, despite their different involvement in drug sales. Thus, there is little support for the hypothesis that drug selling by gangs as a collective act implies a formal organizational structure. Few members of "party gangs," a

group with significant involvement in drug sales, reported that there was an organizational structure or social processes within their gangs. Formal organization exists for both "serious delinquents" and "organizations," despite their distinct patterns of drug use and differences in their involvement in drug selling. These patterns are typical of gang variation even within homogeneous social areas. What we simply may be seeing in these data are two distinct patterns of violence and drug involvement among cohesive gangs: the "fighting" gang, for whom drug use is an accompaniment to gang life, and the gang whose violence may be systemically related to their drug selling and use.

Conventional values also exist alongside deviant ones within gangs, regardless of their orientation toward crime and drug involvement. Most (over 87%) members of "serious delinquents," "organizations," and "social gangs" expressed interest in work, though many (over 40%) were unemployed for the prior six months. Most (over 58%) respondents from these three gang types value school. Although most individuals in all groups value work, few (no more than 34%) think that the gang values work. The gang apparently values education, however. The disparity between individual and collective gang norms on work may reflect either marginal participation of working members in their gang or simply the gang's realistic view of the limited work opportunities in their neighborhoods. The desire of members to work may reflect either a social bond or an economic imperative. Ironically, the "party gang," the strongest drug subculture but the least delinquent gang type, seems to be the most socially isolated in terms of conventional social values and beliefs.

For all gang types, parents are a negligible influence in their lives as gang members or as adolescents. Others have found similar weaknesses in parental influence over inner-city youths (Fagan et al., 1986). This may reflect the later developmental stages of respondents, when parental influence naturally is limited, but it also may reflect the general limitations on families in inner cities (Edelman, 1987; Wilson, 1987). Finally, these results are unequivocal about the absence of intergenerational parental influence on gangs.

Social Processes

The results in Table 6 suggest an association between gang organization and their involvement in violence and drugs. The social processes within gangs that maintain the influence of these structures and cohesion among its members are examined in Table 7. Like many other facets of gang life, the maintenance of cohesion involves complex social processes. Spergel (1989) suggests that gang leaders use delinquent activities to mobilize the gang and sustain group cohesion. Klein (1971) views gang cohesion and delinquency as interactive, though cohesion often preceded delinquent activities and may be associated with collective and individual gang delinquency. Others argue that delinquency is related to status conflicts within gangs, and that gang delinquency may serve to restore cohesion that is threatened by conflict (Short and Strodtbeck, 1965). Unfortunately, there has been

little critical review of gang research on cohesion and process to clarify these views. Table 7 examines differences between gang types for four social processes that reflect gang cohesion.

Four processes were examined: process and reason for getting involved in the gang, the types of rules violations that provoke sanctions, and the types of sanctions for breaking rules. Responses for specific items within each of these processes were analyzed using a multiple response procedure (SPSS, 1988). This routine maps responses for items that have more than one value for each case. Table 7 shows the percentage of gang members reporting whether each of several specific features of each social process existed in their gang. This method provides comparisons of the existence of each social process, but it does not provide tests of statistical significance.

The processes for getting involved in gangs showed little consistent pattern. They reflect the generally informal social processes of gang affiliation, regardless of the extent of gang involvement in substance use or non-drug crimes. Initiation has various meanings, ranging from formal rites of initiation (e.g., fighting other gangs, running a gauntlet, participating in a shooting) to simply hanging around and being accepted by key members of the gang. Specific questions abut processes of initiation revealed no significant differences across gang types. There were few reports of drafting or formal recruitment for any types.

As for reasons for getting involved, members of "organizations" more often reported that there were specific reasons for joining the gang. The attractions of gang life for the most seriously criminal youths in a neighborhood reflect the weakness (or absence) of conventional social institutions in those social areas and, conversely, the strength of gangs as institutions of social control and opportunity. The social immersion of its members within the gang is much greater. The gangs seem to fulfill the basic social needs that more formal social institutions and processes fulfill elsewhere.

In general, the processes for joining gangs and reasons for getting involved

TABLE 7 Social Processes and Codes within Gangs, by Type of Gang

	Gang Type			
	1	2	3	4
Process of Getting Involved				
I had friends in the gang	30.8%	70.0%	56.4%	53.8%
I was recruited by leaders	2.6	10.0	9.1	10.3
I partied with gang members	12.8	30.0	21.8	30.8
I hung out with gang members	51.3	20.0	45.5	38.5
I had business with gang members	17.9	20.0	20.0	12.8
Reason for Joining Gang				
It gave me status and identity	20.5	10.0	26.9	32.5
I was protected from other gangs	28.2	20.0	21.2	35.0
It gave me some good friends	15.4	20.0	17.3	27.5
It gave me a family feeling	33.3	10.0	17.3	30.0
To protect the neighborhood	28.2	50.0	17.3	27.5
I could meet girls	7.7	30.0	15.4	30.0
Violations That Provoke Sanctions				
Take someone's woman	19.5	11.1	21.4	42.5
Insult a neighbor or homeboy	12.2	0	14.3	27.5
Rip off a gang member	48.8	77.8	50.0	65.0
Use another gang's name, etc.	39.0	44.4	53.6	55.0
Snitch on a gang member	56.1	33.3	80.4	60.0
Chicken out in a fight	34.1	33.3	64.3	57.5
Fight with a neighbor or homeboy	4.9	0	16.1	20.0
Sanctions for Breaking Rules				
Nothing happens	61.1	55.6	24.5	35.0
The leader decides sanction	13.9	11.1	28.3	40.0
You have to defend the gang's name	11.1	11.1	24.5	27.5
You have to steal for the gang	8.3	22.2	7.5	20.0
You have to fight someone	11.1	22.2	28.3	47.5
You get beat up by the gang	16.7	0	32.1	40.0

NOTE: Percentages exceed 100% due to multiple responses within items.

describe a multifaceted process that reflects natural opportunities for adolescent social interaction more than any formal recruitment process. There were several motivating influences for joining the gang. Joining may be a calculated act by some youths for protection, status, or economic opportunity. It also may reflect normative processes of adolescent development in specific neighborhoods with strong gang activity. For others, gangs may offer social supports and roles missing from their daily routines outside gang life. Researchers have long cited reports from gang members of the strong social and personal pleasure they derive from the "family feeling" of gang solidarity (e.g., Keiser, 1969). Whether gangs fulfill the role of family for their members, or provide an added dimension of familism beyond their natural families, is unclear from this study.

The use of force as punishment for violating gang codes was more often reported among the two more violent gang types. Of the possible violations listed, over 50% of the gang members reported that most of these acts would provoke a sanction within each of these two gang types. For the two other gang types, fewer than half the acts would provoke a response by more than a minority of their members. Similar trends were found for the specific sanctions. Members of the two more violent gangs more often reported that violent sanctions were used in their gangs, though by less than half of the members. Sanctions in general, violent or not, were rarely reported among "social" and "party" gangs.

Overall, the attractions of gang life and processes for enforcing gang norms and rules were most salient within the two more violent gangs. Comparison of the four social processes across gang types suggests that the gang types differed primarily in the existence of formal rules or norms that might provoke a sanction, and the existence of sanctions for breaking rules. Norms were in strongest evidence among "organizations" and "serious delinquents."

Thus, the gangs with the most extensive involvement in substance use, drug sales, and violent crimes may be the most formally organized groups among a cohort of loosely affiliated gangs.

CONCLUSIONS

The complexity of the drug-crime relationship among gang members is typical of its equally complex relationship among inner-city youths. The patterns of drug use and crime among gangs suggest a skewed and spurious relationship. There is a positive association between drug involvement and serious collective gang acts, again similar to nongang urban youths. Also, members of gangs with greater involvement in substance use and drug selling more often reported that social processes were evident in their gangs to maintain and enforce gang rules and behavioral codes. The data support the contention that substance use and delinquency among gangs occur in gangs with well-developed organizational structures and social norms.

Drug use is widespread and normative among gangs, regardless of city, the extent or nature of collective violence, or their organization or social processes. Serious and violent behaviors occur among a majority of the gangs. Drug use occurs, however, both independently of other crimes and also as part of a general pattern of deviant behavior. Gang delinquency did not occur in the absence of drugs. The factors that shape and influence gang membership may result in joint patterns of drug use and violence, but also in drug use that is not accompanied by collective gang violence.

Patterns of drug selling also reveal a complex relationship with other gang behaviors. Serious crime and violence occur regardless of the prevalence of drug dealing within the gang. All gangs were involved to some extent in drug dealing, but it was most prevalent among gangs that were involved more heavily in PCP, heroin, and cocaine, regardless of their involvement in violence. Thus, involvement in use and sales of the most serious substance, does not necessarily increase the frequency or severity of violent behavior. And there remains a small group of gangs who are heavily involved in drug use and dealing but avoid collective violence.

The complex and ambiguous patterns of delinquency and drug use or selling among gangs differ from patterns observed among adult offenders. The high risk among adult men of systemic violence from involvement in drug trafficking (Chaiken and Chaiken, 1989; Goldstein, 1985) does not appear to apply equally to all gang types or members. Some incidents no doubt are precipitated by disputes over drug sales or selling territories, but the majority of violent incidents do not appear to involve drug sales. Rather, they continue to be part of the status, territorial, and other gang conflicts that historically have fueled gang violence.

The discovery of similar gang types in three cities suggests some generalized social processes supportive of gang behaviors in urban areas. Thus, the important comparison of gang delinquency with nongang delinquency reaffirms the disproportionate involvement of gang members in delinquency. The patterns of delinquent and drug use behaviors among gang members are consistent with patterns observed among institutionalized delinquents and among the most serious and chronic offenders in general population studies. But the comparison also suggests that gangs are a marginal population in their neighborhoods, just as the institutionalized and multiple offenders in other studies were a small proportion of the adolescents in other social areas. This is not surprising—most urban youths do not join gangs (Baker, 1988),[14] and among those who describe themselves as gang members, their involvement ranges from fringe to core. It is likely that only a small percentage of gang members are "core" members (Klein and Maxson, 1989; Spergel, 1989). Thus, core gang members, who have the highest rates and severity of violence, are a marginal group within an already marginal population.

Social organization and other processes of gang cohesion offer only partial explanations of why gangs differ in violence or drug involvement. The transience of membership and leadership cliques and continuation suggest further that gang cohesion may have limited influence on behaviors. Curry and Spergel (1988) suggest that ecological factors, including residential transience, also are important influences on gang activity for Chicago gangs. Baker's (1988) interviews with African-American gang members in Los Angeles offer important clues to how urban form shapes gang cohesion and conflicts. The proliferation of gangs in urban areas with haphazard turf lines, routine activities that place gang members in frequent contact with other gangs and also on others' territory, access to weapons and income from crimes, all contribute to increases in different types of conflicts and opportunities for violence. The frequent contacts between gangs create frequent occasions for both prolonged organized assaults by one group of gang members, "gangbangs," and less organized attacks by individual gang members settling individual conflicts. Conflicts over drug territory are only one of many circumstances that may lead to collective gang violence.

In addition to urban topography, the social ecology of urban areas influences gang participation and patterns of violence. The marginality of the social areas with the highest rates of gang conflict suggests that these also are areas with the weakest social institutions. Thrasher (1927) noted nearly half a century ago that gangs could arise under conditions of social disorganization that in turn created social instability. Curry and Spergel (1988) linked these processes to residential mobility, poverty, and other socioeconomic variables. Several recent studies (Laub, 1983; Sampson, 1987, 1986; Shannon, 1984; Weis and Sederstrom, 1981) have linked social ecological factors with weakened formal and informal social controls and

higher rates of adolescent violence. Thrasher (1927) noted the isolation from the surrounding society of "interstitial areas," where weak social institutions failed to provide effective social controls. Thus, variation in gang violence may reflect the extent of their social embedment in ecological areas that are cut off from normative social and economic influences.

Social isolation of gangs from both legitimate economic opportunity and routine interactions with mainstream society, and the limited influence of viable social controls, may lead to the development and ossification of gangs in a closed social system. In this context, the socialization of adolescents becomes skewed toward processes that sustain gangs as the dominate sources of social status and values, economic opportunities, affiliation, protection, and social control. Gang members in such areas may become inured to violence and also lose sight of other social norms or cultures. Lacking formal or informal social controls or opportunities, gangs may become the primary social influence. The undue reliance of inner-city youths on gang structures for basic social roles and opportunities may neutralize other conventional influences. Thus, one plausible explanation for variation in gang violence may lie in the relative social and economic isolation of their milieu and in the specific influence of social and legal controls and economic and criminal opportunities within those areas. Violence within gangs may reflect both the marginalization of gang members and the marginalization of the neighborhood itself.

APPENDIX:
SELF-REPORTED OFFENSE-SPECIFIC SCALES

Felony Assault

Beat someone up so badly they probably needed a doctor

Forced someone to have sexual relations with them

Shot someone

Minor Assault

Hit an adult or other youth in the neighborhood

Robbery
  Grabbed a purse and ran with it

  Used physical force to get money, drugs, or something else from someone

  Used a weapon to get something from someone

Felony Theft
  Bought stolen goods

  Taken things from a store worth more than $50

  Broken into a car to get something

  Broken into a building and taken something

  Taken a stranger's car without permission

Minor Theft
  Taken something from somebody's wallet or purse

  Stolen money from parents or other family members

  Stolen something at school

Vandalism
  Purposely damaged or destroyed property belonging to your school

  Purposely damaged or destroyed property not belonging to you or your family

Illegal Services
  Sold marijuana

  Sold angel dust, downers, speed, coke, or heroin

  Sold something you had stolen

Weapons
  Carried a weapon with the intention of using it in a fight

  Threatened an adult with a weapon

Extortion
  Threatened to hurt someone unless given something

  Threatened an adult

Drug Sales
  Sold weed (marijuana) or PCP cigarettes

  Sold angel dust, downers, speed, coke, or heroin

Alcohol Use
  Drank beer or wine

  Drank gin, vodka, or other liquor

Marijuana
  Smoked marijuana

PCP or Psychedelics
  Smoked sherms or used dust

  Used acid

Speed or Barbiturates
  Used downers, barbs, reds, speed, uppers, or other pills

Cocaine
  Snorted or shot cocaine, smoked crack

Heroin or other opiates
  Snorted or smoked heroin, smoked or ate opium, shot heroin

Notes

1. Vigil (1988) notes that these patterns are confined to substances that enhance gang social processes—alcohol, marijuana, and phencyclidine (PCP). Among Chicano gangs, heroin involvement is seen as a betrayal of the gang and the barrio: one cannot be loyal to his or her addiction and the addict ("tecato") culture and maintain loyalty to the gang.

2. Although drug use and violence share common etiological processes, they are equally likely to appear independently or together.

3. Temporal order must be considered in these relationships. Drug selling, particularly of rock cocaine or crack, is a relatively recent event for African-American gangs in Los Angeles. Gang violence preceded their involvement in rock trafficking. However, the Detroit findings (e.g., Cooper, 1987) suggest that violence in drug-selling organizations developed simultaneously with their formation, though it existed in other Detroit gangs long before crack was available in the city.

4. A-level metropolitan areas have populations greater than 1,000,000; B-level areas, populations of 250,000 to 1,000,000. Analyses determined the homogeneity of the study neighborhoods with respect to their ecological characteristics. This procedure was necessary to determine whether samples from different cities could be aggregated. The census tract for each respondent's neighborhood was recorded, and 10 variables were extracted from 1980 census data. These variables represented the domains identified by Laub and Hindelang (1981) as sources of social area effects that explain differences in serious juvenile crime: demographic, labor force, poverty, and housing characteristics. Two validation checks were made. First, analysis-of-variance comparisons were made to determine whether the social area characteristics for the samples were comparable; 6 of 10 census variables were comparable. Second, two comparability checks were conducted to determine the homogeneity of samples across sites. Chi-square analyses of demographic

and socioeconomic variables were used to compare sample characteristics; the results were not statistically significant. Also, means for selected explanatory and demographic variables were compared for each site versus the pooled sample from the remaining sites to determine if the exclusion of any site affected the pooled distribution of the inner-city sample.

5. In such procedures, subjects are often asked to nominate "someone just like you."

6. The intermediary agencies asked prospective volunteers if they had contact with gang members in their neighborhoods; they declined offers of assistance from those who either had been victims of gang violence or who personally knew active gang members.

7. The number of gang members involved in specific behaviors was not asked. This decision was intended to protect respondents against reprisals from other gangs and to minimize their disclosure of information that might attract the attention of law enforcement agencies and thus discourage truthful reporting.

8. Also, felony assault was more prevalent than minor assault as both a collective and individual act. In general adolescent samples (e.g., Elliott and Huizinga, 1984), minor assault and minor theft are more prevalent and frequent, respectively, than felony assault and felony theft. In inner-city adolescent samples (e.g., Fagan et al., 1986), similar trends were found among institutionalized male delinquents and school dropouts. The differences for this sample may reflect actual differences between gang members and other adolescents, sampling artifacts (the inclusion of only males in the sample), design artifacts (item and index construction that emphasized more serious criminal acts), and enhancements by gang members in reports of their behaviors.

9. In those samples, 13% identified themselves as gang members.

10. In other words, the loss of critical information from truncating positively skewed distributions may alter the actual meaning and interpretation of this unique feature of delinquency data (see Elliott and Huizinga, 1983).

11. See Fagan et al. (1986) for an item-scale mapping.

12. This is the threshold used by Dunford and Elliott (1984), Elliott and Huizinga (1984), and Fagan et al. (1987, in press) to classify "multiple-index" offenders from others in typological schemes using self-reported annual frequencies.

13. Comparisons of the mean age of gang members in each type established the age independence of the types and rejected the hypothesis that the types simply were similar gangs at different stages of organizational development.

14. Baker (1988) cites Los Angeles Police Department intelligence that estimates the gang population among African-American males at 25,000, or 25% of the city's estimated population of 100,000 African-American males between the ages of 15 and 24.

References

ALDENDERFER, MARK S. AND ROGER K. BLASHFIELD
1984   Cluster Analysis. Beverly Hills, Calif: Sage.

ANDERSON, NANCY AND ORLANDO RODRIGUEZ
1984   Conceptual issues in the study of Hispanic delinquency. Research Bulletin: 7:2–5. Hispanic Research Center. New York: Fordham University.

BAKER, ROBERT
1988   Homeboys: Players in a deadly drama. Los Angeles Times, June 26.

BIERNACKI, PATRICK AND DAN WALDORF
1981   Snowball sampling: Problems and techniques of chain referral sampling. Sociological Methods and Research 10(2):141–163.

BLACK, DONALD
1983   Crime as social control. American Sociological Review 48:34–45.

BOOKIN-WEINER, HEDY AND RUTH HOROWITZ
1983   The end of the youth gang: Fad or fact? Criminology 21(4):585–602.

CAMPBELL, ANNE
1984   The Girls in the Gang. New Brunswick, N.J.: Rutgers University Press.

CERNKOVICH, STEPHEN A., PEGGY C. GIORDANO, AND MEREDITH D. PUGH
1986   Chronic offenders: The missing cases in self-report delinquency research. Journal of Criminal Law and Criminology 76:684–704.

CHAIKEN, JAN AND MARCIA CHAIKEN
1989   Drug use and predatory crime. In James Q. Wilson and Michael Tonry (eds.), Drugs and Crime—Crime and Justice: An Annual Review of Research. Vol. 13. Chicago: University of Chicago Press.

CHIN, KO-LIN
1986   Chinese triad societies, tongs, organized crime, and street gangs in Asia and the United States. Ph.D. dissertation, University of Pennsylvania.

COOPER, BARRY M.
1987   Motor city breakdown. Village Voice, December 1:23–35.

CURRY, G. DAVID AND IRVING A. SPERGEL
1988   Gang homicide, delinquency, and community. Criminology 26:381–406.

DOLAN, EDWARD F. AND SHAN FINNEY
1984   Youth Gangs. New York: Simon & Schuster.

DUNDFORD, FRANKLYN W. AND DELBERT S. ELLIOTT
1984   Identifying career offenders using self-reported data. Journal of Research in Crime and Delinquency 21:57–86.

EDELMAN, MARIAN W.
1987   Families in Peril. Cambridge, Mass.: Harvard University Press.

ELLIOTT, DELBERT S., AND DAVID HUIZINGA
1983   Social class and delinquent behavior in a national youth panel. Criminology 21:149–177.

1984 The Relationship Between Delinquent Behavior and ADM Problems. National Youth Survey Report No. 28. Institute for Behavioral Studies. Boulder: University of Colorado.

ELLIOTT, DELBERT S., DAVID HUIZINGA, AND SUZANNE AGETON
1985 Explaining Delinquency and Drug Abuse. Beverly Hills, Calif.: Sage.

ERLANGER, HOWARD S.
1979 Estrangement, machismo and gang violence. Social Science Quarterly 60(3):235–248.

FAGAN, JEFFREY A., ELIZABETH S. PIPER, AND YU-TEH CHENG
1987 Contributions of victimization to delinquency in inner cities. Journal of Criminal Law and Criminology 78(3):586–613.

FAGAN, JEFFREY A., ELIZABETH S. PIPER, AND MELINDA MOORE
1986 Violent delinquents and urban youth. Criminology 23:439–466.

FAGAN, JEFFREY A., JOSEPH G. WEIS, AND YU-TEH CHENG
In press Drug use and delinquency among inner city students. Journal of Drug Issues 19(4).

FELDMAN, HARVEY W., MICHAEL AGAR, AND GEORGE BESCHNER (EDS.)
1979 Angel Dust: An Ethnographic Study of PCP Uses. Lexington, Mass.: Lexington Books.

FELDMAN, HARVEY W., JERRY MANDEL, AND ALLEN FIELDS
1985 In the Neighborhood: A strategy for delivering early intervention services to young drug users in their natural environments. In Alfred S. Friedman and George Beschner (eds.), Treatment Services for Adolescent Substance Users. Rockville, MD: National Institute of Drug Abuse.

FIELDS, ALLEN
1985 Weedslingers: Young black marijuana dealers. In George Beschner and Alfred S. Friedman (eds.), Teen Drug Use. Lexington, Mass.: Lexington Books.

GANDOSSY, ROBERT P., JAY WILLIAMS, J. COHEN, AND HENRICK HARDWOOD
1980 Drugs and Crime: A Survey and Analysis of the Literature. Washington, D.C.: National Institute of Justice.

GOLDSTEIN, PAUL J.
1985 The drugs-violence nexus: A tri-partite conceptual framework. Journal of Drug Issues 15: 493–506.

HAGEDORN, JOHN
1988 People and Folk: Gangs, Crime and the Underclass in a Rustbelt City. Chicago: Lakeview Press.

HINDELANG, MICHAEL, TRAVIS HIRSCHI, AND JOSEPH G. WEIS
1981 Measuring Delinquency. Beverly Hills, Calif.: Sage.

HOROWITZ, RUTH
1983 Honor and the American Dream: Culture and Identity in a Chicano Community. New Brunswick, N.J.: Rutgers University Press.
1987 Community tolerance of gang violence. Social Problems 34(5):437–450.

JOHNSON, BRUCE D., PAUL J. GOLDSTEIN, EDWARD PREBLE, JAMES SCHMEIDLER, DOUGLAS LIPTON, BARRY SPUNT, AND THOMAS MILLER
1985 Taking Care of Business: The Economics of Crime by Heroin Abusers. Lexington, Mass.: Lexington Books.

JOHNSTON, LLOYD D., PATRICK M. O'MALLEY, AND JERROLD G. BACHMAN
1985 Use of Licit and Illicit Drugs by America's High School Students: 1975–1984. Rockville, Md.: National Institute on Drug Abuse.

KEISER, R. LINCOLN
1969 The Vice Lords: Warriors of the Street. New York: Holt, Rinehart & Winston.

KLEIN, MALCOLM W.
1969 Gang cohesiveness, delinquency, and a street-work program. Journal of Research in Crime and Delinquency 6:135–166.
1971 Street Gangs and Street Workers. Englewood Cliffs, N.J.: Prentice-Hall.
1985 Gang involvement in cocaine rock trafficking. Grant application to the National Institute of Justice. University of Southern California, Social Science Research Institute, Los Angeles.

KLEIN, MALCOLM W. AND LOIS Y. CRAWFORD
1967 Groups, gangs, and cohesiveness. Journal of Research in Crime and Delinquency 4:63–75.

KLEIN, MALCOLM W. AND CHERYL L. MAXSON
1989 Street gang violence. In Marvin E. Wolfgang and Neil A. Weiner (eds.), Violent Crime, Violent Criminals. Newbury Park, Calif.: Sage.

KLEIN, MALCOLM W., CHERYL L. MAXSON, AND LEA CUNNINGHAM
1988 Gang Involvement in Cocaine Rock Trafficking. Final Report to the National Institute of Justice. Social Science Research Institute. Los Angeles: University of Southern California.

LAUB, JOHN
1983 Urbanism, race and crime. Journal of Research in Crime and Delinquency 20:183–198.

LAUB, JOHN AND MICHAEL J. HINDELANG
1981 Juvenile Criminal Behavior in Urban, Suburban, and Rural Areas. Washington, D.C.: Office of Juvenile Justice and Delinquency Prevention.

MAXSON, CHERYL L., AND MALCOLM W. KLEIN
1983 Gangs: Why we couldn't stay away. In James Kleugel (ed.), Evaluating Juvenile Justice. Beverly Hills, Calif.: Sage.

MAXSON, CHERYL L., MARGARET A. GORDON, AND MALCOLM W. KLEIN
1985 Differences between gang and non-gang homicides. Criminology 23:209–222.

MIECZKOWSKI, THOMAS
1986 Geeking up and throwing down: Heroin street life in Detroit. Criminology 24:645–666.

MILLER, WALTER B.
1975 Violence by Youth Gangs and Young Groups as a Crime Problem in Major American Cities. Report to the National Institute for Juvenile Justice and Delinquency Prevention. Washington, D.C.: U.S. Department of Justice.

MOORE, JOAN W.
1978   Home Boys. New Brunswick, N.J.: Rutgers University Press.

MORASH, MERRY
1983   Gangs, groups and delinquency. British Journal of Criminology 23:309–331.

PENNELL, SUSAN AND CHRISTINE CURTIS
1982   Juvenile Violence and Gang-Related Crimes. San Diego: San Diego Association of Governments.

PIPER, ELIZABETH S.
1985   Violent crime by juveniles: The lone wolf or the wolfpack? Paper presented at the annual meeting of the American Society of Criminology, San Diego.

RECKTENWALD, WILLIAM AND NATHANIEL SHEPPARD, JR.
1984   Series on youth gangs in Chicago. Chicago Tribune, July 29 and 30, 1984.

REISS, ALBERT J., JR.
1986   Co-offending influences on criminal careers. In Alfred Blumstein, Jacqueline Cohen, Jeffrey A. Roth, and Christy A. Visher (eds.), Career Criminals and Criminal Careers. Vol. 2. Washington, D.C.: National Academy Press.

SAMPSON, ROBERT J.
1986   Crime in cities: The effects of formal and informal social control. In Albert J. Reiss, Jr., and Michael Tonry (eds.), Crime and Justice: An Annual Review of Research. Vol. 8. Communities and Crime. Chicago: University of Chicago Press.
1987   Urban Black violence: The effect of male joblessness and family disruption. American Journal of Sociology 93(2):348–382.

SCHWENDINGER, HERMAN AND JULIA SCHWENDINGER
1985   Adolescent Subcultures and Delinquency. New York: Praeger.

SHANNON, LYLE W.
1984   The Development of Serious Criminal Careers and the Delinquent Neighborhood. Office of Juvenile Justice and Delinquency Prevention. Washington, D.C.: U.S. Department of Justice.

SHAW, CLIFFORD R. AND HENRY D. MCKAY
1943   Juvenile Delinquency in Urban Areas. Chicago: University of Chicago Press.

SHORT, JAMES F. AND FRED L. STRODTBECK
1965   Group Process and Gang Delinquency. Chicago: University of Chicago Press.

SPERGEL, IRVING A.
1966   Street Gang Work: Theory and Practice. Reading Mass.: Addison-Wesley.
1984   Violent gangs in Chicago: In search of social policy. Social Service Review June: 199–226.
1989   Youth gangs: Continuity and change. In Norval Morris and Michael Tonry (eds.), Crime and Justice: An Annual Review of Research. Vol. 12. Chicago: University of Chicago Press.

SPSS, INC.
1988   SPSS-X Users Guide, 3rd ed. Chicago: SPSS, Inc.

STUMPHAUZER, JEROME S., ESTEBAN V. VELOZ, AND THOMAS W. AIKEN
1981   Violence by street gangs: East side story? In Robert B. Stuart (ed.), Violent Behavior: Social Learning Approaches to Prediction, Management, and Treatment. New York: Brunner-Mazel.

SUTTLES, GERALD D.
1968   The Social Order of the Slum. Chicago: University of Chicago Press.

THIO, ALEX
1983 Deviant Behavior. 2nd ed. Boston: Houghton Muffin.

THRASHER, FREDERICK M.
1927   The Gang: A Study of One Thousand Three Hundred Thirteen Gangs in Chicago. Chicago: University of Chicago Press.

TRACY, PAUL E.
1979   Subcultural Delinquency: A Comparison of the Incidence and Seriousness of Gang and Nongang Member Offensivity. Center for Studies in Criminology and Criminal Law. Philadelphia: University of Philadelphia.

TRACY, PAUL E. AND ELIZABETH S. PIPER
1984   Gang membership and violent offending: Preliminary results from the 1958 cohort study. Paper presented at the annual meeting of the American Society of Criminology, Cincinnati.

VIGIL, JAMES DIEGO
1988   Barrio Gangs. Austin: University of Texas Press.

WEIS, JOSEPH G. AND JOHN SEDERSTROM
1981   The Prevention of Serious Delinquency: What to Do? Washington, D.C.: Government Printing Office.

WHITE, HELENE R., ROBERT J. PANDINA, AND RANDY L. LAGRANGE
1987   Longitudinal predictors of serious substance abuse and delinquency. Criminology 25(3):715–740.

WHYTE, WILLIAM F.
1943   Street Corner Society. Chicago: University of Chicago Press.

WILSON, WILLIAM J.
1987   The Truly Disadvantaged. Chicago: University of Chicago Press.

WISH, ERIC D. AND BRUCE D. JOHNSON
1986   The impact of substance abuse on criminal careers. In Alfred Blumstein, Jacqueline Cohen, Jeffrey A. Roth, and Christy A. Visher (eds.), Criminal Careers and Career Criminals. Vol. 2. Washington, D.C.: National Academy Press.

WOLFGANG, MARVIN E., ROBERT M. FIGLIO, AND THORSTEN SELLIN
1972   Delinquency in a Birth Cohort. Chicago: University of Chicago Press.

YABLONSKY, LEWIS
1963   The Violent Gang. New York: Macmillan.

QUESTIONS FOR DISCUSSION

1. Discuss the common characteristics of drug use and drug dealing among juvenile gangs.

2. List and describe the four types of gangs identified by Fagan.

3. Explain the social organization of gangs.

4. What are the social processes that reflect gang cohesion?

5. What social conditions cause gangs to isolate themselves into their own closed social system?

APPLICATIONS

1. Were there any identifiable juvenile gangs or groups of kids in your high school that hung out or ran together? Which of these groups were regularly violating the law? In what ways did these gangs or groups violate the law?

2. You have been asked to provide recommendations that will reduce gang involvement and drug use among teenagers. Based on the information and research in this article, what would you recommend?

KEY TERMS

anomaly something different, abnormal, or peculiar.

atrophy degeneration or progressive decline.

contingent dependent on or conditioned by something else.

endemic characteristic of or peculiar to a defined area, locality, or social grouping.

inextricable incapable of being disentangled, untied, or disconnected.

inured accepting something that is undesirable.

iterative partitioning a statistical procedure whereby repeated dividing of categories using a sequence of operations yields results successively closer to the desired results.

mediate to interpose or come between two parties or entities for the purpose of reconciliation.

ossification the process of becoming rigidly conventional and opposed to change.

reify to regard something abstract as a material or concrete entity.

truncated when something is cut short or curtailed.

validity the state of something being well grounded, justifiable, or logically correct.

20

Girls, Guys, and Gangs:
The Changing Social Context
of Female Delinquency

Peggy C. Giordano

The historic and widely held assumption that delinquency was predominantly masculine in gender has had important implications both in the kind of theoretical work which has dominated the delinquency literature as well as in the continued choice of males as preferred subjects of empirical research. Psychological or "personal problems" explanations have generally been marshalled to explain female delinquency. It has also been assumed that sexual offenses, incorrigibility and "running away" make up the delinquent repertoire of girls, and that their involvement in more serious offenses is quite limited.

Even when sociological variables have been studied they have typically been interpreted within a psychological framework. For example, while it is widely recognized that coming from a broken home is related to a higher incidence of delinquency, this variable is thought to have an even greater impact in the case of girls. Studies show a more profound sense of loneliness and low self-esteem in girls who have a poor home life[1] or even a psychological reaction against the absent or inadequate father.[2]

Other studies may include social variables, but nevertheless perpetuate the conception that female delinquency is primarily an adaptation to personal problems. These studies deal with the theory, which was first suggested by Cohen,[3] that delinquency in females may be associated with a girl's inability to establish a good relationship with the opposite sex. While for males, long range goals center around achieving success and acquiring material possessions, the primary goal for females is thought to be "catching a man." Thus, the classic Mertonian model, if somewhat stripped of its structural components, can then be applied to understanding female delinquency (usually sexual in character) as a form of "innovation."[4]

The bulk of literature, then, has perpetuated the notion that personal maladjustments characterize the female delinquent—she must have a psychological problem, be unable to adequately perform her proper sex role, or suffer from the ill effects of a bad home life. The recent large increases in both the *number* of adjudicated females and the apparent increased *versatility* of their involvement in crimes, make it far more difficult to account for all female crime in such purely psychological terms. For example, between 1960 and 1973 the arrest rate of females under eighteen years of age increased 265% for all offenses, 393% for violent crimes and 334% for property crimes. This contrasts with increases of 124%, 236% and 82% respectively for males in the same age bracket.[5]

"Girls, Guys, and Gangs: The Changing Social Context of Female Delinquency," *Journal of Criminal Law and Criminology*, 69:1 (1978), pp. 126–132. Reprinted by permission of the author.

Explaining the Increase: Women's Liberation?

A ready explanation for understanding females' involvement and, in particular, these rapidly rising official delinquency statistics is provided by "women's liberation."

Freda Adler's book, *Sisters in Crime*,[6] is one work which suggests a rather direct link between sex role changes and increased delinquency. While this work is important in suggesting changes at various levels of society which may be having an impact on female behavior, these ideas are obscured somewhat by an overall ideological stance which has been taken in relation to the problem. Adler sees the rising crime rate as part of the price society must pay for greater involvement by females at all levels. Women are demanding a bigger piece of the illegitimate as well as the legitimate action. While she does not go so far as to suggest that these women are aligned with the movement itself, casting her argument from a feminist perspective nevertheless imputes "feminst" or "liberated" motives to the criminals.

> Like her legitimate-based sister, the female criminal knows too much to pretend or return to her former role as a second rate criminal confined to "feminine" crimes such as shoplifting and prostitution. She has had a taste of financial victory. In some cases, she has had a taste of blood. Her appetite, however, appears to be only whetted.[7]

We would argue that, important as these sex role changes are, it is a mistake and an oversimplification to suggest such a direct link between the "liberation" of females and increased involvement in crimes. This implies a degree of politicization and commitment on the part of the criminals to which she simply may not adhere. It appears, from what we know about the impact of social movements on various segments of society, that not only is it erroneous to suggest any kind of overt politicization on the part of most female criminals, but it is also an oversimplification to accord any kind of causal, delinquency-inducing status to most attitudinal changes generally associated with the movement. At the very least, recent empirical work demonstrates the necessity for viewing sex role orientation or "liberation" as multi-dimensional and finds a negligible or even negative association between certain indices of liberation and reported delinquency involvement.[8]

Alternative Explanations: Theories of Male Delinquency

In attempting to understand recent changes in female crime patterns, then, it is perhaps more useful to conceive of these women and girls as *recipients* of the effects of broad based as well as micro-level societal changes, rather than themselves being responsible for a new era of sex role equality. We should begin to focus on the ways in which broader changes have filtered down to the point where they have affected the everyday social world of adolescent and particularly lower status girls so that delinquency is one normal outcome. A re-examination of traditionally male theories of delinquency locates particular factors which have generally been associated with delinquent activities on the part of males. To the extent that there have been social changes in the lives of females in these same areas, we should be able to understand and predict increases in female delinquent activity as well.

Aside from labeling and conflict theories which might be invoked to explain recent changes in official *response* to female deviance, control theory, opportunity theory and differential association (or other variations which have emphasized the importance of friendship networks) all implicitly suggest factors which could account for behavioral changes on the part of females. Hirschi's control perspective, which emphasized the notion that delinquency becomes possible when attachment to societal bonds are weakened, has obvious relevance to changing female behavior patterns.[9] Females have traditionally been more protected by and attached to conventional institutions, *i.e.*, school, family, church.[10] A weakening of these bonds to allow a wider range of behavior generally creates new opportunities where deviance is one possibility. Cloward and Ohlin's classic formulation of Delinquency and Opportunity Theory highlights the fact that opportunity in the legitimate as well as the illegitimate arenas is differentially available.[11] A relaxing of curfew and other tight constraints on females creates a whole host of situational contexts in which delinquency may occur (*e.g.*, driving around in a car, going to local hangouts, going to bars "unescorted"). This should have particular relevance in understanding increases in crimes such as drinking, vandalism or drug use where situational factors assume such a crucial role. Jensen and Eve did examine the impact of control variables on female involvement in delinquency, and while such factors were associated with it, they did not completely account for male-female differences.[12] Unfortunately, their use of a sample obtained in 1964–65 may limit the ability to generalize their findings to present day patterns.

However, perhaps most crucial to an understanding of female participation in minor as well as more serious crimes is the role of the *peer group* in transmitting definitions favorable to the violation of law. The importance of group influence on male involvement in delinquency has been amply demonstrated in classic research studies.[13] But the peer group continues to be important in more recent studies. For example, Hirschi's own findings, though emphasizing control variables, suggest the importance of peer influences.[14] The assumption has been that these friendship networks are nonexistent or at least not as important in the lives of adolescent girls. This may have always been a somewhat inaccurate view of the social world of adolescent girls,[15] but clearly peer associations must assume a central role in any attempt to understand recent changing patterns of delinquency involvement. Increases in casual cross-sex socializing (not on a dating basis) could provide reinforcement for behaviors which are illegal, as well as provide opportunities for learning more specifics about some kinds of delinquency. This initial learning may occur in connection with males, but it is hypothesized that there would also be a slowly developing tradition of delinquency among female peers as well. Thus, important changes may be occurring not only because girls are being increasingly exposed to delinquent behavior by

learning about it, but also because of their perception that there would be peer approval for their engaging in unlawful behavior. It is suggested that at the very least the more delinquent, aggressive girls are receiving some kind of reference group support from other females, and possibly from other reference groups as well. This is contrasted with the traditional situation where girls may have curtailed their behavior in part because of concern over what the other girls thought, or because their boyfriends would disapprove.

This article presents the results of a study which examines (in the tradition of countless male-based research efforts) the role of the peer group in understanding the nature of female delinquency. It is hypothesized that it is within the everyday social context of the friendship or gang networks that we can see perhaps the greatest evidence of change, and that these changing peer associations will have a more immediate impact on female crime patterns than that evidenced by any kind of ideological or attitudinal liberation.

STUDY

Methodology

The focus of the present study is largely descriptive. It is concerned with the social context in which females participate in delinquent acts, their perception of the attitudes of others toward their violating the law and the association, if any, between the perceived acceptability of certain kinds of acts and actual involvement in delinquency. A longitudinal design would have been an ideal way to assess the extent of change in female friendship patterns; however, as discussed previously, the few early studies involving females tended to emphasize psychological variables. It is nevertheless thought to be important to determine, using a present day sample, what type of social network seems to be associated with high levels of delinquency involvement on the part of adolescent females. To accomplish this, questionnaires were administered to the total population at a state institution for juvenile offenders (N = 108), and to a comparable sample of eighty-three girls randomly selected from an urban high school in a predominantly lower status area. The high school sample was added to provide a wider range of delinquent involvement—primarily to increase the number who are more "law-abiding." The age range for the institutionalized sample was twelve to nineteen, with a mean age of seventeen; the range for the school sample was fourteen to nineteen, with a mean age of 17.3. Non-whites constituted 50.9% for the institutionalized sample. The school sample included 48.2% non-whites. One of the important limitations of the sample is that the girls came from lower socioeconomic status backgrounds (as indicated by the occupations they list for their parents/guardians) and hence, the findings to be reported cannot be generalized beyond this lower class sample.

A revised version of the Nye-Short self-admitted delinquency test[16] was used to measure the extent of the girls' involvement in delinquent activity. A split-half test for reliability yielded a coefficient of 0.95 for this scale.

Several items derived from the literature on male friendship networks and gangs were used in this study to measure the extent of peer group involvement. Two items were identical to the friendship questions used by Lerman[17] (*Question:* "When you are at home, who do you usually go around with?" *Answer:* Myself, one or two others, or a regular group. *Question:* "How much of your leisure time do you spend with friends?" *Answer:* All, most, or some). Several other single item indicators, which were more descriptive, were also included.

To determine whether changing definitions of what is "acceptable" behavior for females may be accounting for some increase in criminal activity, a series of questions were constructed concerning three reference groups that might be important to the girls. The girls were asked to indicate how various reference groups would react if they were to engage in certain kinds of activity. Three reference groups were selected: "Guys I run around with," "My boyfriend" and "Girls I run around with," realizing that there might be other important reference groups, such as parents. Behavioral items were chosen to rep-

resent independent kinds of actions, some of which might encourage delinquent activity (*e.g.,* "Staying out all night"), and others which were actually illegal (*e.g.,* "Using grass once in a while"). The items chosen dealt with behavior that was traditionally proscribed for females but that it is hypothesized, may be considered more acceptable or even "cool" by today's adolescent subculture. The questions were worded so that there would not be universal disapproval; for example, it is possible to envision approval for one of the items, "Beating up somebody nobody likes," as opposed to something like, "Murdering someone in cold blood." The specific items included were:

Beating up on somebody nobody likes.

Shoplifting.

Running away.

Staying out all night.

Stealing a car for a joy ride.

Making an obscene phone call.

Using a fake I.D. to get in a bar.

Tearing up school property.

Driving around with a bunch of kids.

Using grass once in a while.

Picking up guys.

Total "approval" scores for each reference group were obtained by summing the responses for all eleven items. The split-half reliability coefficient for these items using, "Guys I hang around with," as the reference group was 0.93, for girlfriends, 0.93, and for boyfriends, 0.94.

Results

It should perhaps first be noted that the sample of 108 incarcerated girls did produce a wide range of delinquent activities. One of the initial reasons for administering the questionnaire was to see if girls were indeed primarily involved with status offenses, incorrigibility, and the like, as depicted in the literature, or whether there were girls who had gotten involved in crimes typically considered "masculine." While most of the girls

TABLE 1 Percent of Institutionalized and School Sample Reporting Involvement (One or More Times) in "Serious Delinquent Acts"

	Institutionalized Sample (N = 108)		School Sample (N = 83)	
	N	%	N	%
Stealing items over $50	85	78.3	3	3.6
Taken part in gang fights	60	55.6	15	18.1
Carried a weapon, such as a gun or knife	86	79.6	22	26.4
Fought someone using a weapon	64	59.6	6	7.2
Breaking and entering	68	63.5	3	3.6
Used pills to get high	95	83.3	27	32.5
Tried heroin	47	43.5	1	1.2

in the institution had, in fact, committed many of the "traditional" female offenses (84.2% had run away from home one or more times, 65% had had sexual relations with someone they didn't know too well, and 99.1% had had sexual relations with someone they loved), there was evidence of significant involvement in more serious crimes as well. Table 1 lists the percentage of the sample of 108 girls who had been involved in crimes which had traditionally been considered "masculine" in character, as well as the involvement by girls in the school sample in these crimes.

In addition, 53.7% of the institutionalized group indicated that they had been part of a group of girls that could be called a "gang." Of these, 51.9% indicated that the gang had a name. The names of these gangs (*e.g.,* The Outlaws, the Cobras, Mojos, Loveless, Red Blood, White Knights, East Side Birds, Power) convey neither a particularly "feminine" image, nor suggest a subordinate position to a male gang.

Friendships and Delinquency

The first item which dealt with friendship patterns, "Who do you usually go around with?" had three possible responses—myself, one or two others, or a regular group. An analysis of variance was computed which indicated a statistically significant difference between groups. Those who were part of a regular group were more likely to be delinquent. For the white subsam-

ple, F = 11.65 (p < .001); for the black subsample, F = 4.62 (p < .01). The second item concerned the amount of leisure time spent with the group. A significant positive correlation was found between this variable and the extent of involvement in delinquency (r = .43, p < .001 for whites; r = .22, p < .01 for blacks). That is, the more leisure time spent in the group, the more likely a girl was to be delinquent. Similarly, those who indicated that they had been part of a group of girls that could be called a "gang" were more delinquent than those who said they had not been part of such a group (t = 5.17, p < .001 for whites, t = 3.32, p < .001 for blacks).[18]

The Context in Which Delinquent Acts Occur

In addition to the general association between group involvement and delinquency, which parallels the findings from most male based research studies, it was important to try to specify more clearly the actual social context in which females are likely to commit delinquent acts. Respondents were asked to indicate whether they were more likely to go out with a group of "guys and girls" or with just girls. For the whites, those who indicated they were more likely to go out in a group of guys and girls were significantly more delinquent than those who said they went out more often with girls only (t = 2.40, p < .05). For blacks, however, this question did not appear to differentiate delinquents from non-delinquents.

TABLE 2 **The Social Context in Which "Trouble" is Likely to Occur**

	White (N = 91)*		Blacks (N = 95)**	
	N	%	N	%
Group of girls	17	18.7	33	34.7
A group of guys and girls	25	27.5	21	22.1
A group of guys	28	30.8	15	15.8
One guy	5	5.5	10	10.5
One girlfriend	5	5.5		2.1
By self	8	8.8		12.6
	91		95	

* 3.3% missing data
** 2.1% missing data

In addition, subjects were asked, "When you are out in a group, who would be more likely to start the trouble—a guy or a girl?" While, as expected, most indicated that it would be a male (only 17.6% of the white girls thought a girl might start the trouble), 31.6% of the black girls thought it might be a girl who would be the one to start trouble.

Similarly, Table 2 presents the distribution of responses to an item which asked subject, "Who are you more likely to be with when you get into trouble?" An examination of this table suggests that for whites, "a group of guys" or "guys and girls" provides the social context in which "trouble" will most often occur. While this pattern exists in the black subsample as well, there is a higher percentage of black females that indicated that trouble would be more likely to occur with a group of girls. It should also be noted that an analysis of a different sample group showed that in terms of whom girls actually reported being with when committing particular offenses, the model category was clearly a group of "guys and girls."[19] While this differed somewhat by the nature of the offense, (i.e., it was more likely in the case of robbery (52.7%) or vandalism (54.1%), than for minor theft (28.5%)), and as shown here, by race, it is evident that association with males is somehow tied with many females becoming involved in delinquent acts. It is interesting, however, that this does not *appear* to represent a simple case of the girl adopting a passive role in going along with her boyfriend,

as earlier depictions of the female criminal might lead us to predict.[20] This picture of the girl negatively influenced by the boy with whom she is romantically involved is challenged somewhat by the low percentage of both black and white respondents who felt that trouble would most likely occur with "one guy." Findings regarding the girls' perceptions of how significant others would react if they were involved in various delinquent acts further complicate this image.

Changing Definitions of What Is Acceptable Behavior for Adolescent Girls

Table 3 presents the composite approval scores. This score represents the degree of approval or disapproval the girl thought she would receive from various reference groups if she were to engage in certain behavior. A comparison of the mean scores shows that, in both the white and black subsamples, the highest approval for engaging in these illegal activities came from other girlfriends. Looking at the other reference groups, girls making up the white subsample perceived the least amount of approval from their boyfriends. This lends additional evidence that these girls are not simply following the dictates of a lover when committing delinquent acts. The picture is, however, more complicated in the black subsample. The highest approval score again comes from other girls. However, while the mean approval is lower for

TABLE 3   Reference Group Support for Delinquency and Its Relationship to Actual Self-Reported Involvement (N = 191)

	Mean Approval	Association With Delinquent Activity		Mean Approval	Association With Delinquent Activity	
	White	r	p	Blacks	r	p
Girls I hang around with	29.38	.33	.001	27.00	.29	.01
Guys I hang around with	26.97	.01	.42	24.74	.24	.01
Boyfriend	22.74	.02	.43	26.15	.18	.05

the boyfriend (t = .33 α < N.S.), the gap between the reference groups is narrower. A computation of $E^{2\,21}$ produced a value of 0.86 for the white subsample, 0.23 for the black subsample. This statistic indicates that a much higher percentage of the variance in scores is accounted for by the degree of approval or disapproval from various reference groups in the white subsample as compared to the black subsample. This suggests, then, that the black girls in this sample did not differentiate as sharply between how male and female friends would view their behavior. Also, the meaning of the relatively higher approval score from the boyfriend should be interpreted with some caution, due to the very high variance in that category among black respondents (s^2 = 463.77). This is contrasted with a variance on the girlfriend scales of 174.50, and 201.49 for the male friends scale. Thus, while there may be strong approval by *some* boyfriends, the high variance points to the existence of some girls within this group who perceived much less approval. It is hypothesized that at least some of the girls who thought the boyfriend would be approving may have been thinking of "pimps" when answering those items.

The correlation between the perception of approval from other reference groups and actual delinquency involvement is also presented in Table 3. There are significant correlations, for both black and white subsamples, between extent of approval from other *girlfriends* and actual participation in delinquency. There is also a significant correlation between perception of approval of male friends (r = .24 α <.01) and a weak but significant correlation between a boyfriend's

approval and delinquency in the black subsample (r = .18, α < .05).

The findings regarding the relative importance of *female* approval are interesting, particularly when compared with the earlier findings (see Table 2) that females are quite likely to commit offenses within the context of mixed sex groups. At first this appears to be a contradiction: specifically, that where the whites were more likely to be with males, there does not appear in the white sample to be an important association between approval from males and actual participation in delinquent activity.

However, one possible interpretation of these results is that interaction with males, particularly in a non-romantic way, simply affords the most propitious environment in which girls will *learn* about as well as actually engage in delinquent acts. This does not have to mean that boys are coaxing them into this activity, or that approval from them is a necessary prerequisite. Just as the same sex peer group has offered a source of status and approval in the case of male delinquents, it appears that approval from other girlfriends will also accompany a girl's decision to become involved in delinquent activity.

It could be argued that this approval would be an even greater necessity for girls since their behavior is not as much a part of an established tradition. Therefore, the girls who *do* become involved in delinquency would be likely to first feel that girls in general and themselves in particular are capable of committing certain behavior, that others *like them* (girls) also probably engage in it, and that these girls are not likely to regard them with disdain if they were to engage in that behavior themselves.

SUMMARY AND CONCLUSION

The findings from the present research, which point to an important link between friendship patterns and delinquent involvement, cast further doubt on the assumption that female delinquency represents some kind of personal maladaptation. Rather, for both the white and black subsamples, there was a significant association between group affiliation and self-reported delinquency. Especially in the case of white females, a closer examination of the actual makeup of such friendship networks suggests that groups which include both males and females were particularly conducive to delinquency. Due to the more established tradition of male participation in illegal acts it is likely that girls would, at least to some extent, be learning delinquent modes of behavior from males. This would be particularly important in instances in which there is some technical knowledge involved in committing the act. More research is needed on the particular ways in which association with males exerts this delinquent influence. The pattern *appears* to be more complex than the notion that the boyfriend simply uses the female in an "accomplice" or other passive role while he commits the crime. One index of this is that "trouble" is likely to occur in *groups* which include both males and females. Also, further research should address the important racial differences suggested by this exploratory study; for example, in the black subsample there was a somewhat greater likelihood that "trouble" could involve a group of girls alone. This could represent a difference in the kinds of constraints which may have traditionally been placed on white as compared to black adolescent females. To the extent that the black female has had a longer tradition of independence and freedom of action than has her white counterpart, the less likely it seems that the black female would need to learn techniques, values and motives from "the guys."

Finally, while there were some differences in the social context of black and white participation in delinquency, it was found that for both subsamples the perception of approval from other girlfriends was significantly correlated with actual delinquency involvement. This suggests what may be a crucial element of change. While it is unlikely that girls are or will become immune to what the boys think of their behavior, it is likely that *other girls* are the most important reference group, or at least the group to which they compare themselves. This would be consistent with male subculture theories which have documented the important status-conferring, delinquency inducing influence of the same sex peer group. Girls appear to be no different in this respect.

Notes

1. G. Konopka, *The Adolescent Girl in Conflict* (1966).

2. Barker, Gordon & Adams, *Comparison of the Delinquencies of Boys and Girls*, 53 J. Crim. L.C. & P.S. 470 (1962).

3. A. Cohen, *Delinquent Boys: The Culture of the Gang* (1955).

4. Two researchers have directly tested this theory, but they found that their delinquent sample actually perceived fewer obstacles to marital goals than the control group. *See* Sandhu & Allen, *Female Delinquency: Goal Obstruction and Anomie*, 6 *Can. Rev. Soc. & Anthropology* 107 (1969). And one researcher found that delinquents reported more dates than the non-delinquent sample, but attempted to explain the difference by reference to the "quality" of the dates the delinquents were able to obtain or the sexual favors they may have had to "bestow" in order to get the dates. *See* Morris, *Female Delinquency and Relational Problems*, 43 *Soc. Forces* 82 (1964). Morris also compared the difference in the observers, rating of facial features, figure and grooming between delinquents and non-delinquents but found significant differences only in terms of grooming. *Id.* The importance of this finding, however, is tempered when one considers that the inferior degree of cleanliness and neatness reported may simply be a reflection of middle class interviewer standards and the result may have little to do with the criteria by which boys and girls judge each other as acceptable dating partners.

5. Federal Bureau of Investigation, *Uniform Crime Reports* (Table 28) (1973). The problems with official statistics are well known; however, a recent comparison of self-reported delinquency involvement by girls incarcerated at a state institution in 1960, with the level of involvement reported by a comparable 1975 sample indicates significantly greater involvement in almost every offense category by the 1975 subjects. *See* P. Giordano & S. Cernkovich, Changing Patterns of Female Delinquency (August 30, 1976) (unpublished paper presented at the Annual Meeting of the Society for the Study of Social Problems in New York).

6. F. Adler, *Sisters in Crime: The Rise of the New Female Criminal* (1975).

7. *Id.* at 15.

8. P. Giordano & S. Cernkovich, On Complicating the Relationship Between Liberation and Delinquency (August 11, 1977) (unpublished paper presented at the Annual Meeting of the International Sociological Association Research Committee for the Sociology of Deviance and Social Control, in Dublin, Ireland).

9. *See* T. Hirschi, *Causes of Delinquency* (1969).

10. *See* Parsons, *Age and Sex in the Social Structure of the United States*, 7 Amer. Soc. Rev. 604 (1942).

11. *See* R. Cloward & L. Ohlin, *Delinquency and Opportunity: A Theory of Delinquent Gangs* (1960).

12. *See* Jensen & Eve, *Sex Differences in Delinquency: An Examination of Popular Sociological Explanations*, 13 Criminology 427 (1976).

13. *See* C. Shaw & H. McKay, *Juvenile Delinquency and Urban Areas* (1969); E. Sutherland, *Principles of Criminology* (1934); F. Thrasher, *The Gang* (2d ed. 1936); Cohen & Short, *Research in Delinquent Subcultures*, 14 J. Soc. Issues 20 (1958); Miller, *Lower Class Culture as a Generating Milieu of Gang Delinquency*, 14 J. Soc. Issues 5 (1958).

14. T. Hirschi, *supra* note 9. *See also* R. Akers, *Deviant Behavior: A Social Learning Approach* (1973); Conger, *Social Control & Social Learning Models of Delinquent Behavior*, 14 *Criminology* 17 (1976).

15. In fact, the more general literature on adolescence supports this view. *See* J. Coleman, *The Adolescent Society* (1961); Curtis, *Adolescent Orientations Toward Peers: Variations by Sex, Age and Socioeconomic Status*, 40 *Adolescence* 483 (1975).

16. Nye & Short, *Scaling Delinquent Behavior*, 22 Amer. Soc. Rev. 326 (1957).

17. Lerman, *Gangs, Networks and Subculture Delinquency*, 73 *Amer. J. Soc.* 63 (1967).

18. Similar results for these and subsequent tests were also obtained when the social and institutional samples were computed separately.

19. P. Giordano & S. Cernkovich, *supra* note 8.

20. *See, e.g.*, National Institute of Mental Health, *The Contemporary Woman and Crime*, Public Health Service Pub. No. 161 1975), which suggests: "They have worked under the direction and guidance of men who have been their lovers, husbands, or pimps." *Id.* at 3–4.

21. *See* H. Blalock, *Social Statistics* (2nd ed. 1972).

QUESTIONS FOR DISCUSSION

1. Unlike their male counterparts, explanations for female delinquents have focused primarily on maladaptive behavior or "personal problems." Why is this the case? Provide examples to support your response.

2. Some have argued that as the women's liberation movement expanded, more women moved into traditionally male-dominated roles, both legitimate and illegitimate. Thus, more female delinquency. Giordano argues that this explanation of female delinquency is overly simplistic. Why?

3. Discuss female delinquency and friendship patterns.

APPLICATIONS

1. Giordano suggests that the important reference group for girls is the same-sex peer group. There is evidence that this is also true for boys. Why?

2. According to this article, tendencies toward delinquency are higher in peer groups where both sexes are present. Why? Cite examples from your experiences in high school. Were there any particular groups that were more delinquent than others? Describe the group(s).

KEY TERMS

analysis of variance a statistical technique to analyze data from a randomized design; uses the F-test to determine if there is a significant difference between two or more independent groups.

propitious refers to something being advantageous or conducive.

reference group any social group used by an individual as a standard for evaluating his or her behavior.

repertoire a set of skills, devices, or behaviors that are repeatedly used in social interactions.

21

Players and Ho's

Terry Williams

William Kornblum

I don't exactly fill out a W2 form after I turn a trick.—*Margo Sharp*

Cooksey's, D's Inferno, Club 437, McDonald's, and the mall are familiar hangouts for teenagers in Louisville. The mall is located in downtown Louisville; although it is integrated, it is a meeting place for black youth from all over the city. Many of the teenagers hustle in the pool rooms and discos, peddling marijuana and sex.

For the young women, hustling is synonymous with prostitution. Indeed, in all the cities we studied, prostitution is the main occupation for girls in the underground economy—girls like Donna White, who hustles in Louisville's mall area.

I am 19 years old. About two years ago my parents moved to a little town called Madisonville, Kentucky. I hated that place. But I stayed long enough to finish school at Norman Hopkins [High School]. I wanted to go places and see different things and not stay in that damn place. I wanted to make something out of myself so I left and came here to Louisville. I couldn't find no job for nine months here so I met up with some friends who told me I could hustle and make some money. They said they would show me how. All I had to do was learn.

"Players and Ho's," *Growing Up Poor* (New York: Lexington Books, 1985), pp. 61–72. Reprinted by permission of Lexington Books, an imprint of Macmillan Publishing Company. Copyright © 1985 by Lexington Books.

So I first started hustling in the pool rooms and pushing a few petty drugs. My boyfriend and/or his friend would stand in the pool room or out in the hall and wait till they saw some men, soldiers, businessmen, or whatever, and ask them if they wanted to have some sex. If they said yes, he would steer them over to the pool room and then tell me where to go meet them.

In the Hough district of Cleveland, dilapidated, burned-out structures from the 1960s riots are still visible. The housing consists mainly of single-family units. It is odd to see so many old houses, many in the grand style, decaying, unpainted, and broken. Hough is the ghetto of Cleveland. Its citizens, black and white alike, seem helpless to change it. The community is bankrupt economically, politically, and socially. Many feel that Hough is being punished for the "sins" it committed in the 1960s.

Pearl Varnedoe has worked as a prostitute in the Hough area and downtown near the University of Cleveland since she was fourteen. Pearl left home in order to "make money and live free." She says hustling came easily to her because "my parents had a club that always had pimps, whores, and gamblers in it."

My mother was always beating me. My father tried to make her stop but he couldn't. My mother was always drunk and she couldn't stop that either. My father ran this after-hours club and when I left home I met up with some of them from his joint and they turned me out [set me up as a prostitute]. I always had real big titties and a nice body. As a matter of fact, the vice squad know me on sight and arrest me sometimes just to have something to do. I've been arrested about 21 times. They never knew I was a minor during all the time I spent there. When I went home to check on my father, I found out my mother had been beating my brothers and sisters too. Our neighbor had called in a child-abuse worker to talk to her, she told me she knew about my being on the street and filed a delinquency report with the juvenile authorities.

In Meridian, Mississippi, a large naval base on the outskirts of town has created a thriving market for drugs and sex. Thus the young people in Meridian perceive numerous opportunities in the illegal economy. The young men between the ages of 16 and 20 are the players or pimps, and the young women between the ages of 13 and 20 are the prostitutes—making prostitution the main source of illegal income for youths. Teenagers like Curly and his girls make up the "supply side" of prostitution in Meridian.

Curly is eighteen years old. His hustle is young women. He's a "player" and they are "ho's" or "tricks." (In Meridian "trick" refers to the prostitute or seller of sex; in New York the converse is true—"trick" refers to the buyer of sex.)

I have one or two girls on the street. I still got a couple of them doing things for me. You know I gotta have that paper [money]. The only rule I have is that my main lady don't go out there. The others I have them boosting, tricking, whatever, as long as they keep giving up the money. See, baby, you do what you have to do to survive in this world now. The more money they have, the more I have. They do what they want to to get it. And when I ask them for it, I get it. Sometimes I'll help out if I get hip to someone who wants to make a buy. I'll let them know. But it depends on how much they get and how much I need. But I don't take all of their money. I usually leave them a little. And I don't feel I'm responsible for putting no ho on the street. Look, they are out there trying to be grown. They put themselves out there. If I didn't take their money, they would give it to someone else. Them tricks ain't gonna be

nothing but whores. All I did was fuck them a couple of times and they started giving me money. See, a woman doesn't have to sell her body for a man to pimp her. There are plenty of women that are smart and pretty with good jobs and taking care of men. That's pimping.

Among Curly's "tricks" are Maylee Jones, Clara Thompson, and Dorothea Caddy, aged sixteen, sixteen, and seventeen, respectively. Here's what they have to say about "the life":

Maylee: There ain't no jobs around here. Besides I can make more money doing this. Sometimes I make one hundred or two, sometimes more, sometimes less. If I had a job, I wouldn't make that much. If I could make as much money in a job as I do hustling, I would work. The Navy boys they spend a lot of money. All these old white men do too. Anyway around here they give all the good jobs to the white people.

The most important thing in my life right now is surviving. That's all I believe in. Well, I believe in God but not preachers 'cause all the preachers do is ride around in Cadillacs and wear silk suits.

Clara: I have four boyfriends who give me $15 a week to go to bed with them. I only go out with one of them. The money I get I just spend it on clothes and stuff to get high with. I don't like to do it too much. I think it might do something to me. All the men are young, in their 20s. I give them a bit here and there but they give me the money on time. I like to show my legs and breast. It fascinates me to watch men cream.

Dorothea: I started tricking because I didn't know what time it was. I was at a friend's house getting high and they said, hey, you want to turn a trick for someone? And I said, it depends on the cash, what time, and who. At that time, I needed the money, you know. My boyfriend was there and I didn't know he was no pimp. But he kept encouraging me to do it. Anyway, after that I set my own thing up with one of my girlfriends. I have them [johns] call her. I used to have them call my pimp till I got rid of him. He got mad, but he knew I could fight him if he tried some shit like hitting on me. I didn't need him anymore, you know. I only had him for protection and the first time I went to jail for fighting, the man was out of town. I would make $150 or so and put $75 back and show him the rest, and he would give me $25 of that plus what I had, you know. He didn't know what time it was.

Dorothea dropped out of school in the ninth grade. At seventeen she organized a group of teenage prostitutes and set up a brothel in a fashionable black section of town.

Young women in each of these cities—and in New York as well—are shocked and depressed by the bleakness of their situation. Many do not believe they have a choice between getting a job and hustling. Hustling—meaning prostitution—is the only choice. (Theft and prostitution are often combined, but prostitution is by far the easiest, most convenient, and most profitable form of illegal activity for these teenagers.)

Most girls are recruited into prostitution, but some are tricked, coerced, or charmed into the life. The latter are talked into believing that it is an exciting life complete with fine cars and endless amounts of money. There is a note of self-delusion in some of their comments, like "A lot of the men are lonely and I feel I can help them" or "Most of the time the tricks don't know what time it is, so you can get their money."

While there are adult role models and community institutions that try to steer teenagers away from the life, many find the incentives too strong. Margo Sharp's life as a prostitute in Harlem illustrates the careers young women pursue in the underground economy.

Margo's parents separated when she was four years old. Her mother remarried, and during the ensuing years her father made sporadic appearances. When Margo was twelve or thirteen her mother became embroiled in domestic problems with her stepfather. Arguments and fights were common. Margo's mother began to have relationships with other men, including some of her husband's friends. One of those men had a traumatic impact on Margo.

> My mother had an affair with this man who was later to become my stepfather. Well, he had this friend, best friend no less, who was this little horny Dominican motherfucker. I was 12 years old then and I knew about sex and all of that, although I had never had sex. He would come around the house all the time and even though my mother was seeing my stepfather, this guy would come over sometimes and they would laugh and drink and my stepfather would leave them alone sometimes because he trusted his friend so much. Well, my mother and this little Dominican started to have a thing behind my stepfather's back. And this little motherfucker was so horny, he wound up fucking my mother's best friend too.
>
> Anyhow, one day I was upstairs doing my homework and he comes into my room and tells me he wants to talk to me. I don't remember if anybody was home or not that day, but I assumed he was gonna talk about my mother and their little thing, you know. So he told me to sit on the bed next to him. And I did. Still not thinking anything about it. Well the next thing I know he's taking my blouse off. And all the time he's asking me if I feel anything. Well I don't know why I didn't scream or anything but I just sat there. After he had taken off my panties, the only thought I had in my mind was not to panic. Not to scream because I had read all about how men had killed women and kids molesting them or something, and I wasn't about to say a thing. So he took off my panties and the only thing that stood out in my mind was how big he was. It seemed like he was as big as a tree trunk, I swear to God, I was hurting so bad, I was so sore. I felt, my God, what did he do to me? Well, when it was over, he helped me put back on my clothes and I sat on the bed for a long time just thinking.
>
> I never told my mother anything for two years. And when I did her reaction was typical of women in love. She slapped me. She thought I was lying for years after I told her this. She didn't believe nothing I told her. One day two years later this little bastard drove up to my house to see my mother. Well my mother told me to come out and say hello to him. But I was not too excited about seeing the little fucker ever again. So I refused. But she insisted so I went out to say hello. But when I saw his face I just got angry. The window of the car door was down. And he reached his face out to kiss me and I spat in it. My mother jerked me away and slapped me. But I grabbed her arm and told her I was no kid any more. I was 14 years old and that she had no reason to protect a man who had not only cheated on her by fucking her friend but had cheated on her by fucking her daughter. She didn't believe me. Like I said,

she thought I was lying. She was so in love with this faggot that she didn't believe her own daughter. I hated him for that more than his act against me because it made my relationship with my mother a stormy one for years to come.

Margo was fourteen then. Her mother was unwilling to assume responsibility for her wayward daughter, so she sent Margo to a social worker at the Children's Aid Society. After a series of bad experiences in a variety of schools, Margo finally dropped out. Considered gifted by her teachers, she could not make herself sit still long enough to complete her studies. Instead, she was habitually absent. Her lateness and absenteeism eventually resulted in expulsion.

Margo's attitudes about men were formed early. She was more game than most men could handle. Standing tall and shapely with big eyes and a warm, inquisitive intelligence, she was no child and knew it. After leaving school, she refused to work but always seemed to have money. Her mother occasionally asked her how she was able to get along without working, but Margo always had an explanation.

I would have $200, $300, $400 and my mother knew nothing about it. I wouldn't tell her where I had been. So half the time she didn't know. I didn't buy a lot of stuff or give her money because I was afraid she would ask me where I got it from. I tried to explain it to her one day. I told her a friend of hers, Mr. George, who was about 50 years old had hinted he wanted to have sex with me. So I jokingly told my mom that if he wanted it, it would cost him a hundred bucks. Well, she laughed and said, "Yeah, that's better than giving it to him for free." So in a way, I guess, she didn't really object to what I was doing.

By the time Margo was fifteen she was involved in casual prostitution, averaging two hundred dollars per customer. She was in the life as an "outlaw," that is, without benefit of a pimp. Her method was bit unorthodox. When a man approached her, she would take the money from the transaction and give it to one of her male friends.

Sometimes my friend would look at me funny when I told him to hold the cash. It would be a few hundred dollars. And that I would be back later. I would go to a hotel and after it was over I'd go back to pick up my money. If a guy approached me and said I was beautiful and asked how much would it cost him to have me, I would tell him whatever came to my mind. If he looked well dressed and clean I would say $200, $300, $400. It depended on my mood. If I was real horny, I would react quicker but that didn't mean the price went down. I would just choose someone who I thought was good looking. Someone who I thought would be pleasant to fuck. Sometimes I would get off with these guys but most of the time I would pretend.

At least some liked it enough to pay high prices for it. It started out with offers of $100 or more for an hour or two. When they first started asking me I would decline, and then decided to stop being such a fool. I started accepting, not only money, but gifts, trips, etc. It was sort of like getting your cake and eating it too. I was not only compensated for time, but I was spent time with as well. The sexual acts were sexual acts. But if they brought on a smile, a kiss or hug the morning after, it was worthwhile. I felt not only wanted but needed. At the same time, a lot of lonely hearts were warmed. Call it what you will, I see my actions in a benevolent light. I enjoyed the money, spending highly, indulging in things I wouldn't normally have. The gifts were sweet. They showed a touch more of consideration. The men were usually much older than myself. I, in some cases, portrayed a prized china doll that they flaunted.

Yes, I did get tired of the life at times, but it was an experience, and I learned a lot. I met some very interesting people. I always tried to establish a good rapport with my friends. One never knows who one may need some day. But only as friends. My intimate relationships were always kept separate and never came about from a trick night. It was difficult at times having both a main man and my pastime, but I managed. In some cases, where I felt the person I was dealing with was due more respect, I would cool off my friendly encounters and devote myself to that one person.

For young women like Margo, prostitution becomes a distinctive lifestyle, known as "the life." But for the pimps or players, hustling sex isn't very different from any other kind of hustle. The young man usually has tried a variety of ways of earning money, finally settling on pimping as involving the least effort for the greatest reward. Ray-Ray Southern is typical.

I came to Meridian when I was 11 years old. I went to Oakland Heights Elementary School in the fifth grade. I got along very well with the teachers. We caught the city bus every day to school. I got out of school one day by playing sick and stole a bicycle. I had to go by the babysitter's house to pick up my little sister and brother. They were very happy to see me. My momma came home by the babysitter's house and found out about the bicycle. She asked me where it was and I told her somewhere else, but I didn't know where. Momma took me home and whipped me. The police came and talked to me and we got over that.

About three weeks later our house caught on fire. My sister was smoking a cigarette and threw the butt on the floor. After the fire, we changed schools and I met the wrong type of friends. I had a fight the first day of school. Later on, I stole another bicycle and I didn't get caught. I began to turn out with this girl I was running with. We would do things like stealing, smoking, drinking, and breaking out people's windows.

Everything was happening to me then. My girlfriend and I got caught in the act of love making. My mother was very upset. She wanted to whip me but my dad talked her out of it. She was upset because she didn't know I knew too much about sex. My mother talked to us about it but I wasn't listening. I liked what I was doing. After a few more incidents, we broke up because of her mother. So I met another girl. I was going over there every day. I was going to school but I would play hooky with her. We didn't stay together because all she wanted was sex. The first day of the next term I was kissing this girl and they said I had to go. This happened too many times. So I left because there was too many rules anyhow. You couldn't hold hands, you couldn't talk to white girls, etc.

I got into trouble again and this time they sent me to Columbia Training School. I was there for four months and two weeks. Three months later I was in more trouble— breaking and entering. I got some items out and sold them to the wrong person. I had to go back to the juvenile center. I was out one day and the next one I was in.

I got a job when I got out working at Morrison's [Restaurant] as a cook. But at $1.95 an hour, that's bullshit. At Morrison's they thought they had a real nigger working 'cause I really tried to keep that job. But that damn man [boss] was crazy. He started bitching with me. Now he knows a cook don't wash no damn dishes. I wouldn't do that shuffling routine, so I quit. I started stealing hams and making some money. I would take my girlfriend with me to the supermarket and I'd have a box underneath the cart. We'd walk around filling the box with steaks, pork chops, hams, chickens, all kinds of shit. I'd have tape in my pocket and some stamps with rope. This is so it would look like a package. That don't never fail to work. I'd steal about $1,500 worth of meat and sell it for $800. Sometimes I buy a little weed to sell. I pay $45 for an ounce or $150 for a pound and make more than $300 every three or four days. All I want is a Cadillac, two tons of weed, five pounds of crystal T, a nice house, and be financially well off. I would much rather work than hustle because working is steady. When you work you know where the money is coming from.

We did not find any consistent pattern in the backgrounds of young men who become pimps. Husbands, boyfriends, and transient players all play the role. Young boys sometimes identify with the player image—New York players set standards of dress and lifestyle that are widely imitated—but in most cases the motivation is economic necessity. Frances H., a close observer of the street scene in Meridian, described the situation of teenage pimps in this southern town as follows:

It's not that all these kids want to be players or hustlers. The first thing you think is they don't want to work. That's misleading. Most of them, and I mean the major portion of them, have tried at one time or another to get a job. They have beat down the doors of the unemployment offices. They have been in these stores, dealing with all these crackers who constantly make wisecracks and comments about how dumb they are and stuff like that. And they, rightly so, get tired of it. Then they come back out here on the street and say, "Fuck it. I'll make it any way I can. I'll be a player. I'll be a hustler. I'll be cool. I'll be clean." They want to have that paper. Just like everybody else does. You can't tell 'em they don't know what time it is because they think they do. So it ain't like they ain't tried. It's just that they got tired of all the bullshit. A lot of what this is about is discrimination. It's prejudice against these kids. Them young white boys can go to daddy and say, "I need a job" or "I need money" and get it. But these black kids have to kiss ass and then be told, "Ain't no jobs for you, nigger boy." So you know it ain't about not wanting to work.

The experiences of young people in other regions of the country reveal few differences in lifestyle and some basic similarities in values and outlook toward their immediate future. Most teenagers in the underground economy, regardless of region, maintain the traditional values of work, money, and success. Although these are limited commodities, the youths are as desperate in their search as anyone else.

One thing is clear—teenagers like Ray-Ray will more often than not find illegal opportunities more attractive than legal ones. Those who have had negative experiences in the work place, no matter how brief, will move on to the underground economy and try to forge an identity there. Ray-Ray, however, is the first to admit that he is not going to get rich stealing meat, selling marijuana, or even pimping.

Some teenage hustlers do manage to find jobs. But often they leave within a few months because the demands of the job appear to be too great, especially when hustling seems to offer an easier life. Here's what Margo has to say about her brief career in the nine-to-five world:

> If you're the type that can never be without a job, not having one may cause a problem. I'm not that type. I can live with or without one. I've never been one to worry about work. Occasionally I might find myself in a jam, but I believe things work themselves out and they usually do. Not working doesn't bother me so much as having to do that regular nine to five. I hate straight hours, time clocks and suspicious bosses. I enjoy not having to deal with the same environment and people within that structure on a daily basis. That type of contact, being constant, tires me. I love to free-lance. I enjoy change in work situations. I'm trying other ways to make money, not necessarily legal ways, and I'm open to ideas.

> Not working steadily, I will admit, causes problems for me. Because the cash flow isn't there all the time. Naturally I will find other ways to make up for this lack of money, but the market isn't always open to me. When I say this, I'm speaking of the people I may be with at that particular time in my life, or my access to the street. Making illegal money is a whole different scene. It's part of what I categorized before as free-lancing. Some examples of free-lancing would be anything from hocking your personal property or someone else's, to dealing drugs or selling yourself, borrowing, mediating, touting, you know. If you can do any of these and hold down a tax-paying job, you're alright. But if you can keep this life up and survive from it alone, you're doing better.

> One thing about prostitution, it's a tax-free job. The risk is the thrill. I feel one has to be adventurous, daring, and mischievous to a point. The first thing one has to keep in mind is that you're going to get caught. Not by the authorities, no! That's the last thing in my mind. When I say get caught, I mean by the street. If you're dealing in anything against the law, you always have heavy competition. If your game is good, people want to tear it down. It's a constant battle in the streets for survival. There is a lot of planning, scheming, lying, cheating, and a little bit of fear out there. The fear has to be natural or you're doomed. You have to love danger.

> I hate what society considers normal. So I find other ways of living within this world, without letting it bother me. If it bothers others, that's their problem. Every man for himself. When it comes to money you will find very few are going to help you make it. And if you're the type that helps others, you'll find yourself taken for a sucker. So you resign to helping yourself. The advantages of this street business, hustling, it's on you. You wake up, eat, sleep, you don't punch no clocks, you don't conform to no rules and regulations or courtesy to co-workers, customers, bosses, clients, patients, staff, etc. Best of all, you don't pay taxes either.

Margo's work history includes both legitimate and illegitimate roles. Although she possesses the skills to work in a mainstream occupation, she has not developed the discipline to remain in a job very long. This is partly a result of immaturity. However, it is a well-known fact that few teenagers maintain jobs for more than a few months at a time. It is Margo's street and family values that have kept her at odds with the straight world. Her forays into the regular workaday routine are always of short duration because there is more money to be made on the streets. There is always an available market of older men who will buy her services, yet she sees the weakness of her own game. She knows that a prostitute's life—even a high-class call girl's life—is a short one. She knows she won't always have a youthful face and body. And when things get tough—for instance, after a brutal trick—she looks for work in a regular job. Margo sees no discernible difference between her straightout prostitution and what other women do as secretaries or as wives at home.

Margo's views are not shared by the parents and friends of most of the teenage prostitutes we met. There appears to be a double standard operating in this area: the pimps/players are seen as smooth, slick, and smart, the girls as stupid and dirty. Feelings of revulsion and pity were expressed by some of the parents, while others did not seem to know or care what their children were doing. Many of the girls turned to prostitution after becoming pregnant and being rejected by their boyfriends and parents.

Once a girl enters the life, ties with family and friends are usually broken. It is common practice for a pimp to insist that his girls sever all such relationships. Independent prostitutes like Margo may maintain contact with their friends but tend not to explain to them what they do for a living.

In addition to the availability of prostitution as an option and the perceived disadvantages of straight jobs, certain experiences during childhood and adolescence can lead to a career in prostitution. Rose M. of Hough is a case in point.

Things were okay at home until I turned 13. I moved out when I turned 13 and quit school. My stepfather and I couldn't get along any more. I kept moving in and out until I was 15. My mother didn't mind because I always let her know where I was and went by to see her when my stepfather was at work. I didn't have to worry about supporting myself then. When I was 14 I got put on pro-

bation for not going to school. At 15, when my mother died, my stepfather sent my sister and myself down south to stay with our real father. I didn't like my father so I came back to Cleveland to stay with a friend. I was getting a social security check from my father so I had money.

The girl I was staying with worked the streets. She was only 16. I didn't have to but I started working with her. It was scary but it was a living. I grew up very fast in the streets. I shot dope but I never got hooked. At 16 I got pregnant and left my man. I went to the Safe Space Station, a runaway shelter. The people were really nice. They tried to help, but I was used to being on my own. So I went back to my man and worked until I was seven months. I also shot dope while I was pregnant. The dope only made my baby small.

We moved from place to place after that. Then my stepfather had me put in D.H. and tried to take my baby. I stayed there for ten days, then went to a child-care center for three weeks. I turned 17 in there. The court placed me in the custody of the county. My social worker took me down and got me on welfare. Before that I was still turning tricks. I still worked some even though I was on welfare and got social security because I wasn't used to getting money once a month. I still moved from place to place. My son has never had a stable home until now, and he'll be two next month.

Now I'm 18 and I'm three months pregnant. One thing I promised myself, with this baby I'm not going to go through the things I went through with the first. I feel I have an advantage over most people my age and older because I know and have experienced things they'll never know. The only disadvantage is I don't have as much interest in men like I had. My pimp beat me up and tried to make me have an abortion. But I ran away from him because I was tired of the streets and let myself get pregnant on purpose. I know I wasn't forced to get into the life. Because I used to do it a lot with my girlfriends after school to get money to buy extra clothes. When my mother would ask me where I got the clothes from I would tell her I exchanged them with friends. After my mom died and I wasn't going to my stepfather's anymore, I lived with the rest of the girls at my pimp's stable.

For some teenage girls, incestuous relationships with their fathers and encounters with pimps at school may have started them on the road to prostitution. Kate Strolls is a seventeen-year-old dropout who moved away from home after a series of incidents with her father.

I dropped out of school in the ninth grade. At this point I have no interest in going back. I used to live in the Woodland Projects apartments. It was ugly as hell. It had all these empty houses, old buildings, and winos everywhere. I first hooked up with this pimp at school. I started turning tricks in the afternoon and bringing some of the money home to my mother. She took the money and never asked me where I got it from. She just told me not to get myself killed.

My father moved away after we, my sister and me, got together and told my mother that he had been having sex with both of us and then threatening to kill us if we told anybody. I feel okay about the whole thing but my sister turned real mean and won't talk to nobody. She has no friends and stays at home with my brother even though she is old enough to be on her own. I don't feel that way about men. I just don't develop feelings for them when I'm working. And I prefer to be with women anyhow.

I had this woman stop me one night down on Prospect and give me $100 to go with her. I was scared but, shit, I figured I could outfight the broad if it got too crazy. She had this nice place to stay and all this nice furniture and a man. She turned me out that night.

For many young women, a crucial factor is the lifestyles of the adult women who are closest to them. This was the case for Margo. Her adult role models were her mother, her aunt, and a very close friend of her mother who was active in civil rights, all of whom were rebels and fought private battles at home or public battles against society. Unlike many of the other girls in our study, Margo had a relatively stable home and social environment. She had opportunities to travel, to attend school and do well. But the examples set by her family, her early experiences, and the complexities of her own personality led her to choose the fast life. There is no doubt that young women like Margo could lead successful lives in a professional career were it not for one or two incidents that shaped their life patterns. As she herself explains:

As a baby, not from what I recall, but only hearsay, I was alert, smart, too fast for my britches, and loved to party and drink. One might say that I haven't changed a bit. I was walking at the age of six months, but didn't let go of my bottle till around four years. I was a year old and one still couldn't tell whether I was a girl or a boy, since I still had not grown hair. There was no way to add ribbons, bows or clips to my scalp. So I spent my first year as a child with an undefined sexuality. At eight months my mom was fed up with me, so I say. She claims that it was in my best interest for her to have sent me to my grandparents in South America. This was for a period of three years. I've been told that as a toddler, I spoke too much, knew too much, ate too much, and never liked going to bed on time. I was spoiled, having been the first granddaughter, and yet was very charming and lovable.

At 3½, I was sent back home to my mother, who by this time I'd forgotten. This, of course, was after having traveled throughout South America and the Virgin Islands. I wish they would have saved those trips now. I arrived at Kennedy International Airport via Avianca Airlines, escorted by my aunt, and was received by everyone from a to z that was a member of my family or knew someone in it.

My room was filled with an accumulation of toys over the past three years. Most of them I still have. One that I loved in particular was a teddy bear named Moy-Moy. He used to be white and fluffy, nowadays he is skinned of all his hair, dyed and ripped. One of the dolls I used to have was four feet tall. Now I was a tiny 3½-year-old, so you can imagine in comparison to me this thing was a giant. Sometimes I honestly feel that parents are not practical. An example is that by the time I was five, my father, whom I rarely saw, had given me a collection of dolls from all different nations. By the time I was seven, the collection was destroyed. To this day, my mother still curses me out over it and calls me irresponsible.

I may sound ungrateful, but I'm really not. I really can't complain about my childhood. It's my teen years that I hated the most. I knew my real father as the man who came to give me money, or to take me shopping to buy things. He was very well off and he proved it to me. But I didn't want his fucking money. He deprived me of his presence. He deprived me of his love. What is money to try and replace that? I'll tell ya, it ain't shit. So I threw all of that in his face. I guess that's why he's been so reluctant to contact me now. He knows I hate what he did. All my life I've had negative feelings about my father due to the fact that in my eyes his time was too precious to spend with me. All these years I've denied ever having needed him, loved him, missed him, or wanting him. Now I wonder. I remember when I was real small. He would come in, pick me up, and put me on his shoulders. You see, my father was real tall and skinny and when he would lift me up, it seemed like—oh God—it was to the ceiling. It seemed so high to me. But I would hold my breath and close my eyes and in a few seconds I was on top of the world.

Teenage prostitutes, and the men who exploit them, have developed a negative self-image and considerable hostility toward members of the opposite sex. They are at risk of remaining in the criminal subculture as adults, and if they do not find better role models and opportunities that is the most likely prognosis. But these teenagers, street wise and cynical as they are, are not "lost" or "fallen," even though they may think of themselves in such terms. Timely intervention by caring adults could counteract the experiences that led them into prostitution and could guide them onto more constructive paths to maturity.

QUESTIONS FOR DISCUSSION

1. What motivated these young people to engage in prostitution and/or pimping? Were the motivations the same for the women as for men? If yes, in what ways?

2. Margo saw no difference between prostitution and what other women do as secretaries or wives. Why?

3. The authors suggest that teenage prostitutes and the men who exploit them have a negative self-image and hostility toward members of the opposite sex. Do you agree? Why? Cite examples from this article to support your response.

APPLICATIONS

1. Based on what you have read, what kinds of changes in the social environment might we make to curtail teenage prostitution?

2. If you had an opportunity to talk with Margo about her "life style," what would you tell her to encourage her to make positive changes away from prostitution? (Remember that you and she are more than likely from very different social settings and experiences.)

KEY TERMS

benevolent   marked by good will or disposed to doing good for others.

commodity   an economic good or product.

foray   to make a raid or an invasion for the purpose of obtaining spoils or others' possessions.

revulsion   a sense of utter distaste or repugnance.

self-delusion   a persistent false belief regarding oneself; often results in a bizarre or distorted perception of reality.

underground economy   an unofficial, unsanctioned, or illegal system of exchanging goods and services.

22

The Appearance of Youthful Subculture: A Theoretical Perspective on Deviance

Lynne Richards

A number of theoretical perspectives can be united to form a comprehensive explanation of the formation and dissolution of deviant subcultures. Using this theoretical framework, the role of appearance is herein promulgated as being a primary and contributing factor to this subcultural process. Examining the Teddy Boy subculture of the 1950s and the Hippie subculture of the 1960s, it is shown that appearance factors (1) add credibility to the deviant role; (2) provide a descriptive embodiment of the deviance, to which society reacts; (3) serve as flaunted symbols of deviance in retaliatory counter-pride displays; and (4) contribute cues for imitation by mass society, thereby initiating social repair.

Self-enhancement theory suggests that all human behavior is directed toward constructing and supporting a perception of self that is positive and conducive to esteem (Sirgy, 1982). Thus, deviant behavior can be perceived as merely unconventional or socially unacceptable means for acquiring positive perceptions of the self. Within the investigation delineated herein, this self-enhancement perception of deviance was united with concepts generated by a number of other theoretical perspectives to form a comprehensive interpretation of the formation of deviant

"The Appearance of Youthful Subculture: A Theoretical Perspective on Deviance," *Clothing and Textiles Research Journal*, 6 (Spring 1988): pp. 56–64. Reprinted by permission of the Textile and Apparel Association.

subculture (see Table 1). Ideas concerning the social and psychological functions of appearance were then applied to that theoretical framework, resulting in an explanation in which appearance represented a key ingredient in the subcultural process.

The subsequent theoretical explanation was tested against two real world youthful deviant subcultures: the British Teddy Boys and the American Hippies. These social groups were selected for analysis due to the fact that they were sufficiently remote in time to insure the total completion of the formation and dissolution process while being recent enough for primary data to be adequately available. In addition, the Teddy Boys of Great Britain and the Hippies of America represented two different social class backgrounds, nationalities and decades, thereby providing breadth to the testing of the theoretical explanation.

THE FORMATION OF DEVIANT SUBCULTURE

As noted, self-enhancement theory suggests that all human behavior is aimed at the generation of positive perceptions of the self and self-esteem. Thus, collective social behavior would be that which reinforces self-perceptions for the majority of the members of a social group or, alternately, the self-perceptions of a powerful and controlling minority. Thus, social rules (folkways and mores) rep-

TABLE 1   Theoretical Propositions Employed in the Development of a Comprehensive Explanation of Deviant Subculture Formation

Theoretical Perspective	Proposition
Self-enhancement	All human behavior, including deviant behavior, is directed toward enhancement of self-esteem.
Anomie	Societies promulgate goals and means of goal attainment; such goals and means may not be equally enhancing for all individuals, thereby motivating a search for alternative behavior patterns.
Functional Deviance	Deviance is a necessary component in all societies, serving clearly to distinguish acceptable behavior (which is self-enhancing for the majority) from unacceptable (deviant) behavior.
Cognitive Consistency/ Dissonance	To alleviate mental discomfort caused by conflicting perceptions of others, mental processes are simplified through categorization of individuals as totally conforming or nonconforming, thereby increasing the strength with which the deviant label is applied to nonconformists.
Self-fulfilling Prophesy	The degree to which a nonconformist identifies with a socially promulgated deviant label depends upon the strength with which that label is applied or proclaimed.
Deviant Labeling	If the nonconformist accepts the deviant label, he/she attempts to alleviate social isolation by seeking the companionship of others with a similar label, thereby forming a deviant subcultural group.
Subcultural Leadership	Mass society imitates subcultural behavior, thereby reducing the differences between the subculture and larger society and initiating social repair.

resent behavioral programmers which direct the members of society into those actions which have, in the past, proved successful for maintaining esteem for the majority or controlling minority.

Social roles are learned through socialization, usually beginning in early childhood. The degree to an individual becomes committed to and internalizes social rules is determined by the amount of self-enhancement that accrues from conformity during socialization. Reinforcement of self-esteem received from significant others in response to behavior which conforms to social rules, increases both an individual's desire to repeat the behavior and his/her perceptions of the rightness of that behavior and the corresponding social rule. When the family or society fails to reward compliance with social rules, however, commitment to those rules is subsequently weak (Hewitt, 1970).

Shame is an emotional experience antithetical to self-enhancement. Thus, fear of shame acts as a socio-psychological tool by which individuals are restrained from breaking social rules. For those rules which have been thoroughly internalized during social-

ization, fear of self-shaming may be sufficient to induce continued conformity. However, for those rules evidencing less stringent personal commitment, fear of being caught and experiencing social shame may act as a social deterrent. To decrease the likelihood that social rules will be broken, a society can install intensive socialization mechanisms and thereby create protective barriers (fear of shaming) against non-conformity (Sagarin, 1977).

Deviant rule-breaking occurs when life situations arise for which existing rules are inadequate and when mechanisms are available for circumventing self or social shame. Controlled anonymity or secrecy, lying and self-deception all represent common means for avoiding shame. Those social rules which have been most strongly internalized have the greatest potential for evoking shame when transgressed. Therefore, those same rules require the most substantial amounts of deceit, in the event of rule-breaking, to protect the perception of self from denigration (Sagarin, 1977).

Anomie theory suggests that all societies promulgate specific goals, as well as means by which those goals can be realized. These institutionalized means vary in the degree to which they are effective in the pursuit of socially approved goals. In those societies with ineffective means, social rules may be broken in order to create new avenues for goal realization. For example, lower class individuals may find their pathway to success blocked by discrimination or lack of financial and educational resources. Thus, deviating methods may be adopted in order to obtain the materialistic acquisitions associated with the goal of upward mobility. Deceit mechanisms would be initiated to forestall self or social shaming as a result of the deviance (or rule breaking) (Merton, 1979).

Douglas (1970) maintained that deviance and respectability are two opposing concepts linked together in the same manner as night versus day, goodness versus evil, life versus death. In other words, deviance (rule-breaking) is unacceptable behavior only to the degree to which acceptable behavior has been defined. Similarly, the functionalist theory of deviance contends that deviant behavior is an integral and necessary component of all societies, serving to delineate clearly the boundaries of acceptable behavior (Dentler & Erickson, 1979; Durkheim, 1979).

By adhering to acceptable behavior (rules) a person can perceive the self as being right and thereby enhance self-esteem. However, rightness is only meaningful if there is concurrently a clear definition of wrongness. Individuals are therefore motivated to promulgate actively their own behavior modes as being right and to do so by pointing out opposite behavior modes as being wrong. Thus, labeling others as being deviant serves to upgrade the self-esteem of rule-conformists. The more effectively that opposing individuals can be tagged as deviant and wrong, the more effectively can the positive label of "rule-abiding" be applied to the self.

It can be seen, then, that acts are not deviant in and of themselves. Acts must first be observed by persons who subscribe to an opposing form of rule-governed behavior, after which the acts (and actors) must then be labeled as deviant by members of that audience. Thus, it is the social audience that inadvertently creates deviance by delineating what is considered acceptable versus unacceptable behavior.

Cognitive consistency (or cognitive dissonance) theory suggests that individuals seek ways to alleviate the mental discomfort caused by conflicting information (Mischel, 1968). For example, if an individual is observed committing some form of deviant, rule-breaking behavior, that behavior is perceived as conflicting with the conformity required for group membership. Cognitive dissonance, or discomfort, results from the perception of a group member whose behavior is apparently predictable (rule-conforming) sometimes and unpredictable (rule-breaking) at other times. To reduce this dissonance and foster consistency of expectations, the sometimes nonconformist is perceived as being deviant in general, thereby strengthening the application of the deviant label to the social transgressor. According to Balch and Kelly (1979), deviance becomes a "master status" which overshadows all information to the contrary.

The degree to which a rule-breaking individual identifies with the deviant label (i.e., self-fulfilling prophesy) depends, in part, upon the degree of social conflagration which his/her nonconformity has caused. The greater the number of individuals who voice agreement with the deviant label, as well as the vociferousness with which that label is proclaimed, the more convinced will be the nonconformist that he/she is in fact, deviant. The mass media, by reporting instances of observed deviance to society at large, serves to foster a social outcry against the rule-breaking and subsequent mass labeling of the deviant. In the words of Tannenbaum (1979),

> The person becomes the thing he is described as being: the parents . . . the police . . . the court. . . . their very enthusiasm defeats their aim. The harder they work to reform the evil the greater the evil grows under their hands. The way out is through a refusal to dramatize the evil. The less said about it the better (pp. 162–163).

Mass labeling serves to isolate the deviant from the more conforming members of society. The interactionist or labeling theory of deviance suggests that after an individual acquiesces to a perception of the difference from others, he/she then attempts to alleviate social isolation by seeking the company of persons who are similarly different (Tannenbaum, 1979). The subsequent formation of a deviant subgroup fosters the promulgation of new subcultural rules of conduct supportive of that rule-breaking behavior labeled as deviant by the larger society. Conformity to the social rules of the subculture, defined as right by members of that subgroup, serves to enhance wounded self-perceptions. As with the social rules of the larger society, those of the subculture are likewise enshrouded with a fear of shaming which acts as a deterrent to nonconformity by members of the subculture (Sagarin, 1977).

The presence of subcultures within a society signifies a struggle for supremacy among a number of lifestyles and value systems. Although deviance can be viewed as a creative response to irrelevant, ineffectual social rules, members of society are more likely to perceive nonconformity as a potentially destructive force undermining the security of that which is familiar. Enthusiastic mass media delineations of the activities, lifestyle and appearances associated with the offending subcultures fuel a "moral panic" and lead to an eventual perception of the deviants as "folk devils" (Brake, 1985). Clarke, Hall, Jefferson and Roberts (1976) described a moral panic as,

> . . . a spiral in which the social groups who perceive their world and position threatened, identify a responsible enemy and emerge as the vociferous guardian of traditional values (p. 72).

As the publicized conflict between society and subculture escalates, the deviant group often retaliates against the derisive labeling and ridicule with expressions of aggressive countermoralism. After all, to members of the subculture, those members of the larger society are deviating in regards to subcultural social rules and are thus deserving of social shaming. Corresponding with countershaming are counterpride displays, in which symbols of the deviance are arrogantly flaunted (Sagarin, 1977). Eventu-

ally, seemingly innocuous symbols may, of themselves, become objects of derision which augment a moral panic, due to association with and use by the deviants (Clarke, 1976).

To summarize the aforementioned process of deviant subculture formation, a situation arises within society for which existing social rules of conduct are inadequate, thus creating motivation for not conforming to or breaking those rules. The social rules, however, are protected by a fear of self and/or social shaming, necessitating the generation of defensive deceptions against shame. If the rules are transgressed and if the nonconforming behavior is observed by members of the social audience, society is alerted to the attack against the established social rule structure. Subsequent delineation of the so-called wrong behavior serves to define more clearly the social rules, or right behavior, as adhered to by the majority. The initial perceptions of a deviant act evolve into perceptions of the individual as being deviant. Deviant labeling isolates the individual and encourages the seeking out of others similarly labeled. The subsequent formation of a deviant subgroup results in the generation of new social rules protected by a fear of shaming. As the deviants cohere, the subculture is perceived (by members of the larger society) as being a threat to social stability. Symbols which visually distinguish members of the subculture from members of the larger society serve to accentuate the ensuing social conflict.

As previously discussed, the presence of disparity between socially promulgated goals and means for achieving goals motivates deviant rule-breaking and subsequent formation of subcultures. Brake (1974) has suggested that the specific *nature* of the frustration experienced, due to conflict between goals and means, depends upon the social class background of the actor. For example, a lower class child, having been socialized into the value system of the working class (emphasizing toughness, excitement, autonomy and fate), is confronted in the public schools with the middle class means to success (control of aggression, deferred gratification, respect for property, ambition and responsibility). Being uncommitted to these new prescriptions, the lower class child fails to succeed and the lower class rules which are adopted in early childhood prove ineffectual. On the other hand, a middle class child may be subjected to goal expectations (often the academic or athletic hopes of parents and teachers) which are beyond his/her natural abilities. In other words, no effectual means for success are available, given the excessive goals. Wealthy youth may be promised materialistic goal realization in the form of allowances or inheritances, regardless of individual achievement, thereby negating the value of the means whereby goals are usually obtained (Hewitt, 1970).

Because the frustrations which motivate deviance spring from differing social orientations, the subsequent subcultures tend to reflect specific class identifications. As Rubington and Weinberg (1973) observed, "The crucial condition for the emergence of new cultural forms is the existence . . . of a number of actors with similar patterns of adjustment" (p.233). Likewise, most nonconforming individuals do not deviate from all of the social rules learned during socialization but only from those which somehow pertain to the frustrated need for self-esteem. Thus, some social class rule orientations are carried over into subculture formation, strengthening the identification of the subculture with a particular social class value system.

Individuals who are attracted to subcultural membership select a group which (1) is congruent with their social class and educational background, (2) offers an apparent solution to the conflict between social goals and means of goal attainment, and (3) presents an enhancing identity in regards to self-image. Adolescence is both a time when subcultures seem to have a special attraction and a time for serious searching for identity (Roach, 1969). Especially for lower class youth, a subculture can provide opportunities for acquiring self-enhancement through achieved (rather than ascribed) status.

Brake (1985) and Clarke (1976) have discussed subcultural solutions to social contradictions (between goals and means) as being magical rather than real. In other words, subcultural solutions more frequently reflect pathways to temporary escapism than bona fide alternatives. (In this light, subcultural solutions are congruent with those forms of self-deception used to reduce sensations of nonconformist shame.) The construction of a subcultural identity detached from and in a plane beyond the frustrating reality of class membership, occupation and/or school represents one such magical solution to social inequities. By lifting the subcultural identity out of the social milieu from which it spawned, new and more attainable criteria can be devised for evaluating and enhancing self-perceptions.

Youthful subcultures tend to be masculine oriented and controlled with females acting as peripheral appendages. Brake (1985) suggested that, while males search for alternative identities through subcultural membership, conformity to the social rule of marriage remains of primary importance to many females, especially lower class girls. Therefore, these females tend to maintain a traditional feminine role even within the subculture and to acquiesce to male supremacy. McRobbie and Garber (1976) contended that females have marginal roles in youthful subcultures because they have more central roles within a different range of activities (i.e., home-related). As role alternatives become increasingly available to females, female youth may also participate more fully in the subcultural identity search.

SUBCULTURAL APPEARANCE

Subcultural dress can be perceived to be a form of conspicuous consumption in that clothing is consciously and conspicuously used by members to communicate group identity as well as the values, beliefs and focal concerns of the subculture. In addition, a unique subcultural appearance suggests disassociation from the larger culture while simultaneously acting to unify group members.

As previously discussed, subcultures can provide magical solutions to the inequities of life by lifting the individual out of an identity defined by traditional social class criteria. The new identity revolves around subcultural rules and expectations which are within attainable reach of the members. Subcultural dress serves to add credibility to the new identity while enhancing the unreal or escapist characteristics of the subcultural role. By looking like, as well as acting like, someone from outside the boundaries of the larger culture, the individual proclaims his ineligibility for evaluation under the existing social rule system—a system which, in some way, is perceived to be a threat to self-esteem. Disassociation from the larger social group, then, is communicated through adherence to subcultural dress.

Similarity in dress among members of a subculture serves to designate the boundaries of the group (Clarke, 1976; Clarke et al., 1976). Joseph and Alex (1972) have suggested that through group identification a particular mode of appearance becomes a totemic emblem of that group. A totem, by broad definition, is an object believed to be related to a group and to embody the characteristics of that group. Thus the dress of a subculture is totemic to the degree to which (1) it is perceived to be intrinsic to the subculture and (2) it symbolically reflects the values, beliefs and focal concerns of the group. Brake (1985) used the term "homology" to discuss the close fit between the material objects of a subculture (including items of clothing and adornment) and the characteristic behavior of group members. Behavior, of course, is the outward manifestation of values, beliefs and focal concerns.

As an embodiment of group values, beliefs and focal concerns, the components of subcultural dress reflect symbolic meanings which make statements about the subculture. The specific meanings of subcultural dress may be unintelligible to persons outside the group, however, in that the symbolism may represent a form of "argot" (i.e., the secret jargon of a subgroup) (Brake, 1985). While a subcultural style of appearance may suggest chaos to members of the larger society, to those who are cognizant of the visual jargon, subcultural appearance reveals a meaningful order. The symbolic meanings of subcultural appearance are always most apparent to the initial innovators of a subculture (Hebdige, 1979). For persons who later join, the subcultural appearance symbolizes group identity in general. However, the spe-

cific meanings originally associated with individual components of the subcultural style are less apparent to these late arrivers.

As previously discussed, the frustrations which motivate deviance spring from differing social class situations, and therefore subsequent subcultures tend to reflect specific class identifications. Since most nonconforming individuals do not deviate from all social class rules, some social class orientations are carried over into the subculture. Thus, by reflecting the values, beliefs and focal concerns of the subculture, subcultural dress also contains symbolic components associated with the aspects of the larger parent social class. Hebdige (1979) has maintained that "subcultural styles are mutations and extensions of existing codes rather than the pure expression of creative drives . . . they are meaningful mutations" (pp. 130–131).

It is the *difference* between subcultural dress and that of the larger parent culture that is the most significant visual factor in subcultural style. It is the difference which portrays the separation of the subculture from its parent social class. Greater visual difference between the styles characteristic of the subculture and the larger society suggests greater rapture between the two groups in terms of values, beliefs and focal concerns. It is the *nature* of these appearance differences, however, that symbolizes the reason for the separation or, in other words, which values, beliefs and focal concerns represent the point of contention.

As noted, subcultural dress contains many symbolic components congruent with aspects (including appearance) of the larger parent culture. A "bricoleur" is someone who deliberately rearranges selected symbolic components of language (here, nonverbal language) to create a new and different message (Clarke, 1976). Hebdige (1979) related this concept of bricolage to radical Surrealism, in which the juxtaposition of "two apparently incompatible realities" creates an "explosive junction" (p. 106). Thus, the manipulation of components of dress to juxtapose seemingly incompatible cues (as defined by appearance norms of the larger society) creates a visual explosive junction symbolic of the seeming incompatibility of the two groups and their potentially explosive differences.

Klapp (1972) labeled this subcultural emphasis on visual difference as "style rebellion," defined as the "use of fashion more or less deliberately as symbolic protest, an effort to shock . . ." (p. 330). Thus, style rebellion is merely a form of "counterpride display." The deviant group retaliates against derisive labeling from the larger culture by pridefully flaunting visual symbols of their deviance. Such flaunting of symbols can eventually extend social contempt from the deviant individual to the symbol of deviance. Thus, not unlike the behavior of Pavlov's dog, society begins to exhibit intolerance and persecution at the sight of a visual cue of deviance rather than waiting for observation of the deviant act.

Subculture leadership theory, as it pertains to fashion change, suggests that clothing designers find inspiration in the dress styles of cultural subgroups (Sproles, 1985). This inspiration is then transferred into clothing products for mass consumption. Once subcultural styles are mass consumed, they no longer communicate difference between the subculture and larger society, thereby negating the most important communicative aspect of subcultural dress. In the words of Klapp (1972) "style invasion" threatens the identity of a subculture when "the number of new adopters threatens to swamp the original group and wipe out its boundaries" (p. 332). Style invasion thereby acts to repair the divided social order by reducing the difference factor.

More complete social recuperation, or repair of the divided social order, depends upon 1) the use of subcultural symbols by mass consumers as well as 2) the relabeling of subcultural deviant behavior as being acceptable (Hebdige, 1979). Sagarin (1977) identified this repair process as the pathway by which social rules are changed. A subculture promulgates an exaggerated form of nonconformity into social awareness, eliciting an initial defensive action followed by gradual social acquiescence. Thus, subcultural dress can be perceived as a motivating force behind the change of fashion and appearance norms, introducing seemingly incompatible styles which mass society may initially reject but eventually imitate to some degree.

Working Class Example: The Teddy Boys

"Through the dank mews of Shoreditch and over the littered bomb sites of Stepney slouch some of the nattiest young men in Britain. They are Edwardians—the dead end kids of London." Thus were the Teddy Boys (or Edwardians) introduced by *Newsweek* (Britain: . . . , p. 47) in 1954.

The dreary postwar British environment fostered improved economic opportunities for working class youth. Realizing a little spending money, these youth idled away leisure hours in streetcorner crap games or local dance halls (Britain: . . . , 1954). These activities alone, however, introduced little excitement, status or acclaim into lives overshadowed by the pursuit of dead-end unskilled or semi-skilled jobs.

The Teddy Boys represented an example of working class youth who, socialized into the value and belief systems of lower social strata, found their pursuit of self-enhancement stymied in a world governed by middle class norms. Deviance (rule breaking) and subsequent social labeling fostered the formation of a subculture in which new rules sanctioned nonconformist (and occasionally violent) activities, deemed to be self-enhancing (Great Britain . . . , 1956).

To glamorize their leisure hours, to enhance self-esteems, and in keeping with the trickle-down theory of fashion diffusion (Sproles, 1985), these working class youth adopted a postwar dress style prevalent among young English men of higher social status: the Edwardian suit. This Edwardian costume of the early 1950s represented a reinterpretation of a turn-of-the-century male dress style. The most recognizable feature of the Teddy Boy version included a coat with velvet collar, a narrow tie and slim drainpipe trousers. Lower class affiliation with this Edwardian dress, however, soon motivated the middle and upper classes to abandon the style (Jefferson, 1976). Thus, the Edwardian suit became a symbol of subcultural separation from the larger society by default.

British newspapers faithfully reported Teddy Boy deviance as well as their association with the foppish Edwardian dress (Damage. . . , 1954). The *Tailor and Cutter*, a tailoring trade journal, lamented that

> by a series of vicious coincidences all the old ladies who have been beaten up lately, all the modest young men who have had their faces slashed, and all the poor little pussy cats who have had tin cans tied to their tails have been beset by wicked young dandies in Edwardian clothes (Edwardian? . . . , 1953, p. 2).

These accounts served to confirm the rightness of the larger conforming society by pointing out the wrongness of the youthful deviants. In addition, the descriptions aided in the visual categorization of the deviant. By describing the outer container of the inner deviant nature, the Teddy Boy became a publicly recognizable entity. Contempt for the Teddy Boy's violent acts therefore expanded to encompass the symbol of his deviant group: the Edwardian suit. An editorial writer commented that "no doubt dozens of young men who like to wear drainpipe trousers and bootlace ties are law-abiding but their uniform has been disgraced. They should either discard it or share the disgrace" (Rock & Cohen, 1970, p. 298).

For the Teddy Boys, the Edwardian costume represented a magical solution to their low status position in British society. Donning this male symbol of upper class attire visually separated the Ted from the traditional working class environment. Thus, congruent with the concepts of totemism and homology (i.e., the embodiment of cultural values, beliefs and focal concerns), the Edwardian suit symbolized subcultural frustrations concerning lower class status and subsequent desires for social mobility and self-enhancement opportunities. The coat with velvet collar and narrow tie suggested a lifestyle of leisure, rather than physical labor. The surrealistic explosive junction of incompatible objects could then be perceived as being the placement of a seemingly elegant costume against the backdrop of a working class neighborhood.

A typical Edwardian suit cost about $90, paid in installments from an unskilled or semi-skilled laborer's salary. Although the Ted was not above attacking an enemy with brass studded belts and bicycle chains, care was always taken not to damage the magical (and expensive) Edwardian suit (Lights Out. . . , 1954). If apprehended by the police, Teddy Boys reportedly surrendered without a struggle to avoid spoiling their elegant dress. Why did the Teddy Boys so highly value their costume? According to a British boys' club leader, "It makes him feel smart—important" (Britain: . . . , 1954, p. 48).

Media coverage not only introduced the Teddy Boys to the public but served to introduce the Ted to himself as well (Rock & Cohen, 1970). Social stereotyping clearly delineated just how to dress and behave in order to conform to subcultural Teddy Boy rules. The Edwardian dresser was also informed by newspapers and magazine articles that, due to his clothing choice, he automatically possessed a socially predetermined nature. For example, according to the chairman of the Dartford Juvenile Court, Edwardian suits were ". . . flashy, cheap and nasty, and stamp the wearer as a particularly undesirable type" (Ridiculous. . . , 1954, p. 4). Such deviant labeling and emphasis upon a supposedly uniform style of dress acted to increase solidarity among the Teddy Boys by widening social and visual differences from the larger culture.

The moral panic which ensued isolated Teddy Boyds from the activities of conforming, respectable youth. Exclusion was as much upon the basis of Edwardian appearance, however, as upon evidence of deviant behavior (Town Warns. . . , 1954). For example, the manager of a dance hall in New Cross informed a group of youth: "You cannot come in. You're not properly dressed—and you know it. You will not be allowed in if you wear velvet lapels, drainpipe trousers, slim jim ties or other Teddy Boy outfits" (Rock & Cohen, 1970, p. 298). Similarly, a committee of the Osford City Council recommended that Teddy Boys be banned from dances in the town hall, with decisions for exclusion being made on the basis of "exaggerated Edwardian styles of dress" (Proposed. . . , 1955, p. 4). Thus the mere wearing of *symbols* had become the basis for labeling, isolation and contempt.

British Teddy Boys were most dominant from 1953 through 1955. Thereafter, working class youth began migrating into a diversity of other deviant subcultural groups, donning new esoteric styles. Thus, contrary to the proposed theoretical perspective, visual difference between the Teds and the larger society did not disappear due to subcultural leadership in fashion. The Edwardian suit had been mass produced *before* the Teddy Boys adopted the style, not as a result of their identification with it. This finding has suggested that social repair due to subcultural leadership may not be initiated in cases of lower class deviant groups.

Middle Class Example: The Hippies

The Hippies composed a middle and upper class youthful subculture whose members began "dropping out" of conventional society during the early 1960s. By 1967, there were an estimated 300,000 Hippies in the United States alone (Brown, 1967; Feigelson, 1970). The Hippie movement, paralleling the previously discussed pattern of deviance and subculture formation, emerged from a perceived incompatibility between socially established goals (as reflected in the materialistic American Dream) and means of goal attainment (hard work, deferred gratification and submergence of individualistic identity). However, unlike the Teddy Boy situation (in which the means were ineffectual for realization of socially approved success, Hippies perceived the goals to be incompatible with the perceived high cost of the means. Was "success" worth working always for tomorrow and becoming a cardboard replica of other success-seekers? Rejecting the means for goal attainment and devaluing the goals themselves, the Hippie subculture devised new social rules for experiencing life and evaluating human worth.

Paramount within Hippie philosophy was an insistence upon personal authenticity. Individuals were encouraged to express their true selves, rather than merely to act as mobilizing forces behind a collection of role masks (Berger, 1967). Since social roles help define identity, the Hippie rejection of roles as a component of self led to a shadowy internal perception of personal identity. This lack of well defined identity boundaries, rather than being a source of concern, symbolized for the Hippie a potential for identity growth and expanded, transcendental awareness of self. (According to Willis [1976], this search for true self, through transcendence, also motivated the Hippie use of drugs.) Adherence to prescribed social roles, then, was believed artificially to compartmentalize and to limit self-realization (Willis, 1978).

Congruent with the search for true self was the Hippie emphasis upon unrestrained self-expression or freedom from all inhibition. According to Abbie Hoffman, a Hippie spokesman, the power to forbid was the only thing to be forbidden within the new society (Feigelson, 1970). Similarly, the Hippie movement advocated active participation rather than passive spectating, as applied to all forms of self-expression. A person did not have to be an accomplished artist, musician or dancer before painting, singing or dancing. The personal pleasure derived from self-expression, no matter how crude, far exceeded the value of the resulting product. As stated by Davis (1967), "All men are artists, and who cares that some are better at it than others; we can all have fun!" (p.13).

The emphasis upon the right of all individuals to express and be accepted as their true selves promulgated the underlying theme of love within the Hippie subculture. A true Hippie, one who had successfully realized and internalized the all-accepting doctrine of Hippie philosophy, indiscriminately exuded love for all human beings. In innocence, the Hippies believed that unconditional love would eventually bring societies to realize the errors of their ways; love would cure all social ills (Dropouts. . . , 1967).

> And thus in love we have declared the purpose of our hearts plainly, without flattery, expecting love, and the same sincerity from you, without grumbling, or quarrelling, being Creatures of Your own Image and mould, intending no other matter herein, but to observe the Law of righteous action, endeavoring to shut out of the Creation, the cursed thing, called particular Propriety, which is the cause of all wars, blood-shed, theft, and enslaving Laws, that hold people under misery (Sabine, 1941, p .276).

Thus wrote Gerald Winstanley, a member of the seventeenth century British Diggers. Adopting the Digger name and philosophy of love, the Hippie Diggers (of San Francisco, Los Angeles, Boston and New York) distributed free food to persons in need. They also maintained a Free Store, where anyone (Hippie or non-Hippie) could obtain clothing, furniture, books and other items free of charge (Free Store. . . , 1967). Thus, some Hippies attempted to push their concept of love beyond the realm of mere philosophical rhetoric (The Hippies are. . . , 1967).

The Hippie lifestyle also reflected elected poverty in rebellion against the materialism of the larger culture. Paralleling this with the exploration for identity, Davis (1967) wrote, ". . . they proclaim that happiness and a meaningful life are not to be found in things, but in the cultivation of the self and by an intensive exploration of inner sensibilities with like-minded others" (p.13).

Hippie poverty was augmented by the perception of employment as being a sporadic activity for the purpose of occasionally earning "bread," rather than as a means to self-enhancement (Buff, 1970; Dropouts. . . , 1967). Eight-to-five employment was seen as artificially compartmentalizing time in the same way that roles dissected self-identity. Also undermining commitment to any form of work ethic among the Hippies was the preponderant subcultural enchantment with the here and now (Berger, 1967). At the same time that Hippie youth were questioning the value of sought after goals, they were also facing the fact that future plans could easily be obliterated in a nuclear holocaust. Thus, they were propelled by their environment into stressing the importance of experiencing the immediate moment.

The clothing associated with the Hippie subculture did, at first glance, appear to be a meaningless, unpredictable assortment of diverse items and styles. Males, sporting beards and long hair, dressed in tie-dyed shirts, T-shirts with subcultural logos, leather vests, faded and tattered jeans, army jackets, vintage hats, beads, embroidered headbands, white sheets, diverse theatrical costumes, sandals and/or bare feet. Females, often having waist-length hair, wore long "granny" dresses, jeans, peasant blouses, miniskirts, blanket capes, ragged furs, beads, sandals and/or bare feet. Handmade belts, pendants, wire-rimmed glasses, uniquely colored sunglasses and body paints were adopted by both sexes (Buff, 1970; Dropouts. . . , 1967; Wolf, 1968). Further analysis of such conglomerated appearances, however, reveals the esoteric nature of Hippie dress.

Congruent with the concepts of totemism and homology (i.e., embodiment of cultural values, beliefs and focal concerns), the Hippie appearance symbolically communicated major aspects of the subcultural philosophy. The wide assortment of clothing styles associated with Hippie appearance was, in itself, indicative of the emphasis upon freedom of expression and search for identity. Under the new subcultural rules it was acceptable to appear in any manner of dress as long as that appearance was an authentic expression of the self or search for the self (as opposed to the rule-conforming uniforms behind which the "squares" were believed to hide). Since it was the pleasure of self-expression that was of uppermost importance rather than the end product of that expression, the success of an outfit was defined in terms of its fun rather than by aesthetic or functional criteria.

The conscious election of poverty as a lifestyle (thereby "dropping out" of middle class materialism) often included a conscious selection of appearance cues symbolic of the Hippie identification with the oppressed. Tattered and faded clothing, bare feet, tangled and uncombed hair, and an unwashed body sufficiently separated the Hippie from any suggestion of affluence. Elected poverty, as well as lack of concern for the future, reduced wardrobe planning and maintenance to a minimum. The unpredictable assortment of costume items which made up a particular outfit, rather than being a conscious expression of self, may at times have been a reflection of only those things which were readily available for wear. Wolf (1968) observed that as the Hippie movement progressed and indigence became more fact than choice, the clothing of Hippies began to appear authentically shabby. Increasing numbers of the subculture availed themselves of the Diggers' charity, acquiring nondescript clothing from the bins in the Free Store.

It was the idiosyncratic nature of Hippie dress which most clearly differentiated members of that subculture from the larger society. Although the nature of the difference symbolized the philosophical concerns of the subculture (as discussed above), the mere fact of visual difference represented a conscious effort on the part of subculture to show disassociation from the larger society.

Several aspects of Hippie deviance were of particular interest to the mass media, namely their use of drugs and their liberal sexual attitudes. While publicizing these apparently newsworthy characteristics, the media also served to delineate for society the appearance for deviance. Thus, deviance was provided with an identifiable embodiment (Dropouts. . . , 1967; Inside. . . , 1967).

As occurred with the Teddy Boy and his suit, social contempt for Hippie deviance expanded to encompass the visual appearance of the deviant group. During the ensuing moral panic, the components of Hippie appearance were perceived as symbols of the nonconformist threat against social stability: tattered clothing was indicated as a threat to the traditional work ethic; dirtiness was seen to undermine the traditional definition of respectability; while masculine long hair and beaded jewelry reportedly served to destroy traditional sex roles.

Long hair on men represented an especially pronounced catalyst for social contempt, and the presence of this one visual cue alone became the basis for labeling and isolation. The "Establishment" even initiated a counterattack—a publicity campaign designed to stamp out long hair. Billboards began to appear along American highway, reading "Beautify America: Cut Your Hair." In a retaliatory move against this social derision, the Hippies flaunted their long hair and other symbols of differentness. In such a showing of counterpride display, one Hippie male stated: "If you ask me why I have my hair long, I'd say principally because I like it . . . and to kick society in the bollocks . . . wave my fingers at them . . ." (Willis, 1978, p.96).

Bricolage, the rearrangement of known symbols to create a new message or meaning,

was a common factor in Hippie appearance. No single component of Hippie dress was new, or never before known, but the innovative combination of those components successfully created new messages concerning social and economic philosophy. In many cases, the rearrangement of cues incorporated the Surrealistic combination of seemingly incompatible components (as defined by the appearance norms of the larger society), resulting in an explosive junction. It was the junction of incompatibility which begged for the attention of society and, once obtained, served to flaunt a suggested indifference to social rules. For example, by the standards of society, long hair (a feminine appearance cue) on a male body represented the combination of incongruent factors. As Hippie deviance became more clearly defined and publicly proclaimed, the incompatibility of long hair on a male body became a symbol of explosive incompatibility and polarization between Hippies and non-Hippies. To a similar but often lesser degree, the combination of other incongruent appearance cues served to flaunt the Hippie disregard for social rules: a brocade jacket worn with faded and patched jeans, a heavy wool cape worn in the summer, bare feet in sandals during the winter, a shirt cut from an American flag, or a Roman toga on a twentieth century metropolitan street corner.

Mass media coverage of the Hippie subculture not only served to inflame public indignation but also assisted in the eventual creation of "plastic" (imitation) Hippies (The flowering. . . , 1967; Hippies. . . , 1967; Inside . . . 1967). Youngsters and oldsters alike were provided with a visual formula whereby to flirt with the appearance of liberalism. Weekend Hippies emerged, only to disappear again on Monday mornings. Suggestions of Hippiedom began to peek from the pages of slick, high fashion publications. In keeping with the subcultural leadership theory of fashion change, invasion of the Hippie style had begun (Party. . . , 1967). With a mass consumption of values (i.e., materialism, aggression, etc.) through adoption of an esoteric appearance of differentness. Subsequently, as liberalism became respectable the members of the larger society enhanced self-esteem by emulating the subculture, thereby reducing visual difference between the two groups. Thus, it might be concluded that the trickle down theory of fashion is operative in cases of lower class subculture appearance, whereas the subcultural leadership theory of fashion is most applicable to upper and middle class subcultures. Further studies are needed to test these ideas.

The close ties between appearance cues and the formation of deviant subcultures suggest a relationship between the variability permitted in dress within a given society and the prevalence of subcultures within the same society. One might expect that within those societies which strictly limit variability in dress (i.e., enforce uniform clothing) the formation of deviant subcultures would be correspondingly limited. However, further investigation of subcultural appearance is needed also to ascertain the degree to which subculture formation and dissolution is actually dependent upon these factors.

References

BALCH, R. & KELLY, D.
1979   Reactions to deviance in a junior high school. In D. Kelly (Ed.). *Deviant behavior* (pp. 24–41). New York: St. Martin's Press.

BERGER, B.
1967   December. Hippie morality: More old than new. *Trans-Action*, 5, 19–23.

BRAKE, M.
1974   December. The skinheads. *Youth and Society*, 6, 179–200.

BRAKE, M.
1985   *Comparative youth culture.* London: Routledge & Kegan Paul.

Britain: Foppish Dead-enders
1954   May 17. *Newsweek*, 43, 47–48.

BROWN, J.
1967   *The Hippies.* New York: Time.

BUFF, S.
1970   Greasers, Dupers and Hippies: Three responses to the adult world. In L. Howe (Ed.). *The white majority* (pp. 60–77). New York: Random House.

CLARKE, J.
1976   Style, In S. Hall & Y. Jefferson (Eds.), *Resistance through rituals* (pp. 175–191). London: Hutchinson.

CLARKE, J., HALL, S., JEFFERSON, T. & ROBERTS, B.
1976   Subcultures, cultures and class. In S. Hall & T. Jefferson (Eds.), *Resistance through rituals* (pp. 9–74). London: Hutchinson.

Damage in Southend Train
1954   July 5. *The Times*, p. 3.

DAVIS, F.
1967   December. Why all of us may be Hippies someday. *Trans-Action*, 5, 10–18.

DENTLER, R., & ERIKSON, K.
1979   The functions of deviance in groups. In D. Kelly (Ed.), *Deviant behavior* (pp. 56–69). New York: St. Martin's Press.

DOUGLAS, J.
1970   *Deviance and respectability.* New York: Basic Books.

Dropouts with a Mission
1967   February 6. *Newsweek*, 69, 92–95.

DURKHEIM, E.
1979   The normal and the pathological. In D. Kelly (Ed.), *Deviant behavior* (pp. 51–55). New York: St. Martin's Press.

Edwardian? Cut it Out
1953   November 14. *Daily Herald*, p. 2.

FEIGELSON, N.
1970   *The underground revolution: Hippies, Yippies and others.* New York: Funk & Wagnalls.

The Flowering of the Hippies
1967   September. *Atlantic Monthly, 220,* 63–72.

Free Store
1967   October 14. *New Yorker, 43,* 49–51.

Great Britain: the Teds
1956   September 24. *Time,* 68, 27–28.

HEBDIGE, D.
1979   *Subculture: The meaning of style.* London: Methuen and Co.

Here Comes the Yippies
1968   March 11. *Newsweek,* 71, 68.

HEWITT, J.
1970   *Social stratification and deviant behavior.* New York: Random House.

Hippie—A Passing Fad?
1967   October 23. *U.S. News and World Report, 63,* 42–44.

The Hippies are Coming
1967   June 12. *Newsweek,* 69, 28–29.

Inside the Hippie Revolution
1967   August 23. *Look, 31,* 58–61, 63–64.

JEFFERSON, T.
1976   Cultural responses to the Teds. In S. Hall & T. Jefferson (Eds.), *Resistance through rituals* (pp. 81–86). London: Hutchison.

JOSEPH, N., & ALEX, N.
1972   January. The uniform: A sociological perspective. *American Journal of Sociology,* 77, 719–730.

KLAPP, O.
1972   *Currents and unrest.* New York: Rinehart & Winston.

Lights Out, Petting Aboard Teddy Train
1954   May 24. *Daily Herald*, p. 5.

MCROBBIE, A., & GARBER, J.
1976   Girls and subcultures. In S. Hall & T. Jefferson (Eds.), *Resistance through rituals* (pp. 209–222). London: Hutchinson.

MERTON, R.
1979   Social structure and anomie. In D. Kelly (Ed.), *Deviant behavior* (pp. 110–121). New York: St. Martin's Press.

MISCHEL, W.
1968   *Personality and assessment*, New York: John Wiley & Sons.

PARTY FACE PUT-ON
1967   November 28. *Look*, 31, 52–55. Proposed dance ban on Teddy boys. (1955, September 30). *The Times*, p. 4.

Ridiculous Edwardian Suit
1954   March 25. *The Times*, p. 4.

ROACH, M.
1969   November. Adolescent dress. *Journal of Home Economics*, 61, 693–697.

ROCK, P., & COHEN, S.
1970   The Teddy boy. In V. Bogdanor & R. Skidelsky (Eds.), *The age of affluence, 1951–1964*. London: Macmillan.

RUBINGTON, E. & WEINBERG, M.
1973   *Deviance: The interactionist perspective*. New York: Macmillan.

SABINE, G.
1941   *The works of Gerrard Winstanley*. Ithaca, NY: Cornell University Press.

SAGARIN, E.
1977   *Deviance and social change*. London: Sage.

SIRGY, M.
1982   December. Self concept in consumer behavior: A critical review. *Journal of Consumer Research, 9*, 287–300.

SPROLES, G.
1985   Behavioral science theories of fashion. In M. Solomon (Ed.), *The psychology of fashion* (pp. 55–70). Lexington, MA: D.C. Heath.

TANNENBAUM, F.
1979   Definition and dramatization of evil. In D. Kelly (Ed.), *Deviant behavior* (pp. 160–165). New York: St. Martin's Press.

Town Warns Teddy Hooligans
1954   May 25. *Daily Herald*, p. 5.

WILLIS, P.
1976   The cultural meaning of drug use. In S. Hall & T. Jefferson (Eds.), *Resistance through rituals* (pp. 106–118). London: Hutchinson.

WILLIS, P.
1978   *Profane culture*, London: Routledge & Keagan Paul.

WOLF, L.
1968   *Voices from the love generation*. Boston: Little, Brown and Co.

QUESTIONS FOR DISCUSSION

1. Choose three of the following theoretical propositions and discuss how they explain a youthful subculture:
   a. self-enhancement
   b. anomie
   c. cognitive consistency/dissonance
   d. self-fulfilling prophecy
   e. deviant labeling

2. Discuss how the "Teddy Boys" and the "Hippies" were motivated to create a subculture. What were the similarities and the dissimilarities in how and why these two groups chose their particular style of clothing?

3. Explain how the variability permitted in dress within a given society is related to the prevalence of subcultures within the same society.

APPLICATIONS

1. From your own experiences, how did the clothing styles of students in your high school differ? Were there any specific differences between the students who were considered to be troublemakers and the rest of the class?

2. Based on your experience, why do you believe that clothing styles are so important to adolescents? Cite examples to support your answer.

KEY TERMS

accentuate   to emphasize or intensify something.

acquiesce   to accept, comply, or submit passively.

alleviate   to partially remove or correct; lessening something so that it is more bearable or acceptable.

congruent   when something agrees or coincides.

delineate   to describe or explain in detail.

derisive   expressing ridicule or scorn to show contempt toward another.

esoteric   designed for or understood by only a small group.

foppish   behaving or dressing in a manner considered silly or foolish.

idiosyncratic   a characteristic peculiar to an individual or group.

innocous   when something is not offensive or does not produce feelings of hostility or injury.

juxtapose   placing something side by side with something else.

promulgate   to make something known or public; to put something into action or force.

propriety   appropriateness; conformity in behavior or speech to what is socially acceptable.

retaliatory   reciprocating or repaying for the purpose of revenge.

stymied   when an individual's action has been changed or halted by an obstacle.

transcendental   characterizes something that rises above or goes beyond the limits of what is commonly understood or accepted.

vernacular   the language or expression common to a particular group or class.

PART

IV

INSTITUTIONAL RESPONSES TO JUVENILE DELINQUENCY

*T*he reactions to youth and youth behavior have created a multitude of ideas and programs intended to change either the individual, the social institutions, or the societal reactions toward many youth. Some, such as the creation of public schools, were good ideas and have led to some of the greatest successes in history. Although not a panacea for all social problems, youth involvement in education continues to be a positive foundational aspect of our society. Other ideas and programs are just as meritorious and yet the societal consensus as to how the society should respond to youth and especially youth deviance remains elusive, complex, and frustrating.

Part IV includes seven articles that cover some of the most important institutional responses to youth behavior, and all tend to deal with the issue of status to one degree or another. Should juveniles be treated as adults by the police, the courts, or the correctional systems? Should our reactions to youths be more tolerant than our reactions to adults? Are race, gender, or socioeconomic status more important in determining societal reactions than behavior? These questions and issues not only have shaped the present juvenile justice system but also continue to be some of the most pertinent.

Alan Neigher describes one of the most important legal cases in the history of juvenile justice with his article "The Gault Decision: Due Process and the Juvenile Courts." Neigher examines the case, the decision, and the impact of affording juveniles protections once reserved for "adults only." The impact of the Gault Decision is still being felt, and the due process issue brought forth as a result of the decision grows ever more complicated.

The legal responses often are the most formal and least effective in solving human problems. An interesting example of how the formal or manifest functions of an institution for juveniles is subverted by the informal organizations of both inmates and staff is provided by Barry C. Feld in "A Comparative Analysis of Organizational Structure and Inmate Subcultures in Institutions for Juvenile Offenders."

Kenneth Polk, rather than focusing on juvenile institutions, turns his attention to diverting juveniles away from the formal system in "Juvenile Diversion: A Look at the Record." The issues brought up by Polk include recidivism, sexism, and the power of these diversionary programs.

Diversion away from the formal adult criminal justice system, in many ways, created the juvenile justice system and helps maintain the working assumptions that juveniles are less responsible, less culpable, and indeed, are salvageable. "Juvenile Parole Policy in the United States: Determinate versus Indeterminate Models," by Jose B. Ashford and Craig Winston LeCroy, points out that ideational shifts within the juvenile system since the 1960s have still not lead to the resolution of the aftercare issues. The move toward determinacy has not affected aftercare as much as it has the formalization process in juvenile justice.

When reading "The Saints and the Roughnecks," by William J. Chambliss, keep clearly in mind that societal reactions are often the keys to understanding delinquency. Much delinquency is a result of ascription rather than behavior. Most of us can immediately relate this article to our own teen-aged school days. The societal reaction or labeling perspective gained great momentum in the 1960s, and Chambliss offers insight into the application of this perspective.

The unequal treatment of juveniles based on sex is addressed by Gail Armstrong in "Females under Law—'Protected' but Unequal." She claims that a double standard of morality exists wherein females experience differential sentencing results and in fact are not equal under the law. The way in which justice is applied cannot be discriminatory or justice will not exist.

The last article focuses on the recidivism issue in relation to custody type and indirectly examines the deeper issue of correctional outcome. Anne L. Schneider, in "Restitution and Recidivism Rates of Juvenile Offenders: Results from Four Experimental Studies," examines the effects of restitution on recidivism. Her results were encouraging, and she suggests that further research needs to focus on attitudes and future behaviors. Accepting total responsibility for one's behavior and attitudes underlies much of the success of the juveniles in these experiments.

23

The Gault Decision: Due Process and the Juvenile Courts

Alan Neigher

On May 15, 1967, the Supreme Court of the United States ruled that juvenile courts must grant to children many of the procedural protections required in adult criminal trials by the Bill of Rights. In this, the *Gault*[1] decision, the Supreme Court for the first time considered the constitutional rights of children in juvenile courts.

It is not questioned that *Gault* will have a major impact on the future of juvenile courts in this country, many of which having for years operated under a philosophy that made ordinary procedural safeguards seem evil. It is submitted, however, that the *Gault* decision is neither a panacea for children in trouble nor an onerous burden for juvenile law enforcement officers. The decision will hopefully protect young people from being given indeterminate "correctional" sentences for making allegedly obscene phone calls that no one thinks necessary to verify. The decision may make life a bit more difficult for judges and probation officers. It is clear that at the very least, *Gault* will grant some semblance of consistent legal protection to the child.

But there are some popular misconceptions concerning the scope of *Gault*. As an example, the front page of the May 16, 1967, *New York Times* headlined an otherwise excellent summary of the decision as follows: "High Court Rules Adult Code Holds in Juve-

nile Trials . . . Finds Children Are Entitled to the Basic Protections Given in Bill of Rights."[2] But the decision does not accord to juveniles all of the protections of the Bill of Rights. All juvenile courts—with the exception of the District of Columbia—are, in fact, state courts. The Bill of Rights has not yet been made applicable in its entirety to state criminal proceedings. Further, the *Gault* decision was limited to but a few Bill of Rights issues. This must be kept in mind, although, as will be later noted, the decision was as significant for what it *suggested* as it was for what it actually held as binding legal precedent.

Thus, before the decision may be discussed in terms of its implications for the juvenile courts, a brief examination is in order as to what the "basic protections" of the Bill of Rights are, and whether these protections have been extended to state (and thereby juvenile) proceedings.

Bill of Rights and the Fourteenth Amendment

The Bill of Rights[3] means the first Ten Amendments to the newly written Federal Constitution, proposed to the state legislatures by the First Congress in 1789. The Bill of Rights was intended to be a series of limitations on the three *federal* branches: the Congress, the Executive, and the Judiciary. These proposed limitations were a practical political necessity, to mollify local concern

"The Gault Decision: Due Process and the Juvenile Courts," *Federal Probation*, 31 (December 1967) pp. 8–18. Reprinted by permission of Federal Probation.

over the sanctity of state autonomy in many areas of the law, and thereby speed ratification by the necessary nine state legislatures.

Of these Ten Amendments, six are not directly related to the criminal process. These are the First, Second, Third, Seventh, Ninth, and Tenth. Left for consideration, therefore, are the Fourth, Fifth, Sixth, and Eighth Amendments. And of these four, the Fourth and Eighth were not at issue in *Gault* and will be treated briefly.

Before these Amendments are discussed, the Fourteenth Amendment must be considered because it is closely related to the concept of federalism and because it affects not only those Amendments related to the criminal process, but also the entire Ten Amendments and their applicability to the states.

The Bill of Rights was expressly intended to be a check on federal power. There was nothing in the original Constitution to prevent the states from formulating their own systems of criminal administration, and indeed, the Tenth Amendment provides that "The powers not delegated to the United States by the Constitution; nor prohibited by it to the States, are reserved to the States respectively, or to the people."

After the Civil War, almost a century after the ratification of the Constitution (which included the Bill of Rights), Amendments Thirteen, Fourteen, and Fifteen were enacted, largely for the benefit of the newly emancipated slaves. Amendment Thirteen abolished slavery; Amendment Fifteen provided that race, color, or previous condition of servitude shall not be a disability for voting.

Amendment Fourteen was written partly to assure fair and equitable treatment on the part of state authorities to the newly emancipated. For our purposes, its most pertinent part is Section 1, which provides: ". . . No State shall make or enforce any law which shall abridge the privileges or immunities of citizens of the United States; nor shall any State deprive any person of life, liberty, or property, *without due process of law,* nor deny to any person within its jurisdiction the equal protection of the laws."

Thus, the "due process" clause of the Fifth Amendment was made applicable to the states. However, the vague and sweeping concept of due process was slow in making its impact felt on the states which had been left virtually autonomous in formulating criminal procedures. But in recent years, on a case-by-case basis, the Supreme Court has made *some* of the Bill of Rights protection binding on the states through the due process clause of the Fourteenth Amendment. Of those protections now applicable to the states included are several under those Amendments not relevant to the criminal process (especially freedom of speech under the First Amendment), and these need not be considered here.

The Fourth Amendment was largely a reaction to the Writs of Assistance issued in the colonies prior to the Revolution, which gave British revenue officers nearly unlimited authority to search private dwellings and to seize goods. Consequently, the Fourth Amendment reflects the Founders' jealous regard of the right to privacy—to be secure against unreasonable invasion of one's person, property, and home. The Fourth Amendment now applies in full to both federal and state authorities.

The Fourth Amendment provides for the security of people "in their persons, houses, papers, and effects against unreasonable searches and seizures." The laws pertaining to warrants—for both search and arrest—are too technical to be set out here. Suffice it to say that, as to searches and seizures of property, unless there is consent, individuals and their possessions or dwellings cannot be searched or seized without a warrant, except when this is justified by the surrounding circumstances and is done in a reasonable manner.

The Fourth Amendment prohibits unwarranted and unreasonable arrests, but it does not require that the police obtain a warrant for every arrest. The police may arrest without a warrant where the arresting officer actually sees the commission of a misdemeanor or a felony; also, the arresting officer may arrest without a warrant when he has "probable cause" to believe a felony has been committed. Probable cause is difficult to define precisely, but it may generally be stated that it is the existence of such facts and circumstances as would lead a reasonable person to believe that the suspect to be arrested is guilty of the offense.

Where a warrant must be obtained, it must specifically describe the person to be arrested. A general warrant—one that is to be filled in at the arresting officer's convenience—is not valid. An arrest made pursuant to an invalid warrant is unlawful. A warrant for either arrest or search and seizure may be issued only by a magistrate or judge; police officers have no authority to issue warrants.

The Fifth Amendment

The First Congress included a specific provision regarding grand jury indictments as the first clause of the Fifth Amendment. The purpose of the provision is to insure that persons will not be brought to trial arbitrarily when there is no reasonable basis for believing they are guilty of a crime, and that those who are brought to trial will be adequately informed of the charges against them. The Supreme Court has held that the due process clause of the Fourteenth Amendment does not require a state to provide grand jury indictment, so long as the state provides other means of insuring justice to the accused.

The next clause provides that no person "shall . . . be subject for the same offense to be twice put in jeopardy of life or limb." The Founders' sense of fair play led them to include in the Fifth Amendment the concept that the Government should not be able to harass and persecute a man by trying him repeatedly for the same offense. The double jeopardy prohibition has not yet been binding on the states. However, the states are bound by the due process clause of the Fourteenth Amendment; thus, successive trials which flaunt the principles of justice and fair play are not permitted.

The Fifth Amendment next provides that no person "shall be compelled in any criminal case to be a witness against himself. . . ." The history of inquisition and torture in the Old World gave the Founders ample reason to provide against the idea that a man should be forced to incriminate himself by his own words. The privilege has two aspects: (1) the right to be free from coercion designed to extract a confession; and (2) the right to remain silent without having an inference of guilt drawn from that silence.

Freedom from coerced confessions has long been recognized as basic to due process and neither federal nor state governments may extract a confession by force. Force need not be physical; mental coercion such as threats or interrogation to the point of exhaustion would make a confession coerced, and thereby invalid.

The second aspect of the privilege against self-incrimination is the right to remain silent. This is the right invoked by those who "take the Fifth." This right, too, has recently been extended to apply to the states under the Fourteenth Amendment. A criminal defendant has the right to refuse to testify entirely; his failure to take the stand may not even be commented upon by the prosecution in either the federal or state courts. A witness, on the other hand, must take the stand if called, and must claim the privilege one question at a time. The privilege applies not only to criminal trials, but extends also to those before congressional committees, grand juries, and administrative agencies.[4]

The privilege against self-incrimination was highly relevant to the *Gault* decision.

Following the self-incrimination provision appears the most sweeping concept of American jurisprudence: that no person shall "be deprived of life, liberty or property without due process of law." We have seen that the "due process" concept was later duplicated in the Fourteenth Amendment.

If there exists a legal concept not susceptible of precise definition it is due process. It means justice; it means judicial fair play. It is perhaps the very essence of our constitutional tradition. It is both "substantive" and "procedural"—it prohibits the making of laws that are unfair in themselves, and it prohibits unfair application of the law.

Due process applies to Congress in its law-making authority, and forbids laws that are arbitrary or unreasonable. And when the Executive Branch exercises a law-making or rule-making function, it, too, must exercise substantive due process.

Procedural due process requires that the laws, once made, be applied fairly. It means that an individual has the right to be fairly heard before he stands to lose life, liberty, or property. It requires a fair trial in a criminal case and a hearing by an impartial tribunal in a property case.

Procedural due process considerations were at the heart of the *Gault* decision.

The Sixth Amendment

The Sixth Amendment is of particular importance to the *Gault* decision. Of the entire Bill of Rights, it is the one most particularly concerned with the rights of an accused in a Federal criminal trial. The text of the Sixth Amendment follows:

> In all criminal prosecutions, the accused shall enjoy the right to a speedy and public trial, by an impartial jury of the State and District wherein the crime shall have been committed, which District shall have been previously ascertained by law, *and to be informed of the nature and cause of the accusation; to be confronted with the witnesses against him;* to have compulsory process for obtaining witnesses in his favor, *and to have the assistance of Counsel for his defense.* [Emphasis added.]

The right to a jury trial in criminal prosecutions was considered so important to the Founders that they included the right in the main body of the Constitution as well as in the Bill of Rights: Article III, Section 2, commands that the "Trials of all Crimes, except in Cases of Impeachment, shall be by Jury. . . ."

The Sixth Amendment establishes the basic requirement that the accused be tried by the traditional jury of 12. On the other hand, the states are *not* required to provide trial by jury, although many do by virtue of their own constitutions. Some states provide for juries of 8 or 10, rather than 12. However, the Fourteenth Amendment mandate that the states provide due process requires that whatever form of trial the states do provide must be fair.

Not "all criminal prosecutions" by the Federal Government require jury trials. Military trials, criminal contempt proceedings, or petty offenses punishable by small fines or short periods of imprisonment may be conducted without juries. When the right to jury trial applies, this right may be waived, and the defendant may be tried by a judge alone, where both the defendant and the Government so agree, with the consent of the trial judge.

The Sixth Amendment further provides that "the accused enjoy . . . a speedy and public trial." The history of the Inquisition and the Court of the Star Chamber was not lost on the Founding Fathers. These Courts were notorious for their practices of detaining accused persons for long periods, and interrogating witnesses in secret. The Sixth Amendment provided against these abuses by insuring that the accused has the right to defend himself while witnesses and evidence are still available. The wisdom of this protection is readily apparent if one considers the anxiety involved in a prolonged criminal prosecution. Thus, if an accused is not afforded a speedy trial, he may not be tried at all. As to what constitutes a "speedy trial" suffice it to say that standards of reasonableness must govern. The right to a speedy trial has not yet been held binding upon the states under the Fourteenth Amendment, although an obvious prolongment would probably violate due process.

The right to a *public* trial is a basic right under due process, and this right does extend to defendants in trials conducted by the states. The presence of the public and representatives of the press acts as a guarantee that the court will proceed appropriately. The Supreme Court has not yet determined whether all trials must be freely open to the public or whether circumstances will permit a limitation on the type of spectators allowed.

The next protection afforded under the Sixth Amendment is the right to an impartial jury. The definition of "impartial" as used here has two aspects. First, there must be an opportunity for a cross section of the community to serve as jurors. Exclusion because of race, religion, national origin, or economic status violates the defendant's Sixth Amendment rights, whether the trial be federal or state. The cross-section concept does *not* require that every jury be composed of all the various racial, religious, ethnic, or economic groups of the community. It does prohibit court officials from *systematically* excluding any of these groups.

Second, the right to an impartial jury also involves the problem of publicity surrounding the trial. The First Amendment guarantees of free speech and freedom of the press must be balanced against the accused's right to be accorded a jury that will consider his case with an open mind. Modern communications techniques have added great complexity to this problem. The Supreme Court held in the case of Dr. Sam Sheppard that due process is violated where widespread newspaper publicity saturates the community so as to make it virtually impossible to find a panel of impartial jurors.

The Sixth Amendment next requires that a person be tried by "an impartial jury of the State and District wherein the crime shall have been committed, which District shall have been previously ascertained by law." This provision insures that a person will be tried only in that area where the crime was committed—where evidence and witnesses should be readily available, unless circumstances dictate that an impartial trial can only be had elsewhere. It is also required that Congress define in advance the boundaries of the Districts in which crimes shall be tried. The Supreme Court has not yet dealt with the issue of whether the due process clause of the Fourteenth Amendment limits the states in determining where trials for state offenses may be held.

Of great relevance to the *Gault* decision is the next phrase of the Sixth Amendment, which provides that the accused shall enjoy the right "to be informed of the nature and cause of the accusation." Thus, the accused must be informed of the charges against him sufficiently in advance of the court proceedings to allow him a reasonable opportunity to prepare a defense. Also, such notice must specify the alleged misconduct with reasonable particularity. Again this guarantee obtains, whether the trial be federal or state.

The second clause of the Sixth Amendment also was critical to the *Gault* decision. It provides that the accused shall enjoy the right "to be confronted with the witnesses against him." The philosophy underlying this clause is that the accused should be met by his accusers face-to-face, and be able to subject the testimony of the witnesses against him to cross-examination. The right to confrontation is a basic due process protection and applies to state, as well as to federal courts.

The Sixth Amendment next provides that an accused be entitled to have the court compel witnesses to appear and testify if they are unwilling to come voluntarily. A refusal to so compel witnesses to testify on behalf of the accused violates the right to a fair trial, and consequently offends the due process clause. Although the Supreme Court has not dealt directly with the issue, it does not seem likely that such a basic fair trial protection would bail to be held binding on the states under the Fourteenth Amendment.

Finally, the Sixth Amendment provides that the accused shall "have the assistance of counsel for his defense." There was no right to counsel prior to the enactment of the Bill of Rights, and the accused had to rely on the graces of the trial judge to act as his counsel. The inclusion of this right in the Sixth Amendment reflected the belief of the Founders that most defendants are vastly unprepared to protect themselves against the resources of the state's prosecution machinery. The accused today in both federal and state proceedings has the right to counsel in felony cases, and in misdemeanor cases where the accused is in jeopardy of incarceration. In such cases, the recent *Escobedo* and *Miranda* decisions have extended the right to counsel beyond the trial state; the accused is now entitled to counsel when the investigation focuses upon him so as to attempt to elicit incriminating statements. The reader should note that it is at this point, also, that the Fifth Amendment's privilege against self-incrimination attaches.

The Eighth Amendment

Statutes prohibiting excessive bail and cruel and unusual punishment had been enacted in precolonial England and in the constitutions of a number of colonies. These prohibitions were reflected in the Eighth Amendment which reads: "Excessive bail shall not be required, nor excessive fines imposed, nor cruel and unusual punishment inflicted."

It has not been definitely settled whether the provisions of the Eighth Amendment are applicable to the states under the Fourteenth Amendment.

Bail is a mechanism designed to insure the appearance of a defendant in court; by posting bail, the defendant undertakes to guarantee his appearance in court or else forfeit a sum of money. The amount of bail required is generally set by the magistrate who commits an arrested person to custody. Not every accused person is entitled to bail—military personnel and those accused of capital crimes are generally denied such release. But where the accused is entitled to bail, the Eighth Amendment requires that it not be "excessive." Such factors as the defendant's criminal history, the seriousness of the crime and ability to pay are relevant to the issue of excessiveness. There is generally no right to bail after conviction pending appeal; requests for such bail are left largely to the discretion of the trial judge.

As to the excessive fine provision, it is generally left to Congress to prescribe the limits of fines and to the trial courts to decide what fine should be imposed in a particular case. The Supreme Court has refused to review fines levied by the lower federal courts.

There are no precise standards as to what constitutes cruel and unusual punishment. The death penalty is not of itself cruel and unusual; what is forbidden by very early tradition of Anglo-American law is the infliction of unnecessary pain in the execution of the death sentence.

It is apparent that the Eighth Amendment, like its companions, leaves many problems unanswered, especially because the Eighth Amendment's prohibitions are not yet binding on the states. The law of bail—especially as it applies to the indigent accused—is in a state of re-evaluation. There are those who have argued, in the wake of the Chessman case, that long delay in execution is cruel and unusual punishment; indeed, there are many who argue that by modern standards, the death penalty is itself cruel and unusual punishment.

It is not pretended that the above summary of certain of the Bill of Rights criminal protections is an authoritative treatise. Indeed, entire volumes have been written on some individual Amendments. It is only hoped that the reader be informed of these protections so that the *Gault* decision might be placed in its proper constitutional perspective.

The Case of the "Lewd and Indecent" Phone Call

Gerald and another boy were taken into custody in the morning of June 8, 1964, by the Sheriff of Gila County, Arizona. The police were acting upon a verbal complaint from a Mrs. Cook, a neighbor of the boys, that she received a lewd and indecent phone call. Both of Gerald's parents were at work that morning and no notice of the police action was left at their home. Gerald's mother learned of his being taken to the Children's Detention House only after Gerald's older brother went to look for him at the home of the other boy. At the Detention Home, the mother and brother were told "why Jerry was there" and that a hearing would be held the next day at 3 o'clock.

A petition praying for a hearing was filed on June 9 by an Officer Flagg which recited that "said minor is under the age of 18 years and in need of protection of this Honorable Court [and that] said minor is a delinquent minor." The petition was not served on the Gaults and they first saw it 2 months later.

On June 9, a hearing was held in the chambers of Juvenile Judge McGhee with Gerald, his mother, his brother and the probation officers being present. No formal or informal record of this hearing was made. Judge McGhee questioned Gerald about the telephone calls without advising him of a right to counsel or a privilege against self-incrimination. There is conflicting testimony as to Gerald's answers. Both Officer Flagg and Judge McGhee stated that Gerald admitted making at least one of the indecent remarks while Mrs. Gault recalled that her son only admitted dialing Mrs. Cook's number.

Gerald was released from the detention home without explanation on either the 11th or the 12th (again the memories of Mrs. Gault and Officer Flagg conflict) pending further hearings; a hearing was held before Judge McGhee on June 15th. Mrs. Gault asked that Mrs. Cook be present but was told by the Judge that "she didn't have to be present." Neither the Gaults nor Officer Flagg remembered any admission by Gerald at this proceeding of making the indecent remarks, though the judge did remember Gerald's admitting some of the less serious statements. At the conclusion of the hearing, Gerald was committed as a juvenile delinquent to the State Industrial School "for the period of his minority [6 years] unless sooner discharged by due process of law."

No appeal is permitted under Arizona law in juvenile cases. Gerald filed a writ of habeas corpus with the Supreme Court of Arizona which was referred to the Superior Court for hearing. Among other matters, Judge McGhee testified that he acted under a section of the Arizona Code which defines a "delinquent child" as one who (in the judge's words) is "habitually involved in immoral matters." The basis for the judge's conclusion seemed to be a referral made 2 years earlier concerning Gerald when the boy allegedly had "stolen" a baseball glove "and lied to the Police Department about it." No petition or hearing apparently resulted from this "referral." The judge testified that Gerald had violated the section of the Arizona Criminal Code which provides that a person who "in the presence of or hearing of any woman or child . . . uses vulgar, abusive or obscene language, is guilty of a misdemeanor. . . ." The penalty for an adult convicted under this section is a fine of $5 to $50, or imprisonment for not more than 2 months.

The Superior Court dismissed the habeas corpus petition, and Gerald sought review in the Arizona Supreme Court on many due process grounds. The Arizona Supreme Court affirmed the dismissal of the petition.

The appellants, in their appeal to the United States Supreme Court, did not raise all of the issues brought before the Supreme Court of Arizona. The appeal was based on the argument that the Juvenile Code of Arizona is invalid because, contrary to the due process clause of the Fourteenth Amendment, the juvenile is taken from the custody of his parents and committed to a state institution pursuant to proceedings where the Juvenile Court has virtually unlimited discretion, and in which the following basic rights are denied: Notice of the charges; right to counsel; right to confrontation and cross-examination; privilege against self-incrimination; right to a transcript of the proceedings; and right to appellate review.

These were the questions before the Supreme Court in the *Gault* decision. The Court explicitly noted that other issues passed upon by the Supreme Court of Arizona, but not presented by the appellants to the Supreme Court of the United States, would not be considered. This is consistent with the Court's strict practice of reviewing—if it chooses to review at all—only those issues actually presented to it.

The Decision

The *Gault* decision was handed down May 15, 1967, a little over 5 months after its oral argument was heard by the Supreme Court. Mr. Justice Fortas wrote the opinion for the majority which was, in effect, 8 to 1. Justice Fortas was joined by Chief Justice Warren and Justices Brennan, Clark, and Douglas. Mr. Justice Black concurred with the result but argued that juveniles in jeopardy of confinement be tried in accordance with all of the Bill of Rights protections made applicable to the states by the Fourteenth Amendment.[5] Mr. Justice White concurred with the majority except for Part V concerning self-incrimination, confrontation, and cross-examination which he felt need not be reached, since the decision would be reversed on other grounds.[6] Mr. Justice Harlan concurred in part and dissented in part: he concurred with the majority insofar as it held that Gerald was deprived of due process of law by being denied adequate notice, record of the proceedings, and right to counsel; he dissented on the grounds that the other procedural safeguards imposed by the Court might discourage "efforts to find more satisfactory solutions for the problems of juvenile crime, and may thus now hamper enlightened development of juvenile courts."[7]

Only Mr. Justice Stewart dissented in full. Although acknowledging the shortcomings of many of the juvenile and family courts, he maintained that the procedural safeguards imposed by the decision would abolish the flexibility and informality of juvenile courts and would cause children again to be treated as adults.[8]

In summary form, the decision held as follows:

Notice of Charges.[9]—A petition alleging in general terms that the child is "neglected, dependent or delinquent" is sufficient notice under Arizona law.[10] It is not required that the petition be served upon the parents. No facts need be alleged in the initial petition; the Arizona Supreme Court held that such facts need not be alleged until the close of the initial hearing. No petition at all was served upon Gerald or his parents prior to the initial hearing.

The Arizona Supreme Court rejected Gerald's claim that due process had been denied because of failure to provide adequate notice on the following grounds: that "Mrs. Gault knew the exact nature of the charge against Gerald from the day he was taken to the detention home"; that the Gaults had appeared at the two hearings "without objection"; that advance notice of the specific charges or basis for taking the juvenile into custody and for the hearing is not necessary because "the policy of the juvenile law is to hide youthful errors from the full gaze of the public and bury them in the graveyard of the forgotten past."

The Supreme Court rejected these arguments, noting that the "initial hearing" in this case was in fact a hearing on the merits of the case. The Court stated that even if there was validity to the practice of deferring specific notice on the grounds of protecting the child from the public eye, it must yield to the due process requirement of adequate notice. Therefore, a hearing where a youth's freedom and the parent's right to custody are in jeopardy may not be held unless the child and his parents or guardian be first notified in writing of the specific issues that must be met at that hearing. Such notice must be given at the earliest practicable time and sufficiently in advance of the hearing to

permit preparation. Mere "knowledge" of the kind Mrs. Gault allegedly had of the charges against Gerald does not constitute a waiver of the right to adequate notice because of its lack of particularity.

Right to Counsel.[11]—The Arizona Supreme Court had held that representation of counsel for a minor is discretionary with the trial judge. The Supreme Court disagreed, noting that neither probation officer nor judge can adequately represent the child. Since a proceeding where a child stands to be found "delinquent" and subject to loss of liberty is comparable in gravity to an adult felony prosecution, the juvenile needs the assistance of counsel for the same reasons underlying the inclusion of the right in the Sixth Amendment: The juvenile—even less than the average adult criminal defendant—is not prepared to cope with the complexities of the law or of building an adequate defense. Thus, the due process clause of the Fourteenth Amendment requires that in state proceedings which may result in commitment the child and his parent must be notified of the child's right to be represented by counsel. If they are unable to afford a lawyer, one must be appointed for them.[12]

The Court discounted the holding of the Arizona Supreme Court that since Mrs. Gault knew that she could have appeared with counsel, her failure to do so was a waiver of the right. Notification of the right to counsel plus "specific consideration" of whether to waive the right must precede a valid waiver. Without being expressly advised of the right (and Mrs. Gault was not so advised) there can be no "specific consideration" and thus, no waiver.

Self-Incrimination, Confrontation, and Cross-Examination.[13]—It will be recalled that at the June 9 hearing, Judge McGhee questioned Gerald about the telephone calls without advising him of his right to counsel or his right to remain silent. The judge and Officer Flagg stated that Gerald admitted making at least one of the indecent remarks; Mrs. Gault recalled only that her son admitted dialing Mrs. Cook's number. The Arizona Supreme Court rejected Gerald's contention that he had a right to be advised that he need not incriminate himself, saying that the "necessary flexibility for individualized treatment will be enhanced by a rule which does not require the judge to advise the infant of a privilege against self-incrimination."

The Supreme Court rejected this view and held that any admissions that Gerald allegedly made were improperly obtained in violation of the Fifth Amendment's privilege against self-incrimination. The Court traced the history underlying the privilege, and observed: "one of its purposes is to prevent the State, whether by force or by psychological domination, from overcoming the mind and will of the person under investigation and depriving him of the freedom to decide whether to assist the State in securing his conviction." The Court implied that no less than the freedom from coerced confessions is the importance of the reliability, especially as to alleged admissions or confessions from those of Gerald's age, must undergo careful scrutiny for in the Court's words: "It would indeed be surprising if the privilege against self-incrimination were available to hardened criminals but not to children. The language of the Fifth Amendment, applicable to the States by peration of the Fourteenth Amendment, is unequivocal and without exception. And the scope of the privilege is comprehensive."[14]

The State of Arizona argued that the Fifth Amendment provides only that no person "shall be compelled in any *criminal case* to be a witness against himself" and should therefore not apply through the Fourteenth Amendment to state juvenile proceedings. The Supreme Court held that the privilege is not based upon the *type* of proceeding in which it is involved, "but upon the nature of the statement or admission made, the exposure which it invites." Since the privilege may be invoked in a civil or administrative proceeding, the court noted that it would make no difference whether juvenile proceedings are deemed "civil" or "criminal." The Court took the opportunity to express its disapproval with these labels, and noted that in over half of the states juveniles may be placed in adult penal institutions after findings of delinquency.[15] The Court stated: "For this purpose, at least, commitment is a deprivation of liberty. It is incarceration against one's will, whether it is called 'criminal' or 'civil.' And our Constitution guarantees that no person shall be 'compelled' to be a witness against himself when he is threatened with deprivation of his liberty. . . ."

The Court noted that "special problems may arise with respect to waiver of the privilege by or on behalf of children, and that there may well be some differences in technique—but not in principle—depending upon the age of the child and the presence and competence of parents." And as special care must be taken before the privilege is validly waived, so also must admissions obtained without the presence of counsel be subject to the greatest scrutiny. Here we see the Fifth Amendment's self-incrimination provision to be vitally interwoven with the Sixth Amendment's right to counsel.

The "confession" of Gerald, made without counsel, outside of the presence of his parents, and without advising him of his right to remain silent served as a basis for Judge McGhee's finding of delinquency. Since this "admission" or "confession" was obtained in violation of those rights noted above, the Supreme Court searched for another basis on which the judgment might rest. There was none to be found. There was no sworn testimony. The complainant, Mrs. Cook, did not appear. The Arizona Supreme Court held that "sworn testimony must be required of all witnesses" including those related to the juvenile court system. The Supreme Court held that this is not sufficient: In the absence of a valid confession adequate to support the determination of the Court, confrontation and sworn testimony by witnesses available for cross-examination were essential for a finding of "delinquency" and a subsequent order depriving Gerald of his liberty.[16] The court made it clear, therefore, that an adjudication of "delinquency" or a commitment to an institution is invalid unless the juvenile is afforded the same protections respecting sworn testimony that an adult would receive in a criminal trial.

Appellate Review and Transcript of Proceedings.[17]—The Supreme Court did not specifically decide whether there is a right to appellate review in a juvenile case[18] or whether juvenile courts are required to provide a transcript of the hearings for review, because the decision of the Arizona Supreme Court could be reversed on other grounds. Notwithstanding its failure to rule directly on this issue, the Court pointed out the undesirable consequences of the present case, where: no record of the proceedings was kept; no findings or grounds for basing the juvenile court's conclusions were stated; and the reviewing courts were forced to reconstruct a record while Judge McGhee had the "unseemly duty of testifying under cross-examination as to the events that transpired in the hearings before him."[19]

Epilogue

It should be evident to the reader that the legal precedents handed down by the *Gault* decision are neither numerous nor complex. At any proceeding where a child may be committed to a state institution, that child and his parent or guardian must be given notice in writing of the specific charges against the child sufficiently in advance of the proceedings to permit adequate preparation. The child and his parent must be notified of the child's right to be represented by counsel, and if financial considerations so require, counsel must be appointed for them. The child and his parents or guardian must be advised of the child's right to remain silent. Admission or confessions obtained from the child without the presence of counsel must undergo the greatest scrutiny in order to insure reliability. In the absence of a valid confession, no finding of "delinquency" and no order of commitment of the child for any length of time may be upheld unless such finding is supported by confrontation and sworn testimony of witnesses available for cross-examination.

If indeed the *Gault* decision were significant only for the black-letter law, summarized above, the demands made upon our juvenile judges and probation officers would be rather easy to comply with. The few mandates of *Gault* would eventually become implemented (with, of course, varying degrees of enthusiasm). However, the decision cannot be read solely in the light of its few binding precedents.

Some may recall that it was the same Justice Fortas who wrote for the majority in the *Kent*[20] decision, which a year prior to *Gault* considered the requirement for a valid waiver of "exclusive" jurisdiction of the juvenile court of the District of Columbia so that a youth could be tried in the District's adult criminal court. The essence of *Kent* was that the basic requirements of due process and fairness be met in such a proceeding. But although confined to the narrow issue of waiver proceedings, *Kent* was a prologue to *Gault* insofar as it expressed disenchantment with the course of juvenile justice in this country, which was expressed in an often-quoted sentence: "There is evidence . . . that there may be grounds for concern that the child receives the worst of both worlds: that he gets neither the protections accorded to adults nor the solicitous care and regenerative treatment postulated for children."[21]

With this warning, an alert was sounded in *Kent* for what would become in *Gault* an indictment of the juvenile courts. Despite the limitation of issues actually adjudicated in the decision, *Gault*, taken as a whole, is a comprehensive note of concern over the administration of juvenile justice in this country. Part II of the decision[22] dealing largely with background and history contains 41 footnotes citing materials covering the entire ambit of juvenile justice, from custody to treatment, from probation to psychiatric care, and including numerous books, studies, and articles critical of virtually every aspect of the juvenile process. In Part II the parens patriae doctrine—the concept of the state assuming the role of substitute parent—was challenged on both historical grounds ("its meaning is murky and its historic credentials are of dubious relevance") and on legal grounds ("[T]he constitutional and theoretical basis for this peculiar system is—to say the least—debatable"). The nomenclature attached to "receiving homes" or "industrial schools" did not, in the Court's view, alter the practical reality that these are institutions of confinement where juveniles may for years be deprived of their liberty. The Court was careful to note that the "substitute parents" of the early reformers' ideology have, in fact, become guards, state employees, and fellow juveniles incarcerated for offenses ranging in scope from "waywardness" to rape and murder.

It is therefore apparent to the reader of Part II of the *Gault* decision that the case was not, as the narrow scope of its holding might wrongly suggest, decided in the abstract. Part II was a harsh and critical prelude to the decision. It was tempered with concern for a system of justice that the Court suggests has fallen short of its early hopes and aspirations, and it was laced with documentation of these failings. It is submitted that the marked distaste for the course of juvenile justice in this country, which permeated the decision, was of itself a prologue (as *Kent* was for *Gault*) for further decisions by the Supreme Court extending the due process clause into other aspects of juvenile proceedings. To speculate on the direction of such hypothetical extensions would be indeed foolish. As noted earlier, the Supreme Court selects only a small fraction of those cases submitted to it for review, and of these, only those issues necessary to dispose of a case are actually adjudicated (the appellate review and transcript issue in *Gault* is an example).

For those who are understandably concerned with the present, the *Gault* decision leaves many questions unanswered. Mr. Justice Fortas wrote in *Gault* that "neither the Fourteenth Amendment nor the Bill of Rights is for adults alone." But if indeed they are not for adults only, the Fourteenth Amendment and the Bill of Rights are not yet for children completely. The *Gault* decision did not cover the procedures or constitutional rights applicable to the pre-judicial or post-adjudicative stages of the juvenile process.[23] Thus, the body of law now pertaining to the rights of the adult criminal suspect when he is first brought into custody does not yet apply to the juvenile suspect. It is yet to be decided whether the Fourth Amendment's prohibitions against unreasonable searches and seizures, protections made fully binding upon the states, will affect the kind of evidentiary matter admissible against the child in an adjudicatory proceeding. The Fifth Amendment's right to a grand jury indictment and the double jeopardy prohibition have not yet been made fully binding upon the states by the Supreme Court, and their relevance to juvenile proceedings are uncertain.

One may ponder whether prolonged confinement in a "receiving home" pending a hearing on the merits would violate the Sixth Amendment's guarantee of a *speedy* trial, if this right is held to be firmly binding upon the states. The Sixth Amendment's guarantee to a *public* trial, which is binding upon the states, may have significant implications for juvenile hearings, which have by statute in a large proportion of the states been closed to the public. The Sixth Amendment's guarantee that the accused be entitled to have the court compel witnesses to appear and testify, a right closely related to the right of confrontation, has potential relevance to juvenile hearings, and cannot be ignored (although this right is not yet firmly binding upon the states under the Fourteenth Amendment).

One might further consider the Eighth Amendment and its prohibitions against cruel and unusual punishment, excessive fines, and excessive bail. If any or all of the Eighth Amendment is eventually made binding upon the states, how will the course of juvenile justice be affected? Is it cruel and unusual punishment to deny to a child those safeguards not considered by *Gault* and then subject that child to confinement in an institution of limited treatment facilities? Does unconditional relegation to a "receiving home" pending a hearing infringe on the prohibition against excessive bail?

That these issues may legitimately be framed, in the light of the Supreme Court's refusal in *Gault* to accept the traditional noncriminal label attached to juvenile proceedings is, in the writer's opinion, the greatest significance of the decision. It is not possible to even speculate as to the extent to which the Supreme Court is prepared to go in according to juveniles the procedural safeguards available to adults in criminal proceedings. All that is clear is that the sweeping, intangible concept of due process has at last been officially introduced to our juvenile courts.

Notes

1. *In Re Gault*, 387 U.S. 1 (1967).
2. *New York Times*, May 16, 1967, p. 1, col. 1 (city ed.).

3. For excellent summaries of the entire Constitution from which much of the following material on the Bill of Rights is drawn, see Antieau, *Commentaries on the Constitution of the United States* (1960), and The Younger Lawyers Committee of the Federal Bar Association, *These Unalienable Rights* (1965).

4. The privilege has one notable exception: A person has no right to remain silent if a statute (federal or state) gives him immunity from prosecution—that is, if the government is prevented from prosecuting him on the basis of his testimony.

5. *In Re Gault*, supra note 1, at 59–64.

6. *Id.* at 64–65.

7. *Id.* at 77.

8. *Id.* at 78–81.

9. *Id.* at 31–34.

10. Ariz. Rev. Stat. ANN. tit. 8, 222 (1955).

11. *In Re Gault, supra* note 1, at 34–42.

12. The Court emphasized as "forceful" the Report of the President's Commission on Law Enforcement and Administration of Justice, *The Challenge of Crime in a Free Society*, pp. 86–7 (hereinafter cited as NAT'L CRIMECOMM'N REPORT) (1967), which recommended: "Counsel should be appointed as a matter of course wherever coercive action is a possibility without requiring any affirmative choice by child or parent." In *Re Gault, supra* note 1, at 38–40 n. 65. Also cited was HEW, *Standards for Juvenile and Family Courts*, Children's Bureau Pub. No. 437–1966, p. 57 (1966) (hereinafter cited as *Standards*) which states: "As a component part of a fair hearing required by due process guaranteed under the 14th Amendment, notice of the right to counsel should be required at all hearings and counsel provided upon request when the family is financially unable to employ counsel." In *Re Gault, supra* note 1, at 39.

13. *Id.* at 42–57.

14. The Court cited to this point *Standards, supra* note 12, at 49, for authority that prior to a police interview, the child and his parents should be informed of his right to have legal counsel present and to refuse to answer questions. This provision of the *Standards* also suggests that the parents and child be informed of their right to refuse to be fingerprint-ed, but the Court refused to express any opinion as to fingerprinting as this issue was not before the Court. In *Re Gault, supra* note 1, at 49.

15. HEW, *Delinquent Children in Penal Institutions*, Children's Bureau Pub. No. 415–1964, p. 1 (1964).

16. For this point, the Court again cited *Standards, supra* note 12, at 72–73, which states that all testimony should be under oath and that only competent material and relevant evidence under rules applicable to civil cases should be admitted into evidence. Also cited was, *e.g.*, Note, "Rights and Rehabilitation in Juvenile Courts," 67 Colum. L. Rev. 281, 336 (1967): "Particularly in delinquency cases, where the issue of fact is the commission of a crime, the introduction of hearsay—such as the report of a policeman who did not witness the events—contravenes the purpose underlying the Sixth Amendment right of confrontation." (Footnote omitted.) in *Re Gault, supra* note 1, at 56–57 n. 98.

17. *Id.* at 57–59.

18. The Supreme Court has yet to hold that a state is required to provide any right to appellate review, *Griffin v. Illinois*, 351 U.S. 12, 18 (1956).

19. The Court cited, *e.g., Standards*, supra note 12, at 8, which recommends "written findings of fact, some form or record of the hearing" "and the right to appeal." It recommends verbatim recording of the hearing by stereotypist or mechanical recording. *Id* at 76. Finally, it urges that the judge make clear to the child and family their right to appeal. *Id.* at 78. Also cited was, *e.g.,* NAT'L CRIME COMM'N REPORT, supra note 12, at 86, which states that "records make possible appeals which, even if they do not occur, import by their possibility a healthy atmosphere of accountability." In *Re Gault, supra* note 1, at 58–69, n. 102.

20. *Kent v. United States*, 383 U.S. 541 (1966).

21. *Id.* at 556, citing Handler. "The Juvenile Courts and the Adversary Systems: Problems of Function and Form," 1965 WIS. L. REV. 7 (other citations omitted).

22. *In Re Gault, supra* note 1, at 12–31.

23. *Id.* at 13.

QUESTIONS FOR DISCUSSION

1. The *Gault* Decision afforded juveniles specific protections of the Bill of Rights. What were those protections?

2. What "protections" were adults afforded by the Bill of Rights that juveniles did not receive?

3. Explain what is meant by an "impartial jury."

APPLICATIONS

1. The *Gault* Decision, handed down in 1967, was the first time in American history that the Supreme Court granted procedural protections to juveniles under the Bill of Rights. In your opinion, why did the extension of these rights to juveniles take so long?

2. Since 1967 have any other constitutional rights been extended to or broadened by the Supreme Court? Explain.

KEY TERMS

ambit   refers to a sphere of action or influence; the scope of one's control.

mandate   a directive or requirement.

mollify   to soothe in temper or disposition; to soften or pacify.

nomenclature   designation or description with a particular and agreed-upon set of terms.

onerous   characterizes something that is troublesome or that causes a burden.

panacea   a cure-all; a remedy for all ills or problems.

permeate   to diffuse through or to penetrate.

postulate   to assume or claim to be true, existent, or necessary.

pursuant to   in conformity with or according to a pre-existing condition.

24

A Comparative Analysis of Organizational Structure and Inmate Subcultures in Institutions for Juvenile Offenders

Barry C. Feld

The penological debate over the origins, processes, and characteristics of inmate subcultures in correctional facilities has attributed the qualities of subcultures either to features of the formal organization or to preimprisonment characteristics of the incarcerated offenders.[1] Observers of adult and juvenile correctional facilities confirm the emergence of inmate subcultures within institutions, and most studies of prison cultures document their oppositional qualities ,with the hostility and antagonism between inmates and staff subsumed in an "inmate code."[2]

The two competing explanations of the inmate social system are commonly referred to as the "indigenous origins" model and the "direct importation" model.[3] The former provides a functionalist explanation that relates the values and roles of the subculture to the inmates' responses to problems of adjustment posed by institutional deprivations and conditions of confinement.[4]

Accordingly, the formal organization of the prison shapes the informal inmate social system. While earlier studies of adult maximum-security prisons described a monolithic inmate culture of collective opposition to staff values and goals,[5] more recent studies suggest that a modification of organizational structure in pursuit of treatment goals results in considerably greater variability in the inmate social system and the processes of prisonization.[6]

An alternative interpretation attributes the normative order of adult prisons to the identities, roles, and values held by the inmates before incarceration.[7] Accordingly, inmates' personal characteristics shape the subculture, and in a population of incarcerated offenders an oppositional, criminal value system predominates. Differences in social characteristics such as sex, race, or criminal involvement before incarceration influence both the subculture's qualities and any individual inmate's adaptations to it.[8]

Inmate Violence in Institutions

The prevalence of inmate violence and its significance for stratification, role differentiation, and subcultural processes repre-

"A Comparative Analysis of Organizational Structure and Inmate Subcultures in Institutions for Juvenile Offenders," *Crime and Delinquency*, 27:3 (1981), pp. 336–363. Reprinted by permission of the publisher, Sage Publications, Inc.

sent a recurring theme.[9] However, the relationships between organizational variables, inmate violence, and other characteristics of the subculture have not been adequately explored.

Physical aggression, verbal abuse, or psychological intimidation can be used to create or reestablish relationships of domination and submission within the subculture.[10] Many maxims of the inmate code are attempts to regulate violence and exploitation among inmates, and many of the "argot" roles differentiate inmates on the basis of their use of or response to aggression.[11] For individual inmates, many of the "pains of imprisonment"—material deprivations, sexual isolation, and threats to status, self-esteem, and personal security—cited in functionalist explanations of subcultures can be alleviated by the use of violence. While imprisonment imposes deprivations, violence and exploitation provide at least some inmates with a potential solution, albeit at the expense of other inmates.[12]

The prevalence of inmate violence also reflects characteristics of the incarcerated. Many adult and juvenile inmates are drawn from social backgrounds or cultures that emphasize toughness, manliness, and the protection of one's own physical integrity.[13] Preincarceration experiences equip in different ways inmates from diverse social, economic, criminal, racial, or sexual backgrounds to participate in the violent subcultures within some institutions.[14] Thus, a predisposition to violence among the inmate subculture also reflects influences of cultural importation which organizational features may aggravate or mitigate.

Neither functionalist nor importation explanations alone adequately explain the characteristics of the inmate subculture or an inmate's adaptations to it. The functionalist model does not account for the influence of pre- and postimprisonment variables on inmates' adaptations, while the importation model does not fully explicate the connections between preprison characteristics and the subcultures that arise within institutions that are not custodial or punitive. Although some recent research attempts to integrate the two perspectives by identifying the ways

in which preprison characteristics influence inmates' adaptations to adjustment problems created by the organization,[15] most subculture studies suffer from the common shortcoming of focusing on prisonization within only a single institution. In contrast, a comparison of organizations would permit a fuller exploration of the relationships between formal organizational structure and the ensuing inmate culture, as well as of the influence of preprison characteristics on the adaptations of inmates in diverse settings.[16] Controlling for the effects of preincarceration characteristics on inmates' perceptions and adaptations, this study presents a comparative analysis of the ways in which variations in organizational goals and intervention strategies in institutions for juvenile offenders produce differences in the informal inmate social system.

Organizational features affect the inmate subculture and the prevalence of inmate violence both by creating incentives for inmates to resort to violence and by providing inmates with opportunities to use violence. Organizational variations in the nature and extent of deprivations may motivate inmates in different ways to exploit others. Various organizational control strategies differ in the degree to which they provide an environment conducive to the use of violence to relieve these deprivations. The deprivations and control strategies also influence many other aspects of the subculture. This comparative analysis examines the variations in organizational goals, staff intervention strategies, and social control practices that influence the levels of violence and the structure of the inmate social system.

Correctional Typology

There are several descriptions of the organizational variations in juvenile and adult correctional facilities that can be used as tools to classify systematically and compare the relationships between organizational structure and inmate subculture.[17] A common classification distinguishes juvenile correctional organizations on the basis of their custody or treatment goals,[18] distinguishing differences in goals on the basis of the relative emphases staff place on custody and containment, and on vocational and academic education versus clinical or group treatment.[19] The intervention strategies used to achieve either custodial or therapeutic goals range from group-oriented practices to those more attuned to individuals' characteristics.[20] Group-oriented strategies reflect efforts to change or control an inmate through the group of which he is a member, while individualized methods of intervention focus more directly on the person, without comparable manipulation of the social environment.

Organizational goals—custody or treatment—and strategies of change—group or individual—may vary independently; thus, four different types of correctional organizations may be distinguished on the basis of both their correctional goals and the means used to attain those goals (see Figure 1).

Every juvenile correctional institution confronts the same necessity to explain both what its clients' problems are and how the clients should be rehabilitated.[21] The answers to the questions of cause and cure in turn determine the organizational goals and the intervention strategies and social control practices required to achieve them. The typology in Figure 1 illustrates four different kinds of correctional solutions to the problems of juvenile offenders. It also suggests several interrelated organizational variables: a staff ideology defining inmates and their needs, organizational goals serving those needs, intervention strategies implemented

through programs and social control practices, and the structure of relationships between inmates and staff.

A degree of internal consistency among these organizational variables is necessary. Methods of intervention and social control practices must be complementary, since efforts to ensure compliance that alienate the inmate are incompatible with change strategies requiring commitment on the part of that inmate.[22] Compliance strategies and programs will vary with the correctional goals and inmate changes sought and determine the kinds of relationships staff develop with inmates. Amitai Etzioni's compliance framework provides a basis for a comparative organizational analysis of staff control strategies and inmates' responses in coercive and normative-coercive settings.[23] The primary correctional social control strategies are (1) the threat or use of physical coercion, (2) the threat or use of transfer to less desirable units or isolation cells, (3) the use of a privilege system,[24] and (4) collaboration between inmates and staff, which may be either informal[25] or formal.[26]

Methods

The data for this study were collected in ten cottage units located in four juvenile institutions administered by the Massachusetts Department of Youth Services before the closing of the training schools.[27] A process of institutional decentralization initiated to transform the various cottage settings

FIGURE 1   Correctional Typology

Organizational Means	Organizational Goals	
	Custody	Treatment
Group-Oriented Intervention Strategy	Group Custody Custodial[a] Obedience/Conformity[b] Protective custody[c]	Group Treatment Group treatment[a] Treatment[b] Therapeutic community[c]
Individual-Oriented Intervention Strategy	Individual Custody Educational[a] Reeducation/Development[b] Protective custody[c]	Individual Treatment Psychotherapeutic[a] Treatment[b,c]

a. Organization corresponding to typology in Studt, Messinger, and Wilson, *C-Unit*, p. 12.
b. Organization corresponding to typology in Street, Vinter, and Perrow, *Organization for Treatment*, p. 12.
c. Organization corresponding to typology in Ohlin, "Organizational Reform in Correctional Agencies," p. 1000.

TABLE 1   Inmate Background Characteristics

| | Custody-Oriented Cottages | | | | | Treatment-Oriented Cottages | | | |
| | Group | Individual | | | | Individual | Group | | |
	Cottage 9 (n = 27)	Cottage 8 (n = 15)	Elms (n = 40)	Westview (n = 29)	Lancaster (F) (n = 28+22)[a]	Topsfield (coed) (n = 15)	Sunset (n = 15)	Shirley (n = 16)	"I Belong" (n = 8)
Mean age	15.7	16.3	15.6	15.6	14.9	16.2	15.5	16.3	14.2
Percentage black inmates	19%	27%	35%	21%	11%	32%	25%	19%	25%
Mean age at first juvenile court appearance	12.6	13.2	12.7	13.1	13.1	14.1	12.5	13.8	12.4
Seriousness of present offense (percentage of residents)									
High [b]	24%	36%	35%	27%	9%	0%	23%	21%	29%
Moderate [c]	68	43	60	54	34	60	77	57	43
Low [d]	8	21	5	19	57	40	0	21	28
Prior institutional experience (percentage of residents)	92%	82%	90%	62%	60%	87%	73%	67%	50%

a.   Institutional decentralization and the development of cottage-based programs occurred later and, when this study was conducted, were less complete at the Industrial School for Girls, Lancaster, than at the corresponding male institutions. The school still functioned as a traditional training school without any significant program differentiation by cottage. Separate analysis of inmate and staff data in the two cottages sampled (n = 28 + 22) revealed virtually no differences. Consequently, the Lancaster questionnaire data are presented in the aggregate.

b.   Offenses against the person—murder, manslaughter, rape, assaults, robbery, and the like.

c.   Property offenses—burglary, theft, forgery, unauthorized use of a motor vehicle, and drug offenses.

d.   Misdemeanor-level public misbehavior, such as disorderly conduct, as well as juvenile status offenses.

into small, therapeutic communities[28] provided considerable autonomy and independence for each individual unit. Clinical, vocational, academic, and cottage personnel either formed staff teams or were assigned to cottages to develop coordinated treatment programs. Decentralization resulted in a number of diverse "mini-institutions" in which staff pursued a variety of goals using different intervention strategies.

Since inmate assignments to the various cottages were not randomized, the ten cottages studied were selected to maximize the comparability of inmate populations and the variety of treatment strategies used. The ten cottages studied included seven units for males, two for females,[29] and one coeducational facility, located in four different state institutions. Cottage populations were matched on the basis of age, race, past criminal histories (both official and self-reported), present commitment offense, age at initial contact and number of prior juvenile court appearances, and prior commitments to institutions. The inmate characteristics in the various cottages are summarized in Table 1. The cottages sampled produced comparable inmate groups. Although cottage assign-

ments were not randomized, there was no systematic effort by administrators to match inmate "needs" with particular treatment programs, and the primary determinants were the availability of bed space and the need to maintain a population balance among the various cottages.

In addition to the matching of populations, statistical controls for the effects of background characteristics within each cottage were used to establish cottage comparability. Controls for each background variable were used to determine whether a particular characteristic was systematically associated with differences within each cottage population and whether the differences among cottages were a product of these population differences. In addition to tests for relationships between background variables and attitudes, sign tests were used to allow for interaction effects between inmates' characteristics and cottage treatment strategies. Despite some variations in the respective cottage populations, these techniques support the conclusion that the substantial differences between cottages were not a function of variations in the inmate populations and are properly attributed to the cottages' social structures.[30]

In institutions with young populations (averaging approximately sixteen years of age), who are presumably less committed to criminal careers than are imprisoned adults and who are incarcerated for an average of four months, it is not surprising that background characteristics or preimprisonment experiences are subordinate to the more immediate, organizational imperatives. (Because the sample is not random, no tests of significance are reported.)

Data were collected in each of the ten cottages by a team of five trained researchers who spend about six weeks in each unit administering questionnaires and interview schedules to both staff members and residents. Between 90 and 100 percent of the staff and residents in each cottage completed hour-long closed-ended questionnaires and equally extensive open-ended structural interviews. Most of the researchers' time was spend in participant observation and unstructured interviews, with field notes transcribed onto standardized forms to simplify analysis, coding, and comparison of observations from different settings.

Findings

Organizational Structure

Although the administrators of the Massachusetts Department of Youth Services told the institutional staff to "do good things for kids," they did not specify what the staff members should do or how they should do it. The process of institutional decentralization allowed staff to pursue a variety of goals using diverse treatment strategies within the autonomous cottages. In structuring programs for how their clients should be handled and changed, staff were guided by their own assumptions about the causes of and cures for delinquent behavior. Although there was some diversity among staff within the respective cottages, recruitment, self-selection, and cottage assignments resulted in relatively homogeneous correctional ideologies among cottage personnel; the focus of this study is on the substantial differences among the various units in programs and

goals that emerged and the effects of these differences on the respective inmate cultures.

Cottage Programs and Social Control Strategies

Maximum Security (Group Custody) Cottage Nine was a unit used for juveniles who had run away from the institution and for youths who had committed other disciplinary infractions. About half of all residents escaped from the institution at some time during their stay; there were no significant differences between those who absconded and those who did not. There was no vocational training, academic education, or clinical program in the maximum-security setting. Intervention consisted of punishment and deprivation, with periods of enforced idleness interrupted only for meals, routine clean-up and cottage maintenance. All the cottage activities took place in a highly controlled, structured environment, and virtually all activities occurred in a group setting. Staff attempted to coerce inmate conformity and obedience, and punished recalcitrance or resistance. At a result, a typical three- to four-week stay in Cottage Nine before return to an open cottage was an unpleasant experience which residents had little choice but to endure.

Staff used physical coercion and isolation cells—"the Tombs"—to enforce obedience, conformity, and respect. These techniques were feasible since there was no program in which staff needed to obtain active inmate participation, and the staff's physical domination made coercion practicable. Staff members used their limited repertoire of controls to counter major forms of deviance such as riots and fights, as well as inmate provocation, disrespect, or recalcitrance. They also used mass lockups and other forms of group punishment.

Other control techniques were virtually absent, since there were no amenities or privileges that might be lost, and strategies designed to ensure group control precluded the development of individualized relationships necessary for collaborative controls. The use of coercive tactics alienated inmates, who minimized contacts with staff. Personnel ignored considerable inmate misbehavior that did not challenge their authority, and did not encourage inmates to report deviance that occurred outside the presence of staff members.

Industrial Training School (Individual Custody) Despite considerable program diversity, each of the individual custody settings—Cottage 8, Elms, Westview, and the Lancaster Industrial School for Girls—used vocational training as the primary strategy of change. Most of the trades programs consisted of either institutional maintenance or services for residents—a cafeteria program, laundry program, institutional upkeep, painting, landscaping and groundskeeping, and the like. There were limited academic and clinical programs in some of the cottages. However, individual counseling sessions were not scheduled regularly, and inmates initiated contact with clinical staff primarily to secure a weekend furlough or early parole.

Compared with those in the maximum-security unit, residents of the training school cottages enjoyed greater physical freedom within the institution, which rendered staff control more difficult. Inmate cooperation in the work programs was also problematic. Staff used a privilege system to induce conformity, coupling this with the threat of transfer to more punitive, maximum-security settings. The privilege system was a security-graded progression, with inmates at different levels accorded different privileges or governed by different restrictions. Passage from one level to another reflected the amount of time served and an inmate's general behavior and conformity. Because of the relatively limited privileges available, staff members exercised considerable discretion in the rules they enforced, against whom, and under what circumstances. The staff also collaborated informally with inmate leaders to maintain order, manipulating the privilege system to confer additional status and rewards on the elite. Informal collaboration between staff members and the inmate elite is a common training school control strategy because of the availability of privileges, the discretionary bases upon which rewards are manipulated, and the problems of maintaining order posed by program individualization, the need to secure cooperation, and increased inmate freedom.[31]

Individual Treatment The individual treatment program used all types of clinical treatment, including both individual counselling and individual therapy in a group setting. The cottage program was free and open with few restrictions. Staff minimized deprivations and maximized amenities to encourage inmate commitment and involvement in the clinical process. Staff eschewed universal rules, responding to each inmate or the basis of individualized therapeutic considerations.

Staff relied almost exclusively on a rich privilege system to secure the cooperation and participation of inmates. Although the threat of transfer to a less desirable setting was a possibility, the penalty was never invoked. There was virtually no physical coercion or informal collaboration used to obtain conformity or obedience. In response to inmate deviance, additional clinical sessions were prescribed to reinforce the privilege system—not as sanctions, but to provide additional supports for the recalcitrant resident.

Group Treatment All of the group treatment cottages used a therapeutic community treatment model,[32] which was supplemented with either vocational or academic educational programs. The therapeutic community treatment model used both daily staff-inmate community meetings and group therapy sessions. A daily log provided the agenda for cottage community discussions, with staff and residents encouraged to record incidents that required the community's attention. At these meetings, staff integrated observations of residents on work, school, or cottage living. They then divided the cottage populations into smaller treatment groups and used a type of guided group interaction to deal with interpersonal problems or to resolve issues raised during the community meetings.

Formal collaborations between staff and inmates was the primary means of social control. Staff used the group problem-solving process to define and enforce cottage norms and to mobilize group pressures to deal with specific instances of deviance. Rules and consequences were elaborated in a privilege system that was jointly enforced; each inmate's privileges and freedoms were more dependent upon performance and participation and were less a function of the length of time served than was the case in the more custodial settings. The gradations of privileges and freedom and the responsibilities associated with each level were consistently and energetically enforced.

The strength of the formal collaboration process was the pressure staff placed upon residents to motivate other inmates to change. The concept of "responsibility" was crucial, and residents were responsible both for their own progress and behavior and for that of others. This principle of third-party responsibility provided a therapeutic rationale that significantly transformed subcultural norms governing informing and greatly increased the amount of information received by staff about the inmate group.

The Relationship between Staff Correctional Ideology and Cottage Program Characteristics The differences in correctional programs and control strategies stemmed from various assumptions staff made about appropriate ways to treat inmates. Since staff members were allowed to form their own cottage teams, there was substantial interpersonal and ideological compatibility within units. For purposes of explaining the diversity in the cottage programs and subcultures, the more important differences were among the

different units. (See Table 2 for a presentation of some of the dimensions on which they differed.)

One component of a correctional ideology is the emphasis placed by staff on inmates' obedience, respect for authority, and submission to external controls. Custodial staff were much more concerned with obedience and respect than were treatment personnel, and subscribed more extensively to the use of external controls to achieve inmate conformity.

Cottage staff members also differed in their views of deviance. Personnel in the treatment-oriented cottages attributed delinquency to emotional or psychological problems, while custody staff rejected psychopathology or emotional dysfunction, emphasizing as a cause of delinquency such factors as a youth's exercise of free will, which could be deterred by punishment. Because the custody staff rejected psychological interpretations, they found delinquent or bizarre inmate behavior considerably more difficult to understand than did treatment staff. Staff members also disagreed over whether delinquents were capable of establishing "normal" relationships, with those emphasizing custody far more likely than treatment personnel to regard the inmates in their cottages as "hard-core delinquents" who were dangerous and untrustworthy.

TABLE 2 Selected Indicators of Staff Ideology and Goals (as a percentage of total staff in setting)

| | Custody-Oriented Cottages | | | | | Treatment-Oriented Cottages | | | |
| | Group | Individual | | | | Individual | Group | | |
Scale	Cottage 9 (n = 9)	Cottage 8 (n = 16)	Elms (n = 15)	Westview (n = 10)	Lancaster (F) (n = 14)	Topsfield (coed) (n = 9)	Sunset (n = 5)	Shirley (n = 16)	"I Belong" (n = 8)
Respect for authority	89%	88%	73%	67%	54%	11%	0%	25%	25%
Free will and deterrence	79	81	60	78	50	0	40	38	13
Delinquents cannot be understood	67	75	67	67	43	0	0	19	13
Inmates are dangerous	67	63	47	56	43	0	20	38	13
Conformity to staff orders	56	69	71	63	50	0	20	6	13
Custody-oriented goals	37	34	32	37	38	15	13	21	10
Personnel acting in clinical capacity	0	18	7	10	21	56	20	44	50

NOTE: Each scale contains three or more items, with an interitem correlation greater than .5 and significant at the .001 significance level.

A correctional ideology both rationalizes deviance and its control and describes the end result sought—the "changed" inmate. Institutional behavior provides the staff with an indicator of an inmate's "rehabilitation" and readiness to return to the community. Custody staff strongly preferred inmates who followed orders, kept to themselves, and stayed out of trouble, which reflected their greater emphasis on external conformity rather than internalized controls. Their more negative perceptions of inmates and apprehension about collusion also led the custody staff members to disrupt informal inmate associations and encourage self-isolation, while treatment personnel encouraged inmate involvement with other inmates.

These alternative analyses of delinquency led staffs to pursue different correctional goals. When personnel were asked to choose among various correctional goals for incarcerated delinquents, significantly more of the custody-oriented staff members subscribed to custodial institutional objectives—isolation, respect and discipline, and training and educating—than did treatment personnel. Allocation of institutional resources provides another indicator of organizational goals; in juvenile institutions, personnel are the primary resource. Organizations pursuing custodial goals assign personnel to control and containment, or vocational and educational functions; treatment-oriented organizations, in contrast, assign more staff members to clinical and treatment functions. The greatest proportion of personnel in the custodial cottages served as guards, work supervisors, and academic instructors, while the treatment-oriented cottages assigned a larger percentage of the staff to treatment roles, with a corresponding reduction in purely supervisory personnel.

The Inmate Subcultures

An inmate subculture develops within the confines of a correctional institution, and its norms and values reflect the focal concerns of institutional life and the inmate population. Inmate roles and subculture stratification reflect conformity to or deviation from these norms, and newly entering inmates are socialized into this system and adapt to the expectations of their fellow inmates. The informal social system often mediates the effectiveness of the formal organization, aiding or thwarting staff members in the pursuit of their goals.[33]

A feature of correctional organization that influences the character of the inmate social systems is the extent to which staff members successfully control inmate violence and exploitation. Institutional characteristics influence the prevalence of inmate aggression by varying the levels of deprivation, a condition that gives some inmates an incentive to direct predatory behavior at others, and by providing the opportunities under which such exploitation may be carried out successfully. Inmate violence is directly related to the quality of relations between inmates and staff and to the information available to personnel about the workings of the subculture. Thus, controlling violence is a sine qua non of effective correctional programming and administration.

There was a clear relationship between the type of formal organization and the informal inmate culture. In the punitive, group custody setting, inmates experienced the greatest deprivation and were the most alienated from other inmates and staff members. Inmate alienation prevented the development of effective staff controls and allowed aggressive inmates to exploit their fellows through diverse forms of violent behavior. In the training school settings, the staff members used a privilege system coupled with informal cooperation of the inmate elite to bring potentially aggressive inmates under some degree of control. This reduced the effectiveness of inmate violence and exploitation, although aggression remained the dominant mode of interaction within the subculture. In the treatment-oriented cottages, especially in the group treatment programs, formal collaboration between inmates and staff members reduced the level of inmate violence and provided a therapeutic rationale for informing that made the workings of the subculture more visible to staff. The greater visibility, combined with significantly reduced deprivation, lowered the necessity for and effectiveness of inmate aggression and exploitation and allowed for the emergence of a more positive inmate culture.

Inmate Perceptions of Staff and Inmates Problems of institutional living influence inmates' motives for interaction and the types of solutions they can develop. Just as correctional personnel structure their relationships with inmates, residents attempt to structure and control their relationships with staff and other inmates to resolve the problems of the informal organization. The types of relationships and collective solutions available depend upon the inmates' perceptions of the program, staff, and other inmates. Inmate cooperation with staff augers for a more open, visible, and manageable social system. If staff cannot obtain inmate cooperation through either formal or informal collaboration, then a more closed, subterranean, and violent social system emerges.

Cottage Purposes The cottage goals and programs define the organizational context to which inmates must adapt. Table 3 provides a breakdown of inmates' perceptions of the goals, staff, and other aspects of life in the different cottages. When asked about cottage purposes and staff expectations, residents of the custody-oriented cottages described the cottages as places for punishment, while inmates in the treatment-oriented settings regarded the cottages as places for rehabilitation and for gaining self-awareness. As a further indicator of organizational purposes and adaptive constraints, inmates were asked whether staff encouraged them to conform or to gain insight into their own motivation and behavior. Responding to staff expectations (see Table 26.2), inmates in the custody-oriented settings were more than twice as likely to view the staff as demanding obedience and conformity as were those in the treatment cottages, while the latter were almost three times as likely as the residents of custody-oriented settings to describe staff expectations in terms of treatment and self-understanding.

A corollary of the differences in custodianship and punitiveness was the "pain of imprisonment" that inmates described. While some of the problems inmates confront are inherent in incarceration—loss of liberty, separation from family and friends, increased dependency and submission to authority, and the like—other pains of confinement, such as material deprivations, are attributable to characteristics of a particular setting. By virtually every measure, the inmates in the custody-oriented cottages reported far more extensive and severe problems associated with their confinement—boredom, living with other residents, and material deprivations—than did the inmates in the treatment cottages. These reported differences in institutional amenities resulted from staff actions, since treatment personnel tried to minimize the unpleasant, alienating aspects of incarceration to a greater extent than did custody-oriented staff.

Inmate Perceptions of Staff Inmates' views of staff paralleled staff members' perceptions of inmates. In those settings where staff had negative views of inmates, describing them as dangerous, unreliable, abnormal, or incorrigible, the inmates held correspondingly negative views of staff, regarding them as untrustworthy, unhelpful or indifferent. In those settings where the staff expressed more favorable views of inmates, residents shared more positive views of the staff. Virtually every inmate in the maximum-security setting and over half the inmates in the individual custody settings, as contrasted with only about one-fifth of those in the treatment settings, regarded staff as neither concerned nor helpful. Inmates readily equated punitive programs with unconcerned staff and therapeutic programs with committed staff. Likewise, residents of the custody-oriented cottages initiated fewer contacts with personnel and talked with them less about personal problems than did those in the treatment settings.

Inmate Perceptions of Other Inmates Characteristics of the inmate social system also reflect the extent to which inmates can cooperate with one another to ease the hardship of adjusting to the institution. The residents of the custody-oriented cottages reported substantially lower levels of trust and concern on the part of other inmates than did those in the treatment-oriented settings. Residents

TABLE 3 Selected Indicators of Inmate Attitudes (as a percentage of total residents)

| | Custody-Oriented Cottages | | | | | Treatment-Oriented Cottages | | | |
| | Group | Individual | | | | Individual | Group | | |
	Cottage 9 (n = 27)	Cottage 8 (n = 15)	Elms (n = 40)	Westview (n = 29)	Lancaster (F) (n = 28 + 22)	Topsfield (coed) (n = 15)	Sunset (n = 15)	Shirley (n = 16)	"I Belong" (n = 8)
Inmate perceptions of cottage goals: What is this place trying to do for you?									
Gain understanding	11%	20%	23% (23)[a]	24%	28%	73%	53%	63% (64)	86%
Train and educate	11	7	0 (1)	0	0	13	7	13 (8)	0
Respect for authority	0	13	13 (15)	21	13	13	13	13 (13)	14
Punish for the wrong things they did	78	60	64 (61)	55	60	0	27	13 (15)	0
Staff emphasis									
Obey the rules and don't get into any trouble	63	86	74 (78)	79	73	7	46	43 (37)	0
Understand your personal problems	37	14	26	21	27	93	54	57	100
Staff do not help or care about inmates	96	87	46 (58)	59	51	13	20	25 (18)	0
Positive perception of staff	0	0	39 (30)	35	40	80	73	63 (74)	100
Negative perception of other inmates	70	47	41 (41)	38	51	7	27	25 (21)	0
Regardless of what the adults say, the best way to get along here is—									
Stay out of the way of the adults, but get away with what you can	37	7	23 (18)	17	20	0	13	6 (8)	0
Don't break any rules and keep out of trouble	26	53	54 (54)	55	33	33	27	44 (38)	50
Show that you are really sorry for what you did	0	7	7	10	11	13	13	6	13
Try to get an understanding of yourself	37	33	13 (22)	28	37	53	47	44 (44)	37
Prisonized adoption	59	60	56 (51)	38	53	7	40	13 (21)	0
Approval of informing	7	20	21 (18)	14	36	80	33	50 (51)	88
Positive inmate role	33	33	48 (45)	48	47	64	60	56 (66)	100
Inmate leaders negative	52	73	48 (49)	38	48	13	33	31 (26)	0

a. The numbers in parentheses denote the average percentage of residents in each type of cottage responding as shown to the attitudinal indicator. The responses are mutually exclusive; thus the totals will be 100 percent (with slight variation because of rounding).

of the treatment cottages also reported greater inmate solidarity than did their custody cottage counterparts. Since predatory behavior and subcultural violence were more prevalent in the custody-oriented settings, the differences in inmate perceptions also reflect the extent to which inmates were exploited and victimized by others.

Inmate Adaptations Differences among the programs in staff expectations constitute an additional organizational constraint on inmates' adaptations. Custodial staff emphasized inmate conformity and obedience, whereas treatment staff emphasized gaining insight and solving personal problems (see Table 26.2). In response, inmates in the custody-oriented settings chose either overt conformity and covert deviance or obedience and conformity as adaptive strategies, while those in the treatment-oriented settings chose self-understanding. Similarly, adaptations reflecting elements of prisonization—prompt obedience, conformity, and self-isolation—were chosen by twice as many residents of custody-oriented settings as those in treatment programs, closely paralleling the staff expectations.

Social Structure of the Inmate Subculture Inmates interact more frequently and intensely with residents of their own cottage than they do with those in other settings, and a set of norms and roles based upon those norms govern their interactions with other inmates and staff. Differences in staff intervention practices are strongly related to variations in inmates' perceptions of other inmates, staff, and institutional adaptation, and to corresponding differences in inmate norms, subculture roles, and interaction patterns.

The inmates' and staff's responses to violence and aggression are among the most important determinants of subculture processes. In the absence of effective controls, violence and aggression underlie most interactions within the inmate subculture.[34] Direct action, toughness, and defense of personal integrity are focal concerns of many delinquent inmates,[35] and even a few aggressive inmates can immediately make the control of violence a major concern within the institution. Moreover, the prevalence of violence is closely related to other subcultural norms, particularly those related to informing.

Inmate norms governing interactions with staff and the acceptability of informing personnel of other inmates' activities have been frequently described.[36] Informing and subcultural violence are closely linked, since uncontrolled violence can deter informing, while informing, if properly encouraged by staff, can reduce it. The regulation of the flow of information between inmates and staff thus emerges as a critical determinant of inmate roles and subculture structure.

Inmates' views of staff and inmates and their adaptations to the institution influence the amount of information staff members receive about the inmate social system, which in turn conditions the staff members' ability to control the subcultural violence. Residents of the treatment cottages held relatively favorable views of other inmates and staff. Because of the greater availability of privileges and amenities, they had less incentive to engage in covert deviance to relieve deprivations and thus had less to hide. Almost three times as many inmates in the treatment settings as in the custody-oriented settings approved of informing. In fact, a virtual majority of residents of the former approved of informing.

As indicated previously, the treatment inmates' support for informing stemmed, in part, from the staff members' redefinition of informing as "helping" or "being responsible for others" as part of the treatment program. Formal collaboration reinforced the therapeutic rationale for informing and gave inmates greater protection from intimidation by increasing the visibility of informal pressures by other inmates. By legitimating and fostering informing, staff members received an enormous amount of information about the hidden processes of the subculture, which better enabled them to control inmate violence.

Participant observation and structured interviews provided an insight into "strong-arming" and "bogarting"—the subterranean violence among residents. "You have to fight" was a norm in the custody-oriented cottages, and the levels of verbal abuse and physical violence were considerably higher there than in the treatment-oriented settings. Inmates emphasized toughness, resisting exploitation or provocation, and maintaining one's position in the subculture through physical means. Physical and verbal testing and scuffles were daily occurrences, although actual fights were less frequent. The inmate did not have to be a successful fighter, but a willingness to fight to protect himself, his position, and his property was essential. Fighting and defending against exploitation were as important for female inmates as for males in comparable custodial cottages.

An inmate's readiness and ability to defend personal integrity and property were tested very early during confinement as new residents were subtly or overtly challenged for whatever material goods they possessed. As mentioned above, the greater deprivation in the custody-oriented settings made exploitation a profitable strategy for the more aggressive inmates. Residents who fought back could insulate themselves from chronic exploitation, while failure to do so left them and their possessions vulnerable.

There was significantly less exploitation in the treatment-oriented cottages than in the custody-oriented cottages. The field observers recorded fewer incidents of fights, physical confrontations, or expropriation of property. All the observers commented on the virtual absence here of "ranking"—verbal abuse—as compared with the custody cottages. There was less normative support for fighting, and when it did occur most of the inmates condemned it in the community meetings.

The differences in subcultural violence resulted from the steps staff took to control it. In the custody cottages, inmates retaliated with violence to punish those who informed to staff and to discourage other inmates from doing so. Given their limited social control repertoire, custody staff did not encourage inmates to inform, since it only forced them to confront violent inmates directly. When staff members learned of inmate violence or victimization, they seldom took steps to prevent its recurrence. More frequently, they reinforced the values of the violent subculture by encouraging the resident to fight back and defend himself. In view of the unsympathetic and unsupportive staff response to complaints and the retaliatory inmate violence that followed, inmates had little incentive to cooperate with staff. Custody staff were isolated from the workings of the subculture, and unable to combat the violence that stifled

the flow of information. In the treatment-oriented cottages, formal collaboration and inmate support for informing provided channels of communication and a mechanism for coping with incidents of violence.

While inmate approval of informing afforded greater control over inmate violence, there were differences in other subcultural norms as well. Responses to a series of hypothetical stories concerning common incidents in correctional institutions demonstrated a further contrast in the norms that prevailed in the various cottages. About two-thirds of the inmates in the treatment-oriented settings, as compared with less than half of those in the custody-oriented settings, supported "positive" inmate behavior—cooperation with staff, refusal to aid escapes, and the like.

Different inmate roles and subcultural stratification accompanied the differences in cottage norms. In the more violent custodial cottages, the roles of superior and inferior were allocated on the basis of an inmate's ability to "out-fight, outthink, or out-talk" fellow inmates. Since most inmates were neither complete successes nor complete failures in out-fighting, out-thinking, or out-talking their peers, the distribution of roles resulted in a stratification system with a few aggressive leaders at the top, a few "punks"—chronic victims—at the bottom, and most of the inmates occupying a more intermediate status, neither "one-up" nor "one-down." In the treatment-oriented settings, inmate roles and stratification were not as tied to physical or verbal prowess.

The differences in cottage norms and inmate relations were reflected in the characteristics of the inmate leadership as well. A majority of inmates in the custody-oriented cottages, as contrasted with about one-quarter of the residents of the treatment cottages, described the leaders as filling a negative and violent role in cottage life. Both observations and interviews revealed that leaders were those inmates who "strong-armed" and exploited lower-status inmates. There was greater normative support for negative inmate behavior in these cottages, and the leaders reflected and perpetuated the dominate values of the subculture.

Norms governing violence and informing constrained inmate leaders in the treatment-oriented cottages. Formal collaboration between inmates and staff reduced the leaders' ability to maintain covert physical control over the inmate group, and they played a more positive and supportive role in the institution. Formal collaboration increased their visibility and required that they at least appear to adopt a cooperative attitude in their relations with staff, which enabled other inmates to establish more positive relationships with inmates and staff.

At the bottom of the custody cottages' social structure were the "punks," inmates who were bullied and exploited and who acquiesced in the role of victim. Since the first rule of survival in the violent subculture was to defend oneself, inmates who were unable or unwilling to fight were at the mercy of those who would do so. Punks were chronically victimized, both psychologically and physically, and were the victims of merciless taunting and pummeling. In the custodial settings, the strong norm against informing prevented either the victims or other inmates from revealing what occurred. The inability of staff to control the violence prevented inmates from revealing their victimization and left them at the mercy of their exploiters.

Homosexual rape was the ultimate act of physical aggression by tough cottage leaders against punks. More than exploitative sexual satisfaction, rape entailed conquest and domination of the victim by the aggressor.[37] Every incident of homosexual assault discovered during this study could be analyzed in terms of leader-punk role relationships; such assaults occurred only in the violent custody-oriented cottages.

In the treatment-oriented settings, punks did not suffer as much physical or verbal abuse. Although other inmates regarded them as weak, immature, and lacking self-respect, formal collaboration provided a substantial check on the extent of their victimization. At least by contrast with those custody-oriented settings, low-status inmates in the treatment cottages enjoyed a comparatively benign incarceration experience.

Discussion and Conclusions

Organizational structure has a major effect on the informal inmate social system. The cottage programs varied in both the levels of deprivation and the effectiveness of staff controls and confronted the inmates with markedly different organizations to which to adapt. The respective cottage cultures reflected these differences in inmates' perceptions of cottage purposes and goals, in their adaptations to the institution, in their views of staff and other inmates, and in their norms, values, and interaction patterns.

Punishment and isolation were the reasons given by the inmates in maximum security for their incarceration. They suffered the greatest deprivation within the institution, which gave them the greatest incentive to improve their circumstances through violent exploitation and covert deviance. Staff sought inmate obedience and conformity and used physical control to obtain compliance and suppress challenges to their authority. Inmates were alienated by the staff's repressive controls, and the absence of programs prevented the development of individualized relationships, perpetuating the negative stereotypes of one another held by inmates and staff. Motivated by their poor opinion of inmates, staff attempted to disrupt informal groups. The inmates' isolation hindered them from cooperating with one another in the institutional adjustment or in resisting exploitation, while predatory violence reinforced inmates' negative views of one another. Inmates adapted by isolating themselves, avoiding other inmates and appearing to obey staff. In developing covert deviant solutions to relieve their material deprivation, particularly in exploiting weaker inmates for their possessions, tough inmates reinforced their own dominant status and provided themselves with a measure of safety and security. They discouraged inmate contact that would reveal their own deviant and violent behavior and physically punished inmates who informed to discourage the communication of information that would improve staff control. And the dominance of aggressive inmates reinforced staff efforts to isolate inmates within the culture by making inmates distrustful and fearful of one another. The inmates' ability to use violence determined their various roles within the group, and prevented them from engaging in positive forms of social behavior. The failure of staff to support informing or to control violence forced the inmates to seek accommodation with the primary source of power, the aggressive inmate leaders. This, in turn, reinforced their alienation from one another, precluded collective resistance to aggression, and left each individual inmate at the mercy of those who were more aggressive.

Subculture characteristics in the training school cottages were similar to those in maximum security, although organizational differences reduced the extremes of staff-inmate alienation and antagonism. Program individualization engendered more contacts between staff and inmates that tempered somewhat their negative perceptions of one another. The use of vocational programs required staff to obtain the active cooperation of inmates in productive work. Staff induced at least minimal cooperation and participation in work programs through privileges and rewards that reduced the levels of institutional deprivation. The necessity to obtain voluntary compliance limited the utility of punitive forms of social control, and a privilege system provided staff with a more flexible means of responding to inmates than did the use of force and isolation cells. The forms of adaptation among inmates reflected staff members' primary emphasis on obedience and conformity. Staff informally collaborated with and coopted the potentially violent inmate elite, and thus obtained some control over aggression within the subculture. By coopting the inmate leaders through informal collaboration, staff enlisted their aid in maintaining order within the subculture. In the course of protecting their privileged status, the leaders informally maintained control for staff, suppressed some forms of anti-institutional activities, and reduced the levels of violence within the inmate group. The privileges available reduced the levels of deprivation, and covert inmate deviance declined accordingly. With less to hide,

there was less need among the inmates to restrict contact with staff. Although inmates disapproved of informing, this was not as ruthlessly suppressed as was the case in maximum security. The lesser degree of deprivation and violent exploitation reduced the inmates' isolation and alienation from one another.

The differences in organizational goals and intervention strategies in the treatment-oriented cottages had a significant effect on the inmates' incarceration experience. Staff both elevated treatment expectations over custodial considerations and successfully communicated their expectations to inmates. Rehabilitation, gaining insight, and solving personal problems were seen as the purposes of incarceration, and these goals required change rather than simply conformity. Staff emphasized more rewarding experiences and privileges, and residents of the treatment setting suffered less punishment, deprivation, or alienation than did their custody cottage counterparts. The reduced material deprivation also lowered inmates' incentive to engage in deviant activities within the institution.

In both the individual and group treatment settings, positive contact between staff and inmates was considerable, occurring in individual counseling and through formal collaboration, resulting in markedly more favorable inmate perceptions of staff than in other settings. Formal collaboration allowed inmates and staff to make decisions collectively about cottage life and provided them with a common context in which to meet. Formal collaboration fostered greater equality among staff members, between staff and inmates, and among inmates, and reduced inmates' alienation from staff and encouraged more favorable views of fellow inmates.

Formal collaboration coupled with individual and group treatment increased the visibility of the inmate subculture and provided staff and inmates with a mechanism for controlling inmate violence. Staff provided a rehabilitation-based rationale for informing, enabling the norm governing this behavior to become more positive than was the case in the custody cottages. Equally important, staff members defined the program itself in such a way as to convince the inmates that personnel were committed to treatment rather than punishment.

The increased communication of information enabled staff to control inmate violence, which reinforced this communication. The reduced deprivation, increased freedom, and support provided by formal collaboration for controlling inmate violence combined to foster more positive, less exploitative inmate relationships.

Notes

1. See Hugh Cline, "The Determinants of Normative Patterns in Correctional Institutions," in *Scandinavian Studies in Criminology*, vol. 2, Nils Christie, ed. (Oslo, Norway: Oslo University Press, 1968), pp. 173–84; Barry Schwartz, "Pre-institutional vs. Situational Influence in a Correctional Community," *Journal of Criminal Law, Criminology and Police Science*, December 1971, pp. 532–42; Charles W. Thomas and Samuel C. Foster, "The Importation Model Perspective on Inmate Social Roles," *Sociological Quarterly*, Spring 1973, pp. 226–34; Charles W. Thomas, "Theoretical Perspectives on Alienation in the Inmate Society," *Pacific Sociological Review*, vol. 18 (1975), pp. 483–99; Charles W. Thomas and Matthew Zingraff, "Organizational Structure as a Determinant of Prisonization," *Pacific Sociological Review*, January 1976, p. 98.

2. Donald Clemmer, *The Prison Community* (Boston: Christopher, 1940); Norman S. Hayner and Ellis Ash, "The Prison as a Community," *American Sociological Review*, vol. 4 (1940), pp. 577–83; Howard Polsky, *Cottage 6* (New York: Russell Sage, 1962); David A. Ward and Gene Kassebaum, *Women's Prison: Sex and Social Structure* (Chicago: Aldine, 1965); Clemens Bartollas, Stuart J. Miller, Simon Dinitz, *Juvenile Victimization: The Institutional Paradox* (Beverly Hills, Sage: 1976).

3. Thomas, "Theoretical Perspectives on Alienation in the Inmate Society"; Charles W. Thomas, "Theoretical Perspectives on Prisonization: A Comparison of the Importation and Deprivation Models," *Journal of Criminal Law and Criminology*, March 1977, pp. 135–45.

4. Lloyd W. McCorkle and Richard Korn, "Resocialization with Walls," *Annals of the American Academy of Political and Social Science*, May 1954, pp. 88–98; Gresham Sykes, *Society of Captives* (Princeton, N.J.: Princeton University Press, 1958); Gresham Sykes and Sheldon Messinger, "The Inmate Social System," in *Theoretical Studies in Social Organization of the Prison*, Richard Cloward et al., eds. (New York: Social Science Research Council, 1960), pp. 5–19; Irving Goffman, *Asylums* (Garden City, N.Y.: Anchor, 1961).

5. Haner and Ash, "Prison as a Community"; Clarence Schrag, "Leadership among Prison Inmates," *American Sociological Review*, vol. 19 (1954), pp. 37–42; Clarence Schrag, "Some Foundations for a Theory of Corrections," in *The Prison: Studies in Institutional Organization and Change*, Donald Cressey, ed. (New York: Holt, Rinehart and Winston, 1961), pp. 309–58; Gresham Sykes, "The Corruption of Authority and Rehabilitation," *Social Forces*, vol. 34 (1956), pp. 257–62.

6. Oscar Grusky, "Organizational Goals and the Behavior of Informal Leaders," *American Journal of Sociology*, vol. 65 (1959), pp. 59–67; Oscar Grusky, "Role Conflict in Organizations: A Study of Prison Camp Officials," *Administration Science Quarterly*, March 1959, pp. 452–72; Stanton Wheeler, "Socialization in Correctional Communities," *American Sociological Review*, October 1961, pp. 707–11; Mayer N. Zald, "Organizational Control Structures in Five Correctional Institutions," *American Journal of Sociology*, November 1962, pp. 335–45; Mayer N. Zald, "Comparative Analysis and Measurement of Organizational Goals: The Case of Correctional Institutions of Juveniles, *Sociological Quarterly*, Summer 1963, pp. 206–30; Peter G. Garabedian, "Social Roles and Processes of Socialization in the Prison Community," *Social Problems*, Fall 1963, pp. 139–52; Peter G. Garabedian, "Social Roles in a Correctional Community," *Journal of Criminal Law, Criminology and Police Science*, September 1964, pp. 338–47; Daniel Glaser, *The Effectiveness of a Prison and Parole System* (Indianapolis, Ind.: Bobbs-Merrill, 1964); Mayer N. Zald and David A. Street, "Custody and Treatment in Juvenile Institutions," *Crime and Delinquency*, July 1964, pp. 249–56; Bernard Berk, Organizational Goals and Inmate Organization," *American Journal of Sociology*, March 1966, pp. 522–34; David A. Street, Robert D. Vinter, and Charles Perrow, *Organization for Treatment* (New York: Free Press, 1966); Ronald L. Akers, Norman S. Hayner, and Werner Gruniger, "Homosexual and Drug Behavior in Prison," *Social Problems*, vol. 21 (1974), pp. 410–22; Ronald L. Akers, Norman S. Hayner, and Werner Gruniger, "Prisonization in Five Countries," *Criminology*, February 1977, pp. 527–54; Barry C. Feld, *Neutralizing Inmate Violence: Juvenile Offenders in Institutions* (Cambridge, Mass.: Ballinger, 1977).

7. John Irwin and Donald Cressey, "Thieves, Convicts, and the Inmate Culture," *Social Problems*, Fall 1962, p. 142; Ward and Kassebaum, *Women's Prison*.

8. Ward and Kassebaum, *Women's Prison*; James Jacobs, "Stratification and Conflict among Prison Inmates," *Journal of Law & Criminology*, vol. 66 (1976), p. 476; Leo Carroll, *Hacks, Blacks, and Cons* (Lexington, Mass.: Lexington Books, 1974); Thomas and Foster, "Importation Model Perspective on Inmate Social Roles"; Thomas, "Theoretical Perspectives on Prisonization."

9. Polsky, *Cottage 6*; Bartollas, Miller, and Dinitz, *Juvenile Victimization*; Jacobs "Stratification and Conflict among Prison Inmates."

10. Social control by inmates within the subculture may be maintained by verbal as well as physical manipulation. Verbal assaults—"ranking"—provide a mechanism by which relative status is fixed by verbal rather than physical aggression. Howard Polsky described rankings as "verbal, invidious distinctions based on values important to the group. . . . Ranking fixes antagonistic positions among three or more persons by placing one member in a target position" (Polsky, *Cottage 6*, p. 62). David Matza describes the same process as "sounding," which entails an "imputation of negative characteristics . . . wherein the recipient concurs with the perpetrator in the negative evaluation of the substance of the remark." (David Matza, *Delinquency and Drift* [New York: John Wiley, 1964], p. 43.) This process of verbal denigration is prevalent in female inmate interactions as well (Rose Giallombardo, *Society of Women* [New York: John Wiley, 1966]; Rose Giallombardo, *Social World of Imprisoned Girls* [New York: John Wiley, 1974]). The target of scornful, mocking, or negative statements made in the presence of a social audience can either concur in the negative imputations, establishing subordination, or resist the characterization. Acquiescence or resistance defines relative social status.

11. Sykes, *Society of Captives*; Sykes and Messinger, "Inmate Social System."

12. Polsky, *Cottage 6*; Bartollas, Miller, and Dinitz, *Juvenile Victimization*; Feld, *Neutralizing Inmate Violence*.

13. Walter Miller, "Lower Class Culture as a Generating Milieu of Gang Delinquency," *Journal of Social Issues*, vol. 14, no. 3 (1958), pp. 5–19; Marvin Wolfgang and Franco Ferracuti, *The Subculture of Violence* (London, England: Tavistock, 1967).

14. Jacobs, "Stratification and Conflict among Prison Inmates"; Giallombardo, *Social World of Imprisoned Girls*; Feld, *Neutralizing Inmate Violence*.

15. Charles W. Thomas and Samuel C. Foster, "Prisonization in the Inmate Contraculture," *Social Problems*, Fall 1972, pp. 229–39; Thomas and Foster, "Importation Model Perspective on Inmate Social Roles"; Akers, Hayner, and Gruniger, "Homosexual and Drug Behavior in Prison"; Feld, *Inmate Violence*.

16. Street, Vinter, and Perrow, *Organization for Treatment*; Akers, Hayner, and Gruniger, "Homosexual and Drug Behavior in Prison"; Feld, *Neutralizing Inmate Violence*.

17. Donald R. Cressey, "Prison Organization," in *Handbook of Organizations*, J. March, ed. (Chicago: Rand McNally), pp. 1023–70; Street, Vinter, and Perrow, *Organization for Treatment*; Elliot StudT, Sheldon Messinger, and Thomas Wilson, *C-Unit: Search for Community in Prison* (New York: Russell Sage, 1968).

18. Street, Vinter, and PerroW, *Organization for Treatment*; Lloyd Ohlin, "Organizational Reform in Correctional Agencies," in *Handbook of Criminology*, Daniel Glaser, ed. (Chicago: Rand McNally, 1974), pp. 995–1020; Feld, *Neutralizing Inmate Violence*.

19. Zald, "Organizational Control Structures in Five Correctional Institutions"; Zald, "Comparative Analysis and Measurement of Organizational Goals"; Zald and Street, "Custody and Treatment in Juvenile Institutions."

20. Corresponding to distinctions between custody and treatment, there is also a tension in the organization between tendencies toward bureaucratization and tendencies toward individualization. The pressures of bureaucratization lead personnel to deal with inmates according to gross characteristics. The pull toward individualization leads to nonroutinized treatment with potentially disruptive consequences for the organization. The nonuniform nature of individual behavior results either in individualized, nonroutinized staff responses *or* in an effort to increase predictability through regimentation. While bureaucratization increases regimentation and clearly defined expectations for inmate behavior, individualization requires either specifying norms for every eventuality or delegating discretion and authority to low-level staff to enable them to deal with unpredictable situations and individual variations. The resolution of these countervailing pressures constitutes a primary source of variation in organizations. See Goffman, *Asylums*; Cressey, "Prison Organization."

21. Street, Vinter, and Perrow, *Organization for Treatment*.

22. Amitai Etzioni, *A Comparative Analysis of Complex Organizations* (New York: Free Press, 1961); Amitai Etzioni, *A Comparative Analysis of Complex Organizations* (New York: Free Press, 1975).

23. Ibid.

24. Goffman, *Asylums*.

25. Lacking complete physical domination of inmates, staff members rely upon the inmate elite to maintain social order, in return for which the staff allow the elite certain privileges and immunities. Richard Cloward describes one way in which this process occurs. He notes that the two primary groups in the prison—custodians and inmates—seek, respectively, social order and escape from deprivation. The custodian employs a coercion and inducement, force and incentive to secure order from the inmates, but "in the absence of absolute force, the prisoner must be led to share in the process of social control." Disruptive behavior is avoided by guards who provide access to illegitimate means whereby the prisoners can reduce the deprivation. "The official system accommodates to the inmate system in ways that have the consequence of creating illegitimate opportunity structures." To some extent the guards can determine which prisoners will have access to these opportunities, and in turn these prisoners maintain order for the guards as a means of protecting their own privileged positions. This occurs because "certain prisoners, as they become upwardly mobile in these structures, tend to become progressively conservative. . . . Seeking to entrench their relative advantage over other inmates, they are anxious to suppress any behavior

that might disturb the present arrangements." Richard Cloward, "Social Control in Prison," in *Theoretical Studies in Social Organization of the Prison* (New York: Social Science Research Council, 1960), pp. 20–48.

This process is also described by Richard McCleary, "Communication Patterns as Bases of Systems of Authority and Power," in *Theoretical Studies in Social Organization of the Prison* (New York: Social Science Research Council, 1960), pp. 49–77; Richard McCleary, "The Governmental Process and Informal Social Control," in *The Prison*, Donald Cressey, ed. (New York: Holt, Rinehart and Winston, 1961), pp. 149–88; and Sykes, *Society of Captives*. According to Sykes ("Corruption of Authority and Rehabilitation"), the guards must rely on the inmates to maintain order because of the "lack of a sense of duty among those who are held captive, the obvious fallacies of coercion, the pathetic collection of rewards and punishments to induce compliance, the strong pressures toward the corruption of the guard in the form of friendship, reciprocity, and the transfer of duties into the hands of trusted inmates—all are structural defects in the prison's system of power rather than individual inadequacies." The same processes operate in institutions for juvenile offenders. See Polsky, *Cottage 6*; Feld, *Neutralizing Inmate Violence*; Bartollas, Miller, and Dititz, *Juvenile Victimization*.

26. Formal collaboration between staff and inmates as a means of social control occurs when a social structure allows both to participate, at least to some degree, as members of a common group in defining deviance, determining the appropriate sanctions, or both. Formal collaboration differs from informal collaboration in a number of critical respects. It is explicit and overt, with parties visibly engaged in the process. Since the process is formalized and given organizational sanction, it is legitimate and consistent with the declared principles of the organization, rather than covert, *sub rosa*, and basically subversive of the formal organization. Formal collaboration is universalistic and democratic, with all members of both groups potentially involved, rather than elitist and particularistic, con-

fined only to the inmate leadership.

27. Feld, *Neutralizing Inmate Violence*; Robert Coates, Alden Miller, and Lloyd Ohlin, *Diversity in a Youth Correctional System* (Cambridge, Mass.: Ballinger, 1978); Craig McEwen, *Designing Correctional Organizations for Youth* (Cambridge, Mass.: Ballinger, 1978).

28. Maxwell Jones, *Beyond the Therapeutic Community* (New Haven, Conn.: Yale University Press, 1968); Maxwell Jones, *Social Psychiatry in Practice* (Baltimore, Md.: Penguin Books, 1968).

29. The Lancaster Industrial Schools for Girls was not converted to a decentralized, cottage-based institution to nearly the same degree as were the Shirley Industrial School and the Lyman Schools. It still operated as a traditional training school and there were virtually no differences in the social structure of the individual cottages. Accordingly, questionnaire data from Lancaster are aggregated for tabular presentation.

30. Feld, *Neutralizing Inmate Violence*, pp. 207–11.

31. Polsky, *Cottage 6*; Bartollas, Miller, and Dinitz, *Juvenile Victimization*; Feld, *Neutralizing Inmate Violence*.

32. Jones, *Beyond the Therapeutic Community*; Jones, *Social Psychiatry in Practice*.

33. Sykes and Messinger, "The Inmate Social System"; Sheldon Messinger, "Issues in the Study of the Social System of Prison Inmates," *Issues in Criminology*, vol. 4 (1970), pp. 133–44; Street, Vinter and Perrow, *Organization for Treatment*.

34. Polsky, *Cottage 6*; Bartollas, Miller, and Dinitz, *Juvenile Victimization*; Feld, *Neutralizing Inmate Violence*.

35. Miller, "Lower Class Culture as a Generating Milieu of Gang Delinquency"; Wolfgang and Ferracuti, *Subculture of Violence*.

36. Sykes, *Society of Captives*; McCleary, "Communication Patterns as Bases of Systems of Authority and Power"; McCleary, "Governmental Process and Informal Social Control"; Sykes and Messinger, "Inmate Social System."

37. Susan Brownmiller, *Against Our Will: Men, Women and Rape* (New York: Simon & Schuster, 1975).

QUESTIONS FOR DISCUSSION

1. Discuss the two major competing explanations of the inmate social system.

2. Discuss the characteristics of inmate violence in institutions. Specifically consider the organizational structure and how this affects the social interactions of inmates.

3. Discuss the specific findings of Feld's research pertaining to cottage programs and social control strategies.

APPLICATIONS

1. Assuming that the majority of incarcerated offenders will be returning to society, which

type of treatment strategy or institutional setting, in your opinion, would be the most effective in producing law-abiding and socially responsible individuals. Why?

2. If you were in a position to make decisions about which types of institutional settings to place inmates in, what kinds of settings would you choose? What criteria would you use to decide whether an inmate needed a custody-oriented facility or a treatment-oriented facility?

KEY TERMS

albeit   conceding the fact that; even though.

eschewed   when something is avoided, particularly on moral or practical grounds.

explicate   to give a detailed explanation.

pummel   to physically pound or beat.

recalcitrance   stubborn or obstinate defiance, particularly to authority.

subterranean   existing or working in secret; hidden.

25

Juvenile Diversion: A Look at the Record

Kenneth Polk

What are the accomplishments of juvenile diversion? In their recent review, Binder and Geis (1984) provide a spirited and proactive defense of diversion, noting that many of those finding fault with the concept base their observations on "polemical and ideological conclusions lacking a firm anchorage in fact" (p. 326). In their attempt to "rehabilitate the record of diversion," Binder and Geis (p. 326) express dismay at the fact that the response to diversion seems to be "inconsistent with the actual record." Their conclusion is that the criticisms of diversion originate in the personal motivations of sociologists and are the result of disciplinary narrowness, distrust of the police, and overidentification with the underdog.

That there have been questions raised about the success of diversion, and that the strongest of these seem to come from sociologists, cannot be disputed. Is it possible, however, that the source of these questions resides not so much in the motivations of sociologists, but in the record of diversion itself? A brief review of some of the empirical work on diversion may help to clarify and give shape to the features of the debate opened up by Binder and Geis.

"Juvenile Diversion: A Look at the Record," *Crime and Delinquency*, 30:4 (1989), pp. 648–859. Reprinted by permission of the publisher, Sage Publications, Inc.

Diversion and Subsequent Delinquency

A starting point for many analyses of diversion consists of assessing the outcomes of diversion in terms of its impact on subsequent delinquency. What is that record? It is clearly mixed. There are many studies which show that diversion is successful in reducing subsequent deviance (e.g., Duxbury, 1973; Thornton et al., 1972; Forward et al., 1975; Quay and Love, 1977; Palmer et al., 1978; Palmer and Lewis, 1980). These results are at least equally balanced, however, by findings of no impact. One of the most methodologically rigorous evaluations of diversion concluded that: "The hypothesis that diversion leads to lower rates of subsequent delinquent behavior than traditional processing was not supported" (Elliott et al., 1978: 10). In their review of several California diversion programs, Haapanen and Rudisill report that the programs

> were found to have no measurable effect on the self-report delinquency, the attitudes, the family relations, or the minor misbehavior of their clients. Nor did they have a measurable effect on the official delinquency of their clients over a six-month or twelve-month follow-up period [1980:139].

In their evaluation of several programs in Wisconsin, after making comparisons of records of subsequent delinquency between diversion and control clients, it was concluded by Venezia and Anthony (1978:121) that "none of the comparisons resulted in a significant difference being demonstrated." Similarly, in a review of the outcomes of one diversion program it was concluded that "no strong inference can be made" . . . that diversion "had a significant impact on youths' subsequent delinquent behavior" (Quincy, 1981:127; although it should be noted that this investigation did find consistent positive results on self-report measures of delinquency).

Even more important for the present argument, however, are indications of diversion as having harmful effects. In one analysis of a police diversion program, it was concluded that diversion served to aggravate rather than to deter recidivism (Lincoln, 1976). Elliott and colleagues (1978) report that receiving service, regardless of whether the intervention was in a traditional justice setting or in the diversion agency, resulted in higher levels of perceived labeling and self-report delinquency. Similarly, Lincoln (1977) found that although persons who were diverted had lower rates of recidivism than was true for persons who received a court petition, their rates were also higher than those released outright without any form of service. It further should be noted that these studies suggesting harmful effects of diversion are among the most methodologically rigorous in the diversion literature.

After analyzing this mixed pattern of research, and reviews of evaluations, Alder and Polk (1982:105) suggested that studies showing positive effects "have not stood up under careful scrutiny of their methodology." Binder and Geis profess that it "is inconceivable to us how one can so cavalierly dismiss" the works which show positive results, because this array of research "is no poorer in overall methodology than the array that has produced the negative results upon which the antidiversionists focus their attention" (Binder and Geis, 1984:324–325).

There are three curious features of this response. One, Binder and Geis scrupulously avoid mention of the major empirical investigations which show either negative or harmful effects of diversion. Although they assert that one set of studies is "no poorer," they provide no literature, data, or rationale in support of that assertion. Second, Binder

and Geis fail to inform the reader that at least Alder and Polk cite a basis for their conclusion; namely methodological reviews of diversion research (Alder and Polk, 1982: 105). One of these reviews, after examining a study cited by Binder and Geis as an illustration of the positive effects of diversion, comments:

> The Quay and Love (1977) report presented information on group characteristics, including the mean number of prior arrests for each group within fairly specific categories of offense. Within these narrow categories, the two groups did not differ significantly from one another, and the authors concluded that the two groups were equivalent. However, when the submeans were added together to produce a mean for the total number of priors in each group, the control group mean was 34% higher than that of clients. Given the importance of prior offenses as a predictor of subsequent offenses, this suggests that the groups cannot be compared without taking this difference into account. There were other problems with this study, the most glaring being the different follow-up periods of clients and controls; the control group had a longer period in which to get arrested. If (a) the proportion of youths arrested in each group and (b) the mean number of arrests per individual are standardized with respect to exposure time, the differences between the groups disappear. Given the fact that clients had fewer prior arrests (were better "risks"), this lack of actual difference calls into question the positive treatment effects that were claimed by the authors (Haapanen and Rudisill, 1980:8).

Similarly, Gibbons and Blake (another source cited by Alder and Polk) carry out an analysis of several evaluations of diversion programs, finding such problems in one typical study as too short a time period for impact assessment, the failure to describe the handling of control cases, and an absence of a range of impact data (Gibbons and Blake, 1976:415). This review concludes:

> Clearly, there is insufficient evidence in the nine studies examined here for one to have much confidence in diversion arguments and contentions (Gibbons and Blake, 1976:420).

Third, is not the posture assumed by Binder and Geis at variance with what is generally accepted within the research community? Assume for a moment that the intervention being proposed were some form of medical treatment. What would the response of the scientific community be if there was evidence that suggests that the form of treatment may be either: (1) beneficial, (2) of no benefit, or (3) potentially harmful? How compelling would the argument appear, advanced by an obvious advocate of the treatment, that the research showing positive results is "no poorer in overall methodology" than research showing negative or harmful effects? Would not the rules of evidence which apply in such cases place a particular burden of proof on those who advocate the treatment? Is not some caution to be urged, especially when harm has been found in experimentation? How telling is an attack which makes no reference whatsoever to the data and evidence showing negative or harmful results, and instead leaps immediately to challenging the motives of the researchers?

Diversion and Net-Widening

A major feature of the defense of diversion provided by Binder and Geis is their rejection of the concern that diversion may result in a widening of the net of juvenile justice. Their position seems based in the following propositions:

1. Diversion is beneficial in the sense that many or most clients are helped through the services provided by diversion programs.

2. Because diversion is helpful, then the proposition that doing nothing, rather than doing something, is unacceptable. Being precise, Binder and Geis find the argument that it is more desirable to ignore deviant behavior than to seek remedial help in diversion "a dubious proposition at best and a downright harmful one at worst" (Binder and Geis, 1984:316).

3. Diversion programs in most cases are voluntary because "offenders and their families may refuse services without consequences" (Binder and Geis, 1984:313).

4. When coercion is present, we are reminded that coercion has essentially been invited by the offender's choice of behavior. "If he or she wished to retain maximum freedom of choice, it would have been prudent either to have abstained from the earlier behavior or not to have gotten caught at it" (Binder and Geis, 1984:313).

5. Because there is actual offense behavior at issue, then some form of social control is desirable and probably inevitable. There is nothing pernicious about social control in the view of Binder and Geis because it consists not simply of law, but of etiquette, norms, regulations, customs and ethics, and takes place in the home, street, school, or family. Not only is social control broadly conceived, but so is the notion of an agent of social control, which consists of the following:

> Any person who attempts to influence behavior that is considered unacceptable in a normative sense. This may be a mother, a minister, a friend, indeed anyone with physical or psychological authority, or presumably anyone who interacts with another person, since it is a given of human intercourse that each of us in our actions attempts to influence another to behave in a particular way or to desist from behaving in a certain manner. (Binder and Geis, 1984:316).

For Binder and Geis, given these premises, diversion becomes a reasonable and responsible form of expanding the devices of social control available to a community for coping with adolescent offense behavior and is worthy of an energetic defense. Because diversion is an effective, voluntary, and appropriate response to delinquent behavior, they find no merit in the concern that net-widening may result from diversion, observing instead:

> The phrase "widening the net" is, of course, employed pejoratively, with the intent to evoke an emotional response. It conjures up visions of a mesh net that is thrown over thrashing victims, incapacitating them as they

flail about, desperately seeking to avoid captivity. The net is maneuvered by "agents of social control," another image provoking term, this one carrying a Nazi-like connotation. Both terms are employed for purposes of propaganda rather than to enlighten (Binder and Geis, 1984:315).

Unfortunately, however vivid the imagery, a case rejecting the net-widening argument is built by Binder and Geis which avoids reference to the empirical record. The first two premises are challenged by the evidence of the impact of diversion on subsequent behavior as cited above. If further research confirms either that diversion has no impact or that it is harmful, then the assumption that it is better to do something (in the form of diversion) than to do nothing becomes unsupportable.

Evidence exists which also raises questions about the voluntary nature of diversion services. Early in the development of diversion, Klapmuts (1972) cautioned that if being referred to the diversion program was backed by a threat of referral to court, then the allegedly nonpunitive agency in reality becomes an extension of the justice system and the diversion is a legal fiction. After reviewing the practices of a few diversion programs, Nejelski (1976:410) warned that: "there is a danger that diversion will become a means of expanding coercive intervention in the lives of children and families without proper concern for their rights." A national survey of over 300 youth service bureaus (YSBs), which included more intensive site analyses and interviews with 27 of the diversion agencies, provides some empirical support for such concerns (Polk and Schuchter, 1975:92):

> Data from our field visits suggest that diversionary referrals from court intake and courts to YSBs essentially facilitate deferred prosecution; generally are contingent upon admission of guilt without the advice of counsel; that "voluntary agreements" or consent decrees are obtained under coercive circumstances which vitiate the meaning of voluntariness; that throughout the diversionary and referral process the youth inhabits a legal limbo which increases his vulnerability to subsequent punishment for offenses previously

committed, and which is a much more subtle and pernicious problem than double jeopardy.

A further problem in the viewpoint of Binder and Geis is their undifferentiated view of the sources of social control. In its original intent, as should be clear from the term "diversion," there was a recognition that control within the juvenile justice system should be sharply differentiated from other forms of social control. The basic assumed thrust of diversion would be to shift responsibility and intervention for some individuals who had entered juvenile justice processing outside of that system into some form of nonjustice, community alternative.

A major concern of many of the researchers who write about net-widening is the question of whether this is, in fact, what diversion programs accomplish. Is diversion serving as a process for moving young persons who have "penetrated" the justice network outward and away from that system, or has it become a device for incorporating a whole new class of clients inside an expanding justice system? Some have questioned whether it is offense behavior at all that brings clients to diversion agencies, pointing out that the attributes of diversion referrals (age, sex, reason for referral) suggest that a population quite different from delinquent offenders is being tapped by diversion programs. From his analysis of evaluations and descriptions of over 50 diversion programs, Klein (1979:165) was able to comment that:

> The conclusion seems unavoidable: among projects reporting on the characteristics of diversion clients, no reasonable case can be made that these projects are carrying out diversion as its rationale suggested they should. The bulk of "diversion cases" are young people who are normally counseled and released by the police, if indeed they have any dealings with the police. With clients like these, we cannot truly be testing the efficacy of diversion.

Further, Empey (1982) argues that because a majority of diversion projects have actually been connected with, or even operated by, traditional justice agencies, one of the major functional goals of diversion has been subverted:

> Diversion was supposed to turn the flow of juveniles away from the juvenile justice system and back toward the community. But rather than doing that, several studies reveal that as many as half of all referrals have come, not from police and intake officers, but from schools, welfare agencies, and parents—the very people and institutions that were supposed to be mobilized to serve youth in lieu of legal processing (p. 482).

One of the persons most closely identified with the origins of the concept of diversion has been concerned enough about the control of the diversion process by the justice system to comment that:

> The cooptation of the diversion movement by law enforcement leaves the rather sour conclusion that not only have the purposes of diversion been perverted but, moreover, police power has been extended over youths and types of behavior not previously subjected to control (Lemert, 1981:43).

Perhaps because the discipline makes them more sensitive to the organizational level of analysis, sociologists then become concerned with two issues. One, does the record of diversion show that responsibility for handling of cases is being shifted away from the justice system? When the data indicate that the programs are controlled by justice agencies, that referrals are coming from rather than to schools, families, and other community resources, and that the cases are those that would not under ordinary circumstances come to the attention of justice authorities, then diversion may be functioning in quite a different way than its originators intended and the term would imply.

Second, if clients come to diversion agencies for help with personal and social problems far removed from offense behavior, and if the diversion agency is part of the justice system, then, whatever the motivation, young persons are coming under the control of the justice system for behavior that, prior to the introduction of diversion, would not have led to such control.

The concern for net-widening is, in short, a concern about whether diversion is meeting its original goal of deflecting cases away from juvenile justice processing. A solid, data-grounded argument can be made which suggests that this goal is not being met, and that instead the juvenile justice system, under the banner of diversion, is taking on both more cases and expanded functions (for a recent review, see Blomberg, 1983). It is not a question of whether services should be available for young persons, but one of where those services should be located. The underlying theory of diversion is that both the individuals served and the community itself would be better off if more of the responsibility for youth behavior were shifted to the community and away from juvenile justice. Is it really inappropriate to discuss an apparent inconsistency between what was planned and what resulted when the inconsistency is revealed by data and evidence?

Diversion and Hidden Sexism

The comments of Binder and Geis regarding the suggestion of Alder and Polk (1982; see also Alder, forthcoming) [to] examine such propositions . . . provide a further illustration of their apparent unwillingness to confront the empirical record of diversion. In their statement, Alder and Polk . . . examine such propositions as: diversion clients are more likely to be female than are clients at other points of formal justice processing; the female clients are being referred to diversion programs disproportionately for the same kinds of behaviors (status offenses) that have provoked concern for sexism within the juvenile justice system; diversion programs may be expanding their network of social control; and finally, diversion may increase the probability of further deviance (and, thus, subsequent formal contact with the juvenile justice system). Literature and extensive data are presented to substantiate these points. Alder and Polk warn, however, that the data are not completely consistent with each point of their argument. They are forced to rely on secondary analysis, and data on some key points of a more complete argument chain are not available. Accordingly, they alert the reader to the conjectural nature of the argument. They then observe that if the above observations are accurate (and at least some data are available to support each point), then a reasonable derivative conclusion is that diversion may represent a form of hidden sexism which results in an increase in the number of girls who ultimately come under the control of juvenile justice agencies.

Binder and Geis profess astonishment at this conclusion, and observe that "in truth, virtually the entire argument is conjectural and rhetorical" (1984:324). In what sense is this the case? Do not Alder and Polk present evidence at each point of their argument? Is not the conclusion logically consistent with the premises established? This is not to say that Alder and Polk are correct. Binder and Geis may have discussed how the data cited by Alder and Polk are in error or where in the chain of argumentation leading to the conclusion an important flaw or inconsistency exist. This they did not do. Instead, they observe the following:

> What diversion does, according to Alder and Polk, when it is successful in resolving the family, personal, or school problems of females is to contribute to "sex-role maintenance." When it fails to provide help, then, of course, the intervention may be regarded as unsuccessful, and evidence of inflicted labeling harm (p. 324).

Alder and Polk make no such claims. The reader will look in vain for any reference whatsoever in their work to conditions either where diversion is "successful in resolving . . . problems" or where "it fails to provide help." It is difficult to see how this disturbing misrepresentation of the work of others, or a dismissal of several pages of empirical data as "rhetoric" either meets minimal standards of scholarly fairness or serves to clarify the record of diversion.

Conclusion

The contradictory record of juvenile diversion is not easy to read or interpret. Because individuals will approach the evidence from different experiential bases and differential disciplinary paradigms, some disagreements are probably unavoidable. Consider, for example, the following description of diversion (which can be presumed to come from experience) as seen by Binder and Geis (1984:325):

> Some . . . troubling youngsters will be arrested, some will be referred to probation and the courts. Among the group simply arrested and among those referred upward in the justice system, many will be released or redirected to the community. Among those redirected, at least some would benefit from such services as employment counseling, family counseling, a requirement of restitution, a relationship with a Big Brother or Big Sister, substance abuse education, or even psychotherapy. And that is diversion.

This is, of course, precisely the sense of diversion as it was originally intended (i.e., a process which results in removal of individuals from justice system processing, with supportive community experiences substituted). Because Binder and Geis also see the alternative services as both beneficial and voluntary, the vigor with which they defend diversion becomes more explainable.

Unfortunately, the empirical record suggests that this is not diversion in general practice. Study after study suggests that the programs are often run by, or closely connected to, the justice system, and that most of the clients are not offenders being referred outward, but are youngsters with a variety of personal problems far removed from offense behavior who are being referred into this system. The evidence suggests that a large proportion of the programs may be coercive rather than voluntary. The data on impact do not permit us at this time to reject the hypothesis that the services may be either of no benefit or even harmful to the clients experiencing the diversion program. Several bits of evidence can be woven together to suggest that unanticipated consequences of diversion may be occurring in terms of hidden sexist processes.

Despite their professed desire to explain why the response to diversion is "so inconsistent with the actual record," Binder and Geis themselves choose to ignore that record. Crucial evidence contrary to their position receives no mention. Arguments firmly anchored in fact and data are dismissed as "rhetorical," without presentation of alternative evidence. The concerns about diversion are seen as originating not from the research findings, but from the petty motivations of antidiversionist sociologists. There is an alternative view. Many sociologists, despite what Binder and Geis allege, are firmly committed to the goals of diversion as defined in its original conception. These investigators read the patterns of the empirical record, however, and are dismayed by the drift of diversion from its intended course. They document that drift with data. If Binder and Geis have alternative evidence, they could provide a valuable service by presenting it.

References

ALDER, C.
"Gender bias in juvenile justice." Crime and Delinquency 30 (forthcoming).

ALDER, C. AND K. POLK
"Diversion and hidden sexism." Australian and New Zealand J. of Criminology 15: 100–108 (1982).

BINDER, A. AND G. GEIS
"*Ad Populum* argumentation in criminology: juvenile diversion as rhetoric." Crime and Delinquency, 30:309–333 (1984).

BLOMBERG, T. G.
"Diversions, disparate results, and unresolved questions: an integrative evaluation perspective." J. of Research in Crime and Delinquency 20:24–38 (1983).

DUXBURY, E.
Evaluation of Youth Service Bureaus. Sacramento: California Youth Authority, 1973.

ELLIOTT, D. S., F. W. DUNFORD, AND B. KNOWLES
Diversion: A Study of Alternative Processing Practices. Boulder, CO: Behavioral Research Institute, 1978.

EMPEY, L. T.
American Delinquency: Its Meaning and Construction. Homewood, IL: Dorsey, 1982.

FORWARD, J. R., M. KIRBY, AND K. WILSON
Volunteer Intervention with Court-Diverted Juveniles. Denver: Partners' Court Diversion Program, 1975.

GIBBONS, D. AND G. BLAKE
"Evaluating the impact of juvenile diversion programs." Crime and Delinquency 22:411–420 (1976).

HAAPANEN, R. AND D. RUDISILL
The Evaluation of Youth Service Bureaus: Final Report, Sacramento: California Youth Authority, 1980.

KLAPMUTS, N.
"Children's rights: the legal rights of minors in conflict with law of social custom." Crime and Delinquency Literature (September, 1972).

KLEIN, M. W.
"Deinstitutionalization and diversion of juvenile offenders: a litany of impediments," pp. 145–201 in N. Morris and M. Tonry (eds.), Crime and Justice. Chicago: Univ. of Chicago Press, 1979.

LEMERT, E. M.
"Diversion in juvenile justice: what hath been wrought?" J. of Research in Crime and Delinquency 18:34–46 (1981).

LINCOLN, S. B.
"Juvenile referral and recidivism," in R. M. Carter and M. W. Klein (eds.), Back on the Street: Diversion of Juvenile Offenders. Englewood Cliffs, NJ: Prentice-Hall, 1976.

——— "Recidivism rates of diverted juvenile offenders." Paper presented at the National Conference on Criminal Justice Evaluation, Washington, DC, 1977.

NEJELSKI, P.
"Diversion: the promise and danger." Crime and Delinquency 22: 393–410 (1976).

PALMER, T., M. BOHNSTEDT, AND R. LEWIS
The Evaluation of Juvenile Diversion: Final Report. Sacramento: California Youth Authority, 1978.

PALMER, T. AND R. LEWIS
"A differentiated approach to juvenile diversion." J. of Research in Crime and Delinquency 17:209–277 (1980).

POLK, K. AND A. SCHUCTER
Report: Phase I Assessment of Youth Service Bureaus. A report prepared for the National Institute of Law Enforcement and Criminal Justice, Washington, DC, 1975.

QUAY, H. C. AND C. T. LOVE
"The effect of a juvenile diversion program on rearrests." Criminal Justice and Behavior 4: 377–396 (1977).

QUINCY, R. L.
An Evaluation of the Effectiveness of the Youth Service Bureau Diversion Concept. Unpublished Ph.D. dissertation, Michigan State University at East Lansing, 1981.

THORNTON, W., E. BARRETT, AND L. MUSOLF
The Sacramento County Probation Department 601 Diversion Project. Sacramento: Sacramento County Probation Department, 1972.

VENEZIA, P. AND D. ANTHONY
A Program Level Evaluation of Wisconsin's Youth Service Bureaus. Tuscon, AZ: Associates for Youth Development, 1978.

QUESTIONS FOR DISCUSSION

1. Explain how diversion should ideally be implemented and how, according to this article, it actually is implemented.

2. Explain "net-widening." What are several criticisms of net-widening?

3. Alder and Polk suggest that the practice of diversion for juveniles contains hidden sexism. Why?

APPLICATIONS

1. In your opinion, is diversion an effective mechanism for ensuring that juveniles do not become "hardened" by institutionalization? Why?

2. For what types of juvenile delinquency might we effectively use diversion? Explain.

KEY TERMS

conjectural involving or based on a conclusion deduced or surmised by guesswork.

derivative something made up of or formulated by varying elements.

perjorative something that tends to belittle or disparage.

pernicious highly injurious or destructive.

polemical characterizes something controversial, opposite, or disputed.

26

Juvenile Parole Policy in the United States: Determinate Versus Indeterminate Models

Jose B. Ashford and Craig Winston LeCroy

This paper presents an overview of eight approaches in juvenile parole policy for terminating, extending, and discharging youths from juvenile parole or aftercare. These types were derived from the results of a national survey of juvenile parole policy in the United States. This survey was sent to the departments of correction, youth service bureaus, and legislative service agencies for the 50 states. The survey sought comparative data on trends in substantive and procedural approaches for handling parole duration and discharge issues for juvenile offenders. These trends are evaluated in relation to movements toward formalism in corrections, recent reforms in juvenile sentencing, standards promulgated by various standard-setting groups, and recent shifts in juvenile justice philosophy in the United States.

Since the cases of *Kent v. United States* (1966) and *Gault* (1967), juvenile justice philosophy gradually has shifted toward a fairness or a justice paradigm (Aultman and Wright 1982). This paradigm stresses the fundamental images of "just deserts," equality in sentencing, and crime control. It has ushered in many reforms in sentencing and in release policy (Forst, Fisher and Coates 1985) designed to improve the exercise of judicial and correctional discretion. Most of these reforms advocate using some form of determinate sentencing, presumptive sentencing, or administrative guidelines.

"Juvenile Parole Policy in the United States: Determinate versus Indeterminate Models," *Justice Quarterly*, 10:2 (June 1993), pp. 179–195.

Determinate sentencing refers to any sentencing or disposition system in which the length of a commitment is determined when the initial disposition is imposed (Tonry 1987). Presumptive sentencing, on the other hand, is any scheme entailing a presumed range of dispositions or sentences that are deemed proportionate to the seriousness of the defendant's offense (Singer 1978; Tonry 1987). Administrative guidelines refer to any approaches in sentencing in which agencies establish guidelines or standards that determine a person's length of confinement in a correctional facility.

The specification of the length of a confinement in a determinate sentence does not necessarily mean that the offender will serve the specified duration of the sentence (Singer 1978). In some determinate sentencing systems, offenders still may be released on parole or may receive reductions in the duration of their sentence for good time. In other systems, provisions for supervised release have been abolished or reduced significantly. The function and the role of parole are unclear in this determinate sentencing movement primarily because of the "variety" of determinate sentencing schemes (Singer 1978; von Hirsh and Hanrahan 1981). In particular, considerable confusion surrounds the purpose of the community supervision component of juvenile and adult parole (Clear 1979; von Hirsh and Hanrahan 1984; Wheeler 1978). Does the option of a desert model or of a philosophy of determinate or presumptive sentences necessarily rule out parole supervision (von Hirsch and Hanrahan 1984)? How have the determinacy and accountability movements in sentencing for juveniles affected the minimizing of disparities in duration on parole or aftercare?

Between 1979 and 1980, Forst, Fisher, and Coates (1985) conducted a national survey on juvenile determinate and indeterminate commitment and release practices in the United States. This survey provided invaluable insights into the types of approaches used in juvenile sentencing since the demise of the rehabilitative ideal. Since Forst and his colleagues published the results of their survey, many states have continued to reform their juvenile codes.

> Reformed codes usually include one or more of the following provisions: provisions which broaden the offense age requirements in waiver, allowing a greater number of youth to the criminal court; lowered ages of jurisdiction, which allow the criminal court to routinely handle younger offenders without the need for certification; serious delinquent statutes, which ensure the prolonged incarceration of repeat offenders and sentencing guidelines or administrative guidelines governing institutional exit (Harris and Graff 1988: 66).

Still, it is unclear how parole duration issues are being handled in the reformed and the nonreformed states.

The primary aim of this paper is to examine current trends in juvenile parole policy in view of the inchoate shifts in juvenile sentencing philosophy. In this examination we focus on identifying present variations in determinate and indeterminate approaches to terminating, extending, and discharging youths from parole. We also examine the sources and the patterns of authority involved in the setting of parole standards. This analysis is based on an examination of data from a national survey of youth service bureaus, departments of youth corrections, and legislative service agencies for the 50 states.

Historical Perspective on Juvenile Aftercare or Parole

"Aftercare in the juvenile justice system is the equivalent of parole in the adult criminal justice system" (Siegel and Senna 1985: 512). Traditionally, juvenile aftercare placed greater emphasis on achieving rehabilitative and treatment ends than was necessarily true of adult parole. To some extent, this difference was due to basic jurisprudential differences between the adult and the juvenile justice systems. In the juvenile justice system, authority for parole services is derived primarily from the *parens patriae* powers of the state and from its attendant to social welfare orientation. In contrast, authority for adult parole is derived primarily from the police powers of the state and from its attendant orientation to crime control. Nonetheless, the rationales used to differentiate between these two systems of justice are less sharp today than immediately after the inception of the juvenile court movement.

Some policy makers assume that it is not legitimate to consider all juveniles as victims of social conditions and as needing the protection and care of the state. This viewpoint was emphasized recently in the Model Juvenile Code of the American Legislative Exchange Council (1987). This group advocated holding juveniles responsible for their actions because they are represented dispportionately in current statistics for serious crime. Similarly, Siegel and Senna (1985:viii) pointed out that "those with a law enforcement orientation suggest that efforts to treat children under the concept of parens patriae have neglected the victims of delinquency, and that serious offenders need to be punished rather than rehabilitated." These viewpoints obviously conflict with the original intent of the founders of the juvenile justice system: "Although there is dispute about the motives of the founders—whether they set out to engage in child-saving or in a less benevolent pursuit based on economic and religious beliefs—it is agreed that the movement's basic philosophy was to exempt the young offender from criminal punishment" (Kittrie & Zenoff 1981:308).

Krisberg et al. (1986:26) argue that the current trend in juvenile justice reform reveals "a system growing more formal, restrictive and punitive." It is unclear, however, how these trends are affecting the provision of aftercare services. If rehabilitative ends are being supplanted by punitive objectives, we should expect substantial increases in the formalization of aftercare decision-making processes. These increases are expected primarily because approaches to justice which emphasize principles of punishment generally assume that the ends of justice are served best if decisions are limited by formal criteria. (Daivs 1979; Rothman 1983). Still, it is not clear to what extent punishment has replaced rehabilitation as the raison d'etre in aftercare decision-making processes. Probation and parole officials still justify many of their broad discretionary powers by appealing to rehabilitation (Porter 1980).

"In most states, aftercare is the least developed aspect of correction; in the opinion of many observers, it is less adequate than its counterpart, adult parole" (President's Commission on Law Enforcement and the Administration of Justice 1967:149). This view of juvenile aftercare, presented by the President's Commission on Law Enforcement and the Administration of Justice, was based in part on evidence gathered in a survey of aftercare services in the United States. The findings in this survey showed wide variation in the structure and the program content of juvenile aftercare. It was argued in the Commission's report that their survey revealed "the harsh realities of the nation's failure to come to grips with the juvenile aftercare problem" (Newman 1968:201).

As in the 1960s, the problem with juvenile aftercare in the early 1980s was one of gross neglect (Daum 1981; Simonsen and Gordon 1982). In most jurisdictions, aftercare remained the phase of the correctional process that escaped extensive formalization by correctional authorities (Baird 1981) and intervention by the courts (Bailey and Rothblatt 1982). In fact, aftercare workers in many jurisdictions still had unfettered discretion in making decisions restricting the liberty and the life chances of youths released from correctional institutions. For instance, decisions involving the placement of youths in residential treatment or substitute care were not guided by explicit criteria. Similarly, reclassification or even initial classification decisions were not restricted sufficiently by

explicit standards (Baird 1981). Aftercare workers had the power to employ whatever criteria they deemed appropriate in distributing burdens and benefits (Ashford and LeCroy 1988).

Coffey (1973) observed as early as 1957 that authorities were troubled by the lack of national standards for juvenile parole. Under indeterminate sentencing principles and the rehabilitative ideal, parole agencies and agents were granted broad discretion in making decisions about aftercare supervision, termination, and discharge. These decisions generally were justified by individualized treatment or predictive considerations. Experts in these matters were presumed to be better equipped than either judges or legislators to decide when to terminate parole. It was also assumed that these experts could predict the likelihood of a youth's recidivating while on parole or could determine whether the youth needed further treatment. This confidence of early exponents of parole in professional judgment is illustrated in the following quotation from a historical source in the field:

> As to the length of this trial visit and time when the former offender shall be formally discharged from the custody of the institution, it seems that on account of the greater variety of character disorder with which the reformatory has to deal, and with the great dependence upon the manner in which the former offender conducts himself during the parole, that the time of termination of the parole should rest with this board of experts. It should be for them to determine when the paroled delinquents ought to be returned to the reformatory and when the conduct of any paroled offender was such as to warrant final discharge (Haines 1920: 165–66).

This broad discretion granted to juvenile authorities was not subjected to close scrutiny until the late 1970s. At that time, individuals in academic and policy circles began to examine the aftercare problem. Romig (1978) reviewed eight studies that assessed the effectiveness of juvenile parole. In his review of the literature he found that "in not one of the studies were the results overwhelmingly favorable" (Romig 1978:190). Hudson's (1973) study, which was included in Romig's review, explicitly questioned the effectiveness of traditional parole programming. Hudson reached this position after discovering that low-risk youths released without parole supervision fared as well as youths released with supervision on parole.

Hudson's indictment of the effectiveness of parole supervision was shared by Wheeler (1978). In a study of parole in a midwestern state, Wheeler uncovered several key disparities in the ability of parole to achieve its stated mission. He stated:

> Of the three assumptions of parole, the nature of supervision in the community most dramatically illustrates the negative consequences of the indeterminate parole. Regardless of offense, blacks generally received the longer parole than whites. The same trend of longer parole was observed for younger offenders and females. Also, youth with the least serious offense at commitment were subject to equal or longer supervision in the community than index offenders . . . These research findings present a strong case against continuing the indeterminate sentence. While many lawyers and criminologists agree with this conclusion, correctional practitioners appear highly skeptical of adopting a "fixed" sentence for juveniles (Wheeler 1978:80–82).

On the basis of these findings, Wheeler concluded that indeterminate sentences and juvenile aftercare should be abolished. His recommendations, however, included the suggestion that "authorities may consider making parole services optional" (1978:132).

Wheeler's (1978) recommendation for a just deserts model in sentencing juveniles also was made by the Joint Commission on Juvenile Justice Standards, appointed in 1979 by the Institute of Judicial Administration and the American Bar Association (IJA-ABA). This prestigious group developed a set of juvenile standards for corrections administration that stressed determinate sentences. Melton et al. observed that the IJA/ABA standards were important primarily because they served as a significant "model for the new post-Gault juvenile court" (1987:294).

For its policy on dispositions, this standard-setting group recommended that states classify offense types and limit dispositions

for each class of offense. The IJA/ABA's Standard 2.1 states that "in choosing among statutory permissible disposition, the court should employ the least restrictive category and duration of disposition that is appropriate to the seriousness of the offense . . ." (1980:34). This group was less specific, however, about limits on parole duration because it intended to replace offender-based dispositions with dispositions based on principles of just deserts. As of 1987, no state had adopted the entire code recommended by the IJA/ABA. "Offender-based dispositions are still the rule, except for the most serious offense by the oldest juveniles" (Melton et al. 1987:295–96).

The subject of parole discharge or termination decisions in juvenile justice has received minimal scrutiny. Several standard-setting groups beside the IJA/ABA, however, have developed broad goals and standards to direct policy-making behavior in these areas. The Commission on Accreditation for Corrections of The American Correctional Association (ACA) recommended in Standard 7173 that it is essential for correctional authorities to develop written policy and procedure regarding recommendations for early termination of aftercare.

> The agency should develop . . . criteria for early termination of probation/aftercare. These may include demonstrated successful adjustment in terms of nonarrest and demonstrate stability in terms of home adjustment, school attendance, employment, social relationships, etc. Procedure should include specific time frames and careful case reviews. . . . Supervision should be terminated when it is clear that delivery of services to the youth is no longer required to protect the community or to enhance the youth's overall performance (ACA 1978:34).

In addition, the U.S. government established parole policy guidelines that were designed to "promote a more consistent exercise of discretion and enable fairer and more equitable decision making without removing individual case considerations" (28 C.F.R., Part II, 1990:96). This national parole policy established early termination guidelines from parole supervision for juvenile delinquents and youthful offenders. These guidelines specify that "absent case specific factors to the contrary, termination of supervision shall be considered indicated when:

(i) A parolee originally classified in the very good risk category (pursuant to @ 2.20) has completed two continuous years of supervision free from any indication of new criminal behavior or serious parole violation; and

(ii) A parolee originally classified in other than the very good risk category (pursuant to @ 2.20) has completed three continuous years of supervision free from any indications of new criminal behavior or serious parole violation" (28 C.F.R. Part II,1990:122–23).

These policy guidelines limit the decision-making processes by asserting the principle of a presumed termination of parole. That is, the parolee should be terminated presumptively after serving the minimum period of parole in the absence of specific factors to the contrary. The policy was asserted initially in the Model Penal Code (1968) developed for adult offenders (Morris 1988; Tonry 1988).

The Model Juvenile Justice Court Act (1968) did not subscribe to this principle of a presumed termination of parole at the end of a specified period. It limited commitment dispositions by recommending that commitments should "continue in force for 2 years or until the child is sooner discharged" (36(b)). Unlike the Model Penal Code, the Model Juvenile Justice Court Act advocates a discretionary minimum with a fixed maximum period of supervision. In addition, it includes special standards that allow for the extension of supervision up to a two-year maximum. In 1985 this act officially was renamed the Uniform Law Commissioners' Model Act. The 1987 table for adopting jurisdictions for the Model Act showed that it had not been adopted completely by any of the states.

This review of the literature suggests that since the Model Juvenile Justice Court Act (1968), several standard-setting groups have emphasized the need to limit the duration of sentences for juvenile offenders. Most of these groups have advocated making decision criteria explicit and for setting limits on duration of parole. We do not know, however, how much variation exists mong the states in their policy approaches to parole duration. Furthermore, we do not know to what extent states have chosen to adopt the recommendations of the various national standard-setting groups.

Procedure

Between November 1987 and November 1988 we conducted a national survey to understand the current trends and patterns in juvenile parole/aftercare policy in the United States. This survey consisted of a questionnaire and a request for supporting documentation from the departments of correction, the youth service bureaus, and the legislative service agencies for the 50 states. It requested comparative information on the standards and criteria used to structure the discretion of aftercare decision makers and asked whether these criteria could be found in legislation, administrative rules, or formal agency or departmental procedures. We asked the authorities to respond to six questions. The following question was relevant to this paper:

> Does your state have formal policies and procedures governing the discharge/termination of youth from parole or aftercare services?

If the respondents replied "yes" to this question, they were requested to check boxes indicating where these policies were located. We also asked them to cite appropriate legislation and to enclose relevant statutes or guidelines when appropriate. Finally, we asked the respondents to indicate whether their state had any pending policy or legislation that would address these concerns. Of the 50 states surveyed, we received adequate information from 47, a 94 percent response rate.

We analyzed each of these questionnaires and all supporting documentation. In addition, in spring 1991 we reexamined selected state statutes identified in the survey. We also analyzed secondary sources such as law review articles.

The results of this study cannot be considered an up-to-date account of existing policy because agencies and states are constantly modifying their policy practices. Even so, they represent the best available information since the survey performed by Forst and his colleagues in 1979 and 1980. In fact, this is the first analysis of many of these issues since standards were recommended by several national standard-setting groups in the late 1970s. The findings should benefit policy analysts interested in evaluating the range and variety of approaches to terminating, extending, and discharging youths from supervised release to the community. They present a view of policy practices a decade after significant policy recommendations by juvenile justice authorities.

Findings

We examined all of the materials from the survey to classify state policies affecting the duration of a youth's period on supervised release or aftercare. We used the following variables to classify types of parole; these were derived from the literature on juvenile aftercare and on adult and juvenile sentencing: 1) the amount of discretion allowed to youth service or aftercare workers in making termination and discharge decisions; 2) whether the parole period was determinate or indeterminate; and 3) who set the standards and criteria limiting parole termination or discharge decisions (Forst et al. 1985; Singer 1978; von Hirsch and Hanrahan 1981; Wheeler 1978). Given these variables, we identified eight types of parole supervision:

Type 1 is a determinate parole. In this system, length of parole is related to the period of commitment specified by the committing court. The court commits a youth for a specified period of time and the juvenile may serve a specified portion of this commitment on supervised release in the community. The range of time allowed for supervised release is specified in the initial judicial commitment and is proportionate to the youth's offense. If the youth engages in identified infractions while in the institution, he or she may lose the benefit of supervised release. In these circumstances, the youth will serve in the insti-

tution the specified length of time prescribed in the initial judicial commitment.

Juvenile parole authorities have no discretion to extend the period of supervision beyond the period prescribed in the judicial commitment. As a result, the decision to discharge a youth involves a straightforward computation of time since the beginning of the youth's commitment. This period is commensurate with the offender's offense, prior criminal history, and other factors considered significant by the legislature or sentencing commission. Furthermore, the legislature is the authority that generally sets the standards governing the range of parole duration deemed commensurate with established classes of offenses. Washington was the only state that fit this type of parole. Washington also was one of the few states that had special provisions allowing for voluntary supervision following the expiration of the youth's commitment. This voluntary supervision could last up to six months.

Type 2 is a determinate parole set by administrative agency. In this approach, the parole release date is set immediately after the youth arrives at the institution. This date includes a parole of fixed length that is considered proportionate to the youth's offense classification. This type of approach has much in common with Type 1; parole length in both types is commensurate with the seriousness of the youth's commitment offense and with his or her criminal history. The authority that sets the standards for length of confinement, release dates, and ranges of parole duration is the key distinguishing factor between Type 1 and Type 2. In Type 2, the standards governing the decision to terminate supervision rest with the parole or aftercare agency. Georgia and New Jersey were the only states that belonged to this type. At the time of the survey, Maryland was developing a classification system that prescribed parole lengths proportionate to the youth's classification.

Utah has developed administrative guidelines, but supervision under these guidelines is not determinate. Youths may be kept under supervision because of adjustment difficulties. Nevada also employs a variant of parole duration and supervision that presented some coding difficulties. The statutory language suggests that length of parole is indeterminate. Agency policy developed to implement the statutory language, however, prescribes fixed lengths of supervision and defines three types of discharge that are based on behavioral performance: positive termination, general termination, and negative termination. In Nevada, six months of supervision are prescribed for youths over 18, and nine months under 18. Although these paroles are of fixed lengths, the coders did not believe that Nevada should be coded as a state with determinate parole because the court maintained the discretion to continue youths on parole supervision. Therefore we categorized the fixed period as a presumptive minimum rather than as fixed length.

Type 3 is a presumptive minimum with limits on the extension of the supervision period for a fixed or a determinate length of time. This approach involves the presumption that parole should terminate after the youth completes a minimum period of supervised release. For example, the youth should be terminated presumptively from parole after completing at least six months on supervised release unless established factors or standards indicate otherwise. In effect, the agent or worker cannot depart from the prescribed six-month parole without evidence of behavior that fits standards governing the extension of parole. These specified factors, which limit agents' and workers' authority to extend the period of parole supervision, generally are found in statutes or in agency policies. If the aftercare worker presents evidence of factors indicating a need to extend the parole, this extension is limited to a fixed or determinate period such as six months. For example, supervised release terminates presumptively in Arkansas after six months of supervision, but can be extended only for a maximum of six months.

For the purposes of this study, we considered Type 3 a determinate approach to parole duration. Three states fit the definition for this classification: Arkansas, Kansas, and Mississippi. Presumptive durations in Kansas differed somewhat from those in the other two states. The standard term in Kansas is a presumptive six-month minimum and a maximum of 12 months. Superintendents or directors, however, may set different minimum and maximum lengths of time at the point of release. Another interesting variation in policy was found in Florida, which has a special sentencing provision for youths adjudicated delinquent for first-degree misdemeanurs. For these youths, supervision should terminate presumptively after six months of supervision, but it can be extended for not longer than six additional months.

Type 4 is a presumptive minimum with limits on the extension of supervision for an indeterminate period. This approach also presumes that parole should terminate after a minimum period, absent factors indicating otherwise. In this approach, the discretion to extend parole is limited by explicit standards, but the period of extension is indeterminate. The aftercare worker has the discretion to extend parole supervision for an unspecified length of time until the maximum age for automatic termination of the juvenile court's jurisdiction. Because the presumptive length of parole involves explicit standards governing extensions, we considered this type determinate even though it becomes indeterminate after a finding of poor adjustment on parole. Four state fit the criteria for this classification: Massachusetts, Michigan, Montana, and Nevada.

In Texas the policies include an approach for conventional delinquency commitments that caused some classification difficulties. A youth is committed indeterminately to the Texas Youth Commission until age 18 for conventional acts of delinquency. The institution, however, can release a youth at any time and can place him or her on parole. These youths on parole may be removed from active supervision after they have successfully completed 180 days at the lowest level of supervision. This presumptive discharge occurs after the youth meets the presumptive 180 days free of difficulties at Level 3 supervision. The presumptive discharge is indeterminate, however, because it is contingent on the youth's performance at each level of supervision. Performance difficulties translate into additional time at a given level. As a result, Texas aftercare for conventional commitments was not classified as determinate parole. A similar presumptive element is present in New Mexico; we also coded it under an indeterminate classification, however, because of its discretionary minimum.

Type 5 is a presumptive minimum with discretionary extension of supervision for an indeterminate period. This approach includes the assumption that parole should terminate after a minimum period, but can be extended at the discretion of the supervising authority. No limits are placed on the discretion of aftercare workers to extend the parole. Although the minimum length is specified, the factors allowing for indeterminate extension of supervision up to the maximum period of the commitment or the maximum age for termination are not specified. Because this approach lacks explicit standards limiting the extension of parole, we consider it indeterminate for the purposes of this paper. Five states fit the criteria for this type of parole: Arizona, Florida, New Hampshire, New York, and Pennsylvania. Although New York sets presumptive minimums with discretionary extension of supervision, it also has special determinate sentencing provisions for serious offense categories.

Type 6 is an indeterminate parole with a specified maximum and a discretionary minimum length of supervision. This approach is consistent with the approach advocated by the Model Juvenile Court Act of 1968. It limits the maximum level of commitment, but leaves the length of confinement and the period of supervised release to the discretion of parole authorities. Eleven states fit the criteria emphasizing a specified maximum and a discretionary minimum: Alabama, Colorado, Connecticut, Delaware, Louisiana, New Mexico, North Carolina, North Dakota, Tennessee, Vermont, and Wisconsin. This category encompasses a broad range of philosophies and approaches to determining a youth's readiness for discharge. Some states in this category have not formalized the early release decisions. States such as Wisconsin and Vermont, however, have introduced highly formalized agency policies that structure these decision-making processes.

Type 7 is an indeterminate parole with legal minimum and maximum periods of supervision. In this approach, the parole

authority is granted the discretion to discharge the youth from parole within a broad range of time. That is, the range between the minimum and the maximum term of commitment is much larger than in either Type 1 or Type 2. This approach was dominant in adult sentencing before the determinacy movement in sentencing in the mid-1970s. Seven states fit this classification: Alaska, California, Kentucky, Maine, Ohio, Texas, and Utah. We classified Utah under this option because minimum and maximum ranges in their administrative guidelines are not determinate. That is, their procedures grant authorities the discretion not to release any youth whose behavior does not merit release. In Utah's system, youths are reviewed every three months; the findings of these reviews can affect discharge from parole.

Type 8 is indeterminate or purely discretionary. In this approach, the length of parole is unspecified and there is no legal minimum to limit decisions about discharging a youth from parole. In states in this category, expiration of commitment at the age of majority is the only specified limit. Discharge decisions are based on the discretion of the aftercare staff, who possess the authority to assess the youth's readiness for discharge from parole supervision. Fourteen states fit this classification: Hawaii, Idaho, Illinois, Maryland, Missouri, Nebraska, Oklahoma, Oregon, Rhode Island, South Carolina, South Dakota, Virginia, West Virginia, and Wyoming.

Figure 1 displays the percentages of the distributions of these types of parole across the United States. These results do not include information about special sentencing provisions for serious or nonserious youth offenders. They show that indeterminate approaches to duration of parole supervision remain the dominant type in juvenile aftercare.

Although a number of states have instituted determinate sentencing provisions for serious juvenile offenders, the parole periods under many of these statutes also are subject to substantial discretion and indeterminacy. Of the 47 states surveyed here, 66 percent had standards for discharge from parole in their statutes, 28 percent in administrative

FIGURE 1   Percentages of Parole Types across the United States

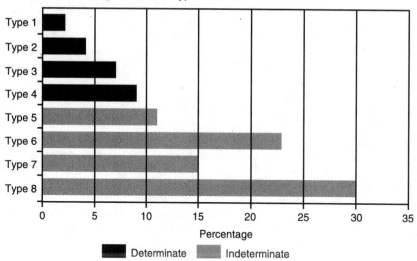

Percentage

■ Determinate   ▓ Indeterminate

rules, and 76 percent in agency policies. Finally, in 19 percent of the states, standards for aftercare policy were located in statutes and in administrative rules.

Discussion

When Washington State enacted its Juvenile Justice Act in 1978, authorities responsible for parole services acknowledged that parole lacked a clear direction in a justice framework. Nonetheless, they took positive steps to avoid the arbitrary termination of aftercare services when commitment orders expired. That is, they confronted the possibility that equal parole lengths for offenses in the same classification "might be detrimental to the rehabilitation of certain youth" (Division of Juvenile Rehabilitation 1987:7). They recommended that youths be entitled to request continued services after completing a length of supervision deemed commensurate with their criminal history, age, and committing offense. Although commensurate approaches to parole length based on principles of desert were advocated by reformers (Wheeler 1978) in the late 1970s and were implemented in Washington State, few states have adopted these recommendations for a desert approach to supervised release. Most states maintain indeterminate approaches to parole supervision.

In addition, few states have adopted fixed or presumptive approaches to parole length. Policy governing length of supervision has been influenced more by principles of crime control and accountability than by principles of consistency or equality in lengths of parole. For example, many states have introduced determinate sentencing provisions that subject youths to extended surveillance and supervision in the community. Thus lengths of parole have not diminished as a result of the determinacy movement. Youths with determinate sentences can be placed on extensive periods of parole supervision. This finding was unexpected primarily because justice models initially were rationalized on the grounds that they would eliminate the unnecessary expansion of the therapeutic state and its disparities in duration (Wheeler 1978). Thus goals of incapacitation and punishment appear to be playing a more important role in policy reforms involving length of parole than are principles of equality or justice.

Similarly, few states have adopted graduated release practices that allow for individualized assessments of a youth's reintegration into the community and readiness for termination from supervision. The states that include systems of levels of parole (Illinois, New Mexico, Texas, Utah) subscribe to various justifying aims ranging from rehabilitative punishment to individualized treatment and rehabilitation. We expected that differentials levels of supervision and formalized procedures for assessing readiness for discharge would play an increased role in discharge decisions, in view of the concerns about discretionary abuses voiced by reformers in the late 1970s. Yet the results of the survey revealed that only a few indeterminate states (e.g., Wisconsin and Vermont) give substantial attention to the results of formal risk, needs, and reassessment instruments. In fact, Vermont is the only state that bases termination decisions strictly on evidence of sufficient rehabilitation as indicated by "a reduction in risk factors and treatment needs." The lack of systems of levels also was unexpected because the National Council of Juvenile and Family Court Judges (1984) recommended the adoption of phased reentry into the community for serious offenders.

Our findings from the survey show that the terms of postrelease supervision in the United States still are justified on multiple grounds. Lengths of supervision vary from jurisdiction to jurisdiction; no clear standard of time presently exists for achieving aftercare objectives. States specify from six months to two years as a minimum period for achieving release objectives. Our results also show that the recommendations of standard-setting groups have not been adopted widely by juvenile justice authorities. In fact, the modal type of parole in the United States remains highly indeterminate and discretionary. In addition, few innovations from the formalization movements in classification and in correctional rule making are influencing state discharge policies. In particular, no state classified under Type 8 has introduced rule-making practices to formalize the decision-making processes involved in their discharge decisions.

Our analysis of state parole policies identifies eight types of approaches to terminating, extending, and discharging youths from supervised release. Although our categorization of some states may be questioned on substantive grounds, our findings are significant primarily in that they illustrate the diversity of parole policies in the United States. This diversity presented obvious coding difficulties. It is reasonable to conclude, however, that the states have no standard approach to reducing disparities in lengths of parole. Furthermore, we find no evidence of a clear trend toward a desert approach to terminating youths from parole supervision.

In sum, postrelease supervision has not been abolished in the juvenile justice system since the onset of the determinacy and the accountability movements. Most states retain some form of supervised release regardless of their philosophy of sentencing. Texas and New York, for example, have passed determinate sentencing provisions, but youths committed under these provisions still may be released on conditional supervision. Although supervised released has been maintained even in determinate-parole jurisdictions such as Washington State, the underlying justification remains unspecified. Few states have articulated a coherent policy that includes the aftercare or parole aspect of the correctional process. As in the late 1960s, aftercare remains the least developed area of the juvenile justice process.

References

AMERICAN CORRECTIONAL ASSOCIATION
1978   *Manual of Standards for Juvenile Probation and Aftercare Services.* Rockville, MD: Commission on Accreditation for Corrections.

AMERICAN LEGISLATIVE EXCHANGE COUNCIL
1987   "Model Juvenile Justice Code" (draft). Claremont, CA: Rose Institute of Justice.

ASHFORD, J.B., AND C.W. LECROY
1988   "Decision-Making for Juvenile Offenders in Aftercare." *Juvenile and Family Court Journal* 39:47–53.

AULTMAN, M.G. AND K.N. WRIGHT
1985   "The Fairness Paradigm: An Evaluation of Change in Juvenile Justice." *Canadian Journal of Criminology* 24:13–24.

BAILEY, F.L. AND H.B. ROTHBLATT
1982   *Handling Juvenile Delinquency Cases.* Rochester, NY: Lawyers Co-operative Publishing Co.

BAIRD, C.S.
1981   "Classifying Juveniles: Making the Most of an Important Management Tool." *Corrections Today* 43:36–41.

CLEAR, T.R.
1979   "Three Dilemmas in Community Supervision." *Prison Journal* 59:2–16.

28 C.F.R., PART II
1987   pp. 91–118.

COFFEY, A.R.
1975   *Juvenile Corrections: Treatment and Rehabilitation.* Englewood Cliffs, NJ: Prentice-Hall.

DAUM, J.M.
1981   "Aftercare: the Neglected Phase of Adolescent Treatment." *Juvenile and Family Court Journal* 32:43–48.

DAVIS, K.C.
1971   *Discretionary Justice: A Preliminary Inquiry,* Urbana: University of Illinois Press.

DIVISION OF JUVENILE REHABILITATION
1987   Juvenile Parole Program Standards. Olympia: Department of Social and Health Services.

FORST, M.L., B.A. FISHER, AND R.B. COATES
1985   "Indeterminate and Determinate Sentencing of Juvenile Delinquents: A National Survey of Approaches to Commitment and Release Decision Making." *Juvenile and Family Court Journal* 36:1–11.

HAINES, T.H.
1920   "Lessons from the Principles Governing the Parole Procedure in Hospitals for the Insane." In *Conference on Social Work,* pp. 159–66. Chicago: University of Chicago Press.

HARRIS, P.M. AND GRAFF L.G.
1988   "A Critique of Juvenile Sentences Reform." *Federal Probation* 52:66–71.

HUDSON, C.H
1973   Summary Report: An Experimental Study of the Different Effects of Parole Supervision for A Group of Adolescent Boys and Girls. Minneapolis: Minnesota Dept. of Corrections.

INSTITUTE OF JUDICIAL ADMINISTRATION/AMERICAN BAR ASSOCIATION
1980   *Dispositions.* Cambridge, MA: Ballinger.

KITTIRE, N.N. AND E.H. ZENOFF
1981   *Sanctions, Sentencing and Corrections: Law, Policy, and Practice.* Mineola, NY: Foundation Press.

KRISBERG, B., J.M. SCHWARTZ, P. LITSKY, AND J. AUSTIN
1986   "The Watershed of Juvenile Justice Reform." *Crime and Delinquency* 32:5–38.

MELTON, G.B., J. PETRILA, N.G. POYTHRESS, AND C. SLOBOGIN
1987   *Psychological Evaluations for the Courts.* New York: Guilford Press.

MODEL JUVENILE JUSTICE COURT ACT
1968   (36).

MODEL PENAL CODE AND COMMENTARIES, PART I
1962

MORRIS, N.
1988   "Sentencing under the Model Penal Code: Balancing the Concerns." *Rutgers Law Journal* 19:811–21.

NATIONAL COUNCIL OF JUVENILE AND FAMILY COURT JUDGES
1984   "The Juvenile Court and Serious Offenders." *Juvenile and Family Court Journal* 35:1–22.

NEWMAN, C.L.
1968   *Sourcebook on Probation, Parole and Pardons.* Springfield, IL: Thomas.

PORTER, J.B.
1983   "Grievance Mechanisms in Community Based Corrections." *Journal of Probation and Parole* 12:29–42.

PRESIDENT'S COMMISSION ON LAW ENFORCEMENT AND THE ADMINISTRATION OF JUSTICE
1967   *Task Force Report: Corrections.* Washington, DC: U.S. Government Printing Office.

ROMIG, D.A.
1978   *Justice for Children.* Lexington, MA: Heath.

ROTHMAN, D.
1986   "Sentencing Reform in Historical Perspective." *Crime and Delinquency* 29:631–51.

SIEGEL, L.J. AND J.J. SENNA
1985   *Juvenile Delinquency: Theory Practice, and Law.* St. Paul: West.

SIMONSEN, C.E. AND M.S. GORDON III
1982   *Juvenile Justice in America.* New York: Macmillan.

SINGER, R.
1978   "In Favor of `Presumptive Sentences' Set by a Sentencing Commission." *Crime and Delinquency* 24:401–27.

TONRY, M.H.
1987   *Sentencing Reform Impacts.* Washington, DC.: National Institute of Justice.
1988   "Sentencing Guidelines and The Model Penal Code." *Rutgers Law Journal* 19:823–47.

VON HIRSH, A. AND K. HANRAHAN
1981   "Determinate Penalty Systems in America: An Overview." *Crime and Delinquency* 27:289–316.
1984   "Abolish Parole." In. R.M. Carter, D. Glaser, and L.T. Wilkins (eds.), *Probation, Parole, and Community Corrections,* pp. 184–94. New York: Wiley.

WHEELER, G.R.
1978   *Counter-Deterrence.* Chicago: Nelson Hall.

Cases Cited

Gault, 387 U.S. 1 at 7 (1967).

Kent v. United States, 383, U.S. 541, 86 S. Ct. 1045, 16 L. Ed. 2d 84 (1966).

QUESTIONS FOR DISCUSSION

1. What are the differences between determinate and indeterminate sentencing? Provide examples of each.

2. What is presumptive sentencing? Give an example of this type of sentencing.

3. Discuss the most common type of juvenile parole in the United States.

APPLICATIONS

1. Aftercare for juveniles is the least developed area of the juvenile justice process. Based on your opinion and what you have read, why is this the case?

2. What kinds of programs and/or activities would you recommend for juveniles during aftercare that would improve their chances of successful reintegration into the community?

KEY TERMS

discretionary when something is left to individual choice or judgment.

explicit expressed without vagueness or ambiguity; leaving nothing questionable or unclear.

implicit not specifically revealed or expressed, but understood in context with something else.

inchoate imperfectly formed or formulated; hazy or unclear.

raison d'etre reason or justification for existence.

recidivism a return or relapse to prison by virtue of the commission of more criminal acts.

supplanted when something is removed and substituted or superceded with something else.

unfettered unrestrained; free.

27

The Saints and the Roughnecks

William J. Chambliss

Eight promising young men—children of good, stable, white upper-middle-class families, active in school affairs, good pre-college students—were some of the most delinquent boys at Hanibal High School. While community residents and parents knew that these boys occasionally sowed a few wild oats, they were totally unaware that sowing wild oats completely occupied the daily routine of these young men. The Saints were constantly occupied with truancy, drinking, wild driving, petty theft and vandalism. Yet not one was officially arrested for any misdeed during the two years I observed them.

This record was particularly surprising in light of my observations during the same two years of another gang of Hanibal High School students, six lower-class white boys known as the Roughnecks. The Roughnecks were constantly in trouble with police and community even though their rate of delinquency was about equal with that of the Saints. What was the cause of this disparity? The result? the following consideration of the activities, social class and community perceptions of both gangs may provide some answers.

The Saints from Monday to Friday

The Saints' principal daily concern was with getting out of school as early as possible. The boys managed to get out of school with

"The Saints and the Roughnecks," *Society*, 11:11 (November–December 1973), pp. 24–31. Reprinted by permission of the author and publisher. Copyright © 1973 by Transaction Publishing.

minimum danger that they would be accused of playing hooky through an elaborate procedure for obtaining "legitimate" release from class. The most common procedure was for one boy to obtain the release of another by fabricating a meeting of some committee, program or recognized club. Charles might raise his hand in his 9:00 chemistry class and ask to be excused—a euphemism for going to the bathroom. Charles would go to Ed's math class and inform the teacher that Ed was needed for a 9:30 rehearsal of the drama club play. The math teacher would recognize Ed and Charles as "good students" involved in numerous school activities and would permit Ed to leave at 9:30. Charles would return to his class, and Ed would go to Tom's English class to obtain his release. Tom would engineer Charles' escape. The strategy would continue until as many of the Saints as possible were freed. After a stealthy trip to the car (which had been parked in a strategic spot), the boys were off for a day of fun.

Over the two years I observed the Saints, this pattern was repeated nearly every day. There were variations on the theme, but in one form or another, the boys used this procedure for getting out of class and then off the school grounds. Rarely did all eight of the Saints manage to leave school at the same time. The average number avoiding school on the days I observed them was five.

Having escaped from the concrete corridors the boys usually went either to a pool hall on the other (lower-class) side of town or to a cafe in the suburbs. Both places were out of the way of people the boys were likely to know (family or school officials), and both provided a source of entertainment. The pool hall entertainment was the generally rough atmosphere, the occasional hustler, the sometimes drunk proprietor and, of course, the game of pool. The cafe's entertainment was provided by the owner. The boys would "accidentally" knock a glass on the floor or spill cola on the counter—not all the time, but enough to be sporting. They would also bend spoons, put salt in sugar bowls and generally tease whoever was working in the cafe. The owner had opened the cafe recently and was dependent on the boys' business which was, in fact, substantial since between the horsing around and the teasing they bought food and drinks.

The Saints on Weekends

On weekends the automobile was even more critical than during the week, for on weekends the Saints went to Big Town—a large city with a population of over a million 25 miles from Hanibal. Every Friday and Saturday night most of the Saints would meet between 8:00 and 8:30 and would go into Big Town. Big Town activities included drinking heavily in taverns or nightclubs, driving drunkenly through the streets, and committing acts of vandalism and playing pranks.

By midnight on Fridays and Saturdays the Saints were usually thoroughly high, and one or two of them were often so drunk they had to be carried to the cars. Then the boys drove around town, calling obscenities to women and girls; occasionally trying (unsuccessfully so far as I could tell) to pick girls up; and driving recklessly through red lights and at high speeds with their lights out. Occasionally they played "chicken." One boy would climb out the back window of the car and across the roof to the driver's side of the car while the car was moving at high speed (between 40 and 50 miles an hour); then the driver would move over and the boy who had just crawled across the car roof would take the driver's seat.

Searching for "fair game" for a prank was the boys' principal activity after they left the tavern. The boys would drive alongside a foot patrolman and ask directions to some street. If the policeman leaned on the car in the course of answering the question, the driver would speed away, causing him to lose his balance. The Saints were careful to play this prank only in an area where they were not going to spend much time and where they could quickly disappear around a corner to avoid having their license plate number taken.

Construction sites and road repair areas were the special province of the Saints' mischief. A soon-to-be repaired hole in the road inevitably invited the Saints to remove lanterns and wooden barricades and put them in the car, leaving the hole unprotected. The boys would find a safe vantage point and wait for an unsuspecting motorist to drive into the hole. Often, though not always, the boys would go up to the motorist and commiserate with him about the dreadful way the city protected its citizenry.

Leaving the scene of the open hole and the motorist, the boys would then go searching for an appropriate place to erect the stolen barricade. An "appropriate place" was often a spot on the highway near a curve in the road where the barricade would not be seen by an oncoming motorist. The boys would wait to watch an unsuspecting motorist attempt to stop and (usually) crash into the wooden barricade. With saintly bearing the boys might offer help and understanding.

A stolen lantern might well find its way onto the back of a police car or hang from a street lamp. Once a lantern served as a prop for a reenactment of the "midnight ride of Paul Revere" until the "play," which was taking place at 2:00 AM in the center of a main street of Big Town, was interrupted by a police car several blocks away. The boys ran, leaving the lanterns on the street, and managed to avoid being apprehended.

Abandoned houses, especially if they were located in out-of-the-way places, were fair game for destruction and spontaneous vandalism. The boys would break windows, remove furniture to the yard and tear it apart, urinate on the walls and scrawl obscenities inside.

Through all the pranks, drinking and reckless driving the boys managed miraculously to avoid being stopped by police. Only twice in two years was I aware that they had been stopped by a Big City policeman. Once was for speeding (which they did every time they drove whether they were drunk or sober), and the driver managed to convince the policeman that it was simply an error. The second time they were stopped they had just left a nightclub and were walking through an alley. Aaron stopped to urinate and the boys began making obscene remarks. A foot patrolman came into the alley, lectured the boys and sent them home. Before the boys got to the car one began talking in a loud voice again. The policeman, who had followed them down the alley, arrested this boy for disturbing the peace and took him to the police station where the other Saints gathered. After paying a $5.00 fine, and with the assurance that there would be no permanent record of the arrest, the boy was released.

The boys had a spirit of frivolity and fun about their escapades. They did not view what they were engaged in as "delinquency," though it surely was by any reasonable definition of that word. They simply viewed themselves as having a little fun and who, they would ask, was really hurt by it? The answer had to be no one, although this fact remains one of the most difficult things to explain about the gang's behavior. Unlikely though it seems, in two years of drinking, driving, carousing and vandalism no one was seriously injured as a result of the Saints' activities.

The Saints in School

The Saints were highly successful in school. The average grade for the group was "B," with two of the boys having close to a straight "A" average. Almost all of the boys were popular and many of them held offices in the school. One of the boys was vice-president of the student body one year. Six of the boys played on athletic teams.

At the end of their senior year, the student body selected ten seniors for special recognition as the "school wheels"; four of the ten were Saints. Teachers and school officials saw no problem with any of these boys and anticipated that they would all "make something of themselves."

How the boys managed to maintain this impression is surprising in view of their actual behavior while in school. Their technique for covering truancy was so successful that teachers did not even realize that the boys were absent from school much of the time. Occasionally, of course, the system would backfire and then the boy was on his own. A boy who was caught would be most contrite, would plead guilty and ask for mercy. He inevitably got the mercy he sought.

Cheating on examinations was rampant, even to the point of orally communicating answers to exams as well as looking at one another's papers. Since none of the group studied, and since they were primarily dependent on one another for help, it is surprising that grades were so high. Teachers contributed to the deception in their admitted inclination to give these boys (and presumably others like them) the benefit of the doubt. When asked how the boys did in school, and when pressed on specific examinations, teachers might admit that they were disappointed in John's performance, but would quickly add that they "knew that he was capable of doing better," so John was given a higher grade than he had actually earned. How often this happened is impossible to know. During the time that I observed the group, I never saw any of the boys take homework home. Teachers may have been "understanding" very regularly.

One exception to the gang's generally good performance was Jerry, who had a "C" average in his junior year, experienced disaster the next year and failed to graduate. Jerry had always been a little more nonchalant than the others about the liberties he took in school. Rather than wait for someone to come get him from class, he would offer his own excuse and leave. Although he probably did not miss any more classes than most of the others in the group, he did not take the requisite pains to cover his absences. Jerry was the only Saint whom I ever heard talk back to a teacher. Although teachers often called him a "cut up" or a "smart kid," they never referred to him as a troublemaker or as a kid headed for trouble. It seems likely, then, that Jerry's failure his senior year and his mediocre performance his junior year were consequences of his not playing the game the proper way (possibly because he was disturbed by his parents' divorce). His teachers regarded him as "immature" and not quite ready to get out of high school.

The Police and the Saints

The local police saw the Saints as good boys who were among the leaders of the youth in the community. Rarely, the boys might be stopped in town for speeding or for running a stop sign. When this happened the boys were always polite, contrite and pled for mercy. As in school, they received the mercy they asked for. None ever received a ticket or was taken into the precinct by the local police.

The situation in Big City, where the boys engaged in most of their delinquency, was only slightly different. The police there did not know the boys at all, although occasionally the boys were stopped by a patrolman. Once they were caught taking a lantern from a construction site. Another time they were stopped for running a stop sign, and on several occasions they were stopped for speeding. Their behavior was as before: contrite, polite and penitent. The urban police, like the local police, accepted their demeanor as sincere. More important, the urban police were convinced that these were good boys just out for a lark.

The Roughnecks

Hanibal townspeople never perceived the Saints' high level of delinquency. The Saints were good boys who just went in for an occasional prank. After all, they were well dressed, well mannered and had nice cars. The Roughnecks were a different story. Although the two gangs of boys were the same age, and both groups engaged in an equal amount of wild-oat sowing, everyone agreed that the not-so-well-dressed, not-so-well-mannered, not-so-rich boys were heading for trouble. Townspeople would say, "You can see the gang members at the drugstore, night after night, leaning against the storefront (sometimes drunk) or slouching

around inside buying cokes, reading magazines, and probably stealing old Mr. Wall blind. When they are outside and girls walk by, even respectable girls, these boys make suggestive remarks. Sometimes their remarks are downright lewd."

From the community's viewpoint, the real indication that these kids were in for trouble was that they were constantly involved with the police. Some of them had been picked up for stealing, mostly small stuff, of course, "but still it's stealing small stuff that leads to big time crimes." "Too bad," people said. "Too bad that these boys couldn't behave like the other kids in town; stay out of trouble, be polite to adults, and look to their future."

The community's impression of the degree to which this group of six boys (ranging in age from 16 to 19) engaged in delinquency was somewhat distorted. In some ways the gang was more delinquent than the community thought; in other ways they were less.

The fighting activities of the group were fairly readily and accurately perceived by almost everyone. At least once a month, the boys would get into some sort of fight, although most fights were scraps between members of the group or involved only one member of the group and some peripheral hanger-on. Only three times in the period of observation did the group fight together: once against a gang from across town, once against two blacks and once against a group of boys from another school. For the first two fights the group went out "looking for trouble"—and they found it both times. The third fight followed a football game and began spontaneously with an argument on the football field between one of the Roughnecks and a member of the opposition's football team.

Jack had a particular propensity for fighting and was involved in most of the brawls. He was a prime mover of the escalation of arguments into fights.

More serious than fighting, had the community been aware of it, was theft. Although almost everyone was aware that the boys occasionally stole things, they did not realize the extent of the activity. Petty stealing was a frequent event for the Roughnecks. Sometimes they stole as a group and coordinated their efforts; other times they stole in pairs. Rarely did they steal alone.

The thefts ranged from very small things like paperback books, comics and ballpoint pens to expensive items like watches. The nature of the thefts varied from time to time. The gang would go through a period of systematically shoplifting items from automobiles or school lockers. Types of thievery varied with the whim of the gang. Some forms of thievery were more profitable than others, but all thefts were for profit, not just thrills.

Roughnecks siphoned gasoline from cars as often as they had access to an automobile, which was not very often. Unlike the Saints, who owned their own cars, the Roughnecks would have to borrow their parents' cars, an event which occurred only eight or nine times a year. The boys claimed to have stolen cars for joy rides from time to time.

Ron committed the most serious of the group's offenses. With an unidentified associate the boy attempted to burglarize a gasoline station. Although this station had been robbed twice previously in the same month, Ron denied any involvement in either of the other thefts. When Ron and his accomplice approached the station, the owner was hiding in the bushes beside the station. He fired both barrels of a double-barreled shotgun at the boys. Ron was severely injured; the other boy ran away and was never caught. Though he remained in critical condition for several months, Ron finally recovered and served six months of the following year in reform school. Upon release from reform school, Ron was put back a grade in school, and began running around with a different gang of boys. The Roughnecks considered the new gang less delinquent than themselves, and during the following year Ron had no more trouble with the police.

The Roughnecks, then, engaged mainly in three types of delinquency: theft, drinking and fighting. Although community members perceived that this gang of kids was delinquent, they mistakenly believed that their illegal activities were primarily drinking, fighting and being a nuisance to passersby. Drinking was limited among the gang members, although it did occur, and theft was much more prevalent than anyone realized.

Drinking would doubtless have been more prevalent had the boys had ready access to liquor. Since they rarely had automobiles at their disposal, they could not travel very far, and the bars in town would not serve them. Most of the boys had little money, and this, too, inhibited their purchase of alcohol. Their major source of liquor was a local drunk who would buy them a fifth if they would give him enough extra to buy himself a pint of whiskey or a bottle of wine.

The community's perception of drinking as prevalent stemmed from the fact that it was the most obvious delinquency the boys engaged in. When one of the boys had been drinking, even a casual observer seeing him on the corner would suspect that he was high.

There was a high level of mutual distrust and dislike between the Roughnecks and the police. The boys felt very strongly that the police were unfair and corrupt. Some evidence existed that the boys were correct in their perception.

The main source of the boys' dislike for the police undoubtedly stemmed from the fact that the police would sporadically harass the group. From the standpoint of the boys, these acts of occasional enforcement of the law were whimsical and uncalled for. It made no sense to them, for example, that the police would come to the corner occasionally and threaten them with arrest for loitering when the night before the boys had been out siphoning gasoline from cars and the police had been nowhere in sight. To the boys, the police were stupid on the one hand, for not being where they should have been and catching the boys in a serious offense, and unfair on the other hand, for trumping up "loitering" charges against them.

From the viewpoint of the police, the situation was quite different. They knew, with all the confidence necessary to be a policeman, that these boys were engaged in criminal activities. They knew this partly from occasionally catching them, mostly from circumstantial evidence ("the boys were around when those tires were slashed"), and partly because the police shared the view of the community in general that this was a bad bunch of boys. The best the police could hope to do was to be sensitive to the fact that these boys were engaged in illegal acts and arrest them whenever there was some evidence that they had been involved. Whether or not the boys had in fact committed a particular act in a particular way was not especially important. The police had a broader view: their job was to stamp out these kids' crimes; the tactics were not as important as the end result.

Over the period that the group was under observation, each member was arrested at least once. Several of the boys were arrested a number of times and spent at least one night in jail. While most were never taken to court, two of the boys were sentenced to six months' incarceration in boys' schools.

The Roughnecks in School

The Roughnecks' behavior in school was not particularly disruptive. During school hours they did not all hang around together, but tended instead to spend most of their time with one or two other members of the gang who were their special buddies. Although every member of the gang attempted to avoid school as much as possible, they were not particularly successful and most of them attended school with surprising regularity. They considered school a burden—something to be gotten through with a minimum of conflict. If they were "bugged" by a particular teacher, it could lead to trouble. One of the boys, Al, once threatened to beat up a teacher and, according to the other boys, the teacher hid under a desk to escape him.

Teachers saw the boys the way the general community did, as heading for trouble, as being uninterested in making something of themselves. Some were also seen as being incapable of meeting the academic standards of the school. Most of the teachers expressed concern for this group of boys and were willing to pass them despite poor performance, in the belief that failing them would only aggravate the problem.

The group of boys had a grade point average just slightly above "C." No one in the group failed either grade, and no one had better than a "C" average. They were very consistent in their achievement or, at least, the teachers were consistent in their perception of the boys' achievement.

Two of the boys were good football players. Herb was acknowledged to be the best player in the school and Jack was almost as good. Both boys were criticized for their failure to abide by training rules, for refusing to come to practice as often as they should, and for not playing their best during practice. What they lacked in sportsmanship they made up for in skill, apparently, and played every game no matter how poorly they had performed in practice or how many practice sessions they had missed.

Two Questions

Why did the community, the school and the police react to the Saints as though they were good, upstanding, nondelinquent youths with bright futures but to the Roughnecks as though they were tough, young criminals who were headed for trouble? Why did the Roughnecks and the Saints in fact have quite different careers after high school—careers which, by and large, lived up to the expectations of the community?

The most obvious explanation for the differences in the community's and law enforcement agencies' reactions to the two gangs is that one group of boys was "more delinquent" than the other. Which group *was* more delinquent? The answer to this question will determine in part how we explain the differential responses to these groups by the members of the community and, particularly, by law enforcement and school officials.

In sheer number of illegal acts, the Saints were the more delinquent. They were truant from school for at least part of the day almost every day of the week. In addition, their drinking and vandalism occurred with surprising regularity. The Roughnecks, in contrast, engaged sporadically in delinquent episodes. While these episodes were frequent, they certainly did not occur on a daily or even a weekly basis.

The difference in frequency of offenses

was probably caused by the Roughnecks' inability to obtain liquor and to manipulate legitimate excuses from school. Since the Roughnecks had less money than the Saints, and teachers carefully supervised their school activities, the Roughnecks' hearts may have been as black as the Saints', but their misdeeds were not nearly as frequent.

There are really no clear-cut criteria by which to measure qualitative differences in antisocial behavior. The most important dimension of the difference is generally referred to as the "seriousness" of the offenses.

If seriousness encompasses the relative economic costs of delinquent acts, then some assessment can be made. The Roughnecks probably stole an average of about $5.00 worth of goods a week. Some weeks the figure was considerably higher, but these times must be balanced against long periods when almost nothing was stolen.

The Saints were more continuously engaged in delinquency but their acts were not for the most part costly to property. Only their vandalism and occasional theft of gasoline would so qualify. Perhaps once or twice a month they would siphon a tankful of gas. The other costly items were street signs, construction lanterns and the like. All of these acts combined probably did not quite average $5.00 a week, partly because much of the stolen equipment was abandoned and presumably could be recovered. The difference in cost of stolen property between the two groups was trivial, but the Roughnecks probably had a slightly more expensive set of activities than did the Saints.

Another meaning of seriousness is the potential threat of physical harm to members of the community and to the boys themselves. The Roughnecks were more prone to physical violence; they not only welcomed an opportunity to fight; they went seeking it. In addition, they fought among themselves frequently. Although the fighting never included deadly weapons, it was still a menace, however minor, to the physical safety of those involved.

The Saints never fought. They avoided physical conflict both inside and outside the group. At the same time, though, the Saints

frequently endangered their own and other people's lives. They did so almost every time they drove a car, especially if they had been drinking. Sober, their driving was risky; under the influence of alcohol it was horrendous. In addition, the Saints endangered the lives of others with their pranks. Street excavations left unmarked were a very serious hazard.

Evaluating the relative seriousness of the two gangs' activities is difficult. The community reacted as though the behavior of the Roughnecks was a problem, and they reacted as though the behavior of the Saints was not. But the members of the community were ignorant of the array of delinquent acts that characterized the Saints' behavior. Although concerned citizens were unaware of much of the Roughnecks' behavior as well, they were much better informed about the Roughnecks' involvement in delinquency than they were about the Saints'.

Visibility

Differential treatment of the two gangs resulted in part because one gang was infinitely more visible than the other. This differential visibility was a direct function of the economic standing of the families. The Saints had access to automobiles and were able to remove themselves from the sight of the community. In as routine a decision as to where to go to have a milkshake after school, the Saints stayed away from the mainstream of community life. Lacking transportation, the Roughnecks could not make it to the edge of town. The center of town was the only practical place for them to meet since their homes were scattered throughout the town and any noncentral meeting place put an undue hardship on some members. Through necessity the Roughnecks congregated in a crowded area where everyone in the community passed frequently, including teachers and law enforcement officers. They could easily see the Roughnecks hanging around the drugstore.

The Roughnecks, of course, made themselves even more visible by making remarks to passersby and by occasionally getting into fights on the corner. Meanwhile, just as regularly, the Saints were either at the cafe on one edge of town or in the pool hall at the other edge of town. Without any particular realization that they were making themselves inconspicuous, the Saints were able to hide their time-wasting. Not only were they removed from the mainstream of traffic, but they were almost always inside a building.

On their escapades the Saints were also relatively invisible, since they left Hanibal and travelled to Big City. Here, too, they were mobile, roaming the city, rarely going to the same area twice.

Demeanor

To the notion of visibility must be added the difference in the responses of group members to outside intervention with their activities. If one of the Saints was confronted with an accusing policeman, even if he felt he was truly innocent of a wrongdoing, his demeanor was apologetic and penitent. A Roughneck's attitude was almost the polar opposite. When confronted with a threatening adult authority, even one who tried to be pleasant, the Roughneck's hostility and disdain were clearly observable. Sometimes he might attempt to put up a veneer of respect, but it was thin and was not accepted as sincere by the authority.

School was no different from the community at large. The Saints could manipulate the system by feigning compliance with the school norms. The availability of cars at school meant that once free from the immediate sight of the teacher, the boys could disappear rapidly. And this escape was well enough planned that no administrator or teacher was nearby when the boys left. A Roughneck who wished to escape for a few hours was in a bind. If it were possible to get free from class, downtown was still a mile away, and even if he arrived there, he was still very visible. Truancy for the Roughnecks meant almost certain detection, while the Saints enjoyed almost complete immunity from sanctions.

Bias

Community members were not aware of the transgressions of the Saints. Even if the Saints had been less discreet, their favorite delinquencies would have been perceived as less serious than those of the Roughnecks.

In the eyes of the police and school officials, a boy who drinks in an alley and stands intoxicated on the street corner is committing a more serious offense than is a boy who drinks to inebriation in a nightclub or a tavern and drives around afterwards in a car. Similarly, a boy who steals a wallet from a store will be viewed as having committed a more serious offense than a boy who steals a lantern from a construction site.

Perceptual bias also operates with respect to the demeanor of the boys in the two groups when they are confronted by adults. It is not simply that adults dislike the posture affected by boys of the Roughneck ilk; more important is the conviction that the posture adopted by the Roughnecks is an indication of their devotion and commitment to deviance as a way of life. The posture becomes a cue, just as the type of the offense is a cue, to the degree to which the known transgressions are indicators of the youths' potential for other problems.

Visibility, demeanor and bias are surface variables which explain the day-to-day operations of the police. Why do these surface variables operate as they do? Why did the police choose to disregard the Saints' delinquencies while breathing down the backs of the Roughnecks?

The answer lies in the class structure of American society and the control of legal institutions by those at the top of the class structure. Obviously, no representative of the upper class drew up the operational chart for the police which led them to look in the ghettoes and on streetcorners—which led them to see the demeanor of lower-class youth as troublesome and that of upper-middle-class youth as tolerable. Rather, the procedures simply developed from experience—experience with irate and influential upper-middle-class parents insisting that their son's vandalism was simply a prank and his drunkenness only a momentary "sowing of wild oats"—experience with cooperative or indifferent, powerless, lower-class parents who acquiesced to the laws' definition of their son's behavior.

Adult Careers of the Saints and the Roughnecks

The community's confidence in the potential of the Saints and the Roughnecks apparently was justified. If anything, the community members underestimated the degree to which these youngsters would turn out "good" or "bad."

Seven of the eight members of the Saints went on to college immediately after high school. Five of the boys graduated from college in four years. The sixth one finished college after two years in the army, and the seventh spent four years in the air force before returning to college and receiving a B.A. degree. Of these seven college graduates, three went on for advanced degrees. One finished law school and is now active in state politics, one finished medical school and is practicing near Hanibal, and one boy is now working for a Ph.D. The other four college graduates entered submanagerial, managerial or executive training positions with larger firms.

The only Saint who did not complete college was Jerry. Jerry had failed to graduate from high school with the other Saints. During his second senior year, after the other Saints had gone on to college, Jerry began to hang around with what several teachers described as a "rough crowd"—the gang that was heir apparent to the Roughnecks. At the end of his second senior year, when he did graduate from high school, Jerry took a job as a used-car salesman, got married and quickly had a child. Although he made several abortive attempts to go to college by attending night school, when I last saw him (ten years after high school) Jerry was unemployed and had been living on unemployment for almost a year. His wife worked as a waitress.

Some of the Roughnecks have lived up to community expectations. A number of them were headed for trouble. A few were not.

Jack and Herb were the athletes among the Roughnecks and their athletic prowess paid off handsomely. Both boys received unsolicited athletic scholarships to college. After Herb received his scholarship (near the end of his senior year), he apparently did an about-face. His demeanor became very similar to that of the Saints. Although he remained a member in good standing of the Roughnecks, he stopped participating in most activities and did not hang around the corner as often.

Jack did not change. If anything, he became more prone to fighting. He even made excuses for accepting the scholarship. He told the other gang members that the school had guaranteed him a "C" average if he would come to play football—an idea that seems far-fetched, even in this day of highly competitive recruiting.

During the summer after graduation from high school, Jack attempted suicide by jumping from a tall building. The jump would certainly have killed most people trying it, but Jack survived. He entered college in the fall and played four years of football. He and Herb graduated in four years, and both are teaching and coaching in high schools. They are married and have stable families. If anything, Jack appears to have a more prestigious position in the community than does Herb, though both are well respected and secure in their positions.

Two of the boys never finished high school. Tommy left at the end of his junior year and went to another state. That summer he was arrested and placed on probation on a manslaughter charge. Three years later he was arrested for murder; he pleaded guilty to second degree murder and is serving a 30-year sentence in the state penitentiary.

Al, the other boy who did not finish high school, also left the state in his senior year. He is serving a life sentence in a state penitentiary for first degree murder.

Wes is a small-time gambler. He finished high school and "bummed around." After several years he made contact with a bookmaker who employed him as a runner. Later he acquired his own area and has been working it ever since. His position among the bookmakers is almost identical to the position he had in the gang; he is always around but no one is really aware of him. He makes no trouble and he does not get into any. Steady, reliable, capable of keeping his mouth closed, he plays the game by the rules, even though the game is an illegal one.

That leaves only Ron. Some of his former friends reported that they had heard he was "driving a truck up north," but no one could provide any concrete information.

Reinforcement

The community responded to the Roughnecks as boys in trouble, and the boys agreed with that perception. Their pattern of deviancy was reinforced, and breaking away from it became increasingly unlikely. Once the boys acquired an image of themselves as deviants, they selected new friends who affirmed that self-image. As that self-conception became more firmly entrenched, they also became willing to try new and more extreme deviances. With their growing alienation came freer expression of disrespect and hostility for representatives of the legitimate society. This disrespect increased the community's negativism, perpetuating the entire process of commitment to deviance. Lack of a commitment to deviance works the same way. In either case, the process will perpetuate itself unless some event (like a scholarship to college or a sudden failure) external to the established relationship intervenes. For two of the Roughnecks (Herb and Jack), receiving college athletic scholarships created new relations and culminated in a break with the established pattern of deviance. In the case of one of the Saints (Jerry), his parents' divorce and his failing to graduate from high school changed some of his other relations. Being held back in school for a year and losing his place among the Saints had sufficient impact on Jerry to alter his self-image and virtually to assure that he would not go on to college as his peers did. Although the experiments of life can rarely be reversed, it seems likely in view of the behavior of the other boys who did not enjoy this special treatment by the school that Jerry, too, would have "become something" had he graduated as anticipated. For Herb and Jack outside intervention worked to their advantage; for Jerry it was his undoing.

Selective perception and labelling—finding, processing and punishing some kinds of criminality and not others—means that visible, poor, nonmobile, outspoken, undiplomatic "tough" kids will be noticed, whether their actions are seriously delinquent or not. Other kids, who have established a reputation for being bright (even though underachieving), disciplined and involved in respectable activities, who are mobile and monied, will be invisible when they deviate from sanctioned activities. They'll sow their wild oats—perhaps even wider and thicker than their lower-class cohorts—but they won't be noticed. When it's time to leave adolescence most will follow the expected path, settling into the ways of the middle class, remembering fondly the delinquent but unnoticed fling of their youth. The Roughnecks and others like them may turn around, too. It is more likely that their noticeable deviance will have been so reinforced by police and community that their lives will be effectively channelled into careers consistent with their adolescent background.

QUESTIONS FOR DISCUSSION

1. In what ways are the Saints and the Roughnecks similar? How are they dissimilar?
2. How does "visibility" affect the delinquent definitions that are applied to the two groups of adolescents?
3. Discuss how money, success in school, and demeanor can influence and insulate being labeled "delinquent" by the community and the police.

APPLICATIONS

1. Draw upon your own experience, and try to recall a positive or negative label that was applied to you.
   a. Who assigned the label to you (friends, parents, a teacher, the police)?
   b. Did the label affect the way you felt about yourself?
   c. Was the label, good or bad, reinforced by others around you?
   d. Do you feel today that your life is a product of the labels that were applied to you and repeatedly reinforced?

2. Try to remember the different groups of student in your high school. Can you think of any groups that were considered to be "saints" or "roughnecks"? Write a short summary about your school describing the characteristics of a saint group and a roughneck group.

KEY TERMS

accomplice someone who aids or abets another person in committing a criminal act.

bias a preconceived or prejudiced belief.

cognitive dissonance a theory that states that individuals strive to maintain internal consistency so that values, beliefs, and opinions maintain consonance. Dissonance occurs when new information does not coincide with an existing perception of the world. To reduce the associated stress caused by this conflict, the individual often redefines or rationalizes the new information to fit existing beliefs.

escapade a breaking loose from restraints; flight from confining rules.

labeling theory a theory that holds that deviant behavior is not a quality of the act a person commits, but rather a consequence of the applications, by others, of rules and sanctions on the offender. Nothing is inherently deviant but only becomes deviant when others apply a deviant label.

reinforcement an event or some reward whose occurrence increases the likelihood that certain behaviors will continue.

social class a category of people who have been grouped together based on one or more common characteristics. A class is a stratum in a societal hierarchy. Classes may be determined by wealth, power, or prestige and other socioeconomic indicators such as income, occupation, and educational attainment.

vagrancy the state of a person who wanders from place to place without a fixed home or livelihood. Usually considered to be a public nuisance. Vagrants often engage in begging, stealing, and even prostitution to obtain income.

28

Females under the Law— "Protected" but Unequal

Gail Armstrong

Graduate Student, Department of Forensic Studies, Indiana University

The sex of the offender is a significant determinant of the length and type of the sentence imposed. Many sentencing statutes and judges make sex distinctions that are transmitted into different sentences for male and female offenders found guilty of the same offense. Sometimes this discrimination on the basis of sex works in favor of females before the law; most of the time it works against them; all of the time, whether the sentence is more lenient or more severe than the one imposed on a male, the misbegotten motive is chivalry or special protectiveness. Our statutes and sentencing practices incorporate a double standard of morality. Males and females are not equal under the law.

Sentencing is a crucial step in the processing of an offender through the criminal justice system. In some cases the sentencing judge may use discretion and choose from several modes of punishment. In other cases this discretionary power is pre-empted by the dictates of the state legislature. Both instances bear evidence of discrimination on the basis of the offender's sex. Women are sentenced both more severely and less severely than men are for the same offenses.

Some states have special sentencing provisions, enacted at the turn of the century to "protect" females, under which the length of a woman's sentence is determined not by the

"Females under the Law—'Protected' but Unequal," *Crime and Delinquency*, 23:2 (1977), pp. 109–120. Reprinted by permission of the publisher, Sage Publications, Inc.

judge but by correctional authorities within the limits set by statute.[1] The result is denial of equal protection for women: under these statutes, female offenders often serve longer sentences than male offenders convicted of the same criminal conduct.[2]

Discrimination in favor of female offenders often occurs when judges have discretionary power. Many judges believe, erroneously, that women are better able than men to reform themselves[3] and that, though given to crimes of passion, they seldom possess the pervasive criminal tendencies that characterize male criminals.[4]

SENTENCING ADULT FEMALES

The Chivalry Factor

Our society is thought to have an especially protective attitude toward women,[5] and it is a widely held belief that women fare much better than men when the trial court has discretion. This selective application of the law is attributed to the "chivalry factor." Pollak states that traditional chivalry in the courtroom has led to acquittals that did not accord with the evidence but rather reflected our cultural attitudes toward women.[6] Compared with men, women are considered to be less liable to be detected, arrested, convicted, and committed, and those who are processed all the way through the criminal justice system are regarded as extraordinarily distasteful or dangerous: "Those who are ultimately sent to prison are the very worst of the total crop."[7]

"Protective" Statutes

In effect today are statutes which reflect the belief that something in the very nature of being a woman justifies her being incarcerated for a longer period than a man would be for the same offense.[8] Between 1869 and 1915, ten states (Indiana, Iowa, Maine, Massachusetts, Minnesota, New Jersey, New York, Ohio, Pennsylvania, and Wisconsin) enacted legislation that created separate facilities for convicted women and established the use of the indeterminate sentence for them, a logical consequence of the legislators' belief that women have psychological characteristics which make longer periods of incarceration necessary.[9] After 1915 three other states (Alabama, Arkansas, and California) enacted sentencing statutes applicable only to women and requiring indeterminate sentences. These statutes usually result in sentences more severe for women than for men guilty of the same offense. Thus there is an interim period during which the male defendant is either under consideration for parole or out on parole, whereas the female defendant remains "protected" in prison, where she is denied a great many fundamental rights.[10]

For example, Iowa law allows women to be confined up to five years for a misdemeanor but, unless an exception is made in the statute defining the particular offense, limits the imprisonment of male misdemeanants to one year.[11] In Maine, women between the ages of seventeen and forty can be sentenced to reformatories for up to three years even if the statutory maximum for the offense is less.[12]

Muncy Act

In Pennsylvania the Muncy Act (1913) required that all women over the age of sixteen who had been convicted of an offense punishable by more than one year in prison must be given a general sentence to the Muncy State Industrial Home for Women. The Muncy Act did not permit the trial judge to use discretion to impose a shorter maximum sentence than the maximum punishment prescribed by law for the offense or to fix a minimum sentence at the expiration of which the female prisoner would be eligible for parole. But he had discretionary power to make these decisions in the case of a male.[13]

Specifically, the Muncy Act discriminated against women in the following ways:

1. A woman could be sentenced to a term of three years even if the maximum was less; a man could not be sentenced over the maximum prescribed by law.

2. A woman was sentenced to the maximum legal penalty if convicted of a crime punishable by more than three years; a man could be sentenced to less than the maximum prescribed by law.

3. A woman could not receive a minimum sentence; not only could a man receive a minimum term but that term could not be more than half the maximum.

4. Under Pennsylvania law, the authority to grant parole lies with the sentencing judge when the sentence is less than two years; it lies with the parole board when the sentence is two years or more. Since all sentences to Muncy were for at least three years, women imprisoned there came under the jurisdiction of the parole board, which does not permit representation by counsel at its hearings.

5. Only if her offense was punishable by a sentence of one year or less could a woman serve the term in a county jail, but she was sent to Muncy, separated from relatives and friends, for the same kind of offense that would have sent a man to the county jail.[14] "Women sentenced under the Act actually spend more than 50 per cent longer in jail than do men sentenced for like offenses. . ."[15].

The philosophy upon which the Muncy Act was originally founded has been expressed as follows:

All delinquent women are sexually immoral and breed feeble-minded bastards; prolonged confinement deters delinquency and impedes sexual immorality; the conclusion drawn from this reasoning is that women should be given indefinite sentences.[16]

Many equal-protection challenges to special sentencing statutes for women have failed because the courts concluded that, since women have a rehabilitative capacity different from men's, they *can* reasonably be sentenced differently. No case in court has ever *shown* that women take longer to be rehabilitated than men do.[17]

Daniels.—On May 3, 1966, Jane Daniels was convicted of robbery in Pennsylvania. The trial court sentenced her to one-to-four years in the Philadelphia County Prison. Thirty-one days later, the judge realized that the Muncy Act deprived him of the power to fix Daniels' term at less than the statutory maximum. He then sent her to the State Industrial Home for Women without fixing a minimum or maximum period of imprisonment. This allowed for the possibility that Daniels would serve ten years (the maximum for robbery) instead of her original maximum of four years.[18]

Theoretically, under the Muncy Act women received discriminatorily favorable treatment with regard to parole. Men were required to sere their minimum sentences before becoming eligible for parole, but women, because their sentences were indeterminate, were eligible for immediate parole. Under her original sentence, Daniels could have been paroled in one year, like a male sentenced to one-to-four years for the same offense.[19] However, under the parole policy of Muncy officials, she would not be paroled for at least three years.

Jane Daniels appealed.[20] The issue presented was the constitutionality of the Muncy Act—specifically, the differences of punishment imposed on male and female offenders convicted of the same offense. Unequal treatment, the United States Supreme Court has said, is permissible only when it is reasonable in the light of its purpose.[21]

Daniels was the first attack ever launched against the Muncy Act. All earlier attacks on similar statutes had failed.[22] Pre-*Daniels* opinions upheld sentencing schemes identical to the Muncy Act and indicated that the indeterminate sentence for female offenders was considered essential to a purpose of reform associated with treatment rather than punishment.[23] In 1946 the Maine Supreme Court, citing a legislative need to experiment with prison reform, upheld an unequal sentencing statute, which provided that women be incarcerated for potentially longer terms than men for identical offenses.[24]

The Pennsylvania Superior Court majority opinion ruled that there was a "rational basis" for the unequal treatment of women committed to Muncy—"i.e., a reasonable connection between the classification by sex and the purpose of the legislation":

> The broad purpose of the legislation was to provide for the punishment and rehabilitation of prisoners. Different types of incarceration for the same crimes are regularly imposed both for classes of individuals (e.g., juveniles, sex offenders, recidivists, criminally insane), as well as among separate individuals where judicial discretion in imposing sentence may be allowed by the legislature. The only requirement for different classes of persons is that the class exhibits characteristics that justify the different treatment. . . . This court is of the opinion that the legislature reasonably cold have concluded that indeterminate sentences should be imposed on women as a class, allowing the time of incarceration to be matched to the necessary treatment in order to provide more effective rehabilitation. Such a conclusion could be based on the physiological and psychological makeup of women, the type of crime committed by women, their relation to the criminal world, their roles in society, their unique vocational skills and pursuits, and their reaction as a class to imprisonment as well as the number and type of women who are sentenced to imprisonment rather than given suspended sentences. Such facts could have led the legislature to conclude that a different manner of punishment and rehabilitation was necessary for women sentenced to confinement. . . .[25]

The majority opinion justified discrimination on the basis of sex, not on the presumption that the Muncy facility provided effective treatment rather than punishment.

The Supreme Court of Pennsylvania unanimously reversed the Superior Court decision on July 1, 1968, saying that there is no difference between the sexes that justifies a shorter maximum sentence for men committing the same offenses as women. It did *not* altogether reject classification by sex.[26]

The inability of the women's reformatory system to offer its inmates a rehabilitative and curative experience—its failure to achieve the penological purposes that might have justified a special sentencing structure—may have been at the bottom of the state Supreme Court's willingness to strike down the sentencing provisions of the Muncy Act as violative of equal protection.[27]

Two weeks after the Pennsylvania Supreme Court handed down this decision, the legislature passed a revision of the Muncy Act. According to the new version, women would not necessarily receive longer maximum sentences than men but were still denied the right to have a minimum sentence set by the judge; consequently, they would remain in prison awaiting parole while men with fixed minimum sentences became eligible for parole.[28] Challenges to the 1968 amendment to the Muncy Act have been unsuccessful.[29]

Douglas.—The *Douglas* case helped persuade the Supreme Court of Pennsylvania to permit an appeal from the superior court decision on *Daniels.* Daisy Douglas and Richard Johnson were convicted of aggravated robbery. Under the Muncy Act, Douglas was sentenced to Muncy for twenty years—the maximum legal penalty; Johnson was sentenced to three-to-ten years in the men's penitentiary. Statistics kept by the Pennsylvania Board of Probation and Parole showed that male parolees convicted of a second equally serious offense were rarely sentenced to the maximum. Douglas filed a petition under Pennsylvania's Post-Conviction Hearing Act, maintaining that her sentence was a denial of her Fourteenth Amendment rights. Her petition was dismissed but her case was consolidated with *Daniels* and was accepted for argument before the Supreme Court of Pennsylvania.[30]

Douglas provided convincing evidence of the discriminatory effect of the Muncy Act. Douglas and Johnson were co-defendants, jointly tried and convicted of the same offense. Johnson, unlike Douglas, had a serious criminal record. Johnson was eligible for parole after three years; under her indeterminate sentence Douglas was technically eligible for parole at any time but in practice would not be eligible for 3½ years. The consolidated appeals of *Douglas* and *Daniels* were successfully argued. Both cases were remanded for resentencing.

Robinson.—In Connecticut, 38-year-old Carrie Robinson pleaded guilty to breach of the peace and resisting arrest. Ordinarily these are misdemeanors carrying maximum terms of one year and six months, respectively.[31] However, under a Connecticut statute,[32] women over sixteen who commit such misdemeanors were to be sentenced to an indefinite term not to exceed three years or to the offense maximum, if longer; the statute allowed women to be sentenced for longer terms than men for identical offenses. Robinson claimed that sentencing only women, not men, to indefinite sentences deprived them of equal protection.

The federal district court decision in *Robinson*[33] struck down the statute, finding it a violation of the equal protection clause of the Fourteenth Amendment. The state argued that the longer terms for women involved treatment and rehabilitation, not punishment; but the court followed the U.S. Supreme Court decision in *In re Gault*,[34] which stated that confinement by any other name is still confinement.

Like *Daniels*, *Robinson* did not reject all sex-based classifications. Some sex-based classifications, it said, are reasonable—e.g., limiting women's working hours. *Robinson* and *Daniels* emphasize that unequal deprivation of a *basic* civil right must be sustained by a valid justification.[35]

Costello and *Chambers.*—In New Jersey, males convicted on gambling charges get minimum-maximum terms in the state prison, and the judge can set the maximum; for identical offenses, females were sentenced (until 1973) to an indeterminate term of up to five years in the Correctional Institution for Women, and the judge had no discretion to lower the maximum.[36] The actual term served by the female offender was determined entirely by the institution's board of managers, while males earned earlier release through "good time" provisions or application to the state parole board.[37]

Mary Costello pleaded guilty in Camden County Court to gambling offenses. She was sentenced to an indeterminate term not to exceed five years at the New Jersey Correctional Institution for Women. For the same offense, a male would probably be sentenced to one-to-two years. Costello appealed, contending that her constitutional rights to equal protection under the law had been violated.[38]

Though New Jersey's sentencing scheme for women was similar to Pennsylvania's and Connecticut's (which had already been held unconstitutional[39]), it was deemed by the court in *Costello* not violative of the equal protection clause of the Fourteenth Amendment. The court cited cases in which sex-based discrimination in sentencing had been found constitutional, even though most of the statutes vindicated in those cases were no longer on the books.

In *State v. Chambers*,[40] a composite of six cases (including *Costello*), each involving females who had been convicted of gambling offenses and had been given indeterminate sentences, the New Jersey Supreme Court held that disparate sentencing based on sex-based classifications violates the equal protection clause of the Fourteenth Amendment. Where a fundamental right of liberty is restrained in conjunction with a classification system based on sex, a state statute is unconstitutional unless a compelling state interest exists. The state's claim that females were better subjects for rehabilitation was insufficient to justify the infringement upon liberty.

COMMITTING JUVENILE FEMALES

The Chivalry Factor

Many believe that female delinquents are not likely to be treated harshly when they come before the courts. Like their adult counterparts, female delinquents are considered to be the beneficiaries of chivalrous treatment. "Our police are inclined to treat unofficially all minor offenses of young girls in order to save them from the social stigma which follows an appearance in court."[41]

Enforcing the Double Standard

Most juvenile courts have broad discretionary powers vested in them by statutes that give them jurisdiction over a wide variety of juvenile activity. Theoretically these statutes apply equally to males and females; actually they are allied in accordance with our double standard of juvenile morality and lend themselves to discriminatory enforcement against females.[42]

Many of the young women who come into contract with the adjudicatory process are "turned in" by their parents or relatives rather than "arrested" by law enforcement officials. The juvenile court is very much concerned with obedience to familial demands. Because of the vastly different parental expectations regarding appropriate behavior for male and female children, there is a corresponding differential response from the juvenile court toward male and female children. Females have a much narrower range of acceptable behavior.[43] For example, in the tradition that a woman's place is in the home, judges often decide that it is delinquent for a young woman, but not a young man, to return home at an "unreasonable" hour.[44]

Most male delinquency consists of statute violation. Most female delinquency involves violation of sex-role expectations *and* is more severely punished than male delinquency. There are basically five offenses that lead to commitment for the juvenile female: (1) running away, (2) incorrigibility, (3) sexual offenses, (4) probation violation, and (5) truancy. Although the official record may read differently, sexual misconduct usually underlies all of these female offenses.[45] A study of 252 young women committed to a correctional school for girls in Wisconsin during the early thirties said that "75.4 per cent had records of sex irregularity. Over 40 per cent of the total number had been promiscuous, and approximately 40 per cent had a history of venereal disease. Sex delinquency was the most frequent offense."[46]

A few years ago in Connecticut a sixteen-year-old girl was sent to the State Farm for Women because her parents and the court agreed that she was "in danger of falling into habits of vice." The law under which she was committed was upheld on the grounds that her commitment was not punishment but a "protective safeguard."[47]

All girls brought into Family Court in New York, including those brought before the court for nonsexual offenses, are given vaginal Wasserman smears to test for venereal disease. This procedure is terrifying for many young girls who have not engaged in sexual activity.[48]

Statistics

More than 50 per cent of the girls—in contrast, only 20 per cent of the boys—are institutionalized for "noncriminal" offenses. Because the offenses committed by girls are not very serious (over one-half are noncriminal) one would expect their dispositions to be shorter than those generally given to boys for criminal offenses. Actually, girls usually get longer dispositions than boys.[49] A 1958 study of 162 training schools throughout the United States showed that the average time served by a juvenile delinquent was 9.7 months. Separating the sexes, the study showed that the average for female delinquents was 12 months; for male delinquents, 9.3 months. In 1962 the overall average for both sexes was 9.5 months (10.8 months for females; 9.2 months for males). In 1964 the overall average declined to 9.3 months. Females averaged 10.7 months; males, 8.2 months.[50]

In 1964, nation-wide statistics put the male-female ratio in juvenile institutions at 3 to 1. The male-female ratio for all juvenile offenses was 4 to 1; for major criminal offenses, 15.3 to 1. There were more juvenile females in institutions than the number of their offenses warranted. "The 'saving' or 'helping' of a girl often justifies more radical and severe 'treatment' than does the punishment of a male law violator."[51]

Statistics published by the Children's Bureau indicate that training schools serving only nonwhite children or only females keep a child for a longer period of time.[52]

Morals Statutes

Juvenile morals statutes are (1) unconstitutionally vague, (2) impermissibly overbroad because they inhibit constitutionally protected behavior, (3) unconstitutionally overbroad because they encourage selective enforcement against female juveniles according to a double standard of sexual morality, and (4) impermissible in that they punish a status.[53]

Most jurisdictions in the United States have statutes that allow a finding of juvenile delinquency when it is established that the defendant engaged in immoral conduct. Few distinctions are made between juveniles according to the grade of offense seriousness. Most jurisdictions lump them all together—all juveniles who break the law are delinquents. Kansas and Illinois are the only states that do not send runaways to state reform schools.[54]

Morality statutes enable the states to place any juvenile under custody for almost any act for a period ranging from six months to eleven years. Vague delinquency provisions based on subjective determinations of "immorality" and unsupported predictions of future criminal conduct have no legal or practical justification. The due process clause of the Fourteenth Amendment requires that statutes provide fair warning. Delinquency statutes should be more precisely defined.[55]

Sex-Neutral Statutes

Courts have been reluctant to rule that juvenile morals statutes are unconstitutionally vague. According to the Texas juvenile morals statute, any child who "habitually so comports himself as to injure or endanger the morals of himself or others" can be adjudged a juvenile delinquent. Because our society believes that *female* sexual morals should be more restricted, such vague statutes will tend to enforce the double standard of morality. Sexual delinquency is the most common offense of female juveniles.

Male juveniles are usually not adjudicated for such behavior and to this extent the vague language incorporated within sex-neutral juvenile morals statutes permits discriminatory enforcement of different sexual standards for males and females.[56]

Sexually Discriminatory Statutes

Juvenile court statutes that differentiate on their face between male and female juveniles fall into three categories:

1. Some juvenile statutes assume that females need more supervision than males and therefore establish higher jurisdictional age limits for females. At the same time, recognizing the earlier emotional maturity of females, many states with such statutes permit females to marry two or three years earlier than males. Jurisdictional statutes providing for higher age limits for females reflect the attitude that young men should be independent and that young women should graduate from parental supervision directly to marriage. These statutes enforce the double standard of morality.[57] Society is obsessed with the notion of protecting unmarried females from themselves.

   Most states are moving toward a common jurisdictional age for both male and female juveniles.[58]

2. The juvenile court system is civil and its purported goal is rehabilitation. Delinquents within the custody of the court may be "treated" by any of several means defined in the disposition and confinement statutes of the state juvenile court act. The integrity of the juvenile court judge determines whether these statutes are applied equally to males and females.[59]

   Several states allow for discrepancies between the permissible length of confinement for female and male juveniles. In New York a female adjudged a "person in need of supervision" may be committed to the state training school to remain until age twenty. A male must be released by age eighteen.[60]

3. A few state legislatures have provided for special treatment of juvenile females. Until recently, Connecticut and Tennessee had provisions in their juvenile codes permitting institutional commitment of any female between certain ages who is leading a "vicious" or "criminal" life.[61] Now, only Tennessee allows juvenile courts to take custody of girls where they may not take charge of boys.[62]

PINS in New York State

The New York State Family Court Act provides:

> Persons in need of supervision means a male less than sixteen years of age and a female less than eighteen years of age who does not attend school in accordance with the provisions of part one of article sixty-five of the education law or who is incorrigible, ungovernable or habitually disobedient and beyond the lawful control of parent or other lawful authority.[63]
>
> Successive extensions [of the original placement] may be granted, but no placement may be made or continued under this section beyond the child's eighteenth birthday, if male, or twentieth birthday, if female.[64]

Under these provisions females are liable for two extra years of original liability and two extra years of placement. It is clear that these provisions deprive females of fundamental rights and liberties.

Court Tests

Courts have applied the equal protection clause to juveniles to invalidate sexually discriminatory juvenile statutes.[65] A statute that distinguishes between two or more classes of people is not always in violation of the equal protection clause of the Fourteenth Amendment. The state must establish that it has a compelling state interest which justifies the law and that the distinctions made by the law are necessary to further its purpose.[66]

The constitutional right to liberty is the major concern in cases challenging sexually discriminatory juvenile statutes. Juvenile laws that discriminate on the basis of sex do affect the liberty of juveniles. The imposition of longer confinement on one sex than on the other is no more permissible with juveniles than it is with adults.[67]

Sex-based discrimination, like racial discrimination, tends to create and perpetuate inferior status and second-class citizenship.[68] In 1972, the United States Supreme Court declared discrimination on the basis of sex to be a "suspect classification."[69]

SENTENCING PROVISIONS THAT DISCRIMINATE AGAINST MALES

Dr. John MacDonald tells the following "apocryphal" story to illustrate "society's divergent attitudes toward the same behavior in males and females":

> If a man walking past an apartment stops to watch a woman undressing before the window, the man is arrested as a peeper. If a woman walking past an apartment stops to watch a man undressing before a window, the man is arrested as an exhibitionist.[70]

It would be a misrepresentation not to mention a few of the rare sentencing provisions that discriminate against males.

1. *Wark.*—A male escapee from the Maine State Prison Farm received a longer sentence for his escape than a woman would have. He asserted that his Fourteenth Amendment rights had thus been violated. Denying his appeal in *Wark v. State*,[71] the court said:

> Viewing statutory provisions for punishment as in part a deterrent to criminal conduct, the legislature could logically and reasonably conclude that a more severe penalty should be imposed upon a male prisoner escaping from the State Prison than upon a woman confined at the "Reformatory" while serving a State Prison sentence who escapes from that institution. We conclude that a classification based on sex under these circumstances is neither arbitrary nor unreasonable but is a proper exercise of legislative discretion which in no way violates the constitutional right to equal protection of the law.[72]

2. *Assault under Arizona Law.*—Under an Arizona law, men are sentenced more severely than women when the victim of the crime is a woman. Arizona defines aggravated assault as an assault made by a male upon a female *or* by a person over age eighteen on a child under fifteen.[73] Under this law, if an adult female spits in the face of another adult female, she will probably be charged with simple assault and pay a $300 fine or serve up to three months. A male who commits the same offense can be charged with aggravated assault and be punished by imprisonment of one to five years and a fine of $100 to $200. North Carolina and Texas have similar assault statutes.[74]

3. *Oklahoma Juvenile Law.*—Under Oklahoma juvenile court law, females who have been adjudged delinquent and have been institutionalized are discharged at age eighteen; males adjudged delinquent and institutionalized are discharged at age twenty-one.[75]

THE EQUAL RIGHTS AMENDMENT

In Oklahoma male delinquents can be confined for a longer period than female delinquents; the reverse is true in New York State. How can the discrepancy between Oklahoma and New York juvenile court laws be rationally justified? Is there some factual difference between males in Oklahoma and males in New York? Or between males and females anywhere that justifies punishment more or less severe for one sex than for the other? Such inconsistencies in our laws demonstrate the need for the proposed Twenty-Seventh Amendment to the U.S. Constitution—the Equal Rights Amendment.

Sexually discriminatory laws and the unequal application of many sex-neutral statutes coerce females to conform to society's conception of the female sex role. It does not make sense, however, to design training programs in domestication for women who have, by breaking the law, shown their reluctance to adjust to an inferior sex role. Yet, institutions for women and girls offer no programs that teach independent trades. Confined females are trained as housekeepers, seamstresses, and waitresses.

Passage of the Equal Rights Amendment would render *any* discrimination on the basis of sex a "suspect classification." this would hold for juveniles as well as adults, for males as well as females. More comprehensive than an extension of the equal protection clause of the Fourteenth Amendment, the Equal Rights Amendment would be a mandate by the American people. But until that amendment is passed and goes into effect (two years after ratification) the equal protection approach should be rigorously pursued to challenge sexually discriminatory statutes.

Conclusion

Special sentencing statutes, sentencing judges, and society's conception of the female sex role are all responsible for the unjust sentencing of females. The disparate sentences received by males and females found guilty of the same offenses provide the most blatant evidence of this unequal treatment. Special sentencing statutes enacted at the turn of the century to "protect" women deny them their fundamental rights. The juvenile justice system enforces society's double standard of morality and severely sanctions only females for "sexual misconduct." These inconsistencies in the application of our laws and in our system of justice can be swiftly diminished and rendered unconstitutional with the passage of the proposed Twenty-Seventh Amendment to the U.S. Constitution. The Equal Rights Amendment can bring us all a *long* way.

Notes

1. Brown, Emerson, Falk, & Freedman, *The Equal Rights Amendment: A Constitutional Basis for Equal Rights for Women,* 80 YALE, L.J. 871, 965 (1971).

2. Clements, *Sex and Sentencing,* 26 Sw. L.J. 890 (1972).

3. *Ibid.*

4. Baab & Furgeson, *Texas Sentencing Practices: A Statistical Study,* 45 TEXAS L. REV. 471, 496–97 (1967).

5. W. Reckless, THE CRIME PROBLEM 99 (4th ed. 1967).

6. O. POLLAK, THE CRIMINALITY OF WOMEN 4 (1950).

7. Kay & Schultz, *Divergence of Attitudes toward Constituted Authorities between Male and Female Felony*

Inmates, in INTERDISCIPLINARY PROBLEMS IN CRIMINOLOGY 209–16 (W. Reckless & C. Newman eds. 1967).

8. Temin, *Discriminatory Sentencing of Women Offenders: The Argument for the ERA in a Nutshell,* 11 AM. CRIM. L. REV. 355 (1973).

9. Clements, *supra* note 2, at 891.

10. Clements, *supra* note 2, at 901.

11. Iowa Code Ann. § 245.7 (1969).

12. Me. Rev. Stat. Ann. tit. 34, § 853–54 (Supp. 1972).

13. Pa. Stat. Ann. tit. 61, ch. 7 (1964).

14. Temin, *supra* note 8.

15. Brief for Appellee at 20–22, Commonwealth v. Daniels, 210 Pa. Super. 156, 232 A.2d 247 (1967).

16. *Id.* at 19.

17. Clements, *supra* note 2.

18. L. KANOWITZ, WOMEN AND THE LAW: THE UNFINISHED REVOLUTION 167 (1969).

19. Gold, *Equal Protection for Juvenile Girls in Need of Supervision in New York State,* 17 N.Y.L.F. 570 (1971).

20. Commonwealth v. Daniels, 210 Pa. Super. 156, 232 A.2d 247 (1967).

21. Calloway, *Constitutional Law—Indeterminate Sentences for Women,* 22 ARK. L. REV. 524 (1968).

22. State v. Heitman, 105 Kan. 136, 181 P. 630 (1919); *Ex parte* Dunkerton, 104 Kan. 481, 179 P. 347 (1919); Platt v. Commonwealth, 256 Mass. 539, 152 N.E. 914 (1926); *Ex parte* Brady, 116 Ohio St. 512, 157 N.E. 69 (1927); *Ex parte* Gosselin, 141 Me. 412, 44 A.2d 882 (1945), *cert. denied sub. nom.* Gosselin v. Kelley, 328 U.S. 817 (1946).

23. Note, *Equal Protection—Longer Sentences for Women than for Males Convicted of the Same Offenses Denies Equal Protection,* 82 HARV. L. REV. 921 (1969).

24. Gosselin v. Kelley, *supra* note 22.

25. Commonwealth v. Daniels, *supra* note 20, 232 A.2d at 251–52.

26. Commonwealth v. Daniels, 243 A.2d 400 (1968).

27. *Supra* note 23.

28. Temin, *supra* note 8.

29. Commonwealth v. Blum, 220 Pa. Super. 703, ——— A.2d ——— (1972); Commonwealth v. Piper, 221 Pa. Super. 187, 289 A.2d 193 (1972).

30. Commonwealth v. Daniels (II), 430 Pa. 642, 243 A.2d 400 (1968).

31. Gold, *supra* note 19.

32. Conn. Gen. Stat. Ann. ch. 309, § 17-360 (1960), as transferred, ch. 323, § 18–65 (Supp. 1972).

33. United States *ex rel.* Robinson v. York, 281 F. Supp. 8 (D. Conn. 1968).

34. 387 U.S. 1 (1967).

35. Kanowitz, *op cit. supra* note 18.

36. N.J. Stat. Ann. § 2A: 164-17 (1971); N.J. Stat. Ann. § 30: 4-155 (Supp. 1973).

37. Lillehaug, *Constitutional Law—Equal Protection–Sex Discrimination in Sentencing Criminal Offenders Is Unconstitutional,* 50 N. DAK L. REV.. 359 (1974).

38. State v. Costello, 59 N.J. 334, 282 A.2d 748 (1971).

39. *See* notes 26 and 33 *supra* and accompanying text.

40. 63 N.J. 287, 307 A.2d 78 (1973).

41. Pollack, *op. cit. supra* note 6.

42. Comment, *Juvenile Delinquency Laws: Juvenile Women and the Double Standard of Morality*, 19 U.C.L.A.L. Rev. 313 (1971).

43. Chesney-Lind, *Judicial Enforcement of the Female Sex Role: The Family Court and the Female Delinquent*, 8 ISSUES IN CRIMINOLOGY 51 (1973).

44. *Supra* note 42.

45. C. VEDDER & D. SOMERVILLE, HE DELINQUENT GIRL 147 (1970).

46. Lumpkin, *Factors in the Commitment of Correctional School Girls in Wisconsin*, 37 AM. J. SOCIOLOGY 222 (1931–32).

47. *To Be Minor and Female*, Ms., August 1972, at 74.

48. *Ibid.*

49. Gold, *supra* note 19.

50. W. LUNDEN, STATISTICS ON DELINQUENTS AND DELINQUENCY 258–59 (1964).

51. Chesney-Lind, *supra* note 43, at 57.

52. Children's Bureau, U.S. Dept. of Health,Education and Welfare, Statistical Series No. 81, Statistics on Public Institutions for Delinquent Children—1964, at 7 (1965).

53. *Supra* note 42.

54. Note, *An Aspect of the Texas Juvenile Delinquency Law—"Morals,"* 24 Sw. S.J. 698 (1970).

55. Note, *Statutory Vagueness in Juvenile Law: The Supreme Court and Mattiello v. Connecticut.* 118 U. PA. L. REV. 152 (1969).

56. *Supra* note 42.

57. Davis & Chaires, *Equal Protection for Juveniles: The Present Status of Sex-based Discrimination in Juvenile Court Laws*, 7 GA. L. REV. 494 (1973).

58. New York's Family Court Act is an exception; it has two provisions which subject females to the authority of the court for a longer period than males. *See* notes 63 and 64 *infra* and accompanying text.

59. Davis & Chaires, *supra* note 57.

60. See notes 63 and 64 *infra* and accompanying text.

61. Conn. Rev. Stat. § 2761 (1949); Tenn. Code Ann. § 37-440 (1955).

62. Davis & Chaires, SUPRA note 57.

63. N.Y. *Judiciary-Family Court Act* § 712(b) (McKinney Supp. 1971).

64. N.Y. *Judiciary-Family Court Act* § 756(c) (McKinney Supp. 1963).

65. *E.g.*, Long v. Robinson, 316 F. Supp. 22 (D. Md. 1970): Lamb v. Brown, 456 F.2d 18 (10th Cir. 1972).

66. Davis & Chaires, *supra* note 57.

67. *Ibid.*

68. *Ibid.*

69. Frontiero v. Richardson, 41 U.S.L.W. 4609, 4613-14 (U.S. May 14, 1972).

70. J. MACDONALD, PSYCHIATRY AND THE CRIMINAL 353 (3rd ed. 1976).

71. 266 A.2d 62 (Me. 1970).

72. *Id.* at 65.

73. Ariz. Rev. Stat. Ann. § 3-245 (1972).

74. Note, *Sex Discrimination in the Criminal Law: The Effect of the ERA*, 11 AM. CRIM. L. REV. 469, 503 (1973).

75. *Okla. Stat. Ann. tit. 10, § 1139(b) (Supp. 1973).*

QUESTIONS FOR DISCUSSION

1. Discuss the "chivalry factor" and its impact on the juvenile justice system.

2. What are the five offenses that lead to commitment for the juvenile female? What do these offenses have in common?

3. Cite examples of enforcement and sentencing disparity for both females and males presented in this article.

APPLICATIONS

1. The author contends that the passage of the Equal Rights Amendment would result in significant changes in the way juvenile females are "protected under the law." Do you agree or disagree with this notion? Why?

2. In your opinion, will America always have a "chivalry factor"? Why?

KEY TERMS

apocryphal   when something is spurious or of doubtful authenticity.

chivalry   the system, spirit, or customs of a knight or king; in this case, chivalry refers to a male-dominated justice system and society.

conjunction the act or instance that two or more elements are combined.

erroneous refers to anything that has been found to have errors in substance or logic.

impede to interfere with or to slow the progress of something.

penitentiary a term applied to early American prisons whose founders were from religious sects. The penitentiary was thought to be a place where offenders could reflect upon their transgressions and repent of their sins.

preempted replaced with something considered to be of greater value or priority.

vindicate to free from allegation or blame by providing a justification or defense.

29

Restitution and Recidivism Rates of Juvenile Offenders: Results from Four Experimental Studies

Anne L. Schneider
Oklahoma State University

One of the major changes in juvenile justice during the past decade has been the increased reliance on restitution as a sanction for juvenile offenders. Although a great deal has been learned during the past 10 years about the operation of restitution programs, much remains unknown regarding its impact on recidivism rates. This report contains the results from four random-assignment experiments conducted simultaneously in four communities: Boise, Idaho, Washington, D.C., Clayton County, Georgia, and Oklahoma County, Oklahoma.

In all four studies, youths were randomly assigned into restitution and into traditional dispositions. On the whole, the results show that restitution may have a small but important effect on recidivism. However, not all programs will be able to achieve this effect, either because of program management and strategy, community circumstances, or other factors.

Youths in the restitution groups never had higher recidivism rates than those in probation or detention conditions. In two of the four studies, the juveniles in restitution clearly had fewer subsequent recontacts with the court during the two-to-three-year follow-up.

"Restitution and Recidivism Rates of Juvenile Offenders: Results from Four Experimental Studies," *Criminology*, 24:3 (1986), pp. 533–552. Reprinted by permission of The American Society of Criminology.

The use of restitution as a sanction for juvenile delinquents is one of the most marked changes in juvenile justice during the past decade. In 1977, a survey of juvenile courts identified fewer than 15 formal restitution programs (Schneider and Schneider, 1977). By 1985, formal programs are known to exist in more than 400 jurisdictions, and more than 35 states now have explicit statutory authority to order restitution—either monetary or community service or both (Schneider, 1985).

The emergence of restitution as a distinct dispositional alternative can be attributed to several factors. For one, restitution is attractive to the proponents of more servere sanctions for juvenile offenders as well as to those who believe that increasingly heavy-handed intervention only exacerbates the delinquency problem (Armstrong, 1980). The former group views restitution as a more servere response than probation, whereas the latter views it as more appropriate than incarceration. The specificity of restitution as well as its emphasis on accountability also have contributed to its popularity among judges and juvenile justice professionals (Beck-Zierdt, 1980; Cannon and Stanford, 1981; Klein and Kramer, 1980).

The second factor contributing to the rapid spread of restitution has been massive federal efforts to improve and expand the use of this disposition. These efforts began during the Carter administration by the Office of Juvenile Justice and Delinquency Prevention and have continued—albeit at a reduced level—during the Reagan administration.[1]

Issues in the Use of Restitution

Restitution has not been without its critics, however. Concerns about restitution have focused on its philosophy, the practical difficulties in implementing restitution programs, and its effectiveness.

From a philosophical perspective, there were initial concerns that restitution would be interpreted as punishment and, even though that interpretation might increase its popularity with the private sector, it could reduce its acceptability with juvenile justice professionals. Treatment-oriented juvenile justice professionals, for example, could thwart the rehabilitative potential of restitution by failing to implement the restitution requirements. It was not at all clear during the early development of programs whether restitution would become a part of the "treatment" perspective or of the "punishment" perspective. Complicating the situation even further was the fact that restitution could be justified from a nonutilitarian perspective grounded in the principles of "justice" and victims rights, thereby avoiding both the "treatment" and "punishment" labels.

What has emerged over the past five years is a growing consensus among juvenile justice professionals that the underlying rationale of restitution is to hold juveniles accountable (to the victims) for the crimes they have committed. This perspective seems to have arisen from the basic logic and practice of restitution throughout the country as literally dozens of programs began focusing on the concepts of accountability and responsibility rather than debating whether restitution is "punishment" or "treatment."

A 1985 survey of restitution programs showed that accountability was by far the most important goal of restitution programs as it was rated 9.7 on a 10-point scale (Schneider, 1985). Treatment of juveniles was rated 7.9 on the same scale; services to victims was rated 7.6, and punishment averaged a 3.3 rating.

From a practical point of view, one of the most pressing issues was how local jurisdictions would finance the development of formal restitution programs once the federal program funds were exhausted. This problem is far from being solved, but the lack of funds to implement new programs almost certainly has contributed to the fact that in may jurisdictions, implementing and monitoring restitution orders has become the primary responsibility of probation officers, replacing their more traditional tasks of counseling and monitoring curfew, school work, and the like.

Another set of practical concerns revolved around whether judges would be willing to order restitution and whether juveniles would be able to pay. This type of issue has become far less prominent over the years as the results from evaluations of the federal programs indicated high completion rates (85%) and overwhelming support from the judiciary. The average order, in most jurisdictions, was slightly over $200 (Schneider, Schneider, Griffith, and Wilson, 1982).

The issue of racial and social class bias was confronted directly by some programs as they sought to obtain subsidies that would insure that no youth was denied the opportunity for restitution (rather than a more severe sanction) solely on the grounds of inability to pay. This practice has continued even beyond the federal funding with programs establishing subsidy funds through private donations, restitution "fines," and state-wide appropriations.

The third issue involves not only whether restitution is effective, but also the criteria against which it should be judged. Proponents of restitution tend to use a justice-based argument: the primary goal of restitution is to hold juveniles accountable for their acts and to return full or partial payment to victims of crimes. When there is no specific victim or no outstanding loss, the goal is to hold the youth accountable through symbolic restitution (community service work).

A strict adherence to justice-based principles would relieve restitution of any responsibility vis-à-vis longer-term effects on the youths. From this perspective, restitution is ordered because it is "right" and "fair" and constitutes a fundamental principle of justice. Most observers of juvenile justice, however, recognize the inherent weaknesses of justifying a dispositional alternative solely on justice-based principles. Any intervention which must rely solely on fairness or justice-based arguments rather than its therapeutic, rehabilitative, or deterrence value, will soon be replaced by a different intervention which promises to reduce the incidence of juvenile crime. Hence, the effect of restitution on recidivism of juvenile offenders will strongly influence the ultimate fate of this alternative.

Restitution and Recidivism

Empirical studies of restitution have been reported only since the late 1970s, and most of these defined the effectiveness of restitution in terms of its impact on victims (Galaway and Hudson, 1978; Hudson and Galaway, 1977). The amount of loss returned, the number of proportion of victims provided with restitution, victim satisfaction with the outcome of the case, and victim perceptions of the fairness or "justice" of the sentence were the common performance indicators included in the early empirical studies.

The first two studies which sought to link restitution with reduced recidivism were both conducted with adult parolees after their release from prison. Heinz, Galaway, and Hudson in 1976 reported that the restitution group had fewer convictions after release than a matched group of incarcerated offenders. Similar results were found by Hudson and Chesney (1978) in their two-year follow-up of adult offenders released from the Minnesota Restitution Center.

In a study conducted by Bonta, Boyle, Motiuk, and Sonnichsen (1983), adult offenders in a restitution program had higher recidivism rates that those in a control group, although the differences were not statistically significant. Both groups were housed in a community resource center, and most persons in both groups were employed. The control program permitted offenders to maintain employment by serving their sentences in the community resource center. The authors point out that the restitution group was a higher-risk group than the others prior to the intervention and that this could have diminished the true impact of the program.

The first two tests of restitution's effect on recidivism of juvenile offenders were undertaken by doctoral candidates. In one of these, conducted by Wax at Washington State, juveniles were randomly assigned into one of three groups: monetary restitution (with the victim present at sentencing), community service restitution, and a control group which had no contact with victims and paid no restitution. No differences in recidivism rates were found to be statistically significant, although restitution was observed to have positive effects on some of the psychological tests (Wax, 1977). The size of the sample in this study, however, was so small (36 total) that the possibility of finding an impact, even if one existed, was exceptionally low.

The second doctoral study examined recidivism rates of approximately 250 offenders in the Tulsa County juvenile restitution program (Guedalia, 1979). Variables found to be significantly related to reduced recidivism were victim contact and restitution orders of less than $100. The latter, of course, could simply be a reflection of a less serious immediate offense (hence the lower amount of the restitution order).

Two recent studies of recidivism rates among juvenile delinquents sentenced to restitution reported positive effects. Cannon and Stanford (1981) found a 19% rearrest rate among restitution cases over a six-month time period compared with a 24% rates for the nonrestitution groups. Hofford (1981) reported an 18% recidivism rate for youths in the juvenile restitution program compared with a 30% rate for those on regular probation.

The results from these studies are instructive, although they are far from being definitive. As is the case with virtually all field research, serious methodological problems confound most of the studies, making it necessary to rely more heavily on replication of findings than on any single study. With the exception of Wax's study and the adult study by Heinz et al. (1976), none achieved a satisfactory degree of equivalence between the comparison group and the recidivism group. In the juvenile studies, little information was provided on whether the groups were equivalent, and multivariate analysis was not conducted in an attempt to hold constant other differences between the groups that could have produced different recidivism rates.

THE EXPERIMENTS

The research reported in this paper is based on experimental studies undertaken simultaneously in four different juvenile court jurisdictions.[2]

Although there were numerous problems involved in establishing the random assignment procedure and insuring the integrity of the data, tests eventually were developed which permitted direct comparisons of restitution against traditional dispositions in Boise, Idaho, Washington, D.C., Clayton County, Georgia, and Oklahoma City, Oklahoma.

Boise, Idaho

The experiment in Boise was structured to provide a comparison of restitution against short-term detention. Youths randomly selected for the treatment group were required to pay monetary restitution to the victims of their crimes or, if there was no outstanding monetary loss, they were required to complete a specified number of community service hours. Juveniles assigned to the control group were sentenced to several successive weekends of detention in a local detention facility. All juveniles were on probation (in addition to their requirements regarding restitution or weekend detention).

The eligible group included all youths referred to court for adjudication on a delinquent offense, except those who were held in detention during their pretrial period. These cases were excluded from eligibility because

the youths had already experienced incarceration, and thus would not represent a proper test of the restitution condition if they later were randomly assigned to it.

After the fact-finding hearing, all youths for whom the charges were substantiated were then randomly assigned either to the restitution or the detention group. At the disposition hearing, the probation officer presented the results of the random selection. The judge was able to either follow the recommendation or give a different disposition. In Boise, the assignment was followed for 89% of those recommended for restitution and for 97% of the detention recommendations.

Case management in Boise was handled by restitution counselors. The average length of time in the restitution program was two months, and the average length of time under court jurisdiction was nine months. Although these youths were technically on probation, there was little if any active supervision by probation officers.

The control group youths were incarcerated for an average of eight days. The incarcerations took place in a local detention facility and usually involved being locked up for several successive weekends. After release from the local facility, the youths were on probation for an average of nine months.

Washington, D.C.

The Washington, D.C., design provided a comparison of victim-offender mediation restitution against probation for a group of serious offenders. One of the eligibility criteria in this study was that the youths have at least one felony conviction.

After the presentence investigation had been completed, the probation officers recommended the youths either for incarceration or for probation. Those recommended for probation were then randomly assigned either into probation or into victim-offender mediation and the restitution program.

The D.C. program rested on the premise that restitution would be effective only if juveniles accepted responsibility for their offenses and were committed to the principal of making amends to the victim. If a youth did not feel responsible for his or her behavior, then restitution was not expected to be effective. Furthermore, serious complications were expected in the mediation sessions if youths were required to participate in this part of the program. Thus, the program wished to permit the youths who had been randomly selected for victim-offender mediation to voluntarily reject their assignment in favor of probation only.

Although this aspect of the program design clearly would create serious problems with the evaluation, it was accepted since it was an integral and "natural" part of their program. A design which did not permit juveniles to choose or reject restitution would not be generalizable after the experiment was over because the program would not continue to operate with youths who had been "coerced" into the mediation process. Furthermore, it is difficult to envision any victim-offender mediation program anywhere in the United States that would require youths or victims to participate. Thus, voluntary participation was essential to the program and to the generalizablity of the research results.

Although various inducements were attempted throughout the program period to encourage juveniles selected for restitution to actually participate in it, there were many refusals—approximately 40%. An analysis of the reasons for the refusals indicated that defense lawyers were an important source of information for the youths and that they were the ones usually suggesting that the youths eschew the restitution/mediation program.

As in the other sites which have "crossovers" or other kinds of violations in the random assignment, the analysis was greatly complicated by these deviations.

Clayton County

The restitution experiment in Clayton County was designed to compare four distinct treatment strategies: restitution, counseling, restitution and counseling combined, and a control condition which consisted of the normal disposition which could be either probation or incarceration. All youths in the first three groups were on probation. Thus,

the actual test was the marginal impact of restitution. An additional feature of this design was the ability to test the marginal impact of counseling.

Cases were randomly assigned into the four conditions after the adjudication hearing. As with the other experiments, the actual placement of the youths into the groups was done by the judge at disposition. The judge could overrule the random assignment, but this was seldom done. Of the cases that were included in the study, 7% received an actual sentence that differed from the randomly assigned one.

The treatments associated with the four groups can be summarized as follows:

Restitution. Youths in this group were ordered at disposition to pay monetary restitution and/or to do community service restitution. Service restitution was more common, involving 60% of the youths. Of the 40% who paid monetary restitutions, slightly more than half found their own jobs and the rest obtained employment through the efforts of the restitution program.

The youths kept some of their earnings—on the average, about 40%. There were no program subsidies in Clayton County, and youths generally were not permitted to pay the restitution from their savings or to have family members assist in the payment. Restitution cases were monitored by restitution case workers who also were responsible for insuring their compliance with normal probation requirements. The average period of supervision was 3.5 months.

Counseling. Juveniles with a counseling disposition were assigned to a mental health therapist on the county social service staff. The counseling consisted of a diagnostic session followed by assignment to one of several special kinds of therapy: recreational, family, and so forth. The average supervision period was 5.6 months.

Restitution and Counseling. For this group, both restitution and mental health therapy were ordered at disposition. The restitution requirements were quite similar to those for the restitution-only group: 63% were ordered to do community service and 44% had monetary restitution requirements. Families were not permitted to pay and most of the youths found employment in private or public sector jobs. These youths were under supervision for an average of 5.8 months.

Control. Any court-approved disposition was considered appropriate for this group, and most were placed on probation (78%). Only 5% were incarcerated, and the remainder either received some other disposition or were dismissed with no sanction.

Oklahoma County

Eligible cases in Oklahoma County included all adjudicated delinquents except those convicted of murder and rape for whom a monetary value could be placed on victim losses. Following the fact-finding hearing, these youths were randomly assigned into one of three groups: the restitution only group; restitution and probation; and a control group which would receive whatever sanction the judge deemed appropriate, so long as it did not include restitution. For those who were to be in either of the restitution groups, program staff developed restitution recommendations which were presented to the judge along with other presentencing information.

One important compromise reached in the negotiation about random assignment was that the judge would be able to sentence youths in any one of the three groups to an incarceration sanction if this was deemed necessary. Although this had an adverse impact on the power of the design (when the youths were left in their assigned groups for the analysis), it does not appear that the effect would be harmful enough to abandon the experiment. Since the youths were randomly assigned into the three groups, each group would contain youths of approximately equal seriousness and would have an approximately equal proportion of their more serious offenders removed for incarceration. This type of "crossover" does not introduce bias into the final groups if the youths are left in their assigned treatment for analysis, but it does reduce the power of the design. Decisions to incarcerate were about equally likely in all three groups: 9% for the restitution-only group were committed to the state for incarceration; 10% of the restitution-plus probation group were given this disposition, and 11% of the control group were committed to the state.

Approximately half of the youths were ordered to pay monetary restitution and the others did community work service.

Randomization

The randomization procedure varied from one program to another, although in each site the procedure guaranteed that any deviations would be immediately obvious. The formulas were all based on some combination of day-of-birth, a random number starter, and a final assignment which allocated cases into groups in accordance with predetermined proportions.

The list of numbers and their assignment was kept by the researchers rather than program staff to insure that persons responsible for identifying the eligible pool would not have prior knowledge of the group to which the youth would be assigned if he or she were determined to be eligible.

The random assignment formulas were not necessarily set to achieve equal number of cases in the treatment and control conditions. Instead, the proportions were established so that the program could take a sufficient number of cases to fulfill its grant obligations and to achieve as nearly an equal distribution of cases as feasible under the circumstances.

METHODOLOGY

Measuring Recidivism

Recidivism was defined as crimes committed after entry into the treatment or control conditions which resulted in contact with the county juvenile or adult court, except incidents which were dismissed due to a lack of evidence or those for which the youth was found not guilty. Crimes that were committed after the immediate offense but before entry into the program were counted as "concurrent" incidents and were not included in the analysis.

A complete search of all juvenile and adult court records was undertaken by a team of trained individuals from the national evaluation group. The follow-up period varied from 22 to 36 months, depending on when the youths entered the program and when the final official records check was conducted.

Multiple measures of recidivism were used to incorporate both the seriousness and frequency of reoffending as well as to minimize possible misinterpretations based on single-indicator analysis. The measures used were:

Prevalence. Prevalence refers to the percentage of juveniles in each group who committed a subsequent offense which resulted in a referral to adult or juvenile court during the follow-up period. Excluded from this figure were any recontacts for which the records definitely established that the case was dismissed for lack of evidence or the youth was found not guilty.

Annual Offense Rate. The annual offense (contact) rate was calculated by summing all of the recontacts for the group, dividing by the time at risk (in days), and then correcting to an average annual rate per 100 youths. Both the pre- and postoffense rates were calculated.

Recontact Frequency. Recontact frequency was used as an individual-level measure of overall recidivism in the regression analyses. Recontact frequency refers to the total number of recontacts for each youth. This is a badly skewed variable, and several transformations were tested in the multiple regression analysis. Although very few differences were noted in the results, the most stable measure was a natural log transformation, and this was employed in the analysis reported here.

Recontact Rate. This is also an individual-level measure used in the multiple regression analysis. It was calculated by dividing the total number of offenses for each youth by the total time at risk, thereby creating an individual-level "rate" of recontact. Juveniles with no reoffenses had differing follow-up periods, however, because they entered the programs at different points in time. A simple rate involves dividing zero reoffenses by the risk time which, of course, produces a score of zero regardless of whether the

youth had six months of time at risk or four years. To distinguish among the nonrecidivists so that those with longer periods of time at risk have lower scores, a small constant (.01) was added to the numerator of this measure.

Seriousness Indices. Three variables representing seriousness were used in the initial data analysis. One of these was an ordinally coded variable representing the most serious offense committed by the juvenile. Violent personal offenses were coded "6," followed by serious property offenses "5," other felony property offenses "4," minor personal offenses "3," minor property offenses "2," and trivial offenses, "1."

The second variable representing seriousness was created by scoring each reoffense in terms of its seriousness and then summing these to obtain an overall measure of frequency and seriousness of reoffense. The final variable was a seriousness rate in which the overall score for each youth was divided by the amount of time at risk, thereby taking into account that youths with longer follow-up periods would be expected to have more reoffenses.

Because these three measures yielded almost identical results and because these results were similar to those produced by the frequency variables, only the last seriousness measure is included in this paper.

In all instances, the rate of reoffending (frequency divided by time at risk) was actually an adjusted rate in which a small constant (.01) was added to the numerator so that the scores of persons who had no recidivist offenses would be scaled in terms of their time at risk.

Establishing Causality

Juveniles were randomly assigned into the program and control conditions in all four sites. In an ideal experiment, the random assignment alone would be sufficient to insure that the statistical measure of program impact was not confounded with other variable. Field experiments, however, seldom meet the rigid requirements of experimental conditions, and the ones in this evaluation were no exception.

The major problem was with cross overs—cases which were assigned to one condition but which ended up in the other. In most of the sites, these cross overs constituted fewer than 5% of the total, but in Washington, D.C., approximately half of the youths randomly selected for the victim offend mediation–restitution program voluntarily decided not to participate and to accept traditional probation instead.

It is always difficult to know what to do with crossover cases, but the analysis here follows the common recommendation, which is to consider a case in the group to which it was assigned, even if the actual treatment was something different. This is generally viewed as a conservative approach due to the expectation that those who violate the random assignment do so to protect the program by "creaming." Hence, the more difficult cases are directed away from the program, leaving only the easier ones. To include all cases, as originally assigned, protects against "creaming."

In the analysis reported below, however, the precaution was also taken of testing all the regression models with the cases in the actual, rather than assigned, groups. The results of these analyses in sites with small numbers of crossovers were no different from the results when the cases were kept in their original groups, and are not reported. However, in Washington, D.C., the crossover group (juveniles who voluntarily selected probation rather thatn restitution) was so sizable that the entire analysis is reported.

For the analysis, bivariate regressions were conducted and, to insure that potentially confounding effects did not interfere with the interpretation, multiple regression analysis also was undertaken in which priors, age, race, school status, and sex were controlled. In all of the regression tests, the independent variable is the treatment/control condition with restitution being scored "zero" and control scored "one."

FINDINGS

Table 1 contains descriptive data for juveniles in the restitution and the control group in all four sites. Table 2 has the results of the multivariate analyses.

Boise

There were no statistically significant differences in the background characteristics of

TABLE 1   Background Characteristics, Prevalence Rates, and Incident Rates [a]

Site	No. Cases	Full-Time Student %	Ethnic Minority %	Gender (Male) %	Repeat Offender %	Age %	Referral Offense Felony %	Months of Followup	Prevalence %	Annual Incident Rate Per 100 Youths Pre	Post
Boise											
Restitution	86	81	5	86	66	15.0	41	22	53	103	86
Detention	95	85	1	84	80	15.3	32	22	59	137	100
Washington, D.C.											
Restitution	143	75	99	97	63	15.4	65	32	53	61	54
Restn. Refused	131	72	98	87	65	15.5	57	31	55	62	52
Probation	137	72	99	91	61	15.5	59	31	63	61	65
Clayton County											
Restitution	73	76	6	86	60	15.1	24	35	49	101	74
Restn. + Counseling	74	82	4	80	43	15.2	40	35	46	55	47
Prob. + Counseling	55	75	4	78	56	15.1	49	36	60	64	84
Probation	55	86	0	80	54	15.2	30	37	52	75	75
Oklahoma County											
Sole Sanction Restn.	104	65	34	91	59	15.2	50	23	49	66	72
Restn. + Prob.	116	69	46	87	59	15.4	48	24	50	56	64
Probation	78	72	32	85	68	15.5	40	24	52	75	74

[a] In all sites, the information on prior and subsequent offenses was based on an official records search of juvenile and adult court records.

youths in the two groups. Most were full-time students (81% and 85%, respectively); the average age was just over 15 years, and more than 80% were males.

The population from which the random assignment was made included primarily serious offenders. In the restitution group, 66% were repeat offenders and 80% were repeaters in the detention group. This difference, which appears to indicate that the detention group contained somewhat more serious offenders than the restitution group, is offset by the fact that 41% of the restitution youths entered the program as a result of a felony conviction compared with 32% of the incarceration group.

The recidivism analysis suggests that the restitution group did somewhat better (that is, had fewer reoffenses), but the differences are not very large and they may have been produced by chance. The observed significance levels in most of the analyses, although favoring the restitution group, were between .25 and .30.

Specifically, in the 22 months of follow-up, 53% of the restitution group had one or more subsequent contacts with the court compared with 59% of the incarceration group. The postprogram annual rate of subsequent contacts per 100 youths was 86 for the restitution group compared with 100 for the incarceration group. Differences of this magnitude would be expected, by chance alone, approximately one fourth to one third of the time.

The multiple regression analysis (see Table 2) indicated a difference of about the same magnitude, but it too would occur by chance about 25% to 30% of the time.

The pre/post comparison shows that the intervention may have slowed the annual offense rate for both groups. The average number of offenses committed, per 100 youths per year, dropped from 103 for the restitution group to 86. For the incarceration group, the annual preprogram rate dropped from 137 to 100. Although maturation of the

TABLE 2   Multiple Regression Analysis of Restitution and Recidivism

Site	Prevalence			Incidence			Seriousness		
	r [a]	bwt [b]	osl [c]	r	bwt	osl	r	bwt	osl
Boise									
(a) Restitution vs. Detention	.05	.44	.27	.02	.02	.33	.04	.04	.29*
Washington, D.C.									
(a) Restitution and Restitution Refused vs. Probation	.08	.10	.04	.07	.10	.05	.02	.05	.25
(b) Restitution vs. Probation	.09	.11	.03	.08	.11	.04	.03	.04	.20
Clayton County									
(a) Restitution vs. Probation	.11	.11	.07	.11	.13	.04	.08	.09	.16
(c) Restitution vs. (Restitution + Counseling)	−.10	−.07	.38	−.09	−.05	.60	.01	.07	.42
(d) Without Counseling vs. With Counseling	.03	−.02	.77	.02	−.03	.69	−.09	−.12	.06
Oklahoma Co.									
(a) Sole-Sanction Restitution vs. (Restitution + Probation)	−.08	.02	.77	−.03	.14	.84	.00	.00	.99
(b) Restitution vs. Probation	.00	.00	.97	.00	.00	.99	.07	.00	.87

[a] The zero-order correlation coefficient.
[b] The standardized regression coefficient (beta weight) with priors, age, race, sex, and school status controlled. Time at risk also was controlled in the equations utilizing prevalence.
[c] The observed significance level (for the restitution variable in the multivariate equation, two-tailed test).
* Positive scores indicate the restitution group did better (that is, had lower recidivism rates). Positive scores in other comparisons indicate the group named first did better.

youths obviously could influence the pre/post change in annual rates, the groups were randomly selected and were about the same age. Hence, the maturation effects should be about the same for both groups and the cross-comparison of pre/post rates yields interesting information. It also should be recalled that the data collected included tracking into adult courts. Thus, there is no cutoff of subsequent incidents as the youths reach 18 years of age.

On balance, the Boise experiment indicates the restitution youths did just as well as those who were in detention and that there was a relatively good probability (about two out of three) that the participation in the restitution program actually yielded a slightly lower recidivism rate. This conclusion, however, must be balanced against the fact that the control group had a higher level of priors before the intervention (but slightly less serious immediate offenses), and the reduction in incidence was actually somewhat higher for the control group.

Washington, D.C.

Referrals to the Washington, D.C., program were serious offenders. More than 60% were repeat offenders, and for approximately 60%, the immediate incident which resulted in their referral was a felony (see Table 1). These youths were predominately black (99%) and male (95%).

There were no statistically significant differences between the restitution and control groups in terms of background characteristics. This held true when the crossovers were grouped with the restitution youths and when they were kept separate. It should be noted, however, that the crossovers contained substantially more females (13%) than either of the other two groups.

The results of the recidivism analysis are interesting, but perplexing. The restitution group (all those randomly assigned restitution, including the "crossovers") had reoffense prevalence rates considerably below the probation group—53% to 63%, a statistically significant difference—and annual reoffense rates similarly lower than the control group (54 to 65). The multiple regression analysis

also shows that the youths assigned to restitution had lower overall contact (both frequency and rates) after controlling for the number of priors, age, race, school status, and sex.

As mentioned previously, substantial treatment contamination occurred in the randomization, with about half of the randomly assigned restitution youths receiving probation instead of restitution. With this issue in mind, three additional sets of multiple regression analyses were conducted. In each instance, different evaluation groups were included or excluded, creating different treatment and comparison groups. In each case, the independent (treatment) variable was dichotomous (scored as zero for the control condition and one for the treatment). These results show the following:

Restitution versus Restitution Refused (Crossovers). This comparison indicates that the restitution group had slightly fewer recidivist offenses, but the differences were not significant.

Restitution versus Probation. In this analysis, the crossovers were omitted entirely and the restitution youths had significantly lower recidivism rates on almost all measures.

Restitution versus Restitution Refused (Plus Probation). The crossovers actually received probation and in these analyses were grouped with the probation youths who were randomly assigned. The restitution group had somewhat better scores on most of the indicators, but the differences were only marginally significant (for example, in the .15 to .25 range).

Three major findings stand out. First, youths who were randomly assigned into restitution—whether they actually participated in it or not—had lower recidivism rates than youths randomly assigned probation. Second, those who actually participated in restitution generally had lower recidivism levels than those in probation. And, third, those who had participated in restitution never had higher rates than those who participated in probation.

Why then did youths who were randomly selected for restitution but refused (the crossovers) have lower recidivism rates that those on probation? Both actually participated in probation. Differences in the background characteristics do not appear to account for these differences.

Perhaps the reason for the differences is that youths selected for restitution were given realistic choices and involvement in the determination of their disposition which the probation youth did not have. All juveniles selected for restitution were presented with two choices of roughly equivalent severity (probation or restitution) and they were allowed some involvement in the process of determining their disposition. It is possible that this choice component allowed them to select a treatment somewhat better suited to their individual interests and motivations and thus one which was more efficacious in impacting their future behaviors.

Clayton County

Clayton County youths were overwhelmingly white (as is the population in that suburban area near Atlanta), approximately 15 years of age, and predominately male (see Table 1). Between one fourth and one half of the youths were referred for felony offenses and most of the others had been involved in misdemeanor property crimes.

The restitution-only group was compared with the restitution-counseling group to determine whether the latter produced any improvement in the successful completion rates. As shown in Table 1, the completion rates were very high for both groups and the small difference observed (86% for restitution-only versus 82% for restitution-counseling) was not statistically significant.

Both restitution groups were somewhat less likely to commit subsequent offenses resulting in court contacts during the three-year follow-up period as 49% of the restitution-only group and 46% of the restitution-counseling group were again referred to court. These figures compare with a 60% and 52% recidivism rates for the two probation groups.

The postprogram offense rates also show similar differences with the restitution groups having lower annual offense rates.

The multiple regression analyses, con-

trolling for number of priors, age, school statues, race, and sex indicate an effect with a high likelihood of being produced by the program (significance levels of .07, .04, and .16 on a two-tailed test). In these tests, the two restitution groups were combined and compared with the two probation groups.

The group reoffense rates before and after the intervention indicate some interesting differences. For the restitution-only group, the preprogram rate was 101 offenses. After the intervention, this dropped to 74. Drops in the postintervention rates of similar magnitudes were not observed for any of the other groups. The restitution and counseling group had a preprogram rate of 55, which dropped only to 47 afterward. The probation and counseling group actually showed an increase from 64 to 84, and the probation only group showed no change (75 to 75).

A second multiple regression analysis was undertaken to determine whether counseling had an impact on recidivism when contrasted with the noncounseling dispositions. For this analysis, both counseling groups were compared with the noncounseling alternatives and no significant differences were found. A final comparison was between the restitution-only condition and restitution-counseling. Again, no significant differences were found.

The results from Clayton County show that youths required to make restitution to their victims either through community service or monetary payments had lower recidivism rates than those given the more traditional juvenile court disposition. These results show that restitution works quite well on its own and that it does not need to be combined with mental health counseling.

Oklahoma County

Most of the juveniles in Oklahoma County were relatively serious offenders: 59% of the restitution youths had one or more priors and 68% of the control youths had a prior record of court contact. Many of the youths entered the experiment as a result of felony convictions: 50% of the sole-sanction group, 48% of the restitution and probation group, and 40% of the probation-only controls.

The groups did not differ on recontact with the court, regardless of the method of measuring recidivism or the type of analysis undertaken. On the average, juveniles in the sole-sanction group committed 140 offenses per 100 youths per year compared with 133 for the restitution and probation group and 150 for the controls. These differences were not great enough to be statistically significant—they were not even close, in fact.

Comparison of the pre- and postrates show that none of the interventions reduced the overall offense rates. In fact, the youths in both restitution groups tended to reoffend slightly more afterward than before whereas the control group continued at the same rate.

The multiple regression analysis effectively removed even the slight differences observed between the groups as the unstandardized regression coefficient with the other variables controlled was .00 in two of the tests and less than .02 in the other.

The findings from this experiment indicate that youths who were given restitution as a sanction, without benefit of probation requirements or probation supervision, were generally as successful as those who received probation along with restitution. Furthermore, the results indicate that youths who received restitution sanctions did no better and no worse than the control group of probation youths in terms of recidivism.

Conclusions

The results from the experiments regarding the effect of restitution on recidivism should be viewed as quite encouraging. In two of the four direct comparisons, approximately 10% fewer of the restitution group were recontacted during the follow-up. An annualized measure of recontact indicated that the restitution program cases produced almost 10 fewer crimes per 100 youth per year than the controls in these two programs (Washington, D.C., and Clayton County, Georgia). The differences in these two sites were great enough to rule out chance variation as a likely cause of the apparent program effect.

In one other jurisdiction—Boise, Idaho—the program youths did better on both measures of recidivism by six percentage points and an annual rate differential of 14 incidents per 100 youths per year. The smaller sample size, however, prevented these differences from achieving statistical significance at the .05 level. The study in Oklahoma County revealed among the three groups no differences of sufficient size to merit policy consideration. These results should not be viewed as inconclusive or as contradictory. Rather, the lesson here is that restitution can have a positive effect on recidivism, but it does not necessarily have this impact under all circumstances.

The reasons for the success of restitution in reducing recidivism—in those instances when it was successful—remain a matter of speculation and theory. As with any effective intervention, it is reasonable to assume that the intervention must have an impact on one or more variables which influence delinquency. And, since the restitution intervention was directed primarily at the juvenile (rather than his or her parents, friends, or neighborhood), it is reasonable to believe that the effect is transmitted through changes in the juvenile's perceptions or attitudes which in turn, alter behavior.

Many possible variables might be cited:

1. Youths who participate in restitution have positive experiences in "real job" situations which not only may provide a positive adult role model, but which also may instill a sense of confidence that the youth can be successful in nondelinquent situations.

2. Restitution may have a less stigmatizing effect on the youth since it offers the juvenile the potential for "paying the debt" and for being "redeemed" for the offense.

3. The youth may have a more realistic understanding of the actual consequences of crime for victims and for the community as a result of being "held accountable" for delinquent acts.

4. Restitution is believed by many program managers to break down the postoffense rationalization (for example, the victim deserved it) and force the offender to confront the true consequences of the crime.

5. It is possible that restitution has a deterrent effect (in the sense of increasing the perception that crimes have consequences which result in costs to the offender).

6. Restitution usually involves a relatively intensive supervision since most of the youths are spending a substantial portion of their free time at work. This may break down the relationship between the youths and other delinquent peers during the supervisory period and perhaps beyond.

Future research needs to focus on the linkages between restitution, attitudes, and subsequent behavior in order to identify how restitution operates to reduce delinquency when, in fact, it has this effect.

Notes

1. The original federal program was intended to involve six or eight juvenile courts and was viewed as a research and development program. When Ira Schwartz became administrator of the Office of Juvenile Justice and Delinquency Prevention, however, the priority given to restitution increased enormously and the program expanded to a 20 million dollar effort eventually involving 85 juvenile courts. A national evaluation was separately funded by the National Institute for Juvenile Justice and Delinquency Prevention. Under the Reagan administration, the emphasis on restitution was temporarily suspended, but was resumed by Alfred Regnery as a major training and technical assistance program (RESTTA, Restitution Education, Specialized Training, and Technical Assistance).

2. The evaluation was conducted at the Institute of Policy Analysis, Eugene, Oregon. The author of this paper was one of the principal investigators of the study, along with Peter R. Schneider. William Griffith, Mike Wilson, and Gordon Bazemore also contributed enormously to the data collection and analysis upon which this paper is based.

References

ARMSTRONG, TROY
1980   Restitution: A sanction for all seasons. Presented at the Fourth Symposium on Restitution and Community Services Sentencing.

BECK-ZIERDT, NATHANIEL
1980   Tri-county juvenile restitution program. Unpublished. St. Paul, MN: Minnesota Crime Control Planning Board Research and Evaluation Unit.

BONTA, JAMES L., JANE BOYLE, LAURENCE L. MOTIUK, AND PAUL SONNICHSEN
1983   Restitution in correctional half-way houses: Victims satisfaction, attitudes and recidivism. Canadian Journal of Correction 20: 140–152.

CANNON, A. AND R.M. STANFORD
1981   Evaluation of the juvenile alternative services project. Unpublished. Florida Department of Health and Rehabilitative Services.

GALAWAY, BURT AND JOE HUDSON (EDS.)
1978   Offender Restitution in Theory and Action. Lexington, MA: Health.

GUEDALIA, LESLIE J.
1979   Predicting recidivism of juvenile delinquents on restitutionary probation from selected background, subject, and program variables. Unpublished doctoral dissertation. Washington, D.C.: American University.

HATFIELD, ELAINE AND MARY K. UTNE
1978   Equity Theory and Restitution Programming. In Burt Galaway and Joe Hudson (eds.), Offender Restitution in Theory and Action. Lexington, MA: Heath.

HEINZ, J., BURT GALAWAY, AND JOE HUDSON
1976   Restitution or parole: A follow-up study of adult offenders. Social Service Review 50: 148–156.

HOFFORD, MERRY
1981   Juvenile restitution program. Unpublished final report. Trident. Charleston, SC: United Way.

HUDSON, JOE AND BURT GALAWAY
1977   A review of the restitution and community-service sanctioning research. In Joe Hudson and Burt Galaways (eds.), Victims, Offenders, and Alternative Sanctions. Lexington, MA: Heath

HUDSON, JOE AND STEVE CHESNEY
1978   Research on restitution: A review and assessment. In Burt Galaway and Joe Hudson (eds.), Offender Restitution in Theory and Action. Toronto: Lexington.

KLEIN, ANDREW R. AND ALBERT L. KRAMER
1980   Earn-It: The Story So Far. Quincy, MA: Earn-It.

SCHNEIDER, ANNE L. (ED.)
1985   Guide to Juvenile Restitution Programs. Washington, D.C.: National Criminal Justice Reference Service and GPO.

SCHNEIDER, ANNE L. AND PETER R. SCHNEIDER
1977   Restitution requirements for juvenile offenders. A survey of practices in American juvenile courts. Juvenile Justice Journal 18: 43–56.

SCHNEIDER, PETER R., ANNE L. SCHNEIDER, WILLIAM GRIFFITH, AND MICHAEL WILSON
1982   Two-Year Report on the National Evaluation of the Juvenile Restitution Initiative: An Overview of Program Performance. Unpublished. Eugene, OR: Institute of Policy Analysis.

WAX, MAX L.
1977   Effects of symbolic restitution and presence of victim on delinquent shoplifter. Unpublished doctoral dissertation. Pullman, WA: Washington State University.

WILSON, MICHAEL J.
1983   The juvenile offender instruments: Administration and a description of findings. Unpublished. Eugene, OR: Institute of Policy Analysis.

QUESTIONS FOR DISCUSSION

1. Why has restitution become more popular as a sentencing alternative?

2. According to this article, how does restitution affect the recidivism rate of the juvenile offenders who were studied?

3. What criteria does the researcher use to measure recidivism?

APPLICATIONS

1. Contact a local juvenile court judge or juvenile probation officer. Find out how often restitution is used as a sentencing option or a condition of probation for the juvenile offenders in your community. What types of restitution are typically utilized?

2. Do you think restitution is an appropriate alternative to other more institutionalized forms of adjudicative action? Why?

KEY TERMS

concurrent   operating or existing at the same time.

efficacious   having the power to produce a desired effect.

exacerbate   to make more bitter, severe, or undesirable.

non-utilitarian   refers to something that is not considered to be useful or good based or its consequences.

substantiate   to establish by proof or competent evidence; to verify.

PART

V

JUVENILE DELINQUENCY
AND PUBLIC POLICY

*T*he current juvenile justice system is an enigma. It is often criticized for failures whose antecedents are to be found outside the system itself. The expectations of reform and a reduction in delinquency are extremely high, yet the resources remain low. Perhaps the most enigmatical feature of the system is the lack of a clear set of goals—a congruent set of expectations in terms of outcomes resulting from policy or program implementations. The complexity of conceptualizing outcomes has been exacerbated by rising violence among juveniles, increased public fear of juvenile crime, and a multitude of political interests. What was once a small system seeking to ameliorate the social ills of neglected, abused, and delinquent youths has become an institution whose charge often vacillates from one extreme to another.

The enigmatic nature of the system should not, however, blind us to the successes of many of the programs and people who struggle daily with issues as real as life and death. One of the great gaps in the research area, and, to a lesser degree, the public perception, is that many young lives are changed in positive ways and these youths go on to good futures. The real issues in this section on policy and future trends encompass much more than the juvenile justice system. This last section presents four articles that focus on the system, youth culture, social change, and significant ideas on how to solve the many problems that contribute to and are caused by juvenile delinquency.

"Rethinking Juvenile Justice," by Barry Krisberg and Ira Schwartz, involves an elaborate assessment of data sources and the implications of policy based on those data. There remains a significant reliability issue in relation to data collection, accounts, and even hidden delinquency. The interface between data and policy is a leading issue in the delinquency field, and juvenile justice reform must begin with improvements in the credibility of data sources.

Hunter Hurst and Louis W. McHardy, in"Juvenile Justice and the Blind Lady," claim that we are setting the stage for another "quick fix'' in the juvenile justice system. Change in the system is inevitable, but there are no easy paths to follow as the complex nature of the issues precludes any panaceas. Certainly, deinstitutionalizing status offenders was a step in the right direction. The structure of juvenile justice administration and delivery remains troublesome, even for the most ardent supporters of the status quo.

The term *gang* often engenders images of youthful mobs roaming the streets of our large cities in search of trouble—angry youths preying on each other and the innocent for money, prestige, or just plain fun. C. Ronald Huff, in "Youth Gangs and Public Policy," claims we may be losing our "human infrastructure" as well as the more highly publicized physical infrastructure in the United States. The recent feminization and juvenilization of poverty are only part of the more complex puzzle of inner-city despair and violence. Subcultural violence is perhaps the single most important issue to the major cities in the United States and appears at times to be epidemic.

Our last selection, "Juvenile Delinquency: Can Social Science Find a Cure?" by Don C. Gibbons, reviews many of the ideas of criminologists over the past century and points out that the causes and cures are much more complex than the simplistic "criminal personality" hypothesis. The refinement of theoretical formulations, data sources, and empirically validated findings all must be improved if the practitioner is to have a positive impact with juveniles.

30

Rethinking Juvenile Justice

Barry Krisberg

Ira Schwartz

Data on juvenile arrests, court processing, and admissions to juvenile correctional facilities offer important information to help rethink juvenile justice policy directions of the last decade. Most striking is the progress in reducing the involvement of status offenders within the juvenile justice system between 1974–1979. Less encouraging is that similar progress was not achieved in the case of delinquent offenders. Moreover, the primary consequence of the removal of status offenders from the juvenile justice system is the large decline in female admissions to public correctional facilities, whereas male admissions were either stable or actually increased from 1974–1979. Also interesting is the leveling off of rates of Part 1 juvenile arrests from 1974–1979: this directly contradicts public perceptions of a steady and alarming increase in serious youth crime.

Preliminary analysis of state trends in rates of admissions to detention and training schools revealed a complex pattern of increases and decreases. This pattern was largely unrelated to the distribution of OJJDP funds. Indeed juvenile correctional admissions are highly concentrated in a few states. An exploratory attempt to explain the large variations in state rates of correctional admissions suggested that most of the variation in detention admissions can be explained by the number of detention beds per 100,000 youth population. For training school admission rates, the number of beds per 100,000 youth population is also the most powerful explanatory variable but nearly two-thirds of the variation in state training school admissions is not explained by bed availability, rates of juvenile arrests for serious crimes, or youth unemployment. Future research should analyze the determinants of the wide disparities between states in rates of detention and training school admissions. Other important areas for further policy investigation are the detaining of juveniles in adult jails and the enormous growth in private residential placements for troubled youth.

"The moral test of government is how it treats those who are in the dawn of life, the children; those who are in the shadows of life, the sick, the needy, and the handicapped."

Hubert H. Humphrey

INTRODUCTION

This is one of the most important periods in our nation's history. Bold proposals have been put forth calling for fundamental changes in our economic and domestic policies and in the relationship and distribution of power between the states and the federal government. Social reforms and programs, some of which had their beginnings nearly a generation ago, are being questioned and re-examined. While the outcomes of this process remain uncertain, few would argue the fact that major changes are underway.

"Rethinking Juvenile Justice," *Crime and Delinquency,* 29:(3) (1983), pp. 333–364. Reprinted by permission of Sage Publications, Inc.

Beginning with the creation of the Children's Bureau in 1912, the federal government has played an increasingly more active role in juvenile delinquency. Now, within the context of broader economic and domestic policy debates, it has been suggested by some that the federal government cease its activities in this area. This proposal has polarized discussion and has served as a barrier to thoughtful assessment.

Nearly a decade ago, after more than five years of exhaustive study on the part of the Senate Subcommittee to Investigate Juvenile Delinquency, Congress concluded ". . . that our present system of juvenile justice is failing miserably." (U.S. Senate Committee on the Judiciary, 1975:3) Congress found large numbers of status offenders and non-offenders locked up in adult jails, detention centers, and training schools. They found overcrowded and understaffed juvenile courts and evidence of abusive practices. They found a critical shortage of alternatives to formal court processing and institutionalization.

Congress responded by enacting the Juvenile Justice and Delinquency Prevention Act of 1974. This legislation was to represent the federal government's ". . . commitment to provide leadership." (U.S. Senate Committee on the Judiciary, 1975:4) It was to serve as a ". . . framework . . ." and a catalyst for better mobilizing the resources of our country ". . . to deal more effectively with juvenile crime and delinquency prevention." (U.S. Senate Committee on the Judiciary 1975:4) "The Act . . . [was] . . . specifically designed to prevent young people from entering our failing juvenile justice system, and to assist communities in developing more sensible and economical alternatives for youngsters already in the juvenile justice system." (U.S. Senate Committee on the Judiciary, 1975:2)

In drafting the Juvenile Justice and Delinquency Prevention Act, its authors recognized that "some youthful offenders must be removed from their communities for society's sake as well as their own." (U.S. Senate Committee on the Judiciary, 1975:2) They felt, however, that the number of such offenders were relatively small, and that ". . . incarceration should be reserved for those youth that cannot be handled by other alternatives."

(U.S. Senate Committee on the Judiciary, 1975:2) It was hoped that the Act would ". . . discourage the use of secure incarceration and detention . . ." (U.S. Senate Committee on the Judiciary, 1975:XXII) and encourage the development and use of ". . . community based alternatives to juvenile detention and correctional facilities." (U.S. Senate Committee on the Judiciary, 1975: XXI)

Clearly, Congress as well as the juvenile justice reformers of the early 1970s, recognized the excessive use and undesirable consequences of institutionalizing youth. It was felt that the Act should mandate the de-institutionalization of all but the most serious offenders as a condition of voluntary participation on the part of states wishing to receive federal funding. But, as with any piece of controversial legislation, compromises had to be made in order to secure its enactment. Consequently, the de-institutionalization mandates were restricted to status offenders and non-offenders. The Act did, however, strongly encourage the development of alternatives for delinquent youth.

This study is primarily concerned with taking stock and reflecting on the de-institutionalization movement within the juvenile justice system. We wish to explore what policy implications have surfaced as a result of this movement. To examine this issue, we assembled and reviewed data from all pertinent national criminal and juvenile justice information systems.

While the data contained in this report are fairly comprehensive and help to further our understanding there are a number of important gaps in our information. For example, there are no reliable data on admissions to detention centers and training schools by race. Also, data on admissions to facilities by offense types are generally unavailable. Staff from the OJJDP and the U.S. Census Bureau have been concerned about these shortcomings and have moved to rectify them by modifying the survey instruments used in the biennial "Children in Custody" survey. These modifications will allow a more comprehensive analysis of the significance of race in juvenile justice decision makling.

Another major gap is the absence of data on juveniles admitted to adult jails. These data are needed to get a complete picture of the numbers of incarcerated youth. Data have been collected regarding the number of juveniles held in adult jails and prisons of a particular day, but comprehensive data on admissions of juveniles to adult correctional facilities are unavailable.

Finally, while there are significant problems with all of the various criminal and juvenile justice information systems, once assembled, we were impressed by what data were available and by the implications these data hold for policy makers. Unfortunately, much of the information that could be helpful has not always been fully accessible in forms either easily understood or usable. These national data sources are important tools for juvenile justice reformers and policy makers. They reveal a sobering picture of the limited achievement of the last decade's reforms. Further, these national data provide a useful array of indicators to stimulate policy evaluations at state and local levels. Such local assessments of juvenile justice reform may encourage a rethinking of juvenile justice and, perhaps, encourage more effective reform strategies.

SOURCES OF DATA

Comprehensive national data about youth crime and its control do not exist. At best, policy analysts can examine only a few independent national data bases to assess national trends. Only a few states such as Utah, Pennsylvania, and Florida have detailed information systems reporting on the flow of youth from arrest to juvenile court disposition. Even these state data bases are relatively new and not easily adapted for research purposes. At present there are only two national data sets from which one can reasonably examine trends to respond to specific policy questions. While these can still produce useful policy data and cues for strategic research opportunities, the analyst must proceed with a healthy respect for the real limitations of available data.

Data On Delinquent Behavior

A first area of concern involves the nature and extent of delinquent behavior

both reported and unreported to law enforcement agencies. This is essentially an unknown area. Only crimes which involve the arrest of a juvenile are recorded at this time. Thus, we may know the number of crimes reported to the police (as reported by the FBI) or the number of reported victimizations (reported in the National Crime Survey), but the proportion of the offenses attributable to youth has not been documented. Official police data do not record crimes by age until a person is taken into custody. Attempts to use the victimization studies such as the National Crime Survey (NCS) to estimate youth crime are limited to: (1) offenses in which the victim actually witnesses the offender, and (2) victim *perceptions* of the offender's age. (McDermott and Hindelang, 1981) These methodological shortcomings cast doubt on the ability of the NCS to yield stable estimates of crime committed by youth.

Still another potential source of national data on the extent of delinquent behavior is the National Youth Survey (NYS) which administers a self-report delinquency questionnaire to a national probability sample of youth. (Elliot, Ageton, and Huizinga, 1980) The NYS was not originally designed to yield national estimates of youth crime but rather to measure the attrition of youth involved in delinquency over a three year period. While it can be adapted to yield national figures on youth crime, the NYS application will require considerable further testing and development of the self report technique. It can yield reliable national data on the extent of youthful criminal behavior.

Arrest Data

Data on the number of youth arrested by police are compiled by the FBI's Uniform Crime Reports (UCR) from approximately 12,000 local and state police agencies across the nation. (Federal Bureau of Investigation, 1980) The UCR classifies offenses into 29 categories. These crime categories are further collapsed into two major categories: Part 1 offenses[1] which are considered to be most serious crimes and the most likely to be reported to police, and Part 2 offenses, which include all other offenses. The UCR also report arrests for juvenile status offenses such as truancy, runaways, ungovernability, etc. Critics of the UCR have pointed out that some Part 2 offenses such as arson may be more serious than Part 1 crimes. Further, there exists variability in the number of police agencies that annually provided data to UCR. While the reporting of Part 1 arrests is reasonably uniform, local practices on reporting Part 2 and status arrests are somewhat less consistent.

Juvenile Court Processing

Juvenile court statistics are gathered by the National Center for Juvenile Justice (NCJJ). (National Center for Juvenile Justice, 1981) Aggregate data are collected from over 80 percent of the nation's juvenile court jurisdictions on: (1) the total number of cases handled, (2) the sex of the youth, and (3) the method of handling (with or without a formal petition). In addition, individual case-based data are collected from states and large jurisdictions supplied juvenile court data from 830 (or 26 percent) of the 3,143 counties in the United States. After a lengthy process of editing to standardize the data elements, the data were analyzed to estimate the rate and characteristics of cases passing through the nation's juvenile court process. While the aggregate data had been collected since 1926, the detailed case-based data were first collected in 1975 with support from OJJDP. The NCJJ case-based data do not report figures for each participating state; only national level statistics are produced. These analyses also include estimates of the nation's use of detention and court dispositions resulting in correctional facility placements. NCJJ's procedures for constructing national estimates based on 26 percent of the nation's juvenile courts are extremely innovative; however, NCJJ warns that the size of sampling errors may be large for more refined data analysis tasks. Thus, small numerical trends must be reviewed with extreme caution.

Juvenile Corrections

The primary national source of data on juvenile corrections is the biennial census on children in public juvenile correctional facilities—known popularly as Children in Custody (CIC). (U.S. Bureau of Census, 1978) Begun in 1971, this series consists of six biennial national surveys administered by the U.S. Census Bureau to all known public juvenile correctional facilities. A special CIC survey was conducted in 1974 to coincide with the implementation of the Juvenile Justice and Delinquency Prevention Act of 1974. In 1979, the survey response rate was 100 percent (1,136 facilities). The response rate has never been lower than 96 percent in any year.

The CIC survey requests data from facility administrators on the number of youth admitted to the facilities, their demographic characteristics, a one-day count of inmates, as well as various budgetary and programmatic facts about each facility. Starting in 1974, survey data were also collected on private juvenile correctional facilities. A major omission of CIC is the number of juveniles held in adult jails. These data, however, are reported as part of the National Census of Jails conducted in 1970 and 1978, and data on juveniles in adult prisons are available for 1978 as part of Abt's monumental study of American prisons and jails. (Abt Associates, 1981)[2]

The CIC series contain a rich source of data about juvenile correctional facilities across the 50 states and the District of Columbia. In most county-by-county level within states. The high response rate as well as preliminary tests of data reliability suggest that CIC holds great potential for future juvenile justice policy research.

How CIC and NCJJ Data Systems Differ

Since the CIC and NCJJ both collect data on detention and placements in correctional facilities, it is useful to examine how these two systems differ from each other. In general, CIC reports a larger universe of activities (i.e., total admissions to a facility per year) and includes admissions caused by agencies in addition to the juvenile court which are not documented through the NCJJ system. Detentions reported by NCJJ include only cases detained while undergoing court processing. Detention admissions in CIC include court-ordered detention, police and other pre-adjudicatory detention, as well as temporary detentions initiated by probation, parole, or other agencies which may not appear in the NCJJ. In 1979, CIC reported 496,526 admissions to detention nationwide, whereas NCJJ reported 249,700 detentions via the court process.

It is important to note that both data systems yield valuable but dramatically different estimates about the use of detention by courts and by other components of the juvenile justice system. Data from NCJJ on court dispositions involving placements in public correctional agencies will differ from CIC statistics on admissions to post-adjudication correctional facilities. CIC juvenile admissions data (for training schools and other commitment facilities) will include initial court commitments, probation and parole violators, inter-facility transfers, and returned AWOLS. Both systems will involve "double-counting" in the sense that individual youths may account for many juvenile court cases or admissions in a year.

Probation and Parole

National data exist for a one day count of the number of juveniles on probation and parole on September 1, 1976. (U.S. Bureau of Census, 1978) This survey documented 328,854 juveniles on probation and 53,347 on parole. No data in this survey are presented on the volume of juvenile admissions to community supervision. Data on client characteristics, on the conditions of supervision, and on the nature of supervising agencies are extremely limited. This lack of data is a significant omission because many studies show that informal and formal probation are the most frequent juvenile justice dispositions. (Krisberg and Austin, 1978) Without more current and comprehensive data on community supervision for juveniles, a major dimension of the juvenile corrections system remains obscured.

Summary

This brief review of available national juvenile justice data sources makes clear the urgent need for better and more reliable data. There are many significant gaps in existing information, and analyses across these data systems must be performed with great care. Our grasp of the statistical contours of juvenile justice in America is not likely to improve greatly in the near future because of the enormous resource investment required to develop more comprehensive data. Plus, the highly decentralized nature of juvenile justice makes centralized and uniform data collection highly problematic. National juvenile justice data that are already available can, however, be employed to guide policy discussions if they are analyzed carefully and cautiously. In the next section, we discuss the key juvenile justice trends reflected in each of the national data sources.

NATIONAL JUVENILE JUSTICE TRENDS

Juvenile Arrest Trends

During the period 1971–1979 the number of youth in age groups under the jurisdiction of the juvenile court declined from 30 million to 28.7 million (a drop of 4.2 percent). In 1971 there were 1.6 million juvenile arrests; by 1974 (the date of the Federal Juvenile Justice and Delinquency Prevention Act), this number had increased 15.7 percent to 1.9 million arrests. From 1974 to 1979, however, total juvenile arrests declined by 3.2 percent to 1.8 million arrests. When considered in proportion to the overall decline in the youth's population, and juvenile arrest rate per 100,000 youth rose by 17.5 percent from 1971 to 1974 but remained unchanged (a decrease of 0.5 percent) from 1974 to 1979.

Arrests for violent offenses also climbed sharply from 1971–1974, leveling off again towards the end of the decade.[3] The rate of violent arrests for 100,000 youth population[4] increased by 36.4 percent from 1971–1974, but grew by only 3.6 percent from 1974–1979. Similarly, the rate of Part 1 arrests rose by one-third in the first part of the 1970s, but increased by a more 0.2 percent in the second half of the decade. The largest declines in arrest figures were for status offenses; with the rate of status arrests dropping by 15.8 percent after 1974. The decline in status offense arrests followed a national effort to reduce the processing of these cases by the juvenile justice system.

Although males are disproportionately represented in all types of juvenile arrests, juvenile arrest rates for males and females were quite similar during the 1970s, mirroring the pattern of sharp increases from 1971–1974 and leveling off from 1974–1979. As described in Table 1, changes in female arrest rates for Part 1 offenses and violent crimes closely paralleled those for males. For example, the female violent arrest rate increased by 35.0 percent over the entire decade; the male violent arrest rate increased by 42.1 percent. From 1974–1979, the rate of female status arrests declined by 13.4 percent, while the male status arrest rate declined by 6.9 percent.

Juvenile Court Trends

As noted earlier, detailed national juvenile court data were first available in 1975 through the NCJJ data base. (see Table 2) In 1975, slightly over 1.4 million cases were disposed of by the nation's juvenile courts. Of this total, 660,867 or 47.0 percent were handled with formal delinquency petitions. From 1975–1979, the rate per 100,000 youth referred to the juvenile court declined by 5.0 percent. In 1979, the proportion of cases handled by petitions was 45.7 percent—virtually identical to the 1975 figure. The rate of cases involving property crimes[5] increased by 17.0 percent from 1975–1979. During this same period, the rate of cases involving crimes against persons[6] was stable (+0.8 percent). By contrast, the rate of status offense cases declined sharply (21.1 percent), a decrease consistent with the decline in arrests for status offenses. Overall, however, both the stability in rates of juvenile court processing and the use of formal petitions do not confirm the hopes of reformers that significant numbers of youth were diverted from formal court processing to other more voluntary community agencies.

Another goal of juvenile justice reformers was to reduce the court's use of detention, partly as a result of the incentives provided by the federal juvenile justice legislation to divert and deinstitutionalize young offenders. Indeed, the rate of detentions per 100,000 youth did decline by 26.9

TABLE 1   Juvenile Arrests by Sex 1971, 1974, 1979

	1971			1974			1979		
	Total Arrests	Arrests Per 100,000	Percent Change 71–74*	Total Arrests	Arrests Per 100,000	Percent Change 74–79*	Total Arrests	Arrests Per 100,000	Percent Change 71–79*
Total Arrests	1,624,310	5414	17.5	1,879,387	6363	−0.5	1,819,673	6329	16.9
Male	1,252,396	4174	18.7	1,463,910	4957	−0.1	1,424,534	4954	18.7
Female	371,914	1240	13.4	415,407	1406	−2.3	395,139	1374	10.8
Part I Arrests	591,909	1973	32.3	771,608	2613	0.2	753,428	2620	32.8
Male	491,076	1637	30.2	630,090	2135	0.3	615,653	2141	30.8
Female	100,833	336	42.4	141,518	479	0	137,775	479	42.5
Status Offense	536,266	1787	7.8	569,481	1928	−15.8	466,885	1624	-9.1
Male	350,966	1170	9.2	377,400	1278	−14.8	313,086	1089	-6.9
Female	185,300	618	5.2	192,081	650	−17.7	153,799	535	−13.4
Violent Arrests	55,093	184	36.4	74,012	251	3.6	74,850	260	41.3
Male	49,214	164	36.0	65,950	223	4.4	66,893	233	42.1
Female	5,879	20	35.0	8,062	27	0	7,957	27	35.0
Eligible Youth Population	30,003,141	—	−1.5	29,534,292	—	-2.6	28,752,877	—	−4.2

SOURCE: Uniform Crime Reports, 1971, 1974, 1979.
* Percent Change denotes change in the juvenile arrest rate per 100,000 youth age 10 to upper age of juvenile court jurisdiction.

Table 2   National Juvenile Court Statistics 1975 and 1979

	1975			1979	
	Total Cases	Cases Per 100,000	Percent Change 75–79	Total Cases	Cases Per 100,000
Cases Disposed Of:	1,406,100	4786	−5.0	1,307,000	4546
With Petition	660,867	2250	−7.7	597,000	2076
Without Petition*	745,233	2537	−2.7	709,800	2569
Status Offense Cases	335,600	1142	−21.1	259,000	901
Property Offense Cases	588,400	2003	17.0	674,200	2345
Person Offense Cases	145,100	494	0.8	143,200	498
Detentions:	349,000	1188	−26.9	249,700	868
Male	245,800	837	−19.5	193,700	674
Female	103,200	351	−44.4	56,000	195
Status Offense Cases	143,000	487	−68.0	44,807	156
Property Offense Cases	108,000	368	4.9	111,100	386
Person Offense Cases	38,200	130	7.7	40,239	140
Eligible Youth Population	29,378,014	—	−2.1	28,752,877	—

*Percent Change denotes change in the juvenile processing rates for 100,000 youth. Population figures are taken from U.S. Census Bureau data for 1970 and 1980.

percent and the female detention rate decreased by 44.4 percent.

Interestingly, NCJJ reported that the rate of detaining status offenders declined by 68.0 percent from 1975–1979. This dramatic decline may well be a direct result of federal policies implemented by OJJDP and its state affiliates. In sharp contrast to the large drop in the status offense detentions however, the detention rates for youth charged with property crimes and person crimes increased during 1975–1979 by 4.9 percent and 7.7 percent, respectively.

Trends In Juvenile Corrections

Admissions to Detention. In 1971 there were 496,526 admissions to detention facilities in the United States. By 1974, total detention admissions increased by 6.5 percent to 529, 075 and then declined by 14.6 percent to 451,810 in 1979. Thus, overall, from 1971–1979 the detention admissions rate per 100,000 youth declined by 5.1 percent, with the most dramatic decline occurring from 1974–1979 (12.3 percent). This 1974–1979 decline is principally accounted for by a drop in admissions of females to detention. Of the 77,265 fewer detention admissions in 1979

compared with 1974, 62,207 or 80.5 percent were females. The drop in the female detention admissions rate was 37.6 percent compared with a 1.4 percent decline in the male detention admissions rate between 1974–1979. Recalling the 15.8 percent drop in the status offense arrest rate from 1974–1979 and the 21.1 percent decline in status offense cases disposed of by juvenile courts from 1975–1979, the sizable decrease in female detention admissions most likely reflects the policies to divert status offenders from the juvenile justice system. Although in general, males are arrested more frequently than females for status offenses, females are more often detained and sent to juvenile correctional facilities for these behaviors. (Chesney-Lind, 1977)

Juveniles Admitted to Training Schools. As shown in Table 3, rates of admissions to training schools were largely unchanged throughout the decade of the 1970s. There were 67,775 training school admissions in 1971; and by 1974, the number of admissions was 67,406. In 1979 there were 65,416 admissions to training schools nationwide—a decline of only 2.9 percent from the admissions reported in 1974. This pattern of stability in national admissions to training schools

TABLE 3   Public Juvenile Detention and Training School Admissions and Expenditures 1971, 1974 1979

	1971			1974			1979		
	Total Admissions	Admissions Per 100,000	Percent Change 71–74*	Total Admissions	Admissions Per 100,000	Percent Change 74–79*	Total Admissions	Admissions Per 100,000	Percent Change 71–79*
Total Admission									
To Detention	496,526	1655	8.2	529,075	1791	−12.3	451,810	1571	−5.1
Male Admissions	349,407	1165	7.9	371,225	1257	−1.4	356,167	1239	6.4
Female Admissions	147,119	490	9.0	157,850	534	−37.6	95,643	333	−32.0
Total Admissions									
To Training Schools	67,775	226	0.9	67,406	228	0.0	65,416	228	0.9
Male Admissions	53,089	177	2.8	53,737	182	8.8	56,972	198	11.9
Female Admissions	14,686	49	−6.1	13,669	46	−37.0	8,444	29	−40.8
Detention Expenditures	$92,110,196	—	41.4	$130,274,470**	—	75.7	$228,848,730	—	148.5
Training School Expenditures	$248,759,346	—	16.9	$290,933,166**	—	37.3	$399,485,111	—	60.6
Eligible Youth Population	30,003,141	—	−1.6	29,534,292	—	−2.6	28,752,877	—	−4.2

*Percent Change denotes change in admissions rate per 100,000 youth.
**1974 Expenditures figures are the average of 1973 and 1975 data.
SOURCE: U.S. Census Bureau, Children in Custody.

actually masks a dramatic decline in the rate of female admissions to training schools. From 1974–1979, the female admissions rate dropped by 37.0 percent, paralleling the decline in female detention admissions. By contrast, the male training school admissions rate *increased* by 8.8 percent. These data lend further support to the view that the accomplishments of the deinstitutionalization movement were largely confined to female status offenders.

Admissions to Private Correctional Facilities. In addition to data on admissions to public juvenile correctional facilities, the CIC collected data on admissions to private correctional facilities beginning in 1974.[7] As shown in Table 4, these figures reveal 42,005 admissions to private facilities in 1974 compared with 49,298 admissions in 1979—an increase of 17.4 percent in total admissions. The rate of male private admissions changed only by 13.0 percent between 1974–1979 compared to a significant increase of 36.0 percent for females, suggesting that females have been transferred from the public correctional system of privately operated facilities. Whether youth are better treated in these private facilities is an issue that demands further investigation.

Correctional Expenditures. National Data sources on juvenile correctional expenditures only report on the operating costs of institutions. They do not report on parole and probation expenditures. Further, since the CIC census of juvenile corrections asks only about operating expenses of facilities; capital improvement, new construction, centralized research, and administrative expenditures are excluded from this analysis. Given these omissions, the following figures on juvenile correctional costs must be viewed as extremely conservative.

In 1971, over $92.1 million were spent on juvenile detention facilities; by 1979, this amount had grown by 148.5 percent to over $228.8 million. Even as detention admissions were declining (by 12.3 percent) between 1974–1979, expenditures for detention rose by 75.7 percent during that same period.

Training school budgets in the United States totaled $248.8 million in 1971, rising to $399.5 million in 1979—an increase of 60.6 percent. Between 1974–1979, when training school admissions remained unchanged, expenditures increased by 37.3 percent. Costs associated with admissions to private correctional facilities are currently not available from national data sources.

TABLE 4   National Juvenile Court Statistics 1975 and 1979

	1975			1979	
	Total Admissions	Admissions Per 100,000	Percent Change 75–79*	Total Admissions	Admissions Per 100,000
Admissions To					
Private Facilities	42,005	142	20.4	49,298	171
Males	27,215	92	13.0	29,771	104
Females	14,790	50	36.0	19,527	68
Admissions To					
Public Facilities	641,857	2,173	−11.0	556,172	1,934
Males	463,247	1,568	−0.8	447,428	1,556
Females	178,610	605	−37.5	108,774	378
Eligible Youth					
Population	29,534,292	—	−2.6	28,752,877	—

Individual State Trends In Juvenile Corrections

While the national-level data on arrests, court processing, and corrections are extremely interesting, they consolidate and therefore mask a broad variety of state and local juvenile justice experiences. For example, forty-four states, voluntarily participate in the 1974 Juvenile Justice Act, received funds: (1) to remove status offenders from secure custody, (2) to separate adults and juveniles in correctional facilities, and (3) to implement certain "advanced techniques" to reduce unnecessary penetration of youth into the juvenile justice system. How these changes impacted specific states and localities is a major public policy question. More complete analyses of inter-jurisdictional juvenile justice data trends may yield better clues to successful strategies for reducing unnecessary youthful incarceration. While it is beyond the scope of this paper fully to examine juvenile justice trends for 51 states[8] or for over 3000 local juvenile court jurisdictions, let us review some examples of this diversity.

State Trends in Detention and Training School Admissions. From 1974–1979, 30 states reported decreases in rates of detention admissions. Fourteen states experienced increased rates of detention admissions, and another seven states[9] did not report detention admissions to CIC because in these jurisdictions, youth are detained in adult jails or other facilities. Wisconsin reported a 66.4 percent decline in its detention admissions rate. Massachusetts and Kentucky experienced drops in detention admissions rate of 51.8 percent and 51.0 percent, respectively. By contrast, Arkansas, Maryland , North Dakota, and South Dakota all showed detention rates that 105.0 percent to 201.8 percent between 1974–1979. Table 5 summarizes these trends by state.

For training school admissions, the states are evenly split. Twenty-five states reported declining rates of training school admissions between 1974–1979 and 25 states reported increases.[10] Vermont experienced a 100 percent decline in its training school admissions rate, while New Mexico, New York, and Texas all reported significant declines in rates of training school admissions during this same period. States reporting sharp increases in training school admission rates include Kentucky, Oregon, Washington, Delaware, and Indiana. Table 6 reports on changes in training school admissions rates for each state.

Trends in Correctional Admissions and Federal Juvenile Justice Policies. A brief examination of individual state trends in rates of admissions to detention centers and training schools yields no obvious patterns. At best these data focus attention on questions for further investigation. One obvious question is the relationship of state trends during 1974–1979 to the amount of funds received from the OJJDP. Combining both special emphasis and formula grant funds awarded

TABLE 5   Changes in Rates of Admissions to Detention by State—1974 and 1979

	1974 to 1979	1974		1979	
	Percent Change	Total Admissions	Admissions Per 100,000	Total Admissions	Admissions Per 100,000
States with Decreasing Detention Rates:					
Wisconsin	−66.4	7,844	1,104	2,499	371
Massachusetts	−51.8	7,928	1,091	3,581	526
Kentucky	−51.0	7,947	1,529	3,841	750
Utah	−42.4	8,698	4,382	5,126	2,525
Alaska	−39.7	309	580	196	350
District of Columbia	−38.3	48,887	5,487	2,545	3,384
Louisiana	−36.6	6,144	1,105	3,793	700
Delaware	−30.4	1,788	2,033	1,192	1,415
Oklahoma	−29.4	3,085	909	2,461	642
Alabama	−27.9	5,348	1,096	4,273	790
Illinois	−25.9	17,262	1,176	11,817	871
Florida	−25.6	33,279	3,331	28,258	2,480
Mississippi	−23.1	3,476	892	2,618	686
Connecticut	−22.4	3,293	960	2,376	745
South Carolina	−22.2	1,287	328	992	256
Georgia	−20.3	17,467	2,607	14,076	2,078
California	−18.9	165,521	5,415	133,285	4,393
Colorado	−18.2	11,628	3,145	9,709	2,572
New Jersey	−17.6	12,996	1,215	10,288	1,001
New York	−16.8	10,468	547	7,981	455
New Mexico	−16.8	4,527	2,366	3,792	1,969
Washington	−16.3	22,279	4,085	18,413	3,420
Michigan	−15.2	19,443	1,528	15,264	1,295
Tennessee	−10.8	14,681	2,353	13,081	2,100
North Carolina	−8.8	3,718	610	3,287	556
Minnesota	−8.1	6,833	1,110	5,876	1,019
Kansas	−7.4	4,338	1,296	3,658	1,199
Arizona	−6.6	9,811	3,026	10,173	2,826
Indiana	−5.2	10,238	1,249	9,180	1,184
Oregon	−3.8	4,431	2,200	7,111	2,116
States with Increasing Detention Rates:					
Pennsylvania	2.6	15,605	901	14,775	925
Iowa	3.0	1,320	304	1,253	313
Texas	10.4	19,129	1,152	21,511	1,271
Missouri	13.5	9,404	1,534	9,905	1,741
Nevada	14.9	3,973	4,948	4,894	5,685
Virginia	15.2	10,373	1,412	11,832	1,626
Hawaii	20.1	1,881	1,513	2,266	1,816
Ohio	22.1	27,538	1,670	30,850	2,039
West Virginia	26.7	1,025	373	1,246	473
Nebraska	50.0	1,152	509	1,599	763
Arkansas	105.0	1,806	578	3,733	1,186
Maryland	179.0	1,207	194	3,282	542
North Dakota	197.3	185	201	609	598
South Dakota	201.8	453	418	1,217	1,260

* Percent change denotes change in rate of admissions per 100,000 youth aged 10 to upper age of Juvenile Court Jurisdiction. Idaho, Maine, Montana, New Hampshire, Rhode Island, Vermont and Wyoming did not report detention admissions one or both years.
SOURCE: U.S. Bureau of Census, *Children in Custody.*

TABLE 6 Changes in Rates of Admissions to Detention by State—1974 and 1979

State	1974 to 1979 Percent* Change	1974 Total Admissions	1974 Admissions Per 100,000	1979 Total Admissions	1979 Admissions Per 100,000
States With Decreasing Training School Rates:					
Vermont	100.0	346	648	0	0
New Mexico	−64.5	933	488	333	173
New York	−58.2	1,725	90	661	38
Texas	−56.9	3,700	223	1,624	96
North Carolina	−47.0	2,740	450	1,408	238
Michigan	−41.5	1,163	91	630	53
Oklahoma	−37.2	843	249	598	156
Florida	−27.5	3,324	333	2,747	241
Colorado	−26.4	560	151	112	116
Illinois	−26.3	2,270	155	1,546	114
South Dakota	−26.0	170	157	421	112
Ohio	−25.0	3,690	224	2,538	168
Rhode Island	−22.4	821	618	605	480
Mississippi	−21.3	861	221	663	174
Minnesota	−18.4	2,404	390	1,837	319
Maryland	−17.0	5,106	822	4,131	682
Tennessee	−16.6	1,962	314	1,633	262
Louisiana	−15.4	1,780	320	1,467	271
New Jersey	−12.9	723	68	605	59
Wisconsin	−10.0	1,269	179	1,082	161
New Hampshire	−9.0	953	854	970	776
Montana	−6.9	416	355	360	331
Connecticut	−6.8	490	143	425	133
Pennsylvania	−2.6	1,446	83	1,300	81
Georgia	−0.7	1,671	249	1,677	248
North Dakota	1.3	165	179	185	182
Idaho	5.8	215	168	231	178
South Carolina	5.8	812	207	851	219
Missouri	11.3	1,192	194	1,231	216
California	12.1	12,201	399	13,573	447
Hawaii	14.7	219	176	252	202
Nevada	15.9	285	355	354	411
Alabama	16.7	517	106	669	124
Maine	24.0	536	362	704	449
Alaska	26.0	993	1,865	1,315	2,249
Virginia	26.5	1,205	164	1,510	208
Arkansas	30.7	659	211	868	276
Utah	31.8	290	146	391	193
Nebraska	44.2	407	180	543	259
West Virginia	58.5	553	201	841	319
Kansas	78.6	526	157	856	281
Arizona	80.8	853	261	1,700	472
Iowa	82.4	662	152	1,112	278
Wyoming	88.1	173	275	358	518
District of Columbia	89.7	959	1,077	1,536	2,043
Indiana	100.2	1,152	140	2,181	281
Delaware	123.8	238	271	510	605
Washington	131.8	378	69	865	161
Oregon	176.3	651	193	1,789	532
Kentucky	717.4	199	38	1,603	313

* Percent change denotes change in rate of admissions per 100,000 youth aged 10 to upper age of Juvenile Court Jurisdiction.
**Massachusetts missing data for 1974.

states from 1975 through 1979, one finds no statistical relationship between OJJDP funds received and progress in reducing rates of detention and training school admissions. The correlation's of OJJDP funds with changing detention and training school rates are $-.08$ and -12, neither of which are statistically significant. Of course, these low correlations cannot be interpreted as measuring the impact of the federal juvenile justice involvement during this period since the only specific deinstitutionalization objective of the 1974 Act involves status offenders and data presented earlier strongly suggest significant progress in removing status offenders from several stages of the juvenile justice system. Yet the null finding (i.e., of no statistical relationship) itself suggests further analyses of the CIC data. For example, the CIC survey reports that public juvenile correctional costs totaled over $842 million in 1979. OJJDP special emphasis and formula grant funds were approximately $75.9 million during that same year. Thus, funds intended to reduce unnecessary incarceration of youth, as well as a number of other congressional goals, represented less than 10 percent of the most conservative estimates of

juvenile correctional facility operational costs. The CIC data also point to the lack of fit between the actual distribution of rates of detention and training school admissions and the block grant funding approach of the Juvenile Justice and Delinquency Prevention Act of 1974.

A block grant funding approach assumes that the distribution of targeted funds is roughly distributed as is the youth population. But examination of individual state variations in rates of admissions to detention and training schools reveals that most admissions are concentrated in a few states, and that often, the less populated jurisdictions have the highest admission rates. For example, in 1979, 29.5 percent of all national detention admissions occurred in California—a state with 10.5 percent of the age/eligible youth population. The top five states in volume of detention admissions (California, Ohio, Florida, Texas, and Washington) accounted for over half the national total volume of detention admissions in 1979. These states, however, received only 24.9 percent of the OJJDP special empasis and formula grant funds. The same pattern holds true for training school admissions in 1979: the top five

TABLE 7 Top 5 States in Volume of Admissions to Detention and Training Schools with OJJDP Special Emphasis and Formula Grants, 1979

State	Admissions				OJJDP Grants			
	Total	Percent of All Admissions	Cumulative Total	Cumulative Percent of All Admissions	Total $	Percent of All $	Cumulative Total $	Cumulative Percent of All $
Admissions to Detention:								
California	133,285	29.5	133,285	29.5%	$6,699,075	8.8	$6,699,075	8.8
Ohio	30,850	6.8	164,135	36.3	3,961,750	5.2	10,660,824	14.0
Florida	28,252	6.3	192,387	42.6	3,180,418	4.2	13,841,242	18.2
Texas	21,511	4.8	213,898	47.4	3,797,000	5.0	17,638,242	23.2
Washington	18,413	4.1	232,311	51.5	1,295,000	1.7	18,933,242	24.9
Admissions to Detention, 51 States	—	—	451,810	100.0	—	—	75,933,261	100
Admissions to Training Schools:								
California	13,573	20.7	13,573	20.7	$6,699,075	8.8	$6,699,075	8.8
Maryland	4,131	6.3	17,704	27.0	1,192,000	1.6	7,891,074	10.4
Florida	2,747	4.2	20,451	31.2	3,180,418	4.2	11,071,492	14.6
Ohio	2,538	3.9	22,989	35.1	3,961,750	5.2	15,033,242	19.8
Indiana	2,181	3.3	25,170	38.4	1,578,000	2.1	16,611,242	21.9
Admissions to Training Schools, 51 States	—	—	65,416	100.0	—	—	75,933,261	100.0

SOURCE: U.S. Bureau of Census, *Children In Custody* Series.

states—California, Maryland, Florida, Ohio, and Indiana—accounted for 38.4 percent of all admissions but received only 21.9 percent of the OJJDP funds (See Table 7).

If one considers the highest rates of admissions to detention and training schools, the discrepancy between high rate jurisdictions and block grant allocations is even more pronounced. In 1979, states with the top 15 rates of admissions received 33.6 percent of the funds. The top fifteen states in training school admission rates reported 46.5 percent of all training school admissions in 1979 but accounted for only 18.8 percent of OJJDP grant funds in that same year. (See Tables 8A and 8B). Potential policy implications of these findings will be discussed later.

State Variations in Detention and Training School Admissions Rates. The analysis of admission rates and OJJDP funds allocations surfaced an even more profound research and policy question: What accounts for the large differences between states in rates of admissions to detention and training schools? Tables 9A and 9B report the top ten states in rates of detention and training school admissions for 1971, 1974, and 1979. These data show that, with few exceptions, the top states

in admissions have been consistent across the decade. Indeed, the rank ordering of state rates of detention and training schools admissions were essentially stable over the period 1971–1979.

Data gathered in the 1979 CIC survey also permit a view of the diversity of uses to which corrections facilities are put. For example, we found that 16 states detained 9,069 youth in training schools in 1979. Likewise, 14 states reported 13,323 admissions to detention centers on a commitment status. In California alone, 10,142 admissions or 7.6 percent of all detention admissions were for purposes of a post-adjudication commitment rather than temporary custody during court processing. These findings allowed us in Table 10 to recompute those 1979 state detention and training school admission rates that reflect a policy of using detention as temporary holding facilities and training schools as post-adjudication placement facilities.

Next, we attempted a very tentative exploration of factors that might account for variation in state rates of detention and training school admissions using 1979 CIC data. Multiple regression techniques were

TABLE 8A　　Top 15 States in Rate of Admissions to Detention with OJJDP Special Emphasis and Formula Grants, 1979

State	Admissions					OJJDP Grants			
	Rate Per 100,000	Total	Percent of All Admissions	Cumulative Total	Cumulative Percent	Total Grants	Percent of Total	Cumulative Total	Cumulative Percent
Detention Admissions:									
Nevada	5685	4,894	1.1	4,894	1.1	$686,998	0.9	$686,998	0.9
California	4393	133,285	29.5	138,179	30.6	6,699,074	8.8	7,386,072	9.7
Washington	3420	18,413	4.1	156,592	34.7	1,295,000	1.7	8,681,072	11.4
District of Columbia	3384	2,545	0.6	159,137	35.3	225,000	0.3	8,906,072	11.7
Arizona	2825	10,173	2.3	169,310	37.6	855,880	1.1	9,761,952	12.8
Colorado	2572	9,709	2.1	179,019	39.7	1,519,345	2.0	11,281,297	14.8
Utah	2525	5,126	1.1	184,145	40.8	430,000	0.6	11,711,297	15.4
Florida	2480	28,252	6.3	212,397	47.1	3,180,418	4.2	14,891,715	19.6
Oregon	2116	7,111	1.6	219,508	48.7	644,000	0.8	15,535,715	20.4
Tennessee	2100	13,081	2.9	232,589	51.6	1,204,000	1.6	16,739,715	22.0
Georgia	2078	14,076	3.1	246,665	54.7	2,239,798	2.9	18,979,513	24.9
Ohio	2039	30,850	6.8	277,515	61.5	3,916,750	5.2	22,941,263	30.1
New Mexico	1969	3,792	0.8	281,307	62.3	386,000	0.5	23,327,263	30.6
Hawaii	1816	2,266	0.5	283,573	62.8	268,000	0.4	23,595,263	31.0
Missouri	1741	9,905	2.2	293,478	65.0	1,948,850	2.6	25,544,113	33.6
Detention Admissions 51 States	1571	—	100.0	451,810	100.0	—	100.0	75,933,261	100.0

SOURCE: U.S. Bureau of Census, *Children in Custody* Series.

TABLE 8B   Top 15 States in Rate of Admissions to Training Schools with OJJDP Special Emphasis and Formula Grants, 1979

State	Admissions					OJJDP Grants			
	Rate Per 100,000	Total	Percent of All Admissions	Cumulative Total	Cumulative Percent	Total Grants	Percent of Total	Cumulative Total	Cumulative Percent
Training Schools:									
Alaska	2349	1,315	2.0	1,315	2.0	$225,000	0.3	$225,000	0.3
District of Columbia	2043	1,536	2.3	2,851	4.3	225,000	0.3	450,000	0.6
New Hampshire	777	970	1.5	3,821	5.8	525,000	0.7	975,000	1.3
Maryland	683	4,131	6.3	7,952	12.1	1,192,000	1.6	2,167,000	2.9
Delaware	605	510	0.8	8,462	12.9	225,000	0.3	2,392,000	3.2
Oregon	532	1,789	2.7	10,251	15.6	644,000	0.8	3,036,000	4.0
Wyoming	518	358	0.5	10,609	16.1	0	0	3,036,000	4.0
Rhode Island	480	605	0.9	11,214	17.0	252,000	0.3	3,288,000	4.3
Arizona	472	1,700	2.6	12,914	19.6	855,880	1.1	4,143,880	5.4
Maine	449	704	1.1	13,618	20.7	313,000	0.4	6,456,880	5.8
California	447	13,573	20.7	27,191	41.4	6,699,074	8.8	11,155,954	14.6
Nevada	411	354	0.5	27,545	41.9	686,998	0.9	11,842,952	15.5
Montana	331	360	0.5	27,905	42.4	227,000	0.3	12,069,952	15.8
West Virginia	319	841	1.3	28,746	43.7	513,000	0.7	12,582,952	16.5
Minnesota	319	1,837	2.8	30,583	46.5	1,736,716	2.3	14,319,668	18.8
Training Admissions 51 States	228	—	100.0	65,416	100.0	—	100.0	75,933,261	100.0

SOURCE: U.S. Bureau of Census, *Children in Custody* Series.

TABLE 9A   Top 10 States in Rate of Admissions to Detention: 1971, 1974, 1979

1971		1974		1979	
State	Rate Per 100,000	State	Rate Per 100,000	State	Rate Per 100,000
1. Nevada	6611	District of Columbia	5487	Nevada	5685
2. District of Columbia	5626	California	5415	California	4393
3. California	5114	Nevada	4948	Washington	3420
4. Florida	3330	Utah	4382	District of Columbia	3384
5. Washington	3013	Washington	4085	Arizona	2826
6. Arizona	2935	Florida	3331	Colorado	2572
7. Georgia	2574	Colorado	3145	Utah	2525
8. Oregon	2496	Arizona	3026	Florida	2480
9. Colorado	2275	Georgia	2607	Oregon	2116
10. Delaware	2200	New Mexico	2366	Tennessee	2100

SOURCE: U.S. Department of Census, *Children in Custody* Series.

employed using such independent variables as violent arrest rates, Part 1 property arrest rates, the bed capacity of each state, and teenage unemployment rates. For rates of detention admissions, these four independent variables explain 81.4 percent of the variation among the states. The number of detention beds per 100,000 youth population explains 76.8 percent of the variation in detention admission rates, with the rate of Part 1 property arrests adding only another 4.1 percent in explanatory power. Neither the violent arrest rate nor the teenage unemployment rates explain much variation in state detention admissions rates.

For training school admission rates, on the other hand, the same independent variables account for 32.9 percent of the state variations. Roughly, two-thirds of the variation among states in training school admis-

TABLE 9B   Top 10 States in Rate of Admissions Training Schools 1971, 1974, 1979

1971		1974		1979	
State	Rate Per 100,000	State	Rate Per 100,000	State	Rate Per 100,000
1. District of Columbia	2313	Alaska	1865	Alaska	2349
2. Alaska	1980	District of Columbia	1077	District of Columbia	2043
3. New Hampshire	736	New Hampshire	854	New Hampshire	777
4. Delaware	666	Maryland	822	Maryland	682
5. Vermont	645	Vermont	648	Delaware	605
6. Nevada	510	Rhode Island	618	Oregon	532
7. Rhode Island	499	New Mexico	488	Wyoming	518
8. Wisconsin	434	North Carolina	450	Rhode Island	480
9. North Carolina	402	California	399	Arizona	472
10. Florida	364	Minnesota	390	Maine	449

SOURCE: U.S. Department of Census, *Children in Custody* Series

TABLE 10   Top 15 States in Rates of Admission to Detention and Training Schools in 1979. Commitments to Detention Excluded. Training School Detainees Added to Detention

State	Rate Per 100,000 Youth	Total Admissions
Detention Admissions:		
District of Columbia	4,875	3,666
Nevada	4,846	4,896
California	4,058	123,143
Washington	3,408	18,348
Arizona	2,826	10,163
Alaska	2,539	1,421
Utah	2,525	5,126
Florida	2,480	28,252
Colorado	2,419	9,133
Oregon	2,116	7,111
Tennessee	2,100	13,081
Georgia	2,063	13,997
Ohio	2,030	30,720
New Mexico	1,969	3,793
Hawaii	1,838	2,266
All States	1,552	446,057
Training School Admissions:		
Delaware	605	510
District of Columbia	552	415
Oregon	532	1,789
Wyoming	518	358
Arizona	473	1,700
California	447	13,573
Nevada	351	354
Montana	331	360
Kentucky	287	1,472
New Hampshire	283	353
Arkansas	276	1,700
Louisiana	271	1,467
Minnesota	268	1,542
Tennessee	262	1,633
Georgia	248	1,677
All States	196	56,347

sion rates is not explained by serious youth crime, youth unemployment, or the availability of beds. Of these factors, the number of training school beds per 100,000 youth population accounts for 27.0 percent of the variation in rates of training school admissions or 82.1 percent of all the variation that is explained by the selected independent variables. Part 1 property arrest rates separately explain 4.5 percent of the variation among the states in training school admission rates. Neither teenage employment nor violent arrest rates significantly boost our explanatory ability.

Summary of Juvenile Justice Trends

Data on juvenile arrests, court processing, and admissions to juvenile correctional facilities offer important information to assess juvenile justice policy directions of the last decade. Most striking is the progress in reducing the involvement of status offenders within the juvenile justice system between 1974–1979. Less encouraging is that similar progress was not achieved in the case of delinquent offenders. Moreover, the primary consequence of removing status offenders from the juvenile justice system was the large decline in female admissions to public correctional facilities while male admissions either remained stable or actually increased from 1974–1979. Also of importance is the leveling off of rates of Part 1 juvenile arrests from 1974–1979: This directly contradicts public perceptions of a steady and alarming increase in serious youth crime.

Preliminary analysis of states trends in rates of admissions to detention and training schools revealed a complex pattern of increases and decreases largely unrelated to the distribution of OJJDP funds. Indeed, juvenile correctional admissions are highly concentrated in a few states. An exploratory attempt to explain the large variations in state rates of correctional admissions suggested the most of that variation in detention admissions could be explained by the number of detention beds per 100,000 youth population. For training school admission rates, the number of beds per 100,000 youth population is also the most powerful explanatory

variable; but nearly two-thirds of the variation in state training school admissions is not explained by bed availability, rates of juvenile arrests for serious crimes, or youth unemployment. Future research should analyze the determinants of the wide disparities between states in rates of detention and training school admissions. Other macro-level variables should be examined and more in-depth micro-level studies should be conducted to understand better the link between availability of beds and admissions to detention centers and training schools.

POLICY CONSIDERATIONS

The data presented in this paper permit a starting point for a thorough and systematic rethinking of juvenile justice. Yet even this first level of analysis suggests a number of immediate policy issues. In our opinion, policy considerations requiring urgent attention are as follows:

1. The removal of status offenders and non-offenders from secure institutions has been one of the more successfull juvenile justice policy thrusts of the 1970s. Reports from state juvenile justice advisory committees, testimony delivered before Congressional committees, and the finding of various studies attest to the success of this initiative. Kobrin and Klein, for example, in their national study of status offender programs, reported significant reduction in status offender admissions to detention centers and training schools. (Kobrin and Klein, 1982) The United States Census Bureau reported a sharp reduction of the number of status offenders held in secure facilities on a particular day in 1979 as compared to the same date in 1977. (U.S. Department of Justice, 1980) The findings of this study are consistent with those of others. There has, for instance, been a substantial decline in the number and rate of female admissions to detention centers and training schools. Because females made up the vast majority of the status offenders and non-

offenders admitted to secure facilities, the decline in female admissions provides additional documentation for what has been achieved. Now, steps must be taken to ensure that the progress that has been made will not be reversed.

2. While the policy thrust to remove status offenders and non-offenders from secure institutions has proven to be a major success, the overall results with respect to de-institutionalization have been far less than what reformers had hoped for. As noted earlier, the decline in the rate of admissions to detention centers from 1971 to 1979 was a modest 5.1 percent. The decline in detention admission rates from 1974 to 1979 was 12.3 percent. Considering the fact that upwards of 40 percent of all youth detained in the early 1970s were status offenders and non-offenders, and considering that large numbers of youth accused of minor and petty delinquent offenses were also detained, the reductions are, at best, disappointing. (U.S. House of Representatives, 1981)

The rate of admissions to training schools has remained relatively constant throughout the decade. There were substantial reductions in the rates of female admissions while rates of male admissions increased. The decline in the rates of female admission were essentially offset by the increases for males.

As stated earlier, one of the major purposes of the Juvenile Justice and Delinquency Prevention Act was to provide states and localities with leadership and resources for the development of programs ". . . to divert juveniles from traditional juvenile justice systems and to provide critically needed alternatives to institutionalization." (Gough, 1976) Implicit in this policy was the assumption that the availability of alternatives would result in reducing input into the system.

Unfortunately, with few exceptions, this has proven not to be the case. Diversion and alternative programs have mushroomed while detention admission rates declined only slightly and training

school admission rates not at all. In fact, many leading juvenile justice researchers and practitioners maintain that one of the unanticipated consequences of the proliferation of alternative programs has been a widening and strengthening act of the "net of social control." (Haugen, 1982)

This study has reported a statistical relationship between correctional admission rates and the number of detention and training school beds per 100,000 youth population. Significantly, admissions rates are relatively unaffected by juvenile arrests and teenage unemployment rates. If detention and training school beds are being used for purposes other than public safety and treatment, this creates a tremendous and perhaps unnecessary expense for taxpayers. This finding is strikingly similar to that of Poulin and his colleagues. (Poulin et al., 1980)

In light of these results, states and localities should adopt and aggressively pursue polices seeking to limit the use of detention and training school placements including, in some instances, closing down such facilities. The potential waste of limited public funds to be spent on the unnecessary confinement of youth becomes even more apparent when considered in light of projected declines in the eligible youth population as well as current fiscal realities.

3. There is a pressing need to develop strategies both to inform and educate the public about the realities of the juvenile crime problem. At present, a huge gap separates the trends in juvenile crime from the public's perception of the problem. The best available evidence suggests that the rate of serious juvenile crime, and violent youth crime in particular, has been relatively stable since the mid 1970s. In contrast, the public perceives that serious juvenile crime has been increasing at a steady and alarming rate. One can hardly expect the development of sound policies with respect to preventing and controlling youth crime

unless and until the public's perception is brought more into line with the reality of the situation.

4. Enormous variation exists between the states in their rates of admissions to detention centers and training schools. These variations have persisted over time and are largely unexplained arrest factors. Needless to say, this disparity raises serious legal and public policy questions regarding due process, equal protection, and the exercise of discretion in the juvenile justice system.

More immediately, the large disparities between the states suggest a need to exert greater monitoring and regulation over discretionary decision making. They further suggest a need to develop mechanisms for the implementation of such things as national standards, dispostional guidelines, and legislative reform.

The problems in juvenile justice are so deep-seated and national in scope that the federal government must continue to play an active role in providing assistance to state and local units of government and public and private agencies and organizations. Accordingly, the federal government should continue:

a. To promote, encourage, and support juvenile justice research. Most importantly, the federal government can play an important role in assisting states and localities in the application of research findings to policy development, in the upgrading of practices, and in program development

b. To collect, analyze, and disseminate data on the juvenile justice system.

c. To serve as an information clearing house and disseminate pertinent data, information, and studies to individuals and organizations throughout the country.

d. To provide technical assistance and consultation.

5. The primary method for distributing funds under the Juvenile Justice and Delinquency Prevention Act is through the formula grant program. This method is essentially a block grant program to states with funds distributed on a per capita youth population basis. The funds can be used in a flexible manner for the development of ". . . more effective education, training, research, prevention, diversion, treatment, and rehabilitation programs in the area of juvenile justice and programs to improve the juvenile justice system." (U.S. Senate committee on the Judiciary, 1975)

The distribution of funds on a per capita youth population basis is an equitable and politically acceptable method for allocating resources. However, this approach has major deficiencies with respect to furthering the goals of de-institutionalization.

Under the block grant system, the states with the largest youth populations receive the bulk of the funds. But with a few notable exceptions, the larger states are not the ones with the highest rates of admissions to detention centers and training schools. In other words, if the goal is to reduce incarceration of youths, the block grant approach does not target resources to where the needs are greatest.

Also, it is clear that the excessive use of detention on the part of a few states is ". . . an enduring phenomenon resistant to change." (Poulin et al., 1980) For example, the states with the highest rates in 1979, were, by and large, the states with the highest rates in 1974 and in 1971.

These findings suggest that the use of block grant strategy as a means of promoting de-institutionalization should be carefully re-examined. Such an assessment should consider the following:

• Can federal fiscal funding incentives be used to bring about substantial changes in state and local policies and practices with respect to de-institutionalization?

• Can resources be targeted to where the needs are greatest? If resources can be targeted, it must be done in such a way as not to appear to serve as an incentive or reward to states with higher rates of incarceration.

6. De-institutionalization polices must be broadened to take into account the interrelatedness of the juvenile justice, child welfare, mental health, and the newly emerging chemical dependency and private youth residential systems. Paul Lerman was one of the first to point out in a systematic way that one gets a distorted view of the impact of de-institutionalization policies by focusing solely on the juvenile system. It seems that ". . . there has emerged, in an unplanned fashion, a new youth-in-trouble system that includes old and new institutions from . . . juvenile correction, child welfare, . . . mental health" (Lerman, 1980:282) and chemical dependency. Lerman suggested that gains made in de-institutionalizing juveniles in the justice system could well be offset by corresponding increases in these other systems. While an assessment of the juvenile institutional trends in the child welfare, mental health, and chemical dependency systems is well beyond the scope and resources of this study, some data supporting Lerman's insights were collected. As reported earlier, there has been a significant increase in female admissions to private correctional settings.

In the state of Minnesota, which ranked 15th in the rate of admissions to training schools in 1979, data were collected at the state and local levels with respect to placements in all of the various youth-caring systems. While is appears that Minnesota's youth-caring systems are plagued with some of the same record keeping and information system problems commonly found elsewhere, the data show a tremendous growth in the numbers of youth placed in residential treatment settings, particularly on a "voluntary" basis. Specifically,

a. In 1976, there were 1,123 juveniles admitted to in-patient psychiatric settings in private hospitals in the Minneapolis/St. Paul Metropolitan Area. They accounted for 46,718 patient days. By 1980 the number of admissions had grown to 1,775, and they account for 74,201 patient days. (Mental Health Data Appendix, 1980)

b. In 1980, there were an estimated 3000 to 4000 juveniles admitted to inpatient chemical dependency treatment programs. Although it is unknown how may juveniles were admitted to such programs in the early 1970s, it is generally assumed that the numbers were substantially less because there were few chemical dependency residential treatment facilities at that time.[11]

c. Between fiscal years 1973 and 1981, the Minnesota Department of Public Welfare reported a substantial increase in the number of juveniles placed in group homes and residential treatment centers for the emotionally disturbed.[12]

In Minnesota, the growth in the number of out of home placements, the reason and methods of referral, and the ultimate impact of these placements on youth raise significant policy questions. One can hypothesize that a "hidden" or private juvenile correctional system has rapidly evolved for disruptive or "acting out" youth who are no longer processed by the public juvenile justice control agencies. Moreover this second system may be vastly expanding the net of youth experiencing some kind of institutional control. The dimensions and nature of this second system of juvenile control should be a major component of future research agendas at both state and federal levels.

7. Any examination of the interrelationship between the various youth-caring systems should take into account the various public and private methods of financing services. In addition to the traditional public and quasi-public funding sources, consideration should be given to the role

and impact of funds emanating from the private health care system.

The private sector has been assuming an increasingly larger role in paying for costs of residential care. Because payments are made through third party reimbursement as part of health insurance coverage, little is known about the nature and extent of services provided and the total dollar amounts involved.

The area of chemical dependency can serve as an example of the potential implications of the role of the private sector. At present, there are 17 states with legislation mandating that private health care insurance provide reimbursement for the cost of chemical dependency treatment as part of their programs. There are some who feel that such requirements serve as strong incentives for promoting the use of in-patient care. They also feel that they are important factors contributing to the escalating costs of health care generally.

8. There is a need to collect comprehensive and reliable data on an ongoing basis concerning juveniles admitted to adult jails and local lock-ups. Rosemary Sarri, in 1974, noted that "an accurate account of the extent of juvenile jailing in the United States does not exist." (Sarri, 1974:4) That statement is just as true today as it was then. Hopefully, the collection of such data could be made part of an existing national criminal or juvenile justice data gathering system. Efforts must also be undertaken to collect data on the "hidden" juvenile justice system.

CONCLUSION

Rethinking juvenile justice involves a process of posing policy questions and reviewing the best available data to formulate answers. It also requires a candid confrontation with both the successes and failures of past reform efforts. But this reassessment may produce new guidelines for more effective reform strategies.

We have learned that available data sources contain important findings that can be used by policy makers and reformers. But there are many other juvenile justice policy concerns not readily answered by available national data. For example, our review of juvenile justice information sources illustrated how little is known about the personal characteristics of the nearly half million children who are annually confined in public juvenile correctional facilities. Not much more is known about youth confined in adult prisons and jails. We lack even basic information about the consequences of juvenile incarceration in terms of public safety. Much more should be known about the impacts of these incarceration experiences on young lives.

The goal of rethinking juvenile justice is to help sustain the reform thrust of the 1970s. Both the goals and strategies of that movement must be carefully reexamined and re-evaluated. Likewise, more analysis should be given to the extreme resistance of the juvenile justice system to constructive reform approaches. This rethinking is not a mere intellectual exercise, it is critical to achieving the unfinished agenda of juvenile justice reform.

Acknowledments

Extensive data retrieval, literature searches, and computational services were provided by Paul Litsky, Theresa Costello, and Dan Haugen. Data for this report were generously provided by staff of the Uniform Crime Reports, National Center for Juvenile Justice, and U.S. Census Bureau. In several instances special data requests for previously unpublished data were provided on short notice. We would especially like to commend Paul Zolbe of the FBI, Rick Meyer and Jim Stephens of the Census Bureau and Howard Snyder of NCJJ.

Helpful suggestions about the strengths and limitations of the data were provided by Charles Laurer and Buddy Howell of OJJDP and Hunter Jurst of NCJJ. Valuable advice for data analysis and interpretation came from Ken Polk, Jim Austin, Solomon Kobrin, Lloyd

Ohlin, Robert Coates, Rosemary Sarri, Delbert Elliott, Brad Smith, Paul Demuro, Jack Calhoun, Robert Figlio, Nancy Anderson, John Korbelick, Jerome Beker, Tom Dewar, Barbara Knudson, Barry Feld, and David Hollister.

Typing and production of graphs were performed by Christy Lord, Jan Casteel, and Dawn Saito.

Finacial support for the research was provided by the Northwest Area Foundation. The Spring Hill Center, the Dayton-Hudson Foundation and the Northwest Area Foundation provided support for sharing and making the study findings available.

Notes

1. Part 1 offenses include criminal homicide, forcible rape, robbery, aggravated assault, burglary, larceny, and auto theft.

2. A National Census of Jails were completed in 1982 but the sampling approach yields nationwide estimates of juveniles held in adult jails but not state-by-state figures.

3. Violent arrests include homicide, rape, robbery, and aggravated assault.

4. Rates are computed for those youth ages 10 to the maximum age of original juvenile court jurisdiction in each state. Adjustments were made if states changed their ages of juvenile court jurisdictions.

5. Property offenses include burglary, auto theft, larceny, vandalism, arson and trespassing.

6. NCJJ defines crime against persons as the UCR violent offenses plus simple assault.

7. Data were also collected on admissions to private shelter facilities but these are excluded from our analysis because these facilities mostly house dependent and neglected youth as well as some status offenders.

8. For this analysis the District of Colombia is treated as a state.

9. Idaho, Maine, Montana, New Hampshire, Rhode Island, Vermont, and Wyoming.

10. Massachusetts failed to report training school admissions in 1973 and 1974 but began reporting these again in 1975.

11. Letter from Cynthia Turner, Ph, D., Director, Planning, Research and Evaluation, State of Minnesota, Department of Public Welfare, Chemical Dependency Program Division, November 6, 1981.

12. The Department of Public Welfare classifies admissions to non-correctional facilities by facility type and by funding category. Funding categories represent more conservative indices of placement trends. Counts within one funding category, emotionally disturbed children, generally include placements in group homes and residential treatment centers, although some similar placements are made under other funding categories. Nevertheless data for the emotionally disturbed category indicate that in fiscal year 1973, 464 placements were funded. In fiscal year 1981, 1959 placements were funded.

References

ABT ASSOCIATES
1981 *American Prisons and Jails.* National Institute of Justice, Washington, D.C.

CHESNEY-LIND, M.
1977 "Judicial Paternalism and the Female Status Offender: Training Women to Know Their Place." *Crime and Delinquency*, April :121–30.

ELLIOTT, D.S., S.S. AGETON, AND D. HUIZINGA
1989 *The National Youth Survey.* Behavioral Research Institute, Boulder, Colorado.

FEDERAL BUREAU OF INVESTIGATION
1980 *Uniform Crime Reports* 1979. U.S. Government Printing Office, Washington, D.C.

GOUGH, A.R.
1976 *Beyond Control: Status Offenders in the Juvenile Court.* Ballinger, Boston, Massachusetts.

HAUGEN, D.
1982 "*Decriminalization.*" University of Minnesota, Minneapolis, Minnesota, unpublished.

KOBRIN, S. AND M. W. KLEIN
1982 *National Evaluation of the Deinstitutionalization of Status Offenders Programs—Executive Summary.* Social Science Research Institute, University of Southern California, Los Angeles, California.

KRISBERG, B. AND J. AUSTIN
1978 *The Children of Ishmael.* Mayfield, Palo Alto, California.

LERMAN, P.
1980 "Trends and Issues in Deinstitutionalization of Youths in Trouble." *Crime and Delinquency*, July 282.

MCDERMOTT, J.M. AND M.J. HINDELANG
1981 *Juvenile Criminal Behavior in the United States: Its Trends and Patterns.* Office of Juvenile Justice and Delinquency Prevention, Washington, D.C.

METROPOLITAN HEALTH BOARD
1980 *Mental Health Index.* Minneapolis, Minnesota.

NATIONAL CENTER FOR JUVENILE JUSTICE
1981 *Delinquency 1978: United States Estimates of Cases Processed by Courts with Juvenile Court Jurisdiction.* Pittsburgh, Pennsylvania.

POULIN, J.E. ET AL.
1980 "Juveniles in Detention Centers and Jails: An Analysis of State Violations during the Mid 1970's." *Reports of National Juvenile Justice Assessment Centers*, U.S. Government Printing Office, Washington, D.C.

SARRI, R.
1974   *Under Lock and Key: Juveniles in Jails and Detention*. National Association of Juvenile Corrections, Ann Arbor, Michigan.

UNITED STATES BUREAU OF THE CENSUS
1978   *Children in Custody*. U.S. Government Printing Office, Washington, D.C.

UNITED STATES BUREAU OF THE CENSUS
1978   *State and Local Probation and Parole Systems*. U.S. Government Printing Office, Washington D.C.

UNITED STATES DEPARTMENT OF JUSTICE
1980   *Children in Custody: Advance Report on the 1979*

Census of Public Juvenile Facilities. Office of Juvenile Justice and Delinquency Prevention, U.S. Government Printing Office, Washington, D.C.

UNITED STATES HOUSE OF REPRESENTATIVES, COMMITTEE ON EDUCATION AND LABOR
1981   *Compilation of the Juvenile Justice Act*. U.S. Government Printing Office, Washington, D.C.

UNITED STATES SENATE COMMITTEE ON THE JUDICIARY
1975   *Ford Administration Stifles Juvenile Justice Policy*. U.S. Government Printing Office, Washington, D.C.

QUESTIONS FOR DISCUSSION

1. List and discuss the various ways that national data on delinquent behavior are collected and disseminated. Which of these sets of data may contain the most accurate data? Why?

2. In your own words, discuss the eight policy recommendations the authors suggest to improve juvenile justice.

3. Which, if any, of the policy recommendations from this article may have no effect on the quality of juvenile justice? Why?

APPLICATIONS

1. Beyond the recommendations presented in this article, what other improvements might we make in juvenile justice with regard to achieving decreases in juvenile delinquency?

2. Some experts would argue that improvements in the justice system will have no impact on juvenile delinquency, but rather will only improve the quality of justice. The justice system only responds "after the fact" to the commission of a delinquent act. The causes of delinquency are based in the society, and it is in the society that the solutions to the delinquency will be found. Do you agree or disagree with this line of reasoning. Why?

KEY TERMS

biennial occurring every two years.

determinants elements that identify the nature of something or that fix or condition an outcome.

disseminate to disperse throughout.

emanate to spring up or come out of a source.

monumental highly significant or outstanding.

pertinent being clearly relevant to the matter at hand.

proliferation reproduction or increase in number.

31

Juvenile Justice and the Blind Lady

Hunter Hurst

Louis W. McHardy

Roscoe Pound called it the highest form of justice. That was 1940 and Mr. Pound was referring to the individualized justice of that bold social experiment known as the juvenile court. In 1967, Justice Fortas of the U.S. Supreme Court called it the worst of both worlds. Mr. Fortas was also talking about the individualized justice of the juvenile court. In 1989, writing for the majority in *Heath A. Wilkins* v. *Missouri,* Justice Scalia said that the Missouri juvenile court's certification procedure ensured individualized consideration of the maturity and moral responsibility of a 16-year-old youth before he was required to stand trial as an adult. The U.S. Supreme Court's determination in this regard was pivotal in its decision to uphold the death penalty imposed on Wilkins by the State of Missouri.

One hundred and twenty years after its informal founding in Suffolk County, Massachusetts, and 92 years after its formal founding in Cook County, Illinois, the U.S. juvenile court and the juvenile justice system it anchors are alive and in many ways surprisingly robust, but the ground is rapidly undulating under its foundations. As we enter the twenty-first century, there are more than a few pressing issues to be resolved in our juvenile justice system.

MISSION

Of the 38 states that articulate a mission for the juvenile court, 37 still assert acting in the interest of the child as the state's primary means of responding to the children who come within its purview, but change is in the wind (Szymanski, 1991a). Arizona, a few years back, passed the so-called PIC Act requiring juvenile courts to impose Progressively Increasing Consequences (PIC) on repeat delinquent offenders. Conceptually, this notion of progressively increasing consequences is more akin to the juvenile court's original concept of "individualized justice" than it is to the criminal court's concept of punishment proportionate to the harm caused by the criminal act. But it does not seem to be exactly what the founders had in mind when they spoke of tailored dispositions that were in the interest of the child. Other states, such as Utah, California, and Minnesota, have departed much farther from tradition by requiring that offenders be held accountable and/or responsible for their criminal law violations, while taking care to avoid any taint of criminality. None of these statutes are very eloquent on just what courts are supposed to do to avoid the taint of criminality while holding juveniles responsible for their "criminal behavior," and as might be expected the issue has become more than a little clouded, as exemplified by the recent actions of the Texas legislature authorizing juvenile courts to

"Juvenile Justice and the Blind Lady," *Federal Probation*, 55:2 (June 1991), pp. 63–68. Reprinted by permission of the publisher and the authors.

impose prison sentences of up to 30 years for certain classes of offenders. Texas courts are also *presumably* supposed to impose these periods of confinement while acting in the best interest of the state's children. Of course, it is at least arguable that it may be in the best interest of the child to sentence him to 30 years in prison, but the logic begins to get brittle somewhere past the age of majority since adult/criminal offenders whom courts sentence to prison for punishment rarely serve 30 years.

If the trend continues in the direction of holding youth accountable for their criminal law violations, we will soon need to re-examine our assumptions about the "criminal responsibility" of juveniles. We cannot continue to hold persons accountable for their criminal behavior without finding them culpable and therefore criminally responsible for their actions. If indeed juveniles are to be held criminally responsible for their behavior, the preferred forum for achieving that goal appears to be the criminal court—the medium that has always been available on a case-by-case waiver or transfer basis, but one that is now increasingly being prescribed by legislatures.

The Protective Side of the Mission

Although ambivalence shrouds the court's mission for delinquents, no such uncertainty exists with regard to neglected, dependent, and abused children. The decade of the eighties has witnessed an unprecedented movement of neglected children into the courtroom. The engine for this movement has been the rapidly disintegrating American family and Public Law 96-272, which requires courts or a court-approved tribunal to periodically review children in placement and assure that reasonable efforts are being made by protective service agents to avoid placement of children in the first instance. Of course, the primary goal of these requirements is to sustain children in their families of origin where possible, but to move with dispatch in finding a permanent home for the child—if efforts to restore the family's functioning fails.

This legislation has added approximately 400,000 cases of children in foster care to the annual dockets of juvenile and family courts in the United States. This sudden increase has not been accompanied by a commensurate increase in resources and, therefore, has strained the court's capacity to the point of breaking. Typically, juvenile and family court judges now spend at least one-half of their bench time hearing such matters, when they were spending less than 20 percent on such cases prior to the advent of Public Law 96-272.

The future portends even more court involvement in protective service matters as states become more and more intrusive into family affairs by default as the family falls apart. Family theorists now insist that there are at least 13 recognizable forms of the family, as contrasted with only three such forms when we entered the decade of the sixties (Taylor, 1985). One clear implication of this rapidly changing social situation is that courts of juvenile jurisdiction are likely to be predominantly courts for protecting children by the turn of the century. In other words, they will be right back where they began 100 years ago but, this time around, the primary basis for their jurisdiction will be neglected, abused, and dependent children rather than delinquents.

STRUCTURE FOR JUVENILE JUSTICE

Before the phenomenon of specialized juvenile courts ever become pervasive in the United States, a court reform movement had already begun that sought to stamp out specialized courts. Fired by the early efforts of the Institute for Judicial Administration, the quest for unified court systems became a passion in the 1970's with the development of the National Center for State Courts and the growth of the Institute for Court Management. For a time in the late seventies, it appeared that specialized courts of all sorts, from water courts in the West to orphans courts in the East, were slated for extinction. But, as it turns out, appearances are often deceiving. As we enter the decade of the nineties, there are only six states that are judged by the National Center for State Courts (1988) to qualify as truly unified court systems. In fact, at the moment, the momentum is in the opposite direction.

One of the trendy movements in court reorganization these days is the discovery of comprehensive family courts. Ironically, this movement begins just as we are interring the remains of the last traditional American family, but such trivialities never seem to phase court reformers. The family court has been around for some time, with the first one established in Toledo, Ohio, in 1914, followed by such communities as Baton Rouge, Louisiana, and Biloxi, Mississippi, in the decade of the fifties. In the late fifties, the then National Council of Juvenile Court Judges, the National Council on Crime and Delinquency, and the U.S. Children's Bureau combined to idealize family courts with a Model Act called the Standard Family Court Act, but the idea never really caught on. New York established a state-wide family court but did not vest it with divorce jurisdiction. Outside of that effort, no other large state attempted to establish family courts until New Jersey in 1982. In the meantime, the District of Columbia, Delaware, Rhode Island, Hawaii, and later South Carolina, had all established their own versions of family courts; but recently the States of Nevada, Missouri, Arizona, and Utah are all considering the establishment of family courts. The State of California recently rejected such a proposal.

In contrast to the family court movement, there is only one state-wide juvenile court in the United States, that being in Utah, though several other states including the State of Louisiana are actively debating the establishment of such courts. Even so, it appears that generic, one-size-fits-all, trial courts are in for rough sledding, at least for the short term. Part of the reason for this trend appears to be the increasing complexity of court management in large urban areas; in fact, the primary reason for the rejection of a proposed family court in the State of California was the perceived difficulty of administering comprehensive family jurisdiction within one institution. California, for some time, has been moving in the direction of even further specialization of its juvenile division of superior court in large urban

areas. Los Angeles County is in the process of building 27 new court facilities to house the juvenile division's "dependency courts." Other large jurisdictions, such as Philadelphia and Detroit, are moving in a similar direction though they have yet to build separate facilities to house the courts. In the words of at least one California trial lawyer, "It is impossible for even the best trained attorney to master all facets of family practice, so it seems implausible that a single court could effectually manage the entire range of jurisdiction" (Mallory, 1991).

ADMINISTRATION OF JUVENILE SERVICES

Juvenile probation is still largely a court-administered service. In spite of—or perhaps because of—the recommendations of sundry national commissions and reform organizations, the judiciary still has either appointing or supervising authority, or both, over juvenile probation officers in 41 of the 50 states (Torbet, 1989). Juvenile probation officers currently number in excess of 20,000, and the workload numbers continue to grow at an annual rate of 400,000 cases not including intake screening, investigation, and predisposition study caseloads (Hurst, 1990a).

While the administration of juvenile probation has been a rather stable phenomenon over the past two decades, the structural reorganization of juvenile corrections, other than probation, has been a rapidly changing phenomenon. As we enter the final decade of this century, there are only 14 states that administer juvenile correctional institutions within a state department of corrections. That number is down from 20 states in 1980. The current trend is in the direction of establishing a state-level department of youth services, or children and youth services, or the equivalent. Thirteen states currently organize their juvenile corrections services in such a manner. However, most state-level juvenile corrections services (23) are administered by the state departments of social service or their equivalents.

In view of the movement to hold juveniles accountable for their "criminal behavior," a movement back toward placing such services within adult departments of correction is to be expected but is not happening yet. It is quite possible that we have begun to recognize that juveniles requiring correctional institutionalization require a substantively different course of remedial action than that required by adult criminals, but in our form of democracy that is quite unlikely. What is more likely is that the current trend toward establishing separate state agencies is the result of a chance confluence between political self-interests and the always safe political harbor of more efficiency in government.

Community-Based Services

This lofty ideal ought to be catalogued under "reforms that failed because everybody liked them but no one bothered to take any action." Community re-integration, community-based services, neighborhood-based services, and the like, caught fire during the Great Society movement of the sixties but crashed and burned along with many of the programs of that era. Community-based services continue to be a part of our rhetoric but not a part of our repertoire. The primary reason for this dilemma is that juvenile correctional services, other than probation, are state-owned and administered, and state-owned services have a way of getting located where the Speaker of the House and the Governor want them located, not where it makes sense to locate them. Those states that have had the most success with achieving community-based services, such as Pennsylvania, have done so because all services for children and families are owned and operated at the local level rather than the state level. In other words, for community-based services to become a reality, they need to be Of the Community, By the Community, and For the Community. That means total local control. That means Home Rule, a feature of our society that has been quietly interred—along with the traditional family.

Another means by which a few states have had some success in building community-based services is through the private services lobby. States—such as Massachusetts, Michigan, and New York—that have a strong private services lobby have built a range of community-based services. Ironically, even though community-based services have never been given a fair test, the logic of the idea remains compelling and has begun to fire rhetoric that transcends community-based and talks about family-based services. So far, unless you live in Scotland, it is just so much talk.

DEINSTITUTIONALIZATION OF STATUS OFFENDERS

Even though labeling as a theory of delinquency causation had largely been discredited by the time the Juvenile Justice and Delinquency Prevention Act was passed in 1974, the logic of that so-called theory permeated the provisions and requirements of the Act (Gove, 1975). Consequently, the Act required that participating states remove status offenders (runaways, truants, ungovernable) from places of secure detention and commitment. More specifically, the Act sought to remove status offenders from all association with delinquent offenders, especially in training schools and detention homes.

Seventeen years after the passage of the Juvenile Justice and Delinquency Prevention Act, states have largely succeeded in removing status offenders from state training schools and have achieved a modicum of success in removing them from pretrial detention facilities. However, the number of status offenders in out-of-home placement has not changed. There was approximately 10,000 such offenders in placement in 1975 and the number was similar in 1987 (Thornberry et al., 1991a). The place of confinement has changed though, with group homes and small residential treatment facilities being the major recipients of status offenders diverted from training schools and detention facilities.

However, the rate of juvenile court referrals for delinquency and status offenses has continued to increase—from 45 per 1,000 eligible youth in 1975 to 57 per 1,000 youth in 1988 (Snyder et al., 1987; Snyder et al., 1990a; and Snyder, 1990b). In 1975, the rate produced 1.4 million such referrals and the same number in 1988. This anomalous appearing situation was caused by a decrease in the eligible child population that equaled the increase in rate of referral. In 1975, status offenders represented 25 percent of the total, or approximately 300,000 referrals. That proportion had decreased slightly to 21 percent by 1988 but status offenders are still very much a part of the juvenile justice system workload.

FORM VERSUS SUBSTANCE

The dynamic tension between Punishing and Acting in the Interest of Children reflected in state codes has significantly affected programs for delinquent youth in the past two decades. Most significantly, Control has been pitted against Rehabilitation, and, recently, Control has been winning.

The use of risk classification instruments has gained wide acceptance in the past 10 years within the juvenile justice system. They are currently being used to screen offenders for placement on probation or placement in the institution, just as they are in the criminal justice system where they have their origins, and they are being used in institutions to segregate security risks and determine facility placement. On the other hand, needs assessment designed to determine the focus of program intervention is beginning to look like a vanishing science.

At the community level, intensive probation is showing signs of becoming the rage of the nineties; however, in today's intensive probation, "intensive tracking" and "electronic monitoring" have replaced family-based case work, home visits, and small group intervention as preferred mediums of dealing with juvenile offenders. Community protection and individual accountability have combined to displace rehabilitation and correction of behavior in both our vocabulary and our programs. "Boot camps," "swamp camps," "gauntlet running," and maximum security institutions are the preferred mediums of community protection. Restitution, community service, fines, and short-term incarceration in secure juvenile detention facilities are the current vogue in accountability.

Competence development, translated as skill development, is as close as we currently come to designing interventions resembling rehabilitation. Literacy training, especially computer literacy, law-related education, G.E.D. training, and skills generally classified as preparation for independent living, i.e., how to open a bank account, rent an apartment, buy groceries, etc., constitute our basic repertoire of competence development.

Character development, building self-esteem, increasing moral reasoning capacity, supporting social maturation, now seem to be notions from a bygone era.

FORCES DRIVING THE CHANGE

At the dawn of the sixties, the term Family still meant a man and a woman living in state-sanctioned matrimony. In the United States, the term was definitive legally and socially. Today, we recognize legally and socially at least 13 new family forms, including the Same-Sex Family and the Room-Mate Family (Taylor, 1985). Galimony and Palimony are now firmly-established trends in family litigation. The rapid evolution of the family has often left today's youth without an established value referent within the family and without mature adult supervision anywhere in their life. These circumstances, combined with a trend in the direction of rapidly increasing so-called Single-Parent Families and Multiple-Career Families, has cast television as the primary baby sitter and socializer of our children.

One of the behavioral outcomes of the foregoing circumstance is the continued escalation in crimes of violence, especially homicide, forcible rape, aggravated assault, and weapons offenses. All four of these crimes by youth have continued to proliferate. For example, in 1965, youth under the age of 18 were arrested at a rate of 5 per 100,000 for the crime of forcible rape; by 1989, the arrest rate had doubled. In 1965, the arrest rate for aggravated assault was 30 per 100,000; by 1989, the rate had tripled. The homicide rate increased four-fold, and the weapons rate increased three-fold (Snyder, 1991).

In addition to rapidly-increasing violence by youth, the juvenile justice system has also faced increased challenges from new types of offenders. In Marvin Wolfgang's (1972) classic study "Delinquency in a Birth Cohort," of all of the male children in the city of Philadelphia who reached age 18 in 1963 only one drug arrest was recorded from birth to age 18. His second birth cohort, born 13 years later and coming of age in 1975, recorded 737 drug arrests (Tracy et al., 1985).

Increased drug use, however, is not the most troubling part of the drug phenomenon for the juvenile justice system today. Drug dealers are. They abound in youth populations throughout the United States. As we enter the nineties, drug dealers, who are frequently no more than 13 or 14 years of age, with almost unlimited access to cash and automatic weapons, are terrorizing neighborhoods and whole communities and do not appear to be the type of delinquent offender that the founders of the juvenile court had in mind when they designed the system to give highest priority to the best interests of the child (Moore, 1991).

Another special population of juvenile offenders currently testing the resilience of the system are gangs that derive a large part of their status from criminal activity. Gangs have long been a part of the urban culture in the United States, but gangs featuring criminal enterprise as a prominent aspect of their dynamics are new to the world of youth. Cities such as Los Angeles and Chicago have had sections of their community terrorized by youth gangs in recent years in a manner reminiscent of nothing that has ever happened in this country before. The drug trade appears to be one of the engines driving gang activity, both from the standpoint of the economic gain to be had from the trade and the social abandon that can come from a good hit.

Of all the juvenile justice system's failures at rehabilitation, none is more prominent than our inability to correct the behavior of rapists. The failure of the juvenile justice system in this regard is also mirrored by the criminal justice system. That failure, combined with the continued escalation in the prevalence of all forms of sexual assault, has placed the system in an increasingly difficult dilemma (Hurst, 1988). Some states are now faced with the need to plan one in five juvenile correctional beds for serious sexual offenders, without any real optimism about our ability to alter the behavior patterns of such offenders (Hurst, 1990b).

The arrest rate for females under the age of 18 for Crime Index offenses increased 10 times as fast in the 1970's and 1980's as did the rate for males (Hurst, 1987). The system had not anticipated this change in the offending patterns of youth and is still trying to cope with the influx by developing specialized programs and modifying staffing patterns to be more responsive to female offenders. This is a trend that does not appear to be likely to reverse itself in the near term.

However, the major force driving the juvenile justice system's response to serious offenders has been the continued emphasis on legal enfranchisement of youth. In our society, rights are—of necessity—balance by corresponding responsibilities. Reformers' zealous pursuit of a full panoply of constitutional rights for juveniles has finally confronted criminal responsibility. It is not clear to these authors whether juveniles are now, have been, or will be able in the future to fully benefit from their new-found rights, but it is painfully apparent that we have concluded that they must be held criminally responsible, diminished capacity for crime and/or freedom notwithstanding.

CONCLUSION

As we approach the end of the 20th century, the pressure on the juvenile justice system to demonstrate the efficacy of individualized justice is greater than at any time in its short history. In state after state, legislative proposals aimed at increasing the number of youth who are subjected to criminal prosecution keep being presented to legislatures and keep passing (Szymanski, 1991b). At times in the past 5 years, our legislative proposals have caused us to appear almost desperate in our pursuit of justice system solutions to the problem of juvenile violence and criminal law violations. In our desperation, we have even begun to pass laws that would make it a crime for parents to produce a delinquent child (Hurst, 1989).

Unless our families suddenly stabilize and our massive congregate school system is broken up into manageable pieces and our neighborhoods regain their sense of community within the near future (and none of these possibilities seems very probable), the juvenile justice system in the 21st century is likely to be characterized by an absence of jurisdiction over most youth age 14 and older charged with a felony crime. This change will not come about for any positive reason but rather because we have grown afraid of our own children and don't seem to know quite what else to do—other than lock them up as criminals.

We have lost much of our optimism about the capacity of youth to change—at a time when the collective need to hurt those who take unfair advantage of their fellow man is at its zenith. Curiously, our penchant for punishing young predators coincides with another social trend that is simultaneously peaking.

Protecting abused, neglected, and otherwise vulnerable children seems morally imperative at the moment. We are also beginning to recognize the insufficiency of adversarial win-lose proceedings as a decision-making medium in such cases. As a consequence, the juvenile court is lurching toward a more fiercely protective posture toward neglected children amid renewed interest in alternative decision-making models such as mediation and collaborative consensus. In many ways, today's juvenile court procedures in abuse and neglect cases are more reminiscent of the equity courts of old (which they replaced) than they are contemporary courts of law. More than a few scholars and accomplished jurists (Moore et al., 1990; Gladstone 1990; and Springer, 1991) are urging significant reforms of the juvenile court, and much of the professional juvenile justice community is sufficiently frustrated with the present system to support reasoned change. The voting public is more than ready for a new "quick fix." Everything seems to be in order for yet another social experiment along the lines of the one launched in Cook County, Illinois, in 1989.

References

Adoption Assistance and Child Welfare Act of 1980
  Public Law 96-272.

BREMNER, R.H. (ED.)
1974   *Children and youth in America: A documentary history.* (Volume III, 1933–1973. Parts 5–7). Cambridge, MA: Harvard University Press

CONFERENCE OF STATE COURT ADMINISTRATORS AND NATIONAL CENTER FOR STATE COURTS
1988   *State court organization, 1987.* Williamsburg, VA: National Center for State Courts.

Gault
1967   In Re, 387 U.S. 1, 87 S. Ct. 1428.

GLADSTONE, W.E.
1990   June 3. Juvenile justice—How to make it work. *Miami Herald*, Viewpoint.

GOVE, W.R. (ED.)
1975   *The labeling of deviance: Evaluating a Perspective.* New York: Holsted.

Heath A. Wilkins v. Missouri
1989   492 U.S. 361, 109 S. Ct. 2969.

HUIZINGA, D., ESBENSEN, F., & WEIHER, A.W.
1991   Are there multiple paths to delinquency? *Journal of Criminal Law and Criminology*, 82(1).

HURST, H.
1987   Sex and crime. *Juvenile and Family Court Newsletter*, 17(4).

HURST, H.
1988   More sex. *Juvenile and Family Court Newsletter*, 19(1).

HURST, H.
1989   Parent responsibility for the crimes of their children. *Juvenile and Family Court Newsletter*, 20(1).

HURST, H.
1990a   Winter. Juvenile probation in retrospect. *Perspectives*. American Probation and Parole.

HURST, H.
1990b   *Juvenile corrections at the close of the twentieth century.* Pittsburgh, PA: National Center for Juvenile Justice.

Juvenile Justice and Delinquency Prevention Act of 1974
  42 U.S.C. 5601.

Kent v. United States
1966   383 U.S. 541, 86 S. Ct. 1045 (1966).

LOEBER, R., STOUTHAMER-LOEBER, M., VAN KAMMEN, W., & FARRINGTON, D.P.
1991   Initiation, escalation and desistance in juvenile offending and their correlates. *Journal of Criminal Law and Criminology*, 82(1).

MALLORY, B.T.
1991   February. Remarks before the Advisory Committee for the Integration of Child and Family Legal Proceedings project, Institute for Court Management/National Center for State Courts, Denver, CO.

MOORE, M., FELD, B.C., GREENWOOD, P.W., & ZIMRING, F.
The future of the juvenile court. Presentations at the 42nd Annual Meeting of the American Society of Criminology, Baltimore, MD.

MOORE, S.
1991   March 16–20. Unpublished remarks at 17th National Conference on Juvenile Justice, Albuquerque, New Mexico.

NATIONAL COUNCIL OF JUVENILE AND FAMILY COURT JUDGES.
1987   Juvenile & Family Court Journal

50th Anniversary Issue 38(2).

NATIONAL PROBATION AND PAROLE ASSOCIATION
1959   (now the National Council on Crime and Delinquency), National Council of Juvenile Court Judges, and U.S. Children's Bureau. *Standard Family Court Act.* New York: National Probation and Parole Association (now the National Council on Crime and Delinquency) 1959.

Progressively Increasing Consequences Act
A.R.S. 8-230.01, July 1, 1984.

SNYDER, H.N., FINNEGAN, T.A., NIMICK, E.H., SICKMUND, M.H., SULLIVAN, D.P., & TIERNEY, N.J.
1987   *Juvenile court statistics 1984.* Washington, DC: U.S. Government Printing Office.

SNYDER, H.N., FINNEGAN, T.A., NIMICK, E.H., SICKMUND, M.H., SULLIVAN, D.P., & TIERNEY, N.J.
1990   *Juvenile court statistics 1988.* Pittsburgh, PA: National Center for Juvenile Justice.

SNYDER, H.N.
1990b   Special Analysis of 1988 Data in the National Juvenile Court Data Archive. National Center for Juvenile Justice.

SNYDER, H.N.
1991   *Arrests of youth 1989.* Pittsburgh, PA: National Center for Juvenile Justice.

SPRINGER, C.E.
1991   Rehabilitating the juvenile court. *Notre Dame Journal of Law, Ethics and Public Policy,* 5(2).

SZYMANSKI, L.A.
1991a   *Juvenile code purpose clauses.* Pittsburgh, PA: National Center for Juvenile Justice.

SZYMANSKI, L.A.
1991b   *1990 update and statutes analysis of juvenile court jurisdiction over children's conduct.* Pittsburgh, PA: National Center for Juvenile Justice.

TAYLOR, L.S.
1985   The family as an adaptable and enduring social unit: a case for assessing delinquent behavior from a family systems perspective. *Today's Delinquent,* 4.

THE PRESIDENT'S COMMISSION ON LAW ENFORCEMENT AND ADMINISTRATION OF JUSTICE
1967   Task Force on Juvenile Delinquency. *Task force report: Juvenile delinquency and youth crime.* Washington, DC: U.S. Government Printing Office.

THORNBERRY, T.P., TOLNAY, S.E., FLANAGAN, T.J., & GLYNN, P.
1991a   *Children in custody 1987: A comparison of public and private juvenile custody facilities.* Washington, DC: Office of Juvenile Justice and Delinquency Prevention.

THORNBERRY, T.P., LIZOTTE, A.J., KROHN, M.D., FARNWORTH, M., & JANG, S.J.
1991b   Testing interactional theory: An examination of reciprocal causal relationships among family, school, and delinquency. *Journal of Criminal Law and Criminology,* 82(1).

TORBET, P.M.
1989   *Organization and administration of juvenile services: Probation, aftercare, and state delinquent institutions.* Pittsburgh, PA: National Center for Juvenile Justice.

TRACY, P.E., WOLFGANG, M.E., & FIGLIO, R.M.
1985   *Delinquency in two birth cohorts.* Washington, DC: Office of Juvenile Justice and Delinquency Prevention.

WOLFGANG, M.E., FIGLIO, F., SELLIN, T.
1972   *Delinquency in a birth cohort.* Chicago, IL: University of Chicago Press.

QUESTIONS FOR DISCUSSION

1. Given that the structure of the family has changed dramatically over the past 30 years, is the family court a realistic and practical way to approach juvenile justice?

2. According to the author, what persistent problems are associated with the administration of the juvenile court?

3. Discuss the tension that exists between punishing a child and acting in the best interest of the child.

APPLICATIONS

1. The author states that "unless our families suddenly stabilize and our massive congregate school system is broken up into manageable pieces and our neighborhoods regain their sense of community within the near future . . ., the juvenile justice system of the 21st century is likely to be characterized by an absence of jurisdiction over most youth age 14 and older charged with a felony crime." In essence we are making the age of

adult criminal culpability lower and lower. In your opinion, is this a dangerous trend? Why?

2. Should we look to the family, schools, churches, and community to find solutions to juvenile delinquency? Why?

KEY TERMS

ambivalence a continual fluctuation or contradiction in attitudes or feelings.

dispatch to send off or away with promptness or speed.

interring the process of burying or depositing in a tomb.

modicum a small portion or a limited quantity.

panoply something forming a protective cover.

penchant a strong inclination or attraction to something.

pervasive that which moves or diffuses throughout something.

portend something that foreshadows a coming event.

shroud a covering for protection or a disguise to conceal.

undulating rising and falling or fluctuating.

32

Youth Gangs and Public Policy

C. Ronald Huff

Recent studies have begun to document the changing organizational forms of youth gangs in the United States. The emergence/re-emergence of these gangs, often accompanied by increased violence and involvement in drug use and/or trafficking, poses major public policy issues. However, little empirical research has been conducted on this subject, and very few studies have been based on interviews with gang members as well as official data and the perspectives of public officials. This article summarizes the results and recommendations of a two-year study of youth gangs in Ohio, focusing primarily on in-depth case studies of Cleveland and Columbus gangs.

Recent studies (Klein and Maxson 1985, Chin 1986, Hagedorn 1988, Fagan 1988) have demonstrated that youth gangs in the United States have developed new, often violent organizational forms. The electronic and print media in many large and medium-sized American cities almost routinely carry accounts (often distorted) of "drug gangs," "Jamaican posses," "drive-by shootings," and other gang-related phenomena. However, research on these emerging/re-emerging gangs has been relatively rare, and studies that include interviews with gang members, as well as the use of official data, have been even more rare. This article summarizes one such study, an analysis of gangs in Ohio, and

presents some public policy recommendations designed to address both the prevention and the control of youth gangs.

The Study

The research on which this article is based took place from April 1986 to May 1988. The research project included in-depth case studies of youth gangs in Cleveland and Columbus, as well as secondary surveys of Ohio's five other large cities (Cincinnati, Toledo, Dayton, Akron, and Youngstown).

Data for the study were collected via the following methods:

1. Interviews with gang members, former gang members, police officers, representatives of community and social service agencies, and school officials in Cleveland and Columbus. To ensure a more representative sample of gang members, some of the interviews were conducted with gang members who had not been apprehended. These interviews generally took place either in members' housing projects or neighborhoods or in neutral locations. They were facilitated by trusted intermediaries who arranged them and accompanied the researchers.[1] Some of these interviews were recorded on audio tape while others, to reduce the interviewees' apprehensions, were summarized by handwritten notes.

2. Field observations of police operations

"Youth Gangs and Public Policy," *Crime and Delinquency*, 35:4 (October 1989), pp. 524–537. Reprinted by permission of the publisher, Sage Publications, Inc.

targeting youth gangs and youth violence.

3. Analyses of secondary data from the Cleveland and Columbus police departments concerning areas believed to be gang-related.

4. Surveys of all 88 county juvenile courts in Ohio, as well as the 7 chiefs of police of Ohio's largest cities and the principals of 66 junior and senior high schools (35 in Cleveland and 31 in Columbus).

Principal Findings

The surveys of school principals in Cleveland and Columbus revealed a moderate level of concern about gangs; little consensus on how to deal with the problem; and much agreement on the role of law enforcement, which is perceived as vitally important in controlling gang behavior in the two cities (law enforcement is viewed as having the primary responsibility).

The surveys of police chiefs of the largest cities in Ohio indicate that several chiefs currently acknowledge some problems with gangs; nearly all state that gangs have been a problem in the past, and all estimate that offenses by youth gangs represent less than 1% of all crime and less than 2% of all juvenile crime.

The case studies confirmed that youth gangs exist in both Cleveland and Columbus. During the course of this study, the primary and secondary data identified more than fifty separately named gangs in Cleveland, some of which undoubtedly were "splinter groups" or "groupies" rather than truly separate and unique gangs. Many of these gangs have either dissipated or merged with each other, leaving fifteen to twenty separate, viable gangs. In Columbus, the study identified more than twenty separately named gangs. However, with the same qualifications noted above, the number of truly separate, viable gangs at present is approximately fifteen. Cincinnati, though not a case study site, also has experienced youth gang problems during the course of this research, including incidents involving the neo-Nazi "Skinheads."

In terms of racial and ethnic identity, it is probable that about 90% of the members of Cleveland and Columbus gangs are black, while the remaining 10% are white and Hispanic. The study identified two Hispanic gangs (on Cleveland's west side). Statewide, police chiefs surveyed also reported that gang membership was more than 90% black, according to their own information.

The age of gang members ranges approximately from ten to thirty (with the most common age range being 14–24), and the larger gangs are stratified by age and sophistication. That is, until one is 16 or 17 years old, he is likely to be in a junior division of the gang. These divisions have their own leadership structures.

Several female "gangs" were identified in Cleveland and Columbus. However, upon closer investigation, these "gangs" were actually more similar to "groupies" whose identity was closely tied to that of male gang allies. Gang membership in Ohio is more than 90% male, according to data generated by this study.

Gangs in Columbus and Cleveland originated in the following ways:

1. Breakdance/"rappin" groups evolved into gangs as a result of intergroup conflict involving dancing, skating, and/or "rappin," competition. This competition would sometimes spill over over into the parking lots of skating rinks, where members frequently had concealed weapons in their cars.

2. Street corners groups similarly evolved into gangs as a result of conflicts with other "corner groups." These groups were more typical of distinctive neighborhoods, such as housing projects. In Cleveland, these groups had a much longer history than in Columbus, although that history has been uneven. Nonetheless, both cities have histories of street corner groups and "street hustling" that predate the current generation of street gangs.

3. Street gang leaders already experienced in gang life moved to Ohio from Chicago or Los Angeles. These more sophisticated leaders were often charismatic fig-

ures who were able to quickly recruit a following from among local youths.

Despite rumors to the contrary, this study produced no solid evidence that any Ohio youth gang is a "chapter" or direct affiliate of a gang in any other city (Chicago, Detroit, or Los Angeles in particular). It is likely that this confusion stems from the "out of state" identities of some gang leaders who moved to Ohio from other states. For the most part, this reflects our society's extensive geographic mobility, coupled with our historic tendency to blame "outsiders" for local problems rather than focus on the root causes (especially poverty and unemployment). However, in the past year Ohio's cities have witnessed the in-migration of "crack" cocaine traffickers from Detroit, Los Angeles, and even Jamaica.

Members of the gangs identified in this study are overwhelmingly drawn from the "urban black underclass" described so well by Wilson (1987) and by Duster (1987). This is true of both Cleveland and Columbus, though for somewhat different reasons. Cleveland, a more heavily industrialized "rust belt" city, has been adversely impacted by the loss of many of its manufacturing jobs and the high unemployment rates it has experienced in the 1980s. Table 1 reflects changes in the poverty status of Cleveland families (including those with children under 18 years of age) from 1970 to 1980, while Table

2 presents the unemployment trend and the loss of manufacturing jobs during that period. Tables 3 and 4 present similar data for Columbus, widely known for its stable, "high-tech," service-oriented economy.

What is compelling about these tables is this: An economically and socially marginal youth who has dropped out of or been expelled from school, and–or is without job skills, is in deep trouble in either Cleveland or Columbus. In Cleveland, he is competing for a rapidly shrinking pool of manufacturing jobs (more than 36,000 of these jobs were lost between 1970 and 1980 alone) and cannot qualify for other jobs. In Columbus, there never were that many manufacturing jobs (in 1970 Columbus has less than one-half as many manufacturing jobs as Cleveland), and the jobs that exist require higher levels of education and job skills. To make matters worse, the military, a traditionally available alternative career path for the poor, is increasingly inaccessible due to the higher quality of applicants generated by an economy with relatively few attractive entry-level positions for unskilled workers.

As these tables reveal, poverty is increasingly victimizing families with children under 18 years of age. With little income to buy the flashy clothes and other consumer goods advertised throughout our society, a poor minority youth may find the "illegitimate opportunities" (Cloward and Ohlin 1960) available through gangs, crime, and drug

TABLE 1   Poverty Status of Families (Cleveland), 1970—1980

	Year 1970	1980	Change 1970—1980	Percent of Change 1970—1980
Number of Families	184,645	143,588	-41,057	-22.2
Number of Families below Poverty Level	24,817	25,926	2,109	8.5
Percent of Families below Poverty Level	13.4%	18.8%		5.4
Families below Poverty Level with Children under 18 Years	18,227	21,754	3,527	19.4
Percent of Families below Poverty Level with Children under 18 Years	9.9%	15.2%		5.3

SOURCE: Bureau of the Census

TABLE 2   Total Unemployment and Loss of Manufacturing Jobs (Cleveland), 1970—1980

| | Year | | Percent of | |
	1970	1980	Change 1970—1980	Change 1970—1980
Civilian Labor Force	303,146	240,538	-62,608	-20.7
Unemployed	15,730	26,359	10,629	67.6
Unemployed as percent of Civilian Labor force	5.2%	11.0%		5.8
Work Force Employed by Manufacturing	107,477	71,055	-36,422	-33.9
Manufacturing Workers as percent of Civilian Labor Force	35.5%	29.5%		-6.0

SOURCE: U.S. Bureau of the Census

TABLE 3   Poverty Status of Families (Columbus), 1970—1980

| | Year | | Percent of | |
	1970	1980	Change 1970—1980	Change 1970—1980
Number of Families	128,594	136,625	8,031	6.2
Number of Families below Poverty Level	12,551	16,482	3,931	31.3
Percent of Families below Poverty Level	9.8%	12.1%		2.3
Families below Poverty Level With Children under 18 Years	9,096	13,265	4,169	45.8
Percent of Families below Poverty Level With Children under 18 Years	7.1%	9.7%		2.6

SOURCE: U.S. Bureau of the Census

TABLE 4   Total Unemployment and Loss of Manufacturing Jobs (Columbus), 1970—1980

| | Year | | Percent of | |
	1970	1980	Change 1970—1980	Change 1970—1980
Civilian Labor Force	227,330	279,727	52,397	23.0
Unemployed	8,647	17,894	9,247	106.9
Unemployed as a percent of Civilian Labor Force	3.8%	6.4%		2.6
Work Force Employed by Manufacturing	50,270	43,709	-6,561	-13.1
Manufacturing Workers as a percent of Civilian Labor Force	22.1%	15.6%		-6.5

SOURCE: U. S. Bureau of the Census

sales more compelling than the legitimate options available to him.

The gangs identified in this study correspond to several loosely-knit typologies:

1. Informal, *hedonistic gangs* whose focal concerns seem to be "getting high" (usually on alcohol and/or marijuana and other drugs) and "having a good time." These gangs occasionally engage in some minor property crime, but tend not to be involved in violent personal crime.

2. *Instrumental gangs* whose focal concerns are more economic and who commit a higher volume of property crimes for economic reasons. Most of these gang members also use alcohol and marijuana; some use "crack" cocaine. In addition, some *individual* members of these gangs sell gangs, but this is not an organized *gang* activity.

3. *Predatory gangs* that commit robberies, street muggings, and other crimes of opportunity (including at least one known group rape). Members of these gangs are more likely to use highly addictive drugs such as "crack" cocaine, and these drugs contribute significantly to their labile, assaultive behavior. Members of these gangs may also sell drugs to finance the purchase of more sophisticated weapons. Although this study produced no hard evidence that any of these gangs is currently a "drug distribution network," they represent a ready-made "target of exploitation" for organized crime or other criminal groups.

Gang members actually spend most of their time engaging in exaggerated versions of typical adolescent behavior (rebelling against authority by skipping school, refusing to do homework, and disobeying parents; wearing clothing and listening to music that sets them apart from most adults; and having a primary allegiance to their peer group instead of their parents or other adults). They appear to "drift" into and out of illegal behavior, as described by Matza (1964), and the frequency and seriousness of their law-violating behavior appear to fit the three loose gang typologies above. The older the members of a gang, the more they seem to drift toward criminality and away from typical adolescent focal concerns.

Law-violating activities committed by youth gangs during the course of this study include theft, auto theft, intimidation and assault in school and on the street, robbery, burglary, rape, group rape, drug use, drug sales, and even murder. To be sure, the more serious the offense, the less frequently it occurs, but gang members do commit all of the above—and more. As one gang member said during his interview, "People may say there's no gangs 'cause they don't see no colors, but if they be robbin' people, shootin' people, and killin' people, they still a gang" (Field Notes 1987).

While three of Ohio's largest cities have youth gangs, until recently only one (Columbus) had officially acknowledged their existence. This research, along with other national studies, suggests that cities experiencing problems with gangs pass through distinct and recognizable stages, and both Cincinnati and Cleveland (until recently) could best be characterized as being in the "official denial" stage. For a variety of reasons, not the least of which is protection of a city's "image," political leaders and others in key leadership roles are reluctant to acknowledge the existence of gangs.

Columbus's emergence from its own denial stage was probably accelerated by several gang-related incidents in 1984 and 1985, including: (1) a challenge issued by a gang leader on a local television news show, followed by his death several days later in a "drive-by shooting" carried out by a rival gang; (2) a gang-related assault on the governor's daughter; and (3) a gang-related assault on the mayor's son.[2]

Official denial of gang problems appears to facilitate victimization by gangs, especially in the public schools. School principals in several Ohio cities are reluctant to acknowledge "gang-related" assaults for fear that such problems may be interpreted as negative reflections on their management abilities. This "political paralysis" appears to encourage gang-related assaults and may send the wrong signals to gang members, implying that they can operate with impunity within the vacuum it creates.

Contrary to much "common wisdom," teachers who demonstrate that they care about a youth and then are firm but fair in their expectations are rarely, if ever, the victims of assault by gang members. Rather, it is those teachers who "back down" and are easily intimidated who are more likely to be the victims of assault. During two years of interviews, *not one* gang member ever said that a teacher who insisted on academic performance (within the context of a caring relationship) was assaulted. Such teachers are respected far more than those perceived as "weak," and "weakness" generally represents a quality to be exploited by gang members in an almost Darwinian fashion, much as they select targets on the street.

On the other hand, *overly* aggressive behavior directed at gang members appears to backfire. Interviews reveal that gang members have an intense dislike for police officers who use unnecessary "strong-arm" tactics in making arrests or questioning them, for example. Gang members indicated that they feel nothing but anger and vengefulness when a police officer behaves "unprofessionally" and that they will seize any subsequent opportunity to "get even."

When asked what they think an officer should do when "baited" in front of other gang members or onlookers, gang members typically respond that an officer should "be professional," perhaps "laugh at him" and walk away rather than fight when challenged. Gang members admit grudging respect for such officers, and this respect appears to be even greater for officers who demonstrate some personal concern for gang members (asking how they're doing when they see them on the streets or admonishing them to stay out of trouble, for example).

Having moved through its "denial stage" rather quickly, Columbus reacted by implementing a comparatively well-balanced, two-pronged approach to the gang problem: (1) active and aggressive enforcement against gang leaders and hard core gang members via the Youth Violence Crime Section, a special 18-officer unit in the Columbus Police Department; and (2) prevention directed at

marginal gang members and would-be members via the Youth Outreach Project, supported by United Way, the Columbus Public Schools, and the Columbus Department of Parks and Recreation. Columbus's approach is perhaps as well-balanced and well-coordinated as any in the nation, though much remains to be accomplished. Two keys to its effectiveness are its unique centralization of all four major gang control functions (intelligence, prevention, enforcement, and investigation) in one police unit (the Youth Violence Crime Section) and that unit's close cooperation with the schools, the courts, the prosecutor's office, the Youth Outreach Project, and other community agencies.

An unanticipated consequence of court-ordered busing in Cleveland and Columbus has been exacerbation of gang conflict in certain schools. Prior to mandatory busing, the gangs that existed were largely neighborhood, "turf"-oriented gangs. As a result of busing, there are now rival gangs at the same schools. Schools were not planned and organized with security in mind and do not readily lend themselves to such concerns. As a result, intimidation and assaults have occurred in certain schools where rival gangs find themselves together.

Busing, along with the ready availability of automobiles and improved freeway systems in our metropolitan areas, has also provided gang members with vastly increased geographic mobility. Gang members described in detail the planning and execution of auto thefts in suburban shopping malls far away from their own homes, for example. The implications for law enforcement are clear: to effectively contain these gang-related offenses, police must have some centralized unit or, at the very least, must share intelligence on gang members and their activities. Whether a department has a gang unit, a juvenile bureau, or a highly decentralized organizational structure, it must identify and be able to recognize gang leaders and members who criss-cross the metropolitan area at will and who may show up at citywide events, such as rock concerts, to "shake down the squares" from the suburbs (intimidate and rob suburbanites coming into the city for such events).

Finally, busing has dramatically changed the meaning of "neighborhood." Forerunners of the current gangs in Cleveland and Columbus were neighborhood street corner groups and "turf"-oriented gangs who fought one another over turf, ethnic and racial conflict, and other issues. Interviews with gang members in both Cleveland and Columbus revealed that "neighborhood" no longer conveys the same kind of meaning, nor does it seem to have much importance to these youths. If still in school, they attend schools with pupils from various neighborhoods. Gang membership is no longer confined to the neighborhood, but involves confederates recruited at school, at skating rinks, and elsewhere throughout the city.

Youth gangs may best be viewed as a symptom of underlying social and economic problems that go far beyond the usual alienation found in youth subcultures in Western nations. The existence of an urban underclass, with its attendant socially disorganized and fragmented living conditions, gives rise to many social pathologies and the gang problem is just one of them. Primary prevention should be heavily emphasized in any strategy addressing youth gangs, yet it is probably the most neglected type of intervention. As a number of police officers have said during this study, "Simply arresting them and locking them up is not the whole answer. We have to figure out a way to reach young kids *before* they get involved with these gangs" (Field Notes 1988). Given the obstacles confronting poor and minority inner city youths, primary prevention programs must address both economic opportunity and neighborhood and family social structures.

For this reason, a two-stage strategy for states is recommended. This strategy, which will require federal assistance, is as follows:

1. In Phase One, a state would commission a study to identify *by zip code* those areas of our cities producing disproportionate numbers of commitments to prison, youth correctional facilities, and mental health facilities, as well as those generating high numbers of public assistance recipients.[3] The total cost of these indicators of social and economic pathology would then be listed for each zip code area. These zip code areas, though not synonymous with "neighborhoods,"[4] would constitute the target areas for special primary prevention efforts.

2. In Phase Two, the state would issue a Request for Proposals for innovative primary prevention approaches to the multiple problems of these zip code areas. Such proposals would address methods of strengthening families and social institutions, improving job opportunities, and otherwise reducing the overwhelming obstacles confronting area residents. Our current failures in these areas of our cities are costing us a great deal of money and even more in human misery and wasted lives. This approach could offer some hope for innovation.

Schools and teacher preparation programs in our colleges and universities should move purposefully to develop teachers who are capable of teaching about and discussing situational ethics in general classrooms. Ethics should not be a special, isolated course, but rather should be integrated at appropriate points during the day as it relates to student dilemmas, student behaviors, history lessons, etc. This proposal is not meant to violate the separation of church and state; the instruction should not be in religion. Rather, it is analogous to the British "Lifeline" series on situational ethics. Other programs, such as Quest, that focus on values and ethics in the school context should also be considered.

Also, schools and teacher preparation programs should heed the findings of this study with respect to gangs' impact in schools. Teachers (and perhaps principals) need to have better assertiveness training and deeper understanding of some guiding principles such as Glasser's Reality Therapy, which emphasizes holding students accountable for their behavior.

As *preventive* measures, states should consider establishing statewide intergovernmental task forces on gangs, organized crime, and narcotics. The enormous profits to be made by selling drugs will be difficult for poor youths to resist. Some of the gangs that now exist may also be easy targets for exploitation by organized crime seeking new narcotics markets. If prevention is to be successful, it will require statewide coordination.

In addition, each large city should establish a local task force that brings together the following components (where they exist): juvenile bureau, youth gang unit, narcotics unit, organized crime unit, school security division, youth outreach project or other social service coordinating program, and juvenile court. Information must be shared on a regular basis if prevention efforts are to be successful in dealing with the potential drug/gang connection.

The increased mobility of gang members requires that police agencies reassess their organizational structures and strongly consider establishing some citywide unit for monitoring gangs and collecting intelligence information. Ideally, the four major gang control functions identified above should be centralized in that unit as much as possible.

Police should be aggressive but professional in dealing with gangs. Gangs must learn that they cannot operate with impunity and that their sense of "invisibility" (which may be a carryover from the well-documented sense of invisibility described by many black citizens in a white-dominated society) is a false one. These aggressive police actions should, however, be targeted solely at the leaders and hard-core members. The marginal members and "wanna be's" can be influenced to redirect their behavior in more positive ways.

For leaders and hard-core gang members who are found delinquent (or, if adults, are found guilty of crimes), but who do not pose threats to pubic safety, the courts should consider the use of intensive probation supplemented by either random, unannounced visits and telephone monitoring or by electronic monitoring. The purpose of this sanction would be to break up street gangs by requiring that hard-core members and leaders be at home unless they are at school, at work, etc.

School boards should develop very clear policies forbidding weapons of any kind to be brought into schools, and these policies should be explained to all students and enforced without exception. Also, there should be a close

working relationship between the schools and the local police, and students should be informed that schools are not "islands" where unlawful behavior is both "invisible" and immune from arrest and prosecution. Weapons offenses, violent assaults, and other serious offenses should be reported to the police.

Schools must make it clear to all that their first obligation is to ensure an environment conducive to learning, and that means one free from intimidation and assault. In some urban schools, administrative concern with school "image" and the administrators'- careers, along with some of the other dynamics of official denial, seem to take precedence over the protection of children.

Traditionally, the school was a place that gang members treated with some respect—a sort of "neutral zone" where gang warfare was largely taboo. In part, this reflected tradition and neighborhood loyalties toward neighborhood schools. The demise of neighborhood schools seems to have significantly dissipated this sense of respect. It also has greatly complicated after-school extracurricular activities, since many students who might want to participate in those activities may have difficulty finding transportation home afterward. Finally, it has reduced the school's perceived importance as a neighborhood center where other kinds of activities occur (parent effectiveness training, continuing education classes, GED classes, job skills workshops, etc.), since the "common denominator" is no longer as clear to many residents.

Urban communities need to re-establish strong neighborhood-based centers and program to tie the residents of inner city areas together in the pursuit of their common concerns. To rebuild a sense of community and collective responsibility, we must begin at the family and neighborhood levels.

Finally, several programs now operating in Ohio and elsewhere offer positive examples of programmatic efforts to address the hopelessness and despair confronting the urban underclass. These include Cleveland's "Scholarship in Escrow" Program. This program was begun because of a concern that about half of all students were dropping out of school, in part because they could see no tangible (i.e., job-related) benefits of a high school diploma. They often had siblings who *had* completed high school, but to no apparent avail; they still had no jobs and none of them could afford college or job training programs.

To counter this lack of incentive, the "Scholarship in Escrow" Program was created by a partnership between the Cleveland Public Schools and representatives of the private sector in metropolitan Cleveland. The program essentially creates a trust fund ($16 million thus far) for all students enrolled in grade 7–12 and credits each of their accounts with ten dollars for every C, twenty dollars for every B, and forty dollars for every A earned in school. The money goes into a scholarship fund, where it earns interest. Each student earning money for grades receives a certificate (somewhat like a stock certificate) indicating the amount earned. Students who graduate from Cleveland public high schools have up to eight years to use their scholarship monies at any Pell Grant-certified college or technical school. The program is based on two rationales: (1) If wealthy families can create trust funds for the future of their children, why cannot we as a society create trust funds for *all* kids? and (2) Since their *future* income will be highly correlated with their educational achievement, why not pay kids for doing well in school now, as an intermediate reinforcement? The program is in its first year of operation, and thus far the superintendent reports that about half of the eligible students are earning money; the other half are earning nothing.

Youth gangs are symptomatic of many of the same social and economic problems as adult crime, mental illness, drug abuse, alcoholism, the surge in homelessness, and multigeneration "welfare families" living in hopelessness and despair. While we are justly concerned with the replacement of our physical infrastructure (roads, bridges, sewers) our *human* infrastructure may be crumbling as well. Our social, educational, and economic infrastructures are not meeting the needs of many children and adults. Increases in the numbers of women and children living in poverty (the "feminization" and "juvenilization" of poverty) are dramatic examples of this recent transformation.

To compete with the seductive lure of drug profits and the grinding despair of poverty, we must reassess our priorities and reaffirm the importance of our neighborhoods by putting in place a number of programs that offer hope, education, job skills, and meaningful lives. It is worth the cost of rebuilding our human infrastructure since it is after all, our children whose lives are being wasted and our cities in which the quality of life is being threatened.

Notes

1. I am especially indebted to Akil Ogbanna, a caseworker with the Home Detention Project of the Cuyahoga County Juvenile Court (Cleveland), and the staff of the Youth Outreach Project (Columbus) for facilitating these interviews, which would otherwise have been impossible.

2. It appears that one of the factors often responsible for moving cities out of the "denial" stage is, unfortunately, a highly publicized assault or homicide involving a highly visible "[V.I.P" in the community (e.g., the governor's daughter and the mayor's son in Columbus; an affluent Asian woman in the Westwood theater district of Los Angeles,; a Honolulu police officer). Generally, the victimization of the poor has not been sufficient to cause this issue to "bubble up" on the political agendas of most American cities.

3. This idea was formulated after learning that the Ohio Department of Youth Services had conducted an internal study analyzing commitments by zip codes. The idea seemed worthy of broader application across multiple social control "systems" (crime, welfare, mental illness, etc.), since zip code information is one of the few common denominators among state government databases, if not the only one.

4. There are several problems inherent in using zip code information; among other things, zip code areas are not uniformly defined, and the populations of those areas are nonuniform. Therefore, any application of this strategy would necessitate some further efforts to standardize these indicators of social pathology on the basis of population size for the purpose of comparing seriousness and developing priority "targets."

References

CHIN, KO-LIN
1986 "Chinese Triad Societies, Tongs, Organized Crime, and Street Gangs in Asia and the United States." Ph.D. dissertation, Wharton School, University of Pennsylvania, Philadelphia.

CLOWARD, RICHARD A. AND LLOYD E. OHLIN
1960 *Delinquency and Opportunity: A Theory of Delinquent Gangs.* New York: The Free Press.

DUSTER, TROY
1987 "Crime, Youth Unemployment, and the Black

Urban Underclass." *Crime & Delinquency* 33: 300–16.

FAGAN, JEFFREY
1988   "The Social Organization of Drug Use and Drug Dealing Among Urban Gangs." Paper presented at the Ohio Conference on Youth Gangs and the Urban Underclass, Ohio State University, Columbus, May 1988. Forthcoming in *Criminology*.

FIELD NOTES
1987   Interview with anonymous juvenile gang member. Cleveland.

FIELD NOTES
1988   Interview with anonymous police officer. Columbus.

HAGEDORN, JOHN M.
1988   *People and Folks: Gangs, Crime and the Underclass in a Rustbelt City.* Chicago: Lake View Press.

KLEIN, MALCOLM W. AND CHERYL L. MAXSON
1985   "Rock Sales' in South Los Angeles." *Sociology and Social Research* 69:561–65.

MATZA, DAVID
1964   *Delinquency and Drift.* New York: John Wiley and Sons.

WILSON, WILLIAM JULIUS
1987   *The Truly Disadvantaged.* Chicago: University of Chicago Press.

QUESTIONS FOR DISCUSSION

1. In the surveys conducted for this research, the author found that the public views law enforcement as having the primary responsibility for curbing gang activity. How is this public view faulty?

2. How has geographic mobility influenced the perpetuation of gangs?

3. List and discuss the gang typology, presented by the author.

4. Why do gangs assault some teachers and not others?

APPLICATIONS

1. Contact a local law enforcement official and find out what is specifically being done to address the gang problem. Are there formalized programs for prevention, rebuilding the city or town infrastructures, and law enforcement in your community? What recommendations would you make to address the problem of gangs in your community?

2. Does the family or church have a role to play in reducing gang activity? If so, what should that role be?

KEY TERMS

charismatic   having an extraordinary power or ability to persuade or charm other people.

dissipate   to cause to spread thin or to scatter.

hedonistic   a characteristic of someone who believes that happiness or pleasure is the sole good or purpose of life.

impunity   exemption or freedom from punishment or negative consequences.

infrastructure   the underlying foundation or basic framework of a system or organization.

33

Juvenile Delinquency: Can Social Science Find a Cure?

Don C. Gibbons

In the first half of this century, criminologists voiced a good deal of optimism regarding the search for the causes of crime and delinquency. Further, they exhibited a good deal of enthusiasm for correctional intervention based upon scientific knowledge. However, although criminological knowledge has grown impressively in the past two or three decades, criminologists have produced many specific findings and conditional proposi-tions but few unequivocal scientific generaliza-tions. In addition, pessimism about treatment has replaced optimism, following the discovery that "nothing works." This article takes stock of the cur-rent state of affairs and offers suggestions regard-ing directions to be pursued.

The task before me in presenting this address is not an easy one. The problem at which I hint is that theorizing and research activities by American criminologists on the causes of youthful misbehavior or on its cure or prevention have been confined almost entirely to American delinquency.[1] Accord-ingly, the question might be asked: What can American criminology contribute to the understanding or treatment of delinquency in other countries? More specifically, do American criminologists have anything to say that might be useful in the Asian-Pacific region of the world?

"Juvenile Delinquency: Can Social Science Find a Cure?" *Crime and Delinquency*, 32 (April 1986), pp. 186–204. Reprinted by permission of Sage Publications, Inc.

I believe that participants in an Asian-Pacific conference can benefit from an exam-ination of American experiences regarding delinquency and attempts to understand and/or control it. Accordingly, I want to comment upon the implications of American social scientific accomplishments in the study of delinquency. But let me hasten to add that many of these remarks have to do more with the limitations of existing knowledge than with a celebration of the discoveries from criminological inquiry.

The Rise of Modern Criminology

When did scientific criminology arise? What are the major directions criminological inquiry on the causes and control of crime and delinquency have taken over the past decades? How much has been learned about the etiology and treatment of lawbreaking? How much remains to be probed by scientific investigation? These are large questions; a full answer to each would require much more time than I have available in this brief address. Regarding the origins of American criminology, suffice it to say that they can be traced to the writings of Parmelee, Gillin, Sutherland, and a few other pioneering fig-ures in the early 1900s (Gibbons, 1979). Juve-nile delinquency received a good deal of attention from sociologists Clifford Shaw, Henry D. McKay, and a few other investiga-tors in the 1930s and 1940s, but it was not until after World War II that research and theorizing on juvenile delinquency became a "growth industry."

The two decades following World War II saw the dramatic expansion of the discipline of sociology. Much optimism was voiced, both about the prospects for scientific sociology generally and for one of its subfields, criminology, more specifically. Most persons educated in this period assumed that once we harnessed the powerful tools of science in the service of social inquiry, we would quickly discover the major causes of lawbreaking and find effective cures for misbehavior and lawbreaking.

One can point to a number of other developments during the 1950s and 1960s, such as the invention of self-report techniques for studying delinquency. Additionally, this period was one in which much optimism for correctional intervention was voiced by criminologists. Many took it as an article of faith that correctional treatment was both desirable and capable of achievement. This faith in the efficacy of treatment seemed to be supported by the results of experiments such as the Highfields project in New Jersey, various experimental treatment ventures conducted by the California Youth Authority, and kindred evidence. My book, *Changing the Lawbreaker* (Gibbons, 1965), was a case in point from this period in which the "rehabilitative ideal" held the allegiance of most American criminologists. That book put forth a detailed version of the "differential treatment" or "different strokes for different folks" argument, in which forms of treatment specific to different offender types were identified.

Criminology has continued to flourish in the United States, as indicated by the growth of organizations such as the American Society of Criminology, which currently has over 1,000 members. It seems fair to say that criminological knowledge has advanced by rather giant strides in the past two or three decades. But on the other hand, criminologists have also come to see that the real world is markedly more complex than they supposed it to be in the 1940s and 1950s. Scientific efforts have not produced unequivocal propositions about the causes of delinquency or about its treatment; rather, we have discovered that few bold and unconditional assertions are warranted from the data at hand. In short, criminologists have become less sanguine and more guarded about the scientific potential of criminological knowledge.

Taking Stock of Criminological Knowledge

Let me begin with some observations on the current state of knowledge regarding the etiology of criminality or delinquency, drawn out of a perusal of textbook contents. Consider first the case of Sutherland's *Criminology*, first published in 1924 and now in its tenth edition, coauthored with Donald Cressey (1978). It is clear from a quick glance at these different editions that criminological theory has grown markedly in sociological sophistication and that the stockpile of research findings has increased at an exponential rate. The same claim can be made about the contents of my general criminology text, first published in 1968, and due to appear in a fifth edition next year, for they also demonstrate the growing explanatory prowess of criminology. Finally, much the same argument can be made regarding delinquency textbooks. My delinquency book first appeared in 1970, with the fourth edition having just been published (Gibbons and Krohn, 1986). The successive editions of it indicate that much has been learned about youthful lawbreaking during the past 15 or 20 years.

However, these remarks about the growth of criminological wisdom need to be qualified. It is unfortunately true that some of our most notable accomplishments in recent decades have involved disconfirmation of hypotheses about lawbreaking and lawbreakers. For example, research findings from the 1960s and 1970s have indicated that most of the claims that were made about gang delinquency by Cohen, Miller, and Cloward and Ohlin are incorrect. Along the same line, we now have a large body of evidence that indicates that the vast majority of juvenile offenders are persons who are free from psychological disturbances, psychiatric opinion notwithstanding, but we are less clear on the question of whether more benign psychological differences contribute to youthful lawbreaking.

I do not mean to suggest that criminological progress has been restricted solely to the accumulation of data that demonstrate that various hypotheses and theories are without foundation in fact. To the contrary, current textbooks and other repositories of knowledge reveal that much has been discovered about factors that play a causal role in lawbreaking. At the same time, these collections of criminological wisdom indicate that our knowledge is incomplete, conditional, and also that many of the tentative conclusions reached by some investigators have been challenged by others. Then, too, ours is a kind of "black box" situation in that although we have identified some of the important factors or influences that are implicated in lawbreaking, there clearly are a host of other causal variables that remain undiscovered and unidentified. Consider the case of predatory crime. The evidence at hand seems to indicate that, in the United States at least, variations in income inequality across American cities have some causal connection to observed levels of predatory criminality. At the same time, this relationship is a relatively weak one that is apparently conditioned by a number of other variables that have yet to be specified. To put the matter in the language of the statistically inclined, the etiological variables that we have uncovered to date separately and jointly explain only a modest portion of the variance in delinquency/nondelinquency.

Let me draw attention to an important recent example that illustrates the limits of criminological science, namely, James Q. Wilson and Richard J. Herrnstein's (1985) *Crime and Human Nature*. This book, authored by two prominent Harvard University scholars, is filled with myriad "facts" about criminality, along with proposals for public policies toward the control of crime. It seems destined to be one of the most influential works on crime and delinquency produced in the 1980s.

Opinions are likely to be divided about this book. On the one hand, its dust jacket contains a number of highly laudatory remarks by other criminological scholars and it has already received very positive reviews in the mass media. On the other hand, some might question the chutzpah or audacity of the authors in their choice of a title for this tome, given that most of the evidence they have examined has to do with criminality in the United States rather than among humans everywhere in the world. Additionally, although Wilson and Herrnstein repeatedly claimed that their intent was to articulate a theory of crime and to review the evidence supporting that theory, they also deliberately restricted their attention to "predatory street crime" and to individuals who engage in "aggressive, violent, or larcenous behavior" or who "hit, rape, murder, steal, or threaten" (Wilson and Herrnstein, 1985:22). Almost entirely missing from their analysis are persons who engage in white-collar crime, mundane lawbreaking, or a number of other varieties of criminality.

Although Wilson and Herrnstein are free to focus their attention on one segment of the crime problem to the exclusion of other portions, they were not justified in redefining the scope of criminology in such a way that large numbers of real-life lawbreakers disappear from criminological scrutiny. Crime is what the criminal law says it is, not what Wilson and Herrnstein chose to single out for attention. Stated another way, Wilson and Herrnstein have engaged in product mislabeling, for their book and their theory did not address crime in its many forms. It was silent on the question of whether their theory applies to patterns of criminality additional to assaults, homicides, rapes, and larcenous acts, but it seems unlikely that Wilson and Herrnstein would contend that physicians who have been involved in Medicare fraud, pharmaceutical manufacturers who have engaged in violation of Food and Drug Administration statutes, and other criminals of that ilk can be accounted for by the theory they set forth in their book.

Leaving aside these larger conceptual issues regarding the Wilson and Herrnstein volume, what can be said about the causal generalizations about predatory street criminals that they have drawn out of the research literature? How convincing is their theory of crime and human nature? Reduced to barest details, their argument is that these persons are uncommonly mesomorphic in bodily build, they exhibit low normal or borderline intelligence, and display atypical personality patterns in the direction of psychopathy, all of which are indicators to Wilson and Herrnstein of constitutional factors in criminality. Further, offenders are from homes characterized by defective "under the roof culture" and are persons who in later life perform poorly in school and in the world of work.

These authors are not entirely wrongheaded. Indeed, their contention that the last word has not been heard on the question of constitutional and biological factors in crime is a point with which many criminologists would concur. Also, I agree that individual psychological differences probably do play a part in lawbreaking and in law abiding conduct. At the same time, I am less persuaded by the evidence they cite from two studies and research on adopted children; moreover, it is likely that a considerable number of other criminologists will also cavil with their conclusions about constitutional factors, based on this evidence. Along the same line, my reading of the literature on psychopathy and on other alleged indicators of personality problems among offenders has led me to conclusions different from those of Wilson and Herrnstein. For example, they noted with favor the Interpersonal Maturity levels theory of Marguerite Q. Warren (1976) involving a scale of delinquent types and detailed recommendations for differential treatment of juvenile offenders that are related to these types. Although this differential treatment "model" provided the guiding theory behind the Community Treatment Project in California and has also been adopted for use in at least one jurisdiction in Australia as well as a number of places in the United States, a number of criminologists have raised questions both about the claims made about juvenile offenders and about the treatment recommendations for them (Beker and Heyman, 1972; Gibbons, 1970).

Another quarrel with Wilson and Herrnstein that many will share concerns their conclusions about the role of schools in the genesis of delinquency as well as the part played by unemployment in both juvenile and adult crime. I do not have time here to develop a full critique of this book, but enough has been said to indicate that considerably less than complete criminological consensus exists regarding the "facts" that these authors discussed.

What accounts for these disagreements between Wilson and Herrnstein and other criminologists regarding the causes of crime? The answer is that although marked growth has occurred in criminology in recent decades, it is still an infant science attempting to grapple with the details of a complicated collection of social phenomena that are caused by a multitude of factors or variables that are intertwined in a number of complex ways. The research studies that have been carried out to date are too few in number, conducted in too few places, and many of them are plagued with methodological deficiencies, all of which results in equivocal findings.

Let me add a few more remarks about the causes of delinquency, before moving on to some observations about treatment or prevention of juvenile lawbreaking.[2] First, it seems doubtful that any single explanatory or causal statement, however complex, accounting for delinquency, can be drawn out of the research evidence. "Delinquency," in American studies, is not a uniformly defined phenomenon that has been investigated by different researchers. One fact that has not always been acknowledged by those who speak of delinquency is that this topic has been "trivialized" by sociologists over the past several decades. Where delinquency once referred, in the work of Shaw and McKay and others, to inner-city neighborhood gangs and delinquent groups who were involved in persistent and serious acts of lawbreaking, more recent investigators, using self-report techniques, have often identified as delinquent, youngsters who have confessed to involvement in one or another relatively innocuous or petty act of misconduct within the past year or so. But it seems doubtful that the Philadelphia youths who appear as delinquents in the cohort studies of Wolfgang et al. (1972) are closely similar to the "delinquents" who turn up in the pages of Hirschi's (1969) study in Richmond, California, or in other self-report investigations.

The picture of fuzzy criminological knowledge I have drawn about adult criminality applies to delinquency as well; that is, causal generalizations about juvenile law-breaking cannot be stated in precise or equivocal terms, nor is there much reason to suppose that all criminologists would be in agreement even on those conditional propositions that can be stated from the research evidence. Consider the 50-odd "propositions" that appear in *Delinquent Behavior.* Among these claims are the following three (Gibbons and Krohn, 1986: 274):

- Strain, as measured by perceptions that occupational and other long-term opportunities are limited, does not appear to be an important factor in producing delinquent conduct. However, the perception of limited opportunities relative to the more immediate concerns of adolescents is related to delinquent behavior.

- Although social bond and its constituent elements are related to the probability of delinquent behavior, other factors must also be taken into account to explain delinquent conduct adequately. For one, those youths who show low levels of social bond are also more likely to associate with others who have committed delinquent acts. In turn, association with delinquent others is strongly related to delinquent behavior, with the result that elements of the social bond are related both directly and indirectly to delinquent behavior.

- Overly aggressive offenders are the product of situations of parental rejection, with the most severe forms of aggression stemming from conditions of early and marked rejection and milder patterns from less marked instances of parental rejection.

The last of these propositions has been drawn out of a large quantity of research evidence; hence there is relatively little disagreement among criminologists about its accuracy. Further, we know a good bit about treatment programs that might be employed in order to reduce "unsocialized aggression" on the part of children and youths. Unfortunately, however, this knowledge does not apply to many delinquents, for the majority of them do not fit the category of overly aggressive child.

The first claim in the preceding list will be recognized as a revised version of theories such as those associated with Cohen and Cloward and Ohlin; however, there is more emphasis upon the discrepancies perceived by youths between their aspirations for good marks in school and the like and their relatively immediate expectations that they are not going to get these good grades, than on expectations that the goals they project for themselves in adulthood are going to be frustrated. The second proposition combines social bonding or control theory, particularly that version created by Hirschi, and hypotheses about the added impact of delinquent associates upon juveniles.

As with the generalization about aggression, there is some research support for the two contentions that, taken together, claim that "strain," control, and associational patterns all contribute in some degree to delinquent conduct. However, these relationships have not yet been so clearly documented that broad consensus exists among criminologists concerning these claims. On the one hand, Hirschi (1979) has argued that little or no explanatory power is gained by attempts to merge variables from other theoretical perspectives such as the learning or strain ones with bond theory. On the other hand, a number of studies, the most recent and impressive of which is by Elliott et al. (1985), seem to show that an integrated theory of this kind is able to account for more of the variance in delinquency and drug use than is bond theory alone.

The causal significance of bond theory has been rendered more muddied by two other studies published in 1985, one by Agnew and the other by Liska and Reed. The first, involving longitudinal data, indicated that bond or control variables only explained about 2% of the variance in delinquency measured at a later point in the lives of the youths studied; the Liska and Reed investigation, involving a non-recursive causal model, reported that involvement in delinquency affected subsequent levels of bonding, as well as the other way around.

Results of Intervention with Delinquents

There is much more that could be included in the commentary upon unsettled issues and unresolved questions in delinquency causation. However, let us move on to examine the status of knowledge regarding efforts to deal with juvenile lawbreaking.

It might be useful to begin with a few brief comments about recent trends in the processing of juvenile offenders in the United States. The National Council on Crime and Delinquency has recently prepared a detailed examination of various kinds of statistical data on delinquency and the processing of youthful lawbreakers, which indicates the following (National Council on Crime and Delinquency, 1984:5):

1. The "at risk" youth population is declining.
2. Juvenile arrests are declining.
3. Juvenile detention populations are increasing.
4. Juvenile training school populations are increasing.
5. In general, fewer youths are entering public facilities but the average length of stay is increasing.
6. Expenditures are increasing.
7. The proportion of incarcerated youth who are Blacks and Hispanics is increasing whereas the White incarcerated youth population is decreasing.

These conclusions, and the statistics behind them, are reflections of a variety of processes and changes going on in the United States, including the following: movement to divert petty offenders and status offenders in particular out of the official machinery; "get tough" policies in some states such as Washington, where a 1977 Juvenile Justice Act mandated the incarceration of serious offenders in training schools; deinstitutionalization programs that have

occurred in Massachusetts, Utah, and some other states; and a number of other developments.

What have the results been from programs of deterrence, incapacitation, prevention, treatment, or control of lawbreaking? These are very large questions, each of which could be discussed at great length. The data that are required in order to answer these queries are not entirely adequate, indeed, data that would answer questions about the impact of some of the recent developments to which I have alluded are nonexistent.

Take the matter of correctional treatment. Although there is a large body of evidence indicating that treatment ventures have not usually reduced recidivism or produced other positive results, some persons continue to find some encouraging signs of treatment success in the data (Jenkins, 1985; Palmer, 1971; Shireman et al., 1978). Nonetheless, there are some general propositions and conclusions about these matters that are in order.

First, most of the evidence on the results of deliberate, planned efforts to increase the impact of correctional treatment or other intervention upon offenders has indicated that these have not been successful (Bailey, 1966; Robison and Smith, 1971; Greenberg, 1977b; Sechrest et al., 1979). The mass of existing studies indicate that few of the treatment programs that have been directed at juvenile or adult offenders have achieved more than very modest results, at best.

The record of treatment failures in juvenile corrections is extensive (Lerman, 1968; Gibbons and Krohn, 1986: 223–268). For example, we know that detached worker or street worker programs designed to wean gang members away from lawbreaking were unsuccessful. Similarly, a number of large-scale efforts to revamp community life, increase opportunity structures for delinquents, and the like, including Mobilization for Youth, the Chicago Area Projects, the Mid-City Project, and a work opportunities program in Seattle, all produced mixed results, at best (Schlossman et al., 1984; Miller, 1962; Brager and Purcell, 1967; Hackler, 1966). Then, too, a number of efforts have been made to create therapeutic milieus in correctional institutions, but to no avail (Jesness, 1965). The record of various and sundry counseling-oriented ventures in the juvenile justice system is a dismal one. Finally, most of the evidence on one of the newest approaches, diversion, indicates that (a) many of these programs have little or no impact upon youths diverted to them, and (b) many of them have resulted in "net widening," which is the opposite of what was intended by the architects of such ventures (Binder and Geis, 1984; Polk, 1984; Decker, 1985; Frazier, 1983).

This kind of bad news continues to come in, as illustrated by a recent report on a controlled experiment in California (Jackson, 1983) involving parole supervision as opposed to outright release of juvenile wards. The results indicated that the discharges and parolees had similar recidivism rates. However, the offenses committed by the parolees were more serious than those of the discharges. Also, parolees who recidivated received harsher sentences than did dischargee recidivists.

As an example of frustrated hopes, consider the case of the Community Treatment Project, conducted over a seven-year period by a California Youth Authority (Palmer, 1974; Lerman, 1975). The central hypothesis of that program was that delinquents who normally are shunted off to training schools could be successfully treated in the community if they were first assigned to Interpersonal Maturity Levels diagnostic types and then provided with intervention programs geared to their particular needs. This was an elaborate social experiment involving random assignment of juveniles either to the community program or to conventional institutional commitment, with the community treatment portion of it representing a highly developed version of the "different strokes for different folks" perspective.

The initial results of this experimental program in the form of parole performance and parole violation rates seemed to favor community treatment. However, subsequent analyses by Lerman (1975) of the Youth Authority's own data on the experiment turned up quite different findings. The differential parole performance by the commu-

nity-treated youths was produced by lenient parole revocation policies on the part of parole officers rather than representing improved parole behavior on the part of the wards. Further, the community-treated youths actually spent more time in custody in juvenile halls than they did in treatment in the community. Finally, because of the small caseloads in the community portion of this experiment, community treatment actually cost more per treated youth than did institutional commitment.

I do not mean to suggest that the evidence is now crystal clear that correctional intervention efforts of one kind or another have all failed to have any impact upon juvenile lawbreaking. Instead, the picture is parallel to the one regarding etiological knowledge presented at the beginning of these remarks. There is some evidence upon which one can draw that seems to suggest that some kinds of treatment or preventive activities may have a payoff. However, these studies are too few in number, as well as often being plagued with methodological problems, to provide the basis for bold and dramatic policy recommendations.

Pursuing this comment a bit further, some criminologists have found some encouragement in the quasi-experimental research study by Murray and Cox (1979), which seemed to indicate that commitment to Illinois state training schools, or alternatively, to a number of other correctional placements outside of institutions, all produced a suppression effect. The youngsters who went through these programs tended to commit fewer delinquent acts in the post-treatment period, even though they did not discontinue lawbreaking entirely. At the same time, some criminologists have found reasons to be somewhat skeptical of the conclusions by Murray and Cox, arguing that desistance from delinquency may have been due to a maturation effect rather than to anything contained in the programs (Lundman, 1984: 198–214). In other words, these boys may have passed through the age period of peak incidence of delinquency during the time they were under supervision.

Advocates of treatment can perhaps find some comfort also in a recent experimental group treatment project in St. Louis (Feldman et al., 1983) that focused upon a variety of kinds of "antisocial" juveniles, some of whom were involved in delinquency. The authors of the report on this study indicate that some antisocial youths were assigned to groups composed of other misbehaving youths; others were put in groups of mixed composition, involving both antisocial and nondelinquent boys; and a control group of nondelinquent boys was also involved. Experienced group counselors apparently managed to bring about behavioral changes on the part of the members of their groups, whereas inexperienced counselors did not produce those results. However, this study contained no evidence on the posttreatment delinquent behavior of the subjects.

These gaps and uncertainties in our knowledge about the impact of intervention upon offenders have not prevented some criminologists from offering strong recommendations for public policy. For example, in a recent volume on public policy and the crime-delinquency problem, Hirschi (1983) set out a blueprint that closely parallels American folk advice: "Spare the rod and spoil the child." According to Hirschi (1983:55), a parent-centered strategy of preventing delinquency is called for in which parents must (1) monitor the child's behavior; (2) recognize deviant behavior when it occurs; and (3) punish such behavior. In this same volume, Jackson Toby (1983) articulated a set of policy recommendations for the control of school violence and school-related delinquency, centering around lowering the age of compulsory school attendance to 15 and relaxation of minimum wage laws so that those who drop out (or are pushed out) of school would have a source of employment, albeit at a very low wage. It is perhaps true, as Toby argued, that the school violence problem would be reduced if large numbers of youths were encouraged to leave school and obtain low-paying jobs in fast food restaurants and the like, but what is less clear is whether such policies would increase the army of young adults who are chronically underemployed or unemployed and who make up the disadvantaged part of the split labor market. Further, it is at least plausible that the policies advocated by Toby would eventually exacerbate the problem of predatory street crime in the United States. For reasons of this kind, a number of criminologists would find much to quarrel with in these "hard-nosed" recommendations.

Where Do We Go from Here?

Richard Lundman (1984) has recently provided a detailed critique of a variety of delinquency control ventures, including efforts to identify predelinquents and engage in preventive intervention with them, diversion projects, postadjudication treatment programs, deterrence-oriented ventures, community treatment efforts, and institutionalization of offenders. His policy recommendations, drawn out of that review and critique, are as follows (Lundman, 1984: 221–238):

1. It is recommended that traditional delinquency prevention efforts be abandoned.

2. It is recommended that diversion be the first response of the juvenile justice system to status and minor offenses.

3. It is recommended that routine probation be retained as the first and most frequent sentencing option of juvenile court judges.

4. It is recommended that efforts to scare juveniles straight be abandoned.

5. It is recommended that community treatment programs be expanded to accommodate nearly all chronic offenders.

6. It is recommended that institutionalization continue to be used as a last resort reserved primarily for chronic offenders adjudicated delinquent for index crimes against persons.

The accumulated evidence about delinquency that fills the pages of delinquency textbooks, as well as the more specific material considered by Lundman in his book, provides considerable underlying support for these broad recommendations. For example, although research has often failed to discover evidence that community treatment ventures are markedly more effective than institutionalization of offenders, the other side of the coin is that the former have generally been shown to be at least as effective as incarceration and at considerably less cost. Accordingly, the recommendation to establish programs such as the National Institute of Justice–sponsored "New Pride" venture (Regnery, 1985) makes a good deal of sense. Project New Pride is a nonresidential, community-based program for juvenile offenders that provides a blend of counseling, alternative schooling, correction of learning disabilities, vocational training, job placement, recreation, and cultural activities.

In my opinion, the most significant recent attempt to rescue rehabilitation and intervention of delinquents is the small book, *One More Chance*, by Greenwood and Zimring (1985). Greenwood and Zimring began with the reasonable argument that those surveys of treatment evaluation studies that have concluded that "nothing works" have failed to look for differences in impact within intervention program types—such as milieu treatment or group counseling. Perhaps some specific efforts have worked while others have been unsuccessful, depending upon whether they were headed by a charismatic, vigorous director and staffed by dedicated workers or contained other positive program elements.

Greenwood and Zimring constructed an eclectic picture of delinquency causation and argued that we need multifaceted treatment approaches that will address these varied causal factors. They then went on to examine a number of specific programs that seem, more on the basis of educated guesswork than hard evidence, to hold particular promise. Certain of these are addressed to chronic or serious offenders and include a number of efforts that are operated by private organizations rather than local or state governments. Other promising intervention efforts were identified for predelinquents or less serious lawbreakers, including programs that strive to teach parenting skills to offenders' parents, intensified schooling programs, and the like.

I am not entirely persuaded by all of the arguments made by Greenwood and Zimring. For example, privately operated programs are difficult to monitor and have sometimes subjected delinquents to highly questionable experiences carried out in the name of treatment. This small volume should not be viewed as a collection of firmly based recipes for treatment of juveniles, nor did the authors make such a claim for it. But there is much food for thought in it for those who are concerned about treatment of offenders.

Concluding Remarks

It should be apparent that the thesis of this essay is not that the search for causes and cures for delinquency should be abandoned because current evidence on these matters is incomplete, controversial, or unclear. To begin with, it would be incorrect to describe our current situation as one of criminological nihilism, in which each person's assertions about causal factors or effective intervention policies carry equal weight. Rather, the evidence at hand is sufficient to demonstrate that some criminological claims are in error whereas others are buttressed by some measure of empirical support. For example, the weight of the evidence is clearly not consistent with Samenow's (1984) contentions about an alleged "criminal personality." In short, Samenow is simply wrong. Contrariwise, there is considerable research support that indicates that social control or social bond variables play some role in delinquency, even though the precise extent to which they do so is not entirely clear. In much the same way, it can be argued that some intervention tactics have been shown to be ineffective whereas research evidence suggests that some other programs hold considerable more promise.

However, we need to refrain from naive scientism. Criminologists should not promise more than can be delivered and policymakers should not look to criminologists for pancreas or other miracle cures for delinquency.

We have little choice but to pursue our efforts to learn more about delinquency through the methods of science and to inform our intervention efforts with the available knowledge. In the years ahead, those who labor at prevention or treatment will need to continue to look to social scientists for guidance on the causes or control of delinquency, while in turn, academically based theorists and researchers ought to redouble their efforts to improve upon the knowledge base employed by justice system workers. Steady, incremental progress in the way of more effective tactics of coping with delinquency will result, it is hoped, as we go about developing intervention programs based on criminological knowledge and conducting careful research evaluations of these programs. But it seems unlikely that we will move ahead by great leaps forward, rather, our progress is likely to be measured in small but significant steps.

Notes

1. In the dozen or so delinquency textbooks currently in print, the phenomena they discuss concern almost entirely youthful misconduct in the United States. My own text (Gibbons and Krohn, 1986) is the only one of these books with an entire chapter given over to an examination of juvenile misconduct around the world. Even so, that chapter is relatively limited in that most of it is devoted to delinquency in England and some other western European countries. A few studies of delinquency in Russia, Argentina, and Taiwan are also mentioned, along with some remarks about juvenile lawbreaking in Ghana, Nigeria, Iraq, and India.

2. This discussion is restricted to mainsteam delinquency theories and research, along with treatment and intervention proposals that flow out of that work. Radical-Marxist theorizing has not been included here. Some of the important radical writings are by Greenberg (1977a), Colvin and Pauly (1983), and Schwendinger and Schwendinger (1979). Those essays locate the main sources of delinquency in structural flaws in the social and economic order of capitalist societies. Prescriptions for the control and amelioration of delinquency have not usually been offered by radical-Marxist theorists, except for the implicit proposal that massive alterations that would create social and economic opportunities for youths are required in the structure of capitalist societies. However, the Schwendingers have articulated a number of recommendations for dealing with delinquency in the United States; most of these, however, seem little different from various liberal proposals, some of which have been noted in this article. Their policy recommendations are considerably less radical than is their analysis of the sources of delinquency.

References

AGNEW, R.
1985   "Social control theory and delinquency: a longitudinal test." *Criminology* 23 (February): 47–61.

BAILEY, W.C.
1966   "An evaluation of 100 studies of correctional outcome." *J. of Criminal Law, Criminology, and Police Sci.* (June): 153–160.

BEKER, J. AND D.S. HEYMAN
1972   "A critical appraisal of the California differential treatment typology of adolescent offenders." *Criminology* (May): 3–59.

BINDER, A. AND G. GEIS
1984   "*Ad populum* argumentation in criminology: juvenile diversion as rhetoric." *Crime & Delinquency* (October): 624–647.

BRAGER, G.A. AND F.P. PURCELL (EDS.)
1967   Community Action Against Poverty, New Haven, CT: *College and Universities Press.*

COLVIN, M. AND J. PAULY
1983   "A critique of criminology: toward an integrated structural-Marxist theory of delinquency production." *Amer. J. of Sociology* 89 (November): 513–551.

DECKER, S.H.
1985   "A systematic analysis of diversion: net widening and beyond." *J. of Criminal Justice* 3: 207–216.

ELLIOTT, D.S., D. HUIZINGA, AND S.S. AGETON
1985   Explaining Delinquency and Drug Use. Beverly Hills, CA: *Sage.*

FELDMAN, R.A., T.E. CAPLINGER, AND J.S. WODARSKI
1983   The St. Louis Conundrum. Englewood Cliffs, NJ: *Prentice-Hall.*

FRAZIER, C.E.
1983   "Evaluation of youth services programs: problems and prospects from a case study." *Youth & Society* (March): 335–362.

GIBBONS, D.C.
1965   Changing the Lawbreaker. Englewood Cliffs, NJ: *Prentice-Hall.*
1968   Society, Crime, and Criminal Careers. Englewood Cliffs, NJ: *Prentice-Hall.*
1970   "Differential treatment of delinquents and interpersonal maturity levels theory: a critique." *Social Service Rev.* 44 (March): 22–33.
1979   The Criminological Enterprise. Englewood Cliffs, NJ: *Prentice-Hall.*

GIBBONS, D.C. AND M.D. KROHN
1986   Delinquent Behavior. Englewood Cliffs, NJ: *Prentice-Hall.*

GREENBERG, D.F.
1977a   "Delinquency and the age structure of society." *Contemporary Crises* 1 (April): 189–224.
1977b   "The correctional effects of corrections," pp. 111–138 in D.F. Greenberg (ed.) Corrections and Punishment. Beverly Hills, CA: *Sage.*

GREENWOOD, P.W. AND F.E. ZIMRING
1985   One More Chance. Santa Monica, CA: *Rand.*

HACKLER, J.C.
1966   "Boys, blisters, and behavior: the impact of a

work program in an urban central area." *J. of Research in Crime and Delinquency* 3 (July): 155–164.

HIRSCHI, T.

1969   Causes of Delinquency. Berkeley: *Univ. of California Press.*

1979   "Separate and unequal is better." *J. of Research in Crime and Delinquency* 16: 34–38.

1983   "Crime and the family," pp. 53–68 in J.Q. Wilson (ed.) Crime and Public Policy. San Francisco: *Institute for Contemporary Studies.*

JACKSON, P.G.

1983   The Paradox of Control. New York: *Praeger.*

JENKINS, R.L.

1985   No Single Cause. College Park, MD: *American Correctional Association.*

JESNESS, C.V.

1965   The Fricot Ranch Study. Sacramento: *Department of the Youth Authority.*

LERMAN, P.

1968   "Evaluative studies of institutions for delinquents: implications for research and social policy." *Social Work* (July): 55–64.

1975   Community Treatment and Social Control. Chicago: *Univ. of Chicago Press.*

LISKA, A.E. AND M.D. REED

1985   "Ties to conventional institutions and delinquency: estimating reciprocal effects." *Amer. Soc. Rev.* 50 (August): 547–560.

LUNDMAN, R.J.

1984   Prevention and Control of Juvenile Delinquency. New York: *Oxford.*

MILLER, W.B.

1962   "The impact of a "total community" delinquency control project." *Social Problems* (Fall): 168–191.

MURRAY, C.A. AND L.A. COX, JR.

1979   Beyond Probation. Beverly Hills, CA: *Sage.*

NATIONAL COUNCIL ON CRIME AND DELINQUENCY

1984   *Rethinking Juvenile Justice:* National Statistical Trends. Minneapolis: University of Minnesota.

PALMER, T.

1971   "Martinson revisited." *J. of Research in Crime and Delinquency* (January): 67–80.

1974   The youth authority's community treatment project." Federal Probation (March): 3–14.

POLK, K.

1984   "Juvenile diversion: a look at the record." *Crime & Delinquency* (October): 648–659.

REGNERY, A.S.

1985   "Introducing new pride." *NIJ Reports* (September): 9–12.

ROBINSON, J. AND G. SMITH

1971   "The effectiveness of correctional programs." *Crime & Delinquency* (January): 67–80.

SAMENOW, S.

1984   The Criminal Mind. New York: *Times Books.*

SCHLOSSMAN, S., G. ZELLMAN, R. SHAVELSON, M. SEDLAK, AND J. COBB

1984   Delinquency Prevention in Chicago: A Fifty-Year Assessment of the Chicago Area Project. Santa Monica, CA: *Rand.*

SCHWENDINGER, H. AND J. SCHWENDINGER

1979   "Delinquency and social reform: a radical perspective," pp. 245–287 in L.T. Empey (ed.) Juvenile Justice: The Progressive Legacy and Current Reforms. Charlottesville, VA: *Univ. Press of Virginia.*

SECHREST, L., S.O. WHITE, AND E.D. BROWN (EDS.)

1979   *The Rehabilitation of Criminal Offenders.* Washington, DC: National Academy of Sciences.

SHIREMAN, C.H., K.B. MANN, C. LARSEN, AND T. YOUNG

1978   "Findings from experiments in treatment in correctional settings." *Social Service Rev.* (March): 38–59.

SUTHERLAND, E.H. AND D.R. CRESSEY

1978   *Criminology,* Philadelphia: Lippincott.

TOBY, J.

1983   "Crime in the schools," pp. 69–88 in J.Q. Wilson (ed.) *Crime and Public Policy.* San Francisco: Institute for Contemporary Problems.

WARREN, M.Q.

1976   "Intervention with juvenile delinquents," pp. 176–204 in M.K. Rosenheim (ed.) Pursuing Justice for the Child. Chicago: *Univ. of Chicago Press.*

WILSON, J.Q. AND R.J. HERRNSTEIN

1985   *Crime and Human Nature.* New York: Simon & Schuster.

WOLFGANG, M.E., R.M. FIGLIO, AND T. SELLIN

1972   Delinquency in a Birth Cohort. Chicago: *Univ. of Chicago Presss.*

QUESTIONS FOR DISCUSSION

1. In your own words, describe the rise of modern criminology.

2. The author is critical of a recent work by Wilson and Herrnstein. Why?

3. Have intervention programs for delinquents been successful? Cite evidence to support your answer.

4. Can solutions to crime and delinquency be found in the social sciences? Why?

APPLICATIONS

1. Canvass several professors who teach sociology or criminal justice. Ask them to provide you with a list of five to ten recommendations they would make to reduce crime. Compare the lists that you obtain and observe the similarities and differences in the responses. If possible, construct a final list which contains the recommendations on which all of the professors agreed. Do these recommendations appear to be plausible?

2. Let us assume that you are the expert. What recommendations would you make for the justice system and society to reduce crime and delinquency?

KEY TERMS

audacity   intrepid boldness or arrogance.

buttressed   strengthened or supported.

cavil   to raise trivial and frivolous objection.

nihilism   a doctrine that denies any objective grounds for truth.

perusal   to examine and consider with great attention and detail.

tome   a volume forming part of a larger work.

unequivocal   leaving no doubt; unquestionable.